Vietnam

To Merle Pribbenow

With pleasure
Admiration
& Appreciation

April 28, 2009

Vietnam

The History of an Unwinnable War, 1945–1975

John Prados

 University Press of Kansas

Published by the University Press of Kansas (Lawrence, Kansas 66045), which was organized by the Kansas Board of Regents and is operated and funded by Emporia State University, Fort Hays State University, Kansas State University, Pittsburg State University, the University of Kansas, and Wichita State University

Library of Congress Cataloging-in-Publication Data

Prados, John.

Vietnam : the history of an unwinnable war, 1945–1975 / John Prados.

p. cm. — (Modern war studies)

Includes bibliographical references and index.

ISBN 978-0-7006-1634-3 (cloth : alk. paper)

1. Vietnam War, 1961–1975—United States. 2. United States—Politics and government— 1945–1989. 3. United States—History—1945– I. Title.

DS558.P743 2009

959.704'3—dc22

                              2008051204

British Library Cataloguing-in-Publication Data is available.

Printed in the United States of America

10 9 8 7 6 5 4 3 2 1

The paper used in this publication is recycled and contains 30 percent postconsumer waste. It is acid free and meets the minimum requirements of the American National Standard for Permanence of Paper for Printed Library Materials Z39.48-1992.

FOR ELLEN

Who saw at the beginning

and carried her candle in the dark

ALSO BY JOHN PRADOS

BATTLE HYMN OF THE REPUBLIC

Mine eyes have seen the glory of the coming of the Lord
He is trampling out the vintage where the grapes of wrath are stored,
He has loosed the fateful lightning of His terrible swift sword
His truth is marching on.

Chorus: Glory! Glory! Hallelujah!
Glory! Glory! Hallelujah!
Glory! Glory! Hallelujah! His truth is marching on.

I have seen Him in the watch-fires of a hundred circling camps
They have builded Him an altar in the evening dews and damps
I can read His righteous sentence by the dim and flaring lamps
His day is marching on.

Chorus

I have read a fiery gospel writ in burnish'd rows of steel
"As ye deal with my contemners, So with you my grace shall deal;"
Let the Hero born of woman, crush the serpent with his heel
Since God is marching on.

Chorus

He has sounded forth the trumpet that shall never call retreat
He is sifting out the hearts of men before His judgment-seat
Oh be swift, my soul, to answer Him! Be jubilant my feet!
Our God is marching on.

Chorus

In the beauty of the lilies Christ was born across the sea,
With a glory in His bosom that transfigures you and me:
As He died to make men holy, let us die to make men free,
While God is marching on.

Chorus

Julia Ward Howe

Contents

Three photograph sections appear following pages 83, 278, and 395.

Preface

After spending years asserting that there was no similarity between Iraq and Vietnam, in August 2007 President George W. Bush switched and began using analogy to Vietnam to explain why the Iraq war needed to be continued. Bush did this without any deep reflection and without taking into account the fact that the Vietnam war is still disputed historical terrain. Never mind the conflations and mischaracterizations of this president's presentation of the past. The fact that he called up Vietnam as justification raises its own questions about the role of that conflict as analogy and the realities behind the mythology that has grown around it. We understand that history unrolls as tragedy and repeats as farce. Vietnam was certainly a tragedy. The question that continues to permeate that conflict, accounting for much of the mythology, is whether it was all inevitable. Was Vietnam an unwinnable war? What does that make Iraq?

Although there have been survey histories of the Vietnam war in the past, current efforts to rely on that conflict as historical analogy for Iraq indicate the need for a fresh review. In addition, most existing accounts were written prior to the declassification of large swaths of records of presidents Richard M. Nixon and Gerald R. Ford, who led the United States during the later phases of the war; these records are especially important because allusions to success in Vietnam are based on that period. This is not to say that earlier events, some as early as the 1950s, were not crucial to the outcome, indicating the necessity for a new broad overview. Histories also pass lightly over certain actions that need to be placed in proper relation to the whole to fully appreciate the unfolding American experience in Vietnam. In particular, this account presents evidence that developments during the Eisenhower administration in 1954–1955 not only conditioned later events but also played a key role in the minds of central actors.

As will become evident, the core argument advanced here is that, whatever the intentions and aims of American leaders, the United States acted within a context defined along political, military, foreign policy, social, and economic dimensions—in effect, an "envelope"—and that envelope narrowed over time due to developments in all those fields. The narrative shows how and why the range of potential choices constricted, as well as which choices were influenced by individual agency, ambition, and misunderstanding of the war's reality or, as the Soviets used to say, the true "correlation of forces."

I believe the Vietnam war remains contested historical terrain in large part because observers have presented "atomized" views. Some write of the agonies of presidents facing crucial decisions at particular moments in time. These accounts emphasize short-range thinking. They frequently allude to long-range impact but still present only a limited slice of the relevant history. Others approach the war as simple military conflict and write of campaigns and battles. With a few exceptions, Americans won all the battles. So how did the United States lose the war? A few accounts combine a battle with a view of the home front, but again, the scope is restricted. Others approach the issue as a technical problem of military doctrine and argue that better strategy and tactics could have led to a different outcome. Some try to explain defeat by focusing on North Vietnam, usually depicted as a warrior state thrusting across international borders and invading the territory of those the United States sought to support. Still others account for the outcome by writing of the American political movement that opposed the war, blaming that for the failure. Variants of that theme include implicating the media in the defeat for not reporting positive news about the war, or charging Congress with running away from its responsibilities and not allocating the necessary funds. What all these visions of Vietnam have in common is that they consider only pieces of the puzzle, extrapolating general conclusions from very narrow bases of evidence. They are atomized views.

There is also an elephant in the room of historical analysis on Vietnam, much as there is with Iraq. That is the *American ally*. Discussions of the troop "surge" in Iraq mention but do not explain why U.S. military action has not been matched by indigenous political progress and then dismiss the subject. In much the same way, accounts of the Vietnam war speak of the Saigon government and its army and mention South Vietnamese aspects when unavoidable, usually the participation of its troops, but they make little serious attempt to understand the limitations of our ally. Nor do they say much about the southern resistance. In Iraq as in Vietnam, Americans substituted hope for the political development of the ally for real analysis of that ally's incentives and social realities. This deliberate donning of blinders inevitably distorts. In Iraq today, this feature contributes to an evolving tragedy. In looking back on Vietnam, it is a fault that led to inaccurate appreciation of the status of the conflict.

There is a third artificiality, at least in the historical debate over Vietnam. This, which may or may not turn out to be true of Iraq, resides in the castigation of the war's political opponents, in the notion that the forces in contention consist of right-thinking supporters of administration policy versus deluded or manipulated opposition elements. This stance prevents debate by preemptively defining the ideological terrain—those agreeing with government policy in the right, the others in some darker place. It also fails to deal with public opinion as a dynamic factor. As a general proposition, opinion tends to follow the flag. Presidents make great headway by simply taking actions that the public rallies around until it learns or feels or knows that the president's course is misguided. In short, apart from the pro and con advocates, the bulk of the public undergoes some transformation that *turns* them against the war. Not recognizing or responding to such changes in itself creates inertia that becomes an obstacle to "progress."

For all these reasons, a fresh analysis of the Vietnam war is necessary. The atomization of the literature has impeded a full understanding. We have narratives of presidents making decisions in which either military or political considerations, or both, have only a backstage presence; they are treated as givens rather than as sets of dynamic forces or, worse, as merely something to mention. Then there are battle histories in which presidents and politics are barely noticed. Virtually all this literature ignores the South Vietnamese, whose struggle lay at the heart of the entire enterprise. And most of it treats the Vietnamese adversary, the Democratic Republic of Vietnam, as mere black box. Hanoi's allies pass with the lightest of touches. Finally, sources on the antiwar movement and various sectors of American society, apart from an initial spate of postwar writing that centered on who did what, when, and where, have been preoccupied with finding scapegoats for defeat. The diplomatic histories tend to focus on either the Johnson or the Nixon period. In contrast, this work aims to bring together the strands of the Vietnam story in a new overview, presenting developments on many fronts as they relate to each other as well as to the whole.

In describing this book to a number of people I have used the term *unified field theory*. By that I mean it attempts to weave an account of both action and context that includes all necessary elements. The theme of individual transformation is also embodied here. Ultimately it is difficult to understand how the mass of a society can adopt some view without seeing that process in action. The domestic politics of Vietnam is a vast canvas, but it is intrinsically necessary to understanding the war, both because of its inherent importance and because U.S. government attempts to counteract the antiwar movement complete the circle of policy and action. I show the roots of that Movement, describe how it evolved, and note significant protests and other events. High points are the focus because, much like the details of military campaigns, any attempt to present a comprehensive account of the welter of efforts would make this book unwieldy. A few stories will have to stand in— both for protest and for combat—for the experiences of many. I apologize in advance to all those who feel that the events in which they participated are slighted here. Many argue that America's war in Vietnam proved to be the most socially divisive U.S. military engagement since the Civil War. In consonance with that, I have drawn many of the chapter titles from a famous Civil

War song whose lyrics eerily evoke various stages of the Vietnam experience: "The Battle Hymn of the Republic."

Individuals aggregate in groups. That transformation needs to be understood too. I chose to focus on one particular group: Vietnam Veterans Against the War (VVAW). This group played a central role at several crucial moments, yet except for accounts that center on the organization itself, it has only a bit part in standard Movement histories. My narrative introduces new evidence of the extent to which the U.S. government initiated an explicit campaign to "get" VVAW, illustrating how the government played simultaneously on the war and antiwar boards. As a veterans' organization, VVAW also furnishes a natural link to another aspect of the narrative—how controversies over the war affected U.S. military forces themselves, ultimately leading back to the nation's ability to carry on a war in Southeast Asia.

The narrative explicitly puts South Vietnam back into the equation, following a number of aspects of Saigon's political, military, and economic development. This war was about the future of South Vietnam, and it is a matter of perplexity that matters Vietnamese receive such short shrift. There are exceptions regarding a few events, such as the coup that toppled Saigon leader Ngo Dinh Diem, and some accounts pay greater attention overall—Stanley Karnow's *Vietnam* is one—but those histories tend to be essentially descriptive. They do not tease out the set of themes that show the dynamics at work. This book does exactly that. It is part narrative history, part interpretive, and it aims to demonstrate why what began as a mote in the eye ended up nearly consuming a great nation.

In addition to South Vietnam, I present material on North Vietnam, China, Russia, and Western Europe in their relation to the Vietnam war. A conscious effort has been made to bring new evidence to bear on the North Vietnamese side. Space precludes this book from being as much of an international history as I would have liked, particularly with regard to the activities of some actors in the Johnson administration's peace feelers and the influence of protest movements in many European lands, but these do receive some attention.

It is also true that existing overviews fail to take into account important bodies of data. In addition to the declassification issue, virtually all the existing survey histories appeared before the availability of White House tapes of five presidents who led the nation during Vietnam, most importantly John F. Kennedy, Lyndon B. Johnson, and Richard M. Nixon. Material such as intelligence records and official histories—including important ones from the Central Intelligence Agency and National Security Agency (which only began to appear in 2006–2008), but military service ones as well—has largely been ignored in previous accounts. And Vietnamese sources from both the South and the North have been notably underutilized, along with a plethora of other material. Incorporating this knowledge is another reason why a fresh overview history is necessary.

As for chronology, my view is that the parameters that set the framework for the war—not so much determining events as establishing the boundaries of the permissible (i.e., the envelope)—were progressively laid down from 1945 to 1955. For that reason, the narrative begins with the end of World War II, treats certain 1954–1955 events in some detail, and follows the American war through to its end. Events during the Johnson and Nixon presidencies are covered in the greatest depth, but other periods are not ignored. I do take advantage of the existing literature; thus, certain events and characters that have been covered in extensive detail elsewhere are treated more briefly. Even for well-known events, however, an effort has been made here to show neglected aspects. Fresh material appears on virtually every facet of the Vietnam war. Most important, this is among the first works to cover the Nixon period based on the emerging documentary record rather than people's impressionistic recollections, and considerable detail is devoted to that era.

This study is based on extensive research, including documentary research in every period covered plus interviews with a wide assortment of the characters involved on every side and at every level. I know, interviewed, participated in conferences with, or have met national security advisers, National Security Council staff, diplomats, secretaries of defense, generals, battalion commanders, grunts, airmen, intelligence officers, and antiwar movement figures; South Vietnamese leaders, generals, soldiers, airmen, and resistance fighters; North Vietnamese diplomats, generals, soldiers, and historians; Australian officers and historians, Canadian and British diplomats, and more.

I am aware of and have used the huge literature on the Vietnam war. There are a variety of historical debates on certain aspects of the war, such as whether Kennedy would have gotten the United States out of Vietnam and what was achieved by the Christmas Bombing of Hanoi, to cite just two examples. Again, these issues are not well developed in the older survey histories. I comment on these debates and on some of the studies that champion them, working the evolving debate into an overview account for the first time. Such discussions are intended to advance the historiography of the war, contributing to the comprehensiveness of this narrative. Ultimately I side with those who consider Vietnam an unwinnable war. I came to that view early, but extensive research and deep analysis confirm that impression.

John Prados
Washington, DC
September 2007

Acknowledgments

Let me begin by acknowledging the example of George McTurnin Kahin, who died eight years ago. Kahin inspired many as the very model of the engaged scholar. Though his field was Indonesia, Kahin remained alert to the wider problems of Southeast Asia and quickly perceived that America's Vietnam war was both a tragedy and a blunder. America's involvement disturbed Kahin so profoundly that he immediately began to delve into these matters and by 1965 was already prepared to stand against the tide of intervention. That year Kahin appeared at a large national teach-in on Vietnam, the one McGeorge Bundy skipped because Lyndon Johnson threatened to fire him. Kahin also spoke against the war in congressional testimony beginning that year. With scholar John Lewis, Kahin published *The United States in Vietnam* in 1967, a work that influenced me and no doubt others. I first met him at Cornell in 1970, where his lack of pretension impressed, and his gracious help to an undergraduate from another school enabled me to raise my own Indochina research to a new level.

Kahin also became an exemplar in the use of declassification to open up the secret record of U.S. history. In the late 1970s and early 1980s, with the release of classified records on Vietnam still at a very early stage, Kahin used the Freedom of Information Act to demand that the State Department simply release all its documents on that matter. The several thousand documents he received formed the basis for his 1986 book *Intervention: How America Became Involved in Vietnam,* which illuminated Lyndon Johnson's 1965 troop decision in a depth never before achieved. All scholars should strive for the integrity and dedication that marked George Kahin and his works on Indonesia as well as Vietnam.

For the present book I am indebted to many, starting with the gracious staffs of the following libraries: Columbia University, the Forty-second Street Library of the New York Public Library, the Library of Congress, the University of California–Berkeley, Texas Tech University, New York University, George Washington University, the Echols Collection of Cornell University, and the Wheaton Regional Library of the Montgomery County Public Library. I received invaluable assistance from archivists at the National Archives and Records Administration (NARA); the presidential libraries of Harry S. Truman, Dwight D. Eisenhower, Lyndon B. Johnson, and Gerald R.

Ford and the Nixon Library Project (both when it was located in a warehouse in northern Virginia and at NARA); and the special collections of the Columbia University Oral History Project, the Library of Congress, the U.S. Army Military History Institute, the University of California–Berkeley, and the Vietnam Center of Texas Tech University. Let me add special thanks to Herbert Pankratz of the Eisenhower Library; Suzanne Forbes and Maura Porter of the Kennedy Library; David C. Humphrey, Nancy Smith, Regina Greenwell, John Wilson, Linda Seelke, and Ted Gittinger of the Johnson Library; Karen Holzhausen and Donna Lehman of the Ford Library; John Taylor of NARA; Richard J. Sommers, John Slonacker, and Pamela Cheney of the U.S. Army Military History Institute; and Steve Maxner, James Ginther, and Ronald Frankum of the Vietnam Center. Some of these persons have gone on to greater things and continue to contribute to American scholarship in valuable ways. I regret to say that John Taylor, an indefatigable font of archival wisdom and a friend, passed away even as I worked on this book. I had been looking forward to presenting him with a copy.

I also want to make special mention of Lewis B. Sorley. Although he did not help me specifically, Colonel Sorley contributed directly to this book and to all future Vietnam scholarship with his painstaking transcriptions of the MACV staff meeting tapes, which are cited liberally in the part of this narrative covering the Nixon years. I ran into Sorley at the Army's Military History Institute while he was engaged in this undertaking, and through my own work with presidential tapes, I am aware of the difficulties of transcription, which are enormous. Thank you. Though our interpretations of the war differ, Sorley is a good friend and has been a fun debating partner on numerous occasions.

For affording me access to their papers, I thank Larry Berman, Daniel Ellsberg, Milton K. Leitenberg, and Douglas Valentine. Ray W. Stubbe graciously provided me with translations of Vietnamese materials on the battle of Khe Sanh. Special thanks are also owed to Merle Pribbenow, who furnished me with some of his extensive translations from the Vietnamese. For specific documents important to this inquiry, I thank William Burr. I am grateful to James Dingeman for providing me with dissertations not encountered elsewhere. I also want to thank Kai Pantin, who helped with printing some of the materials I could not access otherwise, and especially Mary Curry, who actually produced the manuscript text at a critical stage when my computer malfunctioned. For answering questions great and small I thank Gar Alperowitz, James Blight, Robert K. Brigham, McGeorge Bundy, Robert Buzzanco, John M. Carland, Timothy M. Castle, Graham Cosmas, Gloria Emerson, Gerald K. Haines, David Halberstam, William Hammond, George Herring, Melvin Laird, Janet Lang, Theodore Mataxis, Robert S. McNamara, Douglas Pike, James R. Reckner, Marilyn Young, and Howard Zinn. Several of these individuals have since passed away, and I regret their loss.

Colleagues Jeffrey Kimball and Melvin Small read and commented on the manuscript. They helped me sharpen many of the points made here. My companion Ellen Pinzur not only read and commented on the manuscript but also edited it and helped with innumerable questions of fact and language. I stand in great debt to them all. Editor Michael Briggs not only supported this project throughout but also afforded me the time necessary to attend to the myriad tasks required to finish the work—a special thanks. Separately and together, all these persons contributed a great deal to this book. The omissions or errors herein are solely my own.

A Note to the Reader

Given the bitterness that surrounds American memories of the Vietnam war and the broadness of my inquiry in this book, I believe some personal perspective might be helpful. Think of it as full disclosure. To the degree that I have any reputation, it is probably that of an engaged leftist intellectual. But it was in fact Vietnam that brought me here. Surprising as it may sound, as a boy I wanted nothing more than to be a soldier—and not just any soldier, either. I wanted to be the one who understood, the leader who was also a sage, perhaps to shepherd the Army into an age of conflict at any level of violence. John F. Kennedy's ascension to the presidency thrilled me, his inaugural speech suggested we shared a vision, and his call to service against any foe seemed just right. About the time of the movie *The Longest Day* (1962), I decided that General Maxwell D. Taylor, the World War II paratrooper, military adviser to Kennedy in the White House, and then chairman of the Joint Chiefs of Staff, was my model for the kind of officer I wanted to be.

It would not be accurate to say I was an Army brat or that mine was a military family, but it would not be far from true. My father was an Army officer in World War II and Korea. He remained active in the Reserves until retirement. My maternal grandfather was Army too. He fought Aguinaldo in the Philippines and served on the Western Front in the Great War, earning a battlefield commission. My parents met in Leavenworth, Kansas. Grandfather never talked about his wartime experiences and never claimed to have been an officer, but the endless hours I spent playing around the pool at the Fort Leavenworth Officers' Club as a visiting youth carried evident meaning. I played at soldiers, collected armies of toy figurines, built models of military equipment and warships, consumed military histories, and dreamed of going to West Point. I tried to understand the process of combat and taught myself to design and create war games, the kind of board strategy games that still excite the interest of hobbyists across America. Vietnam changed that.

By the early 1960s my father, stymied on Army promotions, had gone into sports journalism. The family moved to San Juan, Puerto Rico, where my father had been hired as the first manager for the city's Hiram Bithorn Stadium, a site for Winter League baseball and a lot more besides. It was from San Juan that I watched my country march into the Vietnam war, something that greatly interested me as an Army wannabe. Coming of political consciousness, I agreed with President Kennedy's policies, thrilled at the exploits of Army heroes such as Captain Roger Donlon at the Nam Dong Special Forces camp in 1965, and thought the enemy would get their due when President Johnson decided to commit American ground forces to South Vietnam. Expecting to serve, I set out to learn everything I could about Vietnam, which was difficult in San Juan because of the limited English-language media and the poor libraries. Nevertheless I plunged into the effort and began by studying the French in Indochina, the immediate antecedents to Americans in Vietnam. I discovered that events in Southeast Asia were a great deal more complex than I had imagined. But my basic stance was the same.

It was actually the 1965 U.S. intervention in the Dominican Republic that first knocked a chink in my ideological armor. San Juan, only a couple of hundred miles away, was a very good platform to witness that event, and it became evident that U.S. moves there belied the aims enunciated by the White House. That raised questions for me, which gradually deepened as I read weekly newsmagazines about the progress in Vietnam, only to see war maps that showed essentially the same situation over a period of three years. Meanwhile, I saw the civil rights protesters as righteous but rejected Vietnam dissenters as wrong—until the Tet offensive. The Johnson administration's claims of approaching victory, capped by the spectacle of a countrywide North Vietnamese offensive, were so disconcerting that I began to question all I thought I knew. Tet was followed in rapid sequence by Johnson's withdrawal from the presidential race, the assassinations of the Reverend Martin Luther King Jr. and Robert F. Kennedy, and a violent eruption at the Democratic National Convention in Chicago. In truth, 1968 was a stunning year.

It was also the year that I began to line up the requisite support for an application to West Point. My father had plentiful and sufficient contacts to sustain such a candidacy. But I had begun to doubt American motives, though I had not joined the ranks of dissenters. Nevertheless, something was not right in the progression from France to America in Vietnam. Those doubts led to some discomfort within my family and to arguments with and estrangement from my father, who supported the war. I gave up the goal of an Army career and the idea of going to the U.S. Military Academy. As I started my senior year in high school I applied to and was accepted at Columbia College, where I originally intended to pursue my studies of French Indochina. There. My cards are on the table. I know that transformation was at the heart of the growth of American opposition to the war in Vietnam because it happened to me.

At an early stage in this project, my editors asked me to write of my own experiences as part of a more limited study focusing on the antiwar movement. I assembled such a narrative. Because that experience is directly relevant to the theme I develop here—the narrowing envelope for American leaders in Vietnam—I have retained portions of that material and present it later in the book. These passages, which are distinguished in the text by being set in italic, illustrate how the Vietnam war affected individual Americans.

Acronyms

AFSC	American Friends Service Committee
AFV	American Friends of Vietnam
ANZUS	Australia, New Zealand–United States (Treaty)
APC	armored personnel carrier
ARVN	Army of the Republic of Vietnam
ASA	Army Security Service
AWOL	absent without leave
CALCAV	Clergy and Laity Concerned about Vietnam
CCI	Citizens Commission of Inquiry
CDEC	Combined Documents Exploitation Center
CIA	Central Intelligence Agency
CICV	Combined Intelligence Center Vietnam
CIDG	Civilian Irregular Defense Group
CINCPAC	Commander in Chief Pacific
CO	conscientious objector
COINTELPRO	Counterintelligence Program
CORDS	Civil Operations and Rural Development Support
COSVN	Central Office for South Vietnam
CREEP	Committee to Re-elect the President
DAO	Defense Attaché Office
DAR	Daughters of the American Revolution
D4M	December 4th Movement
DIA	Defense Intelligence Agency
DMZ	Demilitarized Zone
DRV	Democratic Republic of Vietnam
FBI	Federal Bureau of Investigation
FDR	Franklin Delano Roosevelt
FLM	Front for the Liberation of the Montagnards
FOIA	Freedom of Information Act
FULRO	Front Unifie de Lutte des Races Oprimees
FWF	Free World Forces
GI	government issue (term for a soldier, in use since World War II)
H&I	harassment and interdiction (an artillery tactic)

HES	Hamlet Evaluation Survey
HUAC	House Un-American Activities Committee
ICCS	International Commission for Control and Supervision
ID	identification
IDA	Institute for Defense Analyses
INR	Bureau of Intelligence and Research (State Department)
IRS	Internal Revenue Service
ISA	International Security Affairs (unit of the defense secretary's office)
JCS	Joint Chiefs of Staff
JGS	Joint General Staff
JFK	John Fitzgerald Kennedy
LBJ	Lyndon Baines Johnson
LZ	landing zone
MAAG	Military Assistance Advisory Group
MACSOG	MACV Studies and Observation Group
MACV	Military Assistance Command Vietnam
MAF	Marine Amphibious Force
MIA	missing in action
MP	military police
MSUG	Michigan State University Group
NATO	North Atlantic Treaty Organization
NCO	noncommissioned officer
NIE	National Intelligence Estimate
NLF	National Liberation Front
NPAC	National Peace Action Coalition
NSA	National Security Agency
NSAM	National Security Action Memorandum
NSC	National Security Council
NSDM	National Security Decision Memorandum
NSG	Naval Security Group
NSSM	National Security Study Memorandum
NYPD	New York Police Department
OPLAN	Operations Plan
OSD	Office of the Secretary of Defense
OSS	Office of Strategic Services
PF	Popular Forces
PLAF	People's Liberation Armed Forces
POL	petroleum, oil, and lubricant
POW	prisoner of war
PRC	People's Republic of China
PRU	Provincial Reconnaissance Unit
PSDF	People's Self-Defense Force

PX	post exchange
RF	Regional Forces
RLG	Royal Laotian Government
ROAD	Reorganization Objective Army Division
ROK	Republic of Korea
ROTC	Reserve Officers' Training Corps
RVNAF	Republic of Vietnam Armed Forces
SAC	Strategic Air Command
SAM	surface-to-air missile
SANE	National Committee for a Safe Nuclear Policy
SDS	Students for a Democratic Society
SEAC	Southeast Asia Command (World War II)
SEATO	Southeast Asia Treaty Organization
SGU	Special Guerrilla Unit (CIA Hmong force)
SNCC	Student Nonviolent Coordinating Committee
SOG	Studies and Observation Group (MACV)
SPI	Simulations Publications Inc.
STAG	Student Agitation
SUNY	State University of New York
SVN	South Vietnam
SWP	Socialist Workers' Party
TPF	Tactical Patrol Force (NYPD)
UN	United Nations
UPI	United Press International
VA	Veterans Administration
VFW	Veterans of Foreign Wars
VIG	Vietnam Information Group
VNA	Vietnam National Army
VNAF	Vietnamese Air Force (South Vietnam)
VPA	Vietnam People's Army
VVAW	Vietnam Veterans Against the War
WIEU	Weekly Intelligence Estimate Update
WSAG	Washington Special Actions Group

Vietnam

■ April 1971: Veterans at War

They came in cars, in buses, by train and plane, in their scruffy hundreds, disillusioned veterans of America's war in Vietnam. It was April 1971. Richard Nixon sat in the White House. At his command, U.S. forces in Southeast Asia were supporting an invasion of Laos by the Vietnamese allied to the United States. To avoid the word invasion, the Nixon administration had characterized the Laotian operation as something else, anything else, calling it an incursion, as it had done the previous year in Cambodia. So the veterans styled their march on Washington as an "Incursion into the County of Congress." The events of that week changed the course of the Vietnam war, a change wrought on the banks of the Potomac, not in the paddy fields of South Vietnam.

■ ■ ■ The incursion came as no surprise to the powers that be in the nation's capital. The White House knew by early March there would be a huge antiwar demonstration in Washington on April 24. Intense feeling was palpable. On March 1 a bomb went off on the Senate side of the Capitol. A faction of the Students for a Democratic Society known as the Weathermen took credit. Nixon hung suspended between his preferred war strategy and the American people's evident distaste for that course. Just before the Laotian invasion, polls by the very credible American Institute for Public Opinion showed that 59 percent of Democrats opposed the war and—worse—61 percent of Republicans held identical views. The better-known Gallup poll had the president's approval rating hovering around 50 percent, while the Harris poll showed just a 43 percent favorable rating. H. R. ("Bob") Haldeman, the president's chief of staff, recorded in his diary that Nixon "clearly has sort of a mystic feeling about the Laotian thing."[1] But that operation proved to be an agonizingly slow failure. The president's rating in the Harris poll fell even more.

The Nixon White House, acutely sensitive to any whiff of antiwar activity, doubled and redoubled the stakes in its efforts to neutralize opposition. It employed every tool in its bag of tricks, and they were many. At the Department of Justice, Attorney General John Mitchell enlisted the aid of state and local police forces. Nixon had created a law enforcement assistance program in 1969 to help local jurisdictions. Under the guise of cooperation, Mitchell's officials asked them for information on antiwar activities. The U.S. military monitored dissent in its ranks, which revealed the activities of antiwar veterans who were attempting to reach out to their comrades still on active duty. Meanwhile, the Federal Bureau of Investigation (FBI) had a major operation of its own specifically targeting the antiwar vets.

A group called Vietnam Veterans Against the War (VVAW) was following up public hearings it had held in Detroit in January, where members had exposed a multiplicity of arrogant acts, bad behavior, and even American atrocities they had witnessed as soldiers in Vietnam. One of the group's leaders, a former U.S. Navy officer named John Kerry, had proposed the march on Washington. Kerry's idea was well thought-out; he had come to a national office meeting with a prepared presentation and a poster-board display. California coordinator Barry Romo suggested calling the action "Dewey Canyon III," in a reference to the Laotian invasion.[2] A period of planning and fund-raising ensued. Now the veterans' incursion loomed, scheduled for the four days immediately prior to the big national protest. The veterans made no secret of their intentions. Their March 1971 newsletter encouraged attendance and jocularly warned, "No air cover will be provided (despite the forty members of a crash and rescue helicopter unit in 'Nam who have joined VVAW) so bring [your] own ponchos, sleeping bags, old uniforms and medals."[3] From the beginning they emphasized that the march would be a peaceful protest.

The FBI kept Washington officials apprised. The Bureau had many sources of information. For one thing, FBI special agents were avid scavengers, pocketing every paper found at a VVAW office and every leaflet from a demonstration. Garbage cans and mailboxes outside offices were fountains of data. Undercover operatives had infiltrated the veterans. The agents sought data from local police departments that had their own channels into VVAW. Not that the vets were doing anything in secret—indeed, plans for an encampment in Washington, combined with lobbying efforts and demonstrations, constituted an organizing tool for VVAW. Nevertheless, declassified FBI records show that the Nixon administration knew the basics more than two weeks before Kerry announced Dewey Canyon at a news conference in the office of Massachusetts congressman Michael J. Harrington on March 16. The FBI had detailed knowledge of the plans by the end of March, and it followed subsequent changes.

That was not all. The vets hoped to put 5,000 comrades on the ground in Washington. The Bureau did its best to prevent that. According to FBI records, special agents in Indianapolis and elsewhere used contacts with car rental companies to learn of VVAW efforts to hire automobiles for caravans. In New York other FBI agents found out that Ed Damato and Joe Urgo of the VVAW national office had asked the Penn Central Railroad about hiring a special train to transport veterans from Boston and points south to Washington. The vets were told the railroad had no spare equipment. Coaches could be added on scheduled runs, but arrangements had to be made through the national coordinator for the march, Jack Smith, a former Marine sergeant with two tours in Vietnam who lived in New Haven. Before Smith could do anything, it was too late. It is still unknown what kind of pressure Nixon administration operatives put on the Penn Central, but the mere fact of an FBI inquiry often has a chilling effect. Subsequent Bureau reports noted that VVAW had reserved seats on other trains to Washington.

On March 30 the FBI ordered undercover informants among the VVAW's ranks to accompany the veterans on their Washington mission. Bureau headquarters confirmed the orders on April 1. In California, for example, a VVAW organizer recalls one member who dressed in a fatigue shirt with captain's bars but could not produce the document issued to soldiers leaving the military. The man threw himself into march preparations with gusto and flew to Washington with the rest of the California contingent. Once on the ground he disappeared. Special agents in the field reported on the pre-march activities of Kerry, VVAW southeast regional coordinator Scott Camil, and others. Preparatory activities in Albuquerque, Atlanta, Jacksonville, San Francisco, Milwaukee, Kansas City, St. Louis, Indianapolis, Detroit, New York, Boston, Baltimore, and Washington itself were detailed by those cities' FBI offices. The vets' fund-raising for the march was also featured in FBI reports, as were appeals from clergy for food donations to the encampment.

Because the VVAW action required a place for the protesters to stay, this presented a ripe opportunity for obstruction. At first the vets planned to camp on land owned by Georgetown University. Suddenly the administrator who had given permission was fired, and VVAW was told the agreement had been canceled. The vets tried to make an arrangement with American University, but that proposal went nowhere. Then local organizer Mike Phelan tried to obtain a permit for a camp near the Lincoln Memorial. The National Park Service said that obtaining such permission required three months. The incursion was just weeks away. Organizers finally requested The Mall only as a gathering place and a location for nighttime meetings. This search for a campsite became a touchstone of the entire Dewey Canyon III march.

Meanwhile, the vets were beset with all the headaches associated with trying to bring off such an ambitious protest. They sent solicitation letters to at least nine major food companies, including General Foods, Howard Johnson's, Oscar Mayer, and Bird's Eye. A vegetarian collective in Indiana donated some food. Portable toilets were donated. Friendly Washingtonians were asked to house notables but not the vets themselves. A special effort to cultivate Washington and Capitol Hill police included an open letter explaining the vets' purpose, aimed at minimizing friction. Public relations was a huge lacuna that veteran Tim Butz tried to fill. From New York the

VVAW national office sent one of its members, Mike Oliver, to help local organizers.

Phelan tried to get permits for every planned activity as a means of minimizing potential confrontations. Lots of difficulties arose. VVAW wanted to lay a wreath at the Tomb of the Unknown Soldier in Arlington Cemetery, but the Park Service rejected this innocuous event. The Justice Department went to court to block a march near the White House, claiming security problems, even though it had already given permission for the larger march through downtown Washington by the National Peace Action Committee.

The high point of the planned veteran protests was to come on the last day, April 23, where The Mall rose up to the Capitol. The veterans wanted to stage a symbolic ceremony in which they returned their combat medals to the U.S. government. The idea was for them to line up, make whatever statement they wanted, then deposit their medals in a body bag, which VVAW would present to Congress. The group had requested permits for this event plus an opening-day protest on Capitol grounds. Given their other troubles, VVAW expected problems here, especially since Vice President Spiro T. Agnew, as president pro tem of the Senate, controlled the Capitol grounds. Agnew was famously leery of the Movement and had been Nixon's point man for a political offensive against dissent, labeling protesters an "effete corps of impudent snobs."[4]

Issues came to a head on the afternoon of April 15, when the VVAW's Jack Mallory met with officials from the Office of the Vice President. Agnew staffer Alice Lane huffed that Mallory "did not look like a former captain."[5] Mallory, who had been in Vietnam with the 11th Armored Cavalry Regiment and the 1st Cavalry Division (Airmobile) in 1969–1970, swallowed the insult and got down to business. Remarkably, Agnew's people permitted the event, although they refused to approve the climactic medal return, citing security concerns related to the huge antiwar rally scheduled soon after. The vets countered that a number of senators and congressmen were going to participate. Agnew's representative shot back, "The vice-president doesn't care about the senators and congressmen."[6] Surprised at getting anything at all, the vets left with half a loaf. What VVAW did not know that spring afternoon was that Nixon's people thought they had the veterans in a trap.

■ ■ ■ A little after eleven o'clock the next morning, Richard Nixon, a president who actively followed those things that mattered to him, telephoned aide Charles W. ("Chuck") Colson. Sitting back in their White House offices, the two agreed that the latest developments held potential for pro-war "hawks." Referring to the chances of inflaming their supporters, Colson remarked, "Demonstrations are gonna help us there."

"Particularly," Nixon agreed, "since Agnew's allowin' 'em to do it up at the Capitol. That's good. Just let those people up there see those people, right?"

Colson remarked, "If the Vietnam veterans, uh, put on their show this week, it's just gonna make, uh, it's gonna make the hardhats 'n' the . . . rest of our coalition, uh, it's just gonna stiffen their back."

"Right," said Nixon. The president seemed very pleased.

Colson finished, "I hope they put on a little show 'cause, uh . . . it's important that our, our people get that reinforcement."[7]

In fact, the president and his political aide were working a conscious strategy against the protests. Nixon took the lead, defining the terms and aiming to create a situation that would allow him a free hand in the Vietnam war. Colson would be his point man, although every official in the Nixon White House contributed. As early as January, legal counsel John Dean had begun collecting information on demonstrations in the spring, and in February, about the time VVAW decided to carry out Dewey Canyon, the White House considered creating a task force to plan countermeasures. This led to the so-called Intelligence Evaluation Committee, an interagency group chaired by Robert C. Mardian, the assistant attorney general in charge of the Justice Department's Internal Security Division.

Haldeman rode herd on all this. He monitored the paper flow and floated ideas, lining up the main options. Chief domestic adviser John Ehrlichman worked on specifics, such things as protest permits and security arrangements. Speechwriters Patrick J. Buchanan and Ray Price suggested ways to polish Nixon's image, for example, contacting a student who in early March had sent a letter decrying the protesters' tactics.

Colson made suggestions too. On March 2 he advised Nixon to telephone singer Frank Sinatra, whom he saw as being disenchanted with the liberals. "Sinatra has the makings of another Al Capp," Colson wrote, referring to a prominent cartoonist who had spiraled from the Left to the Right. "Most of our Hollywood friends believe that Sinatra is the most influential celebrity in the country because if he goes, so go many other prominent figures, particularly new young stars."[8] Nixon made the call and later instructed aides to make Sinatra a present of a golf ball. The administration also approached the dairy industry with promises of milk price supports to solidify the backing of American farmers. Nixon mollified big business, too, ordering the Justice Department to drop antitrust suits against the corporate giant International Telephone and Telegraph. On March 25 Nixon met a group of college student government representatives to receive a resolution voted by the National Student Congress, which Colson had bragged some months earlier was "back" under administration "control."[9] Reminded by Colson that "poll data indicates that we do not stand well politically with the 18–20 year old vote" (hardly a surprise) and that "a better organized effort is necessary," Nixon met with Haldeman, Colson, and administration youth envoy Robert Finch for a strategizing session in his hideaway office at the Old Executive Office Building on April 7.[10] The sudden reappearance of Finch, a close adviser during and after the 1968 campaign but who had long been frozen out of the president's councils, is indicative of White House fears.

But the major elements of the Nixon effort were two: an attempt to minimize the impact of the veterans' march, on the one hand, and the creation of a counterweight in the form of labor supporters from the construction industry—"Hard Hats," in Nixon speak—on the other. The alliance with the Hard Hats had been a special project of Colson's, partly to offset growing disaffection with the war by American labor, and partly to project an image of mass public support. Labor backing had begun to disintegrate. At Colson's behest, Nixon massaged Hard Hat leaders with a phone call to Peter Brennan, president of the New York Building Trades Union, in early March. But the Hard Hats were souring too. Colson believed that this was due to cuts in federal payments for construction. The president admonished him to show statistics demonstrating the opposite. The White House hoped the Hard Hats would neutralize the protesters.

As veterans began their trek to Washington, the White House paid close attention. Colson and Nixon discussed the upcoming protests over the phone the evening before the crucial VVAW-Agnew meeting on the Capitol permits. Their conversation not only reviewed tactics they expected the vets to use, including "guerrilla theater," but also covered Colson initiatives from the creation of a group of *pro*-war veterans to talk of the Hard Hats. Colson reported back to Nixon the next day and again on April 16. They scheduled a White House meeting to discuss the Hard Hat strategy, for which Colson prepared by speaking to labor leaders. As for the vets, the White House coaxed a statement out of Alfred Chamie, national commander of the American Legion. Though not as strident as what Colson had hoped for, it deplored "another Washington demonstration, however altruistic may be the motives of the sponsoring organization."[11] On the seventeenth Nixon discussed Agnew's permit with J. Edgar Hoover, director of the FBI. Once the VVAW action began, focus shifted to new countermeasures. On April 20 Nixon and Colson resolved to charge that VVAW vets were phonies, not veterans at all, encouraging press coverage of that charge, and to get groups such as the American Legion and Veterans of Foreign Wars (VFW) to denounce the protest. Then, as VVAW did its thing, Colson actually met labor leader Brennan at the White House.

President Nixon had no intention of sticking around through the protests. On the afternoon of April 23, as the vets threw away their medals, he left to visit daughter Julie in Virginia Beach. After dinner Nixon went on to Camp David. But before leaving Washington the president held a lengthy discussion of the VVAW demonstration with aides. Then he placed no fewer than three telephone calls to Herbert R. Rainwater of the VFW, encouraging him to demand airtime on the television networks equal to that given to coverage of the VVAW protesters, so that Rainwater could defend Nixon's war policy. Then the president phoned Dean and ordered that he be kept up-to-date on the vets' activities. Dean ended up sending hourly situation reports.

Rainwater's statement would say, "I realize the remnants of uniform, the toy guns, and spilled red ink are colorful and considered newsworthy—but I question the value of this type of publicity to the American people."[12] Unknown to Rainwater, White House officials privately considered him a clown.

Meanwhile, the other big issue for the White House had already come to a head: the Vietnam veterans were in fact camping on The Mall, in defiance of court orders that were Nixon's responsibility to enforce. The administration had brought Army regulars to the capital and had plenty more security forces. What would it do?

■ ■ ■ All through the day on Sunday, April 18, veterans trickled into Washington. As darkness fell, around 900 vets had registered with organizers. The small turnout initially sparked much soul-searching. VVAW was not that well known, despite the full-page ad it had taken out in the *New York Times* and the one donated by *Playboy*. The group had demanded that participants bring proof of their military service, undoubtedly dissuading some who might have participated. Also, the spring had been a cold one. There were many possible explanations. Numbers gradually built: there were 1,100 by the next day, and ultimately 2,300 were counted. Historians of VVAW calculate that including those who came for only one or two days, several thousand veterans may have attended. Though this fell short of hopes, such concerns were swept away.

The drama began at Arlington Cemetery on April 19. The vets marched across Memorial Bridge to the cemetery shortly after sunrise. There were a few problems with rush-hour traffic. Then they were denied access. The veterans were accompanied by four Gold Star Mothers—women whose sons or husbands had died in Vietnam—including one whose boy was actually buried in Arlington. The National Park Service closed and chained the gates, unprecedented in Park Service history. VVAW national officer Al Hubbard used a megaphone to denounce "the insensitivity of the government and the military."[13] One frustrated veteran hurled a toy rifle at the gate. It shattered. Another threw a mess kit. Seeking out the ground at the base of the hill where the Tomb of the Unknown Soldier is located, the vets held their memorial service, presided over by the Reverend Jackson Day, an Army chaplain who had served in Vietnam. Then vets and the Gold Star Mothers laid two wreaths at the gate. Some wanted to storm the fence, but others backed them down, arguing that a fight at the cemetery would make them the bad guys. Among the voices of moderation were John Kerry and Scott Camil.

The marchers retraced their steps and, recrossing the Potomac River, stepped down The Mall in cadence, chanting, "Bring our brothers home!" Along the way they passed women of the Daughters of the American Revolution (DAR), which was holding its convention in Washington. "Son," one woman called out, "I don't think what you're doing is good for the troops."

"Lady, we *are* the troops," the veteran replied.[14]

Pointedly, President Nixon addressed the DAR convention but had nothing whatever to do with the antiwar veterans. The United States would stop the war, he said, when there was "a South Vietnam able to defend itself against communist aggression."[15]

Reaching the Capitol steps, the veterans rallied there. Four members of Congress addressed the crowd: liberal Republican Paul McCloskey and Democrat Don Edwards from California, and Democrat Bella Abzug and Republican Ogden R. Reid from New York. On behalf of the VVAW executive committee, veteran and organization founder Jan Barry presented sixteen demands for ending the Vietnam conflict. Afterward most vets returned to The Mall and established a campsite at the heart of this esplanade, close to Congress. Some began lobbying efforts that very afternoon. VVAW garnered tremendous media attention; notably, Walter Cronkite featured the veterans as his lead story on the widely watched *CBS Evening News.*

The VVAW campsite challenged the Nixon administration. The vets had sued the Department of the Interior to permit their marches and their camp. The previous Friday the Justice Department had sought a restraining order prohibiting a camp on The Mall, which was granted by Judge George L. Hart of the U.S. District Court. On Monday lawyers for VVAW appealed that order to the U.S. Court of Appeals for the District of Columbia. The veterans were being prevented from holding their encampment despite contrary precedent—the Poor People's March and the Boy Scouts of America had previously used the exact same area. The appeals court reversed Hart's order, effectively granting VVAW its camp permit. The administration immediately went to the Supreme Court to reinstate the restraining order, with Assistant Attorney General L. Patrick Gray certifying that the government stood ready to enforce it.

Solicitor General Erwin N. Griswold argued before the Supreme Court on April 21 that the VVAW encampment "would cause a serious problem to maintaining public order and could lead to substantial public health hazards with inevitable environmental pollution."[16] Thus the veterans were faced with the possibility of arrest simply for their presence on The Mall. A long and earnest debate ensued, and in a late-night vote, the vets decided to stay. The vote was pretty close, and a motion to make it unanimous carried easily. With them were sympathetic legislators, including Massachusetts senator

Edward Kennedy, New York congressman Ed Koch, and others, acting as a sort of human shield.[17] Visitors also included soldiers of the 3rd U.S. Infantry Regiment, the Old Guard, which mounts the honor guard at the Tomb of the Unknowns.

Relying on their military experience, the vets set up a security perimeter. As Air Force veteran Joe Urgo, a member of the national staff, stood his watch in the early-morning hours, some men with short-cropped hair approached and told him they were active-duty GIs from Fort Bragg.

"I'm one of the organizers of this," Urgo replied. "How do you boys like it?"

One of them answered, "You know, we're on alert to put you down."

"So what're you going to do?" the VVAW man asked.

"Don't worry," they assured Urgo, "the trucks will never roll. We put sugar in the gas tanks."[18]

The vets made their camp. The Park Police, which had put up an observation post to peer across The Mall, told VVAW that they would certainly not arrest anyone who was not sleeping, so the veterans tried to pull an all-nighter. Lots of coffee went down that night. Some vets did not make it, but no one was touched. The next morning the *Washington Daily News* headlined: "VETS OVERRULE SUPREME COURT."[19]

Much of that morning the Nixon White House frantically considered what to do about the defiant vets. Nixon finally ordered Mitchell not to use the police. As Haldeman recorded, "Our decision ended up to be that we just continue negotiating and try to negotiate the issue to death."[20] Vets demonstrated outside the Supreme Court, culminating in the only arrests of Dewey Canyon III—125 persons, including Barry Romo. But Mitchell had to ask that the injunction be lifted. Furious at the administration's failure to deliver on its promise of enforcement, Chief Justice Warren Burger sent the matter back to Judge Hart. He was angry, too, telling Justice Department lawyers, "This Court feels that one equal, coordinate branch of government, the Judiciary, has been dangerously and improperly used by another." The courts had been "degraded by this whole affair." Hart thundered, "If you did not wish to enforce that deadline, you should have come to this Court and had that injunction dissolved and removed."[21] The judge did precisely that. Nixon suffered an embarrassing defeat.

Amid the legal and political maneuvering, VVAW proceeded with its lobbying and demonstrations. Guerrilla theater, in which protesters played character roles to illustrate their concerns, figured prominently. A typical VVAW skit was a mock patrol randomly grabbing people off the street on suspicion of being enemy guerrillas. Teams of vets pulled off such skits all around Washington. Veteran Bill Crandell led one guerrilla theater team that played on the steps of the Capitol to great effect. Inside the building, veterans had varying success. Jan Barry was insulted by the congressman from his district. Texas vet Terry DuBose discovered that Senator John Tower would not even open the door to him. John Lindquist saw Wisconsin Democratic representative David R. Obey, who was against the war, and conservative Democrat Clement J. Zablocki, a hawk—an encounter that went down only half as badly as expected. In the hallway Lindquist, a former Marine who had driven trucks to Khe Sanh in supply convoys, witnessed an incident as strange as he had ever seen. Around the corner came General Leonard F. Chapman, the Marine Corps commandant, in full uniform on a Capitol Hill mission to perform the trick of testifying that the Corps had come in under budget and would be returning money to the U.S. Treasury. A vet challenged Chapman in the hearing room and promptly unclipped the Purple Heart from his fatigues, slapping it down on the table in front of the general. Chapman grimaced and fled down a side corridor.

On April 21, while the vets' lobbying was in full swing, Nixon called Colson from the Lincoln Sitting Room of the White House. The president wanted to know how Colson's meeting with the Hard Hats had gone. "What do they think of these, uh, these, uh, that crowd on The Mall down there?" he asked.

Colson laughed. He reported that the construction workers thought the vets were real bums and had asked, "How do you keep people like this off the streets?" However, the Hard Hats were not going to do anything overt.

Nixon agreed. "That's right. They ought, they shouldn't fight veterans."

Colson thought the Hard Hats were also partly dissuaded by the thought that the VVAWers actually *were* veterans, but then added, "Of course, we know they're not."

Nixon shot back, "A lot of 'em aren't, yeah."[22]

The lobbying efforts, guerrilla theater, a smaller return march to Arlington (which actually got into the cemetery), a spontaneous nighttime candlelight procession around the White House, and other VVAW actions impressed many. The White House countered, with press secretary Ron Ziegler quoting Nixon's claim that only a few of the protesters were real Vietnam veterans. The vets were ready for that one. When a wire service reporter went to the campsite to check, she would be shown a host of service records that proved the opposite. The one big mistake came from the VVAW's own organizer Al Hubbard, who had said on television that he was a former captain in the Air Force. Nixon's people looked up Hubbard's file and discovered he had only been a sergeant, then leaked this to broadcaster Lawrence Spivak. Hubbard had to acknowledge the fact. But this was the only case the White House could find to bolster Nixon's claim, and Hubbard was, in fact, a veteran.

Any embarrassment caused by the "phony veteran" problem was more than wiped out by the powerful statement John Kerry made before the Senate Foreign Relations Committee on April 22. There he posed the basic issue squarely:

In our opinion, and from our experience, there is nothing in South Vietnam which could happen that realistically threatens the United States of America. And to attempt to justify the loss of one American life in Vietnam, Cambodia, or Laos by linking such loss to the preservation of freedom, which those misfits supposedly abuse,[23] is to us the height of criminal hypocrisy, and it is that kind of hypocrisy which we feel has torn this country apart.

Kerry argued that the veterans had found Vietnam's conflict to be a civil war. Many Vietnamese saw no difference between communism and democracy, he said. "They only want to work in rice paddies without helicopters strafing them and bombs with napalm burning their villages." The VVAW spokesman decried the profligate U.S. use of firepower, calling it a war crime; the falsification of "body counts"; and the poor service provided by the Veterans Administration and its hospitals to returned veterans. "Where are the leaders of our country?" Kerry asked. The commanders had, in effect, deserted the troops. "How do you ask a man to be the last man to die in Vietnam? How do you ask a man to be the last man to die for a mistake?"[24]

The next day the veterans staged their medal giveback ceremony. Through Agnew, Nixon's people had contrived to have a wood and wire wall erected on the Capitol steps to prevent access. That backfired. Maine senator Edmund Muskie and others appeared and acknowledged the veterans' contributions. Muskie, expecting to be a presidential candidate in 1972, had taken up the antiwar banner. Denied entrance to the Capitol, the vets changed their plans. Instead of filling a body bag with medals, they stepped up to the wall, made individual statements, and threw their medals over it. One iconic photograph of the Vietnam war era came from this demonstration: angry veteran Rusty Staub hurling his medals full tilt. John Kerry tossed decoration ribbons and some medals given to him by vets who could not attend. Inquiries with the Capitol Police, historians of Congress, and the Capitol architect in the 1990s revealed that no one knows what happened to the medals. In any case, the ceremony proved as powerful as the Kerry testimony. The veterans left Washington, Bill Crandell recalls, feeling they had "moved the town."[25]

■ ■ ■ The vets may have been exhilarated, but they were not safe. Colson continued his dirty tricks. Back in New York, Hubbard would be arrested at another protest within a couple of weeks. Colson and Nixon chortled on May 5 when the aide reported Hubbard's arrest. Colson also leaked claims that Kerry had left The Mall and stayed in comfort at the Georgetown home of a Washington socialite, dining at fine restaurants. A Detroit reporter was given the information, and his article was then sent anonymously to hundreds of Movement figures, using plain envelopes. Not just top VVAW members were vulnerable. Upon his return to California, veteran Steve Miller was arrested almost immediately, not for protesting but because an FBI informant had planted drugs in his refrigerator.

When the vets came to Washington, the Vietnam war was a conflict that had been waged by American presidents on several fronts. One, in Southeast Asia, remained an affair of military proportions—soldiers on patrol, planes loosing bombs or ferrying troops, delicate alliances with the Saigon government. Another front, waged across conference tables and in back corridors, involved international diplomacy, from peace talks to appeals for help. The third front was at home, in America, where presidents struggled to retain the political upper hand for the war they wanted to conduct. Dewey Canyon III changed that. Henceforth there would be two *wars,* and the second of these the Nixon White House waged directly against Americans—veterans most prominently, but many others too. That represented a marked escalation of the political struggle over Vietnam.

The Laotian invasion and the vets' incursion on Washington did not start the new war. Harbingers of the shift had been in the air, and Lyndon Johnson had set the gears in motion. But Richard Nixon's frustration drove him to take more extreme measures, and the protest demonstrations sparked by Laos became the new war's biggest battle. Now the president went beyond political tactics, using the instruments of governmental power to strike directly at those Americans perceived as opposed to his policies.

Never had the veterans of America's legions fought their government over an issue of war and peace. Only once, amid the desperation of the Great Depression, had veterans marched on Washington—in June 1932—but then the issues had been benefits and bread and butter, not U.S. foreign policy. This was different. Never in the history of the United States had a government conducted political warfare against its own citizens. How had American politics come to this turn? Now there were opposing camps, each convinced that the future of the Republic depended on adopting the course it advocated, each determined to fight to the finish. How, indeed, had it come to this? The answers lie in the bitter roots of the Vietnam war.

1   A Splendid Little War

Long before there was a government in conflict with its people, there was a distant war in Asia that had nothing to do with Vietnam. That beginning was a nexus, a moment when nothing was determined and events might have taken many different directions. War in Southeast Asia did not amount to even a mote in Washington's eye. The story traces back to the height of the great global conflict called the "Good War," World War II, when Vietnam, Cambodia, and Laos, collectively known as French Indochina, were occupied by Japan. From President Franklin D. Roosevelt on down, Americans focused on defeating the totalitarians, Hitler's Germany and Imperial Japan. Vietnam figured at most tangentially. At one point in early 1945 the famous American aircraft carrier fleet, Task Force 38, entered the South China Sea to make air raids against Japanese naval and air forces in Indochina. The Office of Strategic Services, forerunner of the Central Intelligence Agency, ran an escape network in Indochina to rescue Allied airmen downed in southern China. And Allied intelligence services of the Southeast Asia Command (SEAC), including British and Free French operatives, worked there to link up with former French colonial officials and military men ousted by the Japanese. That was it. No armies crisscrossed Indochina; no battles took place—except between the French and Japanese or between the French and certain revolutionaries fighting for the independence of Vietnam. There lies the genesis of this conflict, which at first could be seen as a splendid little French war.

Roosevelt held the reins when America had its first opportunity to steer clear of what was to come. But that chance would be lost because of developments in the war, relations among the Allies, and FDR's own failing health. Roosevelt's instincts were sound. He foresaw the end of the old order of empires and colonies, of which Indochina had been one, and set the example even before the war by preparing to accept the independence of the Philippines, a U.S. territory since the Spanish-American War. Roosevelt also saw security interests in French Indochina: in a sense, the Pacific part of the world war had begun there, where weak colonial authorities had been unable to resist Japanese encroachments.

President Roosevelt championed a system of collective security based on a United Nations, envisioning UN trusteeship for Indochina. He spoke of that informally to British diplomats in 1942 and then openly at the inter-Allied conferences at Cairo and Tehran in late 1943. On the latter occasion Russian leader Josef Stalin remarked that the Allies ought not to expend blood and treasure to restore French colonial rule. Roosevelt expressed fierce agreement. After Tehran he told diplomats that he was laboring to prevent a French return.

Great Britain had the greatest colonial empire of all. It was the British, not the French, who were the hidden enemy and stumbling block. Sir Winston Churchill led the British government and committed himself to preserving the empire. Britain was also America's key ally. Though Churchill despised Charles de Gaulle and the Free French, he could hardly collaborate in dismantling the French empire while preserving Britain's. The Free French also made Churchill's choice easier, with a 1944 colonial conference in Brazzaville, Congo, where they proclaimed a liberalized empire christened the French Union. Local autonomy and a greater voice in French policy would replace tight control. After Brazzaville Churchill broadened his support, instructing his SEAC commander to accept increasing French participation.

FDR's policy aimed to marginalize France. His approach to Indochina should be seen primarily in that context. Although Roosevelt expressed sympathy for the Vietnamese, Laotians, and Cambodians who had lived under French rule, his fundamental view was only somewhat less patronizing than the colonials'. Churchill's opposition complicated FDR's task. Meanwhile, the war situation developed in a way that made French cooperation increasingly important. As the Allies invaded northwestern Europe at Normandy in June 1944, soon restoring a French government under de Gaulle, their military resources were stretched thin. By the end of that year the British were disbanding formations to strengthen others, while the United States was combing out its rear service units, air forces, and every available staff to put more troops on the ground. The reconstituted French army then became the largest untapped pool of Allied military manpower.

The campaign against Germany constituted only half the war. Looming ahead was the need to invade Japan. These decisions were made when the existence of the atomic bomb remained a closely held secret and those few who knew about it had no idea whether the weapon would work—long before any were dropped on Japan. The problem was to gather enough troops in the Far East for an invasion. In late 1944 the French government offered to contribute an Expeditionary Corps to the Pacific campaign. The French certainly anticipated that positioning forces in the Far East would provide them with the means to return to Indochina.

Roosevelt died of a cerebral hemorrhage on April 12, 1945. Some treat FDR's death as an opening for the French to reinsert themselves in Indochina. That is too simplistic. The anticolonial rhetoric had already weakened. European experts in the State Department, emphasizing the need to rehabilitate France, were asserting themselves. Roosevelt had been forced into a rearguard action—rather than pressing trusteeship for Indochina, he had been reduced to insisting that *no* immediate decision be made. The logic is inexorable: a serious Roosevelt anticolonial policy required preventing French military forces from appearing in the Far East. Instead, that force was accepted. The key decision involved the ships necessary to move French troops, and that decision would be made by an Allied board in January 1945. FDR could have blocked that action, but he did not. The troops began to sail from Marseilles in March, just as Japan overthrew the French administration in Indochina.[1]

■ ■ ■ The Japanese and Vietnamese set the stage for the first act. Increasingly beleaguered in the Pacific war, Japan worried about Allied moves on many fronts, Indochina among them. An Allied invasion there remained a possibility. If that happened, the French colonial forces were likely to join with the invaders. To forestall this, on March 9, 1945, the Japanese overthrew the colonial governor. In a short, sharp military campaign, the Japanese army either compelled surrender of the French colonial troops or drove them across the border into southern China. Next came the turn of the Vietnamese. The French administration operated in tandem with a Vietnamese monarchy (and Cambodian and Lao ones, too) that, formally, the French were merely protecting. For years, decades even, nationalist and then communist sentiment had grown in Indochina, fanned by colonial excesses. Since about the 1920s the growth of this movement had accelerated. The Indochinese Communist Party formed in 1929. There were abortive revolts in Vietnam in the 1930s. The French military and police repeatedly broke up nationalist plots until the Japanese swept into Indochina, after which the colonial security services were greatly hampered. The Japanese themselves followed a policy of encouraging Asian nationalisms as a counterweight to the European colonialists. For its part, the French administration made certain concessions to nationalists that it considered friendly in order to preserve control in the face of Japanese occupation. The net result was that World War II witnessed a huge shift in the political development of Indochina, Vietnam particularly.[2]

The nationalists took advantage of the French colonial programs, from Boy Scouts to bike races, to assemble a core of modernist activists. Of all the nationalists, the Indochinese Communist Party was the best prepared for this. Leaders such as Ho Chi Minh and Vo Nguyen Giap moved back and forth across the Chinese border, established bases in caves in the northern Vietnamese mountains, and began to build networks throughout the country. In 1941 they created a united front group, the Vietminh (*Viet Nam Doc Lap Dong Minh Hoi*), disguising communist dominance and emphasizing the struggle for independence (*doc lap*) from France. Vietminh cadres spread the message while leaders sought outside support, initially from Nationalist China. The Chinese never quite made up their minds about the Vietminh, sometimes helping them, sometimes imprisoning Ho and other figures. But the Vietminh were successful enough to set up a standing committee at a village quite close to the French colonial capital, Hanoi. French troops began military operations aimed at the Vietminh as early as 1943 but were unable to eliminate them. On December 22, 1944, under Vo Nguyen Giap, the Vietminh formed the Vietnam People's Army, an armed force that grew slowly but gradually cleared whole districts in the mountains. By the time of the Japanese coup the Vietminh had a true base area.

At this point American operatives from the Office of Strategic Services (OSS) arrived on the scene. The Americans had several purposes. They sought data on the Japanese and on Indochina itself, established contacts with the French that might be of use to them, and set up rescue networks for Allied pilots. The OSS ran one agent network out of China. The first OSS officer to land in the country arrived in late March 1945 at Dien Bien Phu, joining a French column that would retreat to China. A full team followed in April, but it was driven across the border after clashes with the Japanese. From the moment of the Japanese coup, Vietnamese, not French, sources offered the best potential for accomplishing OSS aims in Indochina.

By then Ho Chi Minh had direct contact with OSS officers in China, who actually introduced him to the U.S. China commander, General Claire Chennault, at a meeting in Kunming. Ho trekked with another OSS team into northern Vietnam a few weeks later. From then on Americans resided with the Vietminh, trained a few as radio operators, and provided some weapons. The Americans and Vietnamese were friendly even though OSS officers such as Charles Fenn and Rene Dufourneaux knew that Ho was, in fact, a communist. At one point the Vietnamese leader became sick, and treatment by OSS medic Paul Hoagland saved his life. Hoagland belonged to an OSS "Deer" Mission under Major Allison Thomas that arrived in mid-July. For the Vietminh, OSS ties enabled them to claim a relationship with the powerful United States, an important political advantage.[3]

As the days passed, Japanese power waned visibly. News of the atomic bombs dropped on Japan galvanized the Vietminh. On August 12 they determined to stage a general uprising in Vietnam. Ho, Giap, Truong Chinh, and other leaders led columns toward Hanoi. Local committees organized peasants throughout the country. On August 16 Ho Chi Minh declared himself president of a provisional government of an independent Vietnam, which became the Democratic Republic of Vietnam (DRV). Responding to the patriotic mood, the French satrap Emperor Bao Dai abdicated in favor of Ho's government. Vietminh columns actually arrived at Hanoi on August 19, and cadres quickly created the administrative structures of government. This became Vietnam's August Revolution.[4] Neither that summer's famine nor the political jockeying of other nationalist groups shook Vietminh dominance. Any French return would involve dealings with the DRV government, not simply a reinforcement of the French colonial structure.

■ ■ ■ Japan's surrender on August 15 made it necessary to disarm Japanese garrisons throughout China, Southeast Asia, and the Pacific. The Allies had a plan for that. With regard to Indochina, the scheme provided for temporary occupation by Nationalist Chinese in the north and British forces in the south. This arrangement turned out to have important political implications. It set off a chain of events that led from the August Revolution to a Vietnamese war of independence against France.

In the north the Nationalist Chinese were not averse to cooperating with the DRV. Chinese commanders saw an opportunity to enrich themselves. The Vietminh were glad to oblige, using Chinese entrepreneurs to obtain weapons and medicines for the Vietnam People's Army (the Japanese also gave the Vietminh some weapons rather than handing them over to Chinese enemies). The Chinese occupation effectively gave Ho Chi Minh half a year to consolidate control. During part of this time the OSS teams were still present, and U.S. officers Captain Archimedes L. A. Patti and General Phillip Gallagher attended the official ceremonies marking the foundation of the DRV. Again, the Americans helped confer a certain patina of international knowledge, if not recognition, on Ho Chi Minh's government.

Events in the south developed very differently. Disarming the Japanese there fell to Lord Mountbatten's SEAC. Mountbatten had a host of responsibilities in an area that encompassed a significant portion of the surface of the globe. He had to preserve the British position in India, complete the Burma campaign, and reoccupy Malaya—and those were merely London's imperial interests. SEAC also had to insert forces into Indonesia (then the Dutch East Indies) as well as Indochina.[5] Mountbatten could spare only a few troops for the former French colony—specifically, General Douglas D. Gracey's 20th Indian Division, which began arriving at Saigon by air in early September. Stepping off his plane at Saigon's Tan Son Nhut airport, Gracey spoke only to the Japanese and hardly acknowledged the presence of a Vietminh delegation on hand to greet him. That foreshadowed what was to come.

General Gracey's problems were a microcosm of the SEAC's. He began with just a couple of thousand troops; the bulk of his division, following by sea, was not expected for several weeks. Riots rent the city days before Gracey's Gurkha soldiers arrived. Merely establishing order in Saigon posed a formidable obstacle, and he had to do the same for all of southern Indochina. Gracey adopted expedients. Instead of disarming 4,000 Japanese troops, for weeks he used them to impose security under Allied command. A token French unit, a company of commandos, had landed with Gracey, and the general used them as the nucleus for another force, which was greatly expanded after September 12, when the British liberated and rearmed some 1,400 French colonial troops whom the Japanese had imprisoned. French soldiers and colonists, freed from the Japanese yoke, went on a rampage. Vietnamese protests were met with force. Instead of treating with the Vietnamese, General Gracey treated them as lawbreakers, a situation exacerbated when the Frenchman who had been designated temporary high commissioner issued a proclamation that foresaw a new governor-general and an administration little changed from that of the prewar colony.[6]

The Vietminh were not as well established in the southern part of Vietnam, called Cochin China or *Nambo*. They did have weapons, though, mostly of British origin and possibly obtained from intercepted supply drops to the underground network SEAC had earlier tried to create.[7] But there were other political groups, including a significant one of communist Trotskyites, competing for popular support. The latter were especially strong in Saigon. The rioting of September 1945 gave General Gracey a reason to suppress them. The French certainly appreciated that, but so did the Vietminh—their principal competition was thereby neutralized. Gracey declared martial law on September 21. The following night French troops carried out a coup de force, occupying city hall, the police and Sureté headquarters, the treasury, and other key buildings, raising the French flag. The Vietnamese responded with a general strike, and in one neighborhood they seized several hundred French hostages, killing half of them.

As in the north, there was an OSS team in Saigon, led by Lieutenant Colonel A. Peter Dewey. The OSS contingent had flown in from Rangoon even before the first of Gracey's soldiers arrived, and it quickly ran into trouble with the general, who rejected any political role for the OSS. He viewed the OSS as useful for securing Allied prisoners and gathering evidence for war crimes trials. From both Saigon and Hanoi the OSS warned Washington that the occupiers were laying the groundwork for reassertion of the French colonial regime. Colonel Dewey offered himself as intermediary to the Vietminh in Saigon, but both the British and French snubbed him, and Gracey ordered him to leave. Dewey's last report warned, "Cochinchina is burning, the French and British are finished here, and we ought to clear out of Southeast Asia."[8] On September 26, while passing a roadblock between Tan Son Nhut and American headquarters, Dewey was killed by Vietnamese, who no longer bothered distinguishing Americans from other whites. Dewey became the first U.S. combat death of the war. His name is *not* recorded on the wall of the Vietnam Veterans Memorial.

The French Expeditionary Corps that President Roosevelt had failed to keep out of the Far East began arriving in Vietnam just days later. The battleship *Richelieu* docked at Vung Tau carrying major units, while a smaller detachment reached Saigon aboard the vessel *Triomphant*. Paris had appointed a commander in chief, Marshal Philippe Leclerc, who landed at Tan Son Nhut on October 5, the day after the first of his troops. From then on, Gracey's mission became one of handing over the secure zone he had created. On October 9 Paris and London agreed the Expeditionary Corps would take over from SEAC, and the British recognized full French sovereignty. French troops established themselves, then began pushing into the rest of southern Vietnam, fighting Vietminh whenever they encountered them. Some Vietminh bands were already estimated to be as large as a thousand fighters.

■ ■ ■ America's second chance to avoid the Indochina war was squandered by President Harry S. Truman, FDR's vice president and successor. OSS reports squarely posed the alternatives: the United States could be for colonialism or against it. But those reports never reached Truman's desk, and he had little use for that agency anyway, abolishing it in September 1945. America's diplomats were as aware of the possibilities as the spooks were, and the State Department split along lines that could have been anticipated: The Far Eastern Bureau under Assistant Secretary John Carter Vincent, along with Abbot Low Moffat's Southeast Asia desk, agreed with Dewey. The European Bureau, as it had in FDR's time, favored sustaining French aspirations and helping to rebuild that nation's self-respect and grandeur. James C. Dunn expressed the Europeanist view within weeks of Truman's arrival in the Oval Office when he wrote to the secretary of state, "We have no right to dictate to France nor take away her territory."[9]

President Truman was a Europeanist himself and retained fond memories of France from his service there during World War I. In addition, it was primarily in Europe that Truman faced his thorniest challenge: what to do about Russia. The wartime alliance had begun to fray, with the Soviets assuming a dominant position in Eastern Europe and making trouble over the occupation of defeated Germany. Soviet leader Josef Stalin worried Truman, and their July 1945 summit meeting at Potsdam only reinforced his concern. Some officials and opinion makers were already pressing for the United States to adopt the goal of stopping the spread of communism, personified by Stalin and led by Moscow. Already the Cold War had begun to cast its shadow.

Charles de Gaulle was not above taking advantage of those trends: France had a strong communist party, and a powerful socialist one as well. De Gaulle told American diplomats that his nation might go communist if America obstructed it. Although Truman faced down de Gaulle over some things—French border claims in Italy and occupation demands for Germany, being two examples—he had reasons not to look too closely at the

French empire, including Indochina. At Potsdam the Allies ratified the Japanese surrender arrangements that put SEAC in charge of southern Indochina, clearing the way for a French return. That October, as Marshal Leclerc deployed his troops around Saigon, Truman declared: "[The] U.S. has no thought of opposing the reestablishment of French control in Indochina and no official statement by [the] U.S. [government] has questioned even by implication French sovereignty over Indochina."[10]

There were some qualifiers, to be sure. Washington assumed that French claims to have the allegiance of the Indochinese would be borne out, and it also carefully stated that there was *no* U.S. policy to *assist* France in regaining control—but there it was. American ships would not carry French troops to Indochina, but Paris could rely on the British, plus its own resources, for that. Within months there were 65,000 French soldiers in Indochina.

France had lain supine at the end of the war, and Washington had possessed unimagined leverage over Paris. As the leader of a superpower, Truman essentially traded U.S. concerns regarding Indochina for French support on European, especially German, policy. That was his choice, but it is legitimately open to question: How much was French support in Germany worth in 1945 (as opposed to a few years later)? And how far could France have afforded to deviate from U.S. policy at that time?[11] In addition, Truman sought no analysis of what impact the Franco-Vietnamese conflict, whose beginnings were already visible, might have on the United States.

Meanwhile, in Indochina, the French had to enter the north to complete their return. That meant dealing with Ho Chi Minh's DRV. To their credit, the French negotiated an agreement, signed on March 6, 1946, by Ho Chi Minh for the DRV and Jean Sainteny for France. That agreement, simultaneous with Chinese withdrawal from the north, explicitly affirmed that "the French Government recognizes the Vietnamese Republic as a Free State having its own Parliament, its own Army and its own Finances." Vietnam would be part of the Indochinese Federation and the French Union, and north and south would be reunited according to "decisions taken by the populations consulted by referendum." Diplomatic relations, future law, and French interests would be determined at talks held following the French return.[12] Leclerc's troops landed after the signing of the accord and entered Hanoi on March 18.

Thus the Franco-Vietnamese agreement of March 1946 needed to be "perfected" by further negotiations. It turned out that perfecting the details of Vietnamese autonomy, independence, sovereignty, or whatever would be the great enterprise of the last phase of French Indochina. It would not be accomplished in 1946. A combination of officials determined not to yield, military officers anxious to "get" the Vietminh, and Vietnamese suspicions of French motives derailed every initiative. French motives *were* suspect. Even when dealing with regimes the French themselves had created, Paris refused to perfect Vietnamese independence right through 1953–1954, the final months of the Franco-Vietnamese war. This was long after insisting that the conflict was really about the Cold War, not the Vietnamese revolution. Three successive sets of talks failed. Then an incident occurred at Haiphong, where shelling by French warships killed thousands of Vietnamese. After that, the die had been cast. On December 19, 1946, Vietminh attacked the French in Hanoi and elsewhere, igniting the war that continued until Dien Bien Phu.

Ho Chi Minh and the Vietnamese gave Truman a further opportunity to mediate the conflict in a way that could have avoided war. Beginning in February 1946 Ho sent Truman a series of letters appealing for support of Indochinese independence. The detailed record of what happened to these letters seems to have been lost, but Truman never replied. After the Haiphong incident the State Department instructed its consul in Hanoi to "KEEP IN MIND HO'S CLEAR RECORD AS AGENT INTERNATIONAL COMMUNISM" and took Paris's side, emphasizing responsibilities to keep the peace while ignoring Vietnamese fury at the French use of force.[13] After the battle of Hanoi the DRV contrived by several means to put its record of Paris's intransigence and its claims of French provocation in U.S. hands. The government in Washington did more than fail to reply. Top American officials explicitly told the French that the administration had no objection to their actions. Thus evaporated a third opportunity to avoid war.

The weight of blame lies in Paris, not Washington. French high commissioner Georges Thierry d'Argenlieu condemned agreements with the DRV as a new Munich and led efforts to avoid concessions. De Gaulle went along. When his administration gave way to a new government under a socialist only days before the outbreak of hostilities, a key message from Ho Chi Minh to Leon Blum, the new prime minister, was inexplicably delayed in transit at d'Argenlieu's headquarters, long enough for fighting to begin. Blum made efforts to restore peace, but as would happen repeatedly, France proved unwilling to make the concessions that might have made a difference. The advocates of war were in the driver's seat. As a prominent French historian concludes, "Hesitating between firmness and concession, continuing a Gaullist policy of French presence which failed to take into account either the realities of the post-war context or the strength of nationalist sentiment, and unable to secure obedience from its military and civil representatives, the Republic became embroiled in a hopeless war."[14]

Aside from the dynamism and strength of the Vietnamese revolution, a major reason for the hopelessness of the French war lay in France's weakness. The first couple of military budgets for Indochina sufficed to show Paris that it lacked the money for this war. The French looked to the United States for a solution: reframing Indochina as a piece of the Cold War might induce Washington to pick up the tab. Paris proved quite adept at doing that, yet from the standpoint of French national interest, that success was a trap. It locked France into a war that it could not win and could not solve, despite a growing toll in blood and gold, so long as it refused to make the necessary political accommodation. This error was not born of ignorance. The progression would be foreseen: Marshal Leclerc, who retired after his Indochina command, returned in early 1947 to survey the possibilities. The Leclerc report warned that half a million troops—an impossible number—would be needed for France to prosecute the war. The "capital problem" was political, he noted, "a question of coming to terms with an awakening xenophobic nationalism." Leclerc also declared, "Anti-communism will be a useless tool as long as the problem of nationalism remains unsolved."[15] Paris did not listen. Indochina became the "Dirty War."

Susceptibility to French importuning led Washington down the road to American involvement. The United States began with some skepticism, at least taking on board the Vietnamese narrative of descent into chaos. In January 1947 the French were told that U.S. arms sales would be permitted for metropolitan France but not for Indochina. But a few months later American officials in Paris and Indochina were told, "We cannot conceive set-backs to long-range interests [of] France which would not also be setbacks to our own."[16] Meanwhile, Washington became consumed with its conflict with Moscow. A July 1948 State Department analysis of Ho Chi Minh admitted that the United States "has no evidence of direct link between Ho and Moscow but assumes it exists."[17]

The net result was that Washington felt constrained to confer favors on the French in an effort to demonstrate goodwill. Thus the United States declared as "war surplus"—and gave to the French in Indochina—enough airborne equipment to sustain French paratroops for several years. Similarly, in 1949 the United States gave Paris several naval vessels that French crews sailed directly to Indochina to join the fleet there. Truman thus sacrificed leverage and bears additional responsibility in that he failed to think through these issues, effectively putting the United States in a position to be manipulated.

By May 1949 Paris had contrived an alternative of sorts. In its drive to erect some Vietnamese political entity to compete with the Vietminh, the French negotiated with the former emperor Bao Dai and reached an agreement that recognized Vietnamese independence "within the French Union." It accorded autonomy to a State of Vietnam, with terms to be agreed on later. The United States established a formal military aid program that did not include Indochina but had a Far Eastern component that could potentially help France offset the cost of Indochina. In December, as France finalized accords to govern the State of Vietnam, policy reviews by Truman's National Security Council looked ahead to groupings of anticommunist states in East Asia. Once the accords were ratified, Truman promptly recognized the State of Vietnam on February 8, 1950, and three months later provided aid to the associated states and to the French.

Thus by 1950 President Truman had implemented decisions that brought the United States into war in Vietnam, coming full circle from the anticolonial policy of World War II to one supporting a French neocolonial state. This is a good place to spend a moment on theories of the U.S. engagement in Indochina, of which there are many. Given the record of choices made by presidents, at the most basic level the United States simply marched into a quagmire, as Arthur M. Schlesinger Jr. famously argued. Really, though, that is descriptive, not analytical. The question is why, and explanations vary. Some rely on models of presidential decision making or bureaucratic politics. On a higher theoretical plane are those who trace the cause to some form of imperialism, whether economic (seeking to secure Indochinese resources) or political-military (extending a fabric of U.S. control over this region of East Asia). Then there is the argument that the United States had assumed a stance of opposing revolutionary movements of any form, wherever encountered. American rhetoric and official pronouncements lent great weight to Cold War explanations, and these have predominated. An independent thread of analysis also exists that the Vietnamese revolution was a given, that it occurred without regard to U.S. actions and was going to proceed no matter what choices American presidents made. For present purposes it is sufficient to postulate that presidents had Cold War motives, but the Vietnamese revolution was indeed foreordained—had there not been a Cold War, there would still have been revolution in Vietnam.[18]

American decisions from then on only increased aid, not changing course but deepening U.S. involvement. The onset of the Korean war undoubtedly made the U.S. course irreversible. National Security Council policy reviews confirmed this approach several times between 1950 and 1952. In slightly more than one year Indochina received its first $100 million; thereafter aid quickly rose to $100 million *per* year plus more for the associated states, but still not enough for the French. In mid-1952, embarking on an initiative to create a force of light infantry for the Vietnamese national army, Paris asked Washington to bankroll this effort.

When Dwight D. Eisenhower became president in January 1953, the United States was already paying 40 percent of the cost of the French war. By then France had tired of the conflict. Political opposition to the war had grown steadily since the late 1940s, when dockworkers at Marseilles refused to load ships bound for Indochina. There had been a mutiny among French army draftees who feared being sent to Indochina, and the use of draftees in the war had been prohibited by the National Assembly. Opinion polls showed substantial opposition. The fighting seemed deadlocked except that the Vietminh had gradually become stronger, fielding regular forces to match the Expeditionary Corps, which suffered major defeats in 1950. At that time the People's Republic of China, the Chinese state created after the communist victory in the civil war there, began to assist the DRV. The Soviet Union followed suit.

By 1953 France was about ready to abandon its Vietnam war. The cabinet of Joseph Laniel entered office that summer, and it instructed the French commander in chief to stabilize the situation as a basis for seeking a negotiated settlement. That commander, General Henri Navarre, planned to accomplish this by means of a series of offensives. France asked the United States for extra aid to finance the Navarre Plan. The Vietminh countered, sending troops into the Annamite Mountains toward Laos, a maneuver that had particularly irritated the French when first tried the previous spring. Sure enough, General Navarre tried to block them, dropping airborne troops into the upland valley of Dien Bien Phu. Navarre created an "air-land base" at Dien Bien Phu with, as he saw it, the capability to stop the Vietminh. Ho Chi Minh, Vo Nguyen Giap, and their Chinese advisers realized it might be possible to trap a large contingent of the Expeditionary Corps far away from it bases. Navarre thought he could use Dien Bien Phu as an anvil on which to hammer the Vietminh into submission. These moves set the stage for the battle that ended the French war.

Diplomacy had moved off dead center. A conference at Berlin in January 1954 gathered the foreign ministers of the World War II alliance for the first time since the onset of the Cold War. Their decision to hold another international conference at Geneva became the most important result. That meeting would consider Far Eastern issues, including Indochina and Korea. The Geneva conference was scheduled to begin in late April. By then the siege of Dien Bien Phu would be in full swing. Geneva and Dien Bien Phu, aside from their other effects, carried U.S. involvement in the Vietnam conflict to a whole new level.

For Washington, the decade between 1944 and the eve of the Geneva conference witnessed an important evolution in the status of Vietnam issues. Franklin D. Roosevelt had had the luxury of making up his mind in a climate where little weight, either military *or* political, attached to Vietnam or to Indochina as a whole. FDR had been pushed by alliance relations, but politically he had had a free hand. That situation changed under Harry S. Truman. In particular, the fall of Nationalist China to communist revolutionaries wedged open the seam of American foreign policy. Opponents accused Truman of "losing" China. The ferocious Cold War competition set up a Manichean debate, leading Truman to extensive internal "loyalty" programs and other measures that nevertheless failed to protect against McCarthyist charges of being "soft" on communism. The advent of the Korean war added to the entire complex of issues. Truman no longer had a free hand, and Dwight D. Eisenhower's policy space narrowed further.

Eisenhower might have had the opportunity to turn America away from conflict in Vietnam, except that such a choice was illusory for him, at least before Dien Bien Phu. This president believed in the Cold War arguments that had progressively constrained Truman, and he resorted to rhetoric that envisioned "rolling back" the Iron Curtain. Eisenhower's diaries contain ruminations that decry French colonialism in Indochina, and his administration's declaratory policy was to encourage the French to accord full independence to the Indochinese states. But in every instance in which Washington had to choose between cutting support to disingenuous French governments that had not fulfilled their promises and backing the French war, Eisenhower did the latter. He would end the Korean war but extend the effort to contain China, another Cold War stake. Vietnam became a piece on that chessboard, a country on China's periphery whose revolutionaries were seen as making common cause with Beijing. Thus Eisenhower signed on to fund the Navarre Plan, and he stood at the center of what followed. Only a crisis would afford the chance to break free of the stranglehold. Dien Bien Phu brought about that very possibility. What happened there starkly illustrates how America entered the tunnel that the Vietnam conflict became.

March–July 1954: Dien Bien Phu, Geneva, and the Harnessing of American Power

Late in the afternoon of March 13, 1954, Vietminh artillery guns, brought up through the mountain country by dint of stupendous effort, emplaced at Dien Bien Phu at the price of backbreaking manual labor, opened fire on the French fortress. Its defenders, confident the Vietminh would not have artillery, or if they did that it would never survive French counterfire, were stunned. Dien Bien Phu's airstrip, instantly threatened, soon became altogether useless. That night one of the entrenched camp's fortified complexes, held by a full battalion of the Foreign Legion, fell to the revolutionaries. A couple of nights later a second strongpoint fell too. General Navarre sent paratroops to reinforce Dien Bien Phu, but it was evident the Vietminh posed a real threat to the entrenched camp. The French would need to withstand a prolonged siege for Navarre to win the battle. Paris waited less than a week before appealing to Washington for help.

General Paul Ely led this mission to the Americans. Chief of the General Staff of National Defense, the French equivalent of the American Joint Chiefs of Staff (JCS), Ely could answer U.S. questions at the highest level. He landed at New York on March 20 on a commercial airline flight, to be immediately taken aboard a military aircraft and flown to Washington. There he met Paris's delegate to the North Atlantic Treaty Organization (NATO) Standing Council, General Jean Valluy, who had presided over the beginning of the French war during his time as Indochina commander. Valluy stood alongside Ely's American opposite number, Admiral Arthur W. Radford, chairman of the JCS. The military leaders began talks that very night at Radford's quarters in Fort Myers.

Paris knew, even if the Americans did not, that France had reached the end of its tether. But, jealous of their prerogatives, the French were not giving anything away. President Eisenhower needed to convince them that he stood foursquare behind Paris while somehow simultaneously crafting relationships with the Indochinese states the French had created. Suspicious of military aid independently given to the associated states, particularly the Vietnamese, the French erected obstacles wherever possible. But now they were fully extended and could not finance the Vietnamese army—expanding rapidly—without the United States. The French could not even meet their own basic staffing needs and had prevailed on the Americans to lend them mechanics to maintain French combat aircraft in Indochina.

Meanwhile, Eisenhower needed French help on a key European alliance issue. Ambitious force goals set by NATO to meet the threat of Soviet military power could not be achieved without rearming Germany, a measure that aroused dark fears in Paris. French concerns were assuaged by the formula for a so-called European Defense Community, and the treaty creating it was before the French National Assembly for ratification. Once again U.S. diplomacy in Europe posed problems for Southeast Asia policy. The president faced a Gordian knot in this situation.

Politics in the United States had also begun to foreclose options. The controversy over who had "lost" China, which Republicans had emphasized in the 1952 campaign, easily extended to Indochina. Eisenhower, along with John Foster Dulles, his secretary of state, were certainly determined to avoid a repeat. Pundits frequently drew parallels to the Munich crisis before World War II, and any mention of the "Munich analogy" automatically brought certain precepts to mind. The argument was that by attempting a peaceful resolution and making concessions to an aggressive power, the West had invited war rather than avoided it. The Munich analogy posited force as preferable to concession in resolving disputes with an ideological enemy.

In the heat of battle the French took full advantage of every argument. General Ely's agenda included asking for more bombers and transport planes, parachutes for air supply, extended tours for the U.S. mechanics already working with the French, and other technical aid. The French also wanted guarantees in the event of Chinese intervention. Admiral Radford took that last item and broadened it, suggesting that American aircraft could hit the Vietminh around Dien Bien Phu and neutralize them. This proposal came to be called Operation Vulture.

An American fleet cruised off Indochina. It included two aircraft carriers whose planes could contribute mightily to any attack. Later, when tactical nuclear weapons briefly figured in U.S. planning, the carriers became even more necessary since they carried these munitions. The U.S. Air Force also expected to use its heavy B-29 bombers. Under Radford's formula, once the French government made a formal request for intervention, these forces could launch a series of strikes on Vietminh positions. Other members of the Joint Chiefs opposed any attack, at least until they rendered written opinions. Then the Air Force submitted a qualified "yes," and the Navy advocated posturing in such a way as to signal the capabilities of U.S. forces.[1]

These events in the spring of 1954 remain poorly understood even five decades later. Most accounts follow the template laid down a few months afterward by reporter Chalmers Roberts, who published an article titled "The Day We Didn't Go to War."[2] Roberts understood that President Eisenhower stood ready to intervene, provided the action came as part of a joint international effort and that the French finally "perfected" the independence of the State of Vietnam. Roberts credits top congressional leaders, meeting with Secretary Dulles and Admiral Radford on April 3, with posing these conditions in a way that created insurmountable problems for the White House. Much subsequent scholarship has centered on identifying Washington's failed approaches to various allies or the obstacles that supposedly dissuaded Eisenhower.[3]

In this view, Eisenhower was willing to be led, and either Radford or Dulles seized the initiative. Dulles gave a speech on March 29 calling for "united action," the clarion call for an international effort, and approached the other powers. Eisenhower briefly considered the intervention, but his doubts began to increase from early April on. The congressional briefing marked a spike in the president's misgivings, and true reluctance set in after a meeting with the JCS on April 5, where the Army objected that bombing would not be sufficient and that ground forces would have to be sent as well. The French delivered their formal request that day, but with the project already dead. As Ike put it in his 1963 memoir, "there was nothing in these preconditions or in this congressional viewpoint with which I could disagree; my judgment entirely coincided with theirs."[4] In interviews in 1964 and 1967 Eisenhower asserted his total opposition to intervention.

But this version of events cannot account for the ferocity of efforts to implement the scheme. First, Eisenhower was never the passive actor portrayed here. He reworked the draft of the "united action" speech himself and inserted wording that strengthened the text.[5] On April 1 the president convened an off-the-record meeting in the Oval Office, something Ike did only when great events were afoot, and he hinted to outsiders that action in Indochina was forthcoming. He held another Oval Office meeting to *prepare* for the congressional briefing. Dulles, who phoned the president soon after that meeting, *did not* interpret its result as scotching the plan, telling Eisenhower, "on the whole it went pretty well."[6] In fact, in preparing his own account of these events, Roberts questioned numerous legislators and notes, "Their replies made clear that Congress would, in the end, have done what Eisenhower asked, provided he had asked for it forcefully and explained the facts and their relation to the national interest."[7]

Meanwhile, President Eisenhower sent a letter to British prime minister Sir Winston Churchill to appeal the British rejection of intervention. Again, he reviewed the text of that letter and, in addition to changing the State Department's prose, he suggested inserting references to Churchill's own pre–World War II experiences, as reflected in the British leader's account of those years, now used to allude to Dien Bien Phu.

Eisenhower's diaries contain jottings that show his awareness of how the colonialist origin of the Franco-Vietnamese war had hampered the French, both in combat and in their efforts to erect a state that represented a credible noncommunist alternative to the Vietminh. But in the summer of 1953, as Ike considered whether to fund the Navarre Plan, Republican senator Barry Goldwater offered an amendment to the military aid bill that would have made funding contingent on France's granting full independence to Vietnam and the other associated states. Eisenhower *opposed* the Goldwater amendment and defeated it. Now, faced with Dien Bien Phu, Eisenhower's insights on colonialism were reflected palely, if at all, in actual U.S. policy. Instead, Eisenhower used the Munich analogy, explicitly, in his letter to Churchill: "If I may refer again to history; we failed to halt Hirohito, Mussolini and Hitler by not acting in unity and in time. That marked the beginning of many years of stark tragedy and desperate peril. May it not be that our nations have learned something from that lesson?"[8]

Despite British opposition—and that of many U.S. military leaders—on April 6 the president ordered officials to focus on obtaining London's backing plus creating a regional alliance to sustain united action. At a news conference on April 7 Eisenhower posed a stark warning, postulating what became the infamous "Domino Theory." Referring to the impact the fall of French Indochina would have, Eisenhower said, "You have a row of dominos, you knock over the first one, and what will happen to the last one is the certainty that it will go over very quickly."[9] A reporter gave the president a chance to make a forthright declaration rejecting colonialism, but Ike refused it. Instead he responded, "I can't say that the associated states want independence in the same sense that the United States is independent. I do not know what they want." His answer undercut the proposition that anticolonialism was anything more than a rhetorical pillar for U.S. policy.[10]

During the next several weeks, in separate trips to Europe, both Dulles and Radford did their best to enlist the British. In a notorious episode, Dulles apparently offered to "lend" the French tactical nuclear weapons that might neutralize the Vietminh. Eisenhower had discussed such an action.[11] On April 15 Vice President Richard M. Nixon made a speech widely interpreted as a trial balloon for U.S. intervention, saying that it might be time to seize the moment and act to save Asia. Eisenhower subsequently telephoned Nixon and congratulated him. The day Nixon spoke, the secretary of defense ordered the military to prepare necessary plans for action and have them ready by mid-May. Following the Nixon speech, pollsters for the first time measured public opinion on intervention in Indochina, only to find that 68 percent of Americans opposed it, adding public disapproval to political doubts and diplomatic obstacles. Yet the planning continued long past the expiration of the occasion for action, since Dien Bien Phu itself fell on May 7. At the beginning of June Eisenhower still spoke of unilateral U.S. intervention if the Chinese joined the conflict.[12] These were not the actions of a president unalterably opposed to entering the war.[13]

What accounts for Eisenhower's pursuit of these schemes, despite all obstacles? It is now clear that much more important than congressional doubts was Washington's desire to avoid a negotiated settlement of the Franco-Vietnamese war at an international conference at Geneva. As a result of the declassification of documents in many countries, it is possible to conclude that Geneva had been seen as a way to settle the Indochina issue. Of course the French were looking for a way out. The Vietminh were tired too, and Vietnamese documents show that Ho Chi Minh and his comrades both anticipated an offer at Geneva and were prepared to settle for a temporary division of their country. Chinese documents show the expectation of a truce based on such a division. Both the Vietnamese and the Chinese anticipated roughly the specific demarcation line that ultimately emerged. British documents also show that America's closest ally was prepared to accept this outcome.[14]

Historian George Herring divined the basic structure of this situation long ago, writing in *America's Longest War* that the Eisenhower administration "probably hoped there would be no agreement, and during the first five weeks of the conference it kept alive the prospect of military intervention."[15] This can now be affirmed from a host of evidence. Those who argue that U.S. actions at the time of Dien Bien Phu were aimed at creating a regional alliance by *posturing* for intervention either do not deal with this evidence or discount it.[16] Such accounts also typically exaggerate Dulles's freedom of action. Regional alliance represented a consolation prize, not the primary goal. The real alternatives in the spring of 1954 were U.S. escalation versus acquiescence in a negotiated settlement. The role of alliance lay in buttressing the U.S. position behind and around Indochina after that settlement.

But escalation was not really possible. *All* U.S. intervention schemes at the time of Dien Bien Phu presupposed that France would continue to fight. The fall of the entrenched camp brought the immediate collapse of the Laniel government (and parliamentary defeat of the European Defense Community treaty). Pierre Mendes-France, Paris's next prime minister, promised to achieve an agreement or resign. He even set a deadline. Defeated at Dien Bien Phu, the French naturally had a poor negotiating position, equivalent to playing a hand of cards with the two of clubs and the three of diamonds, according to the outgoing foreign minister.[17] The French were finished. As for the United States, Army chief of staff General Matthew B. Ridgway made it abundantly clear to Eisenhower that available forces could not substitute for the French, and Vietnam lacked the port facilities and infrastructure to sustain the required American forces.[18] No alternative to a Geneva settlement actually existed.

The best Eisenhower could manage was a public relations stunt. He awarded the Presidential Medal of Freedom, America's highest civilian award, to Genevieve de Galard Taraube, a French nurse stranded at the entrenched camp when her plane could not take off. She had become known as the "Angel of Dien Bien Phu" for her ministrations to the wounded. Permitted to leave in a casualty evacuation at the end of the battle, Galard came to America. In July she was treated to a ticker-tape parade in New York City attended by a quarter million people, and she addressed a joint session of Congress, the first foreign citizen to do so since the Marquis de Lafayette.

■ ■ ■ The Dien Bien Phu crisis took place at a time when American presidents still had the ability to chart an independent course in Vietnam. Eisenhower could have walked away from the Navarre Plan. He did not. In the spring of 1954 Ike could have supported a negotiated settlement. He did not do that either. Until intervention became an issue, there had been no significant public opinion on Indochina. Indeed, by pressing the actions he did, President Eisenhower contributed mightily to the creation of American opinion on Southeast Asia. Apart from anything else, it can be argued that U.S. presidents would have retained greater freedom of choice for a longer time had there never been a scheme to intervene in Indochina at this time.

In addition, the Geneva settlement afforded the United States the opportunity for a graceful exit from the morass. Although the United States had opened relations with the states of Indochina, its primary commitment had been to the French. Why did Washington keep its shoulder to the wheel? Economic reasons have to be judged secondary. The emergent Vietnam, a minor producer of a few raw materials, would lack economic importance until the discovery of offshore oil deposits decades later. Nor were the Indochinese nations lucrative markets for American products. The United States sought no bases, and the Joint Chiefs of Staff had argued that Indochina was devoid of important strategic objectives, derailing another possible rationale. On the geostrategic plane, President Eisenhower had some sympathy for the Domino Theory, but this served primarily as justification, not cause. After Geneva there arose the chance to take over from the French and "do it right," which perhaps had a certain psychological importance, but a minor one. The anticommunism of the State of Vietnam fit with the U.S. international stance—again, a relatively minor consideration. The clearest way in which supporting Vietnam could serve U.S. objectives lay in its potential contribution to isolating communist China. Eisenhower's commitment to combating China—a Cold War consideration—was the inevitable element in policy, support for South Vietnam the contingent one. Once Dwight D. Eisenhower made that choice, reversing it became increasingly difficult for him and virtually impossible for his successors. Vietnam acquired inevitability.

Many who would play crucial roles in the Vietnam war were present at this creation and drew lessons from it. That included every man who would inhabit the Oval Office. John F. Kennedy was the junior senator from Massachusetts. Lyndon B. Johnson, the Senate minority leader, was the senior senator from Texas. The vice president, of course, was Richard M. Nixon. And Gerald R. Ford had represented Michigan's Fifth District in the House of Representatives since 1948. It is important to ask what Dien Bien Phu and Geneva meant to them. Decisions those presidents made cannot be properly understood without appreciating their positions, the lessons they drew, or the commitments they made during this crisis.

Kennedy takes pride of place, since he would be Eisenhower's immediate successor. By 1954 John Fitzgerald Kennedy at least knew something about Vietnam. As a fresh-faced, recently minted congressman, Kennedy had visited Indochina several years earlier, at the height of France's effort to energize the nationalists without endowing them with much in the way of sovereignty. JFK traveled the land for several weeks, picking up hints of Vietnamese frustration plus a bill of particulars from U.S. economic aid chief Edmund Gullion, whom Marshal DeLattre, the French commander at the time, regarded as a virtual enemy. Kennedy was impressed that even in Saigon, where the French claimed to have broken Vietminh power, the sound of gunfire punctuated the night. His brother Bobby believed the trip affected JFK greatly.

Upon his return to the States, Kennedy made a couple of speeches on Indochina, ones that staked out a sophisticated position on nationalism, recognized the French position as colonialist, and openly marked the pro-French regime as a puppet government. Kennedy spoke out against imposing Western values and institutions and feared that Americans were being identified too closely with the French. In 1952 Supreme Court Justice William O. Douglas introduced Kennedy and Senator Mike Mansfield of Montana, who had an abiding interest in Asia, to a fifty-one-year-old Vietnamese nationalist, Ngo Dinh Diem. JFK identified with Diem, who was Catholic like himself, and saw him as representative of those who had not been tainted by ties to the French. A year later, during the fight over Goldwater's aid-for-independence condition on U.S. support, Kennedy, now a senator, offered amendments to attract Democratic backing for the initiative. When JFK feared that Eisenhower was maneuvering for war, he gave another speech extolling the nationalist alternative. Kennedy stood ready to lend weight to such an initiative. One appeared soon enough.

Lyndon Baines Johnson has been misrepresented in the standard version of the 1954 crisis. Because that narrative exaggerates congressional objections to U.S. intervention and ignores the tradition of a bipartisan foreign policy that held sway in 1954, the questions Johnson raised are interpreted as efforts to stymie the plan. But LBJ was minority leader in the Senate and expected to work *with* the Eisenhower team in securing bipartisan support for whatever the president chose to do. Johnson asked Dulles about the allies who had been lined up for U.S. intervention—a question LBJ knew would be asked by senators, and one that had been vital in the Korean war, when Johnson himself had raised it during the Truman-MacArthur controversy over extending that conflict to China. Immediately after the Dulles-Radford briefing in April 1954, Senator Johnson took the temperature of his Democratic colleagues on intervention, and he reported those results to the White House. Equally important is what LBJ *did not* say: he *never* spoke out against the intervention scheme. In fact, the day after the April briefing, LBJ used the fact of the Indochina war, which some feared might affect world tin supplies, as a reason to allocate federal funds to keep open a tin smelter in Texas—one of his few public speeches referring to the crisis.

Lyndon Johnson's position was not the one historians often attribute to him. Less publicly but quite openly, Johnson's newsletters to his Texas constituents consistently *supported* U.S. intervention, repeatedly making the case for it. The April 3 meeting was reflected in LBJ's newsletter of the fifteenth, which advised that in Indochina "we are at the crossroads" and spoke of the need for "hard decisions—the kind that will tax our determination and willpower." He warned that the fall of Indochina "would be disastrous to all our plans in Asia"—language very close to what Richard Nixon used in his trial balloon speech the same day. On the ally question—Johnson's supposed objection to intervention—he noted, "Shall we continue without clear assurances that others will join us? Or shall we withdraw altogether and fall back upon the concept of Fortress America?" LBJ's answer was implicit. He even raised the specter of falling dominos, writing, "ultimately, we might be driven out of the Pacific itself!" The punctuation was Johnson's.[19]

This is but one example. Johnson's newsletters went out twice a month. From that day through the conclusion of the Geneva conference, LBJ's newsletters repeatedly framed intervention from the perspective of the need to act. Even after the fall of Dien Bien Phu, which the senator conceded was a major setback, he thundered, "*we are ready at any time to cooperate in the preservation of our country.*" Again, the emphasis was LBJ's. His stance is all the more significant because *Johnson was bucking his constituency.* A survey of letters written by Texas voters reveals that the overwhelming majority of LBJ's constituents rejected intervention. Yet even after Dien Bien Phu, Johnson was ready to go for broke.

As vice president, Richard Nixon actually sat in Eisenhower's councils. He favored intervention and did what he could to bring it about. Except for Admiral Radford, Nixon was the only one of Eisenhower's advisers who had actually been to Indochina, visiting during the early implementation of the Navarre Plan. He and Eisenhower privately discussed giving the French atomic bombs to save Dien Bien Phu, and Nixon complained in his diary when Ike's determination seemed to flag. The lessons Nixon drew from the crisis concerned how difficult it was to get the U.S. military to take decisive action, the value of generating uncertainty in the mind of an adversary, and the potential of relying on naval and air forces. These too would be reflected in due course in Nixon's own administration.[20]

Gerald R. Ford left the fewest tracks. Congress never voted or held a floor debate on Dien Bien Phu, and Ford had little opportunity to be heard. But ten years later, at the time of the Gulf of Tonkin crisis—a manufactured rather than a real one—Ford was quick to demand that the United States take command, not merely advise the Saigon government. His aggressive response suggests that Ford saw the 1954 crisis as a missed opportunity.[21]

■ ■ ■ Aside from those who would be president, many other people destined for important roles in America's Vietnam tragedy observed Dien Bien Phu from their own vantage points, a number of them quite closely. Ngo Dinh Diem had spent more than two years in America, mostly at Maryknoll seminaries in Lakewood, New Jersey, and Yonkers, New York. He left in the spring of 1953 for a cloister in Belgium but commuted frequently to Paris, where he saw events unfold from the French side, close to the Vietnamese expatriate community and to Emperor Bao Dai at Cannes. Dean Rusk, Truman's assistant secretary of state for Far Eastern affairs, headed a foundation, the Rockefeller Brothers Fund. Sugar magnate and occasional diplomat Ellsworth Bunker watched from the humanitarian perspective of the American Red Cross, which he headed and which might face a relief mission in Indochina.

Many key field commanders of the American war had front-row seats. William C. Westmoreland, then a brigadier general, was secretary to General Ridgway's staff, whose intervention studies had so effectively torpedoed Eisenhower's schemes. Also there was Major General James M. Gavin, who came away with a healthy skepticism. Frederick C. Weyand, who would be Army chief of staff when the American war ended, served as military assistant to the secretary of the Army, whose memos to Pentagon chiefs solidly backed Ridgway. General Maxwell D. Taylor headed the U.S. Eighth Army in Korea, which would have furnished the bulk of forces for any move in Indochina. Bruce Palmer, a lieutenant colonel in Europe, had just completed a tour as aide to General Alfred Gruenther, to whom he remained close and who corresponded from Paris with another good friend—Dwight D. Eisenhower. Ulysses S. Grant Sharp, a Navy captain, was senior operations staffer for the Pacific Fleet, controlling the naval forces that would have had a primary role in Operation Vulture.

Others inhabited the world of the military war colleges, all of which closely monitored U.S. strategy. They included Army great Creighton V. Abrams and Marine officer Robert E. Cushman Jr., who would become national security adviser to Vice President Nixon. Way down the line, Dien Bien Phu affected even Daniel Ellsberg, then a junior officer in training to lead a Marine platoon. His drill sergeant told him they had better clean their rifles, as they could expect to deploy to Indochina very soon.

The first important rift among Americans over Vietnam developed not when the veterans marched on Washington but when a president and his senior commanders clashed at the time of Dien Bien Phu. The schemes of 1954 marked the onset of differences over the desirable versus the possible within Washington's inner sanctum. General Ridgway and those who sided with him pointed to a lack of capability for the sweeping actions others wanted. Eisenhower, whose policy was to reduce conventional military power under his "New Look" strategy, had helped create those shortfalls. But the president nevertheless signaled his determination to call the shots—he effectively fired Ridgway a year later by refusing to extend the general's term as Army chief of staff.[22] With the Geneva conference the political-military cleavage became muted, but it was not resolved. Once the conflict escalated, these differences returned to help shape the American war.

■ ■ ■ Geneva resulted in a pair of agreements. One, directly between the French and the Vietminh, set a cease-fire; provided for a "Provisional Military Demarcation Line" plus a demilitarized zone, roughly across the seventeenth parallel of latitude; created two "regroupment zones," one each in North and South Vietnam; and laid down strictures prohibiting the introduction of foreign troops or bases, mandating a French withdrawal from North Vietnam and an exchange of prisoners, plus creating an International Commission for Supervision and Control to monitor those provisions. The document expected but did not detail an election to reunify Vietnam. The second piece of the framework was a final declaration by most of the participants—a consensus document not formally signed or voted on—that recognized the agreement and stipulated "general elections will be held in July 1956, under the supervision of an international commission," with arrangements to be made by consultations between "the competent representative authorities" of the two regroupment zones in North and South Vietnam.[23]

Several points require comment. First is the fact that the agreements provided for an election to reunite Vietnam under a single government. Second—an element that would be seized on in subsequent years to claim the legitimacy of continued warfare—the main territorial provisions were contained in the cease-fire agreement between the French and Vietminh military, not in the final declaration among the nation-states. Third, the promise of elections existed in a declaration that lacked the force of an international treaty. These arguments are weakened by the fact that the cease-fire document had been the product of official French and Vietnamese military negotiators duly delegated by their respective governments, thus indeed endowing it with international status. Also, although the final declaration contained the major provisions for an election, the existence of that arrangement had been explicitly recognized by language in the cease-fire agreement.

Equally important, nowhere did Geneva create "nations" in North and South Vietnam. Rather, the entities were specifically created as "regroupment zones," and national status was explicitly *denied* them. They were to be reunited by a political process and *then* become a nation. Most legal arguments Washington adduced to justify its war would be founded on an assertion that South Vietnam was a nation-state with full sovereign rights. This was simply not true. Rather than belabor that point, it is better to note that once the Vietnam war became controversial, its shaky legal basis furnished a ready objection for those who protested it.

The third pillar in justifying the war was the regional alliance called the Southeast Asia Treaty Organization (SEATO). This too existed because of Dien Bien Phu—it was the result of the Eisenhower-Dulles push for united action. In the heat of crisis there had been no possibility of lining up allies, but over a longer time and without pressure for intervention, Dulles succeeded in cobbling together a league of sorts. But SEATO had little in common with the NATO alliance on which it was modeled. It had no standing forces other than staff committees, and the treaty, signed at Manila in late 1954, contained no obligation to take action beyond considering appeals for help. Moreover, the Geneva agreements prohibited the two Vietnams from belonging to alliances, so South Vietnam was not a member. In a device too clever by half, Dulles arranged for the South, run by a government in Saigon, to be a SEATO "protocol" state. That turned out to be a completely ambiguous position affording even less standing to demand collective action. Justifications for war based on alleged SEATO obligations remained hollow ones.

Washington could not abide the Geneva agreements. Its reticence became one reason the conference's final declaration did not take the form of a treaty. Dulles attended the opening of the meeting but then withdrew, leaving U.S. participation to subordinates. He used his presence in Europe to make one last push for intervention and then left, never to return. Chester L. Cooper, a Central Intelligence Agency officer and one of about 200 on the U.S. delegation, notes, "It was no secret, even within the rank and file of the American delegation, that President Eisenhower and his secretary of state had little taste for what was in store."[24] But as much as Washington wished to forestall a communist victory in the Far East, it had no possibility of doing so. Once the negotiations came up with the formula of a demarcation line, the subsequent, protracted talks all centered on where to put it. American negotiators had some influence on provisions for an international control commission, but that was about it.

The Eisenhower-Dulles response to diplomatic progress was to disassociate the United States from the resulting agreement. When the Geneva negotiations were finalized, Undersecretary of State Walter Bedell Smith made a unilateral statement in behalf of the United States. That declaration took note of the agreements, promised that the United States would not threaten or use force to "disturb" them, asserted support for the unity of divided states through "free elections, supervised by the United Nations," backed the State of Vietnam, and said that the United States would view any violation "as seriously threatening international peace and security."[25]

This face-saving device of 1954, like other aspects of this whole situation, would come back to bite. Recognizing the Geneva agreements conceded their international legal significance. The solemn vow not to disturb their implementation would be broken by U.S. subversion of reunification elections, as will be seen. And American use of force in Southeast Asia in the 1960s constituted the very sort of violation the Eisenhower administration had publicly renounced. Contrary to later apologists, the United States did indeed make promises at Geneva that it then broke, and its declaration did not nullify the agreements or justify war. Worse, legal arguments for war that were based on Geneva put the United States in a position of relying on agreements that Washington had abstained from and had been the first to breach. The attempted evasion became more grist for the mill of controversy.

Also disassociating itself from the Geneva agreements was the State of Vietnam. Only at this point—the very nadir of their military fortunes—did the French finally "perfect" the Vietnamese political entity soon known as South Vietnam. By treaty, Paris recognized the State of Vietnam as fully independent and sovereign on May 29; another, coupled treaty a few days later associated the State of Vietnam with the French Union. In fact, however, South Vietnam did not gain sovereignty. For one thing, France had previously recognized another state—the Democratic Republic of Vietnam—occupying the same territory. In addition, these treaties were only initialed; they were never signed or ratified by either the Republic of France or the State of Vietnam. As legal instruments they were worthless. South Vietnam was not a country.

Meanwhile, Emperor Bao Dai dismissed his government's cabinet after Dien Bien Phu and sought a more credible nationalist, appointing Ngo Dinh Diem the new prime minister. Bao Dai met Diem at his villa in Cannes on June 18, and the latter arrived in Saigon on the twenty-sixth. From the beginning Diem tried to act as if his state possessed the legal status it lacked, starting with forging an independent policy for Geneva. Diem's foreign minister rejected the creation of zones but presented a full position only on July 19, when the agreements had already assumed final form. His statements at the last session of the conference solemnly protested key aspects and the fact that Saigon's views had not been incorporated; he finished by asserting that his government "reserves for itself complete liberty of action."[26] Diem denounced the agreements in similar terms the day after the Geneva conference ended.[27]

Dwight D. Eisenhower's actions during the year that followed Dien Bien Phu leave little doubt that he felt intense guilt in the wake of the collapse of his intervention schemes. The crisis had the effect of harnessing American power in the service of a nascent South Vietnamese state. It also pitted the United States against France in a competition for influence in the new Saigon. The spring and summer of 1954 proved crucial to the subsequent American experience in Vietnam.

The Dien Bien Phu crisis and its aftermath also brought into play most of the characters and factors that later operated in the Southeast Asian conflict. The legal framework of Geneva and the sunset of French control; the alliance structure, such as it was; the American commitment to action; the beginnings of cleavage between U.S. political and military leaders; and the preconditioning of the individuals who would serve as president of the United States throughout the war—all were the products of Dien Bien Phu. The issues would play out over years of agony, and some ecstasy, starting right in Saigon.

2   Many Roads to Quagmire (1954–1960)

In the aftermath of Geneva the scene shifted to Saigon. This period proved crucial in structuring the parameters of the American war. These events have not attracted a great deal of attention, but they remain key. Basic records from the Eisenhower administration were not available until the mid-1980s, and vital documents remained classified until the late 1990s. These lay bare motivations, goals, and secret machinations. The events themselves were quite plain. Ngo Dinh Diem preoccupied himself with consolidating power, with reunification posing an obvious threat to him. President Eisenhower threw the weight of the United States behind Diem and abandoned the conditions for support that he himself set. The end result would be the United States complicit with South Vietnam in open violation of the Geneva agreements, without leverage, and committed to a Saigon whose leader recognized no need for any course different from the one he pursued. Events unfolded with increasing inevitability.

Meanwhile, developments in the United States during this era created social and political conditions that assumed increasing importance as Vietnam moved toward the center of American policy a decade later. These conditions had nothing to do with Vietnam, the war, or national security, but they created a style of expression, a form of activity, and a propensity to direct political action that would affect American leaders as much as traditional politics, adding a second constraint on presidential action. Dwight D. Eisenhower presided over this evolution, both in Vietnam and at home, and created the foundation for what came after. It is not possible to understand why Vietnam turned out the way it did without knowing this.

■ ■ ■ All these events lay in the future when Ngo Dinh Diem returned to Saigon. Standing on the tarmac at Tan Son Nhut air base observing Diem's arrival, U.S. Air Force Colonel Edward G. Lansdale decided Diem would need help. On assignment with the Central Intelligence Agency (CIA), Lansdale had supervised U.S. nation-building efforts in the Philippines in the early 1950s, and now he had been sent to Vietnam with a special CIA unit to exploit conditions arising from the French war and the Geneva agreements. The colonel fashioned suggestions on everything from land reform to political action, and with the ambassador's permission, he took a State Department officer as an interpreter and went to see Diem. Lansdale found the prime minister writing at a desk in Doc Lap (Independence) Palace, as Diem had renamed the emperor's palace in Saigon. The brash colonel, a former advertising executive, went right up and introduced himself, striking up a conversation focused on his proposed reforms. Soon Lansdale became a virtual daily presence in Diem's office.

That Colonel Lansdale's talk of reform reflected Washington policy was hardly accidental. President Eisenhower had waited only a few weeks after Geneva to reorient the U.S. approach, which dominated discussions at several meetings of his National Security Council (NSC) and would be formalized in the paper NSC-5429/2, "U.S. Policies Toward Post-Geneva Vietnam." Under this new policy, the United States would complete the creation of the SEATO alliance and help Diem's government broaden its base with economic and political reforms. The policy also envisioned what amounted to a coup d'état, with Diem electing an assembly and promulgating a constitution—actions that would require the Saigon leader to terminate Bao Dai's State of Vietnam. Success here would transform what had been known during the French war as the "Bao Dai solution" into what boosters would soon be calling the "Diem experiment."

Acknowledging the fact that the Saigon regime was a French dependency, NSC-5429 anticipated encouraging France to grant total independence, working to "disassociate" the French from levers of control, and cooperating with them militarily only as necessary to create South Vietnamese military forces capable of providing internal security. But the policy also recognized the continuing presence of the French Expeditionary Corps as essential to Saigon's security.[1]

Policy debates in Washington reveal the continuing rift between diplomats and the military over America's direction. There were major differences over the size of the South Vietnamese armed forces the United States should support, their purpose, the creation of an American training program, and the extent to which the United States ought to cooperate with France in this enterprise. Absent a strong Saigon government, the JCS thought it "hopeless" to initiate military training; they also differed with Secretary Dulles on whether the South Vietnamese army should be oriented to conventional warfare or counterinsurgency.[2]

The dispute over military aid pointed right back to the issue of Saigon political reforms. This necessity—soon a constant refrain in American formulas for progress in Vietnam—was squarely posed at the outset, within weeks of Geneva. That U.S. envoys could not induce Vietnamese rulers to move on this issue says volumes about Washington's real leverage in Saigon. Eisenhower, viewing this situation in its original circumstances, was about to set a pattern that endured for two decades.

President Eisenhower would be acutely aware of conditions in Saigon. Ambassador Donald R. Heath had spent years as minister of a U.S. legation under French proconsuls; he was supportive of the Vietnamese but not blind. He also had several good observers on staff, all of them able to see the machinations in the South Vietnamese capital. The French postured to preserve their privileges, plotting with the South Vietnamese military to obstruct Diem. Vietnamese nationalists outside Diem's circle angled for power. Plots bubbled in every café along Tu Do, the fashionable Saigon avenue that had been the Rue Catinat in colonial days. The American embassy reported all this in exhaustive detail, along with speculations on which Vietnamese would be suitable in a broadened Diem government.

Ike did not pay all that much attention. He permitted himself to be diverted by the post-Geneva evacuations from North Vietnam, which Washington quickly began to view as an opportunity to score propaganda points by inducing the Vietnamese to "vote with their feet" by leaving the soon-to-be-communist North. The U.S. military had had a contingency plan for evacuating Tonkin since 1952, and it was dusted off at the time of Dien Bien Phu. In fact, news of the fall of the entrenched camp reached the JCS in Washington as Admiral Radford and his colleagues were discussing this evacuation plan. A week after Geneva the United States was asked to donate thousands of large tents for the refugees, and on August 5 Diem formally requested U.S. help to move the refugees. The first American ship docked in North Vietnam on August 10.

A numbers game ensued, with the aim being to generate as many refugees as possible. A key task of Lansdale's CIA mission, in fact, would be to maximize this flow by scaring the hell out of Vietnamese in the North. There were some successes. A majority of the people in the Catholic provinces of Phat Diem and Bui Chu left, fearful that the Vietminh would not permit them to practice their religion. On August 22 Eisenhower jumped into the fray with a press release declaring, "Free Vietnam is a country with ample land resources for the resettlement of almost any number of Vietnamese who desire to flee from Communist domination."[3]

Operation Passage to Freedom has entered the lore of Vietnam as an American initiative and an exodus of Vietnamese civilians, with figures of 1 million or 2 million refugees bandied about. Eisenhower gave it every possible resource, reviewing progress at the NSC on October 22. Several months later, as the effort petered out, the responsible U.S. naval commander noted that the "predicted great influx of refugees have failed to materialize."[4] The real number who went south—still large—stood at 625,000 as of February 1955 according to a U.S. embassy summary, but they were not all civilians, and they were not all carried by the United States. French planes and ships took somewhere between one-third and one-half the evacuees, another 50,000 walked, and British vessels transported several tens of thousands. The overall numbers included about 200,000 French or Vietnamese military personnel, 125,000 military dependents, 15,000 to 25,000 Nung tribesmen who had been French auxiliary troops, several thousand former employees of the French administration, their dependents, 25,000 to 40,000 French civilians, and about 45,000 Chinese. Based on these figures, more than 60 percent were people who had no choice. They were not voting with their feet at all.

The evacuees arrived in a land torn by differences. Prime Minister Diem had quickly appointed family members, including his brother Ngo Dinh Nhu, to vital positions. Though styled a counselor, Nhu swiftly began to exert power far beyond his position, whispering in Diem's ear. Lansdale's relationship with Diem, close as it was, paled next to Nhu's. Diem permitted his ministers little leeway, including those for defense and foreign affairs. By the fall of 1954, many already saw a need to restructure the government to include a wider spectrum of Vietnamese politicians. Diem's basic problem was that, as a latecomer on the scene, he lacked any substantial following or indeed any political party. In more than one meeting with Ambassador Heath, Diem promised reforms, but he made no appointments.

Now Eisenhower took things in hand. The day after the NSC had reviewed Operation Passage to Freedom, Eisenhower sent a letter to Diem, informing the prime minister that he was instructing his diplomats to confer with the Vietnamese and examine "how an intelligent program of American aid given directly to your Government can serve to assist Viet-Nam in its present hour of trial." Eisenhower wanted assurances on the use of such aid and went on to specify that "the Government of the United States expects that this aid will be met by performance on the part of the Government of Viet-Nam in undertaking needed reforms."[5] Eisenhower's letter became the basis of American programs. Direct military assistance would be added in January 1955, and shortly thereafter Saigon asked the United States to assume full responsibility for training and equipping the Vietnam National Army (VNA). Not long after his October letter, Eisenhower selected General J. Lawton ("Lightning Joe") Collins, an Army friend and wartime colleague, as his personal representative to South Vietnam—a sort of super-ambassador. Collins knew the French high commissioner, General Paul Ely, and his relationship with the president would command Diem's respect. The next six months became critical to subsequent American involvement.

"If He Failed, Then That Would Be That"

Before leaving for Saigon, General Collins attended an extensive series of briefings. He knew a little of the background—he had been Army chief of staff when Harry Truman first began U.S. military aid—but Collins had been out of the game for several years. He met with Eisenhower, with John Foster Dulles, and with the CIA. In his talk with the CIA on November 2, 1954, clandestine service chief Frank G. Wisner advised

Collins to work closely with Lansdale, remarking that the CIA operative had "been successful in establishing close contacts with both factions, and . . . exploiting these contacts to the fullest extent."[6]

Indeed, Edward Geary Lansdale had just demonstrated his effectiveness. General Nguyen Van Hinh, the chief of staff and most senior Vietnamese officer in the French-trained VNA, was opposed to Diem. Hinh was close to Bao Dai and reliant on the French security services; he acted as their instrument in trying to unseat Diem. Inquiries as to his willingness to resign elicited Hinh's comment that he might fire the prime minister instead. One plot bruited about Saigon was Hinh's—a coup against Prime Minister Diem. Lansdale knew all about it. General Hinh was not certain of the loyalties of his VNA regulars, so he relied on the Vietnamese political-religious sects. These sects were a significant factor in Vietnam then, a collection of syncretistic religious groups (the Cao Dai and Hoa Hao) or political factions (the Binh Xuyen, whom many considered criminals or pirates). All had been armed and paid by the French. Bao Dai had even made a Binh Xuyen officer chief of the Surete. Now the CIA moved to detach these sects from the plot. There are indications of CIA relations with the sects as early as 1952, and those channels were exploited. Lansdale delivered cash for payments that French intelligence had fallen behind on, and he bought off one key faction with a bribe. The United States got the French to give up their support for the sects as of January 1955. Lansdale invited General Hinh and other officers to take a trip to observe counterinsurgency successes in the Philippines. Hinh refused but his deputies went, leaving him without key operatives. Diem then demanded that Bao Dai fire Hinh. The general left and rejoined the French air force.[7]

Collins and Lansdale had a very uncomfortable time together, starting with Collins's first staff meeting. There, by his own account, Lansdale contradicted the president's personal representative, although Collins denied this, asserting that he would never have tolerated such insubordination. The CIA officer thought little of Collins, finding him stupid and rigid and minimally receptive to Lansdale's schemes. But Eisenhower did not suffer fools and had great confidence in Collins, who retained Lansdale when he could have expelled him and listened when he could have ignored him. Collin's papers reveal that he read almost daily reports from Lansdale and others, and he paid attention. Lansdale's commentaries were noticeably more upbeat than most of the others. Nevertheless by early 1955—in less than two months—Collins had come to doubt Diem's viability. These concerns were muted in his initial report to the president, which stated that any Saigon leader would face challenges and that Diem had both good and bad points, but they soon emerged in stark relief.[8]

Meanwhile, Diem, far from broadening his base, worked hard to neutralize opponents, starting with the sects. Once the CIA had driven a wedge between French spooks and the sects, Diem capitalized. When the French services cut off the sects' funding, Diem offered to "integrate" them into the Vietnamese army. This would have meant the end of private armies and thus was never a real choice. But Diem combined that surface policy with secret payoffs to those willing to support him, using an unvouchered CIA fund of 600,000 piasters a month that he controlled. He tried to buy off the Cao Dai and Hoa Hao so as to focus on the Binh Xuyen. This liberal spending became apparent in February when Diem privately asked Collins to loan him another 5 million piasters from U.S. embassy money. Diem got it, and Lansdale served as a conduit. But Diem's maneuver fell flat. The major leaders of the sects forged a common front and demanded reforms and the end of government "dictatorship."

Hoa Hao leaders privately asked the U.S. embassy how Washington might respond to the overthrow of Ngo Dinh Diem. American diplomats discouraged them. Collins also warned Bao Dai against collusion with the sects and tried to ensure that the French would keep their hands off the situation. Lansdale was his instrument there, too.

Meanwhile, Diem made concessions to the VNA to secure its loyalty and ordered plans to crush the sects. It seems the Americans were involved—analyses of the difficulties and advantages of moving against the sects are contained in documents written in both English and French. One undated document, in a typeface common to papers prepared in Lansdale's office, contains a commentary, a draft operations order, and a plan aimed at the Binh Xuyen. The prospective troop list included Diem's personal guard, two paratroop battalions, three Nung light battalions, ten infantry battalions, and two of artillery. When fighting actually broke out later, most of these units, coincidentally or not, would participate.[9]

There is a question of where the United States stood amid all this plotting. Collins felt increasingly uncomfortable with Diem's machinations and frustrated with the predilection for plotting as opposed to broadening Diem's political base. Collins's intelligence adviser (James Cooley, *not* Lansdale) told him, reasonably enough, that the sects would gradually weaken, whereupon Diem could prevail. Patience was all that was needed. Fighting would signal a hard line from the Saigon leader that would complicate nation building in South Vietnam. It is highly unlikely that Collins authorized any coup planning, but the documents are there.

An indication of how the battle lines were drawn on the American side came late in February when Secretary Dulles made his sole visit to Vietnam, returning from a SEATO meeting. The secretary had little time for Collins. Just a week earlier, Foster Dulles's brother, CIA director Allen W. Dulles, had sent an emissary to Saigon with complete knowledge of the agency's covert plans and full decision powers. The CIA could hardly avoid this maelstrom. The available evidence suggests the CIA—and both Dulles brothers—sided with Lansdale, not Eisenhower's personal representative. Political tension erupted into crisis when Diem refused to renew the Binh Xuyen's gambling license for their casino in Cholon. Collins and Ely counseled Diem to be patient. Instead he dismissed the Binh Xuyen police chief. On March 21 the sects countered with a joint ultimatum, supported even by those sect leaders suborned by the CIA and Diem. Lansdale told Diem that Lightning Joe had confronted the waverers to ask why they had professed loyalty but signed the demands. One told Lansdale directly that Diem had not kept his promises.

Prime Minister Diem now ordered up fresh plans to smash the sects, drafted by a young loyalist colonel named Duong Van Minh. Diem handed the draft to Lansdale, and the CIA operative gave it to an American officer for review, telling Saigon's leader he would respond soon. Diem, meanwhile, tried to drive a new wedge between the factions he had bought and the others. Emperor Bao Dai sent messages to both Diem and the sects, appealing for confidence-building measures. Diem strengthened his palace guards, joking to Lansdale that the Binh Xuyen had mortars trained on them at that very moment. On March 26 Diem signaled his intention to push for a climax, telling Lansdale that he would issue orders bringing the police under his direct control throughout Saigon, dissolving the Binh Xuyen army. In Washington, Allen Dulles sent a CIA man to brief his brother. Diem's police prefect tried to take over, only to be barred by the Binh Xuyen. He summoned help. A company of the VNA 6th Airborne Battalion responded, leading to a confrontation. This was defused when the Binh Xuyen vacated the police station, saying they were heeding Bao Dai's appeal. Lansdale warned Diem that he had done nothing to neutralize the Cao Dai or Hoa Hao. In Washington on March 28, Secretary Dulles convened officials to review the situation. Allen Dulles's assistant Richard M. Bissell Jr. represented the CIA.

The sects' united front met just a few hours later. The Cao Dai sent the emperor a message asking him to fire Prime Minister Diem, while the Hoa Hao produced a statement demanding Diem's resignation. The sects agreed to hold a mass demonstration in Saigon to back the demand, after which sect troops would force Diem to step down. Their militance alarmed Trinh Minh The and Nguyen Thanh Phuong, the faction leaders Diem had suborned, and they met with Lansdale in an attempt to distance themselves. The CIA also learned that the Binh Xuyen's orders were to assume defensive positions but fight only if attacked.

Foreign proconsuls Collins and Ely, conferring privately, agreed on many aspects of the sect problem. Ely remarked that the situation had reached an impasse, but the use of force represented "the worst possible solution." Ely said that Diem had mentioned placating the sects by dismissing some of his more objectionable officials and forming a cabinet of "technicians"—an idea Diem had previously tried out on Lansdale. Bao Dai's cooperation would be necessary, and the two proconsuls agreed that France and the United States should jointly approach Bao Dai in Cannes.[10] Collins informed Washington.

That night Saigon went from unrest to crisis. Around midnight the Binh Xuyen staged an armed attack on the Saigon police precinct held by paratroopers of Major Do Cao Tri's 6th Airborne Battalion, backed by some armored cars. They also fired mortar shells at the palace. Major Tri called for reinforcements. The French had responsibility for Saigon's security and ended this outbreak by stopping gasoline and ammunition supplies to all sides. Lansdale later told lurid stories of his run-ins with General Fernand Gambiez, Ely's chief of staff and point man on the sects, including one about countering the Frenchman's attack dog with his own .45-caliber automatic. These stories doubtless emanated from Lansdale's preference that Diem crush the sects. Indeed, his criticism of Collins came from the same place.

Over subsequent days the darkness deepened. The man who resigned was not Diem but Saigon's defense minister. The Americans had not considered him dynamic but had at least been comfortable with him. Diem asked leave to bring fresh VNA troops to Saigon and to shut down police circuits the Binh Xuyen used to communicate. Binh Xuyen commander Bay Vien began marshaling his troops for a showdown in the Saigon region. To many, Diem appeared completely isolated in the face of rising public unrest.

Collins decided that Diem's actions were destroying the potential for a unified government. The Saigon chieftain had run out of time. Collins informed Washington of his opinion and suggested several possibilities for new leadership. Allen Dulles had his CIA analysts respond with a paper rejecting the suggestions, countering that a successor government would be labeled a French puppet regime and that "if the National government gives in, the Sects will have confirmed their position as autonomous power centers," making a central government much more difficult to establish.[11] The timing here suggests that the Dulles brothers were coordinating closely.

On April 4, the same day, John Foster Dulles sent Collins an "Eyes Only" personal message: "I had assumed that a time would come when there would have to be some sort of a showdown to demonstrate the authority of Diem. That, I thought, would be the payoff. If he came through, then the future would be relatively clear. If he failed, then that would be that."[12] Now, in the moment, Dulles could not escape his distaste for the shady Binh Xuyen, which he saw as the worst of the sects. Their corruption blinded him to Diem's megalomania. Three days later, driven to the reluctant conclusion that progress with Diem was impossible, Collins cabled Washington that he *had* to go. Dulles, who had proclaimed his willingness to let the chips fall where they may, instead conspired to undermine the president's man in Saigon.

First, Dulles dallied in responding to Collins's urgent message. There could be no doubt that Saigon was in crisis, that immediate action was necessary, and that the U.S. envoy required instructions. Yet Dulles let four days go by before he sent a reply. In fact, at least three versions of this message were crafted, the last jointly by Dulles and Eisenhower at a White House lunch. Just before that session with the president, Dulles telephoned his brother the CIA director and told him, "It looks like the rug is coming out from under the fellow in Southeast Asia." Dulles did not know if this would get the CIA "in the wrong" with the president. The note taker recorded Allen Dulles's reply (referring to Diem): "He thinks he can adjust things and will look into it." The CIA chief objected to kowtowing to the Binh Xuyen, and the secretary of state sympathized.[13]

As he had with Dulles's "united action" speech in 1954, Eisenhower personally penciled in numerous changes to the message to Collins. Until now, Ike had backed his friend. Even over the weekend, when Secretary Dulles first showed him the cable, Eisenhower had insisted that he could not send someone to deal with this issue and then reject their considered judgment. But as Dulles had told his brother, State had sent Collins several strong messages without swaying him. This was crunch time. At lunch Dulles softened Eisenhower and got him to approve language—following the CIA analysis— that doubted whether Diem could be replaced. On the surface, Dulles accepted Collins's position, but he posed conditions for the embassy's suggested alternatives.[14]

In Saigon CIA station chief Philip Potter and Lansdale fed Collins commentaries designed to show the balance of forces changing in Diem's favor, with the VNA more willing to fight and sect forces beginning to rally to him. Secretary Dulles got President Eisenhower to recall Collins for consultations. Just before Lightning Joe left for Washington, Diem told him that "experience in Vietnam" during the French war "proved compromise to be ineffectual."[15]

On April 18 in Washington, Allen Dulles suddenly phoned his brother with an item—its contents still unknown—so hot that he needed to share it immediately and in person. He rushed to Foster's office. The context suggests this may have been Trinh Minh The's promise to fight the Binh Xuyen, passed along by Lansdale.

Earlier that day Secretary Dulles had defended Diem when the French foreign minister attributed Saigon's crisis to his failure. Foster threatened that the United States would leave Vietnam if Diem were ousted. Dulles now cabled Collins that the French were not supporting Diem and had never really done so, implying that the Vietnamese leader needed to be given a real chance. Any excuse would do.

Collins was no fool. He could smell a fix and sensed that his private understanding with Eisenhower was disintegrating. Collins chose this moment to follow up his January report with a fresh analysis of Diem's ineffectiveness and recommending the United States withdraw support. Collins returned to

Washington on April 22 to make his case, initiating frantic meetings at the State Department, the Pentagon, and the CIA. He lunched with the president. When Ike parroted the line that the lack of French support was what threatened Diem, Collins told him this was not accurate. At Foggy Bottom he held that it would be "a major error in judgment to continue to support a man (Diem) who has demonstrated such a marked inability to understand the political, economic and military problems [of] Vietnam."[16] Collins thought he had won. Cables went to both Paris and Saigon declaring U.S. policy to be the replacement of Diem, spearheaded by Collins and Ely, with a Franco-American approach to Bao Dai in France. But privately Allen Dulles ordered his Board of National Estimates to craft a fresh analysis knocking down Collins's arguments, and he told his brother that the CIA would soon have a critique to counter them.

The ink had hardly dried on the U.S. instructions when fighting resumed in Saigon. A stream of Lansdale cables described the new hostilities. Unlike in March, this time Diem was the unmistakable aggressor. Even as the fighting raged, the Collins approach was up for discussion at the NSC. That morning Secretary Dulles countermanded his instructions, phoning Collins to say that it was unclear whether Diem was falling or emerging a hero. Better to wait and see. Dubious, Collins saw Lansdale's cables characterizing Diem as the indispensable leader. The cables triggered a round of late-night phone conversations as the CIA maneuvered in advance of the NSC meeting. The agency's Far East division chief, George Aurell, informed Kermit Roosevelt, who was standing in that night for Frank Wisner and woke up Allen Dulles with the news. On April 28 Roosevelt offered the NSC a hopeful rendering of Lansdale's cables plus the special estimate the CIA had just completed with its favorable prognosis on Diem. This further strengthened Foster's hand. Lightning Joe answered a few questions. Dulles countered that the United States had "anointed" Diem based on Collins's January report; he blamed Diem's difficulties on the French and the fact that he was from the North and thus suspicious by nature. That was wrong information; actually Diem hailed from central Vietnam. Now Collins spoke: Diem's number was up. Eisenhower, as if Collins had said nothing, averred that it was essential to break the Binh Xuyen. Collins left with theoretical approval of his policy, but Washington was really in a wait-and-see posture.[17]

Collins's assignment was to meet with Ely and collaborate to cool off the situation. He departed Washington on the morning of April 29. Lansdale and Diem had the time Collins was in transit to produce results. Collins's curious twelve-hour layover at Hickam Air Force Base in Hawaii acquires significance here. Briefing the commander in chief Pacific (CINCPAC) was always useful, but with Saigon in dire straits and Collins a man on a mission, he was not the person to update CINCPAC. This stretched his trip to sixty hours—two and a half days.

In Saigon, Diem used the VNA's tanks and artillery to flatten parts of the city and thrust into Cholon, the Binh Xuyen stronghold. Trinh Minh The's intervention strengthened him. Some of the fiercest fighting took place around the so-called Y Bridge at the intersection between the twin cities. A key figure was VNA chief of staff General Nguyen Van Vy, who had risen through the ranks of the French army and seemed to be the only one who could get the French to replenish the VNA's artillery ammunition. Vy was regarded as close to Bao Dai. As the bullets flew, Trinh Minh The's troops arrested General Vy. Do Cao Tri—who had suddenly been promoted to lieutenant colonel and given command of the entire Airborne Brigade—demanded the release of Vy, a fellow paratrooper. When Trinh Minh The refused, Tri told Diem that the army would attack the palace if Vy were not freed. Quietly liberated, Vy fled to Cambodia and went on to Paris.

Before Collins arrived Diem had the upper hand. On May 2 Allen Dulles was able to produce another CIA estimate that observed, "the success of Premier Diem in operations against the Binh Xuyen" had created a "new" situation in which he "dominated." The French and Bao Dai would have "to adapt themselves to a radically new political situation."[18] By May 5 the CIA director could tell the NSC that the Binh Xuyen had largely been driven out of Saigon. By some accounts the weeklong battle involved more troops than fought in Saigon during the 1968 Tet offensive. As many as 20,000 people were left homeless. There were 500 dead and 2,000 wounded. Trinh Minh The, alliance with whom posed certain awkward political problems for Diem, died under mysterious circumstances on May 3. The Collins policy of seeking new leadership became a casualty of the fighting. Some months later, during a global tour of CIA stations, Allen Dulles made a secret visit to Saigon, where Lansdale squired him around town.

■ ■ ■ Thus passed another chance for America to avoid its Vietnam war. Beyond the significant—but ancillary—roles played by such men as John Foster Dulles, Allen W. Dulles, Edward Lansdale, and J. Lawton Collins is that of President Dwight D. Eisenhower. This episode is worth the detail devoted to it precisely because, in the final analysis, it was Eisenhower who passed up this opportunity. Moreover, he acquiesced in a subversion of his own policy process, undermining his personal proconsul. The question that must be asked is why. At the time there were no appreciable political pressures on Eisenhower. The machinations of the Dulles brothers furnished occasion, but the State Department and the CIA were under presidential control, after all, and cleavages with the Pentagon were muted. Public opinion was insignificant. The answer, in my view, goes back to Dien Bien Phu. Indeed, the previous episode was on Eisenhower's mind. In one of the few extracts of Ike's private audio recordings that have been preserved, on February 24, 1955, the president went out of his way to give a visiting journalist a certain version of his actions in the Dien Bien Phu crisis.[19] This was a pregnant moment, with Diem's intransigence already apparent and the struggle between him and the sects about to come out into the open.

The year between the spring of 1954 and that of 1955 proved crucial to setting the U.S. course. It began with the possibility of intervention that would have committed Washington to a war years before that actually happened. Eisenhower worked to enable that scheme and felt guilt at its failure. The Eisenhower letter and Eisenhower's alignment with Ngo Dinh Diem in the sect crisis are best seen in the light of those feelings. No Cold War interests were at stake in the makeup of the Saigon government, and no larger U.S. goals threatened. Opposition to the Geneva-mandated reunification could have been pursued no matter who occupied Doc Lap Palace. Eisenhower made premature promises to Diem in the wake of Dien Bien Phu, then bound himself to that man.

The consequences of Eisenhower's choice affected all future U.S. actions. In October 1954 the president had set explicit conditions for supporting a Saigon leader. In March and April 1955, with that leader having failed to meet those benchmarks, Eisenhower backed him anyway, increasing America's stake by supplanting the French, in the face of specific objections from Ike's own man on the scene. With that act Eisenhower gave up the possibility that Washington could exercise real influence, or "leverage," in Saigon affairs. In Iraq, George W. Bush would do something similar when he forged ahead despite the failure of the Iraqi government to meet the benchmarks on which he had conditioned his "surge" of U.S. forces.

Lack of American leverage in Vietnam would become a matter of perplexity and soul-searching, a huge headache in Washington, and an issue that persisted through the end of the Vietnam war, at least. The leverage problem would be posed quite succinctly in the 1960s by Leslie Gelb in the extensive Department of Defense study known as the "Pentagon Papers." Gelb wrote:

> If U.S. force commitments and the record of [Government of Vietnam (GVN)] non-performance reflect the failure of leverage, what does the record tell us about how leverage could be made to work? Regrettably, the record tells us nothing about that; it merely shows that everything we tried went wrong . . . Attempts at leverage on GVN were seldom thought through and studied carefully. One searches in vain for studies, memoranda or widespread discussion of alternative techniques for leverage and of what our experience shows about how they might work. Pressures against the North, whose results have disappointed us, were a model of planning, foresight, and detailed consideration compared to the subject of pressures on GVN. Yet GVN's failure was the heart of our policy problem throughout the period.[20]

These observations, acute as they are, miss the point that there was a specific moment when Saigon leaders *discovered* they could ignore Washington's demands with impunity. That time came with the sect crisis. By not enforcing U.S. conditions in April 1955, and by increasing its commitment despite Diem's *immobilisme,* Washington gave up the ability to exact behavior in return for its help. Diem learned the lesson well: at each higher level of commitment, the American stake only grew, and unless Washington wished to abandon that investment, it had no choice but to acquiesce either to action or to the lack thereof. Diem's successors were there to see this situation as well. Duong Van Minh played a direct role in these events. Future strongman Nguyen Khanh was brought in to pursue the Binh Xuyen into their swamps. Airman Nguyen Cao Ky led a transport squadron that shuttled VNA troops and Diem officials all over. And Nguyen Van Thieu watched from the perspective of the Military Academy at Dalat, where he was superintendent, feeding graduates into this internecine struggle.

The historical consensus on Dwight D. Eisenhower has changed, moving him up in the ranks of presidents, crediting him with much greater perspicacity exercised with a hidden hand while seeming unconcerned on the surface. But Eisenhower's wisdom failed when it came to Vietnam. If he did not realize the consequences, that failure was direct. If he simply considered Vietnam so insignificant that it did not matter, that was a failure of a different sort. Either way, Eisenhower both tabled the initial stake and set in motion a dynamic that would minimize Washington's influence over the outcome. For these things he bears responsibility.

Supporting Diem amid Social Change

The way the Eisenhower White House and Dulles's State Department played Congress also set a pattern that long endured. Congress was at once ally and foil. In the days of bipartisanship the legislators shared many views with the executive, and even opposition Democrats could be relied on to do Eisenhower's chores. Senator Lyndon Johnson had demonstrated that at Dien Bien Phu. And Ike had able aides, led by "General" Wilton B. Persons, to help him grease the wheels on Capitol Hill. At the same time, administration failures could be shunted onto congressional shoulders. Dien Bien Phu showed that, too. The administration devoted serious attention over the summer of 1954 to crafting a white paper on Eisenhower's deliberations over Dien Bien Phu, and the result would be reviewed not only by the president but also by Secretary Dulles and even the French foreign ministry. Such indulgent self-justification hardly seems necessary, unless Eisenhower was sensitive about the events, as postulated here.[21] The white paper represented the Dulles-Radford congressional consultation as unsuccessful and cited that as the principal reason intervention did not go forward.

Americans' first real knowledge of the inside story of Dien Bien Phu came in the summer and fall of 1954. First, *U.S. News and World Report* published a story on the issue of using ground troops and how General Ridgway had shot it down.[22] The president could be taken here for a fantasist who believed his "New Look" military could succeed without the Army. Then came "The Day We Didn't Go to War," which appeared in a national magazine that September.[23] Its author, Chalmers M. Roberts, was the recently minted chief diplomatic correspondent of the *Washington Post*. His version closely followed the line taken in the (never released) Eisenhower white paper. Here the heroes—or villains, depending on one's view—were the senators and representatives meeting with Dulles and Radford. Eisenhower could have his cake and eat it too, satisfying Cold War stalwarts with his willingness to intervene, yet seeming to acknowledge a legislative role in decisions on war and peace.

Meanwhile, *none* of the congressional characters who figured at Dien Bien Phu were drawn into the administration's inner circle on post-Geneva policy. Instead, Eisenhower and Dulles turned to someone entirely different, Montana senator Mike Mansfield. A Democrat but a neophyte in the Senate, Mansfield had been given a coveted seat on the Foreign Affairs Committee. Earlier he had served in the Philippines and briefly in China as a Marine. Mansfield had been an emissary for FDR in 1944, returning to China on a diplomatic mission. As a Montana congressman and then senator, he became known as an expert on the Far East and first visited Indochina in the fall of 1953, shortly before Richard M. Nixon's tour, where General Henri Navarre treated Mansfield to a briefing on his famous plan.

Senator Mansfield attracted Eisenhower's and Dulles's attention by supporting the big ramp-up of U.S. aid to Indochina for the Navarre Plan, but what made him really attractive now was his enthusiasm for Ngo Dinh Diem. Mansfield first met Diem in May 1953, at the same coming-out luncheon at New York's Yale Club where the Vietnamese politician was introduced to John Kennedy. After Geneva Mansfield enthused over Diem, rejecting arguments about his ineffectiveness. Secretary Dulles cultivated Mansfield, whom he invited to accompany him to Manila for the conference where the SEATO treaty was signed—the only senator so honored. Mansfield went on to Saigon, where he found Diem a virtual recluse. None of this shook his faith. Returning to Manila he told Dulles—who was no doubt glad to hear it—that Diem might be "the last chance" for the right man in Saigon.[24] The senator argued (as Dulles would later, possibly taking his cue from Mansfield) that if Diem fell, the United States should suspend aid to South Vietnam.

Thus, in the heat of the 1955 sect crisis, Senator Mansfield's approach represented the opposite poll to General Collins's. Journalist and scholar Don Oberdorfer, the most knowledgeable student of Mansfield's career, shows that Dulles supplied the senator with copies of Lightning Joe's secret cables and asked for his views. Mansfield's name also came up in conversations between Dulles and Eisenhower and between the Dulles brothers. Mansfield's position was that "the U.S. should stick to its guns in continuing to support Diem." Collins personally met with Mansfield during the former's climactic trip to Washington, without effect. Publicly the senator declared that Diem had "a decent and honest government."[25] Diem gushed thanks in a letter written as his troops cleared Saigon.

■ ■ ■ The end of the French period in Vietnam followed ineluctably. The eclipse of Paris began within weeks of the sect crisis. In early May meetings took place among British, French, and American allies. One phase of that conference concerned Vietnam, directly involving the United States and France. The French prime minister, as a negotiating ploy, spoke of withdrawing the Expeditionary Corps. Before the conversations ended, tentative offers had become firm understandings. The United States reduced its military aid to the French in a way that required withdrawals simply because there was no money. The last French troops left in April 1956. Their departure made America South Vietnam's big brother.[26]

Ngo Dinh Diem capitalized on the transformation to throw off the vestiges of the French-sponsored State of Vietnam. When Bao Dai demanded that Diem come to France—undoubtedly to fire him—he refused. He also spurned the emperor's order to change the army high command. Diem then called a referendum on state power, asking the South Vietnamese people to choose between Bao Dai's or his own government. Diem won the September 1955 referendum with 98 percent of the vote. Multiple accounts show that Lansdale, back at the political action he did so well, helped Diem contrive procedures to ensure victory. Simple peasants were told how to vote, ballots were designed to favor Diem, and his tally in Saigon and elsewhere exceeded the number of registered voters. After this, there was no going back. Senator Mansfield visited again about this time and, in his report to the Foreign Relations Committee, declared, "There is today a reasonable chance of the survival and development of a free Vietnam."[27]

Meanwhile, Washington's latitude for action was becoming constrained, though not from the Left. The first Vietnam activists were pro-Diem agitators. This began with a loose coalition of individuals, primarily figures that Diem had impressed during foreign travels, plus those involved with the first frantic months of Operation Passage to Freedom. Wesley L. Fishel, an academic who had met Diem in Japan in 1950 and arrived in Saigon as an embassy liaison to the Vietnamese leader, would be a prime mover among this crowd. So too was Leo Cherne, chairman of the board of the International Rescue Committee, and his field director, Joseph Buttinger, who organized refugee aid in the South. Catholics were another key group. Francis Cardinal Spellman, who knew Diem from his sojourn in America, appealed for help to Saigon in sermons and weekly radio addresses. Dr. Thomas A. Dooley, a Navy surgeon sent from Yokosuka to run a refugee triage center at Haiphong, became the public face of activism. At the height of the sect crisis Buttinger created the advocacy group American Friends of Vietnam (AFV), with Harold L. Oram its key fund-raiser and cheerleader. AFV president General John ("Iron Mike") O'Daniel had been the top U.S. military adviser. Thus there would be a Vietnam lobby much as there had been a China lobby in Harry Truman's day.[28]

Mansfield, at least, resisted joining them. Apparently concerned at the way his relationship with the administration had leaped the bounds between the executive and legislative branches (hard to conceive in today's power-hungry Washington), Mansfield rejected continuing his de facto policy role. The senator also worried about deepening U.S. commitment, having warned at the time of Dien Bien Phu against America becoming involved in a "nibbling war" in Vietnam.[29] Now Mansfield distanced himself from Dulles, though he preserved amicable ties to the State Department. And while Mansfield continued to support the Diem experiment—to the extent of introducing Diem when he visited Washington and addressed the Senate—the Montana politico played shy. In the summer of 1956 the AFV held its first gala, but Mansfield rejected an invitation to give the keynote speech. (John F. Kennedy spoke instead, terming South Vietnam "a proving ground of democracy," as well as "the finger in the dike" and "the cornerstone of the Free World in Southeast Asia, the keystone in the arch.")[30] Although Mansfield would be listed on the AFV's national board starting a few years later, he could not recall ever having joined it.

For some years AFV stood as the primary, even the sole, public advocacy group involved in Vietnam matters. It held out for steadfast support, lobbied Congress for aid, and hit hard at journalists and others who said anything critical of the Diem government. Some of the members went beyond advocacy. Fishel engaged himself and other professors at Michigan State University in consulting contracts with the Saigon government. The Michigan State group was important in advising Saigon on agricultural programs and police training, among other things. Their activism was of a piece with a new trend in American political development.

■ ■ ■ On another level, AFV represents just one facet of an evolution in American politics that eventually transformed the national landscape. This may be hard to appreciate. The Eisenhower era, after all, is often pictured as a time when conventionality reigned, a period of lost years in economic and social progress punctuated by terrifying Cold War crises. But the antecedents of much that happened in the 1960s were set here. Historian Arthur Marwick, surveying music, culture, and much else besides politics in four countries, has proposed the idea of the "Long 1960s" to denote the period between about 1958 and 1974—in essence, the Vietnam era.[31] In the twenty-first century, with the politics of protest and strident advocacy deeply entrenched, it may be hard to believe that this was not always the case. But in fact the latter half of the 1950s saw the beginnings of what became known as "participatory democracy," fueled by rapid communications; public hopes, fears, and concerns; mass media; and a growing awareness of a gap between official pronouncements and, to borrow a phrase from a later day, facts on the ground.

There had been citizens' movements in the nation's past—the suffragists immediately come to mind, as well as the Bonus Marchers or the America First activists prior to World War II—but never had there been a politics of advocacy and protest. The leading edge of this change had little to do with Vietnam. Rather, it centered on other issues: civil rights and fear of nuclear war.

Lynchings of black Americans had almost stopped in this decade. Some of the last were the outrageous murder of teenager Emmett Till in 1955 and of Mack Parker right out of a jail in 1959, both in Mississippi. The vista opened for desegregation with the May 1954 Supreme Court decision in the case *Brown v. Board of Education.* Civil rights leaders such as the Reverend Martin Luther King Jr., James Farmer, Roy Wilkins, Ralph Abernathy, Bayard Rustin, and others saw the opportunity. Racists saw the threat. Membership in the Ku Klux Klan reached a height not seen in fifty years. Popular resistance to segregation was clearly indicated. Rosa Parks's heroic stand that sparked the 1956 Montgomery bus boycott marked the crystallization of a pattern of mass tactics and deliberate civil disobedience epitomized by the Freedom Riders. The struggle would be long and hard. President Eisenhower lent hope when he deployed Army regulars to enforce desegregation at Central High School in Little Rock in 1957. The need for struggle was not lost on young African Americans such as Stokely Carmichael, then a fourteen-year-old sophomore at the Bronx High School of Science. The civil rights struggle—and the tactics it introduced—would be an important factor in the politics of Vietnam.[32]

What can broadly be called the "peace movement," impelled by the danger of nuclear war, also took a step up. Scientists had experienced guilt over the use of the atomic bomb—their ultimate weapon—at the end of World War II, and fear of nuclear war spread among pacifists and internationalists during the Cold War. At first the solution was seen as world federalism, but the United Nations revealed itself to be a limited quantity, and advocates of the peace movement were tarred by McCarthyism as fellow travelers if not outright communists.[33] Yet nuclear weapons remained a grave and present danger, and the innovation of the hydrogen bomb made the problem worse.

The U.S. test of an H-bomb at Bikini island in the Pacific in March 1954—another event around the time of Dien Bien Phu—contaminated Japanese sailors aboard the fishing boat *Lucky Dragon,* most of whom died of radiation poisoning. The incident not only ignited furor in Japan but also resulted in an outpouring of fear elsewhere, not least in the United States, where "ban the bomb" views quickly emerged. As the administration pursued atmospheric nuclear tests, including of tactical weapons within the United States, opposition sharpened. Beginning in 1957 it became a mass movement. The War Resisters' League, the Women's International League for Peace and Freedom, and the International Fellowship of Reconciliation—all of which became sources of opposition to Vietnam—were reinvigorated. The American Friends Service Committee, a Quaker pacifist group focused largely on private, individual action, gained experience in mass dissent.[34] Taking a cue from the civil rights activists, a coalition of pacifist groups set up the Committee for Nonviolent Action in June 1957 and deliberately attempted to sail small ships into the U.S. nuclear test zone in the Pacific.

The Eisenhower administration clearly saw the political threat of the antinuclear movement. Beginning in 1958 it negotiated with the Soviets for an end to atmospheric testing. Although agreement would only be attained by his successor, Eisenhower declared a moratorium on U.S. atmospheric tests, one that endured through Kennedy's first year in office. Eisenhower's records show that he had sound military and scientific reasons for this test ban, but public pressure was significant as well, particularly after scientists confirmed that radioactive fallout had appeared in cow's milk in places remote from the Nevada test site. Apart from any other effect, the moratorium conveyed the impression that public pressure could yield policy change.[35]

One more thing flowed from the Eisenhower years: the expansion of government surveillance of ordinary citizens exercising constitutionally protected rights. Although President Eisenhower did not initiate these programs and even resisted some attempts to chill public debate (most importantly, those of Senator Joe McCarthy—once again around the time of Dien Bien Phu), surveillance expanded during his presidency. Supposedly aimed at communist subversion, much of the effort focused instead on Americans' attempts to make themselves heard. COINTELPRO, short for "Counterintelligence Program," *was* an Eisenhower product, and it used the FBI not only to find enemy spies but also to identify and actively discredit American citizens. One large FBI operation aimed at the civil rights movement, another at the antinuclear one. Martin Luther King became a victim, but only the tip of the iceberg. When missionary and Nobel Prize winner Albert Schweitzer spoke on the radio and called for the halt of nuclear testing in the summer of 1957, the FBI promptly investigated him. Critic Linus Pauling was denied a passport until winning the Nobel Prize himself in 1954. The FBI conducted a virtual vendetta against physicist Ralph Lapp, a nuclear weapons critic, and its surveillance of the Women's International League for Peace and Freedom significantly increased during the late 1950s. In 1958 the FBI began an intensive inquiry into the National Committee for a Safe Nuclear Policy (SANE). These activities were reported to the White House. Eisenhower never disavowed them; he regarded this as an acceptable part of some "countersubversion" strategy.[36] During the Vietnam war, countersubversion would threaten political expression.

■ ■ ■ Countersubversion remained Ngo Dinh Diem's main business, starting with the sects. The Saigon leader integrated some sect troops into the VNA and ordered it to neutralize the rest. The Binh Xuyen remnants defended the Rung Sat swamps, southeast of Saigon, but the VNA followed, gradually whittling down their strength. Binh Xuyen commander Bay Vien escaped to France. Colonel Duong Van Minh led the pacification of the Hoa Hao provinces, which took a year. Tran Van Soai and his forces surrendered. In May 1956 Ba Cut, one of the most aggressive sect commanders, was captured. He was executed, and others were hanged too. Duong Van Minh became a brigadier general and commander of the military district surrounding Saigon. The strange thing, at least in terms of subversion, is that the Hoa Hao were not even candidates to ally with Ho Chi Minh, since the Vietminh had murdered their patriarch. Yet with Diem's repression, a couple of remaining Hoa Hao battalions eventually did collaborate with a regenerated Vietminh insurgency.

Diem declared a Republic of Vietnam on October 26, 1955, and assumed office as president. That day the VNA became the Army of the Republic of Vietnam (ARVN). With Washington's backing, Diem rejected consultations with Hanoi that were necessary for the upcoming national reunification vote. That vote never took place—a major breach of the Geneva agreements. Instead Diem held an election for an assembly to draft a constitution. He also promulgated an ordinance outlawing political parties, then created quasi-party entities under two of his brothers. One, the Can Lao, became the real backbone of his power. The nepotism that lay at the root of demands for reform reigned stronger than ever. The constitution Diem approved contained an article awarding him power to govern by decree until 1961. The regime then initiated a "Denunciation of Communism" campaign under which anyone suspected of links with the North was swept up. Arrests through 1957 averaged 5,000 a month, with about 150 executed each month. New ordinances outlawed communism, prohibited mass gatherings, and so on.

President Diem did not do all this by himself. His base of support lay in the United States. The Eisenhower administration, abandoning its own preconditions, funneled a steady stream of cash to Saigon, subsidized South Vietnamese imports, and administered a strong military aid program. Official figures show that during this period, corresponding to U.S. fiscal years 1955 through 1961, Washington gave Diem more than $1.5 billion in economic and more than $500 million in military aid.[37] Americans worked with Diem's propaganda apparatus, his economic ministries, and, of course, the South Vietnamese military.

By far the strongest component of the U.S. nonmilitary program was the private-public effort sparkplugged by Michigan State University professor and AFV organizer Wesley Fishel. He and colleagues drafted a proposal for what became the Michigan State University Group (MSUG) as early as October 1954. The chief U.S. aid official in Saigon was opposed to the group, so Eisenhower's acceptance of and payment for the MSUG in the spring of 1955 indicate his determination to make the Diem experiment work. Michigan State advisers labored in Vietnam until June 1962. The original idea to teach civil servants and police and to provide consultants to the Saigon government lost out to security, however. In its time, the MSUG trained 1,500 members of Diem's Surete and 21,000 Civil Guard militiamen, procuring arms, vehicles, and radio equipment. The MSUG also furnished cover for CIA officers, estimated at between 10 and 20 percent of the MSUG's peak staff of about fifty Americans.

Land reform was an area where the MSUG pushed Diem hard, following the prodding of Wolf Ladejinsky, a U.S. mission member rumored to be more than a diplomat. The Saigon leader issued several decrees on land reform starting in early 1955 and culminating in a fall 1956 directive ordering redistribution. Vice President Richard Nixon handed Diem a letter from Eisenhower commending rural change as "*the* pre-condition of meeting the threat of Communism."[38] But what proved to be striking was *how* Diem utilized land reform: Only tiny percentages of peasants saw any benefit. The redistributed land lay overwhelmingly in provinces formerly controlled by the sects or in the Central Highlands, where the tribal minorities known from French times as montagnards were effectively supplanted in key towns and villages by Vietnamese settlers. Diem used land development as a reward system for loyalists, many from the northern diaspora, giving them an interest in the preservation of his regime.

The Americans put $10 million into the land program when it was planned in 1956. According to a montagnard authority, Diem passed along barely $1 million of that money to the upland provinces, and none of it actually trickled down to the tribesmen. By 1959 a total of 125,000 people had been resettled in the Central Highlands, barely 6,000 of them montagnards. By contrast, 17,000 were Vietnamese from the North. As a result, the tribes began to pay attention, and at the beginning of 1955 representatives of a number of them met at the provincial capital Ban Me Thuot to form a Front for the Liberation of the Montagnards (FLM). When Diem went there on

February 22, 1957, for a ceremony to mark the beginning of upland development, an FLM activist tried to assassinate him. The badly aimed bullet wounded the minister of agriculture instead.[39] The montagnards would not be contributors to stability in Diem's South Vietnam.

Diem's major pillar became Vietnamese Catholics—not surprising, given his own religion. An account that cites 900,000 as the number of Vietnamese who fled the north after Geneva puts the Catholics among them at 700,000.[40] The effect was to double the number of Roman Catholics in South Vietnam, but even so, 80 percent or more of the population professed Buddhism in pure or animistic variants. In fact, Buddhism was enjoying a revival that was more than two decades old by this time. By 1962 more than half the pagodas in South Vietnam were either new or recently refurbished, and membership in Buddhist associations had increased by a third. The number of schools training monks more than doubled. Saigon's Xa Loi Pagoda became headquarters for the General Association of Buddhists in 1958, but it represented only six of the sixteen Mahayana denominations, claiming more than 3 million adherents. Both Xa Loi Pagoda and An Quang Pagoda (created in 1951) would be important in events taking place a few years later.

The French had favored the Catholics, and Diem did the same. The congruence between that favoritism and the increase in Catholics from the diaspora shifted Saigon policies further toward what, given Vietnamese regional differences, in some respects constituted an alien minority. Consider the impact on the ARVN: As of 1964 some 48 percent of troops manning the two divisions in the Saigon region were northerners, with a larger proportion of Catholics, whereas the ARVN as a whole was largely Buddhist. Northerners also filled the ranks of the ARVN's elite Airborne units. Among Vietnamese generals—Diem promoted roughly seventy individuals to that rank—northerners did not predominate, but favored classes did: fully one-third of ARVN generals were the sons of landowners, another fifth were the sons of officials, and an additional tenth were from military families—in all, a startling 63.3 percent. Only three ARVN generals were the sons of peasants. Of those who admitted a religious affiliation, the overwhelming majority were Catholics. Just four generals were known to be Buddhists.[41] In short, Diem governed from a rather narrow base.

Given the importance of the military to Diem's power, it should be noted that despite the honors he bestowed and the cash the Americans pumped, his rigidity and arbitrary rule progressively alienated the officers. Most accounts focus on U.S. aid and training plus the dilemmas of choosing what missions the ARVN should be oriented toward. Those are important issues, but the inescapable fact is that the Vietnamese army mounted a full-scale coup d'etat against Diem in November 1960. Thus, in the relatively short time between 1955 and 1960, Diem managed to turn significant elements of his power base against himself. How Diem accomplished that is the real question, and its answer goes right back to the issue of reforms.

The case of Lam Quang Thi is a good one, for Thi, who would rise to become a senior general in the ARVN, was nonpolitical, an artillery expert who never participated in any coup. Scion of a landowning family in the Mekong delta, Thi became an officer under the French, graduating from the Dalat academy and fighting in the last battles of the Franco-Vietnamese war. He greeted the advent of Ngo Dinh Diem warmly. Later Major Thi received advanced artillery training at Fort Sill in the United States and soon found himself an instructor at the ARVN's Command and General Staff College. "By that time," Thi recounts, "my original excitement and hope in Mr. Diem had vanished . . . The problem was, he acted like an emperor. He tolerated no organized opposition; his critics were harassed or arrested. His decrees became laws. He gradually transformed South Vietnam into a quasi-police state where the security apparatus was rigidly controlled by his brother Ngo Dinh Nhu."[42] If Diem could not hold the loyalty of officers like Thi, he was in real trouble.

By the spring of 1960 conditions had reached a fever pitch. At the Caravelle Hotel a group of prominent citizens came together to decry the leader's shortcomings. They included businessmen, former officials, and diplomats, among them Diem associate Tran Kim Tuyen, former head of his intelligence service; Bui Diem, a prominent newspaper publisher; and Nguyen Van Tam, a prime minister under Bao Dai. Tired of unfulfilled promises, the political preserve of the Can Lao, and the puffery of Diem's claims to an articulated philosophy he called "personalism," the Caravelle group issued a manifesto demanding real reform. No Vietnamese newspaper dared print what became known as the Caravelle Manifesto. The AFV did its part, jumping in to refute the manifesto and discredit its authors. Privately, Fishel encouraged Diem to accommodate the Caravelle demands. Diem's effective answer came in the national assembly election he permitted on August 8. The results were even more brazen than those of 1956: all but two of the 123 seats were won by handpicked candidates. Diem allowed only one opposition member and one "independent" to win. Tran Kim Tuyen was exiled as South Vietnamese ambassador to Egypt.

The ARVN delivered an answer on the morning of November 11 that not even the AFV could deny. Three battalions of Colonel Nguyen Chanh Thi's Airborne Brigade, some the same troops that had saved Diem from the sects, plus a battalion of Marines fanned out through Saigon and surrounded Doc Lap Palace. Colonel Thi was one of the ARVN's senior Buddhist officers, but he had fought hard in the sect battles and even became one of Diem's favorites. Although Thi was a thoroughly competent officer, his coup proved oddly tentative. The revolting troops failed to secure the radio station, block the roads against pro-Diem reinforcements, or cut telephones into the palace. Paratroops surrounded it but did not attack, while Colonel Thi sent Diem an ultimatum—to reform. Delay enabled others to take a hand.

General Nguyen Khanh, another Buddhist, did much to save Diem, convincing Thi's associates to talk, carrying their message to the palace, climbing over the back fence, and then staying to help Diem order up loyalist troops. The army was divided. Major Lam Quang Thi, back in Saigon with the ARVN Artillery Command, saw a battalion outside headquarters set up to bombard the palace. Staff chief General Le Van Ty convinced them to hold fire and avoid the destruction and civilian casualties that must surely follow. Lam Quang Thi's younger brother, an ARVN lieutenant, led one of the rebel paratroop companies; his older brother, a tank unit summoned to rescue Diem from My Tho in the delta. In fact, the ARVN division commander for the area, Nguyen Van Thieu, expressed support for the plotters but ultimately responded to the palace summons. General Thieu's troops moved to engage the rebels.

The CIA was all over the November coup. Station chief William E. Colby was only moderately surprised. His home was alongside one of the rebel posts, and he had received warnings from at least one case officer. Colby had CIA people on both sides and took a hand in the talking as well, carrying messages between Ngo Dinh Nhu and the plotters. Talks gained enough time for loyalists to arrive. As they entered Saigon the rebels began to fade away. Nguyen Chanh Thi and some of the plotters escaped to Cambodia. Others were arrested.

A few days after the attempted coup, the AFV sent Diem a telegram of support. But Diem's problems remained. Despite his flimsy base and the clear warning of the coup, Diem continued business as usual. The few changes he made were to tighten security. He now faced a mounting threat—the insurgency that became the American war. His U.S. friends could not make that challenge disappear. Washington stood at the brink of a conflict it hardly understood, at the side of an ally with crippling weaknesses. All this happened on Dwight Eisenhower's watch.

3   Loose the Fateful Lightning (1961–1964)

Theodore H. White, journalist extraordinaire, almost single-handedly established the presidential campaign narrative as a genre of American writing. He began with a big book covering the 1960 election that brought John F. Kennedy to the White House. The book, *The Making of the President, 1960*, followed every candidate, their speeches, campaign stops, the issues, the nominating conventions, the political maneuvers, and the voting.[1] In the thousands of words of text in White's blockbuster, it is remarkable that none of his foreign policy discussions concern Vietnam or Southeast Asia; only Laos is mentioned, once, in passing. The names Ngo Dinh Diem and Ho Chi Minh never appear. This is striking, considering that White spent World War II next door in China as bureau chief for *Time* magazine and had been a don of the Overseas Press Club. It is even more startling in the present context, since three of the five presidential contenders—Kennedy himself, Richard Nixon, and Lyndon B. Johnson—had been involved in the Dien Bien Phu crisis. This inattention is a measure of the minimal importance of Vietnam at that time. Even in televised debates—1960 was a watershed year for that—it hardly mattered. The candidates argued over Cuba and the Taiwan Strait, not the Diem experiment.

Americans worried, but their fears were inchoate. As White put it, "1960 was a year of national concern—but vague, shapeless, unsettling, undefinable." Yet, he noted, those very "atmospherics" were "more than anything else, [what] made it possible for John F. Kennedy's political exertions to triumph."[2] So far as Vietnam is concerned, the problem began to assume a clearer character only days after the election, with the Saigon coup. Then, during the interregnum, while president-elect Kennedy assembled his team, came crisis in Laos. When Eisenhower met Kennedy to review the problems the outgoing president would be handing over, Laos loomed as the key disaster in the making. Vietnam stayed on the back burner—for some people.

For others, that was not true. Among them was Edward G. Lansdale. By this time Lansdale worked at the Pentagon, in the Office of the Secretary of Defense, for a unit that supported intelligence activities of all kinds. Though much of his energy was taken up with preparations for the CIA's Bay of Pigs invasion, he responded with alacrity when superiors sent him to Saigon for a fresh appraisal. Lansdale had already rendered his opinion on the coup attempt; now he focused on broader issues. Reporting three days before Kennedy's inauguration, Lansdale wrote, "1961 promises to be a fateful year for Vietnam." He found that the communists were much further along in their objective of winning back Vietnam south of the Demilitarized Zone than he "had realized from reading the reports received in Washington." He commented that Vietnam was in "critical condition" and recommended that the United States "treat it as a combat area of the Cold War, as an area requiring emergency treatment." Lansdale advised sending a new ambassador with plenipotentiary powers, changing the operating methods of the U.S. mission, and flying closer to South Vietnamese allies.

Yet, even with that sense of tragedy that became America's Vietnam war, myopia endured. Lansdale insisted the only man capable of leading in Saigon was Diem, even while quoting the Vietnamese leader's own remarks that showed how out of touch he was. "If it hadn't been for the dedicated anti-communism of about a million Catholics," Diem had stated, "Vietnam could never have been kept going this long." Diem's own brother, Archbishop Ngo Dinh Thuc, thought otherwise, claiming that the northern Catholics had settled down in their lucrative, favored positions, had gone soft, and no longer wanted to fight.[3]

■ ■ ■ The great mass of Americans knew nothing of this. They saw only the excitement of the Kennedys—the young, dynamic president, the charming first lady, the glitter of Camelot. History tells that it snowed in Washington the day before the inauguration, and it was cold all that week; films of Kennedy taking his oath of office picture the frigid breath he exhaled. But Vietnam lurked behind him as the new president thrilled the nation with his address: "And so my fellow Americans, ask not what the country can do for you, ask what you can do for the country."[4] Kennedy captured the imagination of his countrymen and -women.

Not yet prepared to ask Americans to give their all for South Vietnam, President Kennedy nevertheless responded to Saigon's troubles as a policy problem. As part of a general defense review, Deputy Secretary of Defense Roswell Gilpatric took charge of a panel on Southeast Asia. In the spring of 1961 it reported out a menu of more than forty measures to increase the effectiveness of Saigon's war effort. Kennedy's approach rejected the Eisenhower "New Look" doctrine in favor of a full-spectrum capability that replaced missing links, among them the capacity to respond to guerrilla warfare. JFK became a counterinsurgency enthusiast, ordered senior officials to attend seminars on the subject, and in many respects regarded South Vietnam as a laboratory where theory and practice could be tested in the field. The Gilpatric committee recommendations were largely accepted in that spirit.

The Army of the Republic of Vietnam (ARVN) became the experimental apparatus. Since its inception, the ARVN had been the object of much pulling and hauling in Washington. Right into the Kennedy years, quietly and below the surface, the shape of the ARVN had been the touchstone for differences among U.S. authorities. Perceptive officers wanted to craft a South Vietnamese military suited to internal security and designed for counterinsurgency. Top leadership at the State Department and Eisenhower's minions on the Joint Chiefs of Staff worried about a North Vietnamese invasion across the Demilitarized Zone. They wanted the ARVN trained and equipped for conventional war. The smart money was on the latter choice. Saigon's military establishment, organized in divisions to maneuver with large groups of forces, would be oriented to wars like Korea and World War II.[5]

Of course, this recitation is oversimplified. Washington's military assistance did not follow a pure strategy, due to both U.S. parsimony and Saigon proclivities. On the American side, Eisenhower never committed to the level of aid that could have produced a thoroughly modern conventional force. In particular, the ARVN lacked sufficient tanks and armored vehicles to endow it with capable mobile forces, its scale of artillery equipment was far less than that of comparable U.S. formations, and the Vietnamese Air Force (VNAF) possessed only modest strike and bombardment capabilities. During the 1957–1959 period, the U.S. Military Assistance Advisory Group actually drafted 200 different organizational schemes for the standard ARVN division before ending up with the one implemented.[6] There were seven of these ARVN units in 1961. Washington thought the United States could make good the weaknesses if necessary, but had there ever really been a North Vietnamese invasion, those factors would have come into play and would indeed have driven the need for American intervention, despite the obstacles to that course.

Saigon's desires also shaped the ARVN. The army's origins during the French period played a role, since the Vietnam National Army had been recruited, trained, and based territorially, then operationally focused on territorial sectors. This was good for the ARVN, since it meant that cantonments could be located close to the men's families, reducing the need for leave, travel costs, and other expenses; however, it also made it difficult to move ARVN units to remote areas. Only the general reserve forces—the Airborne and Marines—were truly mobile. That suited Ngo Dinh Diem because it simplified the task of protecting his regime. The nature of the forces made it quite difficult for any disaffected military commander to concentrate troops against Saigon. Diem had only to ensure the loyalty of those few commanders of the general reserves and of formations in the Saigon area—a less formidable challenge. Operational irrationality was a political necessity.[7]

President Diem also felt that political reliability would be improved by shifting the locus of officer training from French military schools to the more technical American ones, and he suspended all ARVN officer training in France in mid-1956, soon after the last of the Expeditionary Corps had left South Vietnam. Given the huge shortfall in officers required for effective leadership, Saigon could have used trained men from wherever it got them.

Washington's Military Assistance Advisory Group (MAAG) was spread thin throughout this period. The Geneva agreements prohibited the introduction of foreign military forces in numbers greater than existed in July 1954, when there had been 342 Americans in MAAG. The Eisenhower administration had devised a succession of subterfuges to exceed those limits—another U.S. violation of the Geneva agreements. "Temporary equipment recovery missions" and the like more than doubled the number of U.S. advisers, and when Kennedy took over, there were 685 members of MAAG. A constant refrain among U.S. advisers would be that the ARVN could be more effective if Americans served with more of its units, at successively ramified levels of the Vietnamese military. Indeed, one of the Gilpatric committee's recommendations was to assign U.S. advisory teams to ARVN units at the regimental level for the first time.

Reviewing this period later, Pentagon analysts concluded that U.S. help had failed to produce an effective ARVN during the period up to 1959. There were many reasons for this failure, among them mistaken perceptions of the threat, an exaggerated view of the value of U.S. methods, political considerations that overrode military objections, and a lack of American leverage. The analysts' language regarding the last point is worth quoting: "The U.S. quickly became so deeply and so overtly committed to the Diem government that any leverage inherent in the assistance program rapidly approached zero."[8]

Military effectiveness was all about fighting the insurgents, and the Vietnam war began there. During Diem's first years there had been no active resistance. About 80,000 Vietminh had gone to North Vietnam after Geneva. There were no precise figures, but it was estimated that between 5,000 and 10,000 former guerrillas remained in the South. Hanoi had stay-behind networks and some arms caches, but no active force. Diem's security measures neutralized most of what remained; certainly the figures for arrests and executions far outnumbered the estimated enemy. North Vietnamese accounts quote letters from southern cadres literally begging for orders to resume fighting. For a long time Hanoi rejected such appeals. Until 1956 the Democratic Republic of Vietnam still hoped for national elections. For several years after that, Hanoi would be preoccupied with internal problems—fostering economic development with few resources proved to be tremendously difficult. In addition, a badly conceived and managed land collectivization program between 1955 and 1957 led to significant upheaval, including popular resistance. By most estimates, as many as 55,000 persons died from hunger, in local revolts, or in security crackdowns as agricultural shortfalls crippled the North.[9]

Meanwhile, Diem's army maintained a permanent offensive against suspected Vietminh, and the number of surviving cadres was reduced by two-thirds. At length, former guerrillas began taking up arms despite the lack of instructions and even orders not to fight. The southern resistance began there and never stopped. Its character should not be misunderstood: these were southerners determined to bring the revolution to Saigon, not North Vietnamese. As late as December 1958, DRV prime minister Pham Van Dong offered to negotiate arms reductions with Saigon. The Diem government, viewing this as propaganda, rejected the suggestion. At a party congress in Hanoi, North Vietnam now decided to help the insurgents. In May 1959 Hanoi ordered specialists from its Vietnam People's Army to create a supply route to the South. That became the origin of the "Ho Chi Minh Trail," which the northerners named the "Truong Son Strategic Supply Route," after the mountains that separated Vietnam from the inland nations of Laos and Cambodia. The first shipments arrived in the South in August 1959. That fall Hanoi added a seaborne component to its supply effort.

Resistance in the South doubled and redoubled, the growth made up almost entirely of southerners. The guerrillas who fought Diem were indigenous. Their impact was felt immediately. The number of kidnappings and assassinations of Diemist officials grew rapidly starting in 1958. Guerrillas, estimated at just 2,500 in 1959—with the ARVN forty times larger—increased to 5,000 late that year and to 12,000 in 1960. Early in 1960 the insurgents stunned the ARVN and its American advisers when a number of units coordinated to attack a regimental headquarters, decimating the army unit, overrunning its base, capturing documents, and burning the barracks. That July two Americans were killed while relaxing after a day's work, the first battle deaths in a new war. Overall incidents, including all manner of attacks, mushroomed from about 600 in 1959 to ten times that in 1961. In Kennedy's first months, the strength of the southern resistance would be estimated at 16,000 to 19,000. Referring to the guerrillas pejoratively as "Vietcong" did nothing to cancel their real power.

As had Eisenhower, Kennedy prematurely committed himself to Ngo Dinh Diem. JFK proceeded on the basis of his favorable memories of Diem from the 1950s, the need to sustain Saigon amid encroaching crisis—exemplified by the Laotian situation—and Eisenhower's advice during the transition. Early on, JFK turned to his deputy national security adviser, Walt W. Rostow, to remark, "This is the worst yet."[10] Court historian Arthur M. Schlesinger defended Kennedy, arguing that perceiving Ho Chi Minh as a nationalist more than a communist would have meant rising above prevailing abstractions, and regardless of the validity, or lack thereof, of the Domino Theory when Ike proposed it, the concept had acquired a certain substance by Kennedy's day. About the U.S. stake in South Vietnam, Schlesinger agreed that "Eisenhower's letter created those interests."[11]

President Kennedy adopted many of the Gilpatric committee's recommendations. To carry the good news, Kennedy sent his vice president, Lyndon Baines Johnson, to Saigon in April 1961. According to Roger Hilsman, who headed State Department intelligence at the time and was close to the Kennedys, LBJ found Diem remote and surrounded by persons less admirable than he, but Johnson nevertheless publicly proclaimed Diem the "Winston Churchill of Southeast Asia."[12] Upon returning, Johnson reported to Kennedy in terms that could have come right out of his 1954 newsletters: "We must decide whether to help these countries to the best of our ability or throw in the towel in the area and pull back our defenses to San Francisco and a 'Fortress America' concept. More important, we would say to the world . . . that we don't live up to our treaties and don't stand by our friends."[13]

Strategic Hamlets and the Vietnam Data Problem

In consonance with the idea of a combat laboratory, Kennedy's program tried out new weapons and tactics in Vietnam's rice paddies. He sent in a covert unit of U.S. combat aircraft, code-named "Farm Gate," an Air Force component of U.S. Special Operations Forces. Army Special Forces, whom JFK first endowed with green berets, were to train a new ARVN elite formation, the Rangers. Kennedy approved a 20,000-man increase in the ARVN as a whole, as well as more South Vietnamese militia. U.S. aid increased to match the higher force levels, as did the U.S. military contingent, which nearly doubled to more than 1,200 by early 1962. American military aid to South Vietnam multiplied even faster.

All these things proved insufficient. In the late summer of 1961 JFK decided to send people he trusted to make a fresh assessment of the situation. Led by General Maxwell D. Taylor, Kennedy's personal military representative, and Walt W. Rostow, the Taylor-Rostow mission that November expressed serious doubts. Arguing that Saigon faced a double crisis of confidence—fear that the United States was not really determined to save Southeast Asia and that Diem's methods would not suffice—Taylor and Rostow recommended a wide range of measures. They wanted not only a U.S. military presence (8,000 soldiers initially, ostensibly for flood relief in the Mekong delta) but also a radical increase in the size of MAAG, combined with overt lifting of the Geneva-imposed "ceiling" on the advisory group; use of American helicopter units to provide airlift for the ARVN in each of its three corps areas (effectively committing Americans to combat, albeit in a support role); a large increase in the militia plus modest growth of the ARVN; and better intelligence, including Americans discreetly inserted directly into the Saigon government structure. Kennedy approved everything except for administrators and combat troops. Schlesinger writes of this period, "Diem's assurances led to little or nothing in the way of performance. This was increasingly the pattern of Washington's relations with the Diem regime."[14]

Some recent scholarship on Vietnam has endeavored to rehabilitate the Ngo family.[15] In this formulation, Diem and Nhu are viewed as conservative modernizers, and an argument is made that Diem actually worked toward a vision of the Vietnamese future based on his philosophy of "personalism." Diem appreciated that liberal capitalism would not work in Vietnam and, with this in mind, tried to gather the resources for modernization by means suitable to Vietnamese society—that is, forcing the peasants to contribute their money and labor. Diem's officials are credited with the insight that Washington-favored reforms, such as a free press and free assembly, were not going to defeat the insurgency. American frustration with the Saigon leadership is castigated as being fueled by misperceptions different only in kind from those of French colonialists.[16]

There can be little doubt that Washington remained mired in its misperceptions of Vietnam throughout the war, but it does not follow that Diem's approach was any more apt—in fact, it was not. All along, the best of the American actors in this tragedy argued for more suitable approaches. Diem's vision, meanwhile, was belied by his actions—or, more properly, his inaction—in the face of the most pressing problems. Diem's failure to eradicate corruption, for example, made efforts at capital formation within the society merely another vehicle for the enrichment of the elite. The same corruption negated much well-intended American aid. As elsewhere, Diem made promises but never reached below the surface. Initiatives that might have built a new Vietnam remained merely rhetorical. Land reform was proclaimed but not enforced. Industrial development plans stayed on paper. Road improvement focused on strategic military highways, not economic infrastructure, linking the Central Highlands to the Da Nang area or Kontum to the Laotian border. Diem's social "reforms," driven by Nhu and his wife, prohibited dancing, public assembly, and political parties; created a private elite and a "republican" youth movement capped by regime thugs; and did little to improve the lives of Vietnamese. If this was "conservative modernism," Vietnam did not need it. The most telling commentary on Vietnamese rejection of the Diemist formula lay in the rapid rise of the southern resistance combined with the growing determination of South Vietnamese loyalists to oust him.

Population resettlement at once illuminates Diem's *immobilisme* and the Americans' illusions, while simultaneously having a direct impact on the rebellion. Classical theories of guerrilla warfare and counterinsurgency hold that liberation movements draw sustenance, protection, and strength from the people, making the insurgents akin to fish swimming in the sea, to follow Mao Zedong's formulation. The favored image in counterinsurgency theory is thus to drain the sea, leaving the fish flopping in the mud to be easily swept up. In practice, this meant isolating the population from the guerrillas. In Malaya in the 1950s the British gave substance to this notion, defeating an ethnic Chinese-based insurgency precisely by close population control. British security expert Sir Robert Thompson, an apostle of the technique, came to Saigon in 1961 to head a British advisory mission and served both Diem and U.S. commanders in South Vietnam, where population control would repeatedly be attempted. The Michigan State University contingent would also be quite active in this regard.

President Diem ordered preparations for resettlement in the Mekong delta in the spring of 1959, implementation that June, and expansion of the concept the following year. Peasants were to be removed to "agrovilles" and later to satellite hamlets. The intent was to separate the peasants from the insurgents, concentrate the people under the watchful eyes of security forces, create new communities, and carry out land reform—all at once and without U.S. assistance. The program was a disaster. Diemist officials conscripted peasants for forced labor to build the agrovilles, including during the harvest season; they demanded villagers spend their own scant money for materials and then treated the inhabitants like prisoners. Resettlement took villagers from their ancestral homes and burial sites—central to Buddhist culture—and obliged them to walk long distances to work the fields instead of living on the land. The new settlements actually gave insurgents a focus for recruitment by concentrating masses of disaffected villagers. The high point of the agrovilles coincided with the takeoff point of the southern resistance. The presidential palace long insisted that problems were due merely to the insensitivity of officials, but Diem did not replace them. In late 1960 the agroville program was canceled.

The next expedient was to fortify villages wherever they lay. This corresponded to Ngo Dinh Nhu's idea of mobilizing youth and expanding a security cordon that could progressively cover the countryside. Experimental efforts in several provinces to create fortified "combat" villages, as well as the CIA–South Vietnamese Village Defense Program in the Central Highlands, were initiated in 1961. Late that year Sir Robert Thompson coined the term *strategic hamlet* when he advocated defended or "strategic" hamlets as part of a plan he proposed for securing the delta. In early 1962 Saigon made strategic hamlets a national program, and Diem appointed Nhu to head it.

Roger Hilsman became a linchpin in selling strategic hamlets to JFK. He learned of Thompson's concept from the U.S. embassy and later heard the gist of it from Sir Robert himself. A paper Hilsman wrote for President Kennedy in early 1962 became the basis for JFK's approval.[17] Almost immediately strategic hamlets became mired in differences, both between U.S. military and civilian leaders and between Washington and Saigon. The military wanted to use them to stymie guerrilla recruitment and devised Operation Sunrise to bodily relocate a series of villages north of Saigon, in the style of the agrovilles. Hilsman opposed that idea, but Nhu and Diem backed it. Operation Sunrise became the first embodiment of strategic hamlets, which quickly took a hit when journalists reported that the new villages were virtual concentration camps.

Diem's defenders argue in retrospect that Americans never appreciated the real significance of strategic hamlets, which were meant to be vehicles for social change and to put the peasants on the front line in defending themselves. This does not track with Hilsman's memoir written in 1967, long before the Vietnam war had even ended. Hilsman cites Thompson thus: "the hamlet scheme and the bureaucratic apparatus that would be created to run it [were to be] the means for a revolutionary change in the peasant's lot— economically, politically, socially, and culturally." Views in Saigon and Washington were no different. Meanwhile, a serious Diemist commitment to the hamlets as agents of social change does not correspond to the consistently low priority Saigon gave them in terms of agricultural assistance, militia weapons, and communications equipment; the failure to carry out local elections; Saigon's siphoning off of aid, requiring the peasants to pay for materials the United States had provided for free; or the fact that no social programs were actually initiated. Vietnamese peasants reacted the same way to strategic hamlets as they had to the agrovilles.

The problem Hilsman anticipated was that the Ngos would overextend the initiative by trying to impose strategic hamlets all over South Vietnam simultaneously. That is precisely what happened. Saigon did not have the money for such a large effort, even with U.S. assistance. In addition, conditions differed widely in various parts of South Vietnam, so the design was not suitable for all forty-four provinces. To meet target goals, Saigon cut corners; in many cases hamlets were simply rechristened as "strategic" or wood palisades were installed around hamlets, and that was that.[18] By April 1963 roughly 6,000 strategic hamlets had been completed, and there were plans for another 2,500 by July, covering the majority of South Vietnam's roughly 14,000 hamlets.

Beyond all the difficulties of what would come to be termed *pacification* was the fact that the stronger these programs became, the more they conflicted with the U.S. military view of how to combat the insurgency, which minimized the importance of the southern resistance. The military, along with certain civilian officials such as Rostow, argued that an outside base— in this case, North Vietnam—was a sine qua non for guerrillas. In that vision, closing the border would drain the sea. Rostow would have gone further and struck the north to dissuade it from helping the insurgents, but he did not get his way. Instead, a host of efforts was attempted to seal the border, including naval patrols off the coast, border scouts and defense camps, and passive defense by minefields. Meanwhile, in the South, American advisers with the ARVN pushed conventional operations that rarely encountered the adversary.

Probably the most important event on the other side during this period was consolidation of the resistance into the National Front for the Liberation of South Vietnam, or, more simply, the National Liberation Front (NLF). Created in Tay Ninh province in December 1960 under a leadership council that included people from many regions and occupations, the NLF represented a united front in the same style as the Vietminh. Its chairman, Nguyen Huu Tho, was a French-trained lawyer who had agitated against colonialism and had been with the resistance since French times. Tho was first imprisoned in 1950. He was not openly a communist, but Diem claimed he was and incarcerated him. Tho was freed by a resistance commando raid. The NLF's striking arm was the People's Liberation Armed Forces (PLAF), the army that Saigon and Washington called the Vietcong. Already in this early period, the PLAF had assumed the character it would retain, with a hierarchy of regular units, provincial local forces, and village-based self-defense forces. The military was matched to a political apparatus in a hierarchy parallel to Saigon's, with leaders at hamlet, village, district, and provincial levels and a wide array of popular organizations designed to enmesh as many Vietnamese as possible in the struggle. Diem talked about broad-based social organizations; the NLF actually created them.

Both the NLF and Hanoi mounted massive propaganda campaigns against strategic hamlets and the American combat techniques they called "special warfare." Some observers interpret these acts as evidence that Diem was winning the war. There *are* indications of concern in Hanoi's official histories. A Central Military-Party Committee directive in mid-1962 ordered the forces in the South to disrupt the strategic hamlet campaign. At the end of that year the DRV Politburo's assessment was that the ARVN's U.S.-backed buildup was outstripping that of the Liberation Front. And in June 1963, meeting again, the Central Military-Party Committee approved a decision to increase the infiltration into South Vietnam.[19] But strategic decisions are made to manage situations and are judged by outcomes, not inputs, which as often as not are wrong. Hanoi had fears aplenty, among them the mass of U.S. power lurking behind the Saigon government. And its appreciation—from the outside—of the effectiveness of Diem's pacification was based more on numbers of strategic hamlets than on any understanding of their coherence or effectiveness. It is noteworthy that the same session of the Central Military-Party Committee that decided to up the infiltration rate felt comfortable with Hanoi's ability to act throughout Indochina, in both Vietnam and Laos. The Vietnam People's Army official history notes that "after a period of difficulties" in late 1962 and early 1963, "the armed struggle movement combined with political struggle in Cochin China began to recover and grow."[20]

It is true that, according to U.S. statistics, the average number of Liberation Front attacks, terrorism, and sabotage incidents, plus detected propaganda efforts, fell between early 1962 and 1963 (from about 550 to 350 attacks a month, for example), while PLAF defections were up (from less than 100 to 375). Pacification statistics claimed that by April 1963, Saigon controlled 53 percent of the villages, a gain of 7 percent; in contrast, NLF control had fallen off a couple of percentage points, and villages where the NLF was ascendant had decreased by almost half.[21] Secretary of Defense Robert McNamara, who visited South Vietnam in mid-1962, came away saying, "Every quantitative measure shows that we're winning the war." The CIA's William Colby, who had left Saigon around that time and by early 1963 headed the agency's Far East Division, carrying the water for the CIA's Vietnam war, argues on this basis that Diem would have turned the corner if he had had two more years in power and would have beat the insurgency a few years after that.[22]

Statistics support both sides of the issue, and even the ones cited here offer an incomplete picture. The Liberation Front activity described in these data began a period of sustained growth in early 1963, although totals remained lower than in the previous year. But numbers of claimed PLAF casualties were down and the ARVN's were up, each by about 20 percent. South Vietnamese weapons losses were also up (in fact, higher than those of the NLF), an indicator of poor combat performance. Stated differently, the NLF was inflicting more losses on the ARVN in fewer attacks. NLF strength increased considerably, with between 22,000 and 25,000 regulars and at least 80,000 guerrillas, despite infiltration rates that remained constant. This indicates very successful recruitment by the southern resistance, which belies the data on reductions in Liberation Front population control.[23]

There is also a very real question about the degree to which these statistics were falsified—made up, guesstimated, or deliberately contrived. The evidence of falsification is overwhelming. Intelligence officer–turned–historian John Newman argues convincingly in his study of Kennedy in Vietnam that the U.S. military engaged in a deliberate effort to demonstrate success through phony statistics and intelligence.[24] Journalist Neil Sheehan, biographer of the legendary U.S. adviser John Paul Vann, shows in excruciating detail how pessimistic reporting from MAAG's best people in the field was suppressed at headquarters, which tended to focus on the positive in its dispatches.[25] Sheehan and other reporters such as David Halberstam, Malcolm Browne, Peter Arnett, and Homer Bigart, among others, were all subjected to attempts at manipulation. JFK even called the publisher of the *New York Times* in an effort to suppress some of Halberstam's articles.[26] CIA officer Harold Ford notes that these war correspondents were "special targets for official pressure."[27]

George W. Allen, a veteran officer with the Defense Intelligence Agency, soon moved to the CIA because he was disgusted with the military's inability to provide objective data. Allen was an old Indochina hand who had cut his teeth on Vietnam at Dien Bien Phu, working on Matt Ridgway's presentation that had helped stymie the Eisenhower intervention. Allen had labored on Vietnam ever since and had encountered the success mentality many times. For instance, sent to Saigon in 1962 to help MAAG develop a better estimate of NLF strength, Allen used all available data and concluded that the PLAF guerrillas alone might have surpassed 100,000 the previous year. But when he proposed that figure, headquarters rejected it.[28]

An especially egregious example of manipulation occurred in the spring of 1963 when the CIA compiled its latest National Intelligence Estimate (NIE). Previous NIEs had retained a healthy skepticism about Vietnam, continuing to warn of Diem's political weaknesses as well as the military uncertainties. Work on this particular NIE began in October 1962. Senior analyst Willard C. Matthias managed its drafting and the coordination among all the relevant agencies, the special feature that made NIEs the considered opinion of the entire U.S. intelligence community. Matthias picked George Carver, formerly of the Saigon station, as lead analyst. Carver had been driven out of South Vietnam by Ngo Dinh Nhu for his role as go-between to rebels during the 1960 coup. Within a month Carver handed Matthias a draft centered on the Cold War angle and concluding that Soviet and Chinese stakes in Vietnam were limited. Matthias, however, wanted an NIE focused on the war, so he and Carver worked up a fresh paper. It found that no satisfactory objective means existed to assess progress, and there were difficult-to-surmount problems with such tactics as strategic hamlets. Progress would be possible only in the context of "radical changes in the methods and personnel of the South Vietnamese government."[29] The Board of National Estimates, corporate manager of the NIEs, changed this language to a more direct indictment of the Saigon regime: "The modus operandi of the Diem government, and particularly its measures to prevent the rise of contenders for political power, have reduced the government's effectiveness, both politically and militarily. We believe that unless radical changes are made in the methods of the government, there is little hope that U.S. involvement can be substantially curtailed or that there will be material and lasting reduction in the Communist threat."[30]

The draft went before the U.S. Intelligence Board on February 27, 1963. There, CIA director John McCone savaged the paper and its drafters, demanding to know why the NIE did not take into account the views of the people who (supposedly) knew what was really going on—the operators. His complaint triggered a round of interviews in which the CIA canvassed those responsible for the war. The final paper, NIE 53-63, issued on April 17, flatly claimed that the NLF's progress had been blunted and the situation was improving; there was reason to expect that the peasantry could be won over, with Diem promising to mend his political fences.[31] The estimate exuded optimism far beyond any sustaining data.

Roger Hilsman's intelligence unit at State would be subjected to identical pressures. By now JFK had promoted Hilsman to assistant secretary for Far Eastern affairs, and deputy Thomas L. Hughes had taken over the Bureau of Intelligence and Research (INR), as the unit was known. That summer, INR analyst Louis Sarris, Hilsman's coauthor on the original strategic hamlets paper, began to study the statistics. By now the gloss had come off the NIE, and McCone had been forced to apologize to his own analysts and issue a pessimistic correction. That did not prevent an outside attack on Sarris's INR paper when it circulated in late October. The Joint Chiefs filed an extensive complaint, which McNamara took to Secretary of State Dean Rusk. McNamara threatened to go to Kennedy unless State agreed that INR would stay out of the military estimates business.[32] Rusk chewed out Hughes and Sarris and mollified McNamara with the promise that future INR papers on these subjects would be coordinated with the Pentagon.[33] By then, all the speculations and warnings about Ngo Dinh Diem's political vulnerabilities had come home to roost.

The Fall of Ngo Dinh Diem

What ultimately shreds the fevered conjecture that Diem could have won the war is his overthrow not by Americans but by Vietnamese. Ngo Dinh Diem's own ham-fisted policies led to this result, and his resistance to reform was just one aspect. Even old friends gave up hope. Wesley Fishel broke with Diem in 1962, convinced the Saigon leader had lost touch. The Michigan State University Group went home. By year's end such stalwarts as Mike Mansfield were telling President Kennedy that Diem was through, and the next summer he argued that supporting Diem was unnecessary to U.S. interests in Southeast Asia. In Vietnam's Central Highlands, where the CIA and Green Berets were working with the montagnards to create a large fighting force, Diem's actions alienated the tribes at an accelerating rate, while Nhu's suspicions of U.S. meddling minimized Saigon's support of the program. One montagnard actually joined the NLF's central committee, and in early 1962 the montagnards set up their own political organization. Later, when Diem released some montagnard activists from jail, he kept back two of the tribes' major leaders.[34] Although villages enlisted in the defense program added to the count of strategic hamlets, in reality, the tribes were spiraling toward a revolt against Saigon. In the lowlands Diem's favoritism toward Catholics did little to endear him to Buddhists, among whom the cinder ignited that began the last act of his reign.

President Kennedy was increasingly concerned about Diem's prospects. Bad data or not, JFK could see little being accomplished. In January 1963 a fight took place at a village called Ap Bac in the delta. This time, despite the

ARVN's considerable numerical superiority, as well as mechanized troops and helicopters courtesy of the United States, a PLAF unit not only stood its ground but actually defeated the attackers, who suffered many casualties. Helicopters and armored personnel carriers were lost. Advisers, including John Paul Vann, in whose sector the battle took place, charged senior South Vietnamese officers with incompetence. Diem replaced neither of the responsible commanders. Kennedy had to notice. If strategic hamlets were to work, they had to be shielded by the ARVN.[35] As for the adversary, the Liberation Front wasted no time exploiting Ap Bac as a psychological success, with propaganda to emulate, or replicate, the victory.

Most important to Saigon was the army. Had Diem spent as much effort prosecuting the war and making his government a dynamic alternative to the NLF as he did countering antipathy toward the Ngo family, the military would have been no problem. Instead, the palace openly played with officer assignments and posts made desirable by opportunities for corruption. Many ARVN officers were committed anticommunists who only wanted to get on with the war.[36] Saigon cafés bubbled with talk of plots. After February 1962, when disgruntled air force pilots tried to kill Diem and Nhu by bombing the palace, both Diem's antics and the talk got darker. Advocates of the "victory" thesis have never managed to explain how the ARVN was going to win the war while Diem was busily engaging it in back-alley political struggle.

A few examples will suffice. Duong Van Minh, who had led the Diemist forces in Saigon during the sect crisis, now headed the ARVN Field Command and was, in effect, its top general. But Diem, worried that army headquarters could control units all over the country, redesigned the system so that corps commanders answered to the palace, leaving Minh little to do. He spent most afternoons playing tennis at the Lido Officers' Club in the nearby town of Gia Dinh. Later Diem shunted "Big" Minh, as he was known, into a meaningless inspector's post. Officers felt that they had been robbed of their top honcho in the fight against the Liberation Front.

Then there was Colonel Pham Van Dong. He *was* a fighter—in French days he would have been called a *baroudeur,* or a barroom brawler. Dong became the first Vietnamese officer in the national army to lead a large combat formation, a mobile group. He had an excellent reputation among U.S. advisers. From 1959 to 1962 Dong served as chief of staff of III Corps, the command that included Saigon. Diem called him in one day and said, "Colonel Dong, I am told you are preparing to make the coup." Dong denied it, but he was sent off to General Minh's staff, then demoted to chief inspector of strategic hamlets. In itself, that assignment reveals something of Diem's regard for strategic hamlets. Dong told American friends that he had been left behind—a comment that also speaks volumes about Diem's war strategy. Many of Dong's subordinates were now his superiors.[37]

Or take the case of Lieutenant Colonel Lam Quang Thi. Basically nonpolitical, Thi had done nothing in the 1960 coup, even though, "by that time, my original excitement and hope in Mr. Diem had vanished."[38] One of Thi's brothers led a unit of the coup, which would have been enough to justify the arrest of Colonel Thi, except for the fact that another brother had commanded the tanks that saved Diem. Despite—or because of—his lack of a role, Colonel Thi was sent to head the artillery section of Minh's staff. Then he was reassigned as an operations staffer to yet another headquarters without troops, the Army Command, which replaced the Field Command.

Such treatment made many enemies for Diem and Nhu. Because there were only a few lucrative or meaningful posts to dispense, over time, there were numerous disgruntled officers for each whose loyalty was bound to the Ngos. Disaffected subordinates could replace loyalists in key units. The air force commander was such a loyalist. But the transport wing commander, Colonel Nguyen Cao Ky, was not. Ky believed that the achievement of higher rank was dependent on party loyalty, as it was in communist countries. Nhu and his henchmen were diverting the American aid intended for strategic hamlets to the black market, but as Ky observed, "at that time even to speak against the Diem regime was dangerous."[39] Ky saw something else too: the same falsification of data that bedeviled Washington being applied in Saigon. One day while shopping at the city's central market, Ky saw police preparing for one of Diem's extremely rare excursions outside the palace. The police, whom Nhu controlled, had instructed merchants that if the president asked about any item they should quote old prices from when Diem first took power. Once Diem got in trouble, Ky not only refused to help the president but also arrested the air force commander.

Colonel Ky, who was a Buddhist, had to be particularly upset by the Buddhist political crisis in the summer of 1963. It began in Hue with Diem's brothers. First, Archbishop Ngo Dinh Thuc, who was celebrating his twenty-fifth anniversary jubilee, held parades through the city that included the carrying of religious flags. Since 1957 there had been laws against the display of any but the South Vietnamese flag. These were not enforced against the Catholics. Then on May 8, Buddhists celebrating the 2,507th birthday of Buddha paraded their own religious banners, and another brother, province chief Ngo Dinh Can, ordered a crackdown. When monk Thich Tri Quang was denied the chance to deliver a birthday message on the radio, some 10,000 Buddhists marched on the radio station, and Can had the police and army break up the demonstration. Major Dan Sy's troops fired on the crowd, and an armored car crushed some of the protesters; eight were killed. Rather than accept responsibility, the Diem government alleged that the violence had been caused by an NLF operative with a hand grenade.

This tragedy led to a cycle of protest, repression, and mobilization—increasingly familiar to Americans of the civil rights movement. Demonstrations soon spread to Saigon. Buddhist elders met with Diem and tabled demands: the government should acknowledge its role, pay compensation, permit display of the Buddhist flag, and prosecute responsible officials. Diem prevaricated. Apologists asserted the NLF argument. Of course, the NLF was going to take advantage of *any* political opening, but that is excuse, not explanation. The fact is that Ngo Dinh Diem refused accommodation. He sided with his brothers and revealed his favoritism for Catholic over Buddhist citizens in an unmistakable fashion.

On May 28 Buddhist monks, called bonzes, held a protest in front of the National Assembly building in Saigon. These demonstrations soon became almost daily events. In early June police used tear gas to break up another protest in Hue. On June 8 Madame Nhu denounced the Buddhists, alleging they had been infiltrated by communists. Several days later bonze Thich Quang Duc immolated himself at a busy Saigon intersection while nuns chanted and burned incense. Efforts to allow cooler heads to prevail were blown when a government commission denied responsibility in the original incident. Nhu mobilized his republican youth, and Madame Nhu famously declared that all the Buddhists had done was to "barbecue a monk."

Saigon's hot summer boiled through August. Then Diem struck. A group of ARVN generals met to ruminate on the Buddhist problem and proposed a crackdown to Nhu; he told them to take the proposal to Diem, who approved it on the night of August 20.[40] The next morning Diem declared martial law and appointed General Ton That Dinh as Saigon regional commander. Ngo Dinh Nhu used security troops under the nominal command of General Dinh, particularly his U.S.-trained and -financed Vietnamese Special Forces, to attack and occupy An Quang and Xa Loi, the key pagodas in Saigon and Hue. An all-day pitched battle ensued at one location. The Ngos probably sealed their fate by trying to place responsibility on the ARVN this time, with Nhu telling the CIA that ten South Vietnamese generals had planned the pagoda raids. Within days, over two different channels, Vietnamese officers were asking what Washington's attitude would be in the event of a coup against Ngo Dinh Diem.

■ ■ ■ The last months of Diem's reign are a jumble of confusion. Starting with the ARVN generals and their renewed determination to oust Diem, Washington's headaches were tremendous. Other threads weave through the tapestry also. One is the question of Kennedy's own resolve and whether he intended to get America out of Vietnam. Some prefer to view JFK as committed to that course. Another matter is the issue of Laos—its role almost entirely ignored yet furnishing key evidence on the question. Washington politics yields another point of evidence.

The coup project against Diem proceeded fitfully. Initial feelers from

ARVN officers triggered frantic soul-searching in Washington. This began with a notorious bureaucratic end run wherein Hilsman took advantage of the absence of many key players to get Kennedy's approval to back the coup in a cabled response to the generals. McCone, McNamara, and Rusk, plus others, combined to quash the initiative, and a countermanding cable was sent. But after a series of White House meetings, JFK finally came back to the same policy. By then the Vietnamese had gotten cold feet, and nothing happened.

Postponement of the coup bought time to pursue other avenues. What the United States wanted was "effective" government in Saigon. That meant Diem had to rid himself of cronies, particularly the Nhus, on whom most U.S. attention focused. But the Saigon leader had promised reforms without delivering countless times before. Kennedy's problem was familiar: lack of leverage. The president decided to pressure Saigon. Nhu would be shorn of the means to claim that the United States backed him. The most visible of those was CIA funding and training for Vietnamese Special Forces. This was terminated, with no effect. Nhu even struck back, orchestrating a pro-Diem demonstration outside the U.S. embassy, giving an interview accusing the *CIA* of fomenting the Buddhist crisis, and then having one of his newspapers blow the cover of the CIA station chief in Saigon. Washington's ultimate form of pressure was to threaten to get out of Vietnam.

Here the quest for leverage intersects with the notion of a "Kennedy withdrawal," which seems to have gained the status of urban myth. There is no question that Kennedy was perplexed. He had certainly been driven far from his hopes for Diem in the 1950s. There are a number of quotations and meditations regarding Kennedy's *desire* to extricate America from the quagmire, and a good-sized list of Kennedy's senior officials all claim that JFK intended to get out after the 1964 election, when he would be in his second term and less vulnerable to political damage. Robert McNamara heads that list, but it includes Roger Hilsman, NSC Southeast Asia staffer Michael Forrestal, and others. John Kenneth Galbraith, Kennedy's ambassador to India, had urged this as well.[41] The withdrawal option, if real, was a further opportunity for America to have avoided its war.

But concrete evidence for the Kennedy withdrawal is sparse and subject to interpretation. There is, however, hard proof for a *McNamara* withdrawal: at a conference in Honolulu in 1962 the secretary of defense ordered plans for a drawdown of U.S. strength to a force level approaching that of the Eisenhower days. This was not a simple thing. In June 1962, about the time of that Honolulu meeting, U.S. troops in South Vietnam already stood at 9,000, and by mid-1963 there were 15,400 American servicemen and -women there. In some versions, the reductions were to be completed by 1965, but planning documents exist with schedules extending to 1968—timed to coincide with a prospective run for the presidency by Robert F. Kennedy. In all cases there was provision for *residual forces,* that is, not a total withdrawal but a restructured U.S. commitment. Most important, every withdrawal scheme was contingent on progress in the war and assumed the defeat of Hanoi and the NLF. The latter point, incidentally, underlines the importance of disputes over Vietnam statistics and data and suggests a motive for McNamara's attack on State Department INR critiques of military progress, which occurred at just the time reductions were being considered. In sum, the record of withdrawal planning indicates an early version of what would eventually be called "Vietnamization," not a U.S. exit from the war.

The situation in Laos is important with regard to the question of a Kennedy withdrawal. Kennedy deserves credit for his approach to Laos: he received a hot potato; quickly understood that conducting a war there, as Eisenhower had advised, was nonsensical; and drew the appropriate conclusion.[42] Kennedy withstood the pressures of his military advisers and officials such as Rostow, who delivered a succession of appeals for active intervention in Laos. Assisted by W. Averell Harriman, JFK then championed an extremely complex negotiation that led to a renewed set of Geneva agreements on Laos in mid-1962. But the neutralization mandated there took hold in name only, and after Geneva, Kennedy acquiesced in covert CIA operations designed to counter the North Vietnamese and Laotian communists. No doubt seen as a way to preserve U.S. options, the CIA maneuvers lent confidence to anticommunist Laotians who conspired to contravene the agreements, while CIA tribal allies initiated attacks on their communist enemies. In the spring of 1963 war resumed in Laos after the murder of a key neutralist minister. Kennedy then entertained a series of *escalation* proposals that summer. He approved the last of these, National Security Action Memorandum (NSAM) 259, just two days before the Vietnamese generals asked about U.S. support for a coup. It is not possible that JFK was unaware of the relationship of Laos to the war in Vietnam, and highly unlikely that Kennedy would escalate in Laos while withdrawing from Vietnam.

The most concrete evidence for the Kennedy withdrawal, to get slightly ahead of our story, comes from meetings in early October, where the president agreed to go ahead with the first tranche of troop reductions, a withdrawal of 1,000 Americans. The NSC meeting where the president pondered this action and the decision document sanctioning the move (NSAM-263) are the supposed proof. But a tape recording of the NSC conversation exists, and JFK's tone and inflection clearly show that he was doubtful and questioning, not affirmatively approving. Conversely, the paper reporting Robert McNamara's and General Maxwell Taylor's conclusions from another fact-finding mission, the subject of this NSC meeting, makes the link between progress and withdrawal, asserting "the military campaign has made great progress."[43] On December 31, 1963, there were 16,300 American troops in Vietnam, roughly 1,000 *more* than at the moment of the presumptive withdrawal decision.[44]

Publicly, Kennedy was straightforward and quite clear. In a television interview with Walter Cronkite of CBS on September 2, JFK referred to Vietnamization, saying, "In the final analysis it is their war. They are the ones who have to win it or lose it." He also spoke directly on the subject of withdrawal: "I don't agree with those who say we should withdraw. That would be a great mistake." A week later in an interview with NBC television, Kennedy affirmed his belief in the Domino Theory and again said, "I think we should stay. We should use our influence in as effective a way as we can, but we should not withdraw."[45] Apart from anything else, for President Kennedy to convey these public messages and then change course and approve withdrawal would have meant significantly increasing his political costs.

This raises the question of leveraging Saigon, to which JFK also alluded. The other way to interpret withdrawal talk is as a device to coerce Diem to dismiss the Nhus. Withdrawal was a means of calling Diem's bluff, Kennedy's biggest stick. Toward mid-September Idaho senator Frank Church drafted a congressional resolution threatening the termination of U.S. military and economic assistance unless Saigon abandoned its repressive policies. Church got JFK's quiet backing, along with State Department help in drafting his resolution. Equally significant, there existed *another* U.S. withdrawal plan—one for total withdrawal, one assembled at exactly the same time by Roger Hilsman. It avowedly formed part of the coercion effort.

In early October members of the Senate Foreign Relations Committee, including Church but also such luminaries as J. William Fulbright and Wayne Morse, visited with JFK. Their questions went to why the United States had not done more. Fulbright asserted that a withdrawal would be unacceptable. In Congress, thus far only Oregon's Morse and South Dakota's George McGovern had called for an end to U.S. involvement, and they were voices in the wilderness. Public opinion remained muted. In the fall of 1963 American Friends of Vietnam (AFV) chairman "Iron Mike" O'Daniel threatened to resign if the organization came out publicly *against* Diem, even though the AFV had ended its open support a year earlier. Madame Nhu later wrote to O'Daniel to denounce AFV as "false friends and traitors."[46] Thus political pressures existed, but their effect was to push Kennedy toward action, not withdrawal.

One purpose of the Taylor-McNamara mission was to encourage Diem to move against Nhu. Colby of the CIA went along with the specific purpose of convincing Nhu to leave; however, Colby's attempt would be scotched by ambassador Henry Cabot Lodge, who forbade him to have any contact with Diem's brother. The Taylor-McNamara mission also looked into prospects for a coup by the generals and found an early coup unlikely. The ARVN generals and South Vietnamese students, who had joined the Buddhist protests, had been neutralized by Nhu's security forces, the mission found. Perhaps with an eye toward the abortive August plot, Taylor and McNamara reported that the generals had little stomach for the attempt. But the day they left Saigon, CIA officer Lucien Conein encountered General Tran Van Don, who arranged for the CIA to be appraised of a coup led by General Duong Van Minh.

One of Minh's options was to murder Diem and his brother. Colby wrote a reply for McCone, which the CIA director sent on October 6, declaring the agency could not encourage or support assassination but had no responsibility to stop every coup. But McCone also counseled Kennedy against overthrowing Diem. He repeated his arguments so often that JFK eventually rebuked him, asking McCone why he was so out of step. But Vice President Lyndon Johnson also opposed the plot, as did Treasury Secretary C. Douglas Dillon, former ambassador Frederick Nolting, and MAAG boss General Paul D. Harkins. Others, like McNamara, were uncomfortable with the use of CIA operative Conein as a channel to the generals. Kennedy instructed the State Department to have Ambassador Lodge neither discourage nor help the plotters.

"Big" Minh, Tran Van Don, and their cohorts needed no help. By late October their preparations were far advanced. Conein got updates. When the Vietnamese wanted money, the equivalent of about $40,000 was stashed away for them in Conein's home safe. He would carry it around in a briefcase during the coup. Washington's last chance to adopt a different course came on October 29, when Kennedy convened his advisers at the White House.[47] This gathering is especially important because Bobby Kennedy, Dean Rusk, John McCone, and Maxwell Taylor *all* expressed reservations (Lyndon Johnson attended but said nothing), but they did not affect JFK's decision. The president's brother, in particular, warned that "we have some very large stakes to balance here" and noted, "it's different from a coup in the Iraq or [a] South American country."[48] Everyone present recognized that the United States would inevitably be linked to the generals' coup, no matter how it turned out. President Kennedy held firm.[49]

General Minh went ahead on November 1. Ngo Dinh Diem, unable to maneuver his way out of this challenge, fled the palace, taking Nhu with him. They surrendered to the plotters the next day and were murdered.[50] The consensus among observers is that the assassinations were ordered by Minh. Certainly one of the killers was Minh's chief bodyguard. Almost all historians of the American war agree that backing the coup froze the United States into a position that made extricating itself from Vietnam nearly impossible. It is fair to ask how John F. Kennedy, if he was serious about American withdrawal, could have agreed to this plot.

■ ■ ■ The question about Kennedy's real attitude cannot be answered by events, for the president himself perished at the hand of an assassin just a few weeks later. After Kennedy was killed in Dallas on November

22, Lyndon Baines Johnson succeeded to the presidency. There is one more piece of evidence, however: NSAM-273. This decision was among the first to plop onto President Johnson's desk after he took the oath of office. It represented deliberations among Kennedy's team at Honolulu between November 20 and 22. A constant refrain had been that Saigon was ineffective because South Vietnamese leaders failed to make the grade; identical measures by Americans would work. The gist of NSAM-273 created a fresh action program, one that included direct pressure against North Vietnam, with key parts under unilateral U.S. control. The document existed in draft form before JFK's death. Once more the question arises how Kennedy could be withdrawing while simultaneously preparing to escalate, this time not in Laos but in Vietnam.

Bill Moyers, among Johnson's closest associates at the time, remembers NSAM-273 coming to LBJ and thought it an ambush.[51] After all, Johnson had never abandoned Diem and thought the coup a mistake. The decision would tie LBJ's hands. In taking over for the fallen president, Johnson had promised to continue Kennedy's policies and even keep JFK's staffers, so LBJ approved NSAM-273. This represented the next-to-last opportunity—if opportunity it had been—to avoid the Vietnam war.

Over the following months U.S. actions focused on making the war effort more effective. The advisory group, reconstituted as the Military Assistance Command Vietnam (MACV), received a new leader, General William C. Westmoreland. But results remained poor. Saigon politics roiled, the generals maneuvered for advantage, while in the countryside the Liberation Front gained ground, particularly in the delta. In late November the PLAF actually captured American prisoners when they overran a Special Forces camp at Hiep Hoa. South Vietnamese weapons losses increased even more after the coup. Liberation Front strength estimates from earlier in 1963 were now termed "conservative," according to CIA experts on December 6.[52] Even military intelligence admitted that the number of PLAF main-force battalions had increased, as had the average strength of its units. Over the first days of 1964 there was a succession of battles in which Saigon forces were either stopped or beaten. In one, a number of American helicopters were damaged; in another, ARVN losses exceeded the enemy's.

Saigon and Washington each had its own response. In Saigon the South Vietnamese military blamed Minh's junta for not consolidating power. Forces under General Nguyen Khanh overthrew Minh. After a week Khanh himself was ousted. He regrouped for a fresh coup and in January 1964 became the new military strongman, though that may be too forceful a term, since Khanh's maneuvers ushered in a period of tremendous political instability: over the next year there were no fewer than seven coups d'etat—some by General Khanh against others, some against Khanh that he defeated, and one that finally threw him out. Unsettled politics affected the war.

In Washington the new game was promoting Saigon's stability. In March 1964 the Joint Chiefs of Staff stated their solution: bomb North Vietnam, mine its harbors, and institute a naval blockade. That program did nothing for stability. Washington instead attempted rhetoric and imagery. Appearing with Khanh in a Mekong village in March 1964, McNamara and Taylor held up his arms like a victorious prizefighter. The NLF disrupted the image, nearly killing McNamara with a bomb planted on a bridge by saboteur Nguyen Van Troi, who was captured and executed. A month later, McNamara told newsmen he was pleased: if people wanted to call Vietnam "McNamara's war," so be it.

But the Americans continued to be aware of Saigon's shakiness. Washington's campaign of covert pressure against the North became the other part of the American response. This started with a secret military campaign called Operations Plan (OPLAN) 34-A, combined with cross-border forays into Laos—a new facet of the effort to seal the South Vietnamese border. Planning began at Honolulu in November 1963, McNamara reviewed the plans that December, and LBJ approved them early in 1964. The CIA and the U.S. military directly controlled the operations. General Khanh was merely informed and asked to furnish commandos for the attacks. Khanh, in search of a unifying theme to solidify his power, began speaking of a "March North."

Meanwhile, LBJ still possessed considerable freedom of action. A late May poll by the American Institute for Public Opinion Research revealed that almost two-thirds of Americans *had given no thought to Vietnam at all.* Among the few who had, the largest single opinion category (6 percent) favored sending a United Nations peacekeeping force. The number of people who favored the existing policy (3 percent) was about the same as those who wanted to either fight or get out (4 percent). The two possible responses that provided for getting tougher and taking definite military action garnered the combined support of 9 percent of poll respondents.[53]

Washington officials began work on what they called "the scenario," a specific project structured to lead to congressional authorization for the use of force in Southeast Asia—the kind of approval Eisenhower had failed to obtain at Dien Bien Phu. They prepared a text. An interagency committee began coordinating all aspects of activity. In June 1964 the Johnson administration contrived to have a Canadian diplomat assigned to the International Control Commission go to Hanoi to threaten North Vietnamese leaders, raising the specter of stronger military action if the Democratic Republic of Vietnam did not abandon the National Liberation Front. DRV prime minister Pham Van Dong would not give an inch, warning that Hanoi would win and that if the United States pushed the war to the North, the people would stand up. The OPLAN 34-A operations were mere pinpricks. But they were against the North, and they were about to lead to a fresh escalation, one entirely by the United States. That happened in the Gulf of Tonkin.

Vietnam Veterans Against the War carry out their "Dewey Canyon III" protest, styled, following Nixon administration rhetoric, as a "limited incursion" into the land of the Congress. Here protesters unfurl their banners on the western side of the Capitol building (Stanley Commisiak).

The VVAW vets had an authoritative voice because they were authentic, not the phonies the Nixon White House sought to paint them. The medals and ribbons worn by this former Marine sergeant from the 3rd Reconnaissance Battalion indicate he had won both the Silver and Bronze Stars for combat actions, had served twice in Vietnam, held two Purple Hearts, the Meritorious Unit Award, and the Combat Action Ribbon, among others (Bernard Edelman).

At the climax of Dewey Canyon III, the veterans hurled medals over a chicken-wire fence hastily erected by Capitol police to keep them from returning their medals to Congress. In one of the iconic photographs of the antiwar movement, former Marine helicopter crewman Rusty Staub throws a gallantry medal over the barrier (Bernard Edelman).

A terrain relief model of the French entrenched camp at Dien Bien Phu that was created by Vietnam People's Army mapmakers. Today, the model is on display at the People's Army Museum in Hanoi (author's collection).

President Dwight D. Eisenhower greets Ngo Dinh Diem at National Airport on May 8, 1957—the third anniversary of the fall of Dien Bien Phu. This would be Diem's only visit to the United States as South Vietnam's leader. Behind Eisenhower, Secretary of State John Foster Dulles greets ambassador Elbridge Durbrow (National Archives).

Journalist David Halberstam coined the phrase "the best and the brightest" to denote the standing of the officials who helped presidents make their Vietnam decisions. Here President Kennedy meets with some of his top officials in the Oval Office on January 3, 1962. From the left, Vice President Lyndon B. Johnson, Kennedy, Secretary of Defense Robert S. McNamara, White House special military representative General Maxwell B. Taylor, and Deputy Secretary of Defense Roswell Gilpatric (Kennedy Library).

A few weeks after February 27, 1962, when Vietnamese air force pilots bombed the Presidential Palace in an attempt to kill him, President Diem staged an elaborate event in Saigon at which the Air Force command renewed its vow of support. The white-uniformed troops presenting arms behind Diem are members of his CIA-sponsored, Filipino-trained Presidential Guard (National Archives).

Madame Nhu, née Tran Le Xuan, the wife of Diem's brother, who increasingly played the role of South Vietnam's First Lady and a key powerbroker, created her own nucleus of support. An important element of that base were the women cadres of the Republican Youth. Founded by Madame Nhu, by late 1962 the group was strong enough to appear in Saigon's national day parade. Lining the street are Presidential Guards and helmeted officers of the National Police, the "White Mice" (U.S. Army).

The South Vietnamese military remained the key factor in all Saigonese political calculations; foremost among them were the paratroops, here passing in review at the October 27, 1962, National Day parade. Paratroops spearheaded Diem's 1955 battle for Saigon, led the 1960 coup, and figured on one side or the other in every coup action except the November 1963 plot that actually toppled Diem (U.S. Army).

Christmas Day 1962. The American Friends of Vietnam were very strong in their support for Ngo Dinh Diem. A principal activist was Francis Cardinal Spellman, a key American prelate. During a tour of South Vietnam's Mekong Delta, Cardinal Spellman toured the streets of My Tho accompanied by a retinue including American and ARVN officers, clergymen, and notables. To Spellman's right is Vietnamese III Corps commander General Huynh Van Cao (U.S. Army).

A little more than a week later, on January 2, 1963, General Cao's troops fought a pitched battle against a much smaller National Liberation Front force at the village of Ap Bac and not only withstood them but inflicted heavy losses and then escaped. The action revealed tactical inflexibility and weak leadership in the ARVN and stunned observers. This aerial view of Ap Bac shows the marks left in the fields by the tracks of the ARVN armored vehicles showing their advances and retreats, demonstrating that they never even reached the village. Two American H-21 helicopters are visible in the center foreground. Five choppers were actually shot down in the action, the worst U.S. loss in the war to date (U.S. Army).

A fateful day, February 7, 1965, when NLF local troops shelled the airbase at Pleiku. Here McGeorge Bundy, flanked by Saigon military strongman General Nguyen Khanh, visit the stricken base. Khanh, who wielded his officer's stick like a baton, was hardly ever without it. Bundy was sickened by the attack. Thinking Hanoi directly responsible, Bundy recommended—and President Lyndon Johnson approved—bombing North Vietnam (U.S. Army).

(Opposite top) Today's hero, tomorrow's traitor, Colonel Tran Ngoc Chau was regarded as an early star of Saigon's pacification program. Chau led Saigon government efforts in two different provinces, headed a cadre training program closely associated with the CIA, and remained close to several Americans, including the CIA's William Colby and RAND's Daniel Ellsberg. Chau later fell afoul of former colleague Nguyen Van Thieu and was abandoned by the Americans during the last days of Saigon. Here, on February 13, 1963, as chief of Ben Tre province, Chau and his staff brief Vietnamese air force pilots on hotspots in their area. His American advisers sit next to him (U.S. Army).

(Opposite bottom) A strategic hamlet in Long An province in the spring of 1963. The defenses of this typical village position, clearly insufficient to resist any serious attack, were built around one of the old French guard towers that dotted the countryside, considered death traps in the French war. Hanoi's fears of the hamlets were real but exaggerated. The most dynamic U.S. pacification program at the time, the strategic hamlets were controlled by Diem's brother Ngo Dinh Nhu. The American solution for the military deficiencies of the hamlets was to equip them with radios to call for help. The U.S. 34th Signal Battalion installed the radios in Long An (U.S. Army).

The American ground war followed swiftly upon the bombing, with U.S. troops flooding into South Vietnam starting from the summer of 1965. Taken from a helicopter lined up to land on the tarmac just visible at the bottom, this picture of An Khe taken in August 1965 shows the beginnings of what became the huge rear base of the 1st Cavalry Division (Airmobile). The division's units began staging through An Khe about two months subsequent to this photograph (U.S. Army).

Planning the Vietnam War became a constant concern for President Johnson and his National Security Council. Here, on January 29, 1966, LBJ reviews peace feelers plus data on North Vietnamese infiltration during the Christmas bombing halt and considers fresh military actions. Army chief of staff General Harold Johnson proposes—and he uses the word explicitly—a "surge" of additional troops. NSC staffer Chester Cooper changes the easel display as the president looks on. Johnson is flanked by Dean Rusk and Robert McNamara. McGeorge Bundy sits at the far end of the table, and Vice President Hubert Humphrey is across from LBJ. CIA director Richard Helms is in the end chair left of Cooper (LBJ Library).

■ August 1964: The Last Mystery of the Tonkin Gulf

Much of this story has become familiar. An attack on an American destroyer took place on the high seas on August 2, 1964, in the Gulf of Tonkin. The warship, the USS *Maddox*, was carrying out a top-secret spy mission to record North Vietnamese radio and radar signals. The destroyer carried extra crew and equipment—a van packed with electronic gear—for this purpose. As the *Maddox* steamed into the Gulf of Tonkin, OPLAN 34-A raiders from a U.S.-led South Vietnamese Special Operations force bombarded two islands off the North Vietnamese coast. The raiders' fast boats passed the *Maddox* as she entered the Gulf.[1] On Taiwan, U.S. naval commanders and representatives of the National Security Agency (NSA), responsible for signals intelligence, and the Naval Security Group (NSG), which carried out activities on behalf of the NSA (and had a detachment aboard the Maddox for this cruise), briefed the destroyer's commanders to expect no hostile response and did not tell them about the raids.[2] The *Maddox* cruise would be the fifth patrol by a U.S. destroyer off the DRV coast since December 1962. These operations were code-named Desoto patrols.

North Vietnamese leaders in Hanoi made no decisions in this matter. Rather, a local naval commander ordered torpedo boats to the islands. The *Maddox* approached the North Vietnamese coast a number of times just after the 34-A raids and was quickly discovered and pursued by the DRV torpedo boats. They found her on the afternoon of August 2. By that time, Captain John J. Herrick, the mission commander aboard the *Maddox*, had the ship back in international waters. The North Vietnamese attacked anyway.

In Washington, President Lyndon Johnson insisted that the *Maddox* had been passing innocently through international waters and ordered the warship *back* into the Gulf, reinforced by a second destroyer, the USS *C. Turner Joy*. The *Maddox* continued to intercept DRV communications—more than a thousand messages during its cruise—including some on Vietnamese naval channels. Lieutenant Gerrell D. Moore, the NSG detachment commander, informed Herrick of these messages and others, among them an alert order for night action sent to two patrol vessels. A chronic stutterer, Moore had a little trouble warning the captain, but the mission commander took it in and promptly fired off a message to higher authorities requesting instructions. He was told to carry on.

Again, Captain Herrick was not informed of OPLAN 34-A activities, which on August 3 included raids by three boats on DRV coastal targets, a radar facility at Vinh Son, and the guard post at the mouth of the Ron River.

During the night of August 3–4, the *Maddox* and *Turner Joy* thought they were being attacked. Lookouts imagined they had seen boats; radar and sonar operators thought they had detected targets. The ships fired a total of 249 five-inch and 123 three-inch shells at the supposed enemy. Lieutenant Commander Robert C. Barnhart Jr., skipper of the *Turner Joy,* believed he had seen smoke and interpreted it as a damaged enemy craft. Captain Herrick, less certain, followed the hasty action reports with a dispatch questioning whether any of this had really happened except for the initial radar contact. American aircraft sent from the carriers *Ticonderoga* and *Constellation* saw nothing. North Vietnam denied making any attacks. But Washington, insisting it was defending the legal principle of innocent passage on the high seas, struck the DRV with 64 jet fighter-bombers from its aircraft carriers. On August 7 Congress passed the Tonkin Gulf Resolution (Public Law 98-104), authorizing the president to use armed force in Southeast Asia.

It is now generally accepted that there was no naval action in the Gulf of Tonkin on the night of August 3–4. The reality of the "battle," immediately called into question by Hanoi, was controversial from the outset. Testifying before the Senate Foreign Relations Committee in favor of the congressional resolution, Secretary McNamara insisted that plentiful evidence proved the administration's version of events. Yet soon afterward, President Johnson was quoted as telling associates that the Navy might have been shooting at whales up in the Gulf of Tonkin.[3] The dispute roiled through the war years, and the evidence was heavily disputed when the Foreign Relations Committee held an unprecedented reexamination in 1968. Congress repealed the Tonkin Gulf Resolution in 1971.

Some observers continued to insist that the battle of August 4 had really happened. But the "evidence" evaporated over time. It was reduced, in the end, to the NSA radio intercepts. That worked until 1997, when McNamara visited Hanoi to confer with former DRV officials, including General Vo Nguyen Giap. McNamara himself finally accepted the second Tonkin incident as an illusion after Giap's assurances that no Vietnamese naval units had made any such attacks that night.[4] Years earlier I had written of "mysteries" in the official account of the two incidents that showed how the portrayal of the second one could not have been accurate.[5] In 2002 the NSA examined the intercept evidence in detail, found a host of traffic that had not been taken into account at the time, and discovered that mistranslations and errors in accounting for the time necessary to transmit intercepts from the field to Washington were the likely source of a U.S. misunderstanding.

NSA chronologies compiled shortly afterward had ignored the discrepant information, emphasized the mistaken material, and then been relied on to defend the U.S. role. In 2005–2006 the NSA finally declassified the full set of its Tonkin Gulf intercepts, which reveal translation and dating problems with the August 4 messages. The NSA's own official historians now agree that the engagement was illusory. The agency's official history volume on Vietnam, declassified in 2007, repeats this analysis.[6]

Fresh evidence has also come to light—the emergence of audiotapes of President Johnson's phone calls. The mass of this evidence confronts us with a new mystery, the final mystery, of the Tonkin Gulf. The tapes demonstrate that the president had grave doubts about Vietnam long before the Tonkin Gulf incident. Yet he forged ahead in a way that committed the United States more deeply to war. The final mystery is why Lyndon Johnson did this.

■ ■ ■ Word of the August 2 incident reached Washington in a little over twenty minutes. It was then shortly after 4:00 a.m. in the nation's capital. The Pentagon's initial effort focused on confirmation. Details were sent to the White House Situation Room, which reported to LBJ in his East Wing bedroom shortly before he had breakfast at 9:00 a.m. About 10:30, President Johnson convened his senior advisers and intelligence experts. Thomas L. Hughes, director of the State Department's Bureau of Intelligence and Research, briefed the group and explicitly connected the 34-A operations and the naval encounter. The group correctly surmised that only North Vietnamese local commanders had been involved. Johnson decided to continue the Desoto patrol and reinforce it. He also had the State Department make a public protest. Johnson announced these actions at a press conference the next morning.

In his memoir *The Vantage Point*, Lyndon Johnson pretends that the 34-A operations were carried out only by the "South Vietnamese" (not U.S.) navy and were "not connected to our patrol."[7] LBJ asserted this at the time, as did McNamara in congressional testimony. Both claims were false. In fact, the administration realized the interrelation quite clearly, as evidenced by the Hughes briefing. In addition, in a telephone call on the morning of August 3, McGeorge Bundy, LBJ's national security adviser, told Undersecretary of State George W. Ball (according to Ball's notes) that "he was persuaded, without having gotten to the root of the thing, that it's a reaction to the 34 enterprise the day before."[8] The president himself said the same thing to Robert Anderson, a businessman and former Eisenhower official, when they talked that morning. "There have been some covert operations up in that area that we have been carrying on," Johnson said, "so I imagine they [the North Vietnamese] wanted to put a stop to it."[9] Less than an hour later LBJ spoke to McNamara about setting up a briefing for congressional leaders.

This time it was McNamara who brought up the link: "I think that I should also, or we should also at that time [at the briefing], Mr. President, explain this Op Plan 34-A, these covert operations. There's no question but what that had bearing on."[10] In short, from the president on down, officials were well aware of the connection between 34-A and the Desoto patrol, and they knew Hanoi had been provoked.

President Johnson nevertheless coupled orders to resume the Desoto patrol with instructions to dust off contingency plans for air attacks on the DRV. These had been developed in the spring as part of "the scenario," which was intended to build a basis for the attacks through a sixteen-day political and diplomatic buildup. On the afternoon of August 3, McNamara spoke to Johnson by phone and reported that he would be meeting with the Joint Chiefs of Staff to review attack plans; he advised that congressional leaders be informed, and LBJ agreed.[11] That evening the president gathered top aides to take another look at the rules of engagement. Subordinates preparing McNamara for that encounter surmised the discussion might include air strikes.

Early on the morning of August 4 the latest NSA intercept arrived. Recorded by a listening post at Phu Bai, this message from the Haiphong naval district alerted a patrol boat for night action, telling its commander that a second boat had similar orders and that the command was trying to find fuel so that a torpedo boat could also participate.[12] (The full record of NSA intercepts now shows that the North Vietnamese "night action" related to the salvaging of boats damaged in the previous battle, that the volume of messages had greatly decreased since August 2, that tracking reports on the U.S. warships had virtually disappeared, that the key message purporting to be an attack order had been mistranslated, and that other NSA stations never recorded the message Phu Bai took to be a combat order.)

At 8:35 AM Washington time, Captain Herrick reported radar sightings of ships and aircraft in the Tonkin Gulf. Based on this information, less than an hour later, McNamara and senior aides were reviewing options such as bombing DRV naval bases, oil storage facilities, airfields, or factories or possibly mining harbors. McNamara phoned LBJ to discuss the situation at 9:43 AM.

LBJ did not want to be merely reactive. "What I was thinking about when I was eating breakfast," Johnson said, was that "when they move on us, and they shoot at us, I think we not only ought to shoot at them, but almost simultaneously . . . pull one of these things that . . . you've been doing."[13] It sounds like Johnson was thinking of more 34-A raids, and he went on to talk of hitting a bridge or even three targets at once. He and McNamara agreed to revisit the idea at lunch.

Just over an hour later, McNamara called to report that the destroyers had sighted two vessels and three aircraft. McNamara said he had an aircraft carrier to back up the Desoto vessels and another en route from Hong Kong, providing "ample forces to respond not only to these attacks . . . but also to retaliate should you wish to do so against targets on the land." The U.S. action was already taking shape. "When I come over at noontime," McNamara remarked, "I'll bring you a list of alternative target systems."[14]

That list was the main subject when the Joint Chiefs conferred with McNamara, Rusk, Bundy, and others at 11:40 AM in McNamara's Pentagon dining room. He and the Chiefs agreed to present five possibilities—four of them quick, sharp attacks, and one for the mining of harbors. Following a private conversation in his office, McNamara and the civilian officials left for the White House, where they joined LBJ's National Security Council (NSC) and the secretary described the supposed attack going on in the Gulf of Tonkin.

McNamara told the Council that military options were not yet ready. That was artfully misleading. McNamara had them in his pocket and was simply waiting for a more private moment during lunch with LBJ. Johnson knew that McNamara had the options. Bundy's notes from that "Tuesday Lunch," as these encounters were called in the Johnson years, indicate that Rusk did most of the talking. The administration wanted an action that was sharply limited (thus rejecting, after brief mention, the mining of harbors) so as to make Hanoi seem responsible for any escalation. Talk of a response by means of 34-A simply disappeared. Much of the discussion dealt with details, everything from the need to inform LBJ's opponent in the election that year, Arizona senator Barry Goldwater, to the timing and precise set of targets to be hit.

One of Mac Bundy's handwritten notes further confirms Washington's awareness of the link between the provocative 34-A operations and the Desoto patrol. "What is 34-A role in all this?" Bundy wrote. In his precise hand, Bundy then provided the answer: "*Must* be *cause,* no other is rational. But not a sufficient cause."[15] In a memorandum Bundy compiled for press aide George Reedy a few days afterward, Mac noted that consensus had developed swiftly; the discussion "was marked by thoroughness, clarity, and an absence of significant disagreement."[16]

Meanwhile, McNamara returned to the Pentagon and conveyed LBJ's orders. The rest is history. There were minor glitches in timing, another meeting of the NSC that evening specifically on the Tonkin Gulf, a session with congressional leaders where Johnson announced his decision, an LBJ phone call to Goldwater, and a late-night television address to the nation in which the president revealed his actions.

Shift scenes to the Pentagon. McNamara managed the department through a central staff known as the Office of the Secretary of Defense (OSD). It had sections to ride herd on everything from the minutiae of weapons development to monitoring the readiness of the armed forces. McNamara even had a small unit known as International Security Affairs (ISA) to track national security policy, a sort of counterpart to the NSC staff or the State Department. On August 4, 1964, a fresh expert joined ISA as special assistant to its director, Assistant Secretary of Defense John T. McNaughton. The newly minted aide, Daniel Ellsberg, was an expert from the Rand Corporation, a prominent defense policy think tank.

Ellsberg read the secret cables in which the details of the supposed naval battle were reported. In addition to noting that the dispatches were arriving extraordinarily quickly, he noticed something else: the engagement seemed to be going on for a very long time. This was unusual. Naval battles proceed quickly as a rule, consisting of moments of intense combat interspersed with long days of cruising. The real engagement on August 2 had lasted barely half an hour. This time, the stream of cables went on for more than two hours. Then, while McNamara and Johnson remained closeted at Tuesday Lunch, Captain Herrick's dispatch arrived to question the veracity of the whole event. The on-scene commander sent further cables that cast doubt on the battle reports. The doubts impressed Ellsberg, who would be stunned when, in the face of this evidence, President Johnson went on television to denounce North Vietnam for deliberate and naked aggression against U.S. warships on routine patrol.[17] Not alone, Ellsberg began a journey that many took during the Vietnam years, when a gap opened and steadily grew between what the government said it was about and what it actually did. Ellsberg's doubts would have consequences. Here they show that official Washington, if not the public, knew better.

■ ■ ■ In the heat of action the nation rallied. Initial opinion polls showed that 85 percent of respondents approved of Johnson's retaliation. Not even the loss of U.S. aircraft in the strike, nicknamed Pierce Arrow, and the capture of American pilots by North Vietnam made any difference to the public. Opinion on LBJ's handling of Vietnam reversed, from 58 percent questioning administration policy to 72 percent approving it. Anticipating this change, LBJ had turned to Bundy to discuss a congressional resolution to approve the use of force. The national security adviser's older brother, William P. Bundy, chaired the committee that had developed "the scenario" and, among other things, that draft resolution. The lesson of the Truman and Eisenhower administrations—in Korea, Indochina, the Middle East, and off the China coast—had been that such resolutions gave presidents political cover as well as legal authority. Lyndon Johnson had no intention of being without such protection.

"You know that resolution your brother's been talking about?" Johnson asked Bundy. "Well, now's the time to get it through the Congress."[18]

The next morning at a staff meeting, Bundy and LBJ's political aides went over the legislative aspects. According to notes prepared by William Y. Smith, an Air Force officer serving as a military adviser, Bundy admitted the connection between 34-A and Hanoi's response.[19] When aide Douglass Cater expressed doubt about the logic of a resolution, Bundy replied that perhaps it should not be questioned too far. In any case, LBJ would give the final draft to Congress that evening.

On August 6 congressional committees debated the administration's request for a Southeast Asia resolution. The lightning quick response was in complete contrast to Congress's usual pace. McNamara, Rusk, and JCS chairman General Earle Wheeler testified. There, as well as in private consultations between congressional and White House officials, legislators were assured there had been *no* American provocation (no connection to 34-A, as well as no infringement of North Vietnamese waters by the Desoto destroyers) and that the purported attack of August 4 had truly occurred. McNamara went so far as to declare, "Our Navy played absolutely no part in, was not associated with, was not aware of, any South Vietnamese actions, if there were any."[20] He also insisted that the destroyers had been on "routine" patrol. Evidence to the contrary stayed secret.[21]

Important senators helped push the Gulf of Tonkin resolution through the Senate. Senator J. William Fulbright's joint committee meeting lasted less than two hours. The House acted even more quickly—the resolution was approved by the House Armed Services Committee after a hearing lasting just forty minutes. Some experts on congressional history believe that this rapid action was taken to help LBJ "contain" the war in Southeast Asia. The resolution passed the next day. In the House of Representatives the vote was unanimous. In the Senate the vote was 88–2. Senator George McGovern expressed doubts but voted in favor. The two dissenting senators were Wayne Morse of Oregon and Ernest Gruening of New Jersey. The Johnson administration subsequently relied on this resolution as its legal authority for conducting the Vietnam war.

Why did Lyndon Johnson do what he did? This question remains at the heart of the U.S. land war in Asia. LBJ kept no contemporaneous record of his thoughts and intentions. He personally wrote only a handful of reflections while in office, none concerning the Tonkin Gulf. Johnson's memoir is opaque, largely assembled by ghostwriters with a view toward his place in history. He describes the Tonkin Gulf as his second major decision on Vietnam (the first having been to continue Kennedy's policies) but says little as to his rationale.

One answer, often postulated, puts Johnson's action in the context of the 1964 election. His opponent Goldwater favored escalation and posed a challenge to LBJ on national security issues. The Tonkin Gulf decision showed Johnson standing strong, and he also benefited from the American people rallying around the flag.

This interpretation has merit but does not account for LBJ's premeditated push for "the scenario." With language crafted in advance, the resolution seems less political cover and more like the open-ended justification for war that it became. Johnson's care to secure this measure is then a key maneuver in laying the foundation for waging aggressive war. This explanation, in turn, fails to account for the evidence of LBJ's grave doubts about the Southeast Asian conflict. In conversations with former Senate colleague Richard Russell, State Department adviser Walt W. Rostow, and occasionally McNamara, LBJ was much less certain. He wavered between fierce determination and an acute awareness that Vietnam might not be winnable and should not be fought. The question of why needs further refinement: why did Johnson permit his doubts to be overcome by a desire to fight?

Useful insight into Johnson's actions in 1964 can be gleaned from at least three sets of evidence. Personal involvement is at issue in all three. First comes Dien Bien Phu. The collapse of the French showed LBJ that his willingness to support intervention in their behalf had been misplaced. Johnson subsequently changed tacks—one of the reasons he backed Ngo Dinh Diem's successor. The second source derives from Johnson's May 1961 mission to Saigon as a token of U.S. support for Diem. While there, Johnson acquired a stake in Vietnam policy, and what he expressed then was virtually identical to some of his statements at the time of Dien Bien Phu, now substituting Diem for the French. Finally, slightly more than two years later, came Diem's ouster, which LBJ opposed. Johnson's push for authority in 1964 is related to his frustration at losing the policy debate over the Diem coup. He now sought a freedom of action that had been lacking. In the previous instances, Johnson believed that the United States had not done enough, bringing him to the Tonkin Gulf with a determination to get things right. This provides a clue to why the response option utilizing 34-A operations was instantly dropped in favor of an open attack. Herein also lies the origin of the advance preparation of a congressional resolution *and* the notion of using it as an open-ended authorization rather than a sanction for a specific act of force. America's Vietnam war sharpened as a direct result.

■ ■ ■ The day of the alleged second incident in the Gulf of Tonkin, August 4, 1964, is important for another reason—one that starts to bring the American people more into the picture. Lyndon Johnson had to divide his time that day between the Vietnam crisis and one in the state of Mississippi, where three civil rights workers had disappeared in the town of Meridian in June, shortly after white separatists burned down the Mount Zion Church. The bodies of the three men were found by the FBI on August 4. LBJ spent much of the day on the phone with the FBI, the governor of Mississippi, and White House officials, discussing how to handle these events and when and how to approach the families of the slain activists.

Civil rights leaders had been anticipating the discovery and held a memorial service for the men in the ruins of Mount Zion Church. Robert Moses, a leader of the Student Nonviolent Coordinating Committee, spoke at the service and held up a newspaper, its banner headline trumpeting Johnson's bombing of North Vietnam. Bitterly Moses told listeners that the government was willing to use force in Vietnam while tolerating white supremacists in Mississippi, where federal marshals could have protected the civil rights workers and the African Americans trying to exercise their rights. A young historian in the audience, Howard Zinn, noted the bitterness and the connection. He would soon be focusing on Vietnam himself.

Just as there were a few doubters in Congress, so too there were some among the public. On August 6, as Congress quickly passed its resolution, a thousand Americans rallied in New York's Washington Square to mark the atomic bombing of Hiroshima. Some of their placards made the same connection as had Bob Moses. One read, "UNITED STATES TROOPS BELONG IN MISSISSIPPI, NOT VIETNAM." Among the speakers at the rally, socialist Norman Thomas and civil rights leader Bayard Rustin both denounced the Vietnam war. A few weeks later in Atlantic City, where the Democratic Party held its convention nominating Lyndon Johnson for the party's 1964 presidential ticket, about 400 demonstrators held an all-day vigil to protest war in Vietnam.

Senators Morse and Gruening; activists Moses, Thomas, and Rustin; and the protesters of August represented the leading edge of political ferment. Driven by concern about the direction of the nation, by pacifism, by doubts about the Johnson administration's explanations for its actions in the Gulf of Tonkin, or by wider concern over the growing U.S. commitment in Vietnam, these dissenters would be the advance guard for what eventually became a movement.

Thus, even in its early stages, the U.S. war in Vietnam had already planted seeds that would grow into a huge opposition. Lyndon Johnson and his colleagues dismissed those feeble protests. If LBJ thought about it at all, he undoubtedly comforted himself with the favorable opinion polls. But several factors that would become central were already visible in microcosm: American leaders and military commanders acted as if military force could be applied precisely and with predictable effects, even though they had little real strategy for the war; leaders made only minor efforts to build a national consensus; they reacted to questioning by denial, even when the questions' premises were correct; and leaders convinced themselves their decisions would carry along the public, indefinitely if necessary. The cumulative stance—which Senator Fulbright later characterized as "the arrogance of power"—would eventually confine presidents to an increasingly narrow range of choice, defining the later course of the war.

4   Burnished Rows of Steel (1964–1965)

The Gulf of Tonkin incident put Vietnam on the map for Americans. According to poll figures, those who had paid no attention dropped by half. Briefly, in August 1964, support for greater use of force mounted to just under the majority, although by the election it had declined (24 percent favored fighting, 9 percent getting out, and 15 percent either fighting or getting out). But Vietnam remained a minor issue in a much larger political tapestry. The choices were posed for Americans not by opinion polls but in the presidential election.

Lyndon Johnson's campaign centered on peace—or at least nuclear peace—with nonintervention in Vietnam implied. The war LBJ wanted to fight was against poverty. Johnson ran a television ad darkly hinting that a vote for his opponent would be one for nuclear confrontation, featuring a little girl picking flower petals and then suddenly dissolving into the mushroom cloud of an exploding thermonuclear weapon. Johnson openly declared that nuclear war could not be won. He privately approached the Soviets to propose a nuclear freeze, which went nowhere in 1964 but would be almost identical to the first arms control agreement with Moscow obtained by the Nixon administration eight years later.

On Vietnam, Johnson reprised statements from the spring. He declared that the United States sought no wider war, that he did not want American boys to fight an Asian war, and—as Jack Kennedy had also said—that the war was Saigon's to win or lose. LBJ explicitly claimed he was trying to prevent war. Political aide Jack Valenti heard the president tell top advisers he wanted to be sure he had not gone too deeply into Vietnam to back out. Republican opponent Senator Barry Goldwater posed the stark alternative, charging that Johnson was soft on communism, his presidency drifting toward defeat and sowing a wind of weakness. In March Goldwater called for victory in Vietnam. In June the Republican candidate suggested that tactical nuclear weapons could be used to defoliate the South Vietnamese borderlands and that bombing North Vietnam could stop supplies to the insurgents in the South. At the Republican convention Goldwater thundered that "extremism in the defense of liberty is no vice."[1] Johnson openly excoriated Goldwater for advocating the bombing of North Vietnam. In South Carolina days before the election, LBJ told voters their job was to elect a candidate who could avoid war.

President Johnson won convincingly. In a landslide vote, LBJ's 61.1 percent plurality amounted to the widest margin yet in an American presidential election. Goldwater won only six states, including his home state of Arizona; the rest were Deep South states fighting the federal government tooth and nail over civil rights.

Whatever else is said about the 1964 election, its results were no mandate for war in Vietnam. Americans who voted for LBJ were blissfully unaware of the disconnect between Johnson's campaign rhetoric and the private deliberations of the president and his war managers. Instead, the election spurred peace advocates, who built some momentum. In some of the first antiwar demonstrations, a couple of hundred SANE members marched in front of the White House in late November, advocating negotiations; a month later in New York City, as many as a thousand people gathered in Washington Square. In a clear confluence between the peace and civil rights movements, that protest had been jointly sponsored by the War Resisters' League, which had recently come out for withdrawal from Vietnam, and the civil rights groups Committee for Nonviolent Action and Fellowship for Reconciliation. Further, an organization that would become a bête noire for many who considered opposition to the war illegitimate, or worse, agreed at its national conference that December to hold an antiwar rally in Washington in the spring. That group, the Students for a Democratic Society (SDS), had focused mostly on civil rights and poverty and would be dipping its feet into war opposition for the first time.

■ ■ ■ Inside the Johnson administration the headaches of Vietnam were unchanged. America was past the stage of freedom to intervene or withdraw. Set on course by Dwight Eisenhower for essentially Cold War reasons, U.S. involvement collided with a Vietnamese revolution at midcourse. John Kennedy had deepened the commitment and assumed a great burden through complicity in the Diem coup. Both Kennedy and Johnson had had opportunities to cut American losses and get out. Both had rejected that. LBJ would have a few more such chances, but his spectrum of possible actions had begun to narrow. The lack of results in the war bedeviled both presidents, with their central dilemma framed as one of how to achieve progress.

Saigon remained unstable. General Khanh put leaders of the Diem coup under house arrest and rode out coup attempts. There were constant rumors in the cafés along Tu Do—not a pretty picture. The United States encouraged Khanh to replace his military junta with a civilian government. Air force commander Nguyen Cao Ky wrote bemusedly, "The Americans recognized that the only group in Vietnam with unity and strength was the military—and on the other hand, because in the U.S. system the military *must* be under civilian control, the Americans expended enormous diplomatic efforts to insist that the Vietnamese military abandon the leadership role."[2] Khanh resisted, restructuring his regime with more civilian ministers but emphasizing the "March North" as a point of unity among Vietnamese. Khanh's close ties with a particular South Vietnamese nationalist group, however, left many suspicious. The Buddhists resumed their protests; the armed forces were restive. In the middle of it all, the CIA/Special Forces–backed montagnards in the Central Highlands began to revolt. The rebellion was defused only with difficult and risky intercessions by brave Green Beret officers. Watching this from MACV, General William Westmoreland observed, "The generals would have ousted Khanh in a moment had they not been aware of how dotingly Washington embraced him."[3]

Khanh's political expedient, the March North, dovetailed with Washington's coercive diplomacy, expressed in OPLAN 34-A. In the middle of the Tonkin Gulf incident, Washington widened the 34-A target list but also instructed the embassy in Saigon to dissuade Khanh from additional strikes. Requests to resume covert operations, which Johnson had halted in the wake of the Tonkin Gulf, began almost immediately. So did demands for more vigorous action. The first discussions about sending U.S. combat units to South Vietnam, to protect air bases there, took place that August. Johnson approved a resumption of Desoto patrols in September, shortly before a coup attempt against Khanh. Advisers recommended that LBJ prepare to respond to any North Vietnamese attacks. General Earle Wheeler reported that the Air Force and Marine Corps believed the time had come for sustained bombing of the North. Lyndon Johnson asked if Vietnam was worth all this. Maxwell Taylor, now U.S. ambassador to Saigon, had just told LBJ that the situation was worsening and answered, "We cannot afford to let Hanoi win, in terms of our overall position in the area and in the world."[4]

Days afterward there came another incident in the Tonkin Gulf when the destroyers *Morton* and *Edwards,* on a new Desoto patrol, thought they were under attack. That dark night in the Gulf had all the attributes of the August affair, with radio intercepts suggesting battle preparations and spurious radar and sonar readings aboard U.S. warships. This time, both the White House and the intelligence community held back from asserting that the North Vietnamese had done anything, although McNamara told the president the attack had been real, a substantial engagement. LBJ responded, "Bob, I have found over the years that we see and we hear and we imagine a lot of things in the form of attacks." He wanted evidence. McNamara related details of the supposed attack. "Well, what is a substantial engagement?" LBJ shot back. "[Does that] mean that *we* could have started it and they just *responded?*"[5]

President Johnson nixed any U.S. strikes. Well might he wonder about shooting at whales in the Gulf.[6]

It would have looked odd, to say the least, had there been a U.S. air strike, given Johnson's campaign rhetoric. His widely quoted speech about not having American boys do the fighting Asians ought to be doing took place in Oklahoma a week later. Then on November 1, two days before the election, came a real NLF attack on the air base at Bien Hoa, just north of Saigon, where U.S. Farmgate aircraft were based. In a mortar bombardment and commando raid, four Americans and two South Vietnamese died; seventy-six persons were wounded (thirty Americans) and half a dozen U.S. B-57 jet bombers were destroyed, with twenty American and South Vietnamese aircraft damaged. The JCS wanted retaliation. President Johnson squelched those demands. But right after the election the gloves came off.

Actors and Agency

In *Dereliction of Duty*, a widely admired book that enjoyed a resurgence once the U.S. military became mired in Iraq, Army officer H. R. McMaster found the armed services, and specifically the Joint Chiefs of Staff, derelict in not clearly telling the president that only decisive action would succeed in Vietnam. The Chiefs were "adept at providing technical information but remained unable to respond to questions that had broad policy implications." Robert McNamara, in this view, moved from a posture of distrusting the JCS to one of deceiving them, while LBJ suppressed the Chiefs' recommendations. Johnson and McNamara, with their "graduated pressure" on Hanoi, created "the illusion that the decisions to attack North Vietnam were alternatives to war rather than war itself," resulting in military planning for failure and then a war without direction.[7] This argument revives the question of Lyndon Johnson's motives, as well as that of the cleavage between U.S. military and civilian leaders already observed here.

One piece of this conundrum is Johnson's real attitude toward war in Vietnam. Unfortunately, that is opaque. His memoirs record events and policies but not private thoughts. Johnson wrote only a few notes for the record and kept no diary as far as we know; his telephone calls are unreliable because the president used the phone to convince, cajole, and otherwise manipulate—as an instrument of politics and diplomacy, as it were. McMaster cites telephone conversations to prove Johnson wanted no war, but not those in which he talked of "touching up" the men in Hanoi. LBJ did indeed say he had never seen such a mess and had no idea what America could get from its commitment. But some conversations go both ways. For example, in March 1964 Chalmers Roberts of the *Washington Post* and a reporter at another paper each wrote about the administration's desire to hit at Hanoi. Johnson quickly surmised the source had been Walt W. Rostow, now heading the

State Department's Policy Planning Council, long an advocate of this course.[8] The president phoned Rostow and told him off for the leak. Johnson then remarked that Rusk's idea man could not have known what the policy *was* because he, LBJ, had not decided it. Their conversation occurred after a Johnson speech in which he had warned Hanoi against playing a "deeply dangerous game," implying forceful action. This could be read as LBJ trying to back Rostow down on aggressive posturing, but also as LBJ preserving the ability to move forward when *he* wanted to.

President Johnson went on to say, at a press conference on March 15, that he shared John F. Kennedy's view that if South Vietnam were lost, all of Southeast Asia would be threatened. And Army chief of staff General Harold K. Johnson, whom LBJ would send on a survey mission early the next year, recounted to General Westmoreland the president's parting words: leaning in, jabbing his breastbone with a finger, Johnson had said, "You get things bubbling, General!"[9]

There is also evidence supporting the view of Johnson as a purposeful war manager. A couple of days prior to LBJ's exchange with Rostow, he had a telephone conversation with McNamara about Vietnam. Johnson sought a simple statement of U.S. purposes that he could commit to memory, and he gave the defense secretary a list of alternatives to work with. The options were as follows: "we could send our own divisions in there and our own Marines in there"; or the United States could stay its hand, which LBJ saw as "let[ting] the commies ... swallow up South Vietnam"; or Washington could withdraw "and say, the hell with you, we're going to have Fortress America" (here again, Johnson's imagery at Dien Bien Phu).[10] Existing policy was not on his list. Similarly, in December 1964 Johnson spoke to one of his oldest and closest friends from the Senate, Georgia's Richard Russell, a congressional power on military matters. Russell said, "I wish we could find some way to get *out* of that, Mr. President." LBJ changed the subject.[11]

As an index of Johnson's slyness on the subject, in *The Vantage Point* he asserts, "during my first year in the White House no formal proposal for an air campaign against North Vietnam came to me as the agreed suggestion of my principal advisers."[12] Here the parsing is remarkable: "formal," "agreed suggestion," "principal advisers." The statement is technically true, since such a proposal would have been contained in a paper of the sort McNamara called a "draft presidential memorandum," and no such document went to LBJ; however, there were several JCS papers on the subject, and the president talked of bombing proposals in his councils. There were also memos by John McCone of the CIA. The phrase "principal advisers" is also cute, since Undersecretary of State George Ball frantically warned against escalation and spent much of October crafting a long paper rejecting the entire proposition, using the analogy of France's disaster in Indochina, among others. Johnson read the paper with interest, but then looked on with equanimity while Bundy, McNamara, and Rusk conspired to scuttle it—another indication of LBJ's ambivalence.

We can take the president at his word that he was most intensely involved in ensuring passage of the Civil Rights Act of 1964 and preparing legislation for the War on Poverty. Johnson would have preferred Vietnam to just go away. He was willing to do things—the minimum necessary—to make that happen. The model of incremental decision making that analysts constructed from the Vietnam experience arose precisely due to that behavior.[13] Sometimes this meant ensuring maximalist options did not reach his desk, and there Johnson worked closely with McNamara, who rode herd on the Chiefs. In 1964 the minimum necessary was "graduated pressure," but it does not follow that LBJ considered this "peace" or that he saw it as an alternative to war. President Johnson himself created the interagency group that drafted "the scenario," whose specific aim was to lay the groundwork for sustained bombing, and he clearly anticipated more robust recommendations. After the Bien Hoa attack, those were inevitable.

As for the Joint Chiefs of Staff, the charge they were derelict is rather thin. This implies that the Chiefs had some deeper wisdom that if they had only been able to force on Johnson would have won the war. The truth is more tragic. The military planned a tragedy because they had no better idea what they were doing than the president himself. At each stage of the war, this one included, the JCS advocated a set of fixed ideas. In 1964 it was "graduated pressure" (not simply a Johnson-McNamara invention), including cross-border operations into Laos. Beginning with the Tonkin Gulf, they added bombing, mining, and then ground troops to the mix. In fact, the troop issue is a good example. When it was talked up in August, LBJ rejected it. In an October JCS memorandum the military wanted a Marine expeditionary brigade to guard bases, but Johnson did not buy that either. After Bien Hoa they renewed the request. The president finally approved the deployment of this force after another NLF attack, the bombing of the Brinks Hotel, a Saigon officers' barracks, on Christmas Eve. When Westmoreland asked for a U.S. airborne brigade as a general reserve for the ARVN, Johnson approved that too. There is no evidence that the Chiefs were even interested in a massive U.S. deployment at this time and none that they had any more innovative military program in mind than the White House. Washington planned a tragedy in unison. Dereliction resides in the maneuvers over who got the play, the credit, and the blame—at both the White House and the Pentagon.

An alternative view is that Johnson was trapped into war, somehow sandbagged by advisers who practically conspired to force him into the conflict. While the war still raged, journalist David Halberstam focused powerful light on JFK's and LBJ's advisers in his book *The Best and the Brightest*.[14] Halberstam meant to personalize the arcane process by which decisions propelled the United States into war, to make "Washington" more than shorthand for the collection of America's war managers. That was important to do. Much of history focuses on broad movements, and the role of individuals is ignored. At a nexus moment, the person with the right skills and contacts can be critical. This would be true in committing America to the Vietnam war.

In Washington in 1964–1965, the individuals in their individual capacities—McNamara with his razor-sharp questions; Bundy, the traffic cop outside the Oval Office; Rusk and his deference to authority; McCone, who never hesitated to leap the bounds of intelligence to advocate policy; Taylor with his can-do approach; and many more—made up a bureaucracy. Together and apart they recommended many things. But it is too easy to elevate the "bureaucracy" to policy determinant. One of the two major decision models to emerge from the Vietnam experience, proposed by political scientists Leslie Gelb and Richard K. Betts, argued that "the system worked" to provide a limited range of options between the unattainable and the unacceptable, guaranteeing that presidents would choose midrange alternatives.[15] Overwhelming Hanoi was unattainable, withdrawal unacceptable, and various degrees of escalation fell somewhere in between. One weakness in this idea was its lack of a driving mechanism. What drove the bureaucrats? The Munich analogy? Some ideological proposition? Too simple by half. Neither the bureaucracy nor its actors held uniform views, nor did they propose identical courses, although they did have certain commonalities in worldview. Yet this bureaucratic politics model informs much analysis of the Vietnam war.

Gareth Porter, for example, writes from this perspective in his most recent investigation of escalation. Porter provides a driving mechanism, which he sees as a shared determination to exert U.S. strategic dominance. For Vietnam, Porter breaks the decisions of November 1963 to January 1965 into a dozen different ones and observes, "There is surely no parallel in modern history to the twelve separate attempts by the national security bureaucracy over a fourteen-month period to get Johnson to authorize the use of military force against the same state."[16] Porter is right that there was an escalatory process that involved a series of choices, but to frame it as a quasi-conspiracy is excessive and ignores Lyndon Johnson's own agency.

Did the bureaucracy speak with the same voice? The Joint Chiefs of Staff, for one, did not, and McMaster takes pains to show them in conflict with McNamara. The defense secretary, in turn, goes to great lengths in his memoir to illuminate his inner doubts, and his draft presidential memoranda of the 1965–1967 period voice those doubts from an early date. Both of the Bundy brothers were ambivalent on Vietnam. Taylor steadfastly opposed troop deployment proposals. In early 1965 Rusk, often regarded as a proponent of force—a "hawk," in the idiom of the day—favored current policy over escalation. So did the NSC staff director for Southeast Asia, Michael Forrestal.

There were others who solidly opposed escalation, most notably George Ball but also line operators such as Paul Kattenberg at State and Clark Clifford, LBJ's éminence grise. Forrestal's associate and successor as "Mr. Vietnam" on the NSC staff, Chester L. Cooper, started out as a hawk but by mid-1964 had begun his transformation into an opponent of the war, to the extent that his "closet dove" position became known to colleagues. Thus, the bureaucracy cannot be elevated to unitary actor. Moreover, doubts were in evidence—not least those of Lyndon Johnson—*before* the major escalatory decisions of this period, and those doubts only grew as the war proceeded.

The other major model of Vietnam decision making centers on presidents and was crafted by Daniel Ellsberg, who called it the "stalemate machine." Presidents operated on the basis of self-interest and utilized a variety of rules, such as not to lose the war before the next election, to avoid a land war in Asia (to the extent possible without breaking the first rule), and to choose actions that minimized the risk of losing South Vietnam.[17] Ellsberg's stalemate machine had the virtue of focusing on the purposefulness of presidents' decisions, but its drawback lay in the notion that presidents could always have their way. Something more was at work. In Porter's Vietnam story, to bring this full circle, Johnson rejected every recommendation to use force except when the bureaucracy denied him vital information—in this construction, the Tonkin Gulf. Yet during his period of analysis, U.S. advisers in South Vietnam increased by more than 7,000; decisions were made to up that number much more; the United States began aerial reconnaissance and then bombing in Laos; 34-A operations were undertaken in North Vietnam (and 34-B activities in Laos);[18] Johnson approved the deployment of an antiaircraft missile battalion then a Marine brigade in Vietnam; aircraft deployments in the combat theater increased substantially; and the United States decisively squashed a Vietnam peace plan proposed by the French government.[19] These were not the acts of a president rejecting force. But they were, in the Gelb-Betts sense, incremental moves. And they were purposeful. It is also reasonable to argue that the specifics satisfied neither the bureaucracy nor the president.

It would be better to describe the process as one of ambivalent men marching into a conflict they did not understand in pursuit of goals they had failed to clarify. LBJ once told speechwriter Richard Goodwin, "They're trying to get me in a war over there. It will destroy me. I turned them down three times last week."[20] So Porter's analysis returns us to the knotty issue of Johnson's intentions. One who saw them at firsthand was Mike Forrestal. In 1964 LBJ wanted a private watchdog on the interagency Vietnam committee and sent Forrestal over to the State Department to chair it. One day, having business with Mac Bundy, Forrestal returned to his old NSC haunts. It was late afternoon. Their work done, the two men were standing in the hallway when President Johnson happened by. LBJ invited them into the Oval Office, where they relaxed over bourbon. The talk got a little loose after a few drinks, and inevitably, Vietnam entered the conversation.

"Don't you think," LBJ asked, referring to hitting North Vietnam, "the time has come to touch them up a little bit?"

It was Forrestal who was hesitant. "Yeah," he replied, "but would it make any difference? It will just make them tougher."

"Well," Johnson shot back, "don't you think if they get tougher, we have to get tougher?"[21]

In the end, it was not just locker-room talk. The president used the identical phrase—"touch them up"—in at least one phone call. And in his 1965 State of the Union speech, Johnson pledged not to abandon the "Eisenhower-Kennedy commitments" to South Vietnam. The morning of that speech Bob McNamara called Mac Bundy to say that the president's statement seemed too strong in light of existing policy. Mac answered that the rhetoric went no further than what had already been said a dozen times. The handwriting was on the wall.

"Pleikus Are like Streetcars"

The beginning of the bombing of North Vietnam illustrates the pattern. As New Year's Day 1965 approached, bombing was coming as certainly as the winter snows that cripple Washington. At the height of the election campaign the previous August, the Joint Chiefs had gone on record that bombing the North had become essential to preventing a complete collapse of the U.S. position. LBJ resisted the recommendation at the time, but in early September he approved preparations for retaliatory bombing—à la Tonkin Gulf—in the event Hanoi responded to graduated military pressure. Johnson then rejected retaliation after the September Desoto patrol incident. But the justification then had been flimsy and the context murky. In October the president approved U.S. bombing missions over the Laotian panhandle, the onset of an air campaign that endured through the end of the Vietnam war.

Then the Liberation Front struck at Bien Hoa just before the election. This kind of attack immediately acquired a name—it was a guerrilla "spectacular." LBJ did nothing, but he appointed William Bundy to lead a fresh search for options. Bundy told his colleagues that "spectaculars" would be the springboard for stronger action. By November 21 Bundy and McNamara's "little State Department" chief, John T. McNaughton, had assembled a paper analyzing three possible courses. The first was to continue graduated pressure; the second, a "fast full squeeze," major attacks on North Vietnam; and the third, called "progressive squeeze and talk"—or later "slow squeeze"—

was supposed to combine military pressure with offers to negotiate. All involved some form of bombing. Security adviser McGeorge Bundy then chaired discussions of the options. Lending further weight to the point that officials' positions changed from day to day, Ball was the only player other than the Joint Chiefs to favor the "fast full squeeze." Far from a conspiracy to sandbag the president into maximum force, the Pentagon Papers argue that McNaughton's full-squeeze language may have been loaded to startle LBJ and dissuade him. The Chiefs tabled a different version of the maximum option they thought more appealing because more controlled, but it turned few heads.

President Johnson mulled this over at the White House on December 1 during a key policy deliberation for which Ambassador Taylor returned from Saigon. LBJ approved a scheme that combined graduated pressure and progressive squeeze in a two-stage program. Washington now had a plan that would begin with retaliatory bombing but transition to a sustained air campaign. In Laos, bombing had already escalated under Operation Barrel Roll, which substituted steady effort for occasional pinpricks. The president, the Bundys, McNaughton, and the rest all accepted the logic and idiom of escalation.

On Christmas Eve came the spectacular at the Brinks Hotel. LBJ rejected retaliation but later noted, "I was persuaded increasingly that our forces deserved the support that air strikes against the source of aggression would represent."[22] The next months were a period of clearing the deck for action. Washington expended considerable energy on the question of American dependents in South Vietnam, vulnerable to terrorism and armed attack if Johnson ramped up his program. The 1,800 dependents, including General Westmoreland's wife Kitsy, were ordered out. LBJ also demanded an expansion of the U.S. effort to enlist allies, the "Many Flags" program. Until then, there had been a number of small advisory missions, such as Sir Robert Thompson's British effort, an Australian advisory group, Filipino engineers, and some humanitarian groups. Now LBJ wanted troops, "Free World Forces," to supplement the ARVN and Westmoreland's MACV, grown to 23,300 Americans.

On January 27, a week after LBJ's inauguration, McGeorge Bundy gave him a memo on behalf of himself and McNamara requesting a private meeting. Bundy's short paper has become known as the "fork in the road" memo. In it—while noting Rusk's specific disagreement—Bundy averred that he and the secretary of defense now believed that the present policy "can only lead to disastrous defeat." One alternative was to use military power "to force a change of Communist policy." The other was to "deploy all our resources along a track of negotiation." Rusk thought the consequences of either escalation or withdrawal so dire that a way had to be found to make current policy effective.[23] Note the lack of unity. Johnson retained his uncertainties—

Cooper's assistant James C. Thomson recalls LBJ as "thrashing around" at this time[24]—but immediately after this meeting, word went out to evacuate noncombatants, and the Joint Chiefs relaxed restrictions on U.S. air strikes inside South Vietnam while ordering another Desoto patrol. LBJ sent Mac Bundy for a look-see in Saigon. Word from the CIA that a high-powered Soviet delegation under Premier Aleksei Kosygin was in Hanoi did not deter the president.

National security adviser Bundy arrived in Saigon on February 4. With him were Chet Cooper of his staff; John McNaughton representing McNamara; Leonard Unger, Bill Bundy's deputy, representing the State Department; and General Andrew Goodpaster for the JCS. Cooper saw Bundy as complacent regarding Saigon strongman Khanh, who had just mounted another coup and overthrown the civilian government he had emplaced only a month earlier. Mac Bundy seemed primarily concerned about the Buddhists, and Cooper labored to bring him together with religious leader Thich Tri Quang. Their session, virtually a séance, left Mac "reeling."[25]

If Bundy's Buddhist encounter was disturbing, he must have really reeled on February 7, when Liberation Front units attacked a U.S. base at Pleiku in the Central Highlands. There, at Camp Holloway, was one of the Army aviation battalions providing mobility to the ARVN. Colonel Theodore Mataxis, senior U.S. adviser to the ARVN's II Corps, had little confidence in base security and had ordered Americans to take turns on watch. That night, guard Jesse Pyle saw the enemy and opened fire. Pyle died in a hail of bullets, but his alert prevented the attackers from laying demolition charges against the wall of a U.S. barracks. The guerrillas threw their explosives on the roof instead, where they still did great damage. Eight Americans died, and more than a hundred were wounded.

Back at Saigon, Bundy grabbed Ambassador Taylor, and both went immediately to MACV headquarters. They saw General Westmoreland at his operations center, and the general takes up the story: "Bundy himself led the discussion, intense, abrupt, at moments a bit arrogant." The MACV commander got the wrong impression of what Mac had been telling the president—he thought Bundy had counseled LBJ that there would be no fighting—but Westmoreland was right that Pleiku "brought us to a kind of Rubicon." This passage ends in a gratuitous fashion: "Perhaps, like numbers of civilians in positions of some governmental authority, once he smelled a little gunpowder he developed a field marshal psychosis."[26] In any case, Bundy telephoned the White House, where the NSC had gathered, and recommended retaliation against North Vietnam.

Bundy had been scheduled to visit the field that day, and he went to Pleiku with Westmoreland and Goodpaster. Mataxis, a former aide to Taylor who had remained close to the general, showed Mac the barracks. On one bunk lay the brain tissue of an American whose head had been split open. Bundy went outside, slumped against the wall, and threw up.

In Washington, President Johnson approved an attack, and his advisers agreed, including Ball. No one held back. Troops were sent to guard important bases. McCone of CIA wanted more dynamic action, systematic attacks against the DRV starting from the Demilitarized Zone and working northward. LBJ invited Senator Mike Mansfield and Congressman Gerald Ford to additional meetings. Mansfield argued in favor of going to the United Nations and against any wider war, raising questions about Hanoi's power, Soviet and Chinese responses, and the apparent unilateral quality of the U.S. decisions. He went back to his office to put his objections on paper. Ford complained that the administration seemed to be stopping halfway, executing only some of the recommended air strikes. He wanted no mere retaliation. Senator Everett Dirksen worried about morale and asked about an American withdrawal. McGeorge Bundy replied with the "standard argument," as McCone recorded, evidently a reference to the Domino Theory.[27] Thus Washington deliberated escalation while employing boilerplate arguments to reject an exit strategy, another eerie prefiguring of the Iraq war.

The uniform impression at the White House was that the Pleiku attack was Hanoi's signal that Washington should back off and get out, or it would suffer even greater losses. No intervention would be tolerated. Many years later, at a conference in Hanoi in 1997, Vietnamese and American officials, military officers, and historians gathered to discuss lost opportunities of the Vietnam war. There, one of the Vietnamese officers revealed that he had initiated and led the Pleiku attack; Hanoi had been informed only after the fact. He had never heard of McGeorge Bundy and had no idea that Johnson's man was in South Vietnam. Cooper, also at the conference, opined that if LBJ had known, it would have made no difference. Washington had been wound *that* tight.[28]

In Operation Flaming Dart, fifty U.S. aircraft struck several DRV barracks. As at the Tonkin Gulf, one plane was shot down and an American pilot captured. A parallel raid by Saigon's warplanes, ordered by Commodore Nguyen Cao Ky, hit another barracks and a Vietnam People's Army (VPA) communications center. Ky had set up a new elite, all-volunteer squadron for this attack and led the twenty-four planes, even though he had just learned to fly this type of aircraft, the A-1E Skyraider, and had almost no flight time in it. A couple of days later the NLF struck back, setting off an explosive charge at another U.S. barracks in the coastal town of Qui Nhon, where planes were also based. A second "tit for tat" response, Flaming Dart II, hit North Vietnam.

By then, Bundy had left Saigon. Winging over the Pacific, he penned a paper for LBJ, arguing that the stakes were high, the U.S. investment large, and defeat inevitable without new action. In an annex Bundy recommended graduated and continuing reprisals. Johnson asked the JCS to plan for ongoing attacks. In the heat of the moment after the Qui Nhon attack, LBJ approved the program without much deliberation. He rejected objections from Mansfield, as well as Ball's warning to be careful of the Chinese and a final appeal to submit the issue to the United Nations. When Vice President Hubert H. Humphrey advised caution, LBJ shut him up and then punished the vice president, a member of the NSC by law, excluding Humphrey from NSC meetings for more than a year. The sustained bombing became Operation Rolling Thunder, the air campaign against North Vietnam.

Regular Rolling Thunder attacks started at the beginning of March. Around that time newspaper reporter David Halberstam, now a White House correspondent, encountered Mac Bundy in the White House barbershop, where he was about to get a shave. Halberstam knew the security adviser, having taken Bundy's course at Harvard. He spoke up.

"Mac," Halberstam asked, "what was the difference between Pleiku and the other incidents?"

Bundy thought a moment before replying. "Pleikus are like streetcars," he said.[29]

Indeed. If it had not been Pleiku it could have been Qui Nhon or Bien Hoa or the Brinks Hotel or the U.S. embassy, which was car-bombed at the end of March in a strike that Hanoi had surely approved. Johnson might have been ambivalent or even deeply troubled about Vietnam, but he was a proud man and not about to run from a fight, whether he perceived it accurately or not. LBJ was not mousetrapped into Vietnam. He marched into war, head held high.

■ ■ ■ The same thing, less the doubts and uncertainties, can be said for Hanoi. The Democratic Republic of Vietnam had a well-defined goal—reunification of the country—and an absolute belief in its cause. The DRV had been helping the southern resistance since 1959 and, toward that end, had infiltrated Laos and created the Ho Chi Minh Trail. Until now, Hanoi's assistance had relied on Vietnamese from the South who had gone North after Geneva. Infiltration had been steady but limited. In October 1963 Hanoi strengthened its dominance over the Liberation Front by assigning personnel to the Central Office for South Vietnam (COSVN), the headquarters that controlled PLAF troops.

The equation changed further after Diem's overthrow. At the end of 1963 the Ninth Plenum of the Party Central Committee decided to increase DRV support by improving the Ho Chi Minh Trail to accommodate trucks. Hanoi responded to the U.S. "graduated pressure," though not in the way proponents of coercive diplomacy had hoped. Instead, the North Vietnamese decided to send integral units of VPA regulars to the South, beginning with the several regiments of the 325th Division. The selection embodied a certain logic, given that the 325th had been the major VPA formation committed in central and southern Vietnam during the French war, and the same unit had already been used to clear the Ho Chi Minh Trail and help the Pathet Lao. Infiltration continued. According to Hanoi's figures, it sent 40,000 men and women down The Trail before the end of 1963. A quarter of them were cadres—prospective troop leaders or political officers, including 2,000 senior people or technicians. The plenum's orders were not a gambit to avoid defeat but an initiative to secure victory.

The Ninth Plenum also issued orders anticipating a full-scale conflict. The People's Army was to bring its units to wartime strength, with the formations themselves under active command of the General Staff. In March 1964, in a move no doubt influenced by Washington's 34-A covert military pressure, air defenses and coastal units went on wartime alert. Now the VPA created a "front," or operational field command, for the Central Highlands under Military Region 5, the old Interzone 5 of the French war. This controlled several PLAF main-force regiments, including artillery units. On June 1 Colonel General Van Tien Dung, chief of the General Staff, widened the combat alert to all units. At that time the People's Army began sending antiaircraft units to Laos to defend the Ho Chi Minh Trail. Antiaircraft battalions that formed parts of VPA divisions were moved to the southern DRV for the same purpose.

As far as can be determined from available sources, Hanoi's decision took place in September 1964. At the time of the Tonkin Gulf incident, the old approach still prevailed—ad hoc collections of cadres and specialists dispersed throughout the NLF forces. But now Hanoi assembled 400 men for its Infiltration Group 53, which deployed just below the Demilitarized Zone and stayed together, becoming the 808th Battalion. It was a short step from sending a constituted unit to dispatching a major formation. The Politburo made the call. Hanoi prepared the 325th Division for war. Its 95th Regiment left on the long march in November. Two more regiments of the 325th plus one from the VPA's flagship unit, the 308th Division, along with artillery and the 545th "Viet Bac" Battalion, an elite combat intelligence unit, became the precursors of a steady stream. They went to the Central Highlands, the first of the regulars who reinforced and eventually overshadowed the PLAF. General Nguyen Chi Thanh, a key member of the Military-Party Committee, trekked south to take up the reins at COSVN.

Kosygin's visit to Hanoi marked a departure. The Soviet leader brought senior commanders of Soviet air defense troops, and among the military aid measures agreed on was the provision of surface-to-air missiles to North Vietnam. The beginning of U.S. bombing just as Kosygin and the North Vietnamese were pondering these matters only added to their urgency.

In early 1965 the Southeast Asian conflict attained a new level. The southern resistance inflicted a serious defeat on the ARVN in the coastal plain at a town called Binh Gia. The PLAF first overran the town, then waited out Saigon's reaction force and chopped up two South Vietnamese battalions, one an elite Marine unit. Hanoi's attacks on Americans figured in a sustained offensive in the Central Highlands. Pleiku became the first battle action of the northern troops. The United States started its Rolling Thunder bombing. Only a week later a northerner of the 325th Division was captured near Pleiku. Several weeks afterward, another soldier from the division's other major unit, the 101st Regiment, defected to the ARVN at Kontum. Washington had its first concrete evidence of direct North Vietnamese participation.

■ ■ ■ The bombing played an extraordinary role for American policy makers. The idea of bombing, proposals for bombing, target lists and bombardment options, the goals of bombing, and the expected results consumed hours of talk and forests of paper for months before Rolling Thunder and for years afterward. Protecting the forces dropping the bombs drove the first U.S. combat deployments. During the war, debate began—and has raged ever since—over the effectiveness of the bombing. That is best engaged later, but an important yet frequently ignored point is that Washington originally began bombing as much to influence Saigon as to coerce Hanoi.

A review of Johnson's deliberations reveals that political instability in Saigon remained a central U.S. concern into 1965. Military strongman Khanh attempted to embrace the same objective as Hanoi—reunification (by means of his March North)—as a device to mobilize support. Bombing, which Washington saw as a low-cost, high-impact measure, had clear relevance to the March North.[30] What is startling about U.S. deliberations is that through these weeks and months, talk ranged back and forth over whether bombing ought to be initiated to increase stability in Saigon, or whether bombing should be delayed, pending a more stable Saigon.

South Vietnamese developments need to be examined because they are critical to this evolution. The junta that overthrew Diem initially enjoyed wide popularity. General "Big" Minh moved to capitalize on that popularity, seizing all Diem family property and the holdings of several Diemist organizations. In early December 1963 the junta also suspended the strategic hamlet program, ordering officials not to demand Vietnamese villagers to contribute; not to force them to perform labor, except for projects of direct benefit to them; and not to oblige peasants to move into strategic hamlets. Existing hamlets were to be provided with the social services that had been lacking.[31] Minh also recruited the Cao Dai sect to fight against the NLF. Except for the suspension of new hamlets, the revised policy was mostly honored in the breach. Every one of South Vietnam's 237 district chiefs was an

ARVN officer. Meanwhile, progress on the battlefield remained remote, symbolized by engagements in Long An province in early January, where an NLF battalion escaped from a strong ARVN encirclement, and in "War Zone C" north of Saigon, where a monthlong operation by a full division of the ARVN netted no results whatever. On January 6 Minh issued a decree according all civil and military powers to his junta.

Meanwhile, after the fall of Diem, France became involved again when President Charles de Gaulle proposed to neutralize Southeast Asia along the lines that were supposed to be working in Laos. The fear of creeping neutralization became an excuse for General Khanh to topple Minh. Khanh became the prime minister on February 8, 1964, and consolidated power in late March, assuming the chairmanship of the board of ARVN generals called the Military Revolutionary Council. Minh was given a sinecure as "supreme adviser," but Minh's junta generals were put under house arrest at Dalat. Then Khanh created an "executive steering committee," effectively making himself strongman. Having done that, Khanh too played the Diem card, ordering the execution of Diem's brother Ngo Dinh Can. The ARVN officer responsible for the suppression of the Buddhist demonstration at Hue was sent to prison. Then Khanh extended conscription, decreeing that South Vietnamese could be drafted for the militia as well as the ARVN.

Beyond the military and certain ultranationalist political parties that emerged from the shadows, the Buddhists now became a political force. ARVN generals suddenly rediscovered their Buddhist roots, converting back from Catholicism. There had been a few Buddhist demonstrations even after the Diem coup, and a few weeks before Khanh took power, the eleven major sects joined in a Unified Vietnam Buddhist Church, with an avowedly political Institute for Secular Affairs led by Thich Tri Quang. The Buddhists would be hobbled by internal cleavages, including charges that Quang functioned as an NLF agent (his brother was an official in Hanoi), but they nevertheless represented a major political force in South Vietnam.[32] In a May 1964 decree, General Khanh elevated Buddhism to the same status as Catholicism, abolishing the Diem-era restrictions on practitioners. A month later there would be a demonstration in Saigon protesting the regime's favoritism toward Buddhists. By late 1964 Quang had become isolated within the hierarchy, and the Unified Church ordered monks to eschew political agitation. That did not work, however, and Buddhist activism continued.

The two key features of the 1964–1966 period in South Vietnamese politics would be the growth of the Vietnamese military role and the definition and shaping of Buddhist influence. The form of expression became the coup d'état. General Khanh's political projects—arresting officers and releasing them, installing governments then overturning them, coups and countercoups, even his March North and certain diplomatic feelers to Hanoi—represented maneuvers within this framework. Many Vietnamese felt uncomfortable, not least ARVN officers. Lam Quang Thi, for example, though somewhat impressed by Khanh, recalled, "I was concerned that the new coup . . . could engender other coups and that these coups and counter-coups, if not stopped, would plunge our country further into political turmoil and would severely hurt our war efforts."[33] He was not alone. Air force leader Nguyen Cao Ky, an enthusiastic participant in several coups, expressed similar misgivings, writing, "My view was that I should stay out of it, that the disagreement was among the ARVN and its generals."[34]

General Khanh unveiled his March North in July at a rally held to denounce the Geneva agreements on their tenth anniversary. A few weeks later, giving the March North a certain substance, Air Commodore Ky told a news conference that Saigon forces were carrying out commando-style raids in the North, and his pilots were training to bomb the DRV. For the Johnson administration, the advantage was that Saigon here assumed responsibility for the 34-A covert operations. But Khanh's political difficulties multiplied. The council of generals promulgated a constitution but withdrew it almost immediately. Khanh tried to accommodate the restive military by holding talks with the generals he had previously arrested. He took advantage of the Tonkin Gulf to declare a state of emergency. Vietnamese students and Buddhists both answered with protests, and one in Hue resulted in the burning of the U.S. Information Agency library there. Khanh promised much greater civilian participation, but in the end he simply reshuffled his junta. Catholic demonstrators marched on the headquarters of the Military Revolutionary Council, and ARVN paratroops quelled the protest. Half a dozen people were killed in these events. Fifty thousand marched in the funeral procession for the slain protesters.

Khanh faced such pressures that he withdrew from the government, pleading a sort of "breakdown," going for a rest cure at Dalat toward the end of August. A civilian replaced him, but the Americans applied tremendous efforts—spearheaded by Ambassador Taylor—to get Khanh back to work. Early in September the strongman plotted again. Making a private arrangement with Buddhist leaders, Khanh returned to the junta, fired the civilian-led cabinet, assumed direct leadership, and appointed General Duong Van Minh head of state.

Ten days later, on September 13, the Catholic General Lam Van Phat and IV Corps commander Duong Van Duc led a coup to get rid of Khanh. Rebel forces soon controlled much of Saigon, including the radio station, where Phat announced Khanh's demise—but too soon. Ambassador Taylor happened to be in Washington. His deputy, U. Alexis Johnson, pleaded with Big Minh not to join the coup and with Phat to abandon it. Johnson considered Khanh brilliant and beguiling but utterly devoid of character, yet the general had been anointed by McNamara and Taylor that spring. Washington rejected Khanh's pleas for military help, but Alex Johnson had each ARVN general under his lash for an hour and a half, cajoling and threatening them. As Johnson put it, "I made it clear to them . . . that Khanh retained American support."[35] Minh proved conciliatory, Phat confused. At MACV, General Westmoreland telephoned around, alerting ARVN commanders and trying to establish who was in on the coup. To get Duc out of the way, Westmoreland had the corps senior adviser ply him with his favorite scotch. Duc had been exiled in Paris and had worked as a waiter until the advent of Khanh and was not averse to this. Colonel Samuel N. Homan lurched into Westy's headquarters at 4:00 AM, saluting, drunk, and slurring, "Sir, mission accomplished!"[36] Probably more important, Commodore Ky intervened with the air force, threatening to strafe Duc's columns on the road from Can Tho. The coup collapsed.

The smoke had barely cleared when, about a week later, the montagnards rebelled in the Central Highlands. Their resentment of Saigon had hardly diminished since Diem, and unlike his treatment of the Buddhists, Khanh's concessions to the tribes were merely cosmetic. Khanh had conferred with tribal leaders that spring and promised to restore French-era administrative practices but had not done it. Montagnards made the same demand of General Nguyen Huu Co, commanding the highlands, with the same result. Meanwhile, in July the montagnards had been in the news in another context, heroically defending the camp at Nam Dong from a Liberation Front attack, along with their U.S. and ARVN Special Forces leaders and some CIA Nung fighters. Captain Roger Donlon won the Medal of Honor in this battle. Tribesmen felt that they were holding up their end of the social contract but Saigon was not reciprocating.

While Khanh negotiated the rapids that led him through the coup, the montagnard nationalist organization FULRO met in Cambodia and decided to rebel. Leaders gave the order on September 19. The first outbreak occurred at the Special Forces camp at Buon Sar Pa the same night. American Green Berets were told this did not concern them and asked not to interfere. The revolt quickly spread to five other camps. Dozens of ARVN Special Forces troopers were massacred and dozens more taken hostage. Green Berets at many camps ignored their own safety to prevent massacres or discourage the revolt. Some offered themselves as hostages in place of Vietnamese. When Khanh learned of the revolt he blamed the Americans for giving the tribes fancy ideas. Anthropologist Gerald Hickey, who worked for the Rand Corporation in South Vietnam and had studied montagnard culture extensively (he had been among the heroes of the Nam Dong battle), briefed Westmoreland and Taylor on the delicacies of the situation. They sent MACV operations deputy General William E. Depuy to Ban Me Thuot. General Khanh himself appeared on September 24. Special Forces chief Colonel John Freund came to negotiate and learned that Khanh had secretly ordered II Corps to attack Buon Sar Pa. Freund managed to get the tribesmen to back down. In October Saigon restored the old French *statut partic-ulière* but still rejected other tribal demands. Thus the Central Highlands remained restive, loyal but on the cusp of revolt. It is not surprising that Hanoi and the NLF could make inroads there.

Political maneuvers continued in Saigon. Mere rumors of a coup brought ARVN troops into the streets in late September. Next Khanh convened the generals and representatives of Buddhists, Catholics, students, and traditional political parties in a High National Council to agree on a provisional government and draft a constitution while he kept control. General Tran Thien Khiem, a junta member, was sent on an open-ended diplomatic mission, effectively into exile. Khanh resigned as prime minister, but the civilian who replaced him soon faced fresh charges of discrimination against Buddhists and old ones of complicity with Diem and even Emperor Bao Dai. Students facing conscription added to the unrest, which rose to the level of scandal when the Sureté announced it had broken up a ring of Khanh's officers who had been selling draft exemptions. There were more demonstrations. On November 26 the government declared martial law. Some saw that as Khanh retaliating against the Sureté, since the decree permitted the army to control the police.

Thich Tri Quang and other Buddhist venerables answered with a hunger strike and more protests against the civilian prime minister. By December 19 Khanh stood ready for another maneuver and launched a coup with Nguyen Cao Ky and other "Young Turk" military leaders. They dissolved the High National Council and replaced it with a military board. Shortly afterward Max Taylor invited the Young Turks to dinner at the embassy, using the occasion to berate them for political involvement. Commodore Ky told Taylor that the food was good but his talk wasted. The day after Christmas the Armed Forces Council extended martial law.

At the beginning of 1965 Saigon tottered on the brink of rebellion. Demonstrators repeatedly ignored martial law strictures. On January 9, pressured by Taylor, the generals agreed to restore civilian rule, but less than three weeks later Khanh mounted a new coup d'état and ousted the civilian government. The Buddhists temporarily subsided while Khanh installed another civilian cabinet. Then there was a failed coup against the strongman himself, led by dissident officers under Colonel Pham Ngoc Thao; though widely considered one of the Young Turks, the colonel would eventually be revealed as a Hanoi intelligence agent. Khanh escaped again, rallying troops who restored him the next day. But a renewed coup, this time led by Ky (changing sides) and General Nguyen Van Thieu, finally bested Khanh. The Armed Forces Council stripped Khanh of his posts as its chairman and commander of the armed forces. He went into exile. Dr. Phan Huy Quat, a man whom Diem had spurned as defense minister in 1955, took office as the head of a civilian cabinet.

This last round of plotting delayed the Rolling Thunder bombing. Keen to get started, Washington could hardly wait. In contrast to the miles of policy papers and days of talk that had characterized Lyndon Johnson's deliberations in 1964, one searches in vain for an explicit proposal for Rolling Thunder, along with the background material and staff work that entailed. In reality, the decision had already been made the previous December. Pleiku provided context. Saigon politics had been the last red light. Once Ky and Thieu seemed secure, the final obstacle disappeared. The American war began in earnest. On March 2, 1965, the first Rolling Thunder mission took wing. There would be many more.

Meanwhile, the deeply unpopular Armed Forces Council dissolved itself. Suddenly an economic crisis erupted, triggered when the NLF cut roads connecting Saigon to the rice fields of the Mekong. Prices went through the roof. Prime Minister Quat dismissed his ministers of the economy and interior. But South Vietnam's chief of state, pushed by Catholics and by those who resented the northerner Quat, refused to approve the dismissals. There was also a problem with another minister, General Nguyen Van Thieu, who felt he had not been properly informed of Quat's moves. Quat sent a close aide, Bui Diem, to placate the general, and Thieu seemed mollified. But the ministerial crisis continued, leading to a late-night confrontation where the generals demanded that Quat explain how he would solve this mess. Exhausted, angry, and disturbed, Quat resigned. The next morning the military announced a new government with Nguyen Van Thieu as chief of state and Nguyen Cao Ky as prime minister. The action came so swiftly that Bui Diem concluded it must have been prepared beforehand by junior officers working for Thieu and Ky.[37] Ky, who promoted himself to air marshal, and Thieu led a Saigon government that endured. That was stability of a sort.

"Not Yet an Organized Opposition"

Amherst, Massachusetts. A typical New England winter. Snow covered the postage stamp–sized common of the town that March day. A handful of citizens stamped their feet in the cold, holding up placards protesting the bombing of North Vietnam. Some passersby expressed support; many did not. This was the dawn of the antiwar movement. In Amherst, Boston, New York, and other cities and towns there would be thousands marching, but now there were just a few. Many linked their opposition to nuclear war with the one suddenly thrust upon them in Vietnam. Others connected the oppression of blacks with the suppression of popular feeling in Vietnam. The antiwar movement had a long way to go, but disquiet existed from the beginning; it was not a phenomenon that started once the United States got into trouble, although that development powerfully affected sentiment. The day after Pleiku, while McGeorge Bundy's plane still winged eastward, the SDS announced an Easter rally in the nation's capital.

More than 1,500 telegrams to the White House commented on LBJ's first retaliatory strikes, opposing them by a ratio of 12–1, a reversal of opinion
since the Tonkin Gulf. Subsequent telegrams piled up at a rate of up to 1,800
a week and again opposed escalation by ratios of 6–1 to 12–1.

Amherst would not be the only manifestation of public protest, nor the
first.[38] Boston may enjoy some distinction there, and again, the connection
would be antinuclear. A number of prominent Boston and Cambridge academics were active in the antinuclear movement; they included the leading
lights at Harvard, MIT, and other schools, among them such figures as
physicist Bernard Feld and linguist Noam Chomsky. It was late 1964. The
group had a sort of a steering committee, its members highly exercised
about what seemed to be happening in Southeast Asia. At the time, not too
much was going on in nuclear matters. Young physicist Milton Leitenberg at
Brandeis, an associate of Feld's, functioned as a sort of staffer to the committee. He too was concerned about Vietnam and had time on his hands. Feld
wanted to engineer some public expression and sent Leitenberg to see
Chomsky. One of them came up with the idea of a full-page ad in a major
newspaper, the *Boston Globe*. Leitenberg drafted a text and, using it, solicited
signatures and donations. The senior people on the committee knew the
Boston elite and took care of Beacon Hill. Before long they had raised
enough money to run the advertisement. The result was "An Open Letter to
President Johnson," published in the *Globe* on December 18, 1964.

Fifty signatories argued, "We believe that we have neither wisdom nor
strength enough to play God's policemen in Southeast Asia." They considered the conflict to be fundamentally a civil war and stated, "we cannot win a
decisive military victory in Vietnam short of all-out war." The United States
was becoming involved in military action "without the American people being fairly informed," and this was not helping the people of South Vietnam.
Under the headline "THE WAR THAT NEVER ENDS," the *Globe* editorialized favorably on the letter, warned of continuing stalemate, and proclaimed it vital
"that public opinion make itself known."[39] The ad eventually appeared in
newspapers in many cities and garnered thousands of signatures.

Boston Brahmin opinion reflected wider developments among the American public. Historian Charles DeBenedetti, an authority on the antiwar
movement, wrote, "By late 1964, there was a significant base of dissent from
Vietnam policy, although there was not yet an organized opposition."[40]
Doubts were first evident among the Old Left, individuals the FBI had been
following for years, but the shift was bigger than that. On the intellectual
plane, the highbrow journals had begun to notice, and the shift was occurring across the political spectrum. Through the 1950s, the conservative *National Review*, vehicle for former CIA operations officer William F. Buckley,
Jr., had viewed the U.S. presence in East Asia through the prism of the loss of
China, later supporting Diem and trying to explain away his foibles. In con-

trast, *Commentary*, long a fellow traveler, opened its pages to Hans Morgenthau's critiques of Johnson's Vietnam policy. The religious center, represented by *Commonweal*, advocated a negotiated settlement, a position soon adopted by many liberal journals, among them the *New Republic*. On the secular side, magazines such as the *Reporter* and the *Saturday Evening Post* focused on reportage, but the stories frequently illustrated policy shortcomings. The Left, typified by the *Nation*, the *Progressive*, and the *New York Review of Books*, remained hostile to LBJ's Vietnam initiatives. The *Nation* was among the early critics of the administration's account of Tonkin Gulf, for example. On the Far Left, with the notable exception of *Dissent*, which opposed an American role in Vietnam as early as the Eisenhower era, organs such as *Partisan Review, Studies on the Left*, and *Liberation* actually devoted little attention to Vietnam. Pleiku and Rolling Thunder stimulated intellectual ferment. Except on the Right and the Far Left, the center of gravity in intellectual opinion moved toward negotiations.[41]

Lyndon Johnson, whose skill at reading the public mind is legendary, was hardly unaware of the discourse. He tried to prepare the ground for sustained bombing, ordering the State Department to issue a white paper. Its principal author was William Jorden, who worked for Walt Rostow on the Policy Planning Council. Jorden could not use the most secret evidence, but the paper contained a welter of data. It was titled "Aggression from the North: The Record of North Vietnam's Campaign to Conquer South Vietnam."[42] Using evidence of Hanoi's infiltration of men and supplies, it tried to build a case that a communist government (the DRV) had set out to deliberately conquer "a sovereign people in a neighboring state." Despite its recitation of the stories of infiltrators and data on weapons entering South Vietnam by sea or from the Ho Chi Minh Trail, the white paper fell flat. It minimized the southern resistance while failing to drive home the case for aggression. The basic difficulty, of course, was that the 1954 Geneva agreements had recognized Vietnam as a unitary state temporarily divided into "regroupment zones," which made it difficult to argue that the conflict was anything other than a civil war. Washington's legal justifications stumbled over this obstacle throughout the war, and the remedy adopted was simply to assert South Vietnam to be an independent nation, a claim that became less and less credible as the United States visibly propped up the Saigon regime.

At the White House, NSC staffer Chester Cooper noted that the white paper "created ripples of support . . . and tidal waves of opposition."[43] Cooper felt it impossible to furnish sufficient evidence of Hanoi's direction to convince both confused nonexperts and sophisticated skeptics. He suffered personally from the effort. Mac Bundy instructed Cooper to publicize the white paper by revealing some of its data in advance to journalist Max Frankel. Cooper did so. He talked to the *New York Times* reporter on "background," thinking that once the white paper came out, the *Times* would feature it prominently. Instead, Frankel made the briefing data into a front-page story in the next day's paper. President Johnson was furious and took it out on the NSC staff. Bundy, who had given Cooper the order, was not pleased either.

As for the white paper's bountiful data, that stumbled over the Vietnam data problem: there was material on both sides of the issue. It took journalist I. F. Stone barely a week to craft an answer to the white paper, which he published on March 8.[44] Stone conceded that the DRV supported the rebellion in the south but noted, this "is no more secret than that the United States supports South Vietnam." He used the paper's own statistics to show that there were few northerners among the infiltrators and that the vast majority of captured weapons were not of communist origin. Stone's critique was widely considered more valid than the white paper itself.

One response to the administration began in the form of the "teach-in" movement. The first teach-in was held at the University of Michigan on the night of March 24. Three thousand persons showed up to be educated on the subject of Vietnam. The event acquired even greater impact after the university president declared that Americans should rely on the pronouncements of Washington, and Michigan officials tried to prevent the teach-in from happening. Teach-ins spread like wildfire, occurring at the University of Wisconsin, University of California–Berkeley, New York University, Chicago, Rutgers, Oregon, Columbia, Harvard, Pennsylvania, University of Massachusetts–Amherst, Goucher, Principia, Marist, and even Flint Junior College. Predictably, the movement went national on the radio. McGeorge Bundy accepted an invitation to speak for the Johnson administration at a televised teach-in, but when the president learned of it he was not happy and chewed Bundy out. Mac recruited Walt Rostow and Zbigniew Brzezinski to speak instead, reciting a long statement prepared by Bundy. Arthur Schlesinger also backed LBJ. Speaking in opposition would be Bernard Fall, Seymour Melman, and Hans Morgenthau. Morgenthau's stance was disturbing, since he had authored a celebrated realist theory of international politics. Vietnam was *that* divisive.

Lyndon Johnson responded personally and within days of the Michigan teach-in. He gave a speech at Johns Hopkins University, alluding to the teach-in by saying that Vietnam was far from quiet college campuses. George Ball, William Bundy, and press aide George Reedy all recalled this gambit as a response to the nascent opposition. The speech was vintage LBJ. Written by Richard Goodwin, then at the apogee of his relationship with Johnson, the text reflected LBJ's desires plus extensive NSC staff work. Johnson waved a stick but offered carrots too. He insisted on the independence of South Vietnam and thundered, "We will not be defeated. We will not grow tired. We will not withdraw, either openly or under the cloak of a meaningless agreement."[45] Then he offered "unconditional" talks, playing to the public on that score. And as a sweetener for Hanoi, Johnson dangled the prospect of a massive effort to harness the Mekong River, similar to the dams and rural electrification projects LBJ had championed early in his career. He had some impact: polls registered 52 percent support for Johnson's Vietnam policy. The Johns Hopkins speech illustrated Johnson's acute ear for public opinion.

Some argue that antiwar sentiment *prolonged* the Vietnam conflict. Most notable is probably Adam Garfinkle, who divides the era into several stages, the first of which extended through 1966. According to this view, if not for antiwar efforts, LBJ's 1965 escalation could have occurred in 1962, 1963, or 1964, presumably a time when the Liberation Front and North Vietnam would have been less able to counter it. As Garfinkle put it, the opposition was well represented in JFK's and LBJ's councils.[46] The core argument is that liberals and antiwar dissidents shared many of the same views. This is unproved. Except for George Ball and Hubert Humphrey, there was no significant objection to the inception of bombing. Garfinkle's work shows no actual linkage between war decisions and the influence of dissent. Other evidence is plentiful that the antiwar movement lacked the cohesion, numbers, or political power to prevent escalation at this time.

Conversely, officials in the Kennedy and Johnson administrations, liberal as they were, hardly let their doubts get in the way and actively worked to prevent contrary views from coalescing. Moreover, muscular intervention was proposed as early as 1961 and rejected on grounds that had nothing to do with dissent. Further, in the decision climate postulated by the "prolonging the war" argument, the contrary option—withdrawal—should have gotten much more of a hearing than it ever did. There is an additional, interesting conflict between this argument and versions of history that propose that the United States had won the war in 1962–1963. If that were true, there was even *less* possibility of a muscular intervention. To the extent the Vietnam data problem led officials to believe that victory was around the corner, this militated against the early intervention in which this school believes.

The Garfinkle hypothesis also implies that earlier U.S. military intervention was feasible and would have succeeded. Neither proposition is demonstrated, and both are highly suspect. Poorly adapted to counterinsurgency as it was in 1965, the U.S. military in 1961–1962 had yet to emerge from the lean budgets of Eisenhower's "New Look"; it was explicitly designed to conduct atomic, not guerrilla, warfare and lacked forces deployable to South Vietnam other than air and naval. A 1964 reform (the "Reorganization Objective Army Division," or ROAD concept) in fact produced combat units far better suited to ground warfare than the structure existing from 1957 on. Meanwhile, the NLF had become well established, and thin and ham-handed U.S. forces in the numbers available were unlikely to add that much capability to the ARVN.

The place to look for understanding at this time was in the White House, not on the streets. This is pointed up by an incident that took place in the summer of 1965. Only continuing presidential sensitivity over events a decade earlier—after Dien Bien Phu—can account for what happened. In Congress, Michigan Republican Melvin R. Laird put together a party-sanctioned booklet on the stakes in Vietnam that tried to highlight Republican and Democratic distinctions. Seeking to demonstrate continuity, Johnson responded at a June press conference, calling attention to Eisenhower's October 1954 letter to Diem, which he read out loud. LBJ would honor those commitments. The Eisenhower letter then became part justification for U.S. actions in the administration's answering pamphlet. At an August press conference of his own, Eisenhower shot back that he had no idea what the Johnson people were talking about. Help to Vietnam meant foreign aid, not military programs. "There was no commitment given in a military context," Eisenhower said.[47] LBJ, who relied on Ike's advice during his troop decision (see later), hit the roof. The former president had either forgotten or was being disingenuous.

As soon as the news appeared, a chagrined Eisenhower telephoned LBJ. He explained the gaffe as a result of reporters trying to make him say that the military plans for what was now happening had started back then. According to the note taker's record, Johnson "doesn't feel that there is any difference between former President Eisenhower and himself." Their purposes were the same. He continued, "That message itself is absolutely correct."[48] President Johnson had press spokesman Bill Moyers say this in a statement he cleared with Eisenhower during their conversation; he also sent General Andrew Goodpaster, a close aide to the former president and now LBJ's go-between, up to Gettysburg to refresh Ike's memory on the 1954 letter. Eisenhower called in reporters, denounced press accounts, and called the charges "rot."[49]

Lyndon Johnson took other purposeful steps to build support. The white paper was one. The most important would be a bridge to the American Friends of Vietnam (AFV). The group had been about to press for more action when LBJ began the bombing. The AFV desisted. The president opened a channel. Chet Cooper, who had been arguing that Johnson's problem lay in his supporters being mostly silent or unorganized, wanted to create a speakers' bureau. Cooper became the contact person, and he was soon reporting that the AFV's Wesley Fishel might pick up the project. Johnson political aide Jack Valenti recruited businessmen to raise funds for the AFV, and Cooper suggested speakers for a Michigan State University rally Fishel organized to counter the teach-ins. This angered some AFV founders, notably Joseph Buttinger, who opposed Rolling Thunder and resigned. Then lack of money forced the AFV to scale back. By early 1966 Cooper had left the NSC staff, and the AFV channel shut down.

Apart from punditry and political speeches, however, there was a new feature on the American scene, one that trended in the other direction. This was the active mobilization of people, most particularly the student movement, gradually growing since Kennedy's day, impelled by civil rights and antinuclear opposition, and greatly spurred in 1964 by a major campus struggle over free speech at the University of California–Berkeley.[50] Its first big manifestation came on April 17, 1965, with the march on Washington sponsored by the SDS. Organizers had predicted a turnout of 10,000 people. Instead, there were somewhere between 15,000 and 25,000. Among the speakers that day—evidence of the antiwar movement's link to the civil rights struggle— was Robert Moses.

Not long afterward, on April 28, President Johnson ordered U.S. intervention in the Dominican Republic, ostensibly to save American citizens caught in the chaos of a coup d'état in Santo Domingo. This turned into a deployment of more than 28,000 troops. LBJ declaimed about Cuban communists, but even the CIA could find no evidence of them. The intervention brought a break between Johnson and longtime ally Senator J. William Fulbright. Fears of U.S. imperial ambition began to color the thinking of antiwar activists. In an article on the SDS march in *Liberation*, Staughton Lynd remarked: "Perhaps next time we should keep going, occupying for a time the rooms from which orders issue, and sending to the people of Vietnam and the Dominican Republic the profound apologies which are due."[51] One day the Movement would come close to doing just that.

Boots on the Ground

In his Johns Hopkins speech, President Johnson had baldly stated that bombing by itself would not settle the Vietnam war. American ground troops were already going to South Vietnam. Behind the scenes, Army chief of staff Harold Johnson had warned LBJ that the conflict might require half a million troops. On April Fools' Day, LBJ approved a change in tactics under which GIs guarding the air bases could carry out offensive actions. On April 6 Johnson signed NSAM-328 expressing that decision, which provided for half a dozen more combat battalions (most of them Marines), logistics forces, a tight lid on news, and more. It had been built around military and civil programs proposed by Max Taylor. LBJ also approved a twelve-point CIA program for covert operations, bringing the agency back into this business less than a year after its covert role had been phased out.

Not long afterward, General Westmoreland put in a bid for Americans to serve as a general reserve behind the ARVN, and Johnson approved deployment of the 173rd Airborne Brigade for that purpose. Then came another powwow of high-level commanders at Honolulu, where MACV tabled a proposal for a total of 175,000 troops (thirty-four combat battalions). According to the authors of the Pentagon Papers, "By that point we were inexorably committed to a military resolution of the insurgency. The problem seemed no longer soluble by any other means."[52] President Johnson engaged in lengthy soul-searching, a process of more than two months' duration.

One question is whether there was a fix on the first play, that is, whether in originally asking for a few troops to guard air bases, the Joint Chiefs and General Westmoreland already had the big troop requests up their sleeves and used the initial move to break the dike. Based on MACV's own command history, the Pentagon Papers analysts determined, "There seems to be sufficient evidence to conclude that General Westmoreland and his staff saw in the deployment of the Marines the beginning of greater things to come."[53] Westmoreland denied this, noting, "I saw my call for marines . . . not as a first step in a growing American commitment but as what I said at the time it was: a way to secure a vital airfield."[54] Defense secretary McNamara sided with him, pointing out that the JCS were themselves divided over strategy and that the administration, not only the military, should have foreseen the need for security once American warplanes were based in South Vietnam.[55] The Pentagon Papers found that the initial deployment of ground troops represented a watershed, a decision without fanfare, with minimal planning.

On June 7 General Westmoreland pushed the troop deployment issue to the forefront with a dispatch that cited Hanoi's commitment of regulars, Liberation Front progress, and continued ARVN deficiencies. He noted: "In order to cope with the situation outlined above, I see no course of action open to us except to reinforce our efforts in SVN with additional U.S. or third-country forces as rapidly as practical during the critical weeks ahead. Additionally, studies must continue and plans develop to deploy even greater forces, if and when required, to attain our objectives."[56]

America's field commander called for the immediate commitment of about 40,000 troops plus another 18,500 South Korean soldiers already slated under LBJ's "More Flags" initiative. Westmoreland wanted a follow-on increment larger than that. McNamara recalled, "Of the thousands of cables I received during my seven years in the Defense Department, this one disturbed me the most."[57] Before the end of June, Westmoreland upped the ante to 200,000 soldiers (forty-four battalions). The MACV commander also sent more cables insisting that massive U.S. troop deployment had become necessary. No more could Vietnam be considered a combat laboratory.

A second issue in the troop decision is the role of President Johnson's deliberations themselves. Again a blizzard of paper flew, documents with such quaint titles as "Vietnam Planning at Close of Business on July 19," and officials spent hours and days closeted with one another. The JCS rendered an opinion, and McNamara commented on the military program. The CIA offered its assessment of McNamara's comments and drafted an intelligence estimate on probable communist reactions. Rusk gave LBJ his opinion in private. Johnson documented the proceedings in an extraordinary fashion, with aides enlisted to compile near-verbatim notes on what was said as the president neared his decision.[58] Viewed from a distance, it seems almost as if the president was ensuring a paper trail that might, ultimately, protect him.

Johnson's treatment of George Ball adds to this impression. On this occasion, as he had several times over the preceding year, the undersecretary of state gave the president a paper opposing the proposal. Ball had already been down this road and had seen Bundy cut him down (Mac once told the president that he ought to listen hard to Ball, then reject his advice). At the time of Pleiku, Ball came to understand that "further frontal opposition would be not only futile but tactically unwise."[59] He contrived to slip LBJ his big paper from 1964, replete with its arguments drawn from French Indochina, through political aide Bill Moyers. When Johnson gathered the NSC principals to discuss the issue, McNamara had erupted with a "pyrotechnic" display of facts to refute Ball.[60] So George began sniping on the margins, resisting each new drop in the bucket. But the prospect of massive deployment smoked him out. Ball crafted a new paper on "keeping the power of decision," which he again got to LBJ through Moyers. Ball advocated a relatively small addition, topping off at 100,000 (the number of troops in Vietnam had already reached 82,000), while telling McNamara and Rusk and possibly the JCS chairman, "you are *not* committing US forces on an open-ended basis" but as a controlled experiment for a period of three months (rather like George W. Bush's "surge" in Iraq in 2007). Ball then would have *ordered* officials to plan for a political settlement and plump for a diplomatic deal. He warned that the United States stood on the threshold of a war that even 500,000 troops might not win, and he again used the French example.[61]

LBJ received this paper just before heading to Camp David for the weekend. On Monday Moyers reported back that the president agreed with most of what Ball had said, would have changed only a few things, and was going to instruct McNamara not to assume he was ready to go overboard on this escalation.

It is not coincidental that on June 30 McGeorge Bundy sent President Johnson a lengthy paper of his own in which he questioned whether France in Indochina in 1954 was "a useful analogy." At nine pages, this memo is among the most detailed the security adviser ever gave the president, and Bundy sought to diminish Ball's French analogy at every turn: France had been at the end of its tether, whereas the United States was not; the force numbers were different; unlike the Vietnamese under the French, "there remains an *impressive resiliency* among the Vietnamese people"; France had been politically unstable, fighting an unpopular war, whereas Americans generally supported the administration (62 percent in the most recent Harris poll). In short, "despite superficial similarities," Johnson's situation was not like that of the French at Dien Bien Phu.[62]

Bundy's analysis contained some elements that Johnson, the "Great Communicator," could not miss. Though conceding that, "in general, the public appears unenthusiastic but reconciled" and that "there is widespread questioning and uneasiness," Bundy maintained that "open skepticism as to our tactics subsides at times of sharp crisis." The security adviser essentially extolled the merits of maintaining a crisis atmosphere. He also argued that the most articulate critics so far were "usually" minorities among their organizations, but he warned of problems arising from the administration's "lack of frankness." Newspaper editorialists and columnists were largely supportive of "a free Vietnam," but Congress had become a source of the "most vocal current comment." LBJ had recently received more dissenting memoranda from Mike Mansfield and heard the criticisms of Wayne Morse, Ernest Gruening, George McGovern, and Frank Church on the Democratic side, as well as Republicans Gerald Ford and Melvin Laird. The president certainly agreed with Bundy's observation about Congress. Overall, Bundy oversimplified the French situation in 1954, overestimated the American political system's capacity to sustain war, and gave Johnson dangerous advice regarding manipulating public opinion through crisis. His wise counsel that vulnerability attached to secrecy LBJ ignored to his peril, for an emerging "credibility gap" became his worst nightmare. In later life, Bundy must have rued the day he wrote that paper.

In any case, McGeorge Bundy had told Johnson things he wanted to hear, and he had responded to a French analogy he knew to be close to LBJ's heart. It was exactly what was needed to win the latest round against George Ball. More Ball papers followed—on a legal basis for terminating American aid to Saigon, on cutting U.S. losses. Mac watched for those too. It was on a proposal to compromise that Bundy counseled LBJ to listen hard, then reject Ball's advice. A number of Vietnam histories and a good chunk of policy analyses have postulated Johnson used Ball as a kind of devil's advocate, the designated bad guy, to ensure every option was aired. But transcripts of the Oval Office and NSC meetings show LBJ working much harder than would be consistent with a devil's advocate model, even baiting Ball to draw him out. Either LBJ was making a record or he truly hoped George Ball could convince others in the room.

Bob McNamara recalled that "the president felt tortured. I sensed it, and others did as well."[63] In particular, McNamara cited Columbia University historian Henry Graff, whom LBJ gave extraordinary access to the White House some months later for a book on Johnson's Tuesday Lunches.[64] But McNamara himself observed that Johnson often resorted to theatrics—the very thing that makes it so difficult to discern his real views. It is thus hard to pinpoint when LBJ's fears became overriding. Was it in 1964, when he blew hot and cold on Vietnam? Now, during the troop decision? Or was it in 1967–1968, when Mac Bundy's vision of American political resilience turned out to be dead wrong?

On July 2 President Johnson had a pair of phone conversations that illustrate this dilemma perfectly. By then the big troop proposal had landed on his desk, together with all the assorted commentary. He spoke to Bob McNamara that morning. McNamara agreed the decision was a "fairly tough" one. Johnson asked for an exploration of several factors, leading with whether the United States, "assuming we do everything we can, to the extent of our resources," could really win. Johnson worried the National Liberation Front could simply continue indefinitely, and he was right. LBJ continued, "And the question is, Do we just want to do it out on a limb by ourselves? I don't know whether those [Pentagon] men have ever [calculated] whether we can win with the kind of training we have, the kind of power, and . . . whether we can have a united support at home." McNamara reassured his president and added in the prospect of a negotiated settlement. A couple of hours later Johnson phoned Dwight D. Eisenhower, telling his predecessor of the troop requests, which might upset such Republicans as Gerald Ford (who, LBJ believed, thought the war could be won by bombing alone). "You've got to go along with your military advisers," Ike replied. "My advice is do what you have to do." Johnson described the differences between his military, which wanted to go all out—"taking all the harbors . . . mining and blowing the hell out of it"—and the more restrained diplomats. Eisenhower answered, in essence, that for negotiations to work, the United States must have a position of advantage. He ended by saying, "I would go ahead and . . . do it as quickly as I could." LBJ enthused, "You're the best chief of staff I've got."[65]

A final strand of evidence concerns the possibility of neutralizing Southeast Asia, as proposed by Charles de Gaulle of France. This had the support of Cambodian ruler Prince Norodom Sihanouk and a degree of backing from other European nations. (At the 1997 conference in Hanoi, the one "missed opportunity" the Vietnamese side admitted to was the chance to have explored this possibility with more alacrity.) The period from the Diem coup to early 1965 has been termed "the long 1963" by one modern observer, who details the proposals for neutralization and the potential for their accomplishment.[66] Perhaps "the long 1963" could be extended to the moment of the troop decision, for the subject returned periodically in U.S. councils until then.

Lyndon Johnson spurned this opportunity. In truth, the circle of rejectionists went beyond the president to include virtually all top U.S. officials. According to Robert McNamara, LBJ spoke against neutralization, "concluding that De Gaulle's approach would lead to a Communist takeover of South Vietnam just as grave as U.S. withdrawal . . . At a minimum we should have pressed De Gaulle to go as far as he could to try and achieve his stated objective. We did not."[67] It remained a cardinal point in U.S. policy throughout to preserve the direct American role and avoid any international approach to Vietnam, including reconvening the Geneva conference or going to the United Nations—both repeatedly suggested and always rejected. Such proposals usually came when officials felt some propaganda or diplomatic advantage might result, and they frequently failed because the U.S. legal position remained shaky. Hanoi might gain more than Washington. Neutralization would certainly have required a new Geneva meeting. American distaste for a proposal emanating from de Gaulle also operated to reduce the possibility of its acceptance.

In South Vietnam there were times under both Diem and Khanh when Saigon attempted direct approaches to either the DRV or the Liberation Front. Whenever that happened, Washington became very sensitive. Neutralization had the same effect. But if Lyndon Johnson had really wanted to find a way to keep American boys from being killed without condemning Asian boys to continue killing one another, a neutralization formula would have been a good solution. The fact that it was never seriously considered not only says something about LBJ but also sheds light on American objectives in Vietnam.

The White House meetings on the troop decision were held in July and had only one possible outcome. Johnson approved the deployment. On July 30 the president went on television and announced to the nation that he would send a large force to South Vietnam, starting with the U.S. airmobile division, with more troops to follow. Johnson did another thing, too. He sent General Goodpaster, whose day job was overseeing the Joint Staff, responsible for all JCS military planning, to South Vietnam to figure out what all those troops might do. Goodpaster's ad hoc study group produced the closest thing to a strategic plan the United States ever elaborated, and, aiming solely at the NLF and VPA main forces, it exhibited the very features that bedeviled America's war effort.[68]

So the American soldiers came, burnished rows of steel bayonets. An amphibious brigade built around the 3rd Marines made its landing as the press watched in March 1965. The 4th Marines and a Marine air wing followed in May, and the 9th Marine Regiment in July. The Army's 173rd Airborne Brigade came from Okinawa, landing in May. The 2nd Brigade, 1st Infantry Division arrived in July. The 1st Cavalry Division (Airmobile) sailed to Vietnam in September, the remainder of the 1st Infantry Division that October, and the 3rd Brigade, 4th Infantry Division before Christmas. Headquarters, logistics commands, and engineer brigades also deployed, beginning a long struggle to ensure that South Vietnam's road and port infrastructure could accommodate all these forces. On December 31, 1965, there were 184,300 American servicemen in South Vietnam. This war was on for real.

5   A Hundred Circling Camps (1965–1967)

Lyndon Johnson no doubt considered his troop decision both urgent and necessary. South Vietnam sagged under the assaults of the National Liberation Front and North Vietnamese. Nguyen Cao Ky recalled, "Things were going poorly, especially in the Central Highlands . . . In past years the monsoon season, which begins in autumn, had signaled the start of a new communist offensive. It was still months before the monsoons, however, and the number and intensity of . . . incidents had increased dramatically . . . In short the enemy was on the verge of cutting South Vietnam into two parts."[1] According to one account, the ARVN high command thought of relocating its headquarters from the capital to the peninsular port of Vung Tau, well suited for close-in defense, and Prime Minister Ky considered abandoning the old imperial capital of Hue, pulling out of the northernmost provinces. General Westmoreland noted, "The enemy was destroying battalions faster than they could be reconstituted and faster than we had planned to organize them under the ARVN's crash build-up program."[2] Without American troops, Westmoreland foresaw quick defeat. He made no claims for victory, but the alternative was disaster.

LBJ made his choice. At Army posts throughout the United States, keen excitement ensued as troop units got orders to prepare for deployment and others were culled for specialists to fill out the ranks of those headed for Vietnam. For the professional military this was the moment, and Vietnam the place, for careers to be made and laurels won. Supremely confident of its capabilities, the military fielded its First Team. The Americans were determined to win.

■ ■ ■ Well might Saigon leaders fear for the Central Highlands. South Vietnamese colonel Nguyen Van Hieu, chief of staff of II Corps, recorded that peasants living in upland strategic hamlets (now called "new life hamlets") and resettlement centers flooded district towns in the foothills. At corps headquarters in Pleiku, food prices rose steeply, doubling in less than six months. The NLF had cut every road connecting the highlands to the rest of Vietnam. Only airplanes linked Pleiku to the outside. Morale plummeted. Hieu looked around him and saw downcast faces. In

June Le Thanh village was overrun. On July 7 the North Vietnamese captured the district town of Dak To, north of Kontum and a key ARVN position. The Vietnam People's Army could not hold the town, but its exploit pointed up the danger. The next day Colonel Hieu and his boss, General Vinh Loc, began a major road-clearing operation. Saigon reinforced II Corps with half a dozen elite battalions, including a Marine group and the Second Airborne Task Force.

The South Vietnamese accounted their operation a success. It featured the first use of B-52 bombers in the highlands and a carefully orchestrated movement of supply convoys that improved Pleiku's situation. But the People's Army struck back, besieging the Special Forces camp at Duc Co. Isolated even after the ARVN's road clearing, Duc Co hovered at the edge of extinction. General Loc defended it because the camp blocked the easiest route to Pleiku from the VPA base camps across the Cambodian border. To scout the area, the Americans lent him Special Forces Detachment B-57, Major Charles Beckwith's Project Delta. Duc Co became its second major operation. Early in August the North Vietnamese closed in and fully invested the camp. Now II Corps committed its two-battalion Airborne Task Force to strengthen Duc Co. Norman Schwarzkopf, the American commander in the Persian Gulf war of 1990–1991, had his first claim to fame as senior adviser to these ARVN paratroops.

General Westmoreland also sent one of the two battalions of his 173rd Airborne Brigade, which freed up enough ARVN troops for II Corps to send a relief column. The Vietnamese Marines, backed by armor and Rangers, made the attempt. They ran into a large-scale ambush carried out by the VPA 32nd Regiment. After a three-day battle the force finally made it to Duc Co, and the ARVN spent the better part of a week sweeping the zone around the camp.

This action served as prelude for what happened upon the arrival of the 1st Cavalry Division (Airmobile), known as "The Cav." Cued by the fighting, General Westmoreland rejected other plans for these troops and sent them straight to the highlands. The Americans already in place secured An Khe in the foothills, which became The Cav's initial base. Hanoi, aiming to study U.S. tactics and methods, chose a head-on battle at another Special Forces camp called Plei Me. "The Front Command launched the Plei Me Campaign," the VPA history notes, "carrying out a plan to besiege a position and annihilate the relief force. Our objective was to deal a painful blow to the puppet army in order to lure the American troops in so that we could kill them."[3] (In the People's Army system, a "front" represented a major regional command, equivalent to an ARVN corps, a U.S. "field force," or the "Marine amphibious force.") Hanoi's Highlands Front, known as the B-3 Front, came under the orders of Chu Huy Man, the DRV's own montagnard. Man had been a prisoner at Kontum during French colonial times. For the Vietminh he had led a division recruited from the mountains along the Chinese border, playing a key role at Dien Bien Phu. Later he held posts dealing with upland minorities and most recently had been in Laos in charge of Hanoi's mission to assist the Pathet Lao. Man came down the Ho Chi Minh Trail in 1964 as chief of the Vietnam Worker's Party General Political Department, responsible for montagnard affairs. Now he was back in the saddle as a combat commander.

General Man put his 33rd Regiment, just arrived from The Trail, into the Plei Me attack. The ambush force would be the 32nd, veterans of Le Thanh and Duc Co. With Pleiku weakened by dispatch of ARVN's relief column, the fresh VPA 66th Regiment would attack General Loc's headquarters. Later, other VPA units would join in to capture Pleiku as a whole. Vietnamese accounts published during the war claimed great success in preserving the operation's secrecy, and postwar histories do not dispute them.

The initial assault captured one of two outposts protecting Plei Me and annihilated a patrol in a satellite position. The Americans applied airpower. Only a sapper attack (a VPA-style commando raid) took place against the camp itself. Vinh Loc sent II Corps reinforcements, a relief force of 1,200 troops with tanks, armored cars, and personnel carriers, plus a couple of guns. The expedition virtually replayed the Duc Co operation. The U.S. command canceled a stand-down for Major Beckwith's Project Delta and got him to Plei Me by October 22, reinforced by two ARVN Airborne Ranger companies. Beckwith took command. The next day and night brought the ambush battle. The lead element of Lieutenant Colonel Nguyen Truong Luat's relief column held off a VPA battalion, but his following force, with the guns and most of his infantry, sustained heavy losses.

Chu Huy Man's calculations went wrong, however. The Cav was now arriving, and the division's 3rd Brigade immediately went into Pleiku. This enabled the ARVN to send its last troops to help Colonel Luat, finally breaking through to Plei Me on October 25. Charlie Beckwith considered himself lucky to get out without a scratch. In pursuit of the People's Army troops fading into the jungle, The Cav's 2nd Battalion, 8th Cavalry airlifted into a landing zone near Plei Me the next day. This began an extensive campaign fought to hunt down Chu Huy Man's men before they could escape. It became known as the Ia Drang (*Ia* is the word for "river" in the local language). Spurred by Westmoreland and Major General Stanley R. Larsen, leader of I Field Force, the command corresponding to Loc's, the 1st Cavalry Division conducted a monthlong operation.

This battle of the Ia Drang valley (actually just a small segment of it) is what most Americans think of when they recall U.S. troops entering South Vietnam. It was popularized by the book and movie *We Were Soldiers Once . . . And Young,* which focuses on a single engagement of the campaign, the heroic stand of Colonel Harold Moore's 1st Battalion, 7th Cavalry at a site called Landing Zone (LZ) X-Ray. The collective memory is dominated by the image of soldiers alighting from helicopters, marching into the nearby jungle, and encountering hordes of charging North Vietnamese. But an examination of veterans' stories, military records, official and popular accounts, and a rich memoir literature conveys a different impression. Moments of sheer terror punctuated an anxious daily existence in which the *potential* for ambush—and the fear of encountering booby traps—alternated with the frustration of navigating the jungle and savannah. Encounters with the enemy brought firefights that were basically delaying actions pending the arrival of reinforcements, aerial support, artillery fire, or all three. For the special operations forces and other combat units sent into remote sectors of "Indian Country," the land inhabited solely by Vietnamese adversaries, help came largely by air and involved complications arising from rules of engagement, location of the action, and availability of forward air control.

Life in the field varied a great deal, depending on where soldiers were operating and at what stage of the war. This is a reason why the second question a Vietnam veteran asks another is usually "When and where were you?" (the first is "What unit?"). Patrols close to bases might actually be accompanied by Vietnamese vendors hawking soda, cigarettes, and candy. Troops on roads enjoyed vehicle transport. But the daily task of clearing roads was some of the most hazardous duty. French soldiers in the previous war had dreaded this necessity, and Americans would too. Serving in the lowlands meant water and mud in the rice paddies. There too, enemy tunnel networks were encountered most often, and tunnel warfare was terrifying.

A large majority of the 2.5 million Americans who served in Vietnam were stationed in the coastal plains and the Mekong delta. Vietnamese were most numerous in the lowlands, so that brought frequent contact with villagers and the kinds of interactions that could evoke the "Ugly American." GIs who dehumanized the Vietnamese as "gooks" or "slopes"—and there were many—impeded counterinsurgency, which aimed at gaining the confidence of Vietnamese. Such pejoratives were often applied to ARVN allies as well. Oddly, this attitude often did not extend to the adversary. Denigrated as Vietcong by the Saigon government, Liberation Front soldiers were generally respected by the Americans, who called them "Victor Charlie," "Mr. Charles," or simply VC. The North Vietnamese were typically the NVA, for North Vietnamese Army, regarded as some of the best light infantry in the world.

In the savannah and highlands, elephant grass sometimes taller than a man could slow progress to a crawl. Ranging the Central Highlands or the uplands of the Annamite mountains below the Demilitarized Zone meant cutting through elephant grass and scaling heavily forested slopes. Triple-layer jungle was the worst, found in the uplands and out toward the border. Heat was pervasive, but in the uplands there could be cold. Combat rations were dreaded, although larger operations featured field kitchens with hot food. During later stages of the war, operations were restricted to areas close to U.S. bases, and the troops were finally confined to the bases themselves in a bid to limit casualties.

Between operations the troops settled into base camps—large posts that might house a brigade or a division—or firebases—smaller installations that controlled the surrounding terrain to support troops on a mission. The Special Forces camps, with their indigenous troops, were another beast. Patrols radiated from these moderately well-defended bases into the hinterland, hoping to dominate the countryside but often settling for scouting out the enemy.

Troops in camp were safer than those outside, but except in the largest, rearmost bases, they were never truly safe, for the NLF and VPA carried out a program of harassment that included mortar and rocket attacks, sapper raids, ground probes, and occasional full-scale assaults. Vietnamese civilians performed a welter of tasks on base, from doing the laundry to carpentry, and there was always the fear that the locals were enemy agents. Air bases and Special Forces camps were especially popular targets for the adversary, offering the possibility of shutting allied eyes in Indian Country. Since most of the "forward operating bases" that served as launch points for special operations into Indian Country were also located at the camps, the enemy's taking them out or isolating them could impede key U.S.–South Vietnamese offensive efforts, the only type of attack, besides bombing, that reached the NLF and VPA in their own base areas.

The strength of the National Liberation Front and its insurgency, particularly once reinforced by the Vietnam People's Army, made it impossible for Washington and Saigon to attain the 10–1 or higher preponderance considered necessary for success in counterinsurgency, even with the addition of Johnson's "Many Flags" third-country troops. Nor could the forces take over Indian Country or permanently occupy the adversary's base areas. Westmoreland, his ARVN colleagues, and other commanders compensated with firepower and tactics. One was to employ so-called harassment and interdiction (H&I) fire—blind bombardment in the hope of inflicting losses or at least preventing movement. The places targeted became known as "free fire zones." Both artillery and aircraft contributed to H&I fire, which soon accounted for much of the artillery ammunition and aerial ordnance expended by U.S. forces.

The primary ground tactic for excursions in Indian Country became the "search and destroy" mission, in which troops entered enemy territory and laid waste to anything deemed valuable. They would also attempt to force a battle, holding the enemy in place while commanders marshaled the capabilities to annihilate them. Closer to allied bases, where pacification and counterinsurgency were critical goals, "clear and hold" tactics were useful. All these tactics were critically affected by the shortage of troops, a problem accentuated by the wide variety of support forces backing U.S. combat troops; as a result, only one rifleman took the field for every seven or eight soldiers in the overall U.S. force.

Getting soldiers to the point of contact was where the helicopter came in. Other methods took more time, giving the enemy an opportunity to evade. The helicopter could quickly insert troops by "air assault" anywhere a suitable landing zone could be found. Of course, the NLF and VPA became adept at reading helicopter movements. Based on knowledge of where combat was in progress, combined with intercepted radio traffic (especially where communications security was sloppy), the adversary had a fair chance of divining the targets of air assaults. The Liberation Front and People's Army also developed their own tactics to counter air assault, designating small units as rear guards to engage the allies, making an LZ a "hot" one, to hold off the attackers long enough for their comrades to escape. Booby traps and other passive defenses could slow down GIs to the same purpose. The VPA became adept at fire tactics that drove the helicopters to higher altitudes (or to very low ones), making an assault more time-consuming (and providing more advance warning) or making the choppers' navigation more difficult.

For both sides these tactics evolved by trial and error, and the Ia Drang campaign began that process. North Vietnamese sources indicate that General Chu Huy Man's command deliberately changed its strategy so as to draw the 1st Cavalry Division into the Ia Drang valley. Most American observers view Ia Drang as a pursuit battle against the People's Army. Major General Douglas Kinnard of The Cav used several novel techniques. For instance, members of the 1st Squadron, 9th Cavalry—who called themselves the "Headhunters"—acted as a sort of aerial scout and strike force, with ground troops for probes once suspicious targets had been identified and gunship helicopters for "aerial artillery." After putting in a brigade to secure Pleiku, Kinnard leapfrogged his Headhunters through it and into Duc Co; from there they ranged over the area and out to the Cambodian border. On November 1 the Headhunters caught up with a VPA battalion licking its wounds at a camp near the mountain massif known as the Chu Pong. Scout troops landed to engage the North Vietnamese. The Cav did what it did so well: used more choppers to pile on troops until the enemy broke. Two days later the Headhunters and some montagnard strikers set overnight ambushes around a new LZ called Mary, catching the VPA and triggering fresh combat. This became the first battle for General Man's 66th Regiment, which had been sent toward the Chu Pong to cache its heavy weapons so the men could march faster. Another action followed on November 6. The Cav then executed another novel procedure made possible by its generous allotment of helicopters: exchanging the entire engaged brigade for a fresh one up from An Khe. This force contained Colonel Moore's 1st Battalion, 7th Cavalry, which in the U.S. Army could trace its lineage to the men who had fought the Sioux under George Armstrong Custer.

Moore's soldiers choppered into Plei Me, known to pilots as the "Tea Plantation," and probed an area at the foot of the Chu Pong. Other units scouted adjacent sectors. The VPA struck back with a sapper raid that apparently went unnoticed by chroniclers of the Ia Drang campaign. In any case, on November 14 the 7th Cavalry air-assaulted into LZ X-Ray, an action critically hampered because The Cav's intense pace left only sixteen choppers for Moore, and the tight jungle around X-Ray permitted simultaneous landing of just eight craft. Waves of helicopters were necessary for the initial lift because of the tight LZ. Robert Mason was a pilot in the second wave, and before they could ground, the LZ was already "hot." Some ships had to abort. More flights were necessary to insert the full battalion, but fighting began before the lift was complete. Three VPA battalions sat on a ridge overlooking the LZ. Moore's troops chased enemy patrols into the jungle, and then the VPA attacked, leaving one portion of grunts separated from the rest, all of them isolated, and some of his men still in the air. The Americans withstood the North Vietnamese assaults and spent an uneasy night. The next morning the enemy struck again. Only after beating off the attack and getting help from another battalion that marched in overland could Moore free his trapped platoon.

Hal Moore's GIs were finally able to fly out on November 17. Given the paucity of choppers, reinforcements from two other Cav battalions had to trek in. They headed for an LZ named Albany, but as they neared it the GIs encountered a tremendous ambush and then a People's Army attack on the new LZ. In some ways the crisis at Albany proved worse than at X-Ray. An hour passed before planes arrived to batter the enemy. Many of the Americans had no idea where they were or where other U.S. forces were. Troops at LZ Albany had to regroup into a final defensive perimeter. By the end of the day they had sustained 40 percent losses.

After the firefight at Albany The Cav switched out its brigades again, moving the unblooded 2nd Brigade into the highlands. At MACV General Westmoreland and his aides gushed about the success, claiming more than 1,500 VPA soldiers dead by body count and the loss of another 2,000-plus estimated. Helicopter pilot Mason recalled that Ia Drang was one of the few early Cav battles where he saw enemy dead lying in the open. General Kinnard also considered Ia Drang a success, validating the air assault tactics that now became a mainstay. But The Cav suffered 305 killed and 524 wounded—the equivalent of a full battalion, 10 percent of its combat strength. Many officers, Hal Moore among them, had little confidence in the "body count" claims. For its part, Hanoi also counted Ia Drang a success, for it suggested the People's Army could stand against the best the Americans could throw at it.

With its mobility, The Cav was in great demand. MACV soon pulled the division out of the highlands and committed it to battle in the central coastal provinces. The ARVN was left to mop up, using its Airborne Task Force, in an operation that caught many VPA soldiers up against the Chu Pong. Colonel Ngo Quang Truong, commanding the ARVN paratroops, showed his military dexterity in this action. Although the ARVN soldiers did well, many Americans found them uninspiring. Before The Cav left, Robert Mason's helicopter unit got the job of moving some ARVN soldiers. Their assignment officer told the pilots to make sure the door gunners kept their weapons trained on the South Vietnamese as they alighted from the choppers. "I was amazed," Mason recalled. "In the months to come I would hear as much about being wary of the ARVNs as I did about the Cong. If neither was to be trusted, who were our allies?"[4]

The War and the World

America's allies were the "Free World Forces" recruited so assiduously by President Johnson. Johnson had begun his "More Flags" program in April 1964, originally to show that many nations were willing to enlist in the Vietnam adventure. Nonmilitary assistance formed the bulk of aid then. But as Washington began pondering combat troops and sought numbers beyond what the United States could deploy, the focus shifted. That December LBJ widened the search for foreign soldiers. He made strenuous efforts in 1965. Westmoreland's forty-four-battalion deployment program already included ten third-country maneuver battalions. This effort became the subject of bilateral diplomacy between Washington and other capitals. At the time, Johnson proved most successful with Australia and the Republic of Korea. A number of countries, including France, lent medical, agricultural, or economic aid. There were also Filipino medical and civic action teams; German, Italian, and Nationalist Chinese medical teams; a small Thai air force observer contingent; and the tiny British advisory mission led by Sir Robert Thompson.

Efforts to build the foreign involvement largely fell flat. With the British, for example, LBJ set security adviser McGeorge Bundy to work on his opposite number, British cabinet secretary Sir Burke Trend, in an attempt to convince London to send at least the Commonwealth infantry brigade it had in Malaysia. The British remained obdurate, even when the United States hinted that support for the British pound sterling, a currency threatened by foreign account deficits, might be contingent on British aid in Vietnam. With some logic but more calculation, London maintained that as a cochair (and presumably guarantor) of the Geneva conference, it could not be a belligerent. Great Britain maintained an embassy in Hanoi, and throughout the war its merchant vessels remained the leading noncommunist traders with North Vietnam.[5]

The other European powers were quite reluctant. Having been forced out of Indochina by the Americans, snubbed when de Gaulle suggested neutralization, and desirous of protecting friendly relations with the People's Republic of China, France was not a candidate for intervention. It too maintained diplomatic ties with Hanoi. Italy saw its role less as participating in the war than as encouraging its settlement. Washington nudged Germany and Japan in the direction of involvement, but both countries, defeated powers in World War II, faced either political or legal obstacles to military involvement. Germany did no more than send medical teams.[6]

Japan's first antiwar protests coincided with the U.S. reprisal bombings after Pleiku. It paid certain war reparations to South Vietnam and made some loans, in all about $56 million, in a program completed in 1965. Tokyo had a thriving foreign trade with the DRV, primarily for Hon Gay coal; however, it curbed those imports under LBJ's pressure. With the Japanese Constitution containing a provision banning foreign military ventures, there could be no question of its contributing to the Free World Forces. Washington faced problems with Tokyo concerning Japanese sovereignty over islands and bases occupied since World War II, so under the circumstances, concerned itself primarily with securing Tokyo's acquiescence in the use of Japanese bases to support its own Vietnam effort.[7]

Possibly Washington's only ideological allies in the war were Australia and New Zealand. Both had similar perspectives on communism that were, on most points, close to that of the United States. A collective defense treaty called ANZUS, one with more teeth than SEATO, linked them to Washington. Australia believed in forward defense—combating the communists in Malaya and Southeast Asia was preferable to fighting them in Queensland. Since July 1962 Australia had had a strong military advisory group in Saigon under Brigadier General "Ted" Serong, numbering almost a hundred in late 1964, when Johnson asked Australia to triple it. Rather than dilute professional forces by drawing off specialists as advisers, Canberra preferred to send a combat unit and offered an infantry battalion, accepted by the Saigon government in April 1965. The 1st Battalion, Royal Australian Regiment, arrived a month later to be posted near Vung Tau. New Zealand added an artillery battery that July. In 1966 the Australians upped their contingent to a full brigade, three battalions with supporting armor and artillery units.

As in the United States, Australia's Vietnam war began in controversy and led to growing public outcry. People suspected political manipulation in the initial agreement to send combat forces. By the time of the Gulf of Tonkin incident, protest rallies had already begun, and telegrams of opposition were sent to President Johnson. A full-page antiwar advertisement first appeared in an Australian newspaper in mid-August 1964, run by the local section of the Women's International League for Peace and Freedom. Parliamentary debate and press reactions were divided but strong, and labor unions opposed the troop commitment, though mildly. A week before the Australian troops went to South Vietnam, a public vigil in opposition took place outside Parliament House in Canberra. The government of Sir Robert Menzies would be LBJ's good ally, but at a growing political cost.[8]

By far the largest foreign contingent would be that of the Republic of Korea (ROK). Under LBJ's original "More Flags," the ROK sent a small group of man-to-man combat instructors. After the program's expansion, bilateral talks between Washington and Seoul led to the dispatch of a major formation, a 2,000-man combat engineer unit—the so-called Dove unit—with infantry attached for security purposes. The Korean National Assembly agreed to this deployment on January 12, 1965. President Park Chung Hee, demonstrating his willingness to meet almost any level of commitment the United States suggested, later offered two full infantry divisions but attached stringent conditions involving U.S. aid to the ROK. This set the tone for the relationship.

American planners steadily expanded their expectations for Korean forces. With President Johnson sending U.S. troops to Vietnam for base defense, in April 1965 the plans called for three ROK battalions in a single regimental combat team. When Washington stepped up to the forty-four-battalion program, nine of ten third-country battalions—a full infantry division—were to be Korean (the last was Australian). LBJ agreed to Park's conditions in May 1965 as details were worked out: the United States would increase economic aid to South Korea, finance the reequipment of ROK forces to replace the ones sent to Vietnam, continue military assistance at previous levels, modernize the full Korean military establishment, defray the pay of the ROK troops in Vietnam, and pay for their transportation costs.

Saigon formally requested ROK troops the same day Nguyen Cao Ky assumed the reins of power. By then, preparations to send the ROK Capital Division—in Vietnam, often called the "Tiger" Division—were well advanced. Its headquarters arrived at the end of September, and a 1st Infantry Regiment plus an ROK Marine brigade in mid-October. They went to Qui Nhon province on the coast below the Central Highlands, even as The Cav fought at Ia Drang. Before the last ROK troops had taken the field, talks were already under way for another division (the 9th), and most of it arrived in September 1966. The ROK forces in South Vietnam totaled about 21,000 at the end of 1965 and 45,000 a year later. They peaked at 50,000 at the end of 1968.

Most versatile of the Free World Forces were the Thais, although their participation began only later. During this early period the Kingdom of Thailand provided special forces to work with the CIA's secret army in Laos, trained some ARVN soldiers in Thailand, and furnished a contingent of fewer than twenty pilots who flew C-47 aircraft for Saigon. Once Dean Rusk provided U.S. security guarantees in early 1963, the kingdom's military rulers agreed to host a network of U.S. bases, constructed between 1964 and 1967. Thus, Thailand's main importance early on was to U.S. air operations over North Vietnam and Laos. But the Thais sent an advisory mission to South Vietnam in 1966, followed the next year by an agreement on troops. A volunteer regiment, the "Queen's Cobras," arrived that September and fought for nearly a year northeast of Bien Hoa. About that time, President Johnson sent Clark Clifford and General Maxwell Taylor to encourage the troop-contributing countries to broaden their involvement, and Thailand agreed to send a full division. These troops, the "Black Panther" Division, began arriving in early 1969. The Thai contingent peaked in 1969–1970 at about 11,600 troops. By that time, Thai pilots were secretly flying combat missions over northern Laos, and Thai artillery—also secretly—supported the CIA in Laos. Infantry followed. By 1972 as many as 20,000 Thai troops were participating in the Laotian war, even as the last Thais left Vietnam. All this remained separate from the counterinsurgency war conducted simultaneously in northeastern Thailand.

Finally there were the Filipinos. The Philippines first became involved in the Vietnamese scene through Ed Lansdale, who had served there before going to South Vietnam. He arranged Filipino guards for Ngo Dinh Diem and later some trainers; he was also involved in Operation Brotherhood, essentially a foreign civic action and psychological warfare program. When the "More Flags" initiative began, the Philippines offered more. In late 1964 Washington and Manila began talks on Filipino combat engineer units. Politics delayed action until after the November 1965 election, which brought Ferdinand Marcos to power. Renegotiation slowed deployment of the Philippines Civic Action Group of three engineer battalions, which reached Vietnam in September 1966. The Filipino force of slightly over 2,000 served through 1968, when it was reduced to less than 1,600, and in 1969 to just a token force.

In sum, Lyndon Johnson worked hard to produce an international coalition but fell short of a true Free World Force. The weaknesses in America's appeals for help trace directly to the shaky legal and moral justifications for war in Vietnam, much as would happen to George W. Bush and his "coalition of the willing" to invade Iraq. The rickety collection of allies Johnson mobilized amounted to a small number of countries, most of which were ready to use America's desperation as a lever to extract U.S. dollars. In an odd way, the paucity of results from Johnson's diplomacy to attract allies mirrored the failure of his efforts to negotiate an end to the war.

■ ■ ■ "We are ready now, as we have always been, to move from the battlefield to the conference table," President Johnson told reporters at the White House on July 26, 1965. He went on: "I have stated publicly many times, again and again, America's willingness to begin unconditional discussions with any government at any place at any time." LBJ asserted that fifteen separate attempts had been made to open talks in concert with forty different nations.[9] These declarations came simultaneously with LBJ's decision to authorize the largest Vietnam escalation to date.

As with LBJ's basic attitude toward the war, these words of peace can be seen in different ways. An unlikely image, especially for 1965, is that of Johnson as a seeker of peace. That picture does, however, fit the evidence that LBJ had doubts about a Vietnam commitment, so it bears mention. But the pattern of Johnson's actions raises questions: the brief bombing pause to make Rolling Thunder seem justified; LBJ's statement itself, in such close conjunction with his troop decision; the Johns Hopkins speech, with its admixture of talk rhetoric and fight imagery; even the president's putting out a number on alleged peace feelers, much as he tried to put a count on America's allies. And that is just the visible record. The actual, secret record of peace feelers adds to the pile of doubt.

First came Washington's use of Canadian diplomat Blair J. Seaborn as emissary for messages to Hanoi in 1964–1965. Seaborn had worked with Henry Cabot Lodge when the latter represented the United States at the United Nations, and Lodge recommended him now. During Seaborn's June 1964 visit to Hanoi, according to the diplomatic volumes of the Pentagon Papers, he warned Prime Minister Pham Van Dong that if the conflict should escalate, "the greatest devastation would of course result for the DRV itself." Dong countered that North Vietnam would win such a contest. Seaborn passed further messages after Pleiku and at the time of Johnson's May 1965 bombing pause. But there was no real negotiating position other than to offer talks and warn Hanoi of dire consequences. Washington's intent was coercive.[10]

Seaborn's final visit came shortly after Hanoi publicized its "Four Points" for an agreement, long the heart of its stance: (1) the United States must withdraw from Indochina, (2) the South Vietnamese people should determine their own affairs, (3) the status of South Vietnam would be characterized by "peace and neutrality," and (4) Vietnam would be reunified. North Vietnamese diplomat Nguyen Duy Trinh told Seaborn that U.S. offers of unconditional negotiations were "deceitful," in view of the American troops in the South and the bombing of the DRV. Seaborn concluded that Hanoi had little interest in talks. Historian George C. Herring observes, "The most important result of the Seaborn missions was probably to afford an additional reason, if one were needed, for subsequent American escalation."[11]

Then there were the peace efforts of UN Secretary-General U Thant. In

February 1965 Thant told the U.S. ambassador he had been urging Hanoi to negotiate and that, according to the Soviets, the DRV would be willing to meet U.S. representatives in Rangoon, Burma (now Yangon, Myanmar). Thant offered as an alternative that the two Vietnams might sit down together. McGeorge Bundy advised Johnson against the idea. Its main result would be an irate phone call to Thant from Dean Rusk denouncing bilateral talks and demanding evidence of Hanoi's sincerity. Thant went public in March, calling for a cease-fire and a multilateral conference, whereupon the United States insisted on positive moves by the DRV. Blair Seaborn's boss, Canadian prime minister Lester Pearson, also gave a speech advocating talks; he suggested that a bombing "pause" might encourage such talks—the apparent stimulus for LBJ's May bombing lull. But by then Thant was reduced to saying, "I strongly hope that there will be a follow-up on the stated willingness of the parties directly involved."[12]

With President Johnson now considering troop deployment and the first U.S. battalions having already landed, public opinion remained divided. Opinion polls in March and early April showed that about a third of Americans favored talks. Negotiations were also a demand of and a rallying point for the SDS march on Washington. LBJ made points with his Johns Hopkins speech, but the teach-ins and combat action in Vietnam kept the issue on the front pages, and Johnson knew, as Americans did not, that escalation proposals were on his desk. More visibility for the diplomatic track seemed necessary to lay the groundwork for troops. LBJ approved the May bombing pause plus Project "Mayflower," the next peace feeler, but certainly *not* at the instigation of his military or intelligence authorities, all of whom assessed the damage inflicted on the DRV as insufficient to drive Hanoi to the bargaining table. The evidence suggests that Johnson was not making an actual effort to jump-start talks.

Given the code name Mayflower on May 12, the feeler sought to use the Soviets to tell Hanoi that the U.S. bombing halt evidenced a desire for peace and to request a response. On the first day of the pause, Johnson made a speech where, without openly referring to the message, he asked Hanoi to consider a political solution. During Seaborn's last Hanoi visit, the Czech ambassador took him aside to say that the DRV had never gotten Washington's message—its man in Moscow had returned the cable to the Russians, ostensibly unopened.

The most concrete feeler of this period actually came to the United States from France. In May, Mai Van Bo, the DRV delegation chief in Paris, told the French that Hanoi's Four Points could be considered subjects for negotiation rather than preconditions. The Quai d'Orsai passed this along speedily, but Washington did nothing. In mid-June Bo went back to the French foreign ministry to ask what had happened. The French could tell him nothing. Bo waited another month, then sent a similar message to Washington through a private citizen. Washington finally responded but kept the contact at a very low level by recruiting retired diplomat Edmund Gullion as its emissary. Gullion and Bo met and got as far as discussing the wording of a communiqué to announce reconvening the Geneva conference, but then Bo broke contact, telling Gullion the air attacks on North Vietnam had to stop for negotiations to begin. Washington, of course, had no intention of permitting another Geneva. Analysts reviewing this episode later for the administration concluded, "The U.S. was sending [Gullion] with the intention of seeking peace from a position of U.S. strength." Gullion took his guidance seriously.[13]

Even the CIA would be drawn into alleged peace efforts in 1966 in a top-secret feeler christened "Elm Tree." The adjective *alleged* is appropriate because some wanted to exploit it simply to induce defections of National Liberation Front adherents, and it would finally be subsumed in a Saigon government "reconciliation" program aimed at exactly that goal. Former strongman Nguyen Khanh played a key role in Elm Tree, approaching Americans to say he had opened channels to the NLF, whose leaders, like those of Saigon, were scions of elite Vietnamese families. When, after soundings by diplomat U. Alexis Johnson, the CIA took over the channel, it evaporated. Elm Tree led nowhere.

Several more feelers occurred between LBJ's troop deployment and late 1966. There would also be another, more extensive U.S. bombing halt, thirty-seven days beginning at Christmas 1965. This represented a strategic choice, not just a publicity ploy. It is an important point because it sheds more light on Lyndon Johnson and has bearing on the charge that the Joint Chiefs of Staff were mere clerks, derelict in their duty. Starting in late October the Chiefs pushed for expanded bombing that would have pleased even Admiral U. S. G. Sharp (see later). Pundits nicknamed this the "sharp blow," and it would have involved a series of strikes—Hanoi, Haiphong, airfields, surface-to-air missile (SAM) sites, roads, and railroads—in a period of just a few days, with at least some targets hit by B-52 bombers. This was the Christmas Bombing seven years before its time, not mere tactical advice. According to General Charles Cooper, then a Marine major and aide to the chief of naval operations, the Chiefs marched into the Oval Office, and LBJ lined them up near the windows. He knew what was up—memoranda on the JCS proposal had circulated, and McNamara had told him the Chiefs were hot under the collar. Johnson did not let them sit down. "We fully realize," General Wheeler told the president, "that what we're going to present today requires a very difficult decision on your part." Johnson listened, then chewed them out royally. The president insulted each man individually, Cooper recalled, and "used the f-word more freely than a marine in boot camp." Then Johnson came to his core concern: "I've got the weight of the Free World on my shoulders and you want me to start World War III."[14]

Thus Johnson had been ready to *fight* to get his way, and he staged this encounter to back his military advisers down. With the pause he inaugurated a sort of peace offensive, weeks of frenetic activity in which U.S. diplomats went everywhere they could think of—from tiny African countries to the Holy See—trying to generate momentum, going through the Hungarians, Russians, Italians, the UN, and other European, African, and Asian countries, three dozen in all. A presidential letter went to every foreign delegation at the United Nations. All this actually led to one contact—"Pinta," the Rangoon meeting with the North Vietnamese—but nothing came of it. Inspired, perhaps, Canadian leader Pearson used retired Canadian envoy Chester A. Ronning in another feeler in the spring of 1966. Ronning thought he had a breakthrough when Pham Van Dong hinted that if the United States stopped bombing, the DRV would negotiate. Washington took a dim view, however, fearing a halt would be seen as acceptance of Hanoi's Four Points, instead demanding that U.S. de-escalation be reciprocated.

Through all this, it was not until January 1966 that the United States even *had* a bargaining position, and then it was crafted mostly for public consumption. There is a disconnect between the conditions posed and LBJ's determination to present them. Secretary Rusk, emulating Woodrow Wilson's Fourteen Points, unveiled 14 Points on Vietnam on January 3, 1966. Rusk may have thought his formula incorporated Hanoi's Four Points, forming a basis for talks, but the U.S. formula indicated little flexibility and minimized the DRV position (its points "could be discussed along with other points that others might wish to propose"). The text explicitly stated, "We are not aware of any initiative which has been taken by Hanoi during the past five years to seek peace." This language failed to acknowledge the Mai Van Bo feeler.[15]

One thing President Johnson did was appoint W. Averell Harriman his special representative for peace talks. This at least made someone responsible for the pathways that might lead to Hanoi. As factotum to backstop him, NSC staffer Chester L. Cooper, who had been ready to leave the White House, was induced to work for Harriman instead. Managing the peace offensive became Harriman's first act, but much of it represented cosmetics. Along with the lack of a U.S. negotiating position, there was no plan for actually conducting talks.[16] Hanoi viewed the bombing halt and peace offensive as a ploy. Its response came in a letter from Ho Chi Minh on January 24, 1966, demanding that the United States accept the DRV's Four Points and unconditionally stop bombing to begin the peace process. Cooper's evaluation of the diplomatic sally is significant: "Where finely tooled instruments were required, we used a sledgehammer. Where confidential and careful advance work was necessary, we proceeded with the subtlety of a Fourth of July parade."[17]

The myriad details lie beyond the scope of this narrative. But note: Johnson concerned himself more with the appearance than the reality of starting talks. In addition, in keeping with an aggressive war strategy, the United States showed no interest in a solution not on its own terms. Most crucial, the key obstacles—the notions of preconditions and the bombing—were on the table at the very beginning of the ground war. And these obstacles were readily visible, known to LBJ and his colleagues. Bombing held particular importance with respect to negotiations. Critics of Johnson's bombing policy treat it in isolation, as if this were a simple strategic bombing campaign. The reality is that bombing and diplomacy were intimately linked, as Rolling Thunder would demonstrate repeatedly. Meanwhile, the public impression remained that of diplomacy entailing much smoke but little fire. That seemed a thin reed, and LBJ's foreign alliances a rickety structure, while the war heated up every day. American politics, already roiled by the bitter struggle over civil rights, sustained a renewed shock from land war in Asia. Social and political forces combined with open war to build steadily toward a climax.

A Gathering Storm

For some in a budding antiwar movement, the storm had already come. Washington increasingly became the focus for those concerned about Vietnam. That soured Lyndon Johnson considerably. The gloom contributed to Chet Cooper's melancholy and his desire to leave the NSC staff. Cooper records, "the atmosphere within the White House was dark and forbidding." He had to be careful about what he said, increasingly resorting to handwritten notes passed to Mac Bundy at meetings rather than considered opinions in papers or memos, which might fall into unfriendly hands. "In the spring of 1965," he notes, "the White House felt like a besieged fortress. Pennsylvania Avenue was crowded and noisy with picketers day and night. Lafayette Park, across the avenue from the White House, had become a virtual campground for taunting protesters." Luci Johnson, the president's daughter, never forgot the "lullaby" that kept her awake night after night: "LBJ. LBJ, how many boys did you kill today?"[18]

Demonstrations outside the White House, the Pentagon, or the U.S. Mission to the United Nations in New York became legion in 1965. Consisting of a few, a dozen, or a hundred protesters, these small events were nickel-and-dime stuff, maybe even penny stuff to professional politicians, but they were the warp and woof of the Movement. The key would be presence, not mass, and it betokened a new style of "grassroots" politics the professionals disdained before they woke up to embrace it. Sponsors in these early days included the War Resisters League, SDS, Women Strike for Peace, Women's International League for Peace and Freedom, Committee for Nonviolent Action, Catholic Worker, and more. The SDS march on Washington became the first mass, multiorganization demonstration, and its unexpected draw hinted at the power of the grass roots. Further evidence was seen when 30,000 attended "Vietnam Day" at Berkeley in May and 18,000 turned up for a teach-in-cum-rally at New York's Madison Square Garden a month later.

Another kind of protest, civil rights protest, also complicated presidential calculations. In August frustrated African Americans rioted in the Watts neighborhood of Los Angeles, leading to a call-up of the National Guard. The Watts riots signaled that the social reform program called the "Great Society," which competed with Vietnam for LBJ's attention, had a long way to go.

For the time being, Johnson countered with his bridge to the American Friends of Vietnam; with his so-called truth squads, which mobilized to speak from every available podium; and with plain prevarication. Protesters' arguments were considered a mere information problem, and White House officials tried to figure out how to cope. The president sent McGeorge Bundy, whom LBJ had forbidden to participate in the first teach-ins, out to battle Hans Morgenthau at a nationally televised teach-in that June. Unlike the earlier events, here Bundy controlled the format and exploited it to belittle the dissenters, quoting Morgenthau's expressed fear in 1961 that communist domination of Laos was a virtual foregone conclusion.[19] Dean Rusk charged antiwar thinkers with "gullibility" and "disregard of plain facts" in April, and in a May speech he supplied a slanted definition of "wars of national liberation"—calling them "any war which furthers the Communist world revolution." In a July 11 interview with ABC Television reporters, the secretary of state asserted that there would be no sanctuary from U.S. attacks in North Vietnam or anywhere else. The CIA commissioned analyst George Carver to write a paper on the nature of the National Liberation Front, which the agency placed in the journal *Foreign Affairs* and then cited as the authoritative source on the subject. Robert McNamara, who met with five antiwar leaders on June 16, dismissed their objections with the comment, "We know things that you don't." He would later write that one cause of U.S. defeat was "profound ignorance of the history, culture, and politics of the people in the area."[20]

Sensing that rhetoric would not suffice, President Johnson also feared charges from the Right, from conservatives and Goldwater Republicans determined to achieve victory. LBJ made his troop decision in the quietest way possible, announcing it in a late-night message to the nation and refusing to seek money from Congress, at least immediately. Early in August White House staffers held a strategy powwow to find ways to sell the war. Aide Douglass Cater advised the president to educate the people and air the issues driving him. Johnson rejected that advice too.[21] The fracas that erupted weeks later over the Eisenhower letter no doubt reinforced LBJ's sense that his course was correct. He must have thought the press already out to get him.

Instead of opening up, Johnson created an interagency committee to manage the flow of information to Americans. That fall the administration set up an active pro-war lobby. This entity, the Committee for an Effective and Durable Peace in Asia, announced on September 9, aimed to build support for LBJ's policy. Its head was Arthur Dean, actually one of the "Wise Men" group of foreign policy advisers, who helped President Johnson when asked and who had recently been consulted on the troop decision. The White House's purposeful action began the spiral of hostility that grew between America's president and its people.

LBJ's measures did not quell opposition to Vietnam. Various accounts of the antiwar movement detail how umbrella coalitions emerged during this period, the most important of them probably the National Coordinating Committee to End the War in Vietnam and the Fifth Avenue Vietnam Peace Parade. In the streets, demonstrations continued, most nickel-and-dime protests, but quite a few larger ones too. The White House became a frequent target, as Chet Cooper's recollections show. On August 8 and 9 more than 350 protesters were arrested outside the White House, charged with blocking access. Days afterward protesters tried to block troop trains en route to the Army port terminal in Oakland. In mid-October came the "First International Days of Protest," a nationwide demonstration in which the largest manifestation of opposition would be the 25,000 people who marched in New York.

Then came November 2. Late that afternoon, in front of the Pentagon's River Entrance and just a hundred yards from the windows of Robert McNamara's office, a Baltimore Quaker named Norman R. Morrison doused himself with kerosene and lit a match, protesting the war in the style of the Buddhist monks in Saigon. Indeed, a monk had burned to death in Saigon just the day before. Morrison immolated himself, at the last moment tossing his fifteen-month-old child, Emily, to other protesters.

McNamara shuddered at this action, considering it a personal tragedy. He reacted to the horror "by bottling up my emotions and avoiding talking about them with anyone—even my family."[22] He would face opposition to LBJ's Vietnam policy from his wife, Margery, and his children. The same was true for many others, from senior officials to junior military officers. Dean Rusk, McGeorge Bundy, the CIA's William Colby, and others shared McNamara's problem, one replicated at family dinner tables throughout the country. The personal costs of LBJ's course did not turn officials away from his policy—yet. This factor is muted in accounts of Vietnam, but its importance grew as the war remained intractable and opposition blossomed. Lyndon Johnson knew of these pressures, and about the grain-of-sand-in-the-seashell irritant of the protests. Although it still seemed minor, the Movement could routinely turn out 4,000 people to picket New York's Waldorf-Astoria Hotel when LBJ attended a dinner there in February 1966. The pot had begun to steam, though not yet to boil.

■ ■ ■ Washington's war decisions were made in a fishbowl, under increasing scrutiny by a concerned public. That might not have been a problem if General Westmoreland's strategy had offered a true path forward. Instead, almost as soon as MACV began deploying troops, the general's staff realized the force was heavily weighted in favor of frontline "grunts," as the GIs were called, lacking the support forces necessary to make them fully effective. Even worse, accelerating deployment revealed that South Vietnam lacked the ports, roads, and airfields necessary to operate the U.S. combat force. As Westmoreland later wrote, "even had South Vietnam been a modern, fully developed country with adequate logistical facilities readily adaptable to military use, troop build-up would have been slow."[23] In fact, a brigade of the U.S. 25th Infantry Division would be airlifted directly to Pleiku to avoid squeezing it through the congested ports. Until the moment American troop strength peaked, several years later, tension between the level of forces and the network to sustain them remained a constant. Westy notes, "men locked in combat cannot long survive without adequate logistic support."[24]

Within weeks of the Ia Drang battles, MACV asked for another 100,000 troops. Forces that General Westmoreland had listed in cables as possible follow-ons were now pegged as necessary. More were requested to "fill out" those already approved. In September the MACV commander wanted twenty-eight fresh battalions; two months later he almost doubled the bid—to fifty-three battalions with commensurate expansion in Free World Forces and a total American deployment of 440,000 men by the end of 1966. Secretary McNamara endorsed the request, which became known as "Program 2."

This would be President Johnson's next significant Vietnam decision. Opposition among his advisers—except on one matter—was minor and involved those who wanted more of one thing or another. For example, General Maxwell Taylor and Air Force chief of staff General John McConnell wanted more bombing of North Vietnam before widening the troop commitment. Pacific theater commander Admiral U. S. G. Sharp wanted more reinforcements to Thailand in connection with the Vietnam buildup. No one suggested that Program 2 be canceled. At a summit meeting with South Vietnamese leaders at Honolulu in February 1966, the president approved the program.

The real problem was not deployment plans but U.S. military resources. Since the beginning of schemes for major combat, the generals had brought up the need to mobilize reserve and National Guard troops for units sent to Vietnam and to fill out the force structure. LBJ saw mobilization as a political problem. The choice begged the question of his legal authority in the absence of a declaration of war and also would have called into question why, if he were mobilizing, LBJ had not asked for greatly increased budgets. Johnson—and McNamara—resisted every proposal for reserve mobilization. That left just one potential solution, the draft.

American men between the ages of eighteen and twenty-six (obligatory service did not apply to women in the 1960s) were subject to military service, familiarly called the "draft." A wartime draft had been instituted during World War II, but none had ever existed in peacetime. That changed in March 1948, and the draft had been reauthorized several times since, requiring men to register for the draft and then be subject to call-up. Administered by the Selective Service System headed by General Louis Hershey, the mechanism worked at the behest of Pentagon planners, who calculated the number of draftees required to fill the ranks. Selective Service then assigned goals to local draft boards, which summoned the requisite number of individuals. The draft is discussed in more detail later, but the force that deployed to Vietnam in 1965 consisted primarily of longtime military professionals with a leavening of draftees. The buildup, combined with Johnson's refusal to mobilize, transformed the U.S. force into one that was increasingly reliant on draftees or volunteers whose decisions to enlist had been driven—in 60 percent of cases, by Pentagon estimates—by the draft. Program 2 was the watershed. In 1966 draft calls jumped from 10,000 men a month to 30,000. Only 16 percent of American battle deaths in 1965 were draftees, but that proportion jumped to 21 percent in 1966 and swelled to more than 33 percent the next year.[25]

In the absence of mobilization, Program 2 had to be stretched out. It took time to turn draftees into soldiers and especially to regroup new men with experienced soldiers in the units sent to Vietnam. In addition, the requirement for support units quickly enmeshed the U.S. Army and Marine Corps in a drive to create engineer, construction, logistics, transportation, helicopter, communications, graves registration, and other specialist formations of all kinds. Detachments pulled from active forces cobbled together provisional units that were rushed out to fill the gap until new ones could be formed. Some of Westmoreland's Program 2 troops did not reach Vietnam until early 1967, and manpower at the end of 1966 would total 385,000. Still, the entire effort portended a steadily expanding war.

■ ■ ■ What Washington could do, Hanoi could do too. Maybe better. With the Vietnam People's Army a less complex, less sophisticated machine, the DRV had fewer obstacles. Hanoi also had no illusion that it was fighting a limited war. It had made its decision to expand efforts—as well as improve the Ho Chi Minh Trail—a year sooner than LBJ, so by late 1965 the work had begun to bear fruit. Both the People's Army and the People's Liberation Armed Forces were upgraded and strengthened to the extent the Ia Drang battle, fierce as it was, represented just one of a series of simultaneous combats. There were other major assaults against the U.S. 1st Infantry Division north of Saigon and in Binh Dinh province on the coastal plain beneath the Central Highlands. Sustaining the field forces were the troops and supplies coming down the Ho Chi Minh Trail, plus a steady effort to land supplies by sea along the coast.

The People's Army expansion would be impressive. At 195,000 men in early 1965, the VPA passed 350,000 that May and reached 400,000 before the end of the year. The army added a second tank regiment and doubled its artillery branch, equipping it with new 130mm guns and rocket launchers. Self-defense and coastal units formed throughout the DRV, with an increase of 600,000 soldiers through 1965 to reach 2 million. The VPA began recalling former enlisted personnel in 1964 and officers the following year.

Under the pressure of Rolling Thunder, and with the help of Soviet and Chinese aid, air defenses multiplied as well. Russian SA-2 SAMs were used to form the 236th Air Defense Missile Regiment in May 1965, with the 238th added a month later; SAM defense of the Hanoi area existed by the fall. Antiaircraft artillery almost tripled, from fourteen battalions to forty-one, with a dozen regiments and many independent units. The People's Air Force formed three regiments of jet interceptors with Soviet-made MIG-17 and MIG-21 aircraft. Radar nets and aerial engagement management units expanded commensurately. This period also saw the introduction of Chinese troops into North Vietnam to assist in antiaircraft and coastal defense and help maintain and improve the DRV's transportation network.

The Ho Chi Minh Trail benefited from systematic improvement efforts. By now it was no longer a collection of tracks and camps but one of roads and bases, called *binh trams*, that serviced passing units. Truck convoys replaced bicycles as the standard conveyances—by 1965 Group 559 operated six truck battalions, compared with just two of bicycles. The *binh trams* were being equipped with vehicle maintenance facilities, antiaircraft defenses, ground security elements, and many modern appurtenances. Separate antiaircraft units were placed at key points, such as the mountain passes where roads crossed from the DRV into the Laotian domain of The Trail. At Xuan Mai, near Hanoi, the People's Army created a training center to prepare units and individuals for the trek. The appointment of Hanoi's transportation minister as commander of Group 559, installed above the officer who had originally created The Trail, denoted the changes.

The regiments of VPA regulars The Cav had encountered at Ia Drang represented only the leading edge. During 1965 Hanoi sent seven full regiments and twenty battalions down The Trail, along with cadres, for a total of 50,000 men. By Vietnamese accounts, that represented an annual deployment of as many troops as had gone South before that time. The Twelfth Plenum of the Central Committee, meeting in Hanoi in late December, judged that despite the American buildup, there had been no net change in the balance of forces.

Hanoi strove to keep it that way. Regiment 18B crossed the DRV border to begin its march in February 1966, the first of fifteen regiments to make the trek that year. Even those 30,000 troops represented just half the total for 1966. That infiltration occurred despite U.S. efforts to stop it. American planes made 4,000 attack sorties (a sortie is a flight by one aircraft) against The Trail in the last quarter of 1965, 8,000 more in January 1966, and another 5,000 sorties in February. The scale of air effort was greater than Rolling Thunder itself during this time. Hanoi had clearly determined to match any escalation by Washington.

■ ■ ■ One reason the Ho Chi Minh Trail was bombed more heavily than the North would be that President Johnson decided to stop Rolling Thunder, a thirty-seven-day pause that became the longest of the war. Here LBJ responded to diverse stimuli. Johnson saw divergent trends in American opinion. On the one hand, a December 1965 poll showed that 65 percent of respondents supported holding the line, and another 28 percent favored carrying the war to North Vietnam even if it meant conflict with China—the conservative challenge. On the other hand, the antiwar movement continued to grow, punctuated by a Thanksgiving weekend march in Washington sponsored by SANE. Its leaders met with NSC staffer Chet Cooper and urged a halt of the bombing long enough to test negotiating possibilities. Since the protest leaders had already—at Cooper's suggestion—actually sent peace appeals to Hanoi, he could hardly refuse to pass their views to the president.

There were other pressures on LBJ as well. Robert McNamara backed General Westmoreland's Program 2 request, verified during his November 1965 visit to Saigon, but the secretary of defense coupled that with his own bid for a bombing halt. At State, Rusk and Ball agreed enthusiastically to the pause. At the NSC, Bundy tepidly backed it. In Congress, Mike Mansfield advocated a peace conference, to which a bombing halt could logically be coupled. Even the Soviets weighed in when their ambassador to Washington, Anatoly Dobrynin, told the White House that should there be a bombing pause, Moscow would do its best to obtain a favorable reaction from Hanoi. Opposition came from the Joint Chiefs, Ambassador Lodge, Admiral Sharp, General Westmoreland, and LBJ's private advisers Clark Clifford and Abe Fortas. At a December 17 White House meeting, McNamara told the president that he could handle the Chiefs if LBJ made a firm decision.

Johnson felt buffeted. By his own account, LBJ reacted with deep skepticism when he first heard the halt proposal. He remembered the summertime pause as a failure and registered the complaints of opponents. At the LBJ Ranch on December 7, Johnson continued to express doubt, but Rusk, McNamara, and Bundy all reassured him. At the climactic meetings on December 17 and 18 LBJ finally agreed, despite Fortas and Clifford, whose "opinions carried weight with me." But LBJ's reluctance is evident in his comment that this amounted to another of "those 51–49 decisions that regularly reach the President's desk and keep him awake late at night," and in his insistence that no public announcement be made except of a brief Christmas truce, which the United States could then quietly extend.[26] Johnson's reluctance is especially apparent from his incremental extensions: first the Christmas truce, then a longer pause, and finally, after a private meeting with McNamara in Texas, the halt, despite the fact that the full program had been laid down in extensive position papers over a period of weeks.[27]

Washington combined its halt with the barren peace offensive already discussed. When CIA intelligence reports showed the North Vietnamese were taking advantage of the halt for troop and supply movements, Johnson ordered resumption of bombing. Rolling Thunder picked up, with 132 attack sorties flown against the DRV on January 31, 1966. Four days later Johnson decided on the Honolulu conference, where he made the final decision on Program 2 and met Saigon leaders Ky and Thieu. That meeting took place on February 6 at the Royal Hawaiian Hotel. Aside from the frenetic activity necessary to take over two prime Hawaiian hotels (the second for guests and the press) at the height of the winter season on two days' notice, the timing shows Johnson's desire to signal U.S. determination.

So what had been LBJ's original intent in halting the aerial assault? Several views can be noted. With the perspective of decades Chester Cooper wrote, "The resumption of bombing and the transparent public relations nature of the so-called search for peace during the halt were troubling."[28] LBJ himself recalled that he had wanted "to explore every possible avenue of settlement before we took additional military measures."[29] The Army's official MACV historian observed, "Fully expecting the diplomatic effort to fail, the president intended the pause primarily to prepare American opinion for the larger war toward which his course was set."[30] It is a reasonable conclusion that the diplomatic effort was the ploy and the deployment plan the president's real business.

Of course, the Saigon leaders attending the instant summit were primarily concerned about the big war. Nguyen Van Thieu left no record. Nguyen Cao Ky recalled making a presentation in which he concentrated on four points he thought the Americans would appreciate: beating the Liberation Front, instituting social reform, building Saigon's economy, and moving toward democracy. Ky's presentation might have been too frank for the president's taste. That night LBJ pulled Ky away from a reception to give him a private scolding. "Everything that we do in public," Johnson told Ky, "whatever we say in public, is just for the public. Let me propose that from now on, every time we want to do something, or we have to discuss something between America and Vietnam, we'll do it at the individual level. Just you and me. Together we'll make the important decisions, things that we don't want the public to know."[31]

Later LBJ had another quiet session with Ky and Thieu together, commenting favorably on Ky's ideas. From this time forward, Johnson became increasingly focused on what he termed Vietnam's "other war," the social and political competition between Saigon and the southern resistance that lay at the heart of what the counterinsurgency theorists called "pacification." Nguyen Cao Ky thus played a role in the president's conversion to a pacification devotee.

Be that as it may, Johnson ended by asking the Saigon leaders to speed up improvements in the South Vietnamese army, the ARVN, which Americans considered ineffective. That remained for the future, however. Almost immediately, Ky and Thieu faced a new political crisis, one that flowed from the alliance of a key ARVN commander with Buddhist factions worried that the Honolulu conference meant a new intensification of the war.

General Nguyen Chanh Thi, commander of the ARVN's I Corps, a zone that included South Vietnam's five northernmost provinces along with Da Nang, Hue, and the Demilitarized Zone, led some of the finest units in the ARVN. Next to Saigon itself, his sector seemed the most vital. General Thi also sat with Prime Minister Ky on the Military Revolutionary Council and was perhaps Ky's most serious rival (other than Thieu, whom Ky then believed he had under control). Ky watched suspiciously as Thi consorted with the Buddhists, especially bonze Thich Tri Quang's group, which advocated a middle way between Saigon's anticommunist war and the NLF's insurgency. Like many ARVN officers, who to one degree or another saw the political Buddhists as a front for communists, Ky held a jaundiced view. Officers on the I Corps staff quietly informed Ky of Thi's Buddhist cavorting.

Early in March Ky decided to relieve Thi of command. That overestimate of his political power and miscalculation of religious feeling created a fresh political crisis. Within twenty-four hours the United Buddhists held protests in Hue and Da Nang, demanding that Ky and Thieu resign. The mayor of Da Nang found himself effectively superseded by a "Military-Civilian Struggle Committee." A general strike paralyzed the city. Students joined the Buddhists in the streets, where roadblocks appeared, with altars and Buddha statues. Ky sent one general to take over, but he lasted just two days. Students seized the Hue radio station, beaming denunciations. This became the Buddhist "Struggle Movement." Demonstrations spread to Qui Nhon, Dalat, Pleiku, Nha Trang, then Saigon itself. There ARVN paratroopers, of whom General Thi was one, even marched in his support. Ky was forced to return Thi to Da Nang to impose order, after which the general refused to resign. Early in April 3,000 men of the ARVN 1st Division, marching behind their military band, paraded in Thi's honor. Ky promoted General Ton That Dinh to I Corps in April, but Dinh could not even assume the command.

Prime Minister Ky's next move would be to replace Thi with General Huynh Van Cao. That proved to be a mistake. Cao, the same officer who had led the ARVN's 1963 debacle at Ap Bac, could not bring himself to act against the Buddhists, whose protests grew. Nguyen Chanh Thi expected to ride the crest of the Buddhist wave. The Americans became heavily embroiled when Ky told MACV of his intention to send Vietnamese Marines to Da Nang to enforce Thi's ouster. Westmoreland refused U.S. aircraft to move the troops, so Ky went through Ambassador Henry Cabot Lodge to obtain this help.[32] As Ky's Marines arrived, artillerymen loyal to Thi trained their cannon on the airfield. Then Thi's troops blocked the road between Da Nang and Hue. Tough ARVN airborne men led by Colonel Ngo Quang Truong cleared the way and surrounded two key Buddhist pagodas, offering amnesty to anyone who left. The Marines got through.

A psychological warfare team with Ky's contingent set up a phony radio station purporting to speak for the Buddhists and made broadcasts designed to spread the idea that the Struggle Movement was a front for the communists. U.S. Marine commander Lieutenant General Lew Walt happened to agree with Ky's phony broadcasts, so he did nothing to obstruct the ARVN psywarriors. Meanwhile, American Marines interposed themselves between the South Vietnamese, ingeniously blocking a bridge to prevent them clashing, and threatened the dissidents with U.S. planes and artillery. Walt ordered these measures, highly unusual among allies in war.

Now Ky sent Colonel Nguyen Ngoc Loan, a trusted operative, to Hue to deal with Huynh Van Cao. Loan had been Ky's chief of staff in the air force, and in 1965 Ky made him National Police chief. That was shortly after Loan and a couple of others had rid the ARVN of Young Turk coup maker (and Hanoi secret agent) Colonel Pham Ngoc Thao, who died by strangulation in a Saigon hospital bed. Arriving in Hue, Loan went to see General Cao, demanding that he move against the Buddhists. Cao's Catholic family lived in Hue, and he feared retribution if the government cracked down. Lew Walt's deputy senior adviser to I Corps, Army colonel Arch Hamblen, was walking toward I Corps headquarters when he spied Cao through a window, listening to Loan while someone held a pistol near the general's head. Hamblen hurried to rescue Cao, who first fled to Walt's command post and then requested asylum at the U.S. consulate in Da Nang. A couple of days later General Cao Van Vien, chief of Saigon's Joint General Staff, supervised Da Nang's takeover by Vietnamese Marine battalions.

Nguyen Cao Ky finally bested Nguyen Chanh Thi with concessions. Ky promised the promulgation of a constitution and the creation of a national assembly. Though Ky watered this down to a constitutional convention and pushed national assembly elections back to 1967, this became the catalyst for such democracy as South Vietnam achieved. An election law advisory panel reported in June, about the time the Buddhist crisis subsided, on rules for the constituent group. Ky openly admits he tried to insert a wedge between Buddhist factions to weaken them. Nguyen Chanh Thi went into exile, much as had Nguyen Khanh, on a meaningless diplomatic mission. The general who replaced Thi, Hoang Xuan Lam, was a Buddhist acceptable to both the Struggle Movement and the military. Lam led I Corps for six years, with disastrous results. The circumstances of his appointment had much to do with his longevity in this post. Ngo Quang Truong, promoted brigadier, received command of the ARVN 1st Division.

Meanwhile, a couple of weeks after the Honolulu summit, LBJ saw Henry Graff, the Columbia University historian. They talked of the "other war" in Vietnam and the Christmas pause and supposed diplomacy but exchanged not a word on either the Program 2 buildup or the Buddhists.[33] LBJ saw the Struggle Movement as deadly serious. He agreed with Ky and noted in his memoirs, "I always believed that if Tri Quang and some of his principal followers were not actively pro-Communist, at least their movement had been deeply penetrated by Hanoi's agents."[34] Yet weeks of turmoil took their toll. By early April Johnson felt frustrated. According to aide Jack Valenti, at a Sunday edition of the Tuesday Lunch held April 2 in the Family Dining Room of the White House, the president told colleagues they should make every effort to keep Ky but "be ready to make terrible choices." He wanted them to prepare a fallback position, talking to the Buddhists while disposing of Tri Quang: "if necessary, get out of I Corps area and even Vietnam."[35] Johnson foresaw making a "stand" in Thailand. Valenti gave the president a paper that analyzed this and other possibilities. At a meeting that night, April 4, LBJ came back to the subject: the "time has come when the alternative is to get out—or do what we need to do to keep the government shored up."[36] Over succeeding weeks, staff put a certain amount of work into the withdrawal option, openly championed only by George Ball, but advocates of force retained the upper hand.[37]

Both the timing and the content of Johnson's comments are significant. Nine months after his fateful decision to engage in the ground war, Lyndon Johnson had been forced to admit that the moment might have arrived when it had become necessary to withdraw. This was, in fact, one of the only times during his presidency that Johnson seriously entertained any thought of leaving Vietnam, and it was developments among South Vietnamese, not opposition in the United States, that brought him to that pass.

The Buddhist troubles not only shook the president; they startled the American people. In March when the crisis began, just under 60 percent supported the war, and a quarter opposed it. By May, when Ky's soldiers occupied Da Nang, the balance had shifted—not decisively, but in an important way. Support for the war had shrunk to less than a majority (49 percent), while opposition had grown to more than a third (36 percent). That third became a core opposition. Antiwar sentiment never declined to much less than that, and in due course it grew. Johnson's personal poll numbers also fell. The Buddhist crisis stripped away a slice of the Saigon government's legitimacy in American eyes, with eventual but fateful consequences. This represented the product of LBJ's staunch support for an ally that progressively seemed less worthy of it. George Bush's backing for an Iraqi government that resisted political accommodation with its people played a similar role in the hardening of American opinion against the Iraq war.

Of course, Johnson did not withdraw from Vietnam. Instead, he did what he could to "nail the coonskin to the wall," continuing the MACV reinforcement program and making new decisions on force. The most important concerned Rolling Thunder, the aerial assault on North Vietnam. It was about to attain new heights of ferocity.

■ ■ ■ At the moment of the Christmas halt, Robert McNamara had told Lyndon Johnson that he could handle the Joint Chiefs of Staff. Although direct evidence still lacks, it is highly probable that McNamara did this by promising the Chiefs that once the halt had run its course, he would back demands for widened bombing. This is in fact what happened. Beginning in late 1965 the JCS had proposed—along with Admiral Sharp at CINCPAC and General Westmoreland at MACV—attacks aimed at North Vietnam's fuel storage and transport system—"petroleum, oil, and lubricants" (POL), in military parlance. Already by October only 10 of the 240 targets on the JCS list outside the Hanoi-Haiphong or border exclusion zones remained to be attacked, yet Rolling Thunder seemed to have achieved little. The air campaign had fallen into a rut. During 1965 North Vietnam had imported roughly 170,000 tons of petroleum products, and the Chiefs were anxious to strike that target. It became a new bombing panacea.

The question of POL attacks was partly subsumed in that of resumed bombing after the Christmas halt and partly folded into a larger strategic debate that dominated the first half of 1966. The Joint Chiefs certainly pushed hard. McNamara discussed POL targets in his advice on the resumption of Rolling Thunder, sent to Johnson in late January. That memo centered on countering infiltration, however, mainly by blocking routes that led to the Ho Chi Minh Trail, to which POL attacks could contribute. But the defense secretary also foresaw an effort so extensive—4,000 sorties per month—that even a proportion of sorties shifted from "armed reconnaissance" interdiction to POL strikes represented a substantial capability. McNamara asked the JCS to assess the feasibility of POL attacks in a specific study. By April, in conjunction with the Defense Intelligence Agency, the Chiefs had that study in hand.

In the meantime, there were changes at the White House. McGeorge Bundy departed, and Walt Rostow replaced him as national security adviser.

Rostow had participated in strategic bombing against Germany in World War II and was a fan of POL. He proved a natural ally for the Chiefs in the POL debate, nudging LBJ as hard as the military and much more effectively, since he had daily access to Johnson. A CIA intelligence estimate in March strengthened the hand of POL advocates by concluding that bombing tactics so far had been flawed. McNamara and Rusk were more reluctant, fearing that effective POL attacks could draw China or the Soviet Union into the Vietnam war.

Admiral Sharp demanded that when bombing resumed, it destroy every significant target in the North, starting with POL. CINCPAC was convinced that Rolling Thunder, carried out that way, could win the war by the end of 1966 and would certainly do so before mid-1967. Sharp thought *heavier* bombing, not pauses, would produce negotiations. He was incensed at the slow approvals for expanding the air war. Much of his memoir is taken up with denunciations of LBJ and McNamara for holding back the aerial assault.[38]

But Rolling Thunder actually moved ahead quite smartly. There were 4,484 attack sorties against the DRV in March and more than 5,000 in April, a new high. There would be 79,000 sorties in all of 1966, dropping no less than 136,000 tons of bombs—over twice the weight of munitions expended the first year. Moreover, the degree of Washington's micromanagement—the main focus of Sharp's complaints—was less than advertised. During the early months, Johnson had already given up approving individual missions, shifting successively to weekly and then biweekly "programs" governing hundreds, and eventually thousands, of sorties. In 1966 LBJ moved to monthly approvals. The focus of the POL debate would be the program for "Rolling Thunder 50," an extensive menu of operations.

Originally, a selection of POL attacks was included in Rolling Thunder 50. But this bombing program landed on Johnson's desk just as the Buddhist crisis heated up. With concern at the White House over whether the United States should withdraw, LBJ did not see this as the moment for an escalatory action such as moving against POL targets, many of which were located near Haiphong or Hanoi, in areas designated as exclusion zones. As an additional safety measure, LBJ increased the size of those zones considerably. POL slipped to Rolling Thunder 51.

Johnson's critics on the air war tend to portray the president much like Adolf Hitler in World War II, pushing pins around on maps of the Russian front to signify orders to individual combat units. The reality was never like that. Rolling Thunder 51 involved 10,000 sorties; Rolling Thunder 52, 13,500. The programs identified long lists of targets and specified sorties to be aimed at each. At that level there was no question of micromanagement. Occasionally targets were taken off the list. Mostly what LBJ did was set parameters. He approved or denied types of weapons or tactics, such as armed reconnaissance versus targeted strikes, or large bombs versus smaller ones or cluster munitions. Johnson set geographic goals too, with many Rolling Thunder programs aimed at different regions of North Vietnam. Exclusion zones were a type of geographic limit. The whole POL debate shows LBJ setting bombing strategy by deciding on a concentration against a given target type. Cases in which specific strikes came to Johnson's attention were primarily those involving previous targets within exclusion zones that were to be reattacked or were being rescheduled after cancellation due to weather or other considerations.

President Johnson's system enabled him to weigh political and diplomatic considerations in a military program. The function of the target lists and exclusion zones related precisely to this. By declaring a halt (or not), expanding or contracting exclusion zones, or authorizing attacks within them, LBJ hoped to signal Hanoi. It could hardly be otherwise, because the goal of Rolling Thunder from the beginning had been to influence the DRV, not simply to hurt it. The damage inflicted, raising the cost of infiltration to North Vietnam, also had this political aim, with military impact an important but collateral consideration. Effectiveness contributed to Westmoreland's attrition strategy, but the aim was never to bomb the DRV back to the Stone Age. Johnson could not hope to obtain a diplomatic effect *except* by varying the violence of Rolling Thunder in some fashion.

Arguments over bombing effectiveness are thus ultimately tangential. The attempt to pin the tail on Johnson also ignores the real flaws in the military's own arrangements. Admiral Sharp at CINCPAC functioned more as bureaucratic manager than field commander, apportioning quotas for attack missions to the Navy, Air Force, and Marine Corps air squadrons. Yes, Sharp fought Washington over rules of engagement, target systems, and aircraft usage (for example, commitment of B-52s to Rolling Thunder), but there is little evidence of CINCPAC developing a fresh strategy for the air campaign. Reliance on specified strikes plus armed reconnaissance continued throughout. Demands to hit Hanoi and Haiphong were about opening up JCS-listed targets, not new strategy. The most important innovations in the air campaign—seeding clouds to cause rain to flood Vietnamese rivers, the inception of an electronic battlefield to help interdict the Ho Chi Minh Trail—came from scientists, not CINCPAC. And in Washington, specifically at the White House, Rostow would be Sharp's closest ally and advocate. The admiral's wholesale condemnation is misplaced.[39]

At the technical level, there were a host of initiatives and improvisations, but these should not be mistaken for strategy. They included the introduction of hot new planes, the adaptation of older ones for night work or electronic countermeasures, efforts to increase bomb loads, tactics that combined slow and fast aircraft, several types of gunships, airborne controllers to spot targets, airborne battle managers to direct large-scale operations, tightly coordinated search and rescue efforts, and more. There were also innovations specifically aimed at the ground war, most prominently the spraying of defoliant—the notorious Agent Orange—along roads and around bases, which began as early as 1962. Improvisations of ways to hit targets were especially prevalent for a time in 1966, when the United States ran short of a dozen kinds of munitions, particularly 500-pound bombs, the most commonly used type. Pilots were furious at being sent out with incomplete bomb loads or none at all. In fact, the Pentagon and CINCPAC, *not Lyndon Johnson*, set load limits to conserve ordnance. Veteran aircrews stationed at Da Nang at the time report their squadrons were practically ready to mutiny over the underarmed sorties. Other munitions, rockets, explosive shells, anything at all usable, were pressed into service to make up the difference. The United States actually paid West Germany a premium to buy back 500-pound bombs sold as surplus a few years earlier.[40] Sortie rates were finally reduced by the high command.

In any case, the air strategy issue for 1966 would be the POL strikes. Prodded by Rostow and Taylor (now LBJ's personal adviser), and with the JCS and Sharp providing support, LBJ edged toward approval. Rostow actually argued that POL strikes would *assist* Johnson's search for negotiations. The debate climaxed late in the spring. The president told the press on June 18, shortly after key deliberations, that heavier bombing was coming. On June 22 the Chiefs sent Admiral Sharp orders to begin POL attacks. The strikes started a week later and reached a high level with Rolling Thunder 51. Reconnaissance photos assessing the damage showed that the bombing was a great success. By late July, when Sharp completed a final strangulation plan, estimated capacities at many DRV oil storage facilities had already fallen by half. CINCPAC and Washington argued, however. U.S. bombing of a Soviet vessel in Haiphong and a pair of intrusions into Chinese airspace raised LBJ's fear of the war spilling over. But in the end, the strikes or the lack of them made no difference. By August Hanoi had shifted its oil from large tank facilities to fifty-five-gallon drums dispersed along roads throughout the country. There was no way to eliminate them. POL bombing had had no discernible effect whatsoever. One more supposedly unbeatable card had fallen to a trump. Admirals and officials knew these secret, inner details. The public saw only broad outlines, like a shadow play, and mostly what the administration wanted it to see. But even the public learned enough for concern. Though the measures were backed by opinion polls, they energized dissenters.

Warplanes, Vietniks, and Grunts

In the era before electronic media, blogs, and the Internet, most Americans did not have access to major daily newspapers, while the television networks had yet to feature Vietnam as a daily story.

Newsweeklies like *Time, Newsweek,* and *U.S. News and World Report* were their fare. These lacked depth, but they were what was available. A survey of this source clearly shows the media on board with the war. One big story came on January 7, 1966, when *Time* named William C. Westmoreland its "Man of the Year" and devoted a little more than six pages to the war. That was the moment of the Christmas halt and LBJ's big peace offensive, which *Time* covered separately in an item it called "The Great Peace Teach-in." Opposition to the Vietnam war would be notably underreported. *Time*'s take on the politics of the day was to write of "Vietniks and isolationists" in contrast to "the great majority of Americans who generally support [Johnson's] Vietnam policy." Even there, though, hints of unease appeared, with the journalists noting that support came "not in many cases without a certain apprehension."[41]

Reporting the Honolulu conference that February, *Time* caught that the event had been scheduled hastily, but the degree of compression was such that the same story covered LBJ's renewal of the bombing, Dwight D. Eisenhower's reaction (the president "has unquestionably made the right decision"), the tail end of the peace offensive—"jawing" at the United Nations—and Vietnam hearings held by the Senate Foreign Relations Committee.[42] There was rather more excitement about action in Vietnam, where MACV threw the 1st Cavalry and the U.S. Marines into a double-pronged attack into the An Lao valley (operations "White Wing" and "Double Eagle"), described as the first division-size offensive of the war, as if Ia Drang had not happened.

Through 1966 the newsweeklies pictured the war as proceeding apace, with U.S. troop numbers constantly growing and progress being made everywhere. That did not match the inner knowledge of the generals or Johnson officials, who were also much more attuned to the growth of opposition to the war. In the spring of 1967 President Johnson summoned General Westmoreland home for consultations, in the course of which the general addressed a joint session of Congress in an attempt to build political support. *Time* called him "the paradigm of the military professional," nodded with approval at Westy's peroration that "we will prevail . . . over the Communist aggressor," and found the war's critics "less vociferous in recent months."[43] At least by then the newsweeklies were reporting protests and made specific mention of Westmoreland's repeated complaints that Hanoi hoped political opposition in the United States would take the wind out of Washington's sails in Vietnam.

Typical stories of this period included one that Hanoi was escalating the war with new types of weapons, a passel of coverage of the Demilitarized Zone and the battle that took place around a strongpoint called Con Thien, the South Vietnamese elections, Moshe Dayan's visit to South Vietnam (he believed that Hanoi could not continue much longer in a war against U.S.

forces),[44] pacification, the air war, and, later in the year, the battles of Dak To and Loc Ninh. Political activity favorable to the Johnson administration often received more prominent treatment than did the opposition. For example, in May 1967 (when public opinion in favor of the war was actually falling), J. William Fulbright and fifteen other senators sent Hanoi "A Plea for Realism" and *Time* opined that "however unhappy or confused about the war, [Americans] agree in greater numbers than ever that it must continue to be fought."[45] Six months later the same Luce publication reported the creation of the Citizens Committee for Peace with Freedom in Vietnam—a prowar lobby directly orchestrated by the Johnson White House that consisted of a handful of establishment figures—as a grassroots nonpartisan group.

When Westmoreland came home in the spring of 1967, his real purpose pertained to LBJ's deliberations on a new reinforcement program. The substance of that request is covered in the next chapter, but the press reported the story when the administration gave it out, not before. In June, about three months after the fact and with the president poised to announce his decision, *U.S. News and World Report* correctly noted the size of the MACV request at between 200,000 and 250,000 troops.[46] Good reporting could furnish a glimmer of another view, such as when *Newsweek* quoted a "McNamara associate" a couple of weeks later saying, "There is a serious question whether we need more troops in Vietnam, even though the military can always justify their requirements. We should be getting more effectiveness out of the South Vietnamese Army rather than deploying more of our own forces."[47] The big national newspapers may have done better on the inner workings of power, but their editorial pages were supportive, and in the newsweeklies, the war was progressing faster and going better than in fact it was.

At the 1997 conference in Hanoi, North Vietnamese diplomats and officers were asked about the DRV's intelligence on Washington decision making. They answered that they had had no agents beyond the Saigon government and had depended on subscriptions to *Time* and *Newsweek* and other publications. The North Vietnamese also obtained the *New York Times* through their embassy in Sweden and pouched the issues to Hanoi, a process that apparently took two weeks. Imagine that: Hanoi had been no better informed on Lyndon Johnson's private thinking than were most people in small-town America! Meanwhile, in late 1967 North Vietnamese defense minister General Vo Nguyen Giap published a book on the future of the war called *Big Victory, Great Task,* which presented some figures on potential U.S. reinforcements to South Vietnam as part of its strategic analysis. Giap used the numbers 200,000 to 250,000. They could have come right out of *U.S. News and World Report.*

The broadest study of U.S. press coverage throughout the Vietnam war, a book by Clarence C. Wyatt, concludes that Washington got most of what it wanted from the press during this period through a policy of inundating journalists with a flood of facts—thus Saigon's infamous "Five O'clock Follies" briefings—putting stories in whatever context the purveyors wanted. Reporters had tons of facts but no clarity. Deadline pressures in the field and some judicious leaning on editors at home did the rest. Most reporters were steeped in the same Cold War mythos as other Americans and willingly played the part of "paper soldiers" in support of the war effort.[48] The Army's official history of its relations with the media reaches similar conclusions.[49] The discrepancies between what journalists were told and what they saw in the field emerged more slowly, and the calamities were yet to come.

■ ■ ■ Vietnam would be only a small part of Lyndon Johnson's State of the Union message of January 12, 1966, but even so, the burden of the conflict was becoming visible. LBJ conceded that due to the war in Vietnam he could not do all he wanted in the War on Poverty. With General Westmoreland demanding troops, the administration out of cash to pay for the war without congressional appropriations, and the Christmas pause there for all to see, LBJ had to make a supplemental request for more than $12 billion. Not long afterward he put another $10 billion into the budget for the coming fiscal year, a deliberate underestimate that Johnson knew would force him into another supplemental request. At budget hearings McNamara had to admit that Saigon had less control of the villages than a year earlier, and the Air Force chief of staff would be obliged to say that the United States was not winning the war. To smooth the way past such discrepant information, Johnson invited senior congressional leaders to the White House for a stroking and grooming session. The president got more than he bargained for. His friend Richard Russell, aligned with those pushing for the POL strikes, had also concluded that carrying out both the war and LBJ's Great Society programs had become impossible. He wanted a choice that Johnson resisted making. Senators Mansfield and Fulbright pressed LBJ not to resume the bombing. After the meeting, the two senators wrote him a letter, signed by more than a dozen colleagues, supporting that position. According to Minnesota's Eugene McCarthy, almost one-third of the full Senate agreed.[50]

Johnson went ahead with the bombing. Fulbright, whether incensed at the president or concerned at LBJ's distancing himself from old congressional colleagues and worried about developments in Vietnam, used his Senate Foreign Relations Committee to hold televised hearings on the war beginning late in January and extending over six days. Here Fulbright made an open break with a president of his own political party and completed his move from conservative Democrat to dissenter. The administration resisted sending witnesses, but Fulbright was able to require Dean Rusk's attendance, since a State Department budget request was before his committee. Rusk tried to invoke secrecy, insisting on executive session to discuss many questions, but Fulbright kept him on the record. Rusk portrayed Hanoi as an aggressor, rejecting contentions that Vietnam's was a civil war, and he generally hewed to strident positions. Having been drawn into the fray, the administration now sent General Maxwell Taylor to do battle; he argued that the loss of South Vietnam would have "grave consequences," setting in motion a "crumbling process . . . for the forces of freedom," an evocation of the Domino Theory. Rusk repeated his performance during a final appearance on February 18, incidentally reiterating that the U.S. "commitment" to Vietnam had been made in 1954 or 1955 by Eisenhower, a veiled reference to the notorious Eisenhower letter, here again used as justification for war.

Another aspect of the Fulbright hearings is that they gave significant voice to opponents of engagement, including another noted general, James M. Gavin, who had once worked for Taylor. Also testifying in opposition was foreign policy guru and former diplomat George F. Kennan.[51] These commentators publicly broke ranks with the uniformed services and foreign policy elite, destroying the pretension that professional opinion stood behind Vietnam strategy.

The most important aspect of the hearings is how they legitimized opposition and helped lay the foundation for dissenters to undermine the credibility of military intervention as foreign policy tool. Some quite substantial Americans, not merely "Vietniks," opposed the war. *Life* magazine called the hearings a "Great Debate," but they did not really rise to that level because the war was not really at stake—Fulbright lacked the power to actually reverse the U.S. course in Vietnam, no matter what happened at his hearings. Historians are divided on this episode. Antiwar movement expert Melvin Small finds, "It is difficult to evaluate the significance of the hearings"; historian Charles DeBenedetti argues, "They did open the ambiguities, contradictions, and uncertainties of administration policy to deliberative review"; and conservative observer Adam Garfinkle notes, "The hearings not only altered the image of opposition to the war, they also got the administration's attention."[52]

Majority opinion still supported LBJ, including the conservatives who would have hit the president had he attempted disengagement. This included much of the press, like it or not. Typical was J. Russell Wiggins, editor (until 1968) of the *Washington Post*—sometimes held out as a bastion of antiwar sentiment—who wrote at the time of Pleiku that the incident (which he, among others, believed had been ordered by Hanoi) demonstrated "with dreadful clarity that South Vietnam is not an isolated battlefield but part of a long war in which the communist world seems determined to continue until every last vestige of Western power and influence has been driven from Asia."[53]

Lyndon Johnson was right to fear a right-wing revolt against withdrawal,

but those who argue the antiwar movement prolonged the conflict miscon-
strue this. First, absent pressure from those denigrated as Vietniks, there
would have been *no* political pressure to counteract escalation demands. The
U.S. buildup proceeded about as quickly as it could have, so it is inaccurate
to claim that intervention could have been more "decisive."[54] Had LBJ been
able to adopt some of the Right's idealized solutions—such as massive
bombing of Hanoi (as in the 1972 Christmas Bombing), at a time when
North Vietnam had warm relations with both Moscow and Beijing—the result would have been the much wider war that Wiggins, for one, claimed to
see and that Johnson dreaded. As described previously, the massive bombing
option had already been explicitly posed, and LBJ had rejected it.

Second and equally important, Johnson may have feared the Right, but he
tried to draw rightists in, to invoke their cooperation. Not so with the Left.
As early as October 1965, when the International Days of Protest occurred,
notes of George Ball's telephone conversations reveal LBJ's personal interest
in stymieing opponents. He had State needle the Justice Department about
applying the Logan Act—a 1799 law that forbids private Americans from
conducting the nation's foreign policy—against groups that encouraged for-
eigners to protest the war at U.S. embassies. Justice thought the idea far-
fetched. Not long afterward LBJ told media figures of his concern that U.S.
protests might be misinterpreted overseas. On October 26, 1965, within a
week of that conversation, the CIA produced an intelligence report titled
"Reactions Abroad to Vietnam Protest Demonstrations in the U.S.," a coinci-
dence that strongly suggests a response to a White House request. The CIA
found that turnouts at foreign demonstrations had been light.[55]

Early in 1966, as protesters planned a new "Vietnam Day," Don Ropa of
the NSC staff monitored it at the White House. Interestingly, like his predecessor Cooper, Ropa was on detail from the CIA. The White House also
followed the organizational evolution of the Movement, including developments such as religious groups' creation of the Clergy and Laity Concerned
about Vietnam (CALCAV). Avid eyes watched poll data. In March a Stanford
poll of 1,474 respondents found 88 percent support for negotiations and 70
percent in favor of a UN cease-fire. Even among those ready to send as many
as 500,000 troops to Vietnam there was 85 percent support for negotiations
and 53 percent for free elections.

In May, as the counterculture magazine *Ramparts* prepared to publish rev-
elatory stories on Vietnam, including an eye-opener on the work of Michigan State University advisers for Diem and as cover for CIA, Johnson
political aide Douglass Cater looked into the magazine and reported to the
president. Later the CIA, upon learning of further *Ramparts* stories directed
at it, would take on the magazine in an attempt to defund or discredit it.

This became the very time when America's internal security services, including local police, the Federal Bureau of Investigation (FBI), and even mil-

itary intelligence, initiated efforts to subvert the peace movement in the guise of gathering information about it. Vietnam Day had been conceived by students at the University of California–Berkeley, the place where the free speech movement had begun. Secret FBI documents opened in 2002 after seventeen years of litigation reveal that the Bureau had kept a "security index" of persons at Berkeley since 1960. In January 1965 FBI director J. Edgar Hoover and CIA chief John McCone concerted a plan to leak derogatory material to conservative trustees on the University of California Board that might eliminate perceived liberals on the faculty and would, at a minimum, harass them. This scheme went so far as to tar university chancellor Clark Kerr as a "pro-communist." The first large student protests at Berkeley happened that September. The following year, when Ronald Reagan ran for governor of California, FBI data were sent to him.[56] The emissary to Reagan would be Charles Brennan, FBI domestic intelligence chief.

The University of California–Irvine became another target. There the intruders were U.S. naval intelligence, and again the evidence emerged in declassified documents years later. Irvine became suspect after May 21, 1966, when the SDS chapter there held an antiwar protest outside El Toro, a nearby Marine air station. The Sixth Counterintelligence Team at El Toro filmed and photographed the protest, recorded license plate numbers, taped speeches ("it is very easy to be antagonistic toward people who disagree with you. Talk with them; try and reason things out"—*that* was subversive?), copied leaflets and handouts, and identified specific individuals, including protest organizer Patty Parmalee. Data on this protest appeared in Parmalee's FBI file when she later got it declassified. FBI special agents appeared on the Irvine campus asking questions about Parmalee, for a more immediate chilling effect.[57]

Investigations carried out by Congress in the 1970s established that the FBI had set up a formal project to counter antiwar radicals only in 1968, but in fact, Hoover had issued a directive in April 1965 ordering intensified coverage of the SDS and one in February 1966 to investigate any university activities linked to supposed "subversive" groups, starting with SDS. A couple of months later the Bureau circulated studies of college unrest in Detroit and Philadelphia, and in May 1966 Hoover directed his field offices to expand their coverage.

The Central Intelligence Agency was not far behind. Langley created Project "Resistance" to keep an eye on the antiwar movement. On March 15, 1966, it circulated a document from the Vietnam Day Committee that had foreseen massive bombing after the Christmas truce and appealed to peace groups everywhere to demand the Johnson administration demonstrate its sincerity with an indefinite cessation of bombing. That summer the CIA gave the White House advance warning of a demonstration there by the Washington Committee to End the War in Vietnam and a heads-up about a planned protest by the Student Nonviolent Coordinating Committee (SNCC) on the occasion of Luci Johnson's wedding.

None of these were big protests. All were of the nickel-and-dime variety, with a couple of hundred demonstrators tops. The big actions of 1966 came that May in New York, when the Fifth Avenue Peace Parade Committee brought together 20,000, and in August when thousands marched on the anniversary of the atomic bombing of Hiroshima. The small demonstration outside the White House on the day Luci Johnson married Patrick J. Nugent amounted to a tiny fragment of the overall canvas, but one embarrassing to the president. One other small demonstration should be mentioned. In November when Secretary McNamara visited Harvard to give a speech, he was confronted by a small contingent of protesters organized by the SDS. In the wake of that experience, McNamara decided to order the review of U.S. involvement in Vietnam that became known as the Pentagon Papers.

No activity seemed too small to escape the attention of government agents. Merely reciting the size of the cache of declassified FBI documents on various groups and individuals (not necessarily the totality of holdings on these entities) gives an impression of the scope of surveillance. As of January 2004 the FBI had released 2,887 pages of documents on the SNCC, 282 on SNCC activist Stokely Carmichael, 11,674 on Malcolm X, 16,659 on Martin Luther King Jr., 967 on Roy Wilkins, 1,296 on Mario Savio of the free speech movement, 1,699 on the CALCAV, and 6,454 on the National Council of Churches. These were just a few of the relevant groups and people, many of them also participants in the civil rights movement—the FBI's primary focus. This was the period of attempts to discredit Martin Luther King. Antiwar figures such as Abbie Hoffman had hardly come into focus, but the FBI would accumulate at least 13,262 pages of material on him too.

The Bureau's tactics also deserve mention. Hoover's monitoring was not limited to standard investigative methods—although the mere appearance of an FBI special agent asking questions about a person could strike fear into those people, their friends, associates, employers, and so on. The Bureau recruited informants inside organizations, running them in much the same fashion as the CIA controlled spies; it also wiretapped telephones, broke into homes and offices (the term of art being "surreptitious entry"; the slang, "black bag job"), and actively sowed dissension by fabricating letters or messages sent to targets or their associates aimed at discrediting them. Many of these methods were inappropriate, but the black bag jobs were outright illegal. Toward the end of 1966 Hoover prohibited them, but not before some 600 operations had been conducted, including 90 break-ins at offices of the Socialist Workers Party (the special agent in charge of the FBI's New York office actually recommended commendations for half a dozen agents responsible for 15 of these burglaries during 1964–1965). Martin Luther King's experience has been extensively recounted, but there was no fish too small to fry. It would have been one thing to employ these tactics against a declared enemy of the United States; it was another thing altogether to use them against Americans exercising constitutionally protected rights.

Despite the surveillance, President Johnson's attempts to massage the American public, and his efforts to downplay the Vietnam conflict, LBJ's poll numbers declined, with negative opinions of him reaching the mid-forties before the end of the year. As midterm elections neared, LBJ found Democratic Party candidates loath to appear with him. The party suffered losses. One of the few bright spots in the picture would be that *Ramparts* editor Robert Scheer was defeated in his run for the House of Representatives. The president did not know he had done well compared to where he would soon be.

■ ■ ■ As 1966 neared its end came an illustration of just how sensitive was the link between peace feelers and the Rolling Thunder air bombardment. A secret approach to Hanoi code-named "Marigold" had begun with contacts between Italian and Polish diplomats and the North Vietnamese; this led to a plan for a Johnson envoy to meet Hanoi representatives in Warsaw under the auspices of the Poles. Everything was in place in early December when U.S. bombers struck near the center of Hanoi. Johnson had approved the air strikes under the Rolling Thunder program, and they had been scheduled weeks earlier but canceled due to bad weather. Because CINCPAC could reschedule strikes without reference to Washington, Admiral Sharp put the mission back up. American warplanes attacked just as the diplomats were about to meet. Some crossed communications involving the Poles prevented salvaging this situation, and another Rolling Thunder restrike near Hanoi led the DRV to recall its envoy. Marigold illustrates exactly why LBJ needed to keep a close eye on the air campaign.[58]

At the 1997 conference in Hanoi, the American delegation spoke to the diplomat who had actually been sent to Warsaw for Marigold. Nguyen Dinh Phuong revealed that he had actually gone bearing detailed instructions for initiating peace talks, including modalities and venues and a précis of a negotiating position. He had waited for several days after the initial missed meeting for the Poles to rearrange it, only to be recalled following the second U.S. bombing. This episode represented a true missed opportunity.

■ ■ ■ These months also saw the coalescence of another piece of the Vietnam problem—the draft and military resistance. As the armed forces sought to fill their ranks, the last quarter of 1965 brought the call-up of 170,000 Americans; another 180,000 young men, facing imminent induction, enlisted to ensure they could pick their assignments. In the spring of

1966 the Selective Service summoned 768,000 men for medical examinations prior to draft reclassification. Demands for manpower drove the Pentagon to relax standards. McNamara is still pilloried for his "Project 100,000," an initiative that accepted recruits who had failed elementary achievement tests. Boxer Muhammad Ali is one example. In 1964 Ali had scored below the charts on the armed forces qualification tests administered as part of the draft physical and had been exempted. In 1966 he would be retested, score just as badly, but be ruled eligible. Ali claimed conscientious objector status as a Muslim cleric. His claim denied, Ali was prosecuted when he failed to report for duty. His case reached the Supreme Court, which ruled that the government had failed to take into account the depth of Ali's religious beliefs.

Draft resistance began. Johnson had signed a bill in the summer of 1965 making the burning of one's draft card a criminal offense. New Yorker David J. Miller promptly torched his in front of the Whitehall induction center in Lower Manhattan. Miller, a student at a Jesuit college, believed the war was wrong both morally and politically, that "it clearly couldn't be right to defend the interests of imperialists within Indochina," and he saw his action as symbolic free speech. The FBI arrested him days later. His case went to the Supreme Court too, which found against Miller in 1968. He served two years in prison.[59] By then there were lots of draft resisters, card burners, and court cases, and Selective Service had become a primal headache for both the White House and the Pentagon.

As the military filled with draftees, many very unhappy at where they were, others became scandalized at what they saw. Many of these men were from minorities and the lower classes because the system effectively selected out youths who had the resources or connections to secure deferments—one historian reframed Vietnam as the "working class war."[60] Military morale began to slide. Suddenly the number of soldiers who went absent without leave (AWOL) or deserted shot up. In 1966 the overall AWOL figure rose to 57.2 per thousand servicemen, and desertions to 14.9 per thousand. The Marine Corps rate stood at 16.1 desertions per thousand. For the Army, the AWOL figure mushroomed to 78 per thousand in 1967; desertions were 21.4 per thousand in the Army and 26.8 in the Marines. Then AWOLs soared even higher in 1968. Drug use increased rapidly too. Military men were not happy, and like Americans at large, they confronted big questions about their attitudes on Vietnam. In a stunning development on June 3, 1966, in Texas, Privates James Johnson, Dennis Mora, and David Samas refused to deploy to Vietnam. They became known as the "Fort Hood Three." Four months later at Fort Jackson, Army doctor Howard Levy stopped training Green Beret medical specialists, refusing to prepare them to perpetrate atrocities. "GI Resistance" to the Vietnam war was born.

■ ■ ■ The pace of both the war and the protests quickened in 1967. At the end of January 2,000 people demonstrated in the cold in front of the White House as CALCAV leaders met with staff to hand over a petition. General Westmoreland carried out a huge, corps-sized offensive north of Saigon. In February Women Strike for Peace mobilized 2,500 protesters who marched up to the Pentagon and pounded on its doors with their shoes. The University of Wisconsin became the locale for strong protests against Dow Chemical, manufacturer of napalm and defoliant chemicals used in the war. Some were arrested. The next day protesters surrounded the offices of the president of the university, trapping him inside.

White House operatives took a hand by engineering the formation of a pro-war advocacy group. In March a letter from a prominent Washington lobbyist to national security adviser Walt Rostow proposed this as part of a public relations strategy. Rostow took the idea to LBJ, who approved it on March 17.[61] Subsequent correspondence shows that the lobbyist took soundings on such a committee at Rostow's behest and came back for instructions based on a detailed concept of what such a group might look like, how it could be funded (start-up costs were estimated at $100,000 minimum, with more for newspaper ads, radio and television time, and so forth), and who might be approached to join it.[62]

Rostow's records show that he discussed the possibility with Nicholas deB. Katzenbach at the Justice Department and John T. McNaughton at the Pentagon and had further conversations with the lobbyist and other associates, including former CIA officer Kermit Roosevelt. On March 27 Rostow lunched with Katzenbach and McNaughton to go over specifics, and on the twenty-ninth he explicitly brought President Johnson into the project, saying, "we concluded that it might be helpful if a group of this kind could publicly throw its weight behind the key elements in your policy." The covert nature of the undertaking Rostow also made explicit: "the enterprise should be organized at some distance from the Government."[63] A similar idea came to LBJ through political aide Harry McPherson, who, like Rostow, told the president, "*there should be no overt White House involvement in this.*"[64] Aides McPherson and John P. Roche monitored this work. The group actually surfaced later that year, alleging that it represented mass opinion and that the antiwar movement was just an isolated fringe. *Time* magazine, at least, reported this as straight news.

Meanwhile, a pair of appearances by Martin Luther King Jr.—one in Beverly Hills, the other at Riverside Church in New York City—brought the civil rights leader out in foursquare opposition to the war. Rostow's office worked hard the day after King's April 4 Riverside Church speech to refute the reverend's main points. By contrast, the Movement celebrated King's adherence. Almost immediately he was made a cochairman of CALCAV. Then came April 15, when parallel marches took place in both San Francisco and New

York, sponsored by the Spring Mobilization to End the War in Vietnam. Huge crowds swarmed in both cities—between 100,000 and 400,000, by various estimates. King appeared again, as did many other civil rights figures and a bevy of antiwar leaders. But in New York's Central Park, some of the most significant attendees were down in the crowd, not up on the speakers' stand. About a dozen Vietnam veterans who had individually decided to come out against the war found one another, most of them under the banner of "Veterans for Peace." A couple of months later they created a new organization and called it the Vietnam Veterans Against the War. It was past time to hear from real Vietnam veterans, for the war was headed to new peaks of ferocity.

6 Trampling Out the Vintage (1967)

There was annoyance in Washington around the New Year. Just after Christmas the *New York Times* began publishing a series of articles by assistant managing editor Harrison E. Salisbury, who spent a fortnight in Hanoi and elsewhere in the DRV, depicting life under the bombs.[1] Grumbling at the White House, pressure on the newspaper, and denunciations by Pentagon spokesmen did not neutralize the stories, which rekindled controversy over civilian casualties of the bombing. The generals had repeatedly assured President Johnson the air attacks were precise and caused few casualties. Salisbury's stories indicated differently. Robert McNamara's press aide Phil G. Goulding saw this as a "national disaster."[2] Following so soon after the collapse of Marigold due to bombing, the dispute could only distress Johnson.

Some in the military turned a jaundiced eye toward the Salisbury trip, believing it provided aid and comfort to the North Vietnamese, a shortsighted view, since his eyewitness reports also had intelligence value to war planners. Moreover, Salisbury played a role of his own in the jockeying to open negotiations. He was accorded an interview with Pham Van Dong, and Hanoi used Salisbury as an emissary. The message undoubtedly embodied what would have been articulated in Warsaw under Marigold—in particular, assurances that Hanoi's Four Points were not preconditions. Salisbury gave the message to Dean Rusk but made no comment on it in his newspaper articles.

As he left Hanoi, Salisbury reported the arrival of two other Americans—Harry S. Ashmore and William C. Baggs, executive vice president and a board member of the Center for the Study for Democratic Institutions, respectively. They had begun a peace project drawing on an encyclical from Pope Paul VI. A Mexican associate visiting China in late 1966 had relayed an invitation to Hanoi, but they delayed their trip when the State Department asked them not to conflict with "other things"—Marigold—in motion at the time.[3] In Hanoi Ashmore and Baggs met senior figures, including Ho Chi Minh. Ho told them a bombing halt was his sole precondition and indicated that the Four Points were items for negotiation. Their notes were certified by a Hanoi official. Back in Washington, Nicholas Katzenbach, now deputy secretary of state, listened to Ashmore and Baggs but cautioned them not to be impatient.

The emissaries were unable to get the United States to respond to Hanoi's feeler, and State Department spokesmen later questioned their veracity and even motives. "There were those in high places," Ashmore and Baggs concluded, "who seemed to regard our open channel to Ho Chi Minh as valuable and who sought to use it . . . but there were also those of equal or higher rank who seemed to be opposed to any kind of exchange with Hanoi."[4]

Unbeknownst to either private emissary, President Johnson had a new peace feeler of his own under way, one that demonstrated their point precisely. This involved the first U.S. move to actually respond to a DRV position. Late in 1966 the administration conceived a formula for a two-phase procedure in which bombing would stop and Hanoi would end infiltration. The United States would appear to stand down its bombers unilaterally but would actually be acting under a private understanding with North Vietnam. Washington would save face by making no acknowledgment, and Hanoi would build U.S. confidence by not taking advantage. The formula became known as "Phase A–Phase B." Talks could follow. This would have been used in Marigold had it not collapsed. Taking up the Salisbury contact, Washington attempted a new feeler code-named "Sunflower." In early January U.S. diplomats in Moscow sent a message through Hanoi's embassy there suggesting a formal channel. Hanoi continued to insist on a bombing halt, but the DRV knew nothing so far of the A–B formula, which Averell Harriman and Chet Cooper, at least, considered capable of breaking the logjam.

There *was* movement. Foreign Minister Nguyen Duy Trinh gave an interview on peace possibilities to Australian journalist Wilfred Burchett, and an article in the newspaper *Nhan Dan* covered the same ground. Both used the more nuanced DRV position on its Four Points. The French government was officially informed that the Trinh statement was significant, and it passed this information on to Washington through its own channels, including visiting senator Robert F. Kennedy. In Hanoi on January 30, Pham Van Dong asked Soviet ambassador Ilya Scherbakov for Moscow's help. Premier Aleksei Kosygin was about to visit the United Kingdom and could ask the British to sound out the United States. Two months earlier Rusk had given Kosygin a paper describing the Phase A–Phase B formula, and of course the Soviets knew of U.S. attempts to contact Hanoi through Moscow. As cochairs of the Geneva conferences in 1954 and 1962, the USSR and the United Kingdom were ideal partners to pursue mediation.

Meanwhile, news of the abortive Marigold feeler had begun to leak. British foreign minister George Brown, who had also been told of Phase A–Phase B and had gone to Moscow to float the formula as his own idea, discovered that both the Poles and the Russians already knew. Brown was furious. The Americans also tabled other cards. In early January the State Department released a version of Rusk's 14 Points that included a brief reference to A–B, though only by publicly linking bombing and infiltration. Chet Cooper flew

to London to console Brown and to Paris to consult Jean Sainteny, whose relations with Ho Chi Minh dated back twenty years, encouraging him to see
Ho on LBJ's behalf. Cooper returned to London for the Kosygin visit, which
took place as Vietnam celebrated Tet, its lunar new year, with a brief bombing pause. Before Kosygin's arrival Cooper spent several days reviewing the
linkage formula with the British.

Premier Kosygin appeared on February 6 and immediately met with
Prime Minister Sir Harold Wilson. Kosygin mentioned the Trinh interview
as evidence of Hanoi's desire to move forward. Wilson presented Phase
A–Phase B. The Soviet leader agreed to forward the proposal. British intelligence had bugged Kosygin's suite at Claridge's Hotel and picked up phone
conversations indicating his optimism. And Kosygin gave an interview
broadly hinting that the Trinh statement by itself was a sufficient basis for
talks.[5]

As in many similar circumstances, Kosygin's going public riled Lyndon
Johnson, who had his press secretary insist on action, not words, from
Hanoi. That set a certain atmosphere for Sunflower. More important, LBJ
had already undercut the entire London channel by sending a personal letter
to Ho Chi Minh through the U.S. embassy in Moscow. That February 8 letter
changed the A–B formula—in fact, reversed it—merely by changing the
tense of a word. It asserted that the United States would stop bombing upon
receiving evidence the DRV had stood down, rather than on an understanding Hanoi *would* desist. The United States thus put its promise in the future
tense and made it conditional—in effect, Phase B–Phase A—a direct challenge to the DRV's insistence that the aerial assault end as a prelude to negotiations. Such a formula not only risked outright rejection; it was the
opposite of what Prime Minister Wilson, acting as Washington's agent, had
told the Soviets. Chester Cooper had seen a draft of the letter to Ho before
leaving the United States. At that time it contained the original A–B formula.
Moreover, at a press conference the day after the Ho letter went out, Rusk reiterated the A–B offer, and UN Ambassador Arthur Goldberg told a university gathering much the same thing. Walt Rostow was the likely architect of
the abrupt switch. Cooper and Wilson were taken completely by surprise.
Wilson had to go back to the Soviets with the reversed position.

The rest of the Kosygin visit degenerated into an effort to salvage something from the calamity. This culminated in the Soviet leader's late-night
visit to Wilson's country residence at Chequers while Cooper hid in the attic,
desperately awaiting an answer to his appeal to the White House for recon-
sideration. Johnson's people refused to reconsider; in fact, they injected a
new urgency, demanding that Hanoi reply within such a short time (within
the span of the Tet cease-fire) that the Russians could hardly move the cables, much less give the DRV a chance to decide. Pressed, the United States
deliberated ad infinitum on extending the deadline—a couple of minor ones

were granted—and construed that as a concession. The United States did not reconsider its reversal of the formula. Personal appeals from Wilson to Johnson brought only reiteration of the U.S. position. The bombing resumed. Hanoi duly rejected Sunflower. Negotiations were further away than ever.

The Johnson administration rationalized its deviation in a couple of ways. One was to cite DRV troop movements—three People's Army divisions were moving into the sector just above the Demilitarized Zone (DMZ).[6] But the moves did not amount to infiltration per se, and U.S. planners were already hedging the DMZ maneuver, accelerating preparations for a defensive barrier along the zone (then called Project 728) while General Westmoreland did the same thing by reinforcing I Corps. The other rationalization was to claim that the American offer included curtailing the U.S. buildup in South Vietnam and therefore went beyond the A–B formula, demanding correspondingly greater reciprocation. That assertion may have looked good in official leaks, but the fact is that the original Phase A–Phase B papers that went through Harriman's interagency coordinating committee in December 1966—more than two months earlier—explicitly provided for the United States "to suspend additional troop movements to Vietnam," *not* as part of any B–A proposal but within the original framework.[7]

Cooper recalled this entire episode as "a dark tale of Washington's shambolic, feckless pursuit of peace."[8] Later in 1967, after a different feeler collapsed, Harvard academic Henry Kissinger (who had worked on the feeler) told historian Arthur Schlesinger Jr. that he had come to believe that "LBJ's resistance to negotiations verges on a sort of madness."[9] Whatever else it shows, Sunflower confirms the impression of private emissaries Ashmore and Baggs that some in the Johnson administration were less interested in peace than others, and for now, they had their way. The die had been cast for more fierce fighting.

"Moving Strongly in Favor of the South Vietnamese"

As William Westmoreland saw it, in the first months after U.S. deployment, he had to use his troops as fire brigades to save pieces of South Vietnam. In 1966 he moved to offensive warfare, using Americans in operations while the ARVN protected pacification programs. The course of the war would never be quite so clear-cut, however; in many places, Americans were involved in pacification, while MACV made sure ARVN units participated in most of the major probes into Indian Country. American offensives through 1966 inflicted many losses on the Liberation Front and the increasing numbers of North Vietnamese who had taken the field, but Westmoreland never succeeded in sweeping away his adversary. And always that enemy remained capable of significant moves of its own.

The many large-scale sweeps of 1966 were dwarfed by a pair of actions

MACV and the ARVN carried out early in the new year. Responding to earlier NLF attacks in Tay Ninh province, and seeking the headquarters of its Fourth Military Region, the thrust also aimed at other suspected base camps and supply caches in War Zone C, the so-called Iron Triangle north of Saigon. An underground base at Cu Chi would soon be discovered right under the noses of the U.S. 25th Infantry Division. Called Operation "Cedar Falls," this action used no fewer than 16,000 U.S. and 14,000 ARVN troops, including the recently arrived tanks of the 11th Armored Cavalry Regiment, elements of two U.S. infantry divisions, plus the 173rd Airborne Brigade. More than 200 prisoners were captured, in addition to many NLF documents, and more than 700 guerrillas were killed. At the peak of the battle U.S. weekly casualties rose to 144 dead, 1,044 wounded, and half a dozen missing.

The sweep also generated negative publicity as journalists witnessed the military's tactics. At Ben Suc the entire populace, herded into resettlement camps, saw their village leveled. This was not the first time such methods had been revealed. Notable examples were film footage by correspondent Morley Safer showing Marines torching villagers' huts, and John Laurence's reports on resettlement during sweeps near the central Vietnamese coast. But Jonathan Schell's articles and book on Ben Suc had such a vivid quality and level of detail that many Americans were horrified. The American unit that captured Ben Suc, the 1st Battalion, 26th Infantry, was led by Lieutenant Colonel Alexander M. Haig Jr. He believed that village was key to the Iron Triangle, but its conquest did nothing to quell NLF resistance. ARVN troops moved in behind Haig's battalion to interrogate peasants and secure Ben Suc, where searchers found extensive tunnels, including a bunker that housed the Front's command for the entire province.

A few weeks later at the University of Wisconsin in Madison, students held a big demonstration against campus recruiters from Dow Chemical, whose napalm and defoliant chemicals (the notorious Agent Orange) had been liberally used in Cedar Falls. This marked a significant passage, in that the Movement began extending protests beyond government to corporations and entities found to be complicit in the war. It is not possible to show a causal relationship between events at Ben Suc and the Madison protests, but the news from Vietnam no doubt added to protesters' numbers and their sense of urgency.

General Westmoreland exploited his first wave with an even larger sweep code-named "Junction City." This time the troops were almost entirely American—twenty-two of twenty-six battalions, with 35,000 men in all. There would not be another endeavor of this magnitude until the invasion of Cambodia. The offensive kicked off about ten days after the collapse of the Sunflower peace feeler. Attempting to block an enemy retreat, the 173rd Airborne Brigade performed what turned out to be the only U.S. mass combat parachute drop of the war. GIs scoured the area for days, finding installations but few opponents. Major fighting developed after about a week. After that the sides traded blows. In late March the NLF showed no hesitation in attacking a U.S. firebase garrisoned by a full artillery battalion plus half an infantry one. Lieutenant Colonel John W. Vessey, the artillery commander, could not fire his guns fast enough to keep the insurgents away and ended up shooting over open sights directly at the oncoming enemy. Another big firefight took place at Ap Gu late in April, where Colonel Haig's battalion held off a major attack. The United States claimed more than 2,200 enemy killed in Junction City.

Both Vessey and Haig would rise to be senior generals, while others who had already attained rank, such as Bernard Rogers, an assistant division commander, and brigade commander Fred Weyand, would play key roles in Vietnam or the postwar U.S. Army. Weyand himself would lead MACV. Haig's battalion, last led by Paul Gorman, became an incubator of Army leadership, with such officers as Max Thurman and George Joulwan, all of whom would win their stars. In a sense the Cedar Falls–Junction City affair amounted to the coming-of-age of a generation of U.S. officers. But their experience was of conventional warfare, not counterinsurgency, at a time when the Vietnam conflict remained an insurgency war. This in itself illustrates the mismatch between U.S. tactics and the center of gravity in the war.[10]

General Westmoreland throughout this period showed special sensitivity regarding I Corps. There the DMZ offered the northerners an avenue into one of the Saigon government's most critical areas, while the mountainous borderlands were always porous, allowing the North Vietnamese to infiltrate with ease. Indeed, in 1966, despite the aggressive U.S. air effort in Laos, the Vietnam People's Army pushed the Ho Chi Minh Trail as far as the Cambodian border. Now Hanoi's bases backed the mountains all the way to the Central Highlands. That March the People's Army also overran the Special Forces camp at A Shau, opening up a valley route that led to Hue while simultaneously denying MACV one of its best jumping-off points for commando missions against The Trail.

No doubt Westmoreland's fears intensified with the Buddhist crisis, for that had virtually stalled ARVN activity in I Corps for months. General Walt's III Marine Amphibious Force (MAF), the corresponding U.S. headquarters, had also been mixed up in these political troubles. As new U.S. units deployed, MACV diverted some arriving Army units to the III MAF area, inserting Army men into what had been a Marine preserve. Westmoreland visited III MAF often and told its leaders to expect more Army troops. In early 1967 he formed several Army brigades into the provisional "Task Force Oregon," later restyled the "Americal," or 23rd Infantry Division. Westy instructed the Marines to strengthen the DMZ sector. Before long, III MAF had its full 3rd Marine Division there. It was in *this* climate that Hanoi conducted its own buildup above the Demilitarized Zone. As Washington held its breath around Tet 1967 and used People's Army reinforcements as a reason to scuttle Sunflower, commanders began probing North Vietnamese positions and bombing around the DMZ to neutralize them. The United States started dropping chemicals along the southern edge of the DMZ to defoliate it. The week after LBJ ended the Tet pause, strike sorties there more than doubled. Sortie rates did not fall below 500 a week until late April.

By then ground troops had engaged in earnest. The Marines made a battalion-size amphibious landing below the DMZ as a spoiling operation. A week after they reembarked, the People's Army hit Quang Tri city in a coordinated attack with four separate assault forces. Right after the Quang Tri attack McNamara revealed plans to protect the DMZ by creating a defense line combining strongpoints with minefields and electronic sensors, backed up by reaction forces and aircraft. At Con Thien, a post west of the city, the VPA began what developed into an extended battle, blasting the place with a thousand artillery shells in a day. On April 24 Marine patrols working their way through the hills near the combat base at Khe Sanh, located near the Laotian border, bumped into North Vietnamese troops in dug-in positions. That led to a series of fights in which Marines cleared the hills. On May 3 the North Vietnamese struck back with an attack on the nearby Lang Vei Special Forces camp. Later that month the VPA conducted sharp attacks and artillery bombardments along the Demilitarized Zone, answered by a Marine-ARVN clearing operation. All this fighting along the DMZ forms the backdrop for one of the key episodes in Lyndon Johnson's stewardship of the war.

■ ■ ■ Announcement of a defense system along the DMZ—one that came to be called the "McNamara Line"—marked a strategic choice by Washington. President Johnson made the decision himself. What few appreciate even today is how close LBJ came to the alternative—an invasion of North Vietnam. The story of how this came about has been shrouded by the atomization of histories of the war, as they center on Johnson, the military, or the antiwar movement. The 1967 decision resulted from initiatives by all the actors in the drama. It represents the first instance in which political constraints actually limited presidential choice, as well as a fundamental shift in LBJ's thinking—his acknowledgment that he had to abandon the goal of "victory" in Vietnam, the idea of putting the coonskin on the wall.

Afflicted by his uncertainties, LBJ had, until now, blown alternately hot and cold on Vietnam strategy. He had laid down markers that circumscribed the boundaries of the conflict: there would be no action that might bring China or the Soviet Union into an expanded war; the ability of Rolling Thunder to function as a diplomatic signaling device would be preserved; the role of the war in U.S. politics would be confined by not seeking a formal declaration or mobilizing the nation; he would not repeat the error of desta-bilizing the Saigon regime. Within that framework, anything went. Johnson wanted—indeed, demanded—strategies that would win. The president's willingness to scuttle the Sunflower feeler shows that in early 1967 he re-mained open to grasping for victory. In his memoir LBJ contends, "by early 1967 most of my advisers and I felt confident that the tide of war was mov-ing strongly in favor of the South Vietnamese."[11]

President Johnson's approval and his occasional active solicitation of new tactics show the same thing. Westmoreland's attrition strategy had been at-tractive because of the reasonable expectation that American forces, with greater weight, firepower, and flexibility than the ARVN, plus their logistical advantages, could inflict much higher casualties on Hanoi and the NLF. The POL bombing had been attractive because proponents portrayed it as a suc-cessful strategic bombing technique from World War II. Johnson himself sought a coherent strategy for the "other war," pacification, because he came to accept the arguments of counterinsurgency theorists, and a strategy for that facet complemented conventional techniques. Johnson had worked the Saigon government angle, meeting its leaders at Honolulu and again at Manila in September 1966, striving to energize the South Vietnamese war ef-fort.

But Johnson's claimed optimism amounted to posturing. Were the war sit-uation really so wonderful, the deployment of North Vietnamese divisions at the DMZ would not have posed the threat the administration clearly took it as. For all the exertion, a glance at the war maps of early 1967 shows the Lib-eration Front and Hanoi controlling the same areas as in 1965; the pacifica-tion data had moved a bare five percentage points in Saigon's favor (and most of this could have been accounted for simply by the refugees packing resettlement camps controlled by the South Vietnamese). During Cedar Falls–Junction City, U.S. troops captured a document with the NLF's own assessment that it controlled a million fewer Vietnamese than in mid-1966, but this situation existed with minimal changes in hamlet control.[12] Mean-while, the infiltration and order of battle estimates indicated the adversary had only grown in power. MACV's 1967 campaign plan explicitly concluded that "despite known losses, [the enemy] has been able to maintain a propor-tional counter buildup to the growth of US . . . forces."[13] Indeed, General Westmoreland relied on these very data in demanding a massive new aug-mentation. The Pentagon Papers describe the Washington atmosphere at this time as one of "hedged public optimism."[14]

The burden of Vietnam had become inescapable. Gone were the days when President Johnson could engage on the sly, failing to disclose the full extent of troop deployments and disguising their budget implications. In his State of the Union address for 1967, Johnson had to ask for a tax surcharge on all Americans to help pay for the war. A request for $12 billion in supplemental funds, plus $21.9 billion for Vietnam in the new fiscal year, followed. Draft calls were up dramatically and increasing, and Selective Service began to eliminate deferments that had shielded graduate students plus families with members already in the military. Opinion polls remained stable but brittle, with slight gains for the antiwar side and fewer respondents who expressed no opinion. Protesters came out in larger numbers. At Stanford University on February 20, Vice President Humphrey had to be physically extricated by his Secret Service detail when protesters surrounded his limousine and began pummeling it.

Congressional backing also weakened. Around the time of Sunflower, LBJ spoke again with the leadership in an attempt to evaluate the potential for replacing the Tonkin Gulf resolution with a more explicit grant of authority. He was told there was no chance of that at all. Instead, opponents of the war attached amendments to the budget supplement, prohibiting the use of monies for operations in the DRV or for augmentation of MACV and supporting negotiations. Although another amendment approved of the U.S. effort, it too backed negotiations. Johnson prevailed on Mike Mansfield to table both in favor of a rider that—Mansfield assured him—consisted entirely of things LBJ himself had said, but this too noted hope for a settlement and deplored expansion of the war. Johnson signed it into law on April 4. He never raised the matter of new authority again.

Another possibility, one that might energize South Vietnam, would be the implantation of democracy. This would be the major focus when LBJ conferred with Thieu and Ky at Guam in March 1967. After U.S. prodding, Saigon leaders had permitted the drafting of a constitution, with presidential elections scheduled for late in the year. But political development only inched ahead while ARVN performance remained lethargic, as illustrated when North Vietnam concentrated forces to attack Quang Tri city. The most visible changes were the builders' final touches on Independence Palace in Saigon. Its reconstruction to an airy, modern Vietnamese design was almost complete, following the bombing of 1962. The new president would have a fancy new home, resplendent with almost as many reception halls as there were members of the Saigon government's cabinet. Remarkably, amid all that space, Saigon's National Security Council would meet in a room right off the entryway, just steps from the entrance to the palace's underground bunker.

In this climate MACV brought forward its latest troop proposal. By now the generals were up to "Program 4." The previous fall the Joint Chiefs of Staff had won approval of a reinforcement program for 1967. Sharp and Westmoreland had asked for enough units and individual augmentations to bring the total to more than 542,000 troops. Analyses by the Office of the Secretary of Defense had questioned some requests, and the Joint Chiefs had shown that the recommended forces would affect U.S. military deployments worldwide. Secretary McNamara went to Vietnam to review the proposal with Westmoreland. McNamara forwarded, and LBJ approved in November 1966, a smaller final recommendation that would bring MACV to 470,000 by June 1968.[15]

At this time, the idea of a DMZ defense line, originally proposed by scientists advising the Pentagon, had been percolating for months and led to a technology program for electronic sensors to enable the United States to extend the barrier across the Laotian panhandle to the Mekong River. McNamara encouraged the exercise. Westmoreland opposed it. The JCS were more ambiguous but took a generally dim view. Impressed by the claims of the technologists, on January 13, 1967, Johnson approved a presidential directive giving the barrier the highest national priority. This order, NSAM-358, was the *only* strategic or programmatic directive LBJ issued on Vietnam during the last four years of his presidency. All his other orders concerned machinery for pacification or methods of selling the war to Americans. Johnson clearly saw the DMZ barrier as one of those fresh concepts he wanted.

Westmoreland responded within days, specifying requirements for the "strongpoint obstacle system," as it would officially be known, and the Joint Chiefs fleshed out the plan over the next month. But the chairman, General Earle Wheeler, invited Westy's views on troop deployments as part of JCS deliberations on how to exert pressure on the enemy. The Chiefs had been pressing LBJ on one of his most sensitive points—the need to mobilize U.S. reserves—and Wheeler likely saw this "Program 5" request as a way to confront the president.

From Saigon, MACV responded with alacrity. Just before the battle of Con Thien, Westmoreland cabled his Program 5 request. He asked for an "optimum force" increase of four and two-thirds divisions plus ten tactical fighter squadrons, in all, a 201,250 increment for an end strength of 671,616 U.S. troops. Westmoreland proposed to send one and a half divisions to I Corps and two to the Central Highlands. Of these, two and one-third divisions were identified as an immediate requirement, a "minimum essential force," to be in place before July 1, 1968. Even that amounted to more than 100,000 troops.[16]

The JCS analyzed Westmoreland's troop request. The Pentagon Papers concluded, "MACV had added little that was new in the way of strategic concept other than to reaffirm their intention to concentrate on certain priority areas."[17] Such a large augmentation hardly seemed necessary if the war was going as well as the administration publicly declared. At a minimum, such a reinforcement demanded detailed examination.

Meanwhile, the Chiefs took the Program 5 request and folded it into a broader analysis of U.S. global military commitments. This became the vehicle for demanding mobilization. Initially completed in late April and refined over succeeding weeks, the Chiefs saw a need for no fewer than twenty-nine

Army and five-plus Marine divisions, which would have created the largest U.S. military establishment since World War II. Later JCS compromises brought the numbers down to a peak Korean war size, but even that amounted to about a one-third increase. No such force could be created without mobilization. In fact, a March JCS study of whether Westmoreland's "minimum essential force" could be moved to Vietnam in one body concluded this could not be done without certain mobilization measures.[18] Lyndon Johnson would have to make the call.

Publicly, Johnson raised the temperature in a speech in Nashville on March 15, ostensibly commemorating the 200th anniversary of the birth of Andrew Jackson. Speaking to the Tennessee legislature, the president seemed combative and spoke of the need "to exact a penalty against North Vietnam for her flagrant violation of the Geneva Accords." LBJ's calm determination seemed to some, including *New York Times* correspondent James Reston, like that of a poker player who had decided to raise the stakes. Reston wrote, "Johnson looks more and more like a man who has decided to go for a military victory in Vietnam, and thinks he can make it."[19] Journalist Marquis W. Childs, reacting to the same speech, wrote that LBJ's "references to ending the war by negotiation have increasingly a perfunctory and repetitious sound as though they were made solely for the record."[20]

The question of new strategies was paramount. There were really only two possibilities: invade North Vietnam and engage Hanoi on its own ground, or invade Laos and shut off the tap for infiltrators by cutting the Ho Chi Minh Trail. Both were considered at this time.

The invasion option should properly be seen as a product of the JCS and Admiral Sharp. On March 17, as LBJ and McNamara headed to Guam to see Ky and Thieu, the Chiefs completed their paper on the movement of a corps-size force, ideal for an invasion. But a survey of options against the DRV prepared for the Guam conference by McNamara's assistant John McNaughton did not even include invasion among the possibilities. Later the JCS also did a conceptual study of a military campaign in North Vietnam that drew in the Chinese and examined how the United States could pursue such operations. The Chiefs hoped Westmoreland would be their champion at Guam and in Washington deliberations. At Guam, though the meeting devoted itself primarily to Saigon political development, South Vietnamese chief of staff General Cao Van Vien presented a plan for the move into Laos to cut the Ho Chi Minh Trail. Westmoreland said little about that but presented his own Program 5 demands. LBJ soon summoned him home for consultations.

Escalation was in the air. Senator Mansfield was concerned enough that, meeting with the editorial board of the *St. Louis Post-Dispatch* on March 17, he warned against an invasion of North Vietnam. The newspaper reported Mansfield's feeling that the president, sincere about keeping the Chinese and

Soviets out of the war, would not go along with any invasion plan, but Mansfield worried about "high-level American military officers in Vietnam" wanting "a coastal landing like that at Inchon in the Korean war." This was not permissible under the Tonkin Gulf resolution, Mansfield asserted, and it would bring China into the war as well as end the Sino-Soviet dispute, both inimical to U.S. policy interests.[21] Columnist Walter Lippmann saw Johnson's Guam conference as ominous. He referred to LBJ's carrot-and-stick technique, "which has become routine since 1965," and worried that "gestures about peace," such as Sunflower, "have been the preludes to an escalation of the war."[22]

Mansfield's warning led antiwar activists to take note, and many were sounded out by organizers desperate to divine LBJ's intentions. Bernard B. Fall, the noted Vietnam expert, had died barely two months earlier, stepping on a mine while accompanying Marines on patrol near Hue. Fall had told a Quaker leader probably just days before his death that if there were an invasion it would likely be on the DRV coast around Vinh; he also noted that there were legal problems preventing the use of Free World Forces such as the Koreans, insufficient ARVN troops, and the Americans were already stretched thin. Fall expressed skepticism about an invasion. Marcus Raskin, Fall's collaborator on a Vietnam reader and a onetime NSC staffer for Jack Kennedy, disagreed. Raskin saw several reasons why invasion might be in the cards. There were leaks about mass troop movements and amphibious exercises. Congressional aide Gar Alperovitz had been told by a friend in the White House that invasion planning was under way. Another source quoted Walt Rostow as saying, "We'll soon have to go North."[23]

Such fears conveyed urgency, and knowing what the protesters did not about actual options, Lyndon Johnson took their demonstrations as a warning. The National Student Association, its covert funding by the CIA about to erupt in a new scandal, adopted an antiwar declaration and met with Secretary Rusk, who dismissed their concerns. Sparkplugged by chaplain William Sloane Coffin, himself a onetime CIA officer, the Yale faculty also went on record against the war. Just as the Sunflower debacle was ending, a petition arrived at the White House signed by 5,000 scientists appealing for an end to the use of chemicals in Vietnam. The protests against Dow Chemical at the University of Wisconsin reflected the same skein of dissent. Shortly afterward Women Strike for Peace mounted its "Shopping Bag Moms" protest at the Pentagon. Resistance to the draft began coming into the open, with demonstrations at Cornell University and elsewhere.

By far the most compelling sign for LBJ, however, was Martin Luther King's emergence among the antiwar ranks, a position King had taken over the objections of his own advisers. Just after returning from Guam, LBJ told an aide he could not understand why King had canceled two successive meetings they had scheduled. The snubs rankled Johnson, who had worked very hard on civil rights and to eradicate poverty with his Great Society programs. When King appeared at Riverside Church to speak against the war, and again at the massive April 15 rally in New York, there could be little doubt of the reason. But LBJ was combative. He chose this moment to make a public announcement that the FBI furnished him with regular reports on the antiwar movement. This interplay continued just as the Program 5 debate came to a head at the White House.[24]

On his way to Washington, General Westmoreland stopped at Da Nang and Honolulu. In both places he gave briefings on plans to invade Laos, one of them a division-size thrust to cut the Ho Chi Minh Trail, but neither as ambitious as ARVN General Vien had advocated at Guam. The Da Nang stop apprised the Marines and the U.S. ambassador to Laos of the plans; in Honolulu the MACV chief spoke to CINCPAC staffs but missed Admiral Sharp, who had preceded him to Washington. Most remember Westmoreland's April 1967 trip as an effort to build public support in a speech to a joint session of Congress (and another in New York), but the strategic debate in Washington far outweighed the public appearance in true importance. This was not lost on everyone—Senator Fulbright commented as Westy arrived that the general's visit presaged escalation. On April 26 Westmoreland probably told the Joint Chiefs of his Laos plan after a private dinner with Wheeler. The next day came the showdown before the president.

Lyndon Johnson held two off-the-record sessions in the Cabinet Room that day.[25] All his war managers were there. Westmoreland reviewed the existing situation, and then Johnson broke at noon to attend to other scheduled commitments. The strategy talk came when the group reconvened at 4:45 PM. Walt Rostow recalled this discussion as one of only two times when he, as national security adviser, ever intervened in a cabinet-level discussion. Rostow actually did more than that, laying out the DRV invasion option.

Prior to the morning meeting Rostow fired off a memo to the president cautioning him against any immediate decisions, providing talking points, and reminding LBJ to have McNamara and Rusk comment on Westmoreland's presentation. America's field commander described the situation sector by sector, nothing much different from what LBJ had heard at Guam and elsewhere. Westmoreland worried about ammunition supplies, expressed his frank dismay "at even the thought of stopping the bombing program," and discussed the "minimum essential force" augmentation. He mentioned contingency plans, saying, "I believe we should confront the DRV with South Vietnamese forces in Laos," and he advised the same for Cambodia. Westmoreland then offered the judgment that "last month we reached the crossover point," meaning that allied forces were now killing more of the enemy than Hanoi and the NLF could replace.

President Johnson wondered why, if that were the case, MACV needed reinforcements. "When we add divisions," LBJ asked, "can't the enemy add divisions? If so, where does it all end?"

Westy answered that Hanoi would probably be able to add only four more divisions, and it might not be able to supply all those troops.

Alluding to China and the Soviet Union, Johnson shot back, "At what point does the enemy ask for volunteers?"

General Westmoreland conceded, "That is a good question."

The United States was not going to lose, the general opined, but progress might be slow, especially at current force levels. McNamara got Westmoreland to say that with existing force levels the war would continue for five more years, versus two if he got his "optimum" force or three with the "minimum essential." Rusk asked about alternatives. Rostow then mentioned both options—possible action in Laos or the DRV invasion. Rusk focused on the bombing alternatives. Westmoreland returned to the Laos option and described his plans for invasion. General Wheeler interjected that the Chiefs were worried about crises elsewhere as well as communist "volunteers" but emphasized that U.S. troops might have to move into Cambodia or Laos or, he said, "We may wish to take offensive action against the DRV with ground troops." The JCS chairman continued, "The bombing campaign is reaching the point where we will have struck all worthwhile fixed targets except the ports."[26]

Between sessions Rostow, working like a demon, wrote another, more extensive memo to LBJ. Now he cautioned against reserve mobilization and linked that judgment directly to American politics. He did not let the force issue get in the way of the offensive options being considered. Rostow's memorandum is worth quoting at length:

> As I see it, it is difficult to ask for the calling up of reserves if we are to do just a bit more of the same. We would be creating a major political crisis in the U.S. without being able to promise an early or decisive result. Westy's plan, as presented to us, was accurately defined as "ladling some water out of the bath tub while the tap is still turned on."
>
> Perhaps that is the best we can do when we consider all the political and military risks.
>
> But, before coming to that decision—and biting a tough bullet at home—we should consider whether there are ways of using our military power to turn off the tap at higher—but acceptable—risk.
>
> For example, we can mine Haiphong and other harbors, which partially closes off, at least, the tap some distance from the bath tub. We can come nearer the bath tub and partially turn it off by:
>
> —landing forces north of the DMZ and cleaning out the three divisions which are their principal instrument for diverting and harassing U.S. forces;

—putting in additional forces to cut the infiltration routes on the ground in Laos just south of the DMZ; or

—we could mount the landings and clean out the 3 divisions and have them come south to assume these blocking positions south of the DMZ, including Laos.

Rostow argued that "the American people—if they are going to be asked for major additional sacrifices of men and money—and additional risk—would rather do something big and hopefully decisive." He did not ignore communist counterintervention or other sore points General Wheeler had cited, and Rostow mentioned the diplomatic and technical difficulties entailed, but he clearly favored his large solution, suggesting that LBJ put aside "the political problems objectively involved" and ask Westy what his plan would be to win the war in the shortest time possible.[27]

When the group reconvened later that Thursday, Johnson asked questions about increasing the ARVN's effectiveness. Westmoreland's impression—a misreading—was that LBJ felt inclined to mobilize but McNamara was reluctant. Then Rostow came into the open, remarking that if additional troops went, "they should be committed in such a way as to gain a spectacular advantage." The amphibious invasion north of the DMZ seemed to him the solution.[28] By his own account, Rostow went to the map set up on an easel in the Cabinet Room and made his case. "On balance," Rostow wrote, he considered the invasion "a more effective way to proceed than going into the difficult terrain of Laos during the dry season, which, in any case, lay a half-year or more in the future." He did not believe the Chinese would intervene if the United States stayed below Vinh, and he claimed—with no basis in the record—that the intelligence estimates supported him.[29] (A few days later, State Department official William P. Bundy commented on ground action in North Vietnam, which he understood as a "contingency thought." Bundy stated, "I would be totally against it, for the simple reason that I believe the chances are 75–25 that it would bring the Chinese truly into the war.")[30]

William Westmoreland then took the floor. He responded that MACV had studied this operation and agreed it could achieve significant results. But an invasion would have to be carried out during the southwest monsoon season, already in progress, which would end in a few months. Since no troops were currently available, it would mean waiting until the spring or summer of 1968. Westy could have said more. The JCS force studies for Program 5 showed that two-thirds of the large landing craft (LSTs) in the Pacific, along with thirty-six more operated by the Military Sea Transport Service, were already providing supply services to MACV. The Navy as a whole did not possess enough amphibious shipping to embark a two-division/wing force of Marines, and more than 20 percent was already in use. In Saigon, State Department expert Douglas Pike had once asked Westy why he did not go for an Inchon-style invasion, and the general had pulled out a map and given an impromptu lecture on shipping, weather, and impossibility. About the meeting with the president, Westmoreland noted, "No one around the table, to include the president, expressed any great enthusiasm for the operation, and the discussion died with only Rostow and me participating."[31]

Meanwhile, implicit even in Rostow's presentation was an understanding that none of this could happen without reinforcements. Yet Walt left the meeting early to write up a fresh memo for the president, enclosing a series of charts summarizing statistics on combat losses—stated four different ways—showing that loss rates had varied little, regardless of the numerical strength of U.S. forces. These data undercut the argument for Program 5. Buttressed by this information, the president postponed his decision. Johnson's new reluctance became evident—he put off the decision for several months and then approved only 45,000 to 50,000 men. In the end, Program 5 came to very little. What there *would* be was more bombing, plus the DMZ barrier—the McNamara Line—a technological solution that required few new U.S. forces and, defensive in nature, threatened no further escalation.

What happened in the White House was invisible to the wider public. Well connected as he was, Arthur M. Schlesinger jotted in his diary on this watershed day, April 27, 1967: "We are reaching some sort of crisis on Vietnam. L.B.J. has evidently decided on a quick and brutal escalation of the war." One point Schlesinger did not miss: "The administration is apparently determined to advance the proposition that dissent is unpatriotic, and has brought General Westmoreland back for this purpose."[32] But the wider public, including Congress, the media, and citizens, drove the final nail into the invasion's coffin. Just four days after the big meeting, columnist Joe Alsop took Rostow aside and asked questions indicating that he knew all about Westmoreland's "minimum essential force" demands. That kind of red flag always sent Lyndon running in the opposite direction. Without the forces, there could be no invasion. Then on May 7 the *St. Louis Post-Dispatch* reported that the administration had been debating an invasion of the North, explicitly mentioning an "Inchon landing."[33] Very quickly politicians began taking positions on the issue. Missouri senator Stuart Symington observed that an invasion would involve the Chinese and have incalculable results. Then a prominent Republican and early candidate for the presidential nomination in 1968, Michigan governor George Romney, told audiences he feared intervention by both the Chinese and the Russians.

Secretary McNamara filed a draft presidential memorandum on May 19 that brought the debate full circle. Among its other points, his paper concluded that in the case of a U.S. invasion of North Vietnam, "we would expect China to respond by entering the war with both ground and air forces," and the Soviets would increase their support to Hanoi. An invasion of Laos he judged similarly unwise.[34] In his commentary on the McNamara paper, Rostow now declared that he agreed: "I do not believe the best use of our forces is to invade Cambodia or Laos. Nor should we decide now to invade the southern part of North Vietnam." Rostow wanted to preserve the option, however, so that Johnson could exercise it the following year.[35] A month later, at the Glassboro summit between President Johnson and Premier Aleksei Kosygin, Anatoly Dobrynin listened as Harriman and other U.S. delegates gave private assurances that Johnson had completely ruled out both invasion and the use of tactical nuclear weapons.[36] Instead of invading the North, Johnson approved an aerial bombardment of the port of Haiphong, along with other targets close to the center of Hanoi.

■ ■ ■ In the North Vietnamese capital, military and party officials were well aware of the dangers of an American invasion. Defense Minister Vo Nguyen Giap built up the People's Army in Vinh Linh, above the DMZ, and presided over a large-scale reorganization of forces throughout the coastal areas as well as air defenses fighting the U.S. bombers. Several naval coastal batteries were refurbished, and the artillery regiments of three VPA divisions reallocated to coast defense. Provincial militias formed "water combat teams" to fight the continuing incursions of U.S.-led "Footboy" (the descendant of OPLAN 34-A) Swift boats and American naval vessels. Militias regrouped the village units into larger formations and built fighting positions at likely landing beaches. Aerial photography confirmed some of these developments for U.S. commanders.

Meanwhile, the stream of reinforcements continued moving through the North Vietnamese panhandle on their way south. A U.S. invasion at Vinh or elsewhere would have put American troops squarely across the pathway sustaining this flow of VPA forces, facilitating Hanoi's ability to concentrate against an invasion. As the Chinese-Vietnamese war of 1979 would show, local Vietnamese troops were capable fighters, and many would have fought a U.S. invasion. The battle area would have been close to North Vietnamese supply sources and villagers hostile to Americans. The resulting ground campaign would necessarily have been conducted entirely within the adversary's air defense environment—something not true of the war in the South, and a situation entirely outside the United States' Vietnam experience. In short, Hanoi's problems would have been *simplified* by an American invasion, even as action confronted DRV allies with the very situation that guaranteed their intervention. When Ashmore and Baggs visited Hanoi in early 1967, they had listened as Colonel Ha Van Lau, the DRV's representative to the International Control Commission, exuded confidence: though Hanoi might have a breaking point, by then, "the matter becomes academic so far as we are concerned, for the Socialist countries would intervene and it would no longer be our war, but the beginning of World War III."[37]

General Giap agreed. He not only appeared at conferences held to emphasize invasion preparations; Giap sounded the same theme in articles later that year, writing that an invasion amounted to assaulting "the mainland of a member country of the socialist camp." In May the *Chicago Daily News* reported that Chinese foreign minister Zhou Enlai had discussed the possibility of committing his nation's combat troops against a U.S. invasion. Although Beijing denied the reports, it turns out that a Hanoi delegation had been visiting China at exactly that moment. Giap had headed the military wing of that group.

In his articles Giap noted, "We have adequately prepared ourselves and are ready to deal destructive blows . . . if they adventurously send infantry troops to the north."[38] He also argued that invasion would increase the dispersion of U.S. forces and facilitate their annihilation. During a postwar interview General Nguyen Xuan Hoang, chief of the VPA's military history institute, told an American that of all the U.S. options, "the landing would have been the most foolhardy. We knew that we could easily defeat as many as a hundred thousand men there."[39]

All this may have denied Washington's option, but Hanoi still needed a strategy of its own. The DRV's system was different, but its deliberations were just as important as Johnson's. By 1967 Ho Chi Minh, aged and infirm, was more patron saint than key player. This would be his last strategic debate. The collective leadership in the Politburo, headed by Pham Van Dong, made the final decisions based on recommendations from subordinates. There were four main channels of advice. One was the Vietnam Workers (Lao Dong) Party itself. Another was the Central Military-Party Committee, which brought together senior cadres and military leaders. Parallel to that stood the General Staff of the Vietnam People's Army, headed by Van Tien Dung. General Giap remained the VPA defense minister. In the South General Nguyen Chi Thanh, top field commander of the Central Office for South Vietnam (COSVN), also suggested strategic approaches.

Western accounts frequently portray Hanoi's decision simplistically, as a contest of wills between Generals Giap and Thanh. In this version Giap argued for protracted warfare in the South, whereas Thanh wanted a full-scale offensive and a general uprising. The truth may never be known, but it is far more nuanced. The most recent analysis, by Vietnamese linguist and former CIA officer Merle Pribbenow, argues that, based on Vietnamese sources, both Giap and Ho opposed the idea of a grand offensive. This view maintains that General Thanh created a contingency plan for such an initiative at COSVN almost as soon as he arrived in the South and that Politburo member Le Duan became its most powerful advocate, pushing steadily for acceptance of the option until, with Thanh's help, he succeeded. In contrast, Vietnamese sources indicate that General Thanh favored the decisive attack but argued for an emphasis on defensive operations in 1966–1967 and that General Giap, though believing Hanoi should start small, backed the concept of the general uprising once "big battles" had crippled the ARVN and American forces. According to Pribbenow's reconstruction, General Van Tien Dung privately colluded with Le Duan to override objections to the plan, including those of Ho Chi Minh, in this version a champion of protracted warfare.[40]

Vo Nguyen Giap numbered among the pro-Soviet faction in the Lao Dong Party, and in fact, the CIA claims some credit for helping isolate him by inserting phony information into party debates when this faction had been curbed earlier in the decade. A purge of senior officers and party officials, even Central Committee members, took place during the last half of 1967. Known to Vietnamese as the "Revisionist Anti-Party Affair," the dispute remains poorly understood. The point of contention has been variously described as between a faction opposed to a strategic offensive versus one in favor, or between groups aligned with Beijing versus pro-Soviet officials. The one clear point is that the victims of the purge included a number of General Giap's associates.[41] Yet the protracted war strategy was Beijing's preference, not Moscow's, and General Thanh was among those who favored the Chinese. Thanh's expertise was political struggle, not military operations, so he should have been more open to protracted war—which emphasized political struggle. But the received history has Thanh advocating a general uprising. However, documents captured during Cedar Falls–Junction City show that Thanh, in fact, spoke in favor of protracted warfare and presided over a study group where the Liberation Front and COSVN agreed that Ia Drang had demonstrated that the NLF and VPA could stand up to American firepower.

Thanh and Van Tien Dung were members of Le Duan's Military-Party Committee; Giap was also, but in the minority. Presumably this gave Thanh the inside track. Dung was part politico, having been commissar of the VPA's 320th Division, and saw alliance with dominant people as his way to the top. Those persons were Le Duan and Le Duc Tho—also pro-Chinese—who were well aware of Mao Zedong's proclivity for protracted war, which Beijing had emphasized in Sino-Vietnamese talks as recently as the previous summer. Duan and Tho held commanding positions after the purge of the pro-Soviet faction. They nevertheless faced the need to compromise with moderates such as Pham Van Dong, who were increasingly concerned about the destruction wrought by U.S. bombing and favored the exploration of diplomacy. The real importance of the collapse of the Marigold and Sunflower feelers—and this cannot be emphasized enough—lay in seeming to show that the Americans were not truly committed to talks, checking

Hanoi's moderates, and opening the way to a military solution. At one level the Tet offensive happened because someone in Washington sabotaged Sunflower.

The evidence suggests these cards were in play from early 1967, and Hanoi was largely united around seeking decisive victory—the real choice being a military versus a diplomatic track, not protracted war versus full-scale attack. A North Vietnamese mission—headed by Pham Van Dong with General Giap as its senior military representative—held successive talks in Beijing, then Moscow, then Beijing again in late March and April, just weeks after the Sunflower fiasco. Several elements of these conversations point to a new direction: coordination among the allies of transport for tripled Soviet military aid; talk of the 1968 dry season as a "crucial moment," with Zhou Enlai stating, "It is possible to defeat the enemy, forcing him to recognize his defeat and to withdraw from Vietnam"; and Zhou's later casual comment that he might visit Hanoi the next year *if* the war were still on, implying some expectation hostilities might end.[42]

Vietnamese sources record that the Politburo and the Central Military-Party Committee discussed a strategy for decisive victory in April 1967, after which General Van Tien Dung sent cadres to the South for an on-the-spot assessment and to encourage field preparations. Several reviews of the concept took place that spring. Cadres, among them General Thanh, were recalled for a policy review, and General Dung is reported as dissatisfied with the original plans, wanting fresh methods and new goals and targets. The Politburo's Thirteenth Plenum approved the approach in June, its resolution calling for a decisive victory gained within a short time. The Central Military-Party Committee reviewed the resolution. Then the People's Army staff began detailed planning. At this point, not earlier, the scheme began to assume its final shape of a countrywide uprising, with Dung providing a briefing on a "general offensive–general uprising" a month later. The General Staff briefing led to a study seminar at the Central Military-Party Committee in late July 1967 and a final review by the Politburo in October. Neither Giap nor Le Duan attended. Giap left for medical treatments in Eastern Europe and the Soviet Union and would not return until after the offensive. Ho Chi Minh too sought treatment, in China. The Politburo is reported to have approved the basic plan but held its "general uprising" component for further study. But the die was cast in December and January, when the Politburo accepted the full plan at final review meetings. According to Ambassador Nguyen Khac Huynh, speaking at the 1997 Hanoi conference on the war, the objective was to win by means of attacking all the big southern towns and cities, not by engaging in a conventional battle as at Dien Bien Phu. Hanoi anticipated three possible outcomes: modest success that might reduce pressure against the North by forcing the United States to concentrate on South

Vietnam; a limited victory, which could be dangerous if it triggered a virulent U.S. reaction, such as expansion into Laos or North Vietnam (again emphasizing defenses against a U.S. invasion); or the hoped-for decisive win.

Over the next months the People's Army made a host of preparations. Sappers, just recently recognized as a service branch of the VPA, were greatly expanded, and the bulk of the force was deployed south. One of the northern sapper battalions combined with two COSVN ones to form the first sapper regiment in VPA history. Four of the finest People's Army infantry divisions were reequipped, retrained, and sent to the DMZ or Khe Sanh sector. Whole divisions infiltrated down The Trail in coordinated fashion for the first time. Units already in the South were strengthened; the main forces were expanded from 204,000 at the end of 1966 to 278,000 a year later, and combat battalions increased from 126 to 190. The Liberation Front also grew. Chinese weapons routed to the far south through the Cambodian port Sihanoukville were now used to arm the NLF, replacing its hodgepodge weaponry with AK-47 assault rifles.

The General Staff and COSVN also reorganized commands and shifted leaders. One key figure who disappeared was General Thanh. While in Hanoi Thanh suffered a heart attack and died at a military hospital. His funeral took place on July 6. Some American authors inaccurately claim that Thanh died from wounds inflicted in a B-52 strike, but VPA Colonel Bui Tin stated that Thanh collapsed after a long night of partying.[43] He was replaced at COSVN by Politburo member Pham Hung and as military leader by Lieutenant General Hoang Van Thai, deputy chief of the General Staff. General Chu Huy Man, the lion of Ia Drang, took up Thai's post in charge of Military Region 5. Major General Hoang Minh Thao assumed command in the Central Highlands, while Major General Tran Van Quang was promoted to lead the forces opposite Hue—what the People's Army called the Tri-Thien region for the southern provinces of Quang Tri and Thua Thien. Earlier Hanoi had set up a special military region for the DMZ. On December 6, 1967, the Central Military-Party Committee separated from this command a Route 9 Front, subordinate to the Tri-Thien region (also known as the B-5 Front), essentially corresponding to the Khe Sanh sector. The Saigon region was reorganized too, a series of subregions like slices of a pie aiming at the center of the South Vietnamese capital. COSVN created two forward commands— one for blocking operations, the other to lead the attack on the city.

The People's Army prepared a multiplicity of training and indoctrination materials for the offensive, including a field manual on tactics to attack fortified positions, a handbook for company commanders, and more. Numerous study groups were held to explain the aims of Resolution 13 and exhort the troops to greater effort. Indeed, General Dung sent his new deputy chief of staff, General Le Trong Tan, and a senior tactics expert, Colonel Le Ngoc

Hien, to the South to appear at these seminars and to confer with key commanders.

Giap had published a series of articles in the fall in the People's Army newspaper *Quan Doi Nhan Dan* and the party organ *Nhan Dan,* interpreting the war situation and furnishing talking points for the political officers' study groups. Collected and republished in the United States a year later under the title *Big Victory, Great Task,* Giap's articles contributed to American confusion over Hanoi's strategic debate. It is correct that Giap extolled the virtues of protracted warfare, but he did so in the context of validating past methods and repeating the line that the VPA and NLF could fight the Americans and win. Almost all the references to protracted war occurred in early portions of the work. Meanwhile, in the West, almost all the attention devoted to Giap's articles came soon after their publication. Thus CIA reports and journalistic treatments in the *New York Times,* the *Economist,* and *Newsweek* appeared when the articles were still a novelty, before Giap had worked up to his prescriptive arguments.[44]

Taken as a whole, Giap's work justified a go-for-broke offensive. He postulated that the United States had been trying to confine the conflict within a limited war framework, implying that a way to counter this could be to escalate. Giap wrote at length of artillery and Special Forces (sappers), two elements the VPA was in the process of introducing in strength. Appeals to coordinate political struggle with guerrilla and conventional operations were significant, in that such a course would be central to the success of a "general uprising." In pregnant phrasing, Giap stated, "The present time is the era of revolutionary storms." He also provided a clear rationale for immediate or near-term action, noting the possibility that President Johnson might send another 100,000 or 200,000 troops to Vietnam, figures that General Westmoreland had used in his Program 5 requests. And Giap was aware of LBJ's approval of an additional 55,000 (dating the writing to August 1967, since it began to appear in September), which would mean the presence of more than half a million troops in Vietnam by mid-1968—thus indicating a need to move before those troops arrived.

General Giap also saw opportunity. Those forces, he noted, represented a mobilization level far beyond initial U.S. forecasts and at variance with American global strategy. Pressing the United States to the wall might force it to yield. The Joint Chiefs of Staff, who were wrestling with the dire possibility of threatening their resignation to force President Johnson to approve national mobilization, would have had to agree.

Finally, Giap predicted the tactics Hanoi and the NLF would actually use. He called military operations a "bugle call" that would encourage the South Vietnamese people "to take advantage of their victories to surge forward"— an evocation of a general uprising. Giap foresaw that the People's Army and

Liberation Armed Forces would harass the enemy repeatedly, destroying units, "scattering the enemy in order to fight him."[45] As shall be seen shortly, this text correlated closely with the series of operations undertaken by Hanoi's forces during the months before the big push.

Vietnamese sources suggest that the real debate was not between Giap and Thanh but between Hanoi and its Tri-Thien leaders. The regional party committee there considered a general uprising premature, requiring more extended preparation. They advised that if an uprising truly represented the correct course, it should be timed for the early summer of 1968 to permit the necessary groundwork. They also asked for reinforcements, in particular, more infantry and artillery. Regional political officer Le Chuong brought Hanoi's answer in early December: All would do as ordained. Leaders should view the general uprising as a process, not a simple battle.[46] The mission of Major General Le Trong Tan and Colonel Le Ngoc Hien was partly to deliver Hanoi's exhortations and final instructions and to hear out the objections of the Tri-Thien leaders. In postwar reflections on 1968, former Tri-Thien commanders faulted themselves for not making their arguments forcefully enough.

Meanwhile, the one thing the debate over the origins of Hanoi's plan fails to find is any significant focus on what had become increasingly salient to President Johnson—political unrest in the United States. The North Vietnamese received delegations of American opponents of the war—Staughton Lynd and Tom Hayden were among the first in early 1966—but they focused on raising consciousness, on what later American presidents would call public diplomacy, not on U.S. political opposition as an element of strategy. Hanoi was *not* commanding the antiwar movement.[47]

Levitation

What the North Vietnamese were dimly aware of came increasingly to center stage in America. General William C. Westmoreland helped set the tone during his April 1967 visit, telling his New York audience of journalists that North Vietnam used "a clever combination of psychological and political warfare." The enemy, Westmoreland added, dwelt in the "hope he can win politically that which he cannot accomplish militarily." The general expressed dismay over "recent unpatriotic acts here at home." Although Westmoreland later professed chagrin at the ensuing storm over his chilling remarks,[48] they came at the moment of Washington's big strategy powwow and were no isolated sally. His remarks followed those of Pacific theater commander Admiral Grant Sharp, who had told a Pentagon news conference a week earlier that the protesters were encouraging Hanoi. Secretary of State Rusk claimed the protesters were backed by a "Communist apparatus" and were prolonging the war. Alabama governor George Wallace called for LBJ to jail "traitors." A pro-war advocacy group, the Support Our

Servicemen Committee, demanded that Congress enact laws against those who gave aid and comfort to the enemy. President Johnson followed suit at a Congressional Medal of Honor presentation that summer, saying that Americans were giving their lives because of antiwar activists.[49]

Such chilling statements helped Johnson by influencing the media to downplay coverage of opposition to the war. But the president did not stop there. He demanded data, investigations—something he could use to charge the protesters *were* a Hanoi or Moscow covert operation. Galvanized by another publicity blow—*Ramparts* magazine published a fresh exposé revealing CIA funding of the National Student Association, a union of college student government officials—the CIA's counterintelligence staff began an inquiry into the leak. The agency crossed the Rubicon of legality, conducting domestic operations that were explicitly prohibited by law. It asked the Internal Revenue Service for a briefing on *Ramparts*'s tax returns (also illegal), looking for anything it could use against the magazine. The FBI intensified COINTELPRO, adding journalists, intellectuals, and even individual writers of protest letters to its target list. The Justice Department had prohibited warrantless wiretapping in 1965, but the attorney general approved such taps against the SDS and SNCC. In April 1966 the FBI initiated the specific surveillance of antiwar activity in Detroit. A Berkeley administrator admitted in the spring of 1967 that the university had given the FBI its files on several students.

In February 1966 the CIA and FBI had agreed between themselves—independently of the law—to an arrangement enabling the CIA to engage in certain domestic operations. Now its Office of Security chief, Howard Osborn, asked if he could use an agency proprietary to identify threats to CIA headquarters by infiltrating dissident groups. Project Resistance became his vehicle. The security effort expanded beyond the CIA proper, with agents infiltrating Women Strike for Peace, the Washington Peace Center, the Congress on Racial Equality, and the SNCC.[50] That summer the Quaker's Friends Committee on National Legislation warned that CIA infiltration threatened the Movement, not to mention American democracy at large, but by then it was too late.

During the summer of 1967 black Americans' frustration at the lack of opportunity in inner-city ghettos and the slow progress of civil rights, after years of marches and even riots, boiled over in widespread urban violence. Detroit was among the cities affected—LBJ wrote that the events there would "remain forever etched in my memory"[51]—but riots in Newark, New Jersey, proved equally destructive. In all there would be upheaval in more than 150 cities and towns across America. President Johnson committed regular Army troops to Detroit and sent Deputy Secretary of Defense Cyrus R. Vance to oversee the restoration of order. The catalysts were different in each place, but the roots the same. When Newark exploded, activist Tom Hayden was outside playing touch football. Hayden had been in the city for several years, part of an SDS project to build a popular movement against racism and poverty. He saw the effects of Vietnam directly: "In 1965–66, as the Vietnam War escalated, I could steadily feel time running out for building an effective movement against discrimination."[52] Meanwhile, within the space of half a dozen years, Newark had been transformed from almost two-thirds white residents to the same proportion of minorities, but with whites still controlling all the levers of political power. The proximate cause of rioting there would be the mayor's determination to appoint another white member to the Board of Education, despite months of warnings from African American leaders. But the mentality of Newark police officials was such that they were convinced Hayden had started all the trouble. Only his football outing saved Hayden from prosecution. But the riots most definitely ended the SDS focus on poverty, because black-white tensions flared so hot that alliances across racial boundaries became impossible. Within months Hayden's focus had shifted to opposing the Vietnam war, and the SDS adopted its first antiwar platform since U.S. troops had started flooding into South Vietnam. That microcosm matched the wider American experience. Lyndon Johnson and Tom Hayden now had at least one thing in common, as did many warriors and war opponents: Vietnam had become the central national problem. Nothing else matched it.

The urban riots had another, even more sinister impact. President Johnson, Attorney General Ramsey Clark, Pentagon officials, and FBI director J. Edgar Hoover all quickly agreed to strengthen domestic intelligence collection and to bring the military into it. The advisory commission Johnson established under Illinois governor Otto Kerner to study the disturbances made the same recommendation, though it did not issue a report until early 1968.[53] The Army set up a task force to identify intelligence needs for civil disturbances, and an obscure unit of Army intelligence called the Counterintelligence Analysis Branch produced a paper identifying individuals and groups that might pose security problems. The Army's general counsel Robert E. Jordan later noted that he and another senior official "were concerned from the outset" by the tone of such reports, particularly the "some[what] inflammatory language, which seemed to draw upon some of the worst of the prose style of . . . FBI subversive reports."[54]

The FBI itself moved quickly after the riots. In his August testimony before the Kerner Commission, FBI director Hoover, whose Bureau had long followed the civil rights movement and targeted many of its participants as "subversives," acknowledged failure. Since late 1966 FBI field offices had had orders to report twice monthly on racial conditions, including on *all* civil rights and black nationalist groups. Hoover now demanded efforts against "vociferous rabble rousers," and the Bureau set up a "Rabble Rouser Index" maintained by the Domestic Intelligence Division under William C. Sullivan. A month later Attorney General Clark canceled LBJ's instructions, issued after the 1965 Watts riots, that had confined FBI race investigations to instances of direct evidence of subversive involvement.[55]

The CIA did not lag far behind. According to director Richard Helms, the president repeatedly pressed him for information. Helms responded by creating a capability to monitor the antiwar movement. On August 15 operations boss Thomas Karamessines asked counterintelligence chief James Angleton to nominate someone to head a unit for "Overseas Coverage of Subversive Student and Related Matters." The unit became the top-secret Special Operations Group. Its chief, Richard Ober, had headed the *Ramparts* leak investigation. He began with the fifty-odd files he had already created plus an index of several hundred names. A couple of weeks later Karamessines ordered CIA stations abroad to begin feeding information to the Ober unit, which used the cryptonym MH/Chaos.

Meanwhile, the antiwar movement carried on what it had christened the "Vietnam Summer." There were appeals for peace talks, for an alliance between student radicals and middle-class voters, and to resist the draft. Spurred by fresh developments—a U.S. aerial campaign aimed at Haiphong harbor and the key bridges and power installations at Hanoi, followed by Robert McNamara's admission before Congress that the bombing had not worked—the Movement redoubled its effort. Accounts of this period are packed with stories of workshops, resolutions, conferences, and slogans. A key feature was the emergence of an umbrella group, the National Mobilization Committee to End the War in Vietnam, formed in Chicago at the end of 1966. It was originally a mixed bag of college activists plus competing communists, socialists, and others. The "Mobe" quickly outgrew its proponents' aims and eclipsed the SDS as a visible source of opposition. According to socialist antiwar activist Fred Halsted, the Mobe brought out the largest contingents for that spring's demonstrations, succeeded in reaching high school students, and overcame old divisions among protest groups.[56] Kirkpatrick Sale, the noted historian of the SDS, concedes that the organization lost its vanguard role on the war, particularly after renouncing additional Washington demonstrations following its 1965 march, but he gives SDS credit for draft resistance: "it is safe to say that without the impetus of SDS as a national organization . . . draft resistance would never have reached the proportions it did."[57] The SDS inspired a mass draft card burning at the April peace rally in New York, which gave the draft much greater national prominence.

Two issues played crucial roles in the disintegration of the political consensus that had enabled presidents to prosecute the Vietnam war. The draft was one. The inequities in terms of who would be drafted, amid the military's demands for more bodies, affected both American youths and their families. Implicated in these inequities were the institutions—notably colleges and universities, but also local police departments and courts, plus municipalities across the nation—that cooperated with the Selective Service. The second issue would be complicity in the war. Corporations producing arms and equipment, as well as universities doing research for the war effort or permitting recruitment by the government and corporations, were all vulnerable. The Wisconsin protests against Dow recruiters were only one example. Protests against secret research were mounted at Chicago, Columbia, New York University, Stanford, and the University of Pennsylvania, to name a few; protesters marched against recruiting at Brown, Columbia, Cornell, Iowa, Iowa State, Missouri, Northern Illinois, San Francisco State, SUNY–New Paltz, Wisconsin, Nebraska, Toledo, and UCLA, among others. Corporations and colleges beset by public protests over time reduced exposure by narrowing cooperation with the government and ultimately exerted their own pressure on Washington. Dow Chemical, for example, eventually stopped making napalm. What began as an irritant became another obstacle to Washington's prosecution of the war.

Draft resistance struck at the war machine by affecting its supply of recruits. Already this movement had been gathering force. In 1966 the newest edition of the Quakers' *Handbook for Conscientious Objectors* sold 11,000 copies in just a few months and went into a second printing. Draft card burnings, which had been scattered and spontaneous, became organized and witnessed by masses of supporters. Stanford held a conference where David Harris, its student body president, encouraged draft resistance, sparking a national movement. Within months more than 2,000 Americans had signed pledges to refuse induction. In October Harris and three colleagues returned their draft cards. Simultaneously, antiwar intellectuals Arthur Waskow and Marcus Raskin released a treatise titled "A Call to Resist Illegitimate Authority." It began with the fact that war had never been declared, followed with an analysis of the dubious legal basis for involvement in Vietnam, then argued that resistance was a citizen's moral duty. Within months that too had acquired thousands of signatories.

Authorities arrested David Harris and others for returning their draft cards—under the Selective Service law, Americans were to be in physical possession of their draft cards at all times. They went to prison, where they were honored by other convicts as political prisoners. Raskin; Dr. Benjamin Spock, the renowned pediatrician and a SANE stalwart; William Sloane Coffin; and others accepted 237 citizens' draft cards, handed over at Arlington Street Church in Boston during the course of "Stop the Draft Week" that October; three times that number were tendered in other protests nationwide. When the group took draft cards at a demonstration in front of the Department of Justice and then attempted to give them to the attorney general, they were arrested on conspiracy charges. Their trial was marred by governmental misconduct—the defendants were bugged, the wiretaps not divulged, and exculpatory evidence suppressed—and their conviction would be over-turned on appeal. In the meantime, on October 26 Selective Service director General Louis Hershey instructed the nation's 4,081 local draft boards that participants in "illegal demonstrations" should be immediately stripped of deferments, reclassified as eligible, and inducted into the service.[58] Such actions put the Johnson administration in the position of openly repressing civil disobedience.

The antiwar movement had also begun building bridges to the Vietnamese. In September a delegation of forty made the trip to Bratislava, Czechoslovakia, to attend a conference organized on the American side by Tom Hayden and Dave Dellinger. They met with a Vietnamese delegation half that size, featuring representatives from both the DRV and the NLF. It was the biggest Vietnamese mission that had appeared in Europe since Geneva 1954. Afterward seven of the Americans toured North Vietnam.[59] Rennie Davis, one of them, an old SDS-er, came away mightily impressed. Davis was being driven down a road when U.S. bombers struck up ahead. He could see the explosions and thought his group would be stranded for a week. Suddenly, shovel-laden peasants emerged from nowhere and patched up the damage. The visiting Americans then attended local meetings, where they were greeted by spontaneous applause. "It could *not* have been programmed," Davis observed. "These people were about something I could not even comprehend."[60]

Another thing that happened that spring would be a call for a fresh mass protest in Washington in October, organized around the theme "Bring the Boys Home." Fred Halsted notes this had been a main goal of the Socialist Workers' Party (SWP) and other socialist delegates to a Mobe meeting in May. That summer the idea took form. At a national conference in Chicago to deliberate strategy—hung between the twin peaks of black militance and 1968 electoral politics—they speculated on a Martin Luther King–Benjamin Spock ticket, but it came to nothing, leaving mass protest as the way forward. Halsted and Mobe official Dave Dellinger recruited activist Jerry Rubin to lead the full-time staff preparing for October. Son of a Teamster labor organizer, Rubin had previously been instrumental in creating the Vietnam Day Committee and in organizing the first big protests at Berkeley. Now he set to work on a Pentagon demonstration to culminate a two-day program.

What would become a collaboration between Rubin and activist Abbie Hoffman began when Rubin, preparing for the Pentagon action, met Hoffman in New York's Greenwich Village. Hoffman had been working on civil rights with the SNCC until that organization, now refocused on black nationalism and its attendant "black power" goals, essentially drummed out its white members. Hoffman had raised eyebrows and attracted international media attention in August when, in a creative evocation of the evils of capitalism, he, Rubin, and Stewart Albert got into the New York Stock Exchange and scattered 1,000 dollar bills from the balcony, causing pandemonium as traders rushed to grab the money. Incredibly, from the perspective of the hundreds of billions squandered in the Wall Street foibles of the early-twenty-first-century economic crash, this stunt halted trading on the Big Board.

Hoffman signed on happily for the Mobe action and became the prime mover for the Pentagon portion of the event. An irreverent scion of the 1960s counterculture, Abbie expressed hope the protesters might "levitate" the Pentagon through the sheer force of their love. It would be "an exorcism to cast out the evil spirits." Hoffman felt contempt for the Old Left, with its fear of protesters with pot and Marxists with flowers in their hair, but he was equally scornful of the SDS, whose members brought their own clean sheets to conferences. Tom Hayden spoke of building a new America. Hoffman's interest went more in the direction of tearing it down, after which a new social order could emerge. As for the October action, he said, "We are throwing everything we have at the Pentagon—that evil hulk that sits like a cancerous death-trap on the beautiful Potomac."[61]

Say what you like about Hoffman's sixties mind-set (he would become more practical later in life, although depression led him to commit suicide in 1989), he managed to wade through many sand traps while preparing this protest. Some fretted at Hoffman's effort to attract the counterculture with ideas such as the levitation. The SDS leadership worried about political correctness—could they be seen in the company of Trotskyists from the SWP?—and ended up giving only nominal support, intending to use the march simply to recruit new members. Socialist Workers and Women Strike for Peace, according to Dellinger, worried about civil disobedience and threatened to withdraw. Fred Halsted denies that. Then there were the sheer problems of logistics. New York alone sent 500 buses—every one had to be paid for in advance. The worst problem came with the Penn Central, which chartered a full passenger train to the parade committee and then tried to renege at the eleventh hour—an action that bore the earmarks of an FBI disruption attempt. When the coalition threatened that their next protest would be at Penn Station and the Port Authority of the City of New York, the train suddenly materialized.

The Johnson administration was well aware of the march and had been since at least August, when the coalition announced its intentions at a press conference. On September 20 President Johnson pondered what to do with a group that included Secretary McNamara, Attorney General Clark, and Undersecretary of State Nicholas Katzenbach. McNamara reported FBI estimates that the marchers would number 40,000 to 50,000 and might "move against" the White House and Capitol in addition to the Pentagon. McNamara prepared to bring in troops and had already organized a planning group under Paul Nitze, deputy secretary of defense. Those at the meeting considered but rejected a court injunction to prohibit the march for which parade permits had already been requested and would be issued two days before the event. A command post would control security, supervised by the Justice Department. All three top officials advised LBJ he should "consider being away from the White House on those days."[62] On October 3 Johnson asked for daily reports on countermeasures and thundered that no bunch of protesters was going to run him out of town.

Numerous other actions aimed to reduce the protest's impact. On September 26 LBJ met with a group of Harvard faculty, emphasizing his reasonableness. Among other things, Johnson told them, "We do not want to invade North Vietnam. We never thought it would bring us military victory."[63] The administration did what it could to encourage expressions of support from Congress and organize competing events, trying to spark simultaneous pro-war demonstrations. Early in October Johnson ordered the CIA and U.S. Information Agency to try to stimulate events abroad that might divert the energies of protesters. It should also be noted that Lyndon Johnson chose this moment—September 29, to be precise—to deliver a speech in San Antonio that renewed his commitment to seek negotiations. Here he made an apparent concession, reestablishing the original Phase A–Phase B formula in public, where it could not be subverted. He softened the requirements to be levied on Hanoi by giving up the demand that the DRV stop supporting the war in the South, asking only that Hanoi restrict itself to the existing level of support. Although the San Antonio speech is usually viewed in the context of negotiations, it had an unmistakable domestic political dimension.

Paul Nitze and Deputy Attorney General Warren Christopher were working on the Washington protest within a week of the first session with LBJ. They treated the event like a military campaign, with forces arrayed in Task Force Washington. Countermeasures took place under the rubric Operation "Cabinet Maker." A nationwide intelligence alert nicknamed "Lantern Spike" began in late September. The Army's 116th Military Intelligence Group (one of McNamara's sources of information at the meeting with the president) already had orders to infiltrate the marchers, and the 108th Group would recruit informants. Nitze recalled later that getting agents into SDS ranks (he may have been using the term to refer to the Mobe as a whole) had not been difficult.

On October 14 the Army Security Service (ASA), a component of the National Security Agency, received orders rescinding a 1963 ban on domestic activity. No objection came from ASA chief Major General Charles J. Denholm. The radio crews were not only to monitor civilian communications during the march but also to be ready to jam them or send deceptive messages. The ASA activated no fewer than thirty-four listening posts for these purposes, most of them right in the Pentagon. The CIA lent a sophisticated communications van plus two technicians to run it. A week later agency director Lieutenant General Marshall S. Carter sent a cable ordering NSA personnel worldwide to report any indications that foreign governments were controlling or advising peace groups; the identities of foreign agents exerting such influence; and the identities of American individuals or groups in contact with them.[64] Carter told other U.S. intelligence chieftains he would inform them of any results. There were none.

Across the land, FBI and Army agents visited train, plane, and bus companies, tracking reservations and charters, obtaining license numbers, and interfering where they could. Ramsey Clark told the president the protesters would try to hire as many as 1,000 buses, but "the indication is that they will only be able to secure about 150"—the FBI must have been working overtime. The FBI, Secret Service, U.S. Marshall Service, Department of Justice, General Services Administration, local police jurisdictions, and the military were all involved in Cabinet Maker. On October 18 Clark advised LBJ he expected fewer than 30,000 protesters.

Underneath the Washington Mall an old gymnasium near the Justice Department was converted into the command post. It would be staffed by several hundred persons, including Nitze and Christopher. The post had TV screens, teleprinters, phone banks, and radio equipment. The District of Columbia deployed 1,500 police, backed by 200 Virginia police and state troopers. The federal government lent 236 U.S. marshals and 140 park police and mobilized the 2,575-man D.C. National Guard. In addition, the Army had 7,861 troops at the Pentagon and brought in a secret reserve—another 2,485 soldiers of the 82nd Airborne Division landed at night by helicopter to avoid giving away the game. They were put in the Pentagon's inner courtyard, out of sight and ready to emerge from any of its transverse corridors. Some 15,000 troops throughout the eastern United States were placed on alert as well.[65]

President Johnson rode out the protest at the White House, ostentatiously attending National City Christian Church that Sunday morning. LBJ's intelligence proved to be wrong. Crowd estimates ranged from 50,000 to more than 100,000. The *Washington Post* reported 55,000 on October 22. There were young and old, men and women, locals and out-of-towners, veterans and active military. A Pentagon official among the marchers kept running into people he knew at The Building. Another encountered his brother, who lived in another city and whom he had never known to express any feelings about the war. A CIA officer found other agency people among the marchers.

The brass decided to surround the Pentagon with a cordon of troops, primarily National Guardsmen. Army officials warned against either overreacting or underreacting, and Nitze put an outer line of U.S. marshals between the protesters and the soldiers. Daniel Ellsberg, now an analyst with the

Rand Corporation, used his Pentagon identification card to cross the picket lines and watch the crowd from the upper floors. Ellsberg had recently finished work on McNamara's review that would become known as the Pentagon Papers. He went up to the third-floor conference room near the secretary's offices. McNamara stood inside, next to the window, and invited Ellsberg to come have a look. Neither spoke. Also at The Building that day were former deputy secretary Cyrus Vance and JCS chairman General Wheeler. Warren Christopher came by later.

"They did it all wrong," Bob McNamara told a journalist years afterward. "The way to have done it would have been Gandhi-like. Had they retained their discipline, they could have achieved their ends. My God, if 50,000 people had been disciplined and I had been the leader I absolutely guarantee you I could have shut down the damn place."[66]

McNamara watched from the roof and circulated through The Building. He recalled women rubbing their breasts against nervous National Guardsmen, moving up close and unzipping their flies; others throwing mud balls or rocks, picket signs or leaflets. Abbie Hoffman noted *one* instance of the unzipping of a fly, but mostly he observed ex-soldiers, girls, students, and priests talking to military policemen. He and his girlfriend made love on the lawn. In Hoffman's stream-of-consciousness account, "Our alternative fantasy will match in zaniness the war in Vietnam."[67] A girl placing a flower stem down the barrel of a soldier's rifle is documented in photographs. Fred Halsted saw burning draft cards, graffiti written on Pentagon walls, and campfires built on The Mall. "It did indeed have the look of a siege about it, with government officials lining the roof of the Pentagon observing the scene."[68] A late-afternoon sally toward a parking ramp was the major bit of militance, but troops stopped the protesters, and only a handful actually made it into The Building. There was nothing to justify the Army's communications intercept effort. At midnight, security forces announced that the protesters' permit had expired and swept the area. There was tear gas, some clubbings, and 675 people were arrested and booked, among them Hoffman and Norman Mailer; another couple hundred were taken into custody but released.

Mailer portrayed the march and the jail experiences of the protesters in his passionate *Armies of the Night*, which won a Pulitzer Prize and affected many Americans' views.[69] Halsted's analysis of the net impact is significant. Direct effects on GIs remained conjectural, but there would be a considerable effect on the Movement: "Before the Pentagon action, the idea of reaching GIs was pressed by a minority. After October 21, 1967, the movement as a whole began to embrace the idea with some enthusiasm."[70]

Equally significant would be the impact on the executive branch of the U.S. government. Abbie Hoffman *did* levitate the Pentagon—or, more accurately, Lyndon Johnson—though not the way he imagined. At a Tuesday

Lunch on November 4, LBJ called the protesters "Communists," claimed he had protected civil liberties since he was nine years old, and rasped, "I'm not going to let the Communists take over this government and they're doing it right now." Johnson wanted to get the story out, and he wanted security measures taken. LBJ had already talked to the attorney general. Helms of the CIA shot back, "Under the laws of this country you cannot prosecute anybody for anything." There was more.

"I've got my belly full of seeing these people put on a Communist plane and shipped all over," Johnson added, referring to the activists who had gone to Bratislava and then on to North Vietnam. "I want someone to carefully look at who leaves this country, where they go, why they are going, and if they're going to Hanoi, how are we going to keep them from getting back."[71]

In the immediate aftermath the Army set up a study group to revise its plans for civil disturbances, while the president ordered a government-wide review of emergency plans and authorities. Military intelligence joined the FBI in widespread surveillance of the Movement, the CIA went to a new level with Project Chaos, and Lyndon Johnson fixated on the opposition as a foreign-controlled threat. The NSA started a watch list of individuals it would monitor under what the agency called "Project Minaret." On that list would go the name of every American who traveled to Hanoi, and soon enough, many more would be added. A great deal of government misconduct followed from the Pentagon levitation.

At a White House meeting to review the events of that weekend, the president took CIA reporting on the Bratislava encounter between antiwar figures and Vietnamese delegates as evidence of foreign control. Johnson then demanded the CIA study the subject. Its paper, presented on November 15, 1967, found no such evidence. LBJ demanded more. But the U.S. government had fielded the equivalent of an infantry division against American citizens, and now it escalated the Vietnam conflict on a second front, within the United States.

A Probing Debate?

Possibly the most notable casualty of all of this would be Robert S. McNamara. The secretary of defense, buffeted by Vietnam, as were all Americans, had shed his early enthusiasm. For some time McNamara's repeated public assertions of confidence had cloaked private doubt. Hoots of derision greeted McNamara when he described this anguish in his 1995 memoir *In Retrospect*,[72] but there is a paper trail. In the last half of 1967 McNamara's pessimism emerged plainly, both within the administration and in public.

War policy to a great degree had been expressed through President Johnson's decisions on General Westmoreland's repeated bids for more troops. Action on each of those augmentations had been framed around formal memoranda from McNamara that took positions on the proposals. As early as the fall of 1965, Mr. McNamara's papers began to show a wavering confidence. In February 1966 at the Honolulu conference, McNamara invited a few reporters up to his hotel room. Stanley Karnow sets the scene:

> His face was grayer and his patent leather hair thinner, and his voice lacked the authority it had when he projected his rosy appraisals in public. The sustained United States air offensive against North Vietnam launched exactly a year before by President Johnson had not succeeded, he told us—and would not. An agrarian society could not be blasted into submission, he said with unusual passion: "No amount of bombing can end the war."[73]

Actions, McNamara warned LBJ, might not yield anticipated results. By May 1967, responding to Westmoreland's 200,000-troop request, McNamara came out against the large solution while also warning of what he saw as false strategic options, like invading the DRV or Laos. This was a far cry from 1964–1965, when he had conspired with Dean Rusk and McGeorge Bundy to keep George Ball's objections from the president.

Secretary McNamara also diverged ever more from Rusk, who remained steadfast in backing force until early 1968. McNamara later referred to the irony of the secretary of defense spearheading negotiating efforts while the secretary of state demanded military action. Peace envoy Harriman recalled McNamara asking, at the height of the aborted Marigold feeler, "why we weren't able to open up channels of communication with Hanoi."[74] The whiz kid would be distressed by the manipulations that destroyed Sunflower, and when the next opportunity arose in mid-1967, he took a central role. French delegates at an international meeting on disarmament approached Harvard professor Henry Kissinger and offered their contacts in Hanoi—one was a personal friend of Ho Chi Minh—to carry messages. This developed into a feeler code-named "Pennsylvania," and McNamara personally dictated some of the messages Kissinger carried to the French intermediaries and later to North Vietnam's Paris representative Mai Van Bo. At the 1997 Hanoi conference on "missed opportunities," McNamara recalled being awoken by the phone at two or three o'clock in the morning for news of Pennsylvania's progress.[75]

This feeler, like others, proved abortive, but it helped crystallize Bob McNamara's doubts. In addition, McNamara was struck by a personal loss, the tragic death of his close collaborator and assistant secretary John T. McNaughton. A key architect of the Vietnam engagement strategy—and the associated Rolling Thunder campaign—McNaughton died in an aircraft accident in late July, shortly after being nominated for secretary of the navy.

The secretary's key differences were with the Joint Chiefs of Staff and Pacific theater commander Admiral Sharp. They came to a head over bombing strategy. Appearing before the Senate Armed Services Committee in early 1967, McNamara expressed doubt that Rolling Thunder had significantly reduced infiltration and certainty that no alternative bombing strategy could do so. General Earle Wheeler told the same hearing that in the opinion of the military, there had been some reduction in infiltration. Inside the administration there were huge battles over target approvals, particularly for installations within the Hanoi-Haiphong exclusion zones. President Johnson approved specific strikes, such as on the thermal power plant in Haiphong, and claims were made as to their effectiveness. But 90 percent of attack sorties were against DRV transport systems or on armed reconnaissance. The big fight was over a small fraction of U.S. capability.

In particular the JCS and Sharp pushed for the bombardment of Hanoi and Haiphong, which McNamara resisted due to his doubts about its effectiveness, the cost in domestic and world opinion, and the fear that Soviet or Chinese ships would be hit, potentially triggering an international incident leading to their intervention. The subject came up at the Guam conference and again during the Program 5 strategy review. In May the Joint Chiefs renewed their demands. McNamara wanted to emphasize attacks south of the twentieth parallel. Within a month, before the actual decision, what he feared happened. Soviet ships were bombed at Haiphong and another port. Fortunately, the Soviets confined themselves to diplomatic protests.

Officials lined up on the recommendations. Newly appointed Saigon ambassador Ellsworth Bunker, who had replaced Cabot Lodge, questioned the efficacy of the bombing but later supported the military. Air Force secretary Dr. Harold Brown backed the existing program. Admiral Sharp argued that the bombing had finally begun to show the real potential of airpower and the time was ripe for "a precisely executed and incisive air campaign."[76] The back-alley fight centered on Rolling Thunder 57 and climaxed when McNamara visited Saigon in July. There, General William W. Momyer, the new Seventh Air Force commander; Admiral Sharp; and Admiral John J. Hyland, Seventh Fleet commander, joined to extol an effort to isolate Haiphong, "apparently with some effect," Momyer later recalled.[77] These and other results of the secretary's trip were presented to LBJ at a meeting on July 12. Commanders had already completed preparations for the aerial assault on Haiphong. After listening to the back-and-forth, Johnson approved but added, ominously, "The U.S. people do think, perhaps, that the war cannot be won."[78]

Admiral Sharp and Air Force chief of staff General John P. McConnell would go to their graves convinced U.S. forces had never been unleashed, that restrictions had crippled airpower. But the truth is not so clear. In fact, Rolling Thunder hit these targets hard. From June to August the proportion of the *entire* bombing effort directed against the Hanoi-Haiphong sector averaged between about 20 and 33 percent of total attack sorties, despite deteriorating weather in August. That amounted to more than 8,500 sorties, with Haiphong enduring more strikes than the capital in both July and August. This was the equivalent of aiming at Haiphong and Hanoi individually an effort equal to *all* of Rolling Thunder in the fall of 1965. Another peak came in October, when almost 2,000 sorties targeted Haiphong and more than 1,400 hit Hanoi—exceeding 35 percent of the Rolling Thunder total. By the end of 1967 only four approved targets within the Haiphong exclusion zone remained untouched, and Washington had approved more than two-thirds of all potential targets there. In his official report on the war a year later, Admiral Sharp himself released figures showing that bombing had reduced Haiphong's cargo handling capacity by more than half, and a whopping 56 percent of trucks and railway cars destroyed by Rolling Thunder in 1967 had been taken out in the Haiphong and Hanoi zones during July and August alone.

There can be no doubt that air commanders had thrown their best punch. Yet Vietnamese infiltration in preparation for the planned offensive in the South increased immensely over the same period.

At the height of all this, a subcommittee of Senator John Stennis's Armed Services Committee gave the generals a platform for an extended attack on McNamara's management of the air war. In a series of hearings through August, all the Joint Chiefs, plus Admiral Sharp and General Momyer, testified. McNamara was sandwiched among them. General Wheeler repeated his judgment that the bombing had reduced movement to the South, "particularly supplies over the last several months."[79] (In White House councils Wheeler argued that Hanoi would view a bombing halt as an aerial Dien Bien Phu, an argument calculated to get LBJ's back up.) Before Congress, Secretary McNamara stuck to his guns, but senators faulted him for micromanaging. Stennis leaked data embarrassing to the secretary, whereupon the White House defended McNamara.

It was in this context, with President Johnson biting the bullet and announcing only minor reinforcements for Westmoreland, that Army chief of staff General Harold K. Johnson contemplated resignation and, in fact, whether he should try to convince the other Chiefs to join him en masse. Such a JCS action would have represented a protest from the Right, which Johnson and, to some extent, McNamara feared more than the Left. But public support for the administration had diminished, dropping below 50 percent in May, subsuming a fall in conservative demands for action. Equally telling, the number of Americans with no opinion also fell—the public had taken sides. By the time of the demonstration at the Pentagon, opposition exceeded support in opinion polls.

Washington had also put much stock in the notion that presidential elections in South Vietnam might convey new legitimacy to the war. By summertime White House meetings were devoting considerable attention to this prospect. LBJ labored mightily to get the Vietnamese elections just right. General Nguyen Van Thieu quickly positioned himself as a candidate. When it looked like Nguyen Cao Ky might challenge Thieu, the United States applied enormous political pressure on Ky, on the South Vietnamese generals who supported military candidates, and anywhere else it seemed useful. Ky, certain that Thieu could not win an election against him, believed the generals were unanimously behind him and that even the Americans, including Ambassador Bunker, preferred him to Thieu. Only Westmoreland differed. But at a crucial meeting Ky made a spur-of-the-moment decision to return to the air force. After appeals from the generals, Ky reluctantly agreed to join Thieu as the vice presidential candidate on a joint ticket.

The CIA hired political consultants to help them, although Washington resisted giving money to the candidates or instituting a formal covert program. Both agency and embassy propagandists served up a diet of information designed to reinforce the Thieu-Ky ticket. The Saigon leaders themselves manipulated the electoral law to maximize their chances, and they were aided by a large field that included ten other candidates, who split the Vietnamese vote. The most formidable opponents, among them former general Duong Van Minh as well as a leading Buddhist, were not permitted to run. The Thieu-Ky ticket captured 34.5 percent of the vote. In second place with 17 percent of the vote was Truong Dinh Dzu, who had advocated a bombing halt and negotiations with the NLF. Along with third-place finisher Phan Khac Suu, the civilian president whose intransigence had brought Ky and Thieu to power, and another candidate, Dzu charged the elections had been rigged. Thus, the elections did not yield the legitimacy Washington had hoped for.

The turbulence did nothing to calm political waters in America. All were affected. Government officials were citizens too. Pentagon bureaucrats regaled one another with talk of intense disaffection among their colleagues. Rusk acquired the reputation of an iron man, but he faced a break with his younger son Richard, a former Marine who turned against the war and in fact joined Vietnam Veterans Against the War. Rusk and his son later jointly wrote the diplomat's memoir, where Rusk admitted to getting through Vietnam on aspirin, scotch, and four packs of cigarettes a day. Top CIA officer William Colby's wife Barbara went on protest marches, and at least one of his children also differed on the war.

Bob McNamara had personal experiences too. In three separate incidents in the summer of 1966, students had shunned McNamara or tried to shout him down at campus appearances, including at elite schools such as Amherst College and New York University. That summer he was accosted at the Seattle airport by a protester, and over the winter there was a similar embarrassing incident at an Aspen restaurant. There were also two attempted arsons at McNamara's Aspen vacation home. Even when entertaining, he had to argue the war with activist Sam Brown, and during dinner with good friend Jackie Kennedy, she pounded his chest and demanded an end to the killing. McNamara's best-known encounter took place at Harvard in November 1966. Hosts and friendly students had had to sneak him through tunnels and down an alleyway and to create diversions to get McNamara in and out unscathed, but there had been a terrifying moment when the secretary had been trapped in a car with protesters all around. It is notable that at Richard Neustadt's defense policy seminar, where McNamara spoke that evening, he replied to a young law student that no secret data justified the war. "There is no such information," he had said. "I base my views on the same information that you read in the *New York Times*. I may receive it a day or two ahead of you, but it is essentially the same."[80]

It was then that McNamara ordered compilation of the Pentagon Papers. He would later write, "I deeply regret that I did not force a probing debate about whether it would ever be possible to forge a winning military effort on a foundation of political quicksand. It became clear then, and I believe it is clear today, that military force—especially when wielded by an outside power—just cannot bring order in a country that cannot govern itself."[81] This thought would echo down the years in the Iraq war.

For a very long time McNamara held his own counsel. He even accomplished the expert's feat of holding two opposing views at the same time without batting an eyelash. Daniel Ellsberg recounts an apposite story from McNamara's October 1966 Vietnam trip. Ellsberg had become ill in Saigon and needed to return to the States, so he hitched a ride on the defense secretary's plane. Ellsberg had just completed a survey of pacification in Mekong delta villages, and during the long flight he showed his latest paper to McNamara. The secretary volunteered that conditions were indeed worse than a year earlier and then agreed with Ellsberg's pessimistic view. When the plane landed at Andrews Air Force Base, McNamara marched down the stairs to the cameras and klieg lights and the crowd of reporters. It was a foggy morning, Ellsberg recalled, but McNamara was clear: he told the world that he was pleased and encouraged by all the progress in Vietnam.[82]

Official records document the same duality. In deliberations on Westmoreland's big troop request, McNamara's presidential memoranda expressed his gloom, but in a meeting with LBJ in July, McNamara told the president, "operations are proceeding well" and "reports on the scene are better than press reports at home."[83] McNamara may well have been referring to a piece in *Time* magazine that depicted the enemy as powerful as it had been a year earlier, if not more so.[84] Clark Clifford quoted McNamara denouncing such stories: "There is no military stalemate in Vietnam!" Pacification, he said, had exceeded his expectations. When Clifford probed further, asking about the growing public view that the war could not be won, McNamara shot back, "For the first time, I feel that if we follow the same program we will win the war and end the fighting." The same was true of the air war. "There is a limit to what the enemy can afford to send to the South," McNamara told Clifford. "We are destroying a significant number of the large units."[85] But a month later the secretary of defense would tell the Stennis hearings, "Enemy operations in the South cannot, on the basis of any reports I have seen, be stopped by air bombardment."[86] McNamara spoke of inflicting losses and held that out as a benefit but kept the view that Hanoi's supply requirements were so small, and the capacity of the Ho Chi Minh Trail so large, that bombing would never stop the flow.

McNamara never discussed his private doubts with Clifford, but he did with Harriman. The two met on July 1, just before McNamara's Saigon trip. McNamara called Rusk much too rigid, "too optimistic over what could be achieved." In fact, Rusk's objectives—which were the military's—could not be attained. Harriman recorded: "Bob McNamara said that (1) it is impossible for us to win the war militarily; (2) that he hoped that the pressure on the President from the hawks wouldn't be so great that the war would be expanded into confrontation with the Soviet Union or China; (3) he felt the most helpful way of ending the war through negotiations would be for Saigon to negotiate with the NLF."[87]

Three days before his testimony to the Stennis subcommittee, McNamara told Harriman that after the South Vietnamese elections, "We must tie our bombing and other military policy to the objective of negotiations."[88]

Mr. McNamara did the same in private. Almost the first thing President Johnson did after the Pentagon demonstration was to invite key legislators to the White House for a confab with his top advisers, including McNamara, Rusk, and Helms. LBJ delivered a soliloquy on why a bombing halt would not lead to negotiations, why the bombers were needed in the war—some North Vietnamese were even talking about another Dien Bien Phu, he said—and how he was not prepared to act "simply on hope." Secretary McNamara jumped in at that point. "We cannot win the war with bombing in the North," he said. "The great danger is to lead our people to think we can win the war overnight with bombing." McNamara spoke in favor of limited action in the north plus operations in South Vietnam. Johnson redirected the conversation. "We do have our differences," LBJ remarked.[89]

Fast-forward to the aftermath of the levitation. McNamara must have been reflecting on his reticence. Also striking was a paper written on October 27 by Johnson's speechwriter and political conscience Harry McPherson. He noted that even middle-of-the-road Democrats who supported the war—"Harry McPhersons in private life"—had grown edgy about the bombing. McPherson feared the bombing had become a surrogate for the whole war, that it rallied world opinion against the United States and created the greatest obstacle to talks. He advised refocusing the air campaign on the portion of North Vietnam just above the DMZ.[90] President Johnson laid on fresh efforts to shore up his position. As part of that, LBJ summoned a blue-ribbon group of former top officials—generals, diplomats, and political advisers—who were to be briefed then render their opinions. That was scheduled for November 2. Ahead of this session with the so-called Wise Men, Johnson held a Tuesday Lunch on Halloween. Suddenly McNamara erupted. "Continuation of our present course of action in Southeast Asia," he averred, "would be dangerous, costly in lives, and unsatisfactory to the American people."[91]

The next day Robert McNamara handed LBJ a nine-page single-spaced paper in which he laid bare his opposition to further escalation and recommended "stabilizing" the war over a fifteen-month period and handing over much of the responsibility to Saigon—the outline for what became Vietnamization. Bombing should be reoriented exactly as McPherson had suggested. The paper argued that U.S. forces were making some progress, but over the long haul, Washington stood no closer to victory, and in the meantime, political opposition could easily outrun military achievements. In retrospect, this was a prescient analysis.

McNamara also raised the timing issue for President Johnson, who faced an election campaign in 1968. Evidently taking his cue from what had been done to George Ball, McNamara showed the paper to no one, especially not to Rusk or Rostow. Clifford was no doubt correct in asserting that McNamara's action was premeditated—he had to have worked up this lengthy proposal over the days since the Pentagon demonstration.[92]

What followed was unprecedented. Not LBJ's ad hominem questioning of McNamara's stability, loyalty, and ties to Bobby Kennedy, but what the president did with the recommendations. They were kept from the Wise Men, who were given bland briefings by the Pentagon and CIA and delivered predictable stay-the-course advice. But inside the administration Lyndon Johnson gave instructions that the paper be retyped to hide the identity of its author and then circulated to senior officials. Clifford and Abe Fortas, who were aware of LBJ's feelings about McNamara, and General Maxwell D. Taylor, who was not, knocked his arguments down hard. Rostow did the same, warning the president against being "pushed off the middle ground you now hold" and allowing the Republicans to "move in and crystallize a majority around a stronger policy." Holding the line might lead to increasing progress. Rusk disputed McNamara's predictions but agreed with some of his recommendations. Significantly, both Rusk and Rostow agreed with McNamara that no invasion of North Vietnam or Laos should be attempted. General Westmoreland opposed both any program of stabilization and any bombing stand-down.[93]

The most striking response to the McNamara stabilization proposal came from Undersecretary of State Katzenbach. He took the Pentagon chief's essential points—that Hanoi would continue fighting and that its military requirements were well within its capabilities—and, like LBJ, began to link North Vietnamese strategy to the antiwar movement in a way Hanoi had not yet done: "The additional costs we can still impose on North Viet-Nam without invading the DRV weigh far less in Hanoi's scales than the value of continuing a fight which they believe we will be prepared to abandon relatively soon." There was, he thought, justification for "Hanoi's belief" that "public and Congressional opinion will not permit the United States to keep meeting immense costs," so that—and Katzenbach underlined this—"*the war can be lost in the United States.*" Warning the United States had objectives "which we cannot prove we are in the process of achieving," the undersecretary saw the alternatives as escalating for a knockout blow or preparing for the "longer pull." Katzenbach's "center position" strategy and the measures he prescribed for carrying it out basically followed McNamara's analysis.

This evokes a question about presidents and the advice they seek. Did Robert McNamara force a probing debate? Certainly Lyndon Johnson treated the McNamara critique in an unusual fashion. And McNamara did furnish LBJ the opportunity for deep reflection. McNamara's pained judgment is that he failed, but the secretary of defense hardly had the ability to force the issue. Johnson did. And Johnson started down that road, demanding his advisers respond to this "anonymous" critique. But LBJ satisfied himself with their, for the most part, tepid arguments and failed to take up Nick Katzenbach's clear warning, drawing only the instrumental, short-term conclusions the president put in his own commentary. Though the president rejected McNamara's analysis he clearly recognized its significance. There is one indication that LBJ went further—the private conversation he had with William Westmoreland signaling that he might withdraw from the White House, if not South Vietnam—but in the main, Johnson reacted by erecting a mountain of rationalization to justify his steady course.

The closest parallel in recent history is George W. Bush and the Iraq war. Beset by a plethora of troubles and yawing failures in war strategy, his policy decisively rejected by the American people, who gave both houses of Congress to the opposition, Bush got his opportunity in late 2006 when an Iraq Survey Group recommended a new strategy, including a reorientation of the effort combined with a gradual withdrawal. Bush made a show of ostentatious consultations, only to reinforce existing policy with his troop "surge." In the fall of 2007, when the surge was scheduled to reach its promised end, Bush orchestrated an elaborate sequence of reports to enable him, again, to hold steady. When security conditions in Baghdad seemed to indicate progress, he hastened to cancel any withdrawals beyond the surge troops and not even all of them. Bush, like LBJ, built a mountain of rationalization, although Johnson, at least, did so privately. Both presidents actively resisted crafting an exit strategy. The parallel with Lyndon Johnson in 1967 is striking.

For present purposes, the crucial point is that the McNamara critique posed to the president of the United States, directly and for the first time, the proposition that the Vietnam war could be lost in America. Far from politics merely constraining Johnson's range of choices, it could determine the outcome. Lyndon Johnson and his predecessors had engaged the nation, but the nature of the war, LBJ's strategic decisions, and the international context made it impossible to win before political factors predominated. The antiwar movement was a consequence of those choices, not their antecedent. Katzenbach put the result quite plainly: "Time is the crucial element at this stage of our involvement in Vietnam. Can the tortoise of progress in Viet-Nam stay ahead of the hare of dissent at home?"[94]

After all this, Lyndon Johnson did something quite unprecedented. He wrote his own memorandum for the record. This document is virtually the only contemporaneous, considered, personal judgment by LBJ on the war. The rest of the Johnson record, huge as it is, consists of off-the-cuff statements at meetings or on the phone or speeches crafted by his staff, massaged as they may have been by the president but nevertheless not his own. Johnson wrote the memo on December 18, just before leaving for Australia. In it he made the McNamara paper his subject, conceding that it raised "fundamental questions of policy with reference to the conduct of the war in Vietnam," declaring that he had studied it "with the utmost care," and adding he had also consulted with "certain advisers," specifically mentioning General Westmoreland and Ambassador Bunker. In his text Johnson ruled out a unilateral bombing halt as a sign of "weakening will," encouraging the "extreme doves" so as to "increase the pressure for withdrawal from those who argue 'bomb or get out.'" He followed Rostow in using a new CIA-run peace feeler through the Liberation Front, one called "Buttercup," as another reason to keep bombing, and LBJ sided with Rusk in saying the United States ought not to announce any policy of "stabilization." But Johnson had also spun out all his thread: "I see no basis for increasing U.S. forces above the current approved level." There would be no wider war on his watch: "As for the movement of U.S. forces across the frontiers of South Vietnam, I am inclined to be extremely reserved."[95]

All that remained was the question of Robert McNamara himself. As Clifford notes, the November 1 paper made it impossible to keep him on the president's team. It happened that the previous spring the defense secretary had run into World Bank president George Woods, who was looking to recruit a successor. McNamara was interested. He had reported the conversation to LBJ but assured the president that he would leave only when he, Johnson, wished it. Unbeknownst to McNamara, Woods had approached Johnson during the summer to ascertain McNamara's availability. LBJ had made no reply at the time. But four weeks after the defense secretary's bombshell paper, Johnson suddenly announced McNamara's appointment to head the World Bank. The former secretary of defense later observed, "I do not know to this day whether I quit or was fired."[96]

■ ■ ■ If there was a way to keep Lyndon Johnson's shoulder to the grindstone, Walt Rostow would find it. The national security adviser had a distinct view and worked hard to sell it, patching up his arguments when they frayed. Rostow actively bolstered LBJ's beliefs too. A favorite Rostow technique was to forward selected pieces of analysis. He did this with documents captured from the North Vietnamese or the NLF when it suited his purposes, with news stories, and with think-tank papers. Among Rostow's favored commentators was Rand Corporation president Henry Rowen, Dan Ellsberg's boss. Rowen tried to put Vietnam in a heroic context, comparing Lyndon Johnson's role to Abraham Lincoln's in the American Civil War. Rostow sent LBJ at least three papers with this identical argument over the space of a couple of years, advancing the notion that the United States was winning and the problem lay simply in getting the word out. In the March 1967 version of Rowen's thesis, Rostow colored in the picture, saying in a cover memorandum, "In short the [Civil War] analogy would call for our pouring it on in Vietnam so that our people can see clearly the end of the road in 1968, even if the end is not fully achieved."[97] By autumn the problem had magnified, and a majority of Americans now believed the war was being lost. Encouraged by Rostow, LBJ hit on the idea of a new interagency group to sell the war, not just any group, but one headed by Rostow himself. Johnson underlined its importance days after the McNamara bombshell when he told his war managers, "It doesn't do any good to win the war over there and lose it over here. We've got to get our story told."[98]

Thus spurred, Rostow's unit, the Vietnam Information Group (VIG), redoubled its efforts. Formed in obscurity that August, this NSC subcommittee played a crucial role and indeed had a certain impact. By dint of focused, sustained moves designed to affect the public, the administration edged past antiwar opinion by a couple of points. At the end of 1967 the polls suggested that Americans might back further escalation. This had the ironic effect of contributing to the disasters of 1968. It is astonishing that the VIG has attracted so little attention.[99]

One reason is that issues and events have been treated as if they occurred autonomously and not according to a script. This is especially puzzling since, in the years after Vietnam, the public's subjection to orchestrated information campaigns has become so commonplace as to acquire a jargon, with terms such as *spin, public diplomacy, branding,* or *rollout* of a policy entering the lexicon. Failure to examine the use of these techniques in the Vietnam era is a notable gap in our knowledge of the period.

A good example is the "order of battle" dispute, which became important to Rostow's group. Order of battle is the military term denoting the specific identification of forces by their component formations, strengths, equipment, and so on. Orders of battle are used by planners of military movements or campaigns, and adversary orders of battle enable intelligence officers to estimate the threat. In Vietnam the order of battle of Hanoi and NLF forces amounted to a key intelligence question, and accounts of the war usually confine it to that arena. But Hanoi's order of battle, combined with infiltration numbers and data on "body count" (losses inflicted on the enemy), underlay claims of progress in the war. This made order of battle estimates as important to the VIG as to senior military commanders.

This is not the place for a detailed recitation of this dispute. Whole books have been written on the subject, and it also featured in a controversial television documentary and possibly the lengthiest and most contentious lawsuit to arise from the Vietnam experience.[100] But a few details are useful here. Captured documents were an important source of intelligence, but these were often imperfectly or incompletely translated. Sam Adams, a CIA analyst who insisted on greater detail, noticed wide discrepancies between U.S. reports on the strength of NLF units in the Mekong and the Liberation Front's reports for its own high command. After some pilot studies, Adams began a wider sampling of captured documents and eventually convinced the CIA that true strength figures for the NLF and Hanoi forces were far greater than those in the order of battle. By early 1967 the CIA was officially pursuing these discrepancies with the military. In March, in a cable dealing with political sensitivities in Washington and how they were affected by MACV's revision of data on enemy attacks, JCS chairman Wheeler put Westmoreland on notice that such data could undercut support for the war. After that, Westmoreland rode herd on MACV order of battle estimates.

An initial dispute took place over a special national intelligence estimate of Vietnamese communist capabilities compiled by the CIA that spring, in which the agency used its order of battle figures rather than MACV's assessment. Differences over the numbers held up the estimate for months. This led to attempts to reconcile the two projections, first at a conference at CIA headquarters and then at another in Saigon. At the second, in September, the CIA tabled its data but acquiesced when MACV officers stonewalled, manipulating the figures and making cosmetic concessions on some types of enemy forces but showing a lower overall number by excluding whole categories of Liberation Front guerrillas and cadres. Agency special assistant for Vietnam, George A. Carver, crafted the final compromise, likely on his own, but some say on the orders of CIA director Helms. The special estimate, published in November, contained lower order of battle figures than even the Carver compromise. It slashed the projected size of enemy combat forces to an overall 208,000 at most—more than 100,000 fewer than previous CIA estimates, and far less than suggested by Adams's and other CIA research (in the 500,000 to 600,000 range). Worse, the estimate's figure of 118,000 for the total of VPA and NLF regulars came in much lower than the 278,000 that Hanoi now tells us it actually had. These numbers would have direct implications for the war.

Carver was a member of Rostow's VIG. It is also significant that participants in the Saigon order of battle conference included MACV's public relations chief. Hardly had the ink dried on the "compromise" when Westmoreland's publicists began working on a press release citing the order of battle figures to enable briefers to claim progress in the war. The VIG massaged this release. Rostow's group went back and forth several times with MACV on the final text. The proposed MACV briefing was discussed at the VIG on October 23, the day after the march on the Pentagon, and at its next two sessions as well. The VIG agreed on publication but remained "concerned about doing this in a manner which would properly represent the actual situation in Vietnam, i.e., the increasing attrition of enemy forces, rather than in a way which would confuse the reporters and lead to unfavorable stories."[101]

On November 9 Secretary McNamara pushed his public relations people at the Pentagon to get the numbers out as soon as possible. Soon the briefing took place, and the figures were all over the press. Reporting to the president on the CIA's estimate with the phony numbers, Rostow was not above telling LBJ that the key conclusion was that "manpower is the major problem confronting the Communists," and although captured documents showed that "guerrilla strength was probably underestimated last year," it had supposedly "declined substantially since."[102] Five days later the VIG discussed how to handle future order of battle figures. Meanwhile, Westmoreland tried to defend the practice of using body counts and told Johnson he had hard evidence that real enemy losses were *greater* than reflected in these soft numbers. Here the top leader of the nation, as much as the public, became the target of manipulated information—afflicted by the Vietnam data problem—in accordance with the preferences of subordinates.

Rostow's group met weekly in the White House Situation Room. There can be no doubt of its centrality to the president's enterprise. Not only did Rostow periodically raise VIG issues with Johnson; he also took guidance from LBJ. The group both organized an information program and coordinated responses, for example, to the battles that raged in South Vietnam in September and October or in defending McNamara against charges he had stymied the Joint Chiefs on the air war. Efforts included neutralizing stories regarding U.S. use of chemical weapons, allegations of torture in interrogations, and charges that U.S. strategy was being driven by election-year politics.

Surfacing the order of battle was just one VIG project. In mid-September Rostow pulled together statistics the president could use in congressional skull sessions. Later that month the VIG drafted a speech to be used to convince officials, using pacification data, that they had a great story to tell. "You and I share a problem," it began. "We have got to find a better way of explaining to the American people how the Viet Nam war is going."[103] The VIG concluded that LBJ himself should not use this text, and there is no evidence it was ever voiced. But the subject—population control data—became a recurring theme at the VIG. One proposal that never took off was to contrive a new white paper on North Vietnam's role in the war, like the ones the State Department had put out in 1964 and 1967. The propaganda wizards eventually settled for a less ambitious paper that became part of State's public information series.

The overarching question of "measures of progress" preoccupied the VIG. Members worked on a proposal to send "potentially helpful academics and intellectuals" to Vietnam and, later, on an office for "control of visitors." Another issue—one LBJ specifically plugged—was to put out the word on South Vietnamese army achievements. Other initiatives included assembling a handbook of captured documents suggesting enemy morale problems, preparing a comparison of the present situation with that in 1965, and selecting stories that could show the accomplishments of combat units. Joint television appearances by Ellsworth Bunker and William Westmoreland in November, and by Robert McNamara with Dean Rusk in early January 1968, were also planned by the VIG. In a television appearance on the CBS program *Face the Nation,* Bunker supplied an image that haunted the White House long afterward. "I think we are beginning to see light at the end of the tunnel," Bunker said.[104]

A project that merits comment is the "blue book," assembled by MACV in November at the direction of Rostow's group. Like the order of battle press release, this document—a compilation of data in chart form, ostensibly prepared for Johnson's cabinet—was actually printed by the White House Situation Room staff, probably by the CIA, which provided many of its personnel. The blue book underwent a continuing process of comment and revision until judged just right. The spiral-bound collection of four- by six-inch charts on blue card stock summarized pacification data, Vietnamese election turnout, North Vietnamese versus friendly troop strength and maneuver battalions, ARVN desertion rate, casualties, enemy defectors, port and airfield construction, and supply tonnage movements. The election chart was inserted on Rostow's specific orders.[105] The blue book's true purpose became evident when it was artfully leaked to the *Los Angeles Times.* The *Christian Science Monitor* received the pacification data in more detail, and *Business Week* turned up with data on enemy attacks and kill ratios, the very statistics Walt Rostow had collected in September.

In mid-October Johnson operatives met with lawyer Abbott Washburn and representatives of the pro-war, White House–inspired National Citizens

Committee for Peace with Freedom in Vietnam, which staged an event to claim widespread public support for the war. The VIG considered what to do about this thread in the Situation Room on October 16. No record of that discussion is currently available.

Vietnam Information Group staff accumulated a morgue file of press clippings that were referred to whenever necessary. One staffer put together anecdotes to use at press briefings and in speeches (among the offerings was a State Department intelligence analysis holding that General Giap sought to fight a "protracted war" and thus his *Big Victory, Great Task* articles acknowledged "there has been little if any progress for the Viet Cong over the past year").[106] Another staffer managed what was, in effect, a "truth squad" operation that countered—the same day—every critical speech appearing in the *Congressional Record*. Others conducted a survey of international attitudes on Vietnam, which found ten governments in open opposition, six neutral in public but privately critical, sixteen noncommittal, four supportive but critical of specific U.S. actions, thirty-nine privately supportive but unwilling to say so, and twenty-two backing Washington (communist bloc nations were not included in the survey). Staff studied the editorial positions of the U.S. press, breaking down opinion in a similar fashion. On November 20 the VIG discussed setting up a database of prominent war critics and the positions they took.

Accounts often note that the administration engaged in a "big sell" of the war,[107] but they fall short of showing just how purposeful those White House efforts were.[108] Journalist Don Oberdorfer, who had recently joined the *Washington Post,* wrote in late November that all the data did not really demonstrate success.[109] He was also the first to delve into the administration's opinion-shaping attempt in his book *Tet!*[110] The reporter interviewed Rostow, by then out of office, and wrote of a "psychological strategy committee" that had worked the issue, but he too failed to capture the full scope. Rostow had in fact worked for a Truman-era NSC unit known as the Psychological Strategy Board, established specifically to manipulate global opinion in the Cold War. This allusion reveals Rostow's attitude in running the VIG. Far from mere public relations, Rostow's VIG in effect conducted psychological warfare against the American people. Just as LBJ's wont for protective security overstepped the bounds of constitutionally protected liberties, now the spin doctors reframed the American polity as object. Both these developments were in place before the end of 1967.

The most insidious piece of what Oberdorfer referred to as Johnson's "success offensive" originated with the CIA. Helms passed on the advice of a congressman who thought that LBJ ought to summon Westmoreland home to reprise his triumphal tour of the spring. Resplendent in his uniform, with his rows of decorations, Westmoreland could claim progress with an authority the White House and Pentagon civilians could not match. There could be no doubt of the purpose here. The summons went out on November 3. Meanwhile, contrary to the VIG's efforts to deny any connection between Johnson's strategy and his political purposes, several days later General Wheeler cabled Westmoreland that the "highest authority is now thinking in terms of assigning priority to those programs which would have a maximum impact on progress in South Vietnam within the next six months."[111] This matched a presidential instruction to the Joint Chiefs to propose measures having the greatest impact within ninety days. One target date corresponded to the first primary of the campaign season, scheduled for New Hampshire in March, the other to the nominating convention.

The showiest piece was Westmoreland's visit home. As the general himself noted, the summons was ostensibly for consultations "but in reality for public relations purposes."[112] The urgency is suggested by the fact that Westmoreland left Vietnam even though at Dak To, in the Central Highlands, Major General William R. Peers's 4th Infantry Division had just stumbled into an intense battle with Hanoi's legions. Westmoreland gave press conferences, testified on Capitol Hill, met privately with Rostow on the McNamara memo, and participated in one White House meeting with the president, but Westy's speech at the National Press Club on November 21 would be the sting. "I am absolutely certain," America's field commander intoned, "that whereas in 1965 the enemy was winning, today he is certainly losing." Hanoi sought to prolong the war, Westmoreland argued, and its desire to force the United States "politically" to stop the bombing was of "essential importance." He foresaw 1968 beginning a new phase, "an important point when the end begins to come into view." Subsequent to that—Westmoreland joined a growing chorus of officials who alluded to handing the war over to the South Vietnamese—American withdrawals could begin.[113] Returning to Saigon, the general told staff that the scheme gave Americans a sense of "some light at the end of the tunnel."[114] The phrase copied Ambassador Bunker, pregnant with consequence.

President Johnson had graciously invited Westmoreland to stay at the White House during his visit, and one event occurred that only the two of them knew about at the time. LBJ took Westy aside late one night, told him that McNamara would be leaving, and asked how GIs might take it if Johnson did not run for reelection. His health was worsening, and the intractable conflict bedeviled him. Westmoreland said nothing then, but the subject would come back soon enough.[115]

◼ ◼ ◼ Thus 1967 was a crucial year for the Vietnam war. Hardly recognized at the time, and little enough since, by its end a host of vital pieces were in place. Lyndon Johnson's crucial markers were evident: there would be limits on U.S. forces and no invasion of North Vietnam or Laos.

Both public and international pressures were pushing the United States toward talks. And Johnson had thoughts of leaving the White House. LBJ had abandoned escalation as a strategy but had also given bombing a chance, and he had unleashed the security services against those who opposed the war. Hanoi had decided on a big offensive and made ready to attack. Public support for the war wavered, with the antiwar movement active and rising, supple enough to accommodate Abbie Hoffman and Jerry Rubin's creation of a Youth International Party—the Yippies—essentially a vehicle to demonstrate the absurdity of the "system." To counter opposition the White House now conducted sustained efforts to mold opinion that set America up for disaster. It is among the great ironies of the war that Lyndon Johnson's success in turning the nation's eye toward victory is measured by the perception of failure in its biggest battle.

Among the South Vietnamese army's general officer corps, Pham Quoc Thuan represented a sort of norm. Close in age to Nguyen Van Thieu, Thuan had been his chief of staff when Thieu commanded an ARVN division. These were the grand old men of the army. Nguyen Cao Ky and his contemporaries were younger, hungrier, ready to take on all comers. Thuan hailed from the North, from Ha Dong, outside Hanoi, where he had been a district chief. He had joined the French-sponsored Vietnam National Army after graduating from the Military Academy at Dalat. Given his Catholic origins, Thuan advanced rapidly, forging enduring links to Thieu. Their wives even developed business ventures together. Now Thuan commanded the ARVN 5th Division. In the South Vietnamese scheme of things, leadership of the 5th was a key post because that unit shielded Saigon, making its political loyalty crucial. Thuan had been an obvious choice. By the fall of 1967 he had held that command for over two years.

General Thuan's division both protected Saigon from prospective coup forces and defended the approaches to the city from the direction of Cambodia. Highway 13, the main road between Saigon and Phnom Penh, ran right through Thuan's sector. That made his 5th Division a natural target for NLF troops seeking to get close to the capital, and events in October 1967 put Thuan on the front line.

The enemy had its own purposes. The Liberation Front was not out to attack Saigon—at least not yet. The Central Office for South Vietnam (COSVN) still had many preparations to make for the general offensive–general uprising. Hanoi had decided this would take place in conjunction with the lunar new year (Tet) at the end of January 1968. Its most important task was reorganization: COSVN needed to refine its control structure, and in October 1967 it created two forward commands as well as focal-point sectors to replace the old military subregions in the Saigon area. Reinforcements needed to be incorporated, including a regiment of People's Army regulars from the Central Highlands, an NLF regiment, half a dozen rocket launcher or mortar units, and an equal number of independent infantry battalions, along with specialist units—including sappers—newly arrived via the Ho Chi Minh Trail. All this shuffling would surely attract attention. Lieutenant General

Hoang Van Thai, who had replaced the deceased Nguyen Chi Thanh as field commander, decided to distract the ARVN's attention by launching a major attack on the troops of General Thuan.

Thai's plan also had another aspect—one Giap had discussed in his articles. The forces in the South had never conducted coordinated operations with troops from different commands. Giap had written of the need for this, and the general offensive required it. Hoang Van Thai intended to give his units practical experience by means of a series of attacks against Loc Ninh, a district capital on Highway 13 about seventy miles north of Saigon. The ARVN 5th Division held Loc Ninh as part of its defense system along the Cambodian border.

Hanoi gave final approval for what has become known as the Tet offensive in October, later confirmed by a party resolution. Part of the scheme's genius lay in the realization that the groundwork could not be laid without Washington and Saigon becoming aware of it. The plan therefore included a deception, an alternative set of expectations the Americans could believe in. In each major war zone Hanoi would battle near the South Vietnamese border, giving the impression it intended to carry out a more conventional operation. The deception began at Loc Ninh, and its first target would be General Thuan.

Hoang Van Thai slated Vo Minh Triet's 271st Regiment to spearhead the attack. Triet would be critically delayed. Searching for food in a local base area, his unit found and ambushed an American battalion. Two companies of Lieutenant Colonel Terry Allen Jr.'s 2nd Battalion, 26th Infantry, were virtually annihilated in this firefight, with fifty-six dead, including Allen himself and the brigade operations officer, seventy-five wounded, and two missing. The battle was chronicled in David Maraniss's book *They Marched into Sunlight*.[1] The NLF could have engulfed the American remnants, but Triet had his own mission. Typically, the MACV spinmeisters played the fight as another victory, albeit a bloody one. The only successful aspect, however, would be that Triet's regiment reached its intended battlefield too late to play its assigned role.

General Thai opened the main action by blooding his new VPA unit, the 88th Regiment, hitting the command post of one of Thuan's ARVN battalions in a sector east of Loc Ninh, along the Song Be (*song* is the Vietnamese word for "river"), on the night of October 27. The VPA troops were repulsed after several assaults. Two nights later the battle moved to Loc Ninh itself.

Nestled in a gently rolling plain in rubber country—many of the 10,000 or so Vietnamese who lived in the district worked for the plantations—Loc Ninh had been little affected by the war. Some plantations had been abandoned, but the largest, the Société des Caoutchoucs d'Extreme-Orient, fully met its schedules. The managers had their compound on a hill overlooking the town, complete with tile-roofed villas, flower beds, manicured lawns, a red-clay tennis court, and a nice-size swimming pool. Loc Ninh also featured a U.S. Special Forces camp, established the previous December to watch the border, held by Detachment A-331 of the 5th Special Forces, with three companies of Vietnamese, Nung, and montagnard irregulars. The camp lay southwest of the plantation, at the edge of Loc Ninh's airstrip. At the other end stood the ARVN district headquarters, encompassing some old French buildings plus more recent bunkers, crowned by an observation tower and surrounded by concertina wire. The district chief, Captain Tran Minh Cong, held sway there, backed by two understrength companies of ARVN Regional Forces, barely 100 men in all.

At 1:15 AM on October 29 the attack began, directed at Captain Cong's position. While a battalion of the NLF 273rd Regiment heaped fire on the Special Forces camp, mortars of the NLF 84th Artillery bombarded all the positions. The 273rd assaulted the district headquarters. Within an hour, the Liberation Front had penetrated the compound. The ARVN retreated into a corner of the post, holding the last positions fiercely. Cong called in artillery fire on top of his own bunker. In all, 611 shells were fired in support. Cong later told reporters he had not been worried: "This is the best bunker in Vietnam, even if you hit it with a B-52."[2] About 100 enemy bodies were left lying on the ground.

At first light the Special Forces detachment sent two companies to disengage the district headquarters, while an ARVN company counterattacked within Loc Ninh town. The notebook of an NLF political officer recorded that the insurgents occupied the town all through the night and for much of the next day. They held a victory ceremony. General Thuan arrived by helicopter with another company of the 9th Regiment of his division from Phu Loi. American troops also came to Loc Ninh, starting with two rifle companies and two artillery batteries of Major General John H. Hay Jr.'s 1st Infantry Division, which set up a firebase near the A-331 camp. Before the day ended they had blasted off another 2,326 rounds. By afternoon the NLF had disappeared, but not before warning citizens they would be back. Townspeople began to flee.

On Halloween COSVN struck again, attacking both the town and the Special Forces camp with the 272nd and 273rd Regiments. Vo Minh Triet's 271st stayed in reserve. This time an NLF battalion surged out of the rubber trees and hit the Green Berets from two directions. They never made it past the barbed wire. Captain Harry Downing's gun crews alone expended 575 shells before dawn, bore-sighting their 105mm howitzer, trimming time fuses to the nub with nail clippers, and shooting so fast the paint on the barrels bubbled and burned from the heat. There were five separate assaults on the town too. Several hundred more bodies were added to the tally. Searchers counting the dead found brand-new Chinese AK-47 assault rifles.

On November 2 came more attacks from both NLF regiments and from two more of the VPA—the 141st and 165th. The Special Forces camp again bore the brunt. Almost 4,000 rounds of artillery, complemented by a B-52 Arc Light strike, flattened the enemy.

Two full battalions of the U.S. 1st Division (joined later by a third), more of General Thuan's soldiers, some from the ARVN 18th Division, and the Green Berets swept the area over the succeeding days. South Vietnamese soldiers washed their uniforms in the swimming pool at the rubber plantation and helped themselves to its wine cellar. The last major contact occurred on November 7. U.S. troops began pulling out the next day. The battle was declared over. In all, defenders benefited from 452 air sorties, 8 Arc Light strikes, and 30,125 rounds of artillery fire. They claimed 900 enemy dead against 50 friendly killed and 234 wounded. *Time* magazine called Loc Ninh the enemy's biggest defeat since the spring, when the hill fights around Khe Sanh had yielded a body count of more than 1,200 adversaries.

Everyone got a little of what they wanted out of Loc Ninh. COSVN had succeeded in coordinating attacks from two different divisions. According to Hanoi's war history, the campaign—which it considered active until December (including two division- and five regiment-size engagements, sixty in all)—"consolidated our offensive springboard north of Saigon and marked a new step forward in the capacity of COSVN's main force soldiers to fight a concentrated battle."[3] MACV could claim a victory too, even though the 1st Division had given up a planned sweep of the Long Nguyen Secret Zone to fight at Loc Ninh. And Lyndon Johnson, who wanted publicity for the new, improved ARVN, could get Walt Rostow's Vietnam Information Group to give out details and induce MACV's public relations people to secure favorable press coverage.

The guns at Loc Ninh had yet to fall silent when a new focal point developed in the Central Highlands. This time the action went to Ray Peers and his 4th Infantry Division. The sector around Dak To had been sensitive for months. In May the Green Berets of Detachment A-244, who had a border surveillance camp there, had encountered signs of VPA presence. After the camp was shelled, Westmoreland had sent his redoubtable fire brigades, the 173rd Airborne and the 1st Cavalry Division, to augment Peers's troops. During the summer there had been repeated contact and some firefights. Now Major General William B. Rosson's corps command, I Field Force, following up new reports of North Vietnamese in Kontum province, wanted to clear them out.

Troops began arriving for the operation on October 28. On November 3, at a height called Hill 1338, a company of the 3rd Battalion, 12th Infantry encountered VPA troops of the 32nd Regiment, an enemy known since the Ia Drang campaign. Contacts multiplied. The battle expanded with fierce actions on Hill 823, Hill 223, Hill 724, and Hill 825, eventually involving several North Vietnamese regiments and a dozen allied battalions, including three ARVN paratroop formations. The worst fighting took place on Hill 875 beginning on November 17; the 173rd Airborne Brigade needed five days to capture it.

The Dak To encounters became a meat grinder for platoon and company officers. The "Sky Soldiers" of the 173rd, with 208 dead and 645 wounded, lost 27 percent of their GIs. Eighty other Americans were killed, as well as 73 South Vietnamese. Le Cao Dai, a People's Army doctor serving at a field hospital with the B-3 Front, Hanoi's command, recorded on November 22: "The enemy admits it is surrounded and cannot evacuate its wounded from our siege. The enemy mobilized paratroopers to break the siege but suffered heavy casualties. Our ground-based firepower prevented their helicopters from landing. Our soldiers have won a resounding victory."[4]

General Westmoreland thought otherwise. At the National Press Club during his visit home, Westmoreland was asked whether the Dak To battle was the "beginning or the end of anything in particular." He replied, "I think it's the beginning of a great defeat for the enemy."[5] The general did not repeat that in his later memoir, but he did write that "spectacular victory" had eluded Hanoi in this battle and that the People's Army had incurred more than 1,400 dead. In a report on the war published in mid-1968, Westmoreland claimed more than 1,600 enemy dead, a number that matched field reports. But General William Rosson doubted the field reports and estimated VPA losses around Dak To at no more than a thousand.[6] And Le Cao Dai's hospital diary makes no reference to the flood of wounded that would have accompanied such battle losses.

General Westmoreland's strategy would be a major reason why the United States was taken by surprise in the coming offensive. Afterward there were assertions that the border battles were Hanoi's bid to pull U.S. troops out of position and that the gambit had failed. But MACV had fed at least three battalions into Loc Ninh and ten to Dak To; the ARVN had sent more. In truth, Westmoreland preferred fighting on the border and advanced a number of reasons why in a December 10 dispatch. Arguing that the VPA had concentrated there in hopes of scoring victories while retaining the ability to pull back to sanctuary, Westy maintained that failure to "violently contest" every sally would yield political, psychological, and economic benefits to his adversary and that the border fights preempted Hanoi's plans, forcing the enemy into battle before it had fully prepared. The MACV commander insisted that U.S. mobility permitted engagement without jeopardizing larger goals; troops could focus on other missions until they were needed, rapidly shift forward, then withdraw after combat. He specifically cited Dak To as a model of this approach. Westmoreland not only stood ready to fight on the border; he was anxious to do so.[7]

These border battles were capped by the most critical one of all, just below the DMZ and out toward Laos, at the Khe Sanh combat base. Marines held that place, their patrols steadily finding stronger enemy forces in the surrounding hills. CIA road-watch teams in Laos, NSA communications intercepts, and aerial reconnaissance also detected a huge surge in traffic along the Ho Chi Minh Trail. The simplest hypothesis was that the People's Army intended to besiege Khe Sanh. Hanoi encouraged that belief and moved up major forces, centered on its 304th and 325th Divisions. On December 6 the Central Military-Party Committee designated leaders for the Route 9 Front. Major General Tran Quy Hai, deputy defense minister under Giap and an alternate member of the Politburo, became the commander. The Front's political officer would be Major General Le Quang Dao, a Central Committee member and deputy director of the VPA General Political Department. Their positions in Hanoi's hierarchy are a clear indication of the importance of this operation, as well as Hanoi's intention to exercise close control at Khe Sanh. The presence of the 304th Division, long the army's prestige unit, and deployed specifically for this mission, provided additional evidence of Khe Sanh's vital role in the scheme for Tet.

General Westmoreland and his MACV intelligence chief, Major General Phillip B. Davidson, had not only aerial reconnaissance data but also communications intercepts. The United States had installed a radio intelligence unit at Khe Sanh in late 1967, and it fed a steady stream of reports up the chain of command. The Route 9 Front headquarters was among those identified. Combat units in battle zones such as Loc Ninh and Dak To also captured documents, including notes of local committee deliberations on Hanoi's plan, notebooks of soldiers commenting on what they had been told by political officers, and eventually notes on, and a copy of, the Lao Dong Party's Resolution 13. A number of these contained the phrase "general offensive–general uprising." Davidson interpreted the intelligence as indicating a full-scale effort to capture Khe Sanh. Westy, entertaining visions of a Dien Bien Phu in reverse, accepted that analysis. Several officers at the CIA's Saigon station filed reports arguing that Hanoi intended a countrywide offensive, but these got no traction. In Washington the agency's special assistant for Vietnam affairs chose to undercut them. George Carver, forwarding the reports to Rostow, added a memo questioning the analysis. Rostow asserted vociferously after the war that the administration had expected the big battle—and both he and Westmoreland cited LBJ's comments to the Australian cabinet during a December visit there—but it was Khe Sanh they expected, not Tet. Typically, senior officers had MACV intelligence staff brief journalists on the alleged enemy plans, among them Don Oberdorfer, who decided he would not miss anything if he used the holiday for a quick trip to report from Laos.

According to a former Defense Intelligence Agency (DIA) analyst, he and his colleagues looked at the data and came to much the same conclusion as the CIA's Saigon station. They drafted a paper stating that Hanoi intended to draw U.S. forces to the Khe Sanh area so the populous lowlands would be left undefended. The analysis never left the building. They presented their findings to the DIA deputy director and recommended that the Joint Chiefs and MACV be sent copies of the paper. The deputy and his aides laughed and asked, "How could you possibly know more about this situation than General Westmoreland?"[8]

As the days passed, Tet loomed. More reports came in of plans to attack specific towns and villages. But each time MACV reframed Hanoi's intent as an offensive at Khe Sanh plus these other maneuvers, rather than a country-wide offensive with Khe Sanh as the sideshow. Eventually the National Security Agency intercepted messages with disturbing implications and warned of upcoming attacks throughout South Vietnam. But the NSA's official history now concludes its warnings were less than advertised. The NSA accepted the same Khe Sanh–plus thesis as the others, and it failed to alert its own personnel of a threat throughout the South or to issue special tasking requirements for ships and stations to collect intercepts on enemy action all over South Vietnam, which would have been congruent with an appreciation of the larger threat. Its warnings did not lead to actions outside the NSA either.[9] Westmoreland—and the White House—continued to focus on Khe Sanh. LBJ even had the CIA build a terrain model of that battlefield to enable him to better visualize the situation there.

Hanoi knew nothing of the inner workings of the U.S. high command, but it proceeded systematically. The Khe Sanh scenario was especially believable because the tactical position seemed like Dien Bien Phu, with a combat base entirely dependent on aerial resupply and air support surrounded, offering the payoff of eliminating a major U.S. force, a goal Giap had mentioned in his articles and the B-3 Front had embodied in its directive for the winter-spring campaign, one of the documents the Americans had captured in the field.

In the years since the war, there has been debate over whether Hanoi really intended Khe Sanh–plus or the countrywide general offensive and general uprising.[10] The evidence continues to mount for the latter. North Vietnamese sources refer specifically to a general offensive, not an all-out attack on Khe Sanh. The B-5 Front, which was responsible for Hue, a focal point, received Politburo and General Staff directives on November 19. The Route 9 Front, a subordinate command, was informed orally by senior Colonel Le Ngoc Hien. General Hai's forces were instructed to initiate preliminary attacks a week before Tet, but they were not told the date for the general offensive. The Khe Sanh sector received priority for supplies, which would have been necessary regardless of the strategic mission, since the troops there were up against a major combat base. But the role assigned by the B-5 Front, in addition to destroying significant allied units, was specifically "to draw in and pin down as many American-[South Vietnamese] forces as possible."[11]

Hanoi leaders debated their final decision on the Tet offensive in December and called a Fourteenth Plenum meeting of the Central Committee for January 1. They prepared a draft resolution. That document, along with Le Duan's speech, are now available. Le Duan's remarks closely paralleled Giap's analysis in *Big Victory, Great Task*. Le Duan told the delegates—as Giap had written—that the United States had become fully extended. He recognized the danger of American escalation arising from Tet, including a possible invasion, but judged this unlikely. Major escalation would require U.S. mobilization—even less likely. Duan provided a lengthy commentary on the evolution of the war and the political situation justifying the general uprising. The uprising would be a process—not open-ended, but not confined to a set number of weeks or months, either. This discussion likely reflected the differences between Hanoi and the Tri-Thien (B-5 Front) leadership. General Tran Van Quang, the B-5 commander, though sick, had come north anyway, his presence noted by Le Duan. The role of Khe Sanh was important but subordinate in both Duan's speech and the Fourteenth Plenum's resolution. U.S. forces could be drawn out and destroyed. But the key task was to "correctly direct the primary attack against the cities"—in effect, putting "a sharp dagger through the throat of the enemy"—coupled with insurrection in rural areas and district capitals. Negotiations could be one outcome. Significantly, there was no mention of the antiwar movement in the United States—not in Le Duan's lengthy exegesis, not in Hanoi's directive. Hanoi expected a political result, but in Vietnam, not the United States.[12]

With the final directives out and the last pieces in place, the long months of preparation were over. The first act came at Khe Sanh. There, on January 20, a battalion of the VPA 95-C Regiment attacked Hill 861, one of the Americans' outlying strongpoints. The next day General Tran Quy Hai's artillery began bombarding the U.S. central position. A lucky hit ignited ammunition at Khe Sanh's main supply dump, leading to a fire and a huge disaster for the Marines. That night the 102nd Regiment of the VPA 304th Division attacked Khe Sanh village, whose defenders held until ordered to retreat by Colonel David Lownds, the overall commander. The next day Westmoreland ordered the Seventh Air Force to initiate a massive bombardment to support Khe Sanh; it became known as "Niagara." The III Marine Amphibious Force sent a fourth battalion to reinforce Lownds, while the ARVN contributed its 37th Ranger Battalion a few days later. The Americans were primed for battle at Khe Sanh. Instead, Tet happened.

■ ■ ■ Brigadier General John A. Chaisson, formerly III MAF operations staff director, had been reassigned in late 1966 to create an operations center for MACV. Chaisson would be quite blunt about Tet. "By about the skin of our teeth we were able to keep the major enemy elements out of

Saigon," he said a year later.[13] There would have been no skin if not for the responsible U.S. corps commander, Lieutenant General Frederick C. Weyand of the II Field Force, which corresponded to the ARVN III and IV Corps and its Capital Military Region. Weyand paid attention when his intelligence officer showed him a curious anomaly. The young captain, Robert Simmons (later a Republican congressman from Connecticut), was reviewing captured documents and noticed the Liberation Front had changed its post office boxes for the Saigon area. Plotting the new setup, Captain Simmons realized that COSVN had realigned its zones so they converged on Saigon. Command areas converging on Saigon—Le Duan had described them as "slices of a grapefruit" to the Fourteenth Plenum—could only mean an effort aimed at the capital. General Weyand agreed. At one of MACV's weekly command conferences and over the phone, Weyand told Westmoreland he was worried about Saigon and proposed to shift units. Between January 11 and Tet, Weyand doubled the number of U.S. battalions within the Saigon zone. Those twenty-seven battalions had much greater firepower than the ARVN in the sector. South Vietnamese generals—accorded full authority for the close-in defense of Saigon only a month earlier—may have groused, but the Americans made much of the difference between victory and defeat at Tet.

Hanoi's mistakes did the rest. The critical ones were of coordination and probably inevitable, given that this was North Vietnam's first attempt at such an ambitious, countrywide operation. To ensure its own Tet celebrations would not be marred, the DRV chose this moment to introduce a new calendar that moved the date of Tet a few days, leaving leaders in the South confused as to the intended timing of "N-Day." In particular, the Interzone V and B-3 Front plans were set to the old calendar. As a result, a number of Tet actions took place a day early, on the night of January 30, including attacks at Nha Trang, Qui Nhon, Da Nang, Pleiku, Kontum, and Hoi An. The multiple events tipped Hanoi's hand, leading General Westmoreland to cancel a Tet cease-fire and place some forces on heightened alert.

Hanoi's planning made Saigon the principal objective, so mistakes made there were of supreme importance. There were two. The first was accelerating the attack. Youth and labor cadres had planned massive street festivals and demonstrations to coincide with the South Vietnamese Tet celebration. The crowds would have served as the core of the Liberation Front's mass uprising and would have enabled commanders to put weight behind the small sapper elements being used for key strikes. The second mistake, required by moving up the date but also by secrecy concerns, was that orders to larger units were issued just twenty-four hours before the attack, forcing many formations to rush to their assault positions. For example, units in Long An province, which furnished most of the larger units that fought in Saigon, needed to march dozens of kilometers. At a minimum, that meant the NLF troops had to leave their heavy weapons behind, greatly reducing their fire-power.

Westmoreland expected attacks before Tet, Phil Davidson afterwards; nei-ther expected them during Tet. The mistimed moves of January 30 led MACV to cancel leaves and order a measure of alert. Now, about twelve hours before the offensive, Westy cabled Washington that the adversary "may not" halt its operations during the holiday.[14] He telephoned senior com-manders. A press release to the effect that the scheduled cease-fire had been canceled was written but never circulated because the Saigon government press office had closed for Tet. The Seventh Air Force went on alert at 12:30 PM. At Chu Lai the 198th Infantry Brigade did the same, recalling patrols and manning bunkers. II Field Force called an alert. Khe Sanh was on alert too.

On the Vietnamese side, President Thieu refused to cancel the cease-fire even when urged to do so by Cao Van Vien and Westmoreland. Half the ARVN was on leave, with some units at only 10 or 20 percent strength. Indi-vidual units took precautions. At the 21st Division in the Mekong delta, General Lam Quang Thi canceled leaves on his own, but soldiers who had al-ready left for the holiday could not be recalled. Bui Diem, Saigon's ambassa-dor in Washington, put it succinctly when he said that although NLF preparations had been known weeks in advance, "The timing and form of the attacks was so audacious that [that] by itself was a surprise."[15]

Despite Hanoi's coordination errors, Tet came as a surprise. The best in-dex of allied preparedness lies in the fact that MACV headquarters at Tan Son Nhut air base was without all its top commanders at the instant of the assault. The routine conditions at "Pentagon East," as the complex was known, left it vulnerable and U.S. forces without leadership at a crucial mo-ment. The staff that had drafted Westmoreland's limited warning to Wash-ington had gone to a Tet party. His intelligence estimates center had just a few officers on duty, and at its ARVN counterpart, all the personnel were gone. Aside from security people, the U.S. embassy had only six Americans on duty that night.

General Westmoreland, at home on Saigon's Tran Quy Hap street, heard the sounds of combat but waited by the telephone for word of develop-ments. General Creighton V. Abrams, MACV deputy commander, was also at home, and even though his house was just down the street from Tan Son Nhut, aides decided not to wake him. Retired general Bruce Clarke was Abrams's houseguest at the time. Chief of staff General Walter T. Kerwin and MACV Studies and Observation Group (MACSOG) commander Major General John K. Singlaub were both at home in the Saigon house they shared. Operations center chief John Chaisson, just returned from leave in Maine, was startled by shooting outside his window. Pacification chief Robert Komer was asleep at home. American public relations czar Barry Zorthian was having a late dinner at his residence. The prescient General

Weyand was away visiting Da Nang, where Marine III MAF commander General Robert E. Cushman slept in his quarters. MACV intelligence chief General Davidson prepared to defend his Saigon house, but no one came; his estimates chief, Colonel Daniel O. Graham, who lived in a bachelor officers' compound in Saigon, ended up participating in a pick-up squad of officers roaming the city streets. Ambassador Ellsworth Bunker, returning to his residence after a party held to celebrate the "light at the end of the tunnel," had to be rescued by Marine guards and hustled into an armored personnel carrier.

Saigon leaders were no better prepared. President Nguyen Van Thieu was at his wife's family home in My Tho in the delta. Vice President Nguyen Cao Ky, who had kept his quarters on Tan Son Nhut, hosted a Tet party for air force and ARVN officers and their wives. Even some who had taken precautions were caught unawares. At Sa Dec, in the delta, 21st Division commander Lam Quang Thi was asleep in his quarters when an aide woke him at 2:00 AM with news that several provincial capitals were under attack. Joint General Staff chief Cao Van Vien? At home in Cholon. He did not reach headquarters until after dawn. Meanwhile, Ky sent his own helicopter to retrieve President Thieu, also in the morning.

Ky quotes Westmoreland as saying, in a 1998 interview, "I knew the attack was coming, but I did not want to let the enemy know I knew."[16] That is certainly a wishful reflection. General Davidson proved more straightforward in conversations, if not in the books he wrote. "There was an element of surprise," Davidson conceded.[17] Bob Komer would be quite blunt. "Boy it was a surprise, lemme tell you," Komer exclaimed. "I was at Westy's elbow."[18] At Ky's house, when partygoers heard gunfire shortly after midnight, they thought it was firecrackers heralding the new year or perhaps soldiers firing their weapons into the air. The picture is not a pretty one for those who would have it that the United States knew all about Tet or, as it is sometimes quaintly put, that the only surprise was the extent of Hanoi's folly.

▨ ▨ ▨ The Vietnamese call it Tet Mau Than, Tet of the Year of the Monkey, in the country's twelve-year animistic calendar cycle. Events did not quite make monkeys of the Americans or the Saigon forces, due partly to Hanoi's inexperience in coordinating operations, partly to rivalries between Liberation Front leaders and those in Hanoi, and also to the sheer disparity in firepower available to the two sides. The quality of American troops, Free World Forces, and South Vietnamese troops also played a role. But by far the biggest reason for Hanoi's eventual failure lay in its miscalculation of the potential for a general uprising in the South.

Tran Bach Dang lived these days in a hut on the outskirts of Saigon. First secretary of the Saigon party organization and an original founder of the

National Front for the Liberation of South Vietnam, Dang had long been in the city under a variety of aliases, from professor to street vendor, moving among its districts with impunity. Evidence indicates that Dang had actually been the NLF figure at the other end of President Johnson's CIA-run peace feeler Buttercup, and at one point his wife had been arrested by the South Vietnamese and then released under American pressure. Dang worked for Nguyen Van Linh and Vo Van Kiet, the COSVN regional party secretary and deputy. While Linh supervised operations outside Saigon, led by General Tran Van Tra's "Vanguard 2" military command, Kiet and Dang were responsible for the city itself, and their "Vanguard 1" group was supposed to attack Saigon from the south and southwest. Because Kiet had COSVN duties as well, Dang became the effective field commander for the most spectacular actions of Tet.

Dang had a penchant for going against the grain. A colleague recalled in later years that he held the distinction of being the only revolutionary fired *twice* by Nguyen Van Linh. At Tet he left Saigon just as many Liberation Front operatives were infiltrating in. A recently arrived American intelligence analyst noticed an awful lot of funerals in the weeks before the attacks, small processions carting bodies for burial. He later realized that the coffins were ideal for smuggling rifles and explosives and that the funerals had been a feature of the NLF supply net. But Dang had gone the other way, in search of a place where he could more easily pull the levers to activate the various threads of his plot. Necessary as that was, the Front would lack a senior officer inside the city with authority to make on-the-spot decisions.

Liberation Front planners also had great need for current information on ARVN and U.S. security procedures. Here Tran Bach Dang's networks proved hugely valuable. For example, one cell met regularly at Ngo Toai's noodle shop Pho Binh (*binh* for "peace") in District 3. The shop stood a mere hundred yards from the Saigon headquarters for U.S. military police. GIs regularly went there to eat. Just listening to the gossip afforded the NLF a window on U.S. security measures throughout the city. Cadres forwarded the intelligence to field commanders. In another intelligence coup, a Front agent and South Vietnamese legislator smuggled one of the field commanders himself onto Tan Son Nhut air base, where they received a guided tour from an unwitting senior Vietnamese air force officer.

Pham Xuan An was the perfect spy. An had built his cover through the years in Saigon, first with the Diem regime's intelligence service, followed by journalism study in the United States and then work for several top-drawer media outlets, currently *Time* magazine. Reporters and even government officials relied on An to interpret Saigon trends and events. He held court every day at the coffee shop Givral, a watering hole for top American and Saigon officials, directly across the street from the hotels that served the foreign journalists, a block away from the Rex, officers' quarters for senior

American military men, only blocks from Independence Palace. When COSVN began its detailed planning for Tet, An's boss, Major Tu Cang, came to Saigon so that An could help him select suitable targets, survey security, and choose landing points and assembly areas. Hanoi's willingness to risk a key agent in this way shows the importance it attached to the Tet plans.[19]

Handpicked commandos of COSVN's 350-man C-10 Sapper Battalion would be Tran Bach Dang's spearhead for a series of attacks on key points in Saigon. What happened at the U.S. embassy was, by far, the most significant action of Tet in terms of impact in the United States. But of greater importance for the general uprising were certain of Dang's other projects, notably strikes on the presidential palace and the radio station, and it is here this account begins.

Independence Palace, four blocks down Thong Nhat Boulevard from the embassy, had largely been an island of tranquility amid the trauma of war. Reopened late in 1966, its construction following a completely new design from architect Ngo Viet Thu, the palace possessed every modern feature from a rooftop helipad to an underground command bunker. Little disturbed its peaceful atmosphere. The previous October the NLF had lobbed a few mortar shells onto the grounds to disrupt the Thieu-Ky inaugural, but that had been the only violent incident at the palace since coup times. Protected by two battalions of presidential guards, other security men, and two tanks, the palace seemed impregnable—until Tet. At 1:30 AM, the Third Commando Team, consisting of fourteen men and a woman in several vehicles, including one packed with explosives, drove up to the gate on Nguyen Du street, where employees usually entered. Challenged, one car sped up to crash the gate but failed. The sappers then fired B-40 rockets but again failed to demolish the gate.

The commando unit at the palace retreated into an uncompleted high-rise across the street and fought South Vietnamese counterattackers. By 5:00 AM eight were dead and four seriously wounded. The others resisted in a firefight that went on for two days. Saigon government troops captured two members of the Third Commando Team and killed the rest except for the female fighter, Doan Thi Anh Tuyet, who escaped. A key element here was Hanoi's decision to change the timing of Tet. Front leaders had expected to stage a massive evening rally of students and youth groups in the Tan Dao gardens behind the palace. They expected tens of thousands to attend. The militants would have surged into the palace through the broken gates. The spectacle would indeed have created the image of a mass uprising and could have triggered similar events elsewhere. But arrangements could not be modified so close to N-Day, and as soon as the offensive began, the Saigon government declared a curfew. The rally never took place.

Dang's final plan called for follow-on units, main-force battalions from Long An province, to move in behind the commandos, attack through the gate, and take over the palace, as well as other key objectives such as the American embassy. But the late attack order critically delayed this force, and Tet festivities affected the Liberation Front too, with many NLF officers and troops celebrating the holiday. The Long An battalions were delayed and understrength, and they lacked their heavy weapons and the 200 metric tons of supplies considered necessary to fuel all the Saigon attacks. The battalions were engaged by ARVN troops of the Fifth Ranger Group much farther down Nguyen Du street and never reached their objectives.

Meanwhile, a dozen sappers of the Fourth Commando Team had been hiding in a house of Tran Phu Cuong, near the radio station. They advanced, disguised as National Police, and quickly overwhelmed the squad of defenders. NLF propaganda broadcasts were not possible, however, because the building housed only the studios, and Lieutenant Colonel Vu Duc Dinh, chief of the transmission complex, cut off the audio feed from the downtown studio. By dawn an ARVN paratroop company arrived to counterattack. The radio was working again for the Saigon government by 7:00 AM. Ten sappers died, and two who were wounded were hidden by Front agents and later smuggled out of the city.

These two failures were key to the collapse of Hanoi's ambitions for an uprising. Other ancillary operations also miscarried. At Vietnamese navy headquarters a dozen sappers in two cars were stopped at a roadblock in Lam Son square. Navy guards challenged them, a firefight erupted, and the naval alert detachment responded instantly. The action ended within minutes. The best the NLF sappers could achieve was to blow a hole in the wall. Two mainforce battalions were supposed to materialize on the opposite bank of the Saigon River, where they could ferry across and flood into the city. But the boats remained tied up at the navy pier, and without the sapper bridgehead, there was no safe place to land. And, like other Long An troops, the units themselves were late.

Of greatest military significance would be the attack at Tan Son Nhut. This strike aimed at Joint General Staff (JGS) headquarters but could have been even more momentous if targets had included the Pentagon East complex as well as the Vietnamese officers' housing, where Vice President Ky lived. Ten American generals were quartered at Tan Son Nhut. Neutralizing this base would have knocked out the nerve center of Saigon's war.

The plan was to hit the base from three sides, with both Tran Bach Dang's Vanguard 1 and the Vanguard 2 troops of General Tran Do supervised by General Tran Van Tra, commander of the PLAF. On the northeastern side of Tan Son Nhut, an assault by the 268th Regiment of Colonel Lam Truyen's NLF 9th Division would distract the defenses. Then the Sixth and Ninth Commando Teams would lead the way, capturing two different gates to break into Tan Son Nhut. From the west another assault aimed to seize Gate 5, which gave access to the runways and aircraft revetments. The follow-up would be Colonel Nguyen Van Nho's task force, combining troops of the NLF's 267th, 269th, and D-16 Battalions, perhaps 1,200 men in all. A small number of aircraft mechanics and pilots, infiltrated down the Ho Chi Minh Trail, were also there, hoping to fly off in captured planes. A second assault would be against Gate 4 near JGS headquarters, the housing area, and MACV. There the 2nd NLF Battalion provided the muscle. Commanders answered to Dang. The Front's Go Mon district battalion was supposed to furnish the reserve echelon, but it too failed to arrive on time.

This operation miscarried for a variety of reasons. The 268th Regiment never made its diversion. As it approached through Go Vap district, where Tran Van Tra's troops were attacking ARVN artillery and armor commands, the regiment got lost. It also had orders to await the arrival of another unit that never showed up and then became embroiled in fighting as the South Vietnamese counterattacked in Go Vap. The regiment retreated after several days. On the base itself the U.S. Air Force unit responsible for ground defense had recently rehearsed its contingency plan for an attack. This helped but could not prevent the NLF from capturing Gate 5 and its protecting Bunker 51 and penetrating almost a half mile into Tan Son Nhut. A ruse involving a taxi, closely followed by a bus full of commandos, overwhelmed the gate guards. Four Americans perished in the bunker. The perimeter was breached in less than twenty minutes. The 267th Battalion reached an interior gate, number 10, close to Pentagon East, but a jeep of Air Force security troops arrived in time to slam it shut, reinforcing the handful of guards. Bruce E. Jones, one of the few MACV intelligence experts on duty that night, grabbed an M-16 rifle and joined the slim ranks of the defenders. They stopped the enemy long enough for more troops to deploy. The U.S. armored cavalry squadron attached to the 25th Division arrived soon after dawn and helped put pressure on Colonel Nho's attackers, who were sealed into a perimeter by Air Force and South Vietnamese troops.

The last assault came at Gate 4, where fate again took a hand. Commandos blasted the gate open with B-40 rockets shortly after 3:00 AM. The first wave of fighters, twenty-seven men under Do Tan Phong, got close to JGS headquarters, but most of the unit entered the ARVN language school and holed up instead of pressing on into the base, probably counting on the Go Mon battalion, delayed until after dawn. Meanwhile, from his home less than a quarter of a mile away, Nguyen Cao Ky phoned military district commander General Le Nguyen Khang, demanding reinforcements. Khang, who had but a single company of troops left, faced many serious threats and wondered if Tan Son Nhut ought to have priority.

"What does it take to become the number-one priority," Ky screamed. "*The enemy is inside the base!* They are less than five hundred meters from my house!"[20]

General Khang relented. A company of the ARVN 8th Airborne Battalion arrived in just ten minutes and engaged the guerrillas in the language school. Tran Bach Dang's district unit from Go Mon arrived, but by then the ARVN had several tanks, and JGS chief Cao Van Vien had released a pair of Marine battalions to join the battle. Low on ammunition, with heavy losses, the sappers made a fighting withdrawal. The ARVN then helped the Americans evict Colonel Nho's troops from their positions around Bunker 51. Late in the day authorities pronounced Tan Son Nhut secure. This had been a closer battle than Tet accounts usually suggest. It was not merely a question of the NLF being able to capture and secure the base, which it could never have held for long. Some judicious demolitions in the JGS compound and MACV headquarters and a shooting spree in the ARVN's senior housing area—not to mention the numerous nearby MACV quarters—would have had a huge effect on the U.S.-Saigon war effort. Had a contingent of top Saigon officers been captured—not least of them Air Marshal Ky—the impact would have been enormous.

With President Thieu out of pocket, Vice President Ky managed the government's countermeasures. He ordered a curfew to keep people off the streets and thanked his lucky stars that the radio station remained in friendly hands to spread the message. Bypassing General Khang, Ky put National Police chief General Nguyen Ngoc Loan in charge. Loan, an air force officer loyal to Ky, commandeered whatever troops he could lay his hands on to regain control of the Saigon area. One of the most damaging moments of Tet occurred when Loan apprehended a Liberation Front officer and summarily executed him with a revolver in front of reporters. Photographer Eddie Adams caught the instant of the bullet's impact on film, and his photo first appeared in the United States on February 2. It would be said in defense of Loan that the NLF cadre had been responsible for killing friends and family, but the picture was emblematic of Saigon's arbitrary methods and its violation of humanitarian standards, prisoner of war regulations, and even intelligence rubrics on gaining important information at critical moments. This photograph became one of the iconic images of the Vietnam war.

Meanwhile, COSVN General Tran Van Tra, from a hamlet on the outskirts of the city, monitored a whole series of combat operations. At Bien Hoa, an air base and headquarters of the ARVN III Corps, the NLF 274th Regiment assaulted but became confused because its assembly point, a rubber plantation, had been cleared away the month before by huge Rome plows. It made no headway. On the airfield a couple of planes were destroyed and seventeen were damaged, but no break-in occurred. At nearby Long Binh, Weyand's headquarters (the general now back in place), the NLF fought to a standstill. Americans of the 199th Infantry Brigade and the 101st Airborne Division were critical in both engagements. The 11th Armored Cavalry, the fabled "Black Horse" regiment, sealed the fate of Bien Hoa's attackers, returning sixty miles from its position to counterattack before nightfall.

These battles, all real and significant, paled next to the tiny assault on the U.S. embassy at Thong Nhat Boulevard, where Ngo Thanh Van's Eleventh Commando Team of seventeen fighters made up the attack force. Disguised as ARVN soldiers, they drove up in a taxi and a truck. Their equipment had been brought into Saigon hidden in shipments of rice and tomatoes. The South Vietnamese police who normally secured the perimeter wall fled. The sappers blasted through the front gate. Marine guards inside barely managed to bar the embassy doors. They mounted a desperate defense. Colonel George Jacobsen, who lived on the embassy grounds (needless to say, at home that night), single-handedly accounted for a number of the sappers. The rest kept up a steady fire until morning, when Americans from the 716th Military Police Battalion attacked from outside while a platoon of paratroopers from the 101st Airborne Division choppered onto the roof to break out of the building. Two wounded sappers were captured; the rest were killed.

Reporters in Saigon quickly learned of the fighting at the embassy, and the first dispatches were sent before dawn. The spectacle of the U.S. embassy under attack was too dramatic to ignore; journalists flocked to cover the battle. Don Oberdorfer, then in Luang Prabang, Laos, quickly rushed back. Oberdorfer decided his MACV briefers had been myopically optimistic.

The pictures and reports from Saigon proved just as shocking at home, especially in view of President Johnson's efforts to convince Americans that light was visible at the end of the tunnel. In fact, early news reached the White House as Walt Rostow entertained four *Washington Post* correspondents. He was about to show them captured documents supporting his thesis that People's Army and Liberation Front morale had disintegrated.

Instead of doing a victory dance, Rostow found himself on the telephone, first to the embassy, then to General Westmoreland directly, as the president demanded to know what the hell was going on. Walt ended up having to apologize to JCS chairman Wheeler for going around the military chain of command and speaking to Westmoreland. The MACV leader, meanwhile, did the cause no good either. After looking around the battered embassy once it was secured, Westy turned to the assembled journalists, declared the damage superficial, and told them these "deceitful" attacks were preliminary to an assault on Khe Sanh. Oberdorfer recorded the reaction: "The reporters could hardly believe their ears. Westmoreland was standing in the ruins and saying everything was great."[21]

But things were not great at all. Smoke was still rising from the embassy and other battle sites, while major fighting continued at Tan Son Nhut, Bien Hoa, Go Vap, and in other places. In fact, throughout South Vietnam the NLF or Hanoi troops had attacked 5 of South Vietnam's autonomous cities, 35 (of 44) provincial capitals, 64 district seats, and 50 other hamlets—166 localities in all. To cite just one example of the countrywide fighting, the battalion of the nascent Americal Division stationed at Tam Ky in I Corps, like some other units, stood ready. At brigade headquarters in Chu Lai, the intelligence officer had been brought into a room where a large tarp covered a sand table map. When the tarp was drawn back, the map, based on top-secret communications intercepts, depicted the People's Army 2nd Division poised to attack throughout the region. Intelligence had no doubt that attack impended. The night of Tet everyone was ready. Some of the Special Forces teams in their village camps nearby had dug in so deeply "it was like Hitler's bunker." They figured if they could hold out for twenty-four hours they would come out okay. Following the messages that night, "the enemy came on like a tsunami," with post after post reporting attacks, then going silent. So many calls for help clogged the radio circuits that the system collapsed.[22]

It was obvious that a "defeated" enemy could have no such capability. Nor did it matter that in almost all these places the combat ended within a day, or else two or three. Nor did it matter that Hanoi had not gotten its precious general uprising. What mattered—a great deal—was that the supposedly defeated adversary could strike anywhere, even in the heart of Saigon, in great force. And that enemy, far from demoralized, fought to the finish.

The point would be driven home at Hue. There General Tran Van Quang's Tri-Thien troops took over the city, Vietnam's traditional imperial capital. Although ARVN defenders were on alert—1st Division scouts had actually seen some of the attack forces leave their camps—only the headquarters was actually located in Hue, and division commander Ngo Quang Truong did not redeploy, leaving little with which to contest the city. At Hue, too, the uprising failed, the populace horrified by the massacre of between 2,500 and 3,500 persons, mostly civilians or families of Saigon government officials. The VPA and its NLF cadres systematically took away people named on lists that had to have been prepared by local networks. (Both sides could play at that game: The CIA's base chief for Hue escaped with a radioman, exfiltrating through enemy lines in James Bond style, dressed in black and carrying exotic gear. He went immediately to the command post of the Marine general leading the response force and handed him a list that, according to a witness, contained thousands of names of NLF sympathizers in the Hue area.) In spite of the lack of popular support, the VPA—here, regulars were the bulk of the force—resisted for weeks in the old imperial capital, in the face of everything U.S. Marines and the ARVN threw at them. At the end, on February 24, VPA troops escaped the doomed Citadel.

Beyond even Hue, the siege of Khe Sanh went on for seventy-seven days. Though nothing happened at the moment of Tet, over the succeeding weeks General Tran Van Hai jabbed when he could. The Special Forces camp at Lang Vei would be overrun on February 7. A succession of assaults against Khe Sanh's outlying strongpoints failed. Westmoreland pelted the enemy with a cascade of bombs in Niagara, tens of thousands of pounds of munitions, including one fabulous B-52 strike directly on the People's Army command post. Hai survived, but his headquarters went off the air for a period of days. On February 17 Hai received orders to make a real effort to attack the Americans. He constructed a trench system to get in close. Constant North Vietnamese bombardments failed to get at Colonel Lownds in his Khe Sanh dugout. Eventually the VPA slunk away to lick its wounds, but only in April could MACV mount the large-scale ground offensive necessary to disengage Khe Sanh.

Tet struck at America—not South Vietnam—with shock and awe. The widespread attacks and the fight for the embassy contradicted all the press releases. Pacification was set back everywhere, as was only too obvious. The infamous photograph of General Loan shooting an NLF cadre challenged any notion that Saigon's was a government of laws and procedures. The battle for Hue refuted the argument that Hanoi had no staying power. The siege of Khe Sanh negated the talk of light at the end of the tunnel. And all this happened on film, recorded by journalists throughout the land and played back every day on America's TV screens and in its print media. Rostow's Vietnam Information Group worked assiduously to counter these developments—I will spare readers the details of these frantic efforts—without effect. Public opinion turned decisively. In February one poll showed 56 percent support for U.S. withdrawal from Vietnam. A month later a Harris poll recorded the view that Tet represented a U.S. failure to attain its objectives in Vietnam.

Forget about victory, CBS anchorman Walter Cronkite told the nation in a February 27 broadcast. "It seems now more certain than ever that the bloody experience of Vietnam will end in a stalemate." Widely considered a bellwether, Cronkite had gone to see for himself and came down hard: "To say that we are closer to victory today is to believe, in the face of the evidence, the optimists who have been wrong in the past."[23] LBJ recognized this pronouncement for what it was. He told associates that when he lost Cronkite, he had lost the country.

Transformation

Administration officials at the time, and successive waves of apologists, have argued that the Tet offensive marked a massive defeat for North Vietnam and the National Liberation Front. General Westmoreland, for example, asserted that Hanoi had put itself in the same position as Germany at the Battle of the Bulge. These same individuals dismissed the political impact in the United States as the product of negative press reporting. Reporter Peter Braestrup opened this vein with his complaints about the work of colleagues.[24] Clarence Wyatt, a historian of Vietnam journalism, called the flaws Braestrup complained about "the product of American journalism and government information policies that had been developing for years."[25] As for eyewitnesses, Ambassador Robert Komer would later reflect, "I knew in one day that whatever had happened out there, Tet had changed absolutely everything in Washington."[26] Komer came to that insight instantly, before the media reporting had appeared. Ambassador Bui Diem comments, "The general feeling was consternation, and I was there during those days in Washington."[27]

"For liberal intellectuals as well as for the general public," writes historian Robert Tomes, "Tet was a shocking, frightening experience which revealed the vulnerability of the American military apparatus in Vietnam."[28] Yet poll data show that in the immediate aftermath the public, as it frequently does, rallied around the flag, with more respondents supporting bombing and thinking themselves hawks. About efforts to handle the media, the Army's official historian actually concludes, "the gloomy reporting of the press had little effect on American public opinion."[29]

The rat pack of reporters may have focused on the embassy, Hue, and Khe Sanh, as Braestrup deplores, but those were crucial stories, and the situation really was problematic, as Washington's secret records show. The month or so following Tet was the only time during the Vietnam war when the JCS chairman and MACV commander held daily conversations by secure phone that were reported directly to the White House. Dispatches spoke of pacification breakdown, and that too was real. The United States rushed reinforcements to South Vietnam, another indication of abnormality. Lazy journalism did not mean the story was made up. General Westmoreland took the occasion to make another demand for massive troop increases—one that promptly leaked—in fact, a repetition of Program 5.

Westmoreland complained in his memoir that the "attitude" of the press contributed to Hanoi's "psychological victory." Reporters wanted him to say "the walls were tumbling down," when he "knew they were not."[30] But no reporter decided to ask for massive augmentation. That was Westmoreland. And it was also Westmoreland who handed the media the jarring juxtaposition, so at odds with the destruction visible all around, of Hanoi at Tet with the Germans at the Battle of the Bulge. Similarly, it had been the White House, not the media, that chose to exaggerate progress for political reasons, creating a disjunction between U.S. descriptions and what people could see for themselves. Johnson's media operation boomeranged, leaving journalists with a sense of betrayal that caused them to question everything thereafter. That began with the revelation that "victory" required such an infusion of reinforcements as to necessitate national mobilization. As Bui Diem put it, "In a sense the shock effect of the enemy offensive was created in part by Washington itself."[31] What transformed views in the United States would be that one-two punch. Blaming the press for Vietnam was like the second Bush administration complaining that the Iraq war was not going well because the media had not reported the "good" stories.

Meanwhile, the argument for military victory has its own flaws, depending on how many losses the adversary sustained. Hanoi and the Liberation Front undoubtedly suffered greatly. The body count for the Saigon area was reportedly more than 13,000, at Hue over 5,000, and between 10,000 and 15,000 at Khe Sanh; the overall total was somewhere between 67,000 and 84,000. But everyone had questions about the body count. Rostow's VIG had even created a subcommittee to look into obtaining better body count data. The true meaning of the losses depends on the size of the adversary force—the very order of battle so manipulated the previous year. If the main-force units aggregated close to 300,000 and the full VPA-NLF complement numbered twice that, and if a large portion of Tet casualties came from NLF ranks—which it did—then the actual attrition suffered by Hanoi was far less than advertised. Indeed, the Vietnamese retained the capability for two more "waves" of this offensive later in the year, ones that were far more punishing to its battle force.

There is also the question of friendly losses. Official statistics show 55,084 enemy dead for January and February 1968. Over the same period there were 3,326 American combat deaths (and 287 other fatalities), along with 7,930 ARVN and 258 Free World Forces (FWF) soldiers killed in action; the wounded numbered 16,947 Americans, 18,270 South Vietnamese, and 532 FWF troops; and 1,474 ARVN plus an undisclosed number of Americans were missing in action, for an aggregate total of 49,024 casualties.[32] Senator George Aiken of Vermont, a Republican with studied views on Vietnam, opined, "If this is failure, I hope the Vietcong never have a major success."[33]

Life magazine captured America's growing discomfort at the beginning of March. "The entire tree of American public opinion about the war," wrote Shana Alexander, "its branches drooping with doves, hawks, eagles, owls, now shudders in the lash of the new firestorm."[34] The Time-Life Corporation had, until very recently, always staunchly supported the Vietnam war. The cascade of events that shattered old wisdoms was being replayed throughout the nation. Something very different would emerge.

■ ■ ■ Officials were not oblivious to developments. Ellsworth Bunker fed Washington a steady stream of upbeat cables. So did Westmoreland. But the clouds were darkening. The CIA's daily reporting from across South Vietnam reflected less optimism. Ed Lansdale, back in Saigon as an embassy counselor—a sort of sounding board for Saigon's generals and politicians—witnessed a stream of backbiting among local allies jockeying for position in the post-Tet environment. The doubts had been planted. Pacification boss Bob Komer, one more time: "It was the Tet shock to the American psyche that made me first think we might lose."[35] Former Green Beret Donald Duncan, already gone over to the antiwar movement, would have agreed. "And then came Tet of 1968," Duncan later reflected. "And in one night the illusion of progress was gone."[36]

Indeed, the American psyche was in the balance. A most startling indicator would be the emergence of the veterans' antiwar movement. Men and women who had served under the flag were especially qualified to speak out on this foreign military adventure. During the early years such a voice had been lacking. Vets first marched together at a Washington protest in November 1965 led by Ed Bloch, a Marine veteran of World War II. A group called Veterans for Peace formed two months later at a meeting held in Chicago, and several hundred appeared at its first peace march. But these vets were overwhelmingly the men of Korea or the world wars. A group of Vietnam veterans began coalescing in the spring of 1967 when a few of them marched with the Veterans for Peace under a banner that read, "Vietnam Veterans Against the War." One of them, Jan Barry, began reaching out to others, concerned that Veterans for Peace had so few Vietnam vets. An organizing meeting took place in his kitchen in New York's East Village on June 1, 1967.

Barry had served in Vietnam during the advisory period and had been stunned by the Diem regime's action against Buddhists in Nha Trang, where he had been stationed. Yet he followed his ambition to become an officer and secured a place at West Point, the first combat veteran of Vietnam appointed to the military academy. He was at West Point when the Gulf of Tonkin incident occurred, souring Barry further. He resigned from the corps of cadets in late 1964 but served out his enlistment, leaving the Army in May 1965. Watching the travails of civil rights activists and the horrors of the Watts riots drove Barry to more critical thinking, but when his girlfriend began attending peace demonstrations, he was not interested. Instead, Barry began reading about Vietnam and its history. He had heard there were Americans back from the war and bitter about it, and he eventually encountered the sole survivor of a squad that had been wiped out in the Ia Drang battle. They shared their personal grief. Barry's first march was the April 15 demonstration where Martin Luther King spoke, which Barry attended simply because he had seen a Veterans for Peace ad. Now Barry became the president of Vietnam Veterans Against the War (VVAW).

The group got meeting space at 156 5th Avenue, where the 5th Avenue Peace Parade Committee was headquartered, and it soon had its own office at 17 East 17th Street. Barry designed a logo for the organization based on the MACV shoulder patch—a bright red shield with a superimposed golden sword bisecting a rampart. For the sword he substituted an upside-down rifle with a helmet on top, the traditional marker for the grave of a hastily buried soldier. VVAW vice president Carl Rogers was a natural at dealing with the media; he and VVAW treasurer Dave Braum, who had been a helicopter crew chief, made an early TV appearance. Rogers had come out against the war soon after returning to "The World," the phrase GIs used to distinguish their life in "The Nam" from that in the States. Rogers denounced the concept of "kill ratios," one of Washington's measures of merit in the war that made killing seem like something sterile. Sheldon Ramsdell, another VVAW founder, was a former sailor and a talented photographer; he documented the group's actions. Green Beret Donald Duncan became another early adherent. Chapters formed in Alabama, California, Oregon, and Texas. A small VVAW group participated with the Veterans for Peace in the Pentagon levitation, and the group raised enough cash to run a full-page ad in the *New York Times* on November 19, 1967. In line with the Johnson administration's increased efforts to tamp down protest, and despite his own misgivings, Secretary of Defense Robert McNamara asked the FBI to investigate the backgrounds of the ad's signers. Similarly, the CIA began looking into whether VVAW was controlled by communists.

Nevertheless, until Tet, VVAW remained, in the words of historian Andrew Hunt, "an organization in search of an identity."[37] Tet shattered preconceptions, led to rapid expansion, and conveyed a new sense of urgency. William Crandell, for example, a former lieutenant in what became the Americal Division, supported the war until he heard General Westmoreland pronounce Tet a great victory. Crandell began organizing, and there were soon chapters at both the University of Ohio and Kent State. Mike McKusker had been a combat journalist with the 1st Marine Division in 1966–1967; he decided to come out against the war after an encounter with Vietnamese Buddhist bonze Thich Nhat Hanh at the airport in Fargo, North Dakota, where they were both stranded by a blizzard. VVAW soon moved back to larger offices at 156 5th Avenue and started a national publication called *Vietnam GI*, edited by Jeff Sharlett. Its maiden issue appeared the month of Tet.

But Tet proved to be more than just an organizational stimulant. It galvanized many serving GIs who later joined VVAW. Joe Urgo, an airman with the 377th Security Police Squadron, had been among the Air Force ground troops behind Bunker 51 at Tan Son Nhut the night of the attack. The bunker had been his duty post, but he had traded off with another airman. Everyone in the bunker died. Also at Tan Son Nhut was Horace Coleman with the 619th Tactical Air Control Squadron, the base's air traffic controllers. Hearing that the U.S. embassy was under attack, Coleman had a helicopter filled with ammo and weapons and sent it downtown. But the crew were newbies and had no idea where they were, and they flew too low to show up on Coleman's radar screen. He had to have a Vietnamese sergeant listen to the airmen describe what they could see and then give them directions from a map. Coleman got the chopper near the embassy, but then it was shot down.

Danny Friedman's assignment was to D Troop of the 17th Cavalry, one of the fire brigades that saved so many beleaguered outposts during those dark days. Friedman's troop intervened at a crucial moment at Bien Hoa. The

11th Armored Cavalry played a key role in saving Tan Son Nhut, and vet David Connolly was with that unit. Larry Rottmann perched over the tunnels of Cu Chi as an information officer with the 25th Infantry Division. John Ketwig, a lieutenant with the 4th Division at Pleiku, spent ten terrifying days in his bunker. Barry Romo was an intelligence officer with the 196th Light Infantry Brigade at Tam Ky.

Farther north, W. D. Ehrhart, a Marine gunner at the battle of Hue, was saved from death by a Japanese fighting for America. Mike McCain was a communications specialist with the 1st Marine Division, Ehrhart's unit. Sergeant Fred Nienke, also with the 1st Marine Division, was appalled at the profligate use of CS gas in the fighting. James Duffy, a helicopter door gunner with the 1st Cavalry Division, had been at Hue too. At Bong Son, Stosh Commisiak of The Cav watched a tremendous light show as explosions and tracer rounds lit the night. Michael Hunter arrived a couple of days after the start of Tet to join The Cav's 5/7 Battalion. He soon witnessed an incident in which medics refused to treat a wounded Vietnamese boy, and the officers did nothing. He participated in the overland expedition to relieve Khe Sanh. So did Lynn Witt, a rifleman with 1st Battalion, 2nd Marines, and Kenneth J. Campbell, a scout with 1st Battalion, 1st Marines, who arrived as his unit mopped up in the ruins of Hue.

Back in The World, Peter Zastrow, then at Officer Candidate School, would be struck by how tightly the Army clammed up. He and his buddies were not even told Tet was going on.

These were merely a few of those who became antiwar vets. Indeed, one of the most significant VVAW actions, a few years afterward, would be a public testimonial on U.S. war crimes in Vietnam. Almost a quarter of the 120 former servicemen who gave witness there had been on the ground, in Vietnam, at Tet.

■ ■ ■ Far above the veterans' pay scale sat Lyndon Johnson. He too lost confidence at Tet. There were very specific antecedents to LBJ's change of heart. Shortly before it, General Westmoreland had sent an overview covering the previous year, expressing his belief in increased success in 1968. On February 12, when the JCS summarized MACV's view of developments, that impression had been transformed. Although Westmoreland remained optimistic and claimed between 30,000 and 40,000 enemy losses, he had to admit uncertainty about new attacks and concede that three-quarters of the enemy regulars had never been engaged. While the public was told the ARVN was fighting very well, LBJ learned that five of its nine paratroop battalions were now rated ineffective, the average ARVN battalion had half or fewer of its soldiers present for duty, and desertions were up. The Chiefs called for more than a division in emergency reinforcements.

One of their options required mobilizing 120,000 reserves. Then there was Khe Sanh. Lyndon Johnson had been a key player in the Dien Bien Phu crisis and was now the commander in chief. The parallel could not resonate more.

President Johnson sent some fresh forces to South Vietnam, but nowhere near what the JCS asked for. He visited the troops before their departure. He also sent General Earle Wheeler to Vietnam for a look-see. Wheeler coordinated new troop requests with General Westmoreland by back-channel cable before his trip, encouraging MACV to ask for everything it could wish for. It appears that the Joint Chiefs chairman still harbored his private agenda of forcing the president into mobilization. Westmoreland demanded a package of new troops totaling 205,000 men. Wheeler then wrote a report backing the MACV request.[38] The huge troop request stunned President Johnson. He ordered newly sworn Secretary of Defense Clark Clifford to carry out an "A to Z" review of the way forward in Vietnam.

Clifford had received Senate confirmation on the very eve of Tet. He had watched uneasily as the attacks rolled in and said nothing when Westy asked for permission to stage a fake invasion of the North Vietnamese coast. "There can be no question," Clifford notes from his authoritative position, "that [Tet] was a turning point in the war." He saw the concentration of enemy losses among the NLF as a negative, simply raising the proportion of better-armed and -trained soldiers among the adversary's main units. "The military reassessment of the Tet Offensive since it ended was incomplete and self-serving," Clifford wrote. He unambiguously attributed defeat not to reporters or the antiwar movement: "Our policy failed because it was based on false premises and false promises."[39] All this is again reminiscent of the Bush administration in Iraq.

Coming to the Pentagon, Clifford had a reputation as a hawk. As recently as in his response to the McNamara cri de coeur, the new defense secretary had dealt savagely with any sign of weakness. But Clark Clifford prided himself on realism and practicality, and he too had seen the beginnings of cracks in the empire. In conversations with McNamara in the summer of 1967, Clifford had expressed his own doubts of victory. That fall LBJ had sent him on a mission to drum up more Free World Forces. Clifford had found the contributing countries quite loath to add to their troop contingents, leaving him puzzled and concerned. Tet served to affirm what they had been saying. Then came Westmoreland's troop request, which moved Johnson to put Clifford in charge of the policy review. The Clifford task force consumed several weeks. It quickly determined to hold reinforcements to those already earmarked and, based on political developments, soon moved on to consider a bombing halt—the very option Clifford had disdained when McNamara suggested it just a few months earlier.

As the administration struggled to find its footing, Lyndon Johnson's political troubles deepened. A sitting U.S. president generally has little difficulty securing his party's nomination for another term, and this had seemed to be the case for LBJ. But the war changed that. Activist Allard Lowenstein, whose roots lay in the civil rights struggle, started a "Dump Johnson" movement. Lowenstein needed someone to put up against LBJ and tried to recruit Bobby Kennedy, who had visible differences with Johnson over Vietnam. Bobby refused to take the plunge, and South Dakota's George S. McGovern also shied away. Minnesota senator Eugene McCarthy accepted, however, and came out swinging. McCarthy was not dynamic, more poet than politico, and the conventional wisdom held he would go nowhere against LBJ's mastery of the party machine. Johnson had not formally stood for reelection yet and would have to win by write-in votes in the primaries, but that did not seem an obstacle. McCarthy became the darling of the antiwar movement, which furnished the volunteers who flooded New Hampshire to work for him in the first primary, "Get Clean for Gene" their slogan. Tet prodded them to do more.

Suddenly America was stunned again, this time by the size of Westmoreland's 205,000 troop request. This news appeared in the *New York Times* on March 10, leaked by persons unknown.[40] One result would be Daniel Ellsberg's final conversion from cold warrior to antiwar activist. Ellsberg, who had become more and more leery, was finally convinced of the need to move the public. He had talked to Kennedy, to small groups of the elite establishment, and to others, but without reaching the public. Ellsberg knew the Joint Chiefs had been pressing for escalation the previous fall, and as a defense analyst with Rand, he had seen General Wheeler's memo with its proposal to add troops to MACV. Ellsberg feared this would lead to an invasion of North Vietnam and war with China. He did not know LBJ shared this view and worried that the president would sign a blank check. He showed the Wheeler paper to Bobby Kennedy—the first time, by Ellsberg's account, that he broke government secrecy rules. But the leak struck him like sun emerging from overcast: only secrecy had made LBJ's strategy possible. That insight led Ellsberg to the biggest leak of all, the Pentagon Papers. When he eventually blew that whistle, it would have a tremendous impact on Johnson's successor.[41]

Lyndon Johnson had been comfortably ahead in the New Hampshire primary, but the troop request revelation led to a fresh spike in his unfavorable ratings. LBJ's advantage over Gene McCarthy dwindled, but not fast enough for him to lose—the primary was just two days later—but the challenger came within a few hundred votes of beating the incumbent president. The result galvanized others. A few days after New Hampshire, Robert Kennedy declared his own candidacy. It had become open season on Lyndon Johnson.

LBJ wrestled with varied dilemmas. Troop reinforcements were just not practical once the request had been made public, especially given the views of Clifford and other top officials. The president decided to replace General Westmoreland instead. He would be promoted to Army chief of staff, replaced at MACV by General Creighton V. Abrams. Meanwhile, after years of holding the line, in early March Dean Rusk reluctantly backed a partial bombing halt to start negotiations. Clifford wanted a full stand-down but chose to lock in Rusk's support and backed his position. LBJ decided to summon the Wise Men once more, incorporating their advice and that of the Clifford task force in a nationally televised speech. Harry McPherson served as lead writer and sat in on many sessions among the ad hoc group, an outgrowth of Clifford's task force, that cobbled together the policy this speech would announce. McPherson thought LBJ bleak and depressed. But, combative as ever, Johnson demanded strident language for the speech. Clifford feared that would tear the nation apart.[42]

The Wise Men met at the State Department on March 25. They heard from top-tier officials, had dinner, then settled down to briefings from the diplomats, military, and CIA. Military briefer General William E. DePuy dutifully presented Tet as a major U.S. victory until challenged by Johnson intimate and UN ambassador Arthur Goldberg, one of the Wise Men. DePuy had claimed that Hanoi and NLF dead numbered 80,000. Goldberg asked about the ratio of wounded to dead. DePuy put that at 3–1, suggesting total enemy casualties of 320,000. The assessed size of Hanoi's force? DePuy said 230,000, maybe 240,000. So, Goldberg asked, "Who the hell is there left for us to be fighting?" The order of battle controversy had struck again—at the highest level of the U.S. government. Then came the CIA's George Carver, who, before leaving CIA headquarters, had actually been taken bodily and shaken by his deputy with the demand that he present the facts honestly. Carver took the floor to say that pacification would take much longer than previously thought. State Department briefer Philip Habib completed the picture, telling the group that Saigon politics was a mess and victory unachievable. The next day, with a few exceptions, the Wise Men told Lyndon Johnson he should take steps to disengage.[43]

President Johnson, shocked, had the briefings repeated for him directly. LBJ recalled himself "bothered" by what he heard but decided they had used "outdated information" and that the most important factor now was the mood of the country.[44] Johnson determined to shift more of the responsibility for the war onto the South Vietnamese. McPherson and Clifford worked to soften LBJ's speech. Rusk and Rostow, deflated by the climactic encounter with the Wise Men, did nothing to stymie this. If one day has to be chosen as the tipping point for U.S. policy, it would be March 25, 1968, the day those data stunned the Wise Men. Lyndon Johnson gave his speech on March 31. He declared that the United States would stop bombing North Vietnam beyond the area above the Demilitarized Zone—the partial bombing halt— and stop the flow of reinforcements. He renewed his commitment to negotiate. Then LBJ went further: "I shall not seek, and I will not accept, the nomination of my party for another term as your president."[45]

■ ■ ■ A few days of breathless anticipation followed. The CIA went into high gear to monitor international reactions to Johnson's reversal and partial bombing halt. Signs were good. The most important audience sat in Hanoi, and there LBJ took special measures, inviting Soviet ambassador Anatoly Dobrynin in for a précis a few hours before going on television. Moscow should tell Hanoi the United States had no desire for a military solution, was open to talks, and would respond to Hanoi's restraint by terminating Rolling Thunder operations. Johnson informed Dobrynin that Averell Harriman would be his personal representative.[46] Dobrynin dutifully passed along these private assurances, as did Moscow in Hanoi. The Russian press took a cautious view. But Radio Hanoi, in a statement on April 3, affirmed the DRV's willingness to send a delegation for negotiations.

The president had less than a day to bask in the glow, and Washington little time to absorb its implications, before domestic trauma engulfed the nation. In Memphis on the evening of April 4, Dr. Martin Luther King, there to support striking African American sanitation workers, was assassinated at his motel by a gunman. A new round of urban riots immediately broke out, a tidal wave that swept across America. There were disturbances in more than a hundred cities and towns, including, Chicago, Washington, and New York. In Washington whole neighborhoods in the northeast quadrant of the city would be burnt. Subsequent aerial photographs showed the area along Georgia Avenue north of the Mall a virtual wasteland. Federal troops and National Guardsmen, over 75,000 of them, were sent to help local police. More than 700 fires were recorded, and 200,000 people were arrested in the riots in which 46 Americans died and 2,600 were injured. On April 10 Clifford directed the U.S. Army to create a permanent task force to cope with civil disturbances and plan contingencies for deploying troops in up to two dozen cities at a time. In Chicago, where Mayor Richard Daley ordered police to shoot to kill, police bashed antiwar protesters when 10,000 marched on April 27, sending 21 demonstrators to the hospital. This action helped reduce the number of demonstrators at the Democratic National Convention in Chicago later that year.

The King assassination affected the war in several ways. It put Johnson on notice that his base, whether on negotiations or on the war, remained unstable. Another impact, largely hidden, would be a loss of morale in federal ranks, reflected in resignations from government service. Applicants for the diplomatic corps had been scheduled to take the foreign service examinations the day the riots began, and some of them now refused. All that talent was lost to the United States.

A third effect, only apparent later, flowed from King's death. The murder canceled the move toward a grand alliance between civil rights and antiwar forces and erected huge barriers to regaining that plateau. King's widow, Coretta Scott King, maintained a consistent antiwar stance, but no African

American leader had King's stature, and most had other ideas. Civil rights leaders focused on the Poor People's Campaign, which brought protesters and a tent city to The Mall in May. But black nationalism eclipsed civil rights, with slogans of black power in ascendance. The draft arguably affected African Americans more than whites, yet after 1968, blacks were noticeably underrepresented in antiwar groups. At the same time, militant black power advocates generated new pressure on the antiwar movement to adopt violent tactics that alienated moderate opponents and retarded the development of opposition overall.

Meanwhile, the riots in the United States became just the first manifestation of a more international upheaval. Australia put a cap on its force in South Vietnam. New Zealand followed suit. If Washington intended further increases in Free World Forces, they would not come from Down Under. In France, where public opinion had been against the war since its inception, opposition to the United States in Vietnam would be an important feature of student and labor unrest that escalated through the early months of 1968 and took the form of student strikes in April and riots and a general strike in May. More than 2,000 protesters and 300 police were injured, and the French government nearly toppled. In Germany the shooting of a student leader led to major riots in April and May, and again, Vietnam was an important focus. Protests took place in Great Britain too. SDS-er Todd Gitlin aptly recorded, "Paris in particular filled the air with the ozone of impending revolution."[47]

All this was in progress when student protests in New York actually shut down Columbia University and roiled American politics. A strong chapter of Students for a Democratic Society existed at Columbia, an outgrowth of antiwar protests that had begun as early as 1965, when students briefly blocked the entrance to a Naval Reserve Officer Training Corps award ceremony. Beginning in 1966 the SDS took the lead in opposing CIA campus recruiting, a manifestation of the opposition that led the CIA to halt all on-campus recruiting efforts nationwide by the end of 1967. Other protests at Columbia singled out Dow Chemical and the Marine Corps, as well as the university's participation in the Institute for Defense Analyses (IDA), a government-private think tank that conducted much of its research through a consortium of universities.[48]

Columbia administrators adamantly ignored student and faculty complaints about these issues plus quality-of-life and community concerns, in particular dormitory conditions and university plans to build a new gymnasium on city-owned parkland. Then SDS activists found evidence Columbia had misled the community regarding government contracts, including with the CIA and IDA. Once officials rejected a petition against IDA involvement signed by 1,500 faculty and students and presented on March 27, 1968, the mood turned explosive. After the university disciplined five SDS members for anti-IDA demonstrations, applying rules that had been ignored in similar instances, if anything, the atmosphere became worse.

Contempt for student opinion would be epitomized by the professor who declared that students' views on war, peace, and the university in its community were no more important than whether they liked strawberries.[49] The revolt was prefigured on April 9 when protesters, led by SDS chapter head Mark Rudd, demonstrated after a memorial service for Martin Luther King. On April 23 IDA war research and the gymnasium were the subjects at the "Sundial" on College Walk, the traditional locale for Columbia rallies. This led to a sit-in at Hamilton Hall, the main classroom building for Columbia College. An occupation of Hamilton followed. The racial split developing swiftly in American protests is shown by the way black students and community people asked the rest to leave the next morning. Ejected, the SDS then took over Low Library, the Columbia administration building. On the second day, architecture students took over their building, Avery Hall, and others occupied Fayerweather Hall, where economics and political science were taught, as well as Mathematics Hall. Swirling around the occupations were students opposed to these tactics, faculty coming out on both sides, and community leaders supporting the Hamilton Hall blockade. The university summoned police, and a siege began that extended through April 30, when New York riot police from the Tactical Patrol Force (TPF) forcibly entered every building not vacated. The violence of the TPF maneuver, in which 143 protesters, bystanders, and even counterprotesters were hurt (over a hundred required hospital treatment) and 712 arrested, shook the Columbia community. The dispute intensified rather than diminished. Support for university president Grayson Kirk evaporated, and classes were suspended. When the university attempted to reopen on May 6, thousands boycotted class. Hamilton Hall was reoccupied and cleared by the TPF again on May 21, with another 138 arrests. Police action radicalized like nothing else. Anyone could be pulled in. Novelist Paul Auster, then a Columbia undergrad, had taken his junior year abroad in Paris, returned late, and gained reinstatement just a few months earlier. Now Auster ended up in the thick of things; he helped occupy a building, suffering injury and arrest at TPF hands. He then disengaged and went on to his literary work. Not so Josephine Duke, a Barnard College student who opened a GI coffeehouse outside Fort Dix, New Jersey.

A major American university had effectively been shut down by the Vietnam war. This had considerable impact. Deputy Secretary of Defense Paul Nitze met one of the Columbia SDS leaders through his daughter and ended up in long conversations with other leftists. Nitze took his impressions into the Johnson administration. Army intelligence promulgated a plan for collecting data on civil disturbances on May 2, and its chief critiqued Justice Department proposals. Military intelligence units also paid attention, with the Army's 432nd Intelligence Group working directly at Columbia. When protesters showed up outside the East 16th Street offices of the Army's 108th Military Intelligence Group, the captain in charge was so shaken he had revolvers issued to duty staff.[50]

On May 14 FBI director J. Edgar Hoover ordered COINTELPRO operations directed at the antiwar movement, on top of those already under way. Declassified FBI reports indicate that the Bureau had at least five informants at Columbia. In line with the FBI initiative, its New York office looked for data to substantiate claims that the New York Police Department had acted responsibly—a futile effort. Washington officials clucked approvingly at Columbia professor Zbigniew Brzezinski's theory that students were motivated by desperation: society had passed them by, becoming technocratic, while they were mired in the past, their protests the "death rattle of historical irrelevants."[51] Anxiety can only have increased as less intense but similar student strikes occurred that spring at several other universities.

Richard Nixon, now positioning himself as the Republican candidate for president in the 1968 election, called the Columbia troubles the "first major skirmish in a revolutionary struggle to seize the universities."[52]

New England SDS regional traveler Eric Mann noted, "The Columbia strike more than any other event . . . has given the radical student movement the belief that we can really change this country."[53] Tom Hayden reminisced, "I had never seen anything quite like this."[54] At the time he wrote in *Ramparts,* "Columbia opened a new stage in the resistance movement which began last fall."[55] Antiwar historian Dan Berger called Columbia a "catalyst for white radicals."[56] Similarly, Jeremy Varon observed, "the use of police violence . . . fed an uncompromising rhetoric of condemnation that compelled the protesters to see political conflict in overtly confrontational terms."[57] The U.S. government thought so too. Paul Auster walked into a rural Massachusetts post office a year later and, scanning the pictures as he waited in line, was stunned to discover that he knew seven of the ten persons on the FBI's Most Wanted list, all from Columbia.

Hanoi certainly noticed the post-Tet political troubles in the United States. Soviet diplomat Anatoly Dobrynin concluded that Johnson's withdrawal from American politics "only consolidated the determination of the North Vietnamese leadership to fight to the end while still hoping the United States would become more flexible if negotiations actually began."[58] In deciding for *Tet Mau Than,* Hanoi had all along seen the general uprising as a "process," implying that it had stages. Politburo instructions to COSVN on April 8 set a policy of fighting while talking, explicitly linking the strategy to the Tet orders in Resolution 13, this time foreseeing "political attacks" that would support "our powerful attacks on the battlefield aimed at securing a major victory."[59] There would be another wave of Tet, and this time Hanoi expected a political outcome.

■ ■ ■ The second wave of Tet attacks turned out far differently than Hanoi anticipated. They converted what had been a costly if ambiguous result into an actual military setback. Halfway through April a senior NLF officer defected. Colonel Tran Van Dac, alias Tam Ha, told the South Vietnamese about the second phase, scheduled for late April but likely to be postponed due to difficult preparations. The offensive began on May 4 around Saigon and again featured assorted attacks throughout the country. There was tough fighting in the capital, where four U.S. battalions fought alongside the ARVN, Police Field Force, and South Vietnamese Marine troops. An initial flurry of attacks was beaten off, then another assault came in late May and June. This time the North Vietnamese and NLF sustained at least 36,000 losses without capturing any key objective. But allied casualties included more than 9,000 dead and as many wounded as the enemy had suffered in dead and defectors combined. The second wave of Tet had been a bloody one. Hanoi historians concede it lost the element of surprise, and NLF troop units were much understrength, disrupted by successive U.S.-ARVN sweeps.

A neglected aspect of the Saigon battle is that it pulled the rug out from under Saigon's flamboyant air marshal and vice president, Nguyen Cao Ky. At a critical juncture a number of Ky's most important loyalists were wiped out. Official South Vietnamese accounts attribute this to friendly fire—a mistaken rocket launch from a U.S. gunship—but Ky himself reported that the culprits were never identified. Ky heard rumors that the gunship had actually been crewed by Colonel Tran Van Hai, the ARVN's Ranger commander and a Thieu man. The casualties included General Loan, who lost his leg; his deputy; the Saigon and district police leaders; and the port director. Ky himself had been asked to visit the Chinese school on Khong Le street where this carnage occurred, but a dream the night before left him afraid for his life, and he stayed in bed that morning. At one stroke Ky lost control of the security apparatus, the local police machinery, and customs enforcement. Ky, who was rumored to traffic in drugs and engage in more common corruption, never recovered. Thieu appointed Colonel Hai to replace Loan as the head of the National Police.

Hanoi made one more try, in August. The third wave employed new tactics, with almost all attacks carried out as bombardments or small-scale sapper assaults. But again the allies were ready. This time the NLF and Hanoi sustained at least 17,000 losses against overall allied casualties totaling about 16,000. Hanoi's history is frank about the offensive's shortcomings:

COSVN and region 5 concluded that all local areas and units had made
efforts, but because the time allotted was short and absolute secrecy had to be
maintained, our preparation of supplies, spiritual preparations, and
preparation of tactics were all insufficient. We were subjective in our

assessment of the situation, especially in assessing the strength of the mass political forces in the urban areas. We had somewhat underestimated the capabilities and reactions of the enemy and had set our goals too high. Our plan for military attacks was too simplistic and our arrangements for carrying out and coordinating combat operations by our forces for coordination between the battlefields and between military attack and the mass uprisings were disjointed . . . When the battle did not progress favorably for our side and when we suffered casualties, rightist thoughts, pessimism, and hesitancy appeared among our forces.

They admit other faults too: "Because we did not reassess the situation in a timely fashion, especially after the development of a number of unfavorable factors in the balance of forces and the progress of the war, we did not move quickly enough to shift the direction of our attacks. We continued to attack the cities, leaving the rural areas open and undefended."[60] The People's Army and NLF suffered serious losses, were unable to keep more than a portion of their forces in the field, and pulled many units back to mountain base areas or into Cambodia.

In the end, *Tet Mau Than* constituted a political defeat for the United States and a military check for the DRV. The second and third waves converted Hanoi's check into a military disaster. But that defeat did not cancel out the American one. Washington could not convert its battlefield advantage into the progress Lyndon Johnson had sought so long. There were many reasons for this failure, beginning with eroding support for the war. There would also be military reasons why the advantage proved fleeting. And that would be true despite Herculean efforts by LBJ, and then a new president, to achieve victory. Again, this story begins in the United States.

7   Terrible Swift Sword (1968–1969)

Chicago. For those thinking back on the events of 1968, the name has just one meaning. Beyond the race riots, beyond the stockyards, Chicago references a tragedy very much akin to what happened at Columbia. Antiwar protesters went to Chicago that August to demonstrate outside the Democratic National Convention. They were met by baton-wielding, bone-crushing police. There would be an official inquest by a special staff led by Daniel Walker and reporting to the National Commission on the Causes and Prevention of Violence. The Walker investigation's conclusion was that there had been a police riot in Chicago, that "police violence was a fact of convention week."[1] Chicago marked an American counterpoint to events in France and West Germany, one that revealed Vietnam's fissures.

Chicago did not happen in isolation. It was the product of tensions building on all sides of the Vietnam imbroglio. One was the increasing militance of the Movement. Todd Gitlin the SDSer had moved to California in late 1967 and found it hard to believe America was ready for change, but he watched the draft protests and responded to Tet with fresh energy. "Attitudes were cheap," he noted, "what counted was *stopping the war.*"[2] Gitlin did not avoid Berkeley in June, when police engaged Trotskyists of the Young Socialist Alliance in street fights along Telegraph Avenue, a disturbance that began with a rally supporting the French student revolt.

Already Eugene McCarthy had stunned political circles with his performance in the New Hampshire primary. Robert F. Kennedy then entered the race. LBJ withdrew. The assassination of Martin Luther King threw the nation into chaos. Bobby Kennedy soldiered on, trying to rebuild bridges between blacks and whites, telling a crowd at the Indianapolis airport, "What we need in America is not division . . . but love, and wisdom, and compassion toward one another." Kennedy's entrance into the campaign generated immense enthusiasm, attracting many who were unmoved by McCarthy. The latter watched some of his own support siphoned off to the younger, more dynamic Kennedy. The two were equally opposed to the war. Bobby won primaries in Indiana, Nebraska, and the District of Columbia, but he still needed traction. McCarthy beat him in Oregon. California became the prize, and Kennedy carried the primary there on June 5. Appearing to claim the laurels, he was gunned down by Sirhan Sirhan.

Robert Kennedy's death raised the hysteria of 1968 to a new level. Todd Gitlin alternated between feeling the murder unthinkable and inevitable. Bernardine Dohrn recorded the death in her appointment calendar. Tom Hayden wept when Kennedy's casket lay on view at St. Patrick's Cathedral. Daniel Ellsberg, in Chicago for a conference on the war, wept too. Several of those at his meeting were in the same state. Thousands of Americans shed tears or stood silently by the tracks as a special funeral train bore Kennedy's body from New York to Washington for burial at Arlington National Cemetery. "I had a sudden vision the war wasn't going to end," Ellsberg ruminated.[3] Movement historian Kirkpatrick Sale wrote that Kennedy's death "came with a kind of fated resignation, another glaring symptom of the national malady."[4] Lyndon Johnson put that thought better: "Robert Kennedy's death seemed to symbolize the irrationality that was besieging our nation and the world."[5]

Events were in the saddle. Electoral and radical politics headed for a showdown in Chicago, where police action would drive liberals closer to the New Left. On the electoral side, Vice President Hubert H. Humphrey had entered the race late in April. Both Kennedy and McCarthy had beaten him by margins of 3–1 or 4–1 in California, but drawing on his own base and LBJ's support, Humphrey swiftly captured the party machinery, gaining delegates. A longtime civil rights champion, Humphrey also had advantages among African Americans. Kennedy had represented a serious challenge, but he was gone. McCarthy failed both to pick up the orphaned Kennedy supporters and to increase his own dynamism. McCarthy arrived for the August convention with a small core of committed delegates. Other liberals fought for an "open convention," hoping to detach Humphrey from his delegate base. They had little success.

The antiwar protesters came with a variety of purposes. Abbie Hoffman's Yippies had made Rennie Davis their main strategist, and Davis wanted a "Festival of Life" in Chicago. The Yippies would ridicule the system by nominating a pig for president. Dave Dellinger's Mobe had serious goals, aiming to use nonviolent resistance to engender a new form of democracy. The SDS went to Chicago too. Some groups were more involved with electoral politics. Fred Halsted observed that Women Strike for Peace and Chicago-area SANE chapters were backing McCarthy. Halsted's own socialists feared protesters being co-opted by Democratic Party reformers.

The veterans went to Chicago as well. Carl Rogers, vice president of the nascent Vietnam Veterans Against the War, went as part of an ad hoc "Veterans for McCarthy" group, which had basically supplanted VVAW. He flew out with pacifist Dellinger. The grizzled activist asked the young, handsome Rogers whether, after the convention, VVAW intended to reconstitute itself. "Probably," Rogers answered. Dellinger, of the Old Left, encouraged him: "You veterans are the most important thing happening in the antiwar movement today."[6] The comment would be prescient.

Todd Gitlin's analysis is that "Chicago became a Gotterdammerung because all the protagonists thought polarization served their larger purposes."[7] This view has a certain plausibility, because New Left groups always had conflicting goals, but it attributes too much to the kaleidoscope of factions. It would be more accurate to say that at Chicago the objectives of all the New Left groups were overtaken by the police riot. Norman Mailer, who pursued his dip into political reporting with a book on the political conventions of 1968, would call it "The Siege of Chicago." For Mailer, "The event was a convention that took place during a continuing five-day battle in the streets and parks of Chicago between some of the minions of the high established, and some of the nihilistic of the young."[8]

The police were primed for a fight. Since the spring, when they used force to break up a demonstration at Chicago's Civic Center, the police had abandoned any pretext of neutrality. And security forces had been planning for the convention for a long time. The Police Intelligence Division's "Red Squad" (known by that name since the 1920s) had divided its attention between civil rights and antiwar groups, but by 1967 it focused more closely on the latter. That fall police actually burglarized the offices of Women Strike for Peace, the Chicago Peace Council, and the Fellowship for Reconciliation. By February 1968 the police department's planning committee had already opened channels to the Secret Service, military intelligence, the National Guard, and convention organizers and hosts. Yippie events were raided and participants arrested. Police intelligence gathered the leaflets the protesters put out, infiltrated the groups, and collated data from elsewhere. In March a large number of police officers were given special training in minimally aggressive crowd-control tactics—which had not mattered a whit at the Civic Center incident. More than a month before the convention, police began openly following black leaders, even though their intelligence indicated that protests would come from elsewhere. The crudity of this security work is exhibited by widespread expressions by police in source materials that the protesters were "hippies," counterculture dropouts who preferred to turn on and tune out, when in fact hippies were elusive recruits for Movement organizers throughout the years of protest.

Mayor Richard Daley contributed to the troubles, pushing through a new municipal ordinance on disorderly conduct, creating difficulties over parade and camping permits, and arranging for a partial mobilization of the National Guard. When a Justice Department official met Daley to apprise him of the protesters' plans, trying to avert violence by ensuring each side knew what the other was up to, the mayor cut him off. "The city of Chicago will take care of the city of Chicago," Daley brusquely said.[9] Days before the convention the mayor thundered that outsiders were the only troublemakers, and he repeatedly included the media. Parade and camping permits that covered the range of planned protest activities were denied, virtually ensuring confrontation if the city enforced its ordinances.

Deputy Superintendent James Rochford commanded police operations throughout the convention. There were 12,000 officers in the Chicago Police Department. Not all of them were involved, but the police presence would be strong. In an ominous concatenation of events, on August 20, days before the convention, Soviet tanks rolled into Czechoslovakia to crush the "Prague Spring." There is no authoritative estimate of the size of the demonstrations in Chicago, but 10,000 is the generally accepted number. The police began acting against protesters the weekend before the Democratic convention, moving into Lincoln Park where the Yippies had their campsite. Police cleared it one night; the next there were ten times as many protesters. Violence began. Protesters forced out of the park carried their anger to the streets, overturning garbage cans, engaging in random vandalism. Police escalated. They gassed crowds a number of times that week. Reporters were clubbed along with protesters. Cameras were broken, notebooks seized; it was open season. Protesters pelted police with empty bottles, rocks, whatever they could find. The scene shifted to Grant Park, near the Conrad Hilton Hotel, convention headquarters for some candidates. Uptown, downtown, from the bus barn to the Polish consulate, police chased people and broke up their marches. When the National Guard deployed, they set up machine guns. Twice police invaded the Hilton, cracking heads among party delegates, campaign staff, and helpers sent to observe the horrors. All this was captured on television, on film, and in reporters' journals. Indeed, protesters at several points chanted, "The Whole World Is Watching!"[10]

It did not matter. Rochford ended up obliged to order his officers to desist, sometimes having to actually pull them off citizens. The Walker report estimated that approximately 1,100 people were injured at Chicago, 400 gassed, and 58 had to be hospitalized. Some 668 were arrested. Of the 192 injuries sustained by police, more than three-quarters occurred on the fourth day, when protesters became enraged. It is almost a footnote to state that the Democratic convention chose Humphrey as its nominee that same day, on the first ballot and by a comfortable margin. McCarthy delayed his departure to make sure his people got out of Chicago safely. As McCarthy's chartered plane took off, the pilot announced, "We are leaving Prague."[11]

Lyndon Johnson's absence did not mean that events in Chicago were of no concern to him. LBJ entertained notions of coming back as a dark horse if the convention deadlocked, and he secretly commissioned both a speech and a laudatory documentary film on his life. LBJ treated Chicago as a sally of invigorated forces to battle dissent. Clark Clifford recorded, "In the weeks preceding the convention, we discussed at length what role, if any, the federal government should play if civil disturbances, which radical groups were threatening, broke out in Chicago."[12] Clifford favored prepositioning Army troops. Attorney General Ramsey Clark, who also repeatedly turned down FBI demands for wiretaps on the Chicago offices of Dellinger's National Mobilization Committee, opposed the troops. Johnson sent them anyway.

Army communications specialists installed and operated a command post next to the amphitheater. They kept an open line to both the Pentagon and the White House. The CIA communications van and specialists were back. Armored personnel carriers were placed at Soldiers' Field, right off Lake Shore Drive, under Secret Service control. Meanwhile, 6,000 troops in full combat gear were airlifted in to reinforce an equal number of Illinois National Guardsmen. In an indication of the growing restiveness within the U.S. armed forces, 31 African American soldiers refused to deploy. At Fort Hood the Army staged a full-scale riot-control exercise involving some 7,500 men. Military police arrested GIs who refused to participate.

The Pentagon followed developments on a daily basis. On August 19, as Chicago was ramping up, intervention plans were fourth on the agenda at Clifford's morning staff meeting. Army deputy secretary David McGiffert gave a detailed briefing on prospects for violence and described how it would be handled. By August 26 Chicago had risen to the top of the agenda, right after the day's review of global security threats. McGiffert again led the discussion. Given that the Soviets had just invaded Czechoslovakia, which some thought could trigger World War III, and the Tet third wave had spiked, that is a telling comment on the importance of Chicago to the Department of Defense.

President Johnson's political maneuvers were no less serious. In the middle of the convention LBJ wanted to go to Chicago to defend himself and perhaps also encourage a draft-Johnson shift. Clifford spent eight hours closeted with Harry McPherson and political adviser Joe Califano, writing a speech for the president. Johnson separately and secretly sent McPherson to California the week before to help with the movie. LBJ finally canceled the trip. When Clifford's morning meeting mulled over Chicago's outcome on August 30, aide George M. Elsey exclaimed, "How fortunate LBJ didn't go!"[13]

Hubert Humphrey needed to create space between himself and Johnson to have any chance in the election. LBJ's pressure dissuaded Humphrey from any speech that broke with the White House on Vietnam, but the candidate resolved to have a peace plank in the party platform. Johnson made that impossible, getting loyalists to ensure the platform conformed to his policy. LBJ had Walt Rostow send a back-channel message to General Abrams, gathering ammunition for surrogates in Chicago, who used it to torpedo the factual basis for Humphrey's Vietnam plank. The defense secretary discovered the ruse when Abrams, guarding his flank, notified Clifford and Ambassador Bunker. Rostow then circulated the same questions to top NSC officials, as if the White House were doing a routine sounding. Rostow claimed that, without bombing, Hanoi's infiltration rate would triple and the United States would have to abandon important posts in the South. But Pentagon data showed that bombing attrition had never exceeded 7 percent, even in 1967, when there had been *no* restrictions on "armed reconnaissance." Analyzing Abrams's cable, Clifford told staff he needed to "bear down hard" on the president, Rostow, and Max Taylor—still LBJ's personal military adviser—"pointing out how terribly dangerous it is—not just to use military stuff in politics but *phony* military stuff whose figures *won't* stand up!"[14] The Vietnam data problem posed a stumbling block to every kind of action.

■ ■ ■ Clark Clifford not only worked hard to keep Lyndon Johnson viable politically; he played a large role in providing Washington the strategy it followed through the rest of the American war. The idea for Vietnamization—indeed, the foundations of the program—were not products of the next administration but innovated by Clifford, approved by Lyndon Johnson, and foisted on Saigon during this same fateful summer of 1968. Creighton Abrams would be a front-row player, but the new MACV commander would have gotten nowhere without Clifford's political savvy, his influence on Johnson, and his steady hand in dealing with the Joint Chiefs of Staff.

Secretary Clifford and General Abrams cemented their alliance when the Pentagon chief visited Saigon in mid-July. LBJ had sent him to find ways to better publicize South Vietnamese army efforts and see if more ARVN troops could be sent to I Corps—pretty standard stuff. As MACV deputy commander, Abrams had been in charge of helping the ARVN and had long wanted a new level of effort. Tet brought some changes—particularly a priority on giving the ARVN M-16 assault rifles—but commitments fell short of what Abrams felt necessary. For his part, Clifford saw the political impact of U.S. casualties and wanted to reduce them. Washington's analyses showed the adversary effectively controlled the loss rate by choosing when to fight, so the practical way to cut losses was to have fewer Americans at risk and let the ARVN do more of the fighting. Clifford focused on the second point for the moment and discovered that, other than the M-16s, little had been ordered for the latest ARVN augmentation of 84,000 troops. He feared that the war was drifting. Clifford's meeting with Thieu also convinced him that Saigon did not want to end the conflict and would not budge so long as a large U.S. expeditionary force protected it. Withdrawals would have the dual benefit of reducing casualties and signaling that Saigon's days of wine and roses were ending.

Later critics, such as Colonel Harry Summers, accused Clark Clifford of duplicity and disloyalty in managing the "A to Z" review and in his subsequent actions.[15] They claim Clifford somehow prevented U.S. forces from exploiting "victory" at Tet. This view distorts to the point of caricature. In fact, for eight months of 1968, Hanoi, not MACV, held the initiative. And the U.S. military still had no operational concept for victory and no strategic reserve deployable without triggering national trauma, as the furor over Westmoreland's troop request demonstrated quite clearly. Moreover, the center of gravity in the war had shifted. Those participants who just *knew*, on the day of Tet, that everything had changed were right. Major escalation was no longer politically sustainable. Clifford rendered a service in recognizing the bankruptcy of strategy and configuring a way to buy time.

Meanwhile, President Johnson called another of his flash summits for Honolulu at the conclusion of the Clifford visit. Thus the secretary left Vietnam in the company of the Saigon leadership, all of them headed to the conference. Clifford privately told LBJ of his concerns. Nguyen Van Thieu, no dummy, caught wind of Clifford's misgivings, very likely from Bunker, and sent his own signal. Visiting an aircraft carrier shortly before the Honolulu summit, Thieu told reporters he foresaw the beginning of U.S. withdrawal. Now he gave Johnson the same message directly: American troops could begin to leave in mid-1969. Thus, before the end of that July 1968 summit, both pillars of what became the Vietnamization program were in place.

Another concern was the third wave of Hanoi's *Tet Mau Than*. For more than a month Washington and Saigon had expected new attacks. The intelligence was solid, but the People's Army had completed its tactical transformation, and the contours of this operation were very different. Americans were left scratching their heads, wondering whether the offensive had really happened. This exercise culminated at a White House meeting where Clifford recited a long series of statistics comparing the scale of enemy activity in August with that of earlier periods, demonstrating that a high point had indeed occurred. Although Hanoi's new tactics limited losses, these remained considerable. Suddenly VPA main-force units began to pull back to base areas in Indian Country or behind the Cambodian border. By mid-September Washington pondered whether this reflected the wounds of Tet or a subtle sign that Hanoi wanted to negotiate. To pursue the enemy would have meant invading neutral Cambodia or exceeding U.S. logistical capabilities in the Central Highlands and other places by deploying massive American forces there, neither a realistic measure. That is where the Summers critique ultimately leads.

An enduring mystery of this period lies in the mind of Lyndon Baines Johnson. Much of what he said publicly, plus his effort to put together a U.S. bargaining position for talks, reflects a commitment to peace. But some of what he did privately—torpedoing the Humphrey peace plank, certain maneuvers with Republican candidate Richard Nixon (discussed later), and rejiggering the war to reduce visibility without impairing effectiveness—suggests a different intent. The March 31 speech can also be read as a device to quiet dissent and buy time for one last roll of the dice. This conundrum reflects Johnson's long ambivalence over Vietnam. There is no direct evidence here, but only a record of LBJ's personal behavior. Here again the anti-war movement takes center stage.

■ ■ ■ A week after his March 31 speech Lyndon Johnson chop-pered to Camp David, the presidential retreat in the Catoctin Mountains. This visit was his first in almost a year, and it was billed as a time to consider a U.S. negotiating strategy. An array of key officials went with or followed LBJ to the secluded northern Maryland hideaway, including Clifford, Rusk, Harriman, Bunker, and Rostow. But the trip was more than a palaver on diplomacy; it was an opportunity for Johnson to get away from the hysteria of rioting in the wake of King's murder and to take refuge from the contro-versies of Vietnam. On this level, the Camp David trip represented LBJ pro-tecting himself, something he did quietly but definitely during his last year in office. The vicissitudes of Vietnam wounded him deeply.

Like many presidents, Lyndon chafed at the security requirements im-posed by his Secret Service White House Detail. Though he had affection for—and a close relationship with—Rufus W. Youngblood, the special agent heading his protective unit, LBJ nevertheless saw the Secret Service as getting in the way of his glad-handing political manner. Youngblood had earned Johnson's confidence when, at the time of the Kennedy assassination, the Se-cret Service agent had leaped on the then vice president to shield him from a potential bullet. LBJ had presided over the ceremony in December 1963 where Youngblood received an exceptional service award. Only a month later Johnson had phoned Youngblood to complain of low morale at the Secret Service and that members of the White House Detail were requesting trans-fers.

Johnson, code-named "VOLUNTEER," became notorious among Secret Ser-vice agents. In June 1964 he complained to another agent, Floyd Boring, that he was humiliated at having to give the detail a day's notice when he wanted to go to New York. At the White House the president sometimes hopped in a car or a boat and told staff just to drive away, leaving the Secret Service to trail VOLUNTEER as best they could. At the LBJ Ranch Johnson did the driving himself, tearing around the hardscrabble at seventy miles per hour with a cooler of beer in the backseat and an open can between his legs. The presi-dent did enough of that on the Ranch to wear out a favored Lincoln Conti-nental convertible every year of his presidency. He told Youngblood the detail did not have the sense to stay back as he gunned the car, then slammed on the brakes, and that he was comfortable with only one agent in his car.

Those were early days. As antiwar sentiment rose, Johnson's behavior changed. VOLUNTEER accepted security more readily, then began restricting his travel. The Secret Service started to run interference between the presi-dent and protesters, and antiwar opposition increasingly fueled supposed threats to the chief executive. When LBJ visited McConnell Air Force Base in November 1966, the Secret Service broke up a demonstration against him, arresting local SDS figures as alleged threats. Other similar instances led to lawsuits. The Secret Service opened an office in Paris for foreign intelligence liaison whose only purpose could have been surveilling the antiwar visitors to Hanoi's mission, since Johnson visited Europe only twice during his presidency—once for the funeral of the German chancellor, the other a visit to Rome.

In fiscal year 1964 (JFK's last), there had been 80 arrests for threats to the president. There were more than 400 in each of fiscal years 1966 and 1967, and the Secret Service took more than 200 individuals into custody in front of the White House and had them committed for psychological observation. The Secret Service intelligence unit, which had typically handled 100 items a month in 1963, was fielding 7,000 a month four years later. The Secret Service also maintained a permanent list of those considered a threat to the president. That file contained 400 names in 1963 but 1,800 in 1967.[16]

During each of his last two years in the White House, LBJ made about forty trips, a dozen of them political. The fact that the number grew only slightly in VOLUNTEER's last year is remarkable, since 1968 was the political year, when the president should have been on the hustings almost every day. Johnson never went to New Hampshire for its primary, never went to Chicago for the convention; he made only one appearance in support of Hubert Humphrey. Special agent Marty Venker, who joined the detail a little later, remarked, "In his last days as President, about the only place where he could safely shake hands was on a military base, with a crowd of soldiers."[17] Similarly, Secret Service historian Richard Melanson records that LBJ became a "political recluse," a man who "holed up in the White House or visited only those few places—mostly military bases—where he might find a friendly audience."[18] These comments get the recluse part right, but they exaggerate the other. In 1967 and 1968 Johnson visited military bases exactly three times each year. But the president visited the LBJ Ranch, on average, once a month in 1967 and no fewer than eighteen times during his final year in office. The president went to Camp David ten times in those two years. His visits to such protected locations during the last half of 1968 were twice as frequent as during the same months of the preceding year.

Nor was VOLUNTEER safe abroad. In the fall of 1967 LBJ traveled to Australia for talks there and for the funeral of Prime Minister Harold Holt. Protesters threw balloons filled with red and green paint at Johnson's motorcade, and his Secret Service detail, led by Youngblood, took the brunt of the barrage. A year later VOLUNTEER complimented the Secret Service at a commemoration, recalling how he had cried inside his car, looking at the special agents "with that paint streaming down their faces, splattered all over them, but their chins up and their President safe."[19]

When he had to be seen, Johnson took extra measures. Press aide George Christian reported, "He was openly self-conscious about his personal protection."[20] The White House ordered a new armored limousine from the Ford Corporation, hand-built with a glass roof so that LBJ could be seen without endangering himself. In November 1967 VOLUNTEER scheduled an address to the National Grange Association meeting in Syracuse, New York. But when Secret Service advance people discovered protesters preparing cups of urine, LBJ canceled the trip. When Johnson went to New York in December for the funeral of Francis Cardinal Spellman, the White House press corps got no advance notice. LBJ landed at a remote location (Floyd Bennett Field on Long Island) and helicoptered to Central Park to avoid a motorcade into the city.

In February 1968, while returning from a trip to salute the troops being sent to reinforce MACV after Tet, LBJ told the press corps he would not be giving much prior warning on his future travels. Sighs turned to groans a week later when VOLUNTEER flew to Dallas on an hour and a half's notice, motored through city traffic in an unmarked car, and continued the trip in the same fashion, announcing each destination just before takeoff. Even this did not prevent LBJ from being confronted by about a hundred demonstrators in Austin when he landed at Bergstrom Air Force Base (today, Austin's international airport). On a trip a week later, VOLUNTEER announced his destination *after* Air Force One was already in flight.

So it went, through the year. LBJ could not enforce the no-notice travel routine, but the Ranch increasingly became his sole or primary destination. On October 17 Johnson returned to New York (again, without notice) for the Alfred E. Smith Memorial Foundation Dinner at the Waldorf-Astoria Hotel, where he appeared with both Hubert Humphrey and Richard Nixon. Observers thought the president witty and whimsical when, in a nod to Nixon, he said, "Pretty soon you won't have Lyndon Johnson to kick around any more." But more tellingly Johnson went on, "I don't think any veteran could appreciate my feelings on this night except maybe General Custer." And most significantly of all, President Johnson described himself as "the resident prisoner of a big white jailhouse."[21] Outside, a double ring of police surrounded the hotel. Soon after, Johnson left for Camp David.

Lyndon Johnson anguished over the war, and this evidence shows him acutely aware of the feelings of Americans. More than any poll numbers, personal experience put the president on notice that some strategic options in Vietnam were just not viable. Another bid for victory stood foremost among them. Negotiations offered the only solution.

October Surprise

Diplomacy had become a major enterprise. Instead of frustrating peace feelers in the dark, the sides were at last communicating.

Hanoi's opening after President Johnson's March 31 speech led first to desultory exchanges on a venue, but the sides finally settled on Paris. By the summer the delegations were meeting regularly. The Americans were led by Averell Harriman and Cyrus Vance; Hanoi's team was headed by Xuan Thuy, with Colonel Ha Van Lau and Mai Van Bo, supervised by Le Duc Tho, who never appeared at the table but hovered in the wings. Progress on preliminaries enabled LBJ and Thieu to discuss their stance at Honolulu in July.

But much of the talking amounted to posturing before world opinion, scoring propaganda points rather than moving toward a settlement. The Democratic Republic of Vietnam still stood on what amounted to Pham Van Dong's old four points, although DRV diplomats said otherwise. Records of Washington's internal deliberations show that its own protestations of flexibility were less than real: a stand-still cease-fire, the only practical way to end the fighting, was unacceptable because this would leave North Vietnamese troops in control of territory in the South. There also remained the problem of the Saigon government and the National Liberation Front, neither of which participated at this stage. Washington concerned itself with Saigon, of course. It was up to Hanoi to insist on the inclusion of the NLF. How a settlement could be forged without their involvement could only be guessed at. Finding out fueled a CIA feeler to the Front.

Secretary Clifford tried to resolve the impasse in September. Clifford wanted to give Hanoi a complete bombing halt in return for Saigon's presence at the bargaining table. The Soviets delivered the message and a favorable reply. Certain conditions became attached as Clifford strove for approval on his own side: Hanoi must cease attacks on South Vietnamese cities and refrain from violating the Demilitarized Zone. Broached with DRV negotiators, this formula led to the first real movement in the negotiations. Exchanges in Paris led to an expectation that this direction could be productive, and in October President Johnson began marathon deliberations. At midmonth he made a final decision. Then the formula crashed and burned in an episode that has become known as the "October Surprise" (the origin of the phrase used to describe all subsequent October surprises that seem to afflict U.S. elections). "If this segment of history had been written as a work of fiction," LBJ would later reflect, "it would have been a comedy." He also noted, "There were so many currents and crosscurrents running that it was hard sometimes to know what was happening and why . . . But it was happening before our eyes, and in real life."[22]

A major obstacle would be the Thieu regime in Saigon. The way the story is understood, Thieu decided he could get a better deal from a Republican successor and conspired to help candidate Richard Nixon. That is part of the story, but incomplete. The truth is that Thieu opposed *any* negotiated solution. Soon after Tet, Thieu had demanded accelerated improvements of the ARVN, and his own plans increased South Vietnamese forces to more than a million troops. That summer he issued a law for full mobilization. Thieu rejected any deal that included a national unity government with the NLF. He wanted a halt to Hanoi's infiltration and its supplies to the Liberation Front. This amounted to a demand for surrender—not a likely outcome. As early as June, speaking to visiting U.S. diplomat Kenneth T. Young, Thieu had remarked, "Many Vietnamese are afraid of an American abandonment of Vietnam or a sell-out in Paris."[23] His point was that Washington should agree to no settlement. Thieu saw clearly enough that the United States could not proceed as before, that negotiation had become inevitable. Saigon could live with that so long as the Americans remained on the offensive militarily and kept up their support. Thieu gambled on military victory eclipsing negotiations. He acquiesced in the beginning of U.S. withdrawal because that, too, had become unavoidable.[24]

What did Nguyen Van Thieu expect? It is significant that, suddenly, coup rumors returned to Saigon. Already in mid-September Thieu had had a conversation with Nguyen Cao Ky in which they mulled over coup dangers. Of course, Ky was the main suspect as instigator, since he was being edged out and his loyalists neutralized or eliminated. The purported source of anxiety—alleged plotting by pacification officers and others in I Corps, retailed by Thieu's National Police chief (who had replaced Ky's man Loan)—lacked any real significance. The meeting amounted to a warning to Ky cloaked in the guise of talk about whether the *Americans* might engineer a coup to move the talks along.[25] Thieu had already deployed ARVN Rangers thickly around the presidential palace. On October 8 he suddenly called a red alert, preparing his troops. No coup transpired. Ky accepted his increasing isolation. But to the extent that Thieu responded to Saigon politics at all, he operated on the assumption that meaningful progress in the peace talks endangered his power. The better deal Thieu expected from Nixon must have been for Washington *not to settle* with Hanoi.

There were sources of inertia in Washington too. Clifford and Harriman might have been enthusiastic and General Abrams resigned, but others were less amenable. Dean Rusk continued to be reluctant, while Bunker took Thieu's side. The Joint Chiefs were uncomfortable but willing to go along. Walt Rostow played a complex game: on the one hand, seeming to adopt the position of his boss, LBJ, who feared leaving office having done nothing to jump-start talks; on the other hand, throwing up obstacles. Rostow became the prime mover in a last-minute demand that Hanoi agree in advance that talks be "meaningful." He advised LBJ to plan for military action in case diplomacy failed, suggesting the predictable options (bombing Cambodian base areas, resuming Rolling Thunder, bombing Hanoi-Haiphong, mining Haiphong, ground attacks in or north of the DMZ). At a crucial moment he ordered the State Department to cut Clifford out of the cable traffic. Clifford's access would be restored when State's top administrator went to Rusk and objected that the secretary of defense could not function without the cables. One reason President Johnson's deliberations went on for more than a month was the struggle to get everyone on board.

Hanoi triggered a headache of its own when it balked at beginning negotiations within days of their announcement. Suddenly the North Vietnamese said they could not ensure the appearance of NLF representatives that quickly. The DRV also wanted the Americans to acknowledge that the bombing halt was "unconditional." Johnson, frustrated and angry, nevertheless persisted. Hanoi abandoned the idea of a formal acknowledgment and gradually moved to the stance that negotiations could begin a few days after a bombing halt. There is also a still murky piece of this history involving the CIA channel, which Liberation Front figures reportedly used to test the water for a deal that might have created a coalition government in Saigon, one that could have joined negotiations—a potential alternative explanation for Thieu's sudden fear of a coup.

Meanwhile, Washington crafted a scheme whereby Hanoi's agreement to Saigon's participation would kick off a series of scheduled events, ending in a joint announcement and the beginning of talks. The action was to begin on October 15. Johnson informed congressional leaders. Then Thieu intervened. A South Vietnamese official told Bunker that Saigon would eventually have to inform the allied nations—those fielding the FWF troops—and in fact Thieu's representative went to them that very day. Thieu claimed he had no idea what had happened, and the allies complained of being blindsided. Thieu demanded time to deliberate. One possibility is that the Saigon leader had learned of maneuvers in the NLF-CIA channel and now sought to retaliate against Washington. Then Hanoi changed the schedule, wanting more time to produce a Liberation Front delegation. Rusk represented the impasse to the media as solely a product of DRV delays, but on October 17 Saigon's foreign minister told the United States that it would not participate in any negotiation where the NLF appeared as a separate entity.[26]

The contention that Richard Nixon's campaign created an October Surprise hinges on timing and content—the exact moment when the Nixon camp and Saigon began their contacts and the content of their discussions. There would be denials later, and to this day, figures such as Melvin R. Laird insist there is nothing to this controversy. It is widely accepted that Nixon received back-channel information from academic Henry Kissinger, whose participation in LBJ peace feelers gave him contacts within the U.S. delegation in Paris as well as at high levels in the administration. Kissinger himself has called the entire narrative a "fairytale."[27]

The real problem with such denials is that independent evidence makes plain there were extensive contacts between the South Vietnamese embassy in Washington and key Nixon figures during the final days of the presidential campaign. Hoover's FBI followed persons entering and leaving the embassy and tapped its telephones. That the contacts occurred is beyond question; the mystery lies in their meaning. But the record of FBI surveillance shows this beginning in late October, *after* LBJ's negotiating initiative had begun to fray.

Lyndon Johnson is part of the problem. During the summer LBJ wavered, ruminating at one point that Nixon might be a better leader for the nation than Humphrey, his own vice president and the candidate of his party. Johnson actually hosted Nixon at the LBJ Ranch on August 10 for a wide-ranging discussion that included much on Vietnam. Notes on the meeting show that Nixon learned LBJ intended to stop the bombing "under [the] right conditions." The Republican candidate asked about Thieu's attitude and whether Hanoi "still" believed the United States had lost the war.[28] Johnson told Clifford later that Nixon had promised not to criticize the administration so long as LBJ did not "soften" his position. The defense secretary thought Nixon had been promoting himself as more sympathetic to Johnson on Vietnam than was Humphrey.[29] The net impression is that the Republican candidate took a hard line, much different from his campaign promise to end the war; had thoughts of reversing the military situation; and was aware of Thieu's misgivings. None of this dissuaded LBJ from keeping Nixon closely informed. Johnson phoned Nixon right away when Humphrey broke decisively with LBJ in a speech at Salt Lake City on September 30, coming out for an end to bombing. The next day Nixon accused Humphrey of "squandering the 'trump card' of a bombing halt by telegraphing to Hanoi what he would do as president."[30] LBJ had at least two more conversations with Nixon before October 16, when LBJ officially informed the candidates of the impending bombing halt and talks.

Then there was Henry Kissinger's inside information. Kissinger called October Surprise a fairytale in the 2003 version of his Vietnam story. But in his original memoir, from which the more recent version is constructed, Kissinger wrote that he had fobbed off Nixon emissaries by stating he would only answer specific foreign policy questions, not provide advice. When introduced to campaign manager John Mitchell in early October, Kissinger rendered the opinion that Hanoi would likely make a deal on the terms Johnson was offering and would do so just before the election. Mitchell, Kissinger noted, "checked that opinion with me once or twice more during the campaign." Kissinger was given a telephone number for Nixon aide H. R. Haldeman and was asked to call "if I ever received hard information."[31] Nixon was much more direct in *his* memoir. He claimed that Haldeman told him of the Kissinger link on September 12, a month earlier than Kissinger maintained, and two weeks later Henry called to report information he had received on a trip to Paris. A few days after that—still in September—Haldeman addressed a note to Nixon with more information Kissinger had given to Mitchell. Kissinger's specific details of limited contact disappeared from his 2003 account.

Richard Nixon thus had data from both LBJ and Kissinger. He also had at least three channels to President Thieu. One lay through his Texas political ally Senator John Tower. A second was rooted in his own staff—John Mitchell and foreign policy chief Richard Allen both had contacts with the South Vietnamese. The third utilized Republican political activist Anna Chennault. All these paths to Saigon went through ambassador Bui Diem, careful to water all flower beds, who kept open lines to both the Johnson administration and its Republican challengers. Chennault, in particular, had previously been asked to be a conduit between Nixon and Thieu. She visited Saigon, by her own account, to present "credentials" to the Saigon leader.[32] Chennault also had close contacts with Thieu's brother, who was Saigon's ambassador to Taiwan. Several weeks before Nixon's LBJ Ranch visit, Chennault met with the candidate at his New York apartment. Bui Diem also attended and spoke privately to both Nixon and Mitchell, giving them Thieu's view on the then-upcoming Honolulu summit. Nixon was thus well positioned to play politics with the Vietnam negotiations before election day.

Henry Kissinger, by Nixon's account, supplied information on October 12 that President Johnson would shortly stop the bombing. Chennault had ample time to pass a message. Thieu began stalling on October 15. Then, on the nineteenth, Thieu widened the breach with a televised speech in which he blasted Hanoi as undeserving of a bombing halt, making public his opposition to NLF representation at talks. President Johnson carried on for another ten days before demanding FBI surveillance.

When the president set the FBI to ferret out these maneuvers, he had already been forced to break a succession of schedules for the joint announcement. Each time Saigon raised some fresh difficulty (Hanoi by now had agreed with the United States to move forward). Johnson ordered FBI surveillance because he suspected chicanery. He also decided to go ahead despite Thieu. Johnson summoned General Abrams home to lend the weight of his reputation to the assertion that the halt would have no adverse impact on the war. Abrams arrived in the dead of night and participated in an unusual 2:00 AM NSC meeting. Johnson announced the bombing halt on October 31. America reacted with joy.

Richard Nixon told an audience at Madison Square Garden that night that he would do nothing to destroy the chance for peace. But privately he instructed speechwriter William Safire to prepare a statement justifying Thieu's opposition and attacking the halt for failure to provide for mutual withdrawal. Nixon had a surrogate, Robert Finch, divulge this to reporters on background, saying on the record only that the halt idea had been hastily conceived. On November 2 FBI wiretaps recorded calls from vice presidential candidate Spiro Agnew's staff to both Bui Diem and Anna Chennault. Publicly Thieu reiterated his opposition. When he was eventually walked back to accepting a formula ("our side–your side") for dealing with anyone on the other side of the table, Saigon began to dispute what shape the table should have, an attempt to ensure the talks would not recognize the existence of the National Liberation Front. Thieu did not send a delegation to Paris until January 1969, and the first talks did not take place until a new president of the United States had been inaugurated.

Humphrey had been polling behind Nixon, but beginning with the Salt Lake City speech, he started to pick up ground. Through the month of October Humphrey closed the gap, and by the time of the bombing halt he was ahead in some polls. The Republican candidate had reason for desperate measures. An opening of negotiations would advantage Humphrey. But with the delays, an operative in the Nixon campaign passed information to LBJ indicating that Nixon's people estimated that Thieu had diminished the value of the bombing halt by a quarter to a third. On election day, November 5, 1968, Richard Nixon won the presidency by half a million votes. Vietnam would become Nixon's war. A strong card in his appeal was the notion, held by many Americans, that Mr. Nixon had a secret plan to end the conflict.

At Full Extension

On November 29, 1968, a group of sixty-eight soldiers graduating from basic training at Fort Jackson, South Carolina, sent president-elect Nixon a petition. The trainees were model soldiers—not a single case of going AWOL, administrative discipline, or court-martial among the lot. The petition noted their fundamental opposition to the war and reminded Nixon of his promise to end it.[33] That the cream of the latest crop of fighters headed for the front was starting its odyssey already against the war was indicative of the sea change in America's stance. If Nixon intended to pursue war termination by force of arms, he was starting from behind, for the instrument the president would wield atrophied by the day.

The armies of this twilight were no longer those of the dawn.[34] The U.S. military was fighting at full extension and had been for a long time. With sixteen Army and three Marine divisions in the entire armed forces, the deployment of a ten-division force to South Vietnam consumed a huge proportion of U.S. combat power. There was a reason why Joint Chiefs kept asking to mobilize the reserves. A multitude of signs betrayed the transformation, ranging from the simple mechanics of recruiting and training the forces to the clearly rising evidence of discontent among the ranks.

The cadre of experienced noncommissioned officers (NCOs) who were the glue that held the forces together was thinning, with the grizzled veterans of World War II and Korea going into retirement and reenlistment down among their successors. This was true for all ranks, with enrollments following completion of a first hitch down to a mere 12 percent by 1970. The Army had already resorted to a variety of NCO programs that took promising trainees, gave them additional leadership instruction, and pushed out "shake and bake" sergeants. The Marine Corps was better off, but not much. Many important jobs—the services called them "military occupational specialties"—were going begging. Communications personnel, generator repairmen, and many others were needed. One solution—also necessitated by U.S. budgetary problems—was to reduce the size of the force. The years 1968–1969 were those of greatest American strength. More than 400,000 servicemen would be cut from the rolls in the twelve-month period starting in mid-1969. By 1972, when the force had been reduced by more than 1.2 million, almost half of all Army occupational specialties remained understaffed.

For officers the situation was worse, with the antiwar movement playing a more direct role. West Point, of course, could not educate everyone needed to run an Army that numbered 1,512,000 men and women in 1969 (the Marines had another 310,000). A few military colleges—Virginia Military Institute, the Citadel, Texas A&M, Norwich University, North Georgia College—complemented the academy, but graduates from all these combined amounted to a fraction of requirements. And there were the losses. The battles around Dak To were very costly for the West Point class of 1966. Then there were the resignations among officers who decided they could not go on anymore. The *Army Times* newspaper of that era used to publish weekly lists of officers killed and of resignations. A typical field-grade officer, a battalion commander with The Cav during his final tour in Vietnam, watched with dismay as his friends' names turned up on one or another of those lists—until the day he too resigned. Perhaps four or five officers soldiered on for every one who left, but they watched the lists too, and they led soldiers who were increasingly shaky themselves. Morale was a problem.

The Reserve Officers' Training Corps (ROTC) plus promotions from the ranks through Officer Candidate School supplied the bulk of junior officers who reached the field. During the 1967–1968 school year there had been 218,000 students in ROTC programs throughout the country. But the ROTC was under heavy pressure from the protesters. There were two dozen serious incidents at ROTC facilities in 1968, ranging from picketing to noisy demonstrations; the number spiraled to 325 the following year, and the spectrum widened to include firebombing. Colleges began terminating their ROTC programs as losses rose into the millions of dollars. Starting in 1969 some thirty-eight ROTC units were forced off campus. Columbia's was one. At Harvard, when president Nathan Pusey defended the university's ROTC unit, his support triggered student protests. By 1971 ROTC enrollment had dwindled to 87,000.

By now the draft had become the major source of enlisted personnel. In each year since Johnson's decision for war, the Selective Service System had drafted more than 300,000 Americans. As of January 27, 1969, the projection for that year was for another 276,000 inductions (286,600 men would actually be drafted). To reach that number the Selective Service had to call more than a million men for physicals and preinduction testing. Of them, 169,000 filed for conscientious objector status. As General Lewis B. Hershey told Nixon that September, attaining the goal essentially meant summoning every potential draftee available each month, from the twenty-six-year-olds at the end of their eligibility to the youths of nineteen just entering that phase. Worse, studies showed that the majority of recruits enlisted for fear of the draft; this was even more true for the National Guard and Reserves—90 percent in 1970. Putting enlistment on a voluntary basis offered the best hope to right the military's malaise. It just might yield soldiers who wanted to fight. The new secretary of defense, Melvin R. Laird, moved to create an all-volunteer Army starting from his first day on the job.

In the meantime, social developments in America were inevitably reflected in the armed forces. The vestiges of racism and rise of black power led to tense relationships among soldiers, particularly on base, though less so in combat. In Vietnam many GIs clustered within circles of comrades divided along racial or ethnic lines. "Hooches" acquired identities—black, white, or Hispanic—with outsiders barely tolerated, or not at all. At the Marines' Camp Lejeune, racial tensions led to a July 1969 riot at the enlisted men's club, where one Marine died and more than a dozen were injured. Difficulties were not confined to the continental United States. There was a riot at Long Binh, northeast of Saigon. A MACV staff conference in June 1969 considered the racial problem. General Creighton Abrams repeatedly touted the magnificent quality of the troops in his command but worried about this. Key subordinates minimized the difficulties, but that meeting alone disclosed incidents that had taken place at Bien Hoa, Pleiku, Qui Nhon, and Cam Ranh, plus vaguely rumored "meetings" at Da Nang.

Later that year the president sent Air Force colonel Frank Borman on a mission to Vietnam. Famous as the mission commander of *Apollo VIII*, the first manned spacecraft to circle the moon, Borman was supposed to buck up morale but also had a special assignment to look into race relations. "Commanders of every unit I visited," Borman reported back, "are extremely concerned about the increasing antagonism of the young black soldiers. These young servicemen are obviously well versed in the most militant black ideology, and their increased aggressiveness is potentially dangerous to the future stability of our Armed Forces."[35]

MACV formed a watch committee whose sole purpose was to keep an eye on the racial situation. The group collected data on incidents initiated by African Americans against whites and on those sparked the other way. The majority of incidents began with blacks' complaints about white comrades. During the first eleven months of 1970 incidents averaged more than one a day, with high points in January (thirty-seven incidents) and September (forty-one incidents). With the exception of the Cambodian invasion, where soldiers understood the purpose of their offensive, peak months of tension corresponded to those when U.S. forces mounted the most battalion-size or larger combat operations.

Soldiers expressed their concerns wherever and however they could. Some GIs formed actual organizations, beginning with the American Serviceman's Union in 1967, created in the hope of attaining redress through collective action. The union, started by a soldier after his court-martial at Fort Polk, grew to over 10,000 members. Several groups of African American GIs, perhaps the best known called De Mau Mau, formed later. The Movement for a Democratic Military, comprising mostly Marine and Navy personnel, began in 1969. Naturally the very notion of military democracy was anathema to commanders, concerned about the preservation of discipline. But the rise and flowering of the GI movement evidenced the inability to maintain the old way of doing business. Off-base GI coffeehouses became centers of social and political interaction and materialized at many posts, including in Germany and Japan. GI newspapers were soon quite widespread. Assembled on the sly—some of them merely mimeographed, others with newspaper-quality production and editing—the GI press expressed the concerns of enlisted men. Though many of these papers put out only a single issue, by 1971 some 144 of them had been identified; a year later another hundred were in existence. One could run down a list of military facilities and find a GI newspaper at almost every one of them.

Commanders' efforts to preserve functional military units ranged from deft to crass. The best leaders listened to their men, gave something when they could, and made intelligent use of discipline. The post commander at Fort Eustis, Virginia, permitted the distribution of GI newspapers within specified hours. Many commanders regarded the mere possession of such literature as an actionable offense. Another commander at Fort Devens, Massachusetts, regularly met with committees representing enlisted men. Other officers cracked down with a whip hand. The military justice system contains levels of severity, with the bottom rung being administrative punishment at the unit level. At worst, this could involve what GIs called an "Article 15"—dismissal from the service—75,000 of which were handed out in 1968–1969. Summary court-martial, the next rung, amounted to formal recognition of a legal indictment, though less serious than a special court-martial. The worst offenses were consigned to a general court-martial, the type of proceeding the public imagines when the term *court-martial* is used. In 1968 there were 252 general courts-martial for willful disobedience or mutiny; that number grew to 382 in 1970 in a much smaller Army. An example of the way broader circumstances conditioned the administration of discipline was the Marine Corps' handling of drug offenses: by 1969, defen-

dants previously subjected to general court-martial were being sent to special courts, with first offenders facing summary courts meting out lesser sen-
tences and fewer consequences.

Even so, events at military prison facilities, crowded with inmates sent
away in an effort to impose discipline, provide more evidence of the decline
in U.S. capabilities. In August 1968, only days after the Democratic National
Convention in Chicago, several hundred prisoners at the Long Binh jail in
South Vietnam staged a major riot. In mid-October, again only days after a
major peace demonstration, more than two dozen inmates at the San Francisco Marine brig known as the Presidio mutinied. These men became
known as the "Presidio 27," and theirs would be the first of fifteen known
mutinies at military incarceration facilities between 1968 and 1972. The brig
at Camp Pendleton had been designed to accommodate 400 persons, was officially rated by the Marine Corps for 612, but rarely held fewer than 800 or
900 inmates. The numbers themselves suggest the shakiness of discipline.

As previously noted, military desertions and the number of GIs going
AWOL increased during the early years of the American war. These trends
became marked as Nixon took office. For the Army and Marine Corps, approximately 70,000 persons deserted in 1969; a similar number deserted the
following year, and it would be higher in 1971 (exceeding 80,000), when the
force was half a million smaller. Including GIs who went AWOL increases
the 1969 figure to over 240,000—20 percent higher than the year of Tet, the
supposed moment of victory. In comparison, there were some 123,000 desertions from the South Vietnamese army that year, *fewer* than in 1968. The
numbers are even more striking because the ARVN figures include those absent without leave. Analysts endlessly mulled over how ARVN desertion
rates indicated a reluctance to fight. What can one say about the American
rates?

The use of drugs by servicemen and -women also needs mention. This
represented a way to tune out the horrors of the moment without doing anything as extreme as going AWOL. In the first year of the U.S. ground war,
MACV investigated barely a hundred drug cases among the entire force, but
a late 1966 survey found that twenty-nine fixed outlets for buying marijuana
existed in the Saigon area alone. Use of drugs among the troops rose rapidly,
especially in 1969 and after, though data indicate that the proportion of GIs
using drugs was no higher than among the general U.S. population. Data
also show that most drug use occurred on base and did not affect combat
operations. Nevertheless, the III Marine Amphibious Force began using
drug-sniffing dogs in 1968, and the Americans and South Vietnamese began
"Operation Intercept" to eradicate marijuana plots at this time. Military police made 11,000 drug arrests in Vietnam during 1969–1970. As an example,
in 1969 the 1st Marine Division recorded 13 murders, 32 aggravated (and 41
simple) assaults, and 2 rapes, but 490 drug-related offenses. The Army

adopted a policy of not prosecuting servicemen for possession or use unless other infractions were involved. Drugs in Vietnam became a specific concern at the Nixon White House. The president actually assigned deputy national security adviser Alexander M. Haig to investigate this problem on a December 1970 visit. Not long afterward the Pentagon began mandatory drug testing of servicemen.

As with civilians facing the draft, servicemen were permitted to apply for status as conscientious objectors (COs). Army CO applications increased 40 percent from 1967 to 1968, then almost doubled the following year, maintaining the same high rate through 1970. Marine CO applications nearly tripled from 1968 to 1969. The military—which often dealt with COs by simply taking away their rifles and sending them back into combat as medics—ridiculed the whole idea. In 1967 just over a quarter of CO applications received Pentagon approval. Such was the shift in the environment that by 1972 the approval rate reached 77 percent. Commanders now believed that if a soldier doubted his role, he could only be less effective in combat.

The COs were persons whose moral or religious principles led to a rejection of war in general, but as in the wider society, specific opposition to the Vietnam war rose in the U.S. military. By 1968 use of the peace sign had become widespread among GIs in Vietnam. Leafleting and demonstrations occurred, more at U.S. and European bases, and the coffeehouses were hotbeds of ferment. A notorious "peace bomb" incident took place in the Bay Area that October, in connection with demonstrations planned by Veterans for Peace. Navy nurse Lieutenant Susan Schnall overflew the Presidio, the aircraft carrier *Ranger,* the Treasure Island navy base, and the Oakland Naval Hospital, dropping leaflets supporting the march. When the protest took place, local commanders held roll call and formation every couple of hours, forcing soldiers to stay on base. Five hundred marched anyway. Court-martialed and dismissed, Lieutenant Schnall became an even more effective activist as a former military person.

In April 1969 antiwar marches were held across the nation as part of a round of Easter protests. GIs led those demonstrations in half a dozen cities. That July, protest came directly to South Vietnam when over a hundred GIs, many of them African Americans, marched through the base and port at Qui Nhon and clashed with police, who stopped them near the airfield by using tear gas. At Thanksgiving a hundred servicemen and -women of the 71st Evacuation Hospital at Pleiku held a silent fast to protest the war and asked that their dinners be given to the poor. There would be more protests later. Equally important, soldiers who began opposing the war would leave the service and become the mainstay of VVAW.

A disturbing new phenomenon would be so-called fragging, the deliberate attempt by GIs to kill their officers or NCOs, as illustrated in Oliver Stone's movie *Platoon*. Previously, leaders who impressed their men as stupid, reckless, or just plain nuts would simply not get the word when their men saw danger, but from 1969 on, there was an actual possibility that such officers would be actively targeted. Typically an officer would be warned, and if he did not mend his ways, he might become the victim of fragging, which often took the form of a fragmentation grenade (hence the term) rolled into his hooch. In the first half of 1969 the III Marine Amphibious Force had 15 fragging incidents, two-thirds in combat units. Only one perpetrator was apprehended. The Army had 126 of these incidents in 1969, more than twice that many the next year, and 333 in 1971, when the MACV ground force was half the size and shrinking rapidly. During one week in December 1970, across MACV as a whole, there were eight "nonhostile deaths" recorded. Case records indicate that three were probable fragging incidents, with a fourth possible one.

All this added up to a ground force with great firepower but uncertain and diminishing combat capability. Soldiers were sick of the system. A typical GI, Roy Miles, told journalists in February 1970, "I feel as if I've been used."[36] Leaders were increasingly concerned about taking the field with their units. Battalion commander David Hackworth, on his third tour in Vietnam (he would serve two more), recalled the atmosphere in 1969: "Anarchy ruled. My unit was composed of 99 percent draftees. They were all good men, but none in their heart of hearts wanted to be there. They just wanted to stay alive and get the hell out . . . Most in the line were the guys from the other side of the tracks: the have-nots and disenfranchised . . . They all knew they were cannon fodder . . . My job was to keep them alive, not win an unwinnable war."[37] Dealing with the men when not on operations became problematic. Passive resistance to orders, a military tradition, became pronounced under these circumstances. "Working it out" became slang for a sort of rough battlefield democracy that emerged, in which officers, NCOs, and GIs somehow reconciled orders and decided how to get through the day in the face of an enemy who could strike at any time, whose traps and mines posed constant threats.

Mutiny, or a large-scale refusal to carry out orders, became an actual possibility. The North Vietnamese newspaper *Vietnam Courier* claimed there were fifteen instances of American units refusing orders during the first half of 1969 alone. A documented incident took place that August near Da Nang, when a company of the 196th Infantry Brigade refused to continue a difficult patrol operation. Its commander was replaced. That November a platoon of the 25th Infantry Division near Cu Chi similarly rejected its mission. Even the best units were affected. It is recorded that elements of the 1st Cavalry Division refused combat *three dozen times* during 1970. Several refusals occurred at the time of the Cambodian incursion, and as many as ten major incidents of this sort were recorded through 1972.[38] Refusals usually came in the context of officers who lacked their men's confidence, making them candidates for fragging. Probably the worst episode of this sort took place in October 1971, when military police actually air-assaulted into a signal site called Praline Mountain to protect an officer who had been repeatedly targeted for fragging. The MPs protected the man for a week until the situation could be rectified.

In short, MACV had become less than the sum of its parts. Commanders differ on the implications of the transformation. Years later, at the Vietnam Center of Texas Tech University, this was discussed among a large audience that included almost two dozen former battalion commanders from this period. Some argued that their troops were fine in the field; it was only in camp that morale became an issue. Some had no problem when they shared the dangers of the field with the troops; difficulties arose for those who tried to fight the war remotely, from command helicopters. Others simply saw their men as less than capable, period. In a show of hands, the commanders divided about evenly on whether they believed their units had been fully able. I have since continued to ask that question of former battalion commanders. The number is currently at about forty, and they still divide roughly evenly. The U.S. military was becoming increasingly brittle. The net result was that if Richard Nixon intended to crush the serpents in Hanoi under his heel, it was unlikely he could obtain that result with ground forces. America's sword remained swift, but it was no longer so terrible.

By early 1967 the U.S. war effort in South Vietnam was at full stride. The MACV command decided to conduct a massive dual-phase offensive north of Saigon called Operations Cedar Falls–Junction City aimed at entrenched Liberation Front forces. Here troops of Battery C, 2nd Battalion, 32nd Artillery in Tay Ninh province fire their 175mm guns in support of the attack forces on February 22, 1967 (U.S. Army).

On Air Force One, March 20, 1967, en route to the Guam summit LBJ confers with top officials. Richard Helms of the CIA is second from the left. General Maxwell D. Taylor, returned to the White House as a special military adviser, sits behind the president. Behind LBJ's desk are Robert McNamara; South Vietnamese General Nguyen Duc Thang, chief of Saigon's pacification program; Dean Rusk; and Walt Rostow (Johnson Library).

Operation Rolling Thunder, the bombing of North Vietnam, became the best-known component of the U.S. air war in Indochina, which actually encompassed huge efforts in many places. Its massive scale is suggested in this photograph, actually of a small strike over Laos—three A-7 Corsairs from the carrier *America* and an equal number of F-4 Phantoms from the *Midway*. [Both types carried bomb loads half again as large as those of a World War II B-17.] In Vietnam even a small air strike could be very destructive (U.S. Navy).

In one of the most striking pictures of the Vietnam air war, the destruction of a North Vietnamese MiG-17 interceptor is seen through the gun camera of "Hambone 2," the F105 Thunderchief flown by Major Ralph L. Kuster Jr. of the 388th Tactical Fighter Wing. Kuster downed this plane on June 2, 1967, during the period of the intense Rolling Thunder bombing aimed at Haiphong (U.S. Air Force).

Americans captured in North Vietnam or sent there up the Ho Chi Minh Trail were imprisoned at the notorious "Hanoi Hilton." This photo shows part of what remained of the Hanoi Hilton in 1997, when it was being torn down to make way for the urban development of Hanoi, including an actual Hilton Hotel (author's collection).

The UH-l helicopter, originally named the Iroquois, became the iconic chopper of Vietnam and the craft referred to by GIs using the colloquialism "slick" for their aerial trucks. UH-ls acquired many roles, including that of gunship, and pioneers in the creation of helicopter battle tactics were the soldiers of the 1st Cavalry Division (Airmobile). One of their most novel units was the 1st Squadron, 9th Cavalry, nicknamed the Headhunters, which combined gunships with scout infantry to find and fix the adversary until heavier units could catch and destroy them. Here a platoon of Headhunters participates in Operation Pershing in May 1967, skimming a plain in Binh Dinh province about thirty miles northeast of An Khe (U.S. Army).

Below the Demilitarized Zone, in 1967 the U.S. installed the defensive system that became known as the McNamara Line. Among its key installations was the strongpoint of Con Thien, 2 miles south of the DMZ, which in the fall became the focus of an extended battle launched by the Vietnam People's Army. This banner, strung atop the command post at Con Thien by a follow-on unit, the 1st Battalion, 1st Marines, shows the high morale of the Americans. Marines suffered over 1,800 casualties, while North Vietnamese dead were estimated at more than 1,100 (U.S. Marines).

At the western end of the McNamara Line stood the U.S. combat base at Khe Sanh. From here reconnaissance patrols radiated into Indian Country, communications intercept units tracked North Vietnamese movements, and the Americans made a start at deploying the technology for the "electronic battlefield." The most exposed position at Khe Sanh was the outpost atop Hill 950, a key observation post for surveillance of the entire sector. Supporting Hill 950 remained a difficult task throughout the occupation and the famous siege of Khe Sanh. Here a chaplain offers Mass using as his altar a blanket spread over boxes of C rations (U.S. Marines).

Antiwar demonstration at the Pentagon on October 22, 1967. President Johnson ordered strenuous security efforts to counter this protest. More than any other single event, the Pentagon action set Lyndon B. Johnson on the course that put the U.S. government squarely in confrontation with the American people, narrowing the envelope for presidential initiatives and moving the public toward rejection of the Vietnam war policy (U.S. Army).

The fiercest of the border battles preceding the Tet Offensive was that which erupted in the Central Highlands around Dak To while General Westmoreland was in the United States to play his part in President Johnson's public relations offensive. Known to U.S. commanders as Operation MacArthur, Dak To featured a series of bloody fights for the surrounding hills. On November 23, 1967, these troopers of the 4th Battalion, 503rd Infantry, 173rd Airborne Brigade move up Hill 875 prior to the final assault. The brigade suffered massive losses in the battle, particularly in the 2/503 (U.S. Army).

In Saigon the Combined Documents Exploitation Center (CDEC) of the Combined Intelligence Center Vietnam provided much of the raw material Washington used for President Johnson's public relations campaign. This view of CDEC's office shows the table used to post the "best hits" among recently captured documents. At Dak To the United States recovered documents referring to Hanoi's Tet offensive plans, yet the evidence was misinterpreted in the months before the attack, as Washington emphasized its claims to winning the war (U.S. Army).

(Opposite below) The Tet Offensive shattered all the carefully nursed claims to victory. Among its most dramatic events was an attack on the U.S. embassy in Saigon. The small commando unit assigned this mission got into the embassy compound and failed to penetrate the building itself, but the mere fact of the attack stunned both the public and the government. Here Americans of the 716th Military Police Battalion, the morning after the assault, patrol the embassy perimeter (U.S. Army).

The climax of President Johnson's victory campaign came at Cam Ranh Bay on December 23, 1967. LBJ tacked a brief "photo op" appearance in South Vietnam onto the Australian trip where he had been so sorely tried by protesters. Here Johnson speaks to American soldiers. On the dais with him are (starting from behind LBJ, to his right) Lieutenant General Stanley R. Larson, William O. Porter, General William C. Westmoreland, Ambassador Ellsworth Bunker, and General Cao Van Vien (National Archives).

South Vietnamese troops in Saigon advance cautiously behind an armored personnel carrier on January 31, 1968, near Bachelor Officers' Quarters No. 3. Such American personnel billets, poorly defended at best, were not attacked at Tet. It was an important flaw in Hanoi's planning for Tet that it failed to provide for the actions that would have done most to cripple the MACV and ARVN commands (U.S. Army).

American mechanized troops stand guard as Vietnamese civilians flee from My Tho in the wake of Tet. President Thieu had been at My Tho the night the offensive began. Far more than an event in Saigon, Hue, or at Khe Sanh, Tet proved an upheaval across all of South Vietnam (U.S. Army).

Renowned television reporter Walter Cronkite came to South Vietnam after Tet to see the situation for himself. Outside Hue during the final days of the battle for that city, Cronkite interviews the commander of the 1st Battalion, 1st Marines. Cronkite later broadcast his conclusion that America was not winning in Vietnam. Lyndon Johnson believed that when he lost Cronkite he lost the country (National Archives).

8   Crush the Serpent under Heel (1969)

Once elected, Richard Milhous Nixon needed to deliver on his campaign promise to end the Vietnam war. Nixon—whose whole political career had been built on Cold War confrontation, who had advocated U.S. intervention at Dien Bien Phu and had spent the mid-1960s attacking Lyndon Johnson for not doing enough—ought not to have been able to fool anyone. But he did. Perhaps the public had become so desperate that by merely saying he had a "plan," people assumed Nixon intended to negotiate an end to the war. The real intent, Henry Kissinger's protestations aside, was to batter Hanoi into conceding defeat at talks. Melvin R. Laird, whom Nixon made his secretary of defense, frankly acknowledges that this was the case.[1]

The handling of the Vietnam policy review conducted by incoming national security adviser Henry Kissinger indicates Nixon's direction. The president-elect ordered Kissinger to ready both a spectrum of options and a set of questions designed to elicit the differences among Washington agencies, field commanders, the Saigon embassy, and so on. Kissinger hired the defense think tank Rand Corporation for this task. Fred Ikle led the study team, and its top analyst was Daniel Ellsberg. After reviewing a plethora of material, interviewing Washington officials, and holding preliminary conversations with Kissinger, Ellsberg wrote a draft listing Vietnam options—together with illustrative questions—on December 20, 1968. He presented these to Kissinger on Christmas Eve and had a revised options paper on January 8, 1969. A number of things changed between the first and final drafts. A section on objectives, added at the head of the paper, specified the aim as ensuring the withdrawal or destruction of North Vietnamese forces in the South and of National Liberation Front infrastructure and forces; plus, it noted, that goal "would mean rejecting a compromise outcome if offered to us and would probably mean our refraining from proposing any compromise terms." Confusing outcomes with tactics, the paper characterized compromise itself as a policy. It also denigrated the withdrawal option as one with "no advocates within the U.S. Government" but that "might become necessary if some of the alternative strategies failed." Given this set of choices, the Vietnam paper clearly favored victory as an objective.[2]

There was more. In Ellsberg's initial formulation, four alternatives were offered (and one more penciled in) for escalation, but the final version added two variants on an invasion of North Vietnam, even though this was expected to require an additional 250,000 U.S. troops with added costs of $6 billion to $9 billion in the war budget. Advocates believed, the paper argued, that "U.S. public opinion and U.S. allies will tolerate this course, especially if DRV proves intransigent at Paris," and that "military victory is probably already on its way in South Vietnam." But the paper correctly judged this opinion as highly speculative and noted that failures at each level of escalation would increase pressure for additional moves. It stated, "U.S. domestic controversy raised by any of these measures and especially by mobilizing reserves could strongly encourage Hanoi to hold out . . . expecting the U.S. ultimately to be forced to withdraw." However, according to this paper, proponents believed that "the *threat* or onset of the higher levels [of escalation] is likely to bring major concessions from DRV, perhaps sufficient for a satisfactory settlement." Meanwhile, the withdrawal option was modified to a partial pullout, leveling off at about 100,000 troops, *excluding* a full U.S. withdrawal.[3]

This version was distributed to those attending the NSC meeting on January 25, the first big Nixon-era Vietnam powwow. By then the language warning of escalation pitfalls had been cut, though the concept of threat remained. The change had much to do with two people. The first was Harvard academic Thomas C. Schelling, Ellsberg's mentor and Kissinger's colleague. Schelling, who sat in on the presentation of the draft paper to Henry, remarked that it lacked strategies for winning or for threats (which lay at the heart of Schelling's theories about force and bargaining). The second person was General Andrew Goodpaster, who had become a sort of general factotum for the Nixon transition team. He took the options paper and gave it final form. In Goodpaster's hands, alternatives inserted merely to cover the waterfront acquired a more concrete character.

Several points need to be made about this exercise. First, the judgments themselves embodied contradictions. For example, although officials believed Hanoi was talking because of its military defeat at Tet, the documents contained a clear sense the DRV could maintain its strength in the field over the foreseeable future, and no expectation that Hanoi might offer the concessions to be expected of a defeated power. Second, although Mr. Nixon wanted to issue the paper on inauguration day—and did so—he never actually chose an option. Nixon went straight to implementation. The use of threat to influence Hanoi became central to his strategy.

The other key point is that arguments about all the options included claims or beliefs about the antiwar movement, what consequences courses of action would have on it, and inferences about the Movement's impact on subsequent strategic choices. In short, Washington now recognized that strategy could no longer be determined in isolation. Richard Nixon knew he was in a race for victory from day one.

Discussion at the National Security Council on January 25, 1969, showed that Nixon was well versed in the essentials. "We do have the internal problem in the U.S.," the president remarked, "and it will be very difficult to continue without some change." Nixon nevertheless felt the best course of action would be to hold on and told the group that achieving a cease-fire ought to be *dropped* as a negotiating goal. Offers of unilateral withdrawals were also to be eliminated. He wanted to "seek ways in which we can change the game," Nixon said, adding, "I visualize that it could take two years to change this thing." General Earle Wheeler warned that draft calls would increase. General Goodpaster suggested making a cease-fire part of restoration of the DMZ. He too worried that "Hanoi will initially also target on the U.S. domestic problem," hoping to "erode U.S. patience and willingness to continue." Nixon wanted six months of strong military action combined with "a good public stance which reflects our efforts to seek peace." He said quite directly that some troops could be brought home after a few months, "as a ploy for more time domestically," and Nixon wanted to clarify exactly how the Soviet Union could deliver Hanoi. After the meeting the president asked Laird for his views on the draft, and he asked the Pentagon to provide advice on transitioning to an all-volunteer military establishment.[4]

As a practical matter, this was Nixon's first opportunity to implement his plan for peace. It is quite clear that his entire thrust ran in the opposite direction from the suppositions of those who, during the 1968 campaign, had imagined that Nixon's plan was to negotiate a solution. The record also shows that Nixon intended to use troop withdrawals to counter antiwar critics. Nixon's concept closely resembled the "Madman Theory" he had articulated to political operative Harry Robbins "Bob" Haldeman—now White House chief of staff. One day, walking along a beach, Nixon told Haldeman he would end the war during his first year, confident he could actually do that. The means? Speaking in the third person, Nixon had said, "They'll believe any threat of force Nixon makes because it's Nixon." His notion of threat, Haldeman affirms, flowed not from academic theorists like Kissinger but from experience in the Eisenhower administration, when Ike was thought to have ended the Korean conflict by threatening escalation—and, of course, there was what Nixon believed to be the lost opportunity of Dien Bien Phu.

Nixon named the concept himself. "I call it the Madman Theory, Bob," Nixon had said. "I want the North Vietnamese to believe I've reached the point where I might do *anything* to stop the war."[5] It is no longer necessary to continue the historical debate that has raged over whether the Madman Theory existed and what it meant.[6] The actual, secret records of the policy documents and the NSC discussions make Nixon's intentions explicit.

Recalling these deliberations, Henry Kissinger would write that officials had been "too demoralized" and the Nixon team too new at that first NSC meeting to extract any "imaginative ideas" for a president eager to hear them.[7] That is debatable. In fact, it was Kissinger himself who short-circuited the discussion of options, telling the Council they could ponder these once everyone had responded to the questions Ellsberg had drafted—the other part of the transition review. Kissinger issued these questions as National Security Study Memorandum (NSSM) 1 and required each element of the bureaucracy—from the JCS to the CIA to the Office of the Secretary of Defense to the embassy in Saigon—to separately detail its views. The imaginative ideas, such as they were, were already in the NSC options paper. Despite all the erasures, emendations, and revisions, one element that remained was the notion of threat—Schelling's calling card, and soon Nixon's mantra. Most important, short-circuit or not, the conversation in the Cabinet Room *had* alluded to the path Nixon would take: avoid a political settlement in Paris; push Hanoi by vigorous near-term military action, combined with Soviet leverage; and play for time with the public by projecting an image of openness to talks, pulling out a few troops, and dealing with the draft. Nixon also spoke of sending a letter to open channels to Prince Sihanouk of Cambodia. Kissinger reinforced the message a few days later, meeting with Secretary Laird and General Wheeler and asking what might be done to signal escalation to Hanoi. As an illustration, Henry mentioned a buildup of amphibious shipping at a South Vietnamese port to suggest an imminent invasion of North Vietnam.

Time was the real issue, and it had become short indeed. The part of the Nixon transition exercise that has attracted the most attention is NSSM-1, answered over a period of weeks. Ellsberg and NSC staffer Winston Lord collaborated on the summary paper that compared the bureaucracy's responses and drew out their themes. Not even the most optimistic respondents assured the president of victory in any tolerable time frame. The optimists estimated 8.3 years would be required to pacify South Vietnam. The pessimists' average came in at 13.4 years or more. But the options papers anticipated the need for an outcome in about two years (five at most), and Nixon had mentioned two when speaking to the NSC. Yet Hanoi drove the pace of fighting, and the ARVN, though judged more effective in 1968, "faces severe motivation, leadership, and desertion problems." Indeed, September 1968—*after* the enemy's military defeat at Tet—marked the latest peak in South Vietnamese desertion. Recent statistics showed North Vietnamese defections down—rather odd for a "defeated" adversary.[8] No matter who was consulted, NSSM-1 afforded no confidence that Nixon had much time.

Haldeman's words are instructive on this point: "From the very first days in office the brilliant Nixon-Kissinger team was confident they could finish, with honor, the most difficult conflict this nation has ever waged . . . Nixon had conceived the 'Madman Theory' as the way to do it. Henry perfected the theory and carried it to the secret series of the Paris peace talks: A threat of egregious military action by an unpredictable U.S. President who hated Communism." But Hanoi stood fast. Says Haldeman, "The reason was clear. No threat, and no offer, could obscure one great fact known to the world at large. The American people had turned against the war."[9]

■ ■ ■ Whatever was going to happen in the paddy fields would take time. This president wanted immediate action. Nixon's drive to smite the enemy led to bombing, an application of aerial firepower to lay the groundwork for his Madman Theory. The effort to apply such force that Hanoi would back down consumed the first year of Nixon's presidency.

According to Kissinger, the option arose "not from a desire to expand the war, but to avoid bombing North Vietnam and yet to blunt an unprovoked offensive." Initial discussions took place on January 30, when he met with JCS chairman Wheeler and Secretary Laird "to explore how we might respond should there be an enemy offensive."[10] But the memorandum of that conversation reveals that the idea had nothing to do with responses to an attack. Instead, Kissinger raised the question of "what could be done in South Vietnam which could convey to the North that there is a new firm hand at the helm."[11] Wheeler suggested operations in the DMZ or ground forays into enemy base areas. But troops were already fully committed, and talk turned to the potential for CIA covert operations in Cambodia. It was Kissinger, again, who asked about stepping up B-52 strikes.

During the transition Nixon had already raised Cambodia and what could be done to destroy Hanoi's forces there. The day after the inauguration he asked the Joint Chiefs for options to stop supplies through Cambodia. This formed the backstory for Nixon's remark at the NSC on January 25. Wheeler and the Chiefs thought little of the preferred alternative, a naval blockade, and had hardly begun working the problem when Nixon spoke out. Secretary of State William P. Rogers dutifully recommended sending the letter to Sihanouk. It is true the prince had begun warming to the United States. In early 1968 the Cambodian leader had told interviewers that if there were North Vietnamese bases in his country, the fault lay with the United States; by year's end he would inform *Washington Post* reporter Stanley Karnow that he looked forward to better relations. Sihanouk released the crew of a U.S. naval craft that had blundered into Cambodia. Phnom Penh also began to obstruct Chinese arms shipments funneled through the port of Sihanoukville to base areas along the Cambodian-Vietnamese border.

Before anything could be done, General Abrams asked for a bomber raid against COSVN, the enemy command center, which U.S. intelligence believed to be in one of the base areas. The Abrams request catapulted Nixon into his first big Vietnam decision, telescoping all the careful planning. On February 18 a MACV briefing team explained the proposal for an Arc Light strike against COSVN, after which Dr. Kissinger sent the president a lengthy paper on the pros and cons of two options, an overt or a covert attack, either of which could be framed as unilateral, responding to provocation, or "officially categorized as a mistake."

In his memoirs Kissinger wrote, "I advised against an unprovoked bombing of the sanctuaries. We should give negotiations a chance, I argued, and seek to maintain public support for our policy."[12] That is not precise. Kissinger recommended against an unprovoked *overt* attack and against an *immediate* covert strike (not because of negotiations but because cables exchanged between Secretary Rogers and Ambassador Bunker had "deprived us" of the option "during the next few weeks without unacceptable risk of compromise"). There was not a word about American public support. In fact, Kissinger's paper insisted there were advantages to "a covert 'accidental' attack against COSVN Headquarters." He advised Nixon to have Abrams bomb right up to the border "to set the stage for a possible covert attack," to plan the actual raid, and to be on the lookout for a "suitable local action" as pretext.[13] Nixon approved on February 22. Nixon and Kissinger were looking for their own Gulf of Tonkin.

President Nixon initially ordered the bombing on February 24, during a trip to Europe. Kissinger issued the execution order aboard Air Force One during a stop in Brussels. Laird and Wheeler warned that those who knew about the messages regarding the bombings might make trouble. Laird's warning, combined with Kissinger's "covert" bombing idea, resulted in the secret bombing of Cambodia. Nixon waited a few weeks while planners designed a scheme to conceal the attacks. The issue of negotiations did not enter the calculus until the second week of March, at which point Kissinger advised the president to move immediately, before there could be private talks, so the bombing would already be under way when they began.[14]

Because of the controversy attached to this bombing, which eventually involved Senate hearings and the near passage of an impeachment charge against Richard Nixon, many key participants later distanced themselves or contrived to minimize their participation. Only one—MACV commander General Creighton V. Abrams—took full responsibility. In fact, Abrams went further. The initial MACV request aimed only at its nemesis, COSVN. But Abrams told a Senate panel in 1973 that he had asked for wider attacks on enemy base areas because he knew troop withdrawals were coming. Abrams wanted to show "evidence of support" for his troops, "their spirit and their morale and their determination." "If you did not do those things," General Abrams related, "you would be courting, in my opinion, disaster for the whole force."[15]

The general's concept is borne out by the records of tape-recorded MACV command conferences that have recently become available. Although the Cambodia bombing is referred to only obliquely, it is clearly the base areas at issue, not COSVN. Incidentally, General Andrew Goodpaster, now in Vietnam as Abrams's deputy, was a key proponent too. Secretary Laird arrived for his first Saigon visit on March 5, emphasizing that the change in administration would afford "a little time here," but that the key was "to develop a national policy that we *can* go to the people with." Laird's concept included protecting the U.S. force, developing the South Vietnamese, and reducing the U.S. commitment, "not only in the form of men, but in casualties and materiel and in dollars." Laird raised the question of B-52s but warned that Pentagon budgets factored in reduced numbers of missions, with additional cuts anticipated for 1970.[16] There was no direct mention of the Cambodia strikes, but Abrams told the Senate that he did have such conversations with Laird at this time.

The MACV commander's concept would be altered in translation. From the beginning Nixon ordered tighter-than-tight security. Operation "Menu" would be conducted under such secrecy it could not possibly have had the morale effect Abrams wanted. Under its control system, B-52s were briefed to strike inside Vietnam; their mission changed while airborne, and they were directed by ground-based radar to the Cambodian target. Paperwork was falsified to indicate attacks in South Vietnam. The JCS automated database did not record the strikes. Targets were developed at MACV, sent to Washington by back channel, turned into mission plans by the Joint Staff, and passed to Secretary Laird, who approved them, presumably after consulting Kissinger. General Wheeler then sent orders directly to the Strategic Air Command. Only selected individuals knew. For example, neither the secretary of the Air Force nor its vice chief of staff were aware of Menu. Laird did tell key legislators, including senators Richard Russell and John C. Stennis. The falsification of reporting became a problem once controversy erupted, because false reporting is an offense under the Uniform Code of Military Justice. Kissinger told Laird on the eve of Menu that Nixon's order to attack neutral Cambodia was "something he cannot ever avow."[17]

In any case, Nixon approved the raids but postponed them, rejecting Kissinger's advice on the desirability of immediate attack. But by his security adviser's account, Nixon was "champing at the bit."[18] On March 15 the NLF fired some rockets into Saigon. Washington took this as a violation of an "understanding" with Hanoi (never formally agreed) that underlay LBJ's final bombing halt. The Nixon White House immediately went into high gear, with the president ordering the bombing and Kissinger privately phoning Laird to prompt him on what to say at a meeting the next afternoon. This encounter, on March 16, was apparently held to afford Secretary Rogers an opportunity to state his objections, based on domestic political grounds and negotiations. Then Nixon responded. "The state of play in Paris is completely sterile," he said. "I am convinced that the only way to move the negotiations off dead center is to do something on the military front. That is something [Hanoi] will understand."[19]

The Menu bombing began with "Breakfast," a strike at one enemy base area in the Fishhook region of Cambodia (the bases were each given their own code names—"Lunch," "Dinner," "Supper," "Dessert," "Snack"). It went in at 2:00 PM, Washington time, on March 17. Almost sixty B-52 bombers loosed 1,386 tons of ordnance on the target.[20] High anticipation at the White House, marked by Nixon checking with Kissinger on the flights of the planes, NSC memos commenting on results, and so on, would be rewarded by reports of many secondary explosions, some more powerful than the bombs that set them off.

"Breakfast" marked the beginning of a real air campaign. In April, when North Korea shot down an American spy plane and an order for direct retaliation was countermanded by Laird,[21] Nixon resorted to more Cambodian bombing instead. Again the NSC memos flew. Afterward the president told General Wheeler he was very pleased. Then the aerial offensive became regularized, averaging a hundred sorties a month into the summer, several hundred monthly after that. About 70,500 tons of bombs fell on Cambodia during 1969, with another 35,300 tons in the first four months of 1970. This represented almost 15 percent of the bomb tonnage dropped on North Vietnam in all of Rolling Thunder.

A week after the first Menu attacks, Jack Walsh of UPI wrote a brief wire-service story on General Abrams's original request to strike COSVN. Another journalist, William Beecher of the *New York Times,* followed up. Beecher had apparently got wind of earlier appeals to bomb Cambodian base areas (Westmoreland had recommended this in December 1967) and did some checking. In Thailand, where one of the B-52 units, the Thirty-third Bombardment Wing of the Strategic Air Command, was stationed, the Thai press ran an early story mentioning the bombing. Beecher confirmed the details. On May 9 his piece "Raids in Cambodia by U.S. Unprotested" appeared in the *Times.* Beecher's story correctly noted base areas as the targets, revealed that the United States was sending Special Forces teams into Cambodia to assess bomb damage, contained an accurate figure for bombs dropped to that point (5,000 tons), and reported the White House's purpose as being "to demonstrate to Hanoi that the Nixon Administration is different and 'tougher' than previous administrations." The only error lay in dating Nixon's decision to January.[22] All Nixon's draconian secrecy had been pointless.

The president went ballistic. At his Key Biscayne, Florida, retreat, Nixon burned up the phone wires with blistering calls to Kissinger and FBI director J. Edgar Hoover. He demanded the leaker's head. Kissinger and Hoover conferred and by that afternoon had tabbed one of Henry's own NSC staff, Morton H. Halperin, as the likely culprit. By 6:20 PM a wiretap had been placed on Halperin's phones. The circle of taps quickly expanded. Kissinger made Alexander Haig his contact person for the wiretap transcripts, which soon filled a White House safe. All the taps were illegal under the 1968 Omnibus Crime Control Act. Within a few scant months of assuming office, Richard Nixon had begun his march down the path of illegality.

Mr. Nixon's War

It likely would have made no difference to Nixon had he known that the Cambodia bombing story had been built on journalistic shoe leather, based on information gleaned in Thailand and not from a White House leak.[23] Such suspicions roiled across this man's mind that he probably would have suspected some other skullduggery afoot. If not that, there were plenty more reasons for action. From the beginning Nixon saw himself as isolated, the target of shadowy bureaucratic forces out to sabotage his initiatives. He would counter his enemies by holding his cards more than close. Nixon conducted policy as a virtual conspiracy. The wiretaps, far from an anomaly, were an excess waiting for an excuse.

Characteristically, within days of assuming office Nixon did something about the "October Surprise" charges left over from the election. What he did was try to pin it on *Lyndon Johnson*, turning it into a conspiracy by LBJ to sabotage the election and throw it to Humphrey. Diplomat Philip Habib would be raked over the coals to shake him down to get evidence against Johnson. Nixon subsequently kept the October Surprise in mind and repeatedly threatened to "out" this alleged Democratic maneuver. In fact, President Johnson's papers contain a file on this episode today precisely because one of Nixon's threats led Walt Rostow to order the documents be brought together. Rostow added his own memo summarizing what he knew of the Nixon campaign's machinations. Clearly LBJ and Rostow intended to use the records if Nixon made any public claim about the October Surprise, which would have been explosive in that era of Watergate.

Bob Haldeman, Nixon's chief of staff until Watergate brought him down, recorded that this president needed to be protected from himself. Nixon was forever firing off orders—as little notes, perhaps, scribbled in the margins of memos or news clippings, on the phone, or blurted out at meetings. The orders often demanded extreme measures. Some White House officials adopted the technique of sitting on certain Nixon orders for a day or two, then asking the president whether he really wanted those things done. Other orders went straight to the "circular file." Kissinger became adept at channeling Nixon's ire, riding the wave in the direction of actions he himself thought desirable. And Nixon's constant demands for "more"—more aggressive Pentagon proposals, more White House control in diplomacy, more sway over the bureaucracy—became a theme in every crisis or negotiation.

Nothing if not complex, Richard Nixon would be the subject of endless efforts to understand the man, by former colleagues as well as observers. At age fifty-six he had reached the stage of life where legacies and accomplishments seemed important, and Nixon had lost two elections before going up against Humphrey. Following his California gubernatorial debacle in 1962 he had lashed out at the press, famously declaring that they wouldn't have "Dick Nixon to kick around any more." Losing the presidency to Kennedy in 1960, he had indulged in similar recriminations in a memoir called *Six Crises,* charging JFK with using secret information about Cuba in a televised debate (untrue). Henry Kissinger was being charitable when he wrote, "generosity of spirit was not one of Nixon's characteristics."[24]

Vindictiveness was a Nixon trait, and it likely played a part in both the post-Cambodia wiretaps and Nixon's soon-to-be "enemies list." But that was just the beginning. The president was also prone to intense suspicion, secretiveness, hypersensitivity, and narcissism. Haldeman, writing his first volume of recollections shortly after the appearance of the science fiction movie *Star Wars,* remarked that the president had treated him like one of the androids in the film. Dr. Arnold Hunschnecker, Nixon's psychiatrist, reportedly believed the president had been emotionally deprived as a child.[25] Bryce Harlow, legendary Republican political operative who worked with Nixon for more than two decades, believed the young Nixon had been "hurt very deeply by someone he trusted . . . hurt so badly he never got over it and never trusted anyone again."[26]

Other aspects of Nixon's character rather suited him to guide American foreign policy. Alexander Haig recalls him as a "living data bank regarding the history, culture, economy, aspirations, secret agenda, and current news and gossip about every important country in the world." What Nixon did not know he studied. And he knew just about everybody on Capitol Hill plus many foreign leaders. Haig found Nixon "brilliantly intelligent."[27] Kissinger agreed that Nixon was knowledgeable and perceptive and thought him decisive and brave too, willing to make decisions that often went against the advice of his experts. Many saw Nixon as painfully shy, fearful of confrontation and willing to do almost anything to avoid it, unable to relax except with family. Speechwriter Ray Price believed Nixon had light and dark sides in contention. Nixon's other key speechwriter, William Safire, saw the president as even more complex, an intellect of many layers constantly in motion. Safire pictured Nixon as "an amalgam of Woodrow Wilson, Niccolo Machiavelli, Teddy Roosevelt, and Shakespeare's Cassius."[28]

A key issue is probity. Was Nixon to be trusted? Entirely apart from these insider pictures, the record in 1969 did not bode well. Nixon's political operations had repeatedly dealt in exaggeration and negative campaigning, the truth of his claims debatable. In his first run for a California congressional seat, he made his opponent out as the tool of communists. The same happened in 1950 when Nixon was elected to the Senate. In between was the notorious episode of the "Pumpkin Papers," in which Nixon, chairman of a panel of the House Un-American Activities Committee (HUAC), "discovered" microfilmed documents hidden in a pumpkin that incriminated HUAC target Alger Hiss. The staged discovery and Nixon's ostentatious return to Washington from a vacation cruise raised questions about the evidence. Then, during Nixon's run for the vice presidency with Eisenhower in 1952, the *New York Post* published allegations of a Nixon slush fund, and Ike nearly threw him off the ticket. Nixon responded with a televised speech in which he obsequiously sought forgiveness, ignoring the central charges while providing irrelevant details about personal expenses and admitting only to accepting the gift of the family dog, named "Checkers" by daughter Tricia. Not least would be Nixon's claim of a plan to end the Vietnam war during his 1968 campaign. Insiders knew plenty more about Richard Nixon, but even the public had food for thought.

In his book *Six Crises,* Nixon alluded to a predilection for framing life as a series of "us versus them" situations. Suspicion and hypersensitivity had free rein in his White House, only this time Richard Nixon had the full resources of the U.S. government at his disposal. This had implications for the Vietnam war as well as for America. The subjects of the FBI wiretaps merely became the first victims.

Journalists, colleagues, family members, scholars, and others have devoted thousands of pages to dissecting Richard Nixon's early life, attempting to divine what made the man. It is safe to say that Nixon was affected by his relationship with his mother; his perceptions of growing up poor in California; the missing father-son relationship, truncated when the former left the family and difficult before that; and his bonds with his four brothers, two of whom died before Dick had established himself. There are also clues in the tortured courtship with his first girlfriend, not to mention the odd relationship between Nixon and Dwight Eisenhower, possibly the closest thing to a father, or at least a political mentor, in Nixon's life. Ike once told journalists he would need days (a couple of weeks, actually) to think of what Nixon had done as vice president. Dick repaid the remark. Cordial enough in his eulogy at Eisenhower's funeral—the former president died two months into Nixon's presidency—in his memoirs Nixon would write that "perhaps the best description I can give of Dwight Eisenhower is that he had a warm smile and icy blue eyes."[29] That was supposed to be complimentary. It was Eisenhower's reserve, his aloofness, the "tempered hard steel" beneath apparent high spirits that Nixon admired. And it was probably not coincidental that, in choosing a passage from his own diaries to capture Ike's decision style, Nixon selected late March 1954, when the Dien Bien Phu crisis had been at its height and the "Vulture" option on the table. Richard Nixon saw himself as hardened too, and he sought to project that image.

The president took office with a war in Vietnam mired in stalemate, an American public soured on the conflict, and an active and surging movement opposing the U.S. course. A negotiated settlement could have been had right then, as Henry Kissinger outlined in a quietly discarded *Foreign Affairs* article.[30] But apart from the complicating factor of Washington's alliance with Saigon, settling would not have displayed strength, constituting a basic reason for Nixon to reject it. That the antiwar movement favored a settlement made that alternative even more unpalatable. This was not the Movement prolonging the war; rather, *this* U.S. leadership refused to take what was on the table and gambled the balance could be reversed. In making that choice, by inclination and by will, Richard Nixon would follow the path of force.

Of course, Nixon faced a basic contradiction in pursuing this strategy. The war had passed a turning point in 1968, like it or not, and for all the damage to Hanoi's armies, the United States could no longer fight the same way. American withdrawal could be slowed or stretched out, but it could not be avoided. The ground forces were a diminishing quantity in terms of capability too. Vietnamization was afoot. Nixon's reliance on naval and air power would be dictated by these factors, but it also represented the preferred posture during Eisenhower's administration, where Nixon had gained his spurs. In a sense, the "Vulture" scheme finally came to fruition in 1969. But now, as at Dien Bien Phu, a reliance on remote striking power contained fatal flaws.

The political knot of Vietnam started with the antiwar movement. In the early days of his presidency Nixon spoke of the "youth problem" and deputized his friend and aide Robert Finch as a sort of ambassador to youth. Given this president's style, the Finch appointment quickly lost any meaning, since the envoy would be frozen out of the Oval Office. After a few months Nixon made Daniel Patrick Moynihan his new point man. But Moynihan, too, amounted to little more than a fact finder. The action stayed in White House hands. A darker and deeper track emerged, already set up, now stoked to a new intensity.

Barely a month after the inaugural, deputy White House counsel Egil Krogh told Hoover's assistant at the FBI that the president opposed student protests—he used the term "disorders"—and wanted the FBI's information on which students benefited from federal scholarship money.[31] At a news conference on March 14, answering a question that had most likely been planted, Nixon declared he was considering terminating financial aid to student protesters. The president softened the pill a week later when he said that the students were properly drawing attention to real social problems, but he restricted that primarily to university issues. Not long afterward Nixon told speechwriters to work up a text that would not be so accommodating. On April 28, before the Chamber of Commerce, the president demanded that colleges discipline student protesters, referring to a "new revolutionary spirit and new revolutionary actions that are taking place on the campuses."[32]

The Nixon White House scrambled to understand the "youth problem." The day after the president's threat to defund students, advisers recommended that Nixon open lines of communication to them. Moynihan told the president that, on this subject at least, U.S. intelligence was deplorable. Nixon asked Kissinger his opinion. The latter met with a delegation of student leaders in late April, but that session backfired when the students used the White House Press Room to declare that efforts at opposition must continue: the administration was not actually moving to end the war. Domestic affairs czar John D. Ehrlichman also had secret meetings with protesters. In May Ehrlichman asked consultant Arthur Burns to use his academic contacts to poll faculty opinion on student concerns. The adviser reported a general feeling that only a small group of protesters existed, most affiliated with the SDS. In itself, this demonstrated Moynihan's proposition on poor intelligence, for protests had long surged past the level Burns suggested, and the SDS, already eclipsed, was about to fracture. Nixon issued formal instructions to Ehrlichman to assemble the best recent literature on the students.

Understanding fell short at 1600 Pennsylvania Avenue. Some, like speechwriter Ray Price, actually considered this a nonproblem and thought it was a mistake to take the protesters seriously. Ehrlichman, ignoring the Movement's strong critique of U.S. imperialism, stated, "these people were not taking seriously the role of the United States in the world." Some at the White House had children of an age to be swept up in the cauldron of these times. Ehrlichman's son announced he was leaving to go live in the woods. "It was," Ehrlichman recalled, "a tough time to be a parent."[33] Others trivialized the Movement. When Harvard erupted in the spring of 1969 and students took over some buildings, Kissinger cracked that in three days no one would know who had done what to whom. When one of Ehrlichman's kids phoned in anguish—all his friends were in the streets protesting—the boy was brought to Washington and accorded a one-on-one with Kissinger, who managed to still his doubts, at least for the moment. Some Kissinger dog-and-pony shows worked better than others. (Laird's son John had fewer doubts; he came out actively against the war and marched in demonstrations.) Roger Morris, a Kissinger aide on the NSC staff, recalled the general feeling about the students: "They were insubstantial and capricious, [we] basically thought it was a Draft protest, [we] thought they were cowardly, [we] thought they were there for frivolous reasons . . . [We] just never took the protest seriously in an intellectual sense."[34]

Not waiting for better information, the Nixon people swung into action. Attorney General John N. Mitchell ordered the FBI to initiate wiretaps without court order against the Black Panthers in February. Ehrlichman aide Tom Huston suggested funneling money to friendly student groups in March. Around this time his boss first advocated creation of a special security unit under White House aegis—the notorious "plumbers" of Watergate fame. The domestic czar and others called on the Internal Revenue Service for data on opponents as well (the IRS began delivering in July, and between then and September 1970 it would review the tax returns of 1,029 organizations and 4,300 individuals). Nixon ordered Ehrlichman to put Huston in charge of gathering intelligence on whether foreign powers controlled the protesters, and Huston asked both the FBI and CIA to report on this matter. He defined "control" so broadly that something seemed certain to turn up. Nothing did. But the fact that neither agency could find any hard evidence did little to allay suspicions. Haldeman continued to believe it even after the war. "I think Hanoi was instigating them to begin with," he told a historian of the antiwar struggle.[35]

What happened when the Army tried to *stop* its domestic spy program shows the direction of the Nixon approach. Operating under a summer 1968 directive, the Army collected a huge array of information and had its plainclothesmen infiltrate widely. Until Army personnel planners asked for an extra 175 slots specifically for these spies, service officials thought that Army intelligence was merely using FBI data. Requests for infiltration were considered covert operations, subject to approval by Secretary of the Army Stanley R. Resor. After a few more disturbing incidents, the deputy secretary and the Army's chief counsel moved to tighten control and phase out domestic intelligence with a directive to the Army's vice chief of staff. In March 1969 chief counsel Robert E. Jorden III went to the Justice Department to request language in a new government-wide directive that would formally assign this collection role to the FBI, precluding military spying.

Jorden failed, despite a series of meetings with Deputy Attorney General Richard Kleindienst. He thought he had made progress when William H. Rehnquist, in charge of Justice's Office of Legal Counsel, wrote a draft that went partway. The Rehnquist draft provided that the Army would act only at the request of Attorney General Mitchell. But Mitchell and Kleindienst changed the order to state that the attorney general would manage *all* domestic intelligence gathering, including the Army's. The Mitchell version went to the White House on April 11. Nixon approved the directive on May 19. Meanwhile, senior officials saw a quarterly report on Army domestic intelligence collection demonstrating that almost 40 percent of the 3,219 spot reports had come from its own agents, not the FBI or elsewhere. The Army stayed in the domestic spy business.

Nixon was pleased when a federal grand jury in Chicago indicted eight antiwar leaders who had participated in the demonstrations the previous summer. The indictment, which came through on March 19, cited violations of several statutes. Ironically, one of them had been authored by Jerry Voorhis, whom Richard Nixon had defeated in his first electoral contest by painting Voorhis as soft on communism.

By now the president was ready for his power play on Hanoi. The connection between the war and Nixon's perception of the opposition is neatly encapsulated by what transpired. He called a summit on the Pacific island of Midway. Before leaving, on June 2 Nixon scribbled his approbation in the margin of a *Wall Street Journal* editorial that argued Abraham Lincoln had taken extreme liberties with the law but had still saved the nation in the Civil War. Nixon departed the next day. He flew on Air Force One to Madison, South Dakota, where he spoke at a small education and technical school, General Beadle State College (soon to be renamed Dakota State College). Nixon felt safe from protesters, but even here a demonstrator turned up, brandishing a poster condemning "America the Insane," headed, of course, with Vietnam. A photo duly appeared in *Time* magazine. In Madison the president laid down the gauntlet. He could have been parroting the *Wall Street Journal.* "We find old standards violated, old values discarded, old precepts ignored," Nixon thundered. "We have the power to strike back, if needed, and to prevail. The nation has survived other attempts at insurrection, we can survive this."[36] The word *insurrection,* applied to the protesters, was disturbing. On the way to Midway Nixon stopped off at Honolulu for a strategy session with military commanders. These were indeed dangerous times.

"He Appeared to Want a Quick Solution"

Of escalation strategy Richard Nixon would write in his memoir, "It was an option we ruled out very early."[37] That sentence cloaks a huge story, one that preoccupied him for many months. And appropriately, the Midway conference, on an island named for its location roughly halfway between North America and Asia, oddly represents about the midpoint of that evolution. Conversation at the administration's first NSC meeting on Vietnam, according to Kissinger's official record, had ruled out any de-escalation.[38] On January 27 Nixon had gone to the Pentagon for a private lunch with Laird and Wheeler, where they mulled over "a program of potential military actions which might jar the North Vietnamese into being more forthcoming at the Paris talks."[39] And Laird and Wheeler had returned the visit, meeting with Kissinger at the White House a few days later to go over the same ground.

By late February the JCS planners had assembled some possible actions, and Laird sent their working paper to Kissinger. The possibilities included the standard options, save that the Pentagon provided for either real or feigned use of each, and it added one for "technical escalation," which from the contents of this appendix appears to be a euphemism for nuclear weapons.[40] The other alternatives were invasion of the North, invasions of Laos or Cambodia, resumed bombing of North Vietnam, and attempted subversion of North Vietnam. Kissinger handed the package to Al Haig, rapidly expanding his role from mere military expert on the NSC staff to Henry's deputy. Once Haig rendered an opinion Kissinger responded to Laird. It was March 3. Again the political constraints were manifest. "I am somewhat concerned," Kissinger wrote Laird, "that the 'realities' of the current domestic and international environment do not lend themselves to the acceptance of these risks at this time." Kissinger returned to the proposals he had pressed on Laird a month before—visible signals of a buildup such as planning conferences or "even the staging of amphibious shipping"—which "could be implemented with less risk of international or domestic turbulence."[41]

Here is where the circle closes. The Nixon White House realized that the politics of Vietnam stood in the way of its preferred option. Rather than abandon his course, Nixon tried to contrive conditions under which it could be carried out. In the first instance this involved concretizing Vietnamization, which Laird did during his Saigon trip. The second element, beginning in mid-March, was the president's counterattack on the antiwar movement. A final ingredient in the mix centered on the Paris negotiations, where Nixon and Kissinger both perceived that the appearance of American flexibility would help gain them freedom of action.

But the problem of an actual U.S. bargaining position remained. One of the Nixon-Kissinger NSSMs had had the object of distilling acceptable provisions for a settlement. Deliberations that spring, culminating in discussions from early April on, boiled the negotiating position down to a series of points. These included a full North Vietnamese withdrawal, no cease-fire that recognized any National Liberation Front territorial control, and political reconciliation if the insurgents laid down their arms. This American position was acceptable to Saigon. Officials surely knew it would be a nonstarter in Hanoi. Privately, Nixon and Kissinger considered certain political guarantees to the NLF, but that went beyond anything agreed on by the bureaucracy and was also ahead of Saigon. In mid-May Mr. Nixon unveiled the position, calling for mutual withdrawal of DRV and U.S. forces over a one-year period. Hanoi insisted Vietnam was one country, its troops under no obligation to withdraw anywhere. That too was predictable. The most sensible conclusion is that Nixon wanted to get what he could out of Hanoi if it agreed, but failing that, he hoped to generate the sense of a process under way that might shield him from criticism.

A dichotomy existed in Washington's use of communications channels. The Nixon administration made the term *linkage* part of its diplomatic lexicon, and it referred to getting the Soviets to do things on behalf of the United States for the sake of Moscow's relationship with Washington. One of these was to deliver Hanoi. At a minimum the Soviets could pass messages to DRV leaders. At their first meeting, on February 21, Kissinger asked Soviet ambassador Anatoly Dobrynin to inform Hanoi that the United States "could not accept a settlement that looked like a military defeat, and . . . was not prepared to accept a settlement immediately followed by the change of government in South Vietnam . . . although they had no objection to a gradual evolution."[42] This was Kissinger's "decent interval," in a nutshell. But the steel behind the rhetoric was that Nixon wanted no part of defeat—and that entailed escalation. Kissinger confirmed this when he told Dobrynin on April 3, in answer to a direct question whether the United States intended to expand the war, that Nixon would end it "one way or the other." Kissinger returned to this theme later, adding that it would be unfortunate if the United States were driven to escalate, since a U.S.-Soviet confrontation over Southeast Asia made no sense.[43] On April 14 Kissinger saw Dobrynin again, remarking that the president had "decided to make one more direct approach on the highest level before drawing the conclusion that the war could only be ended by unilateral means."[44] In the absence of a settlement, he said, "we might take measures that would create a 'complicated situation.'" Dobrynin warned that Moscow's influence in Hanoi was strictly limited.[45] Seeing Dobrynin in June, Kissinger reiterated that Nixon intended to end the war, one way or the other.

The threat loomed. The "one more direct approach"—a visit to Moscow by Cyrus Vance, deputy chief of the U.S. delegation to the Paris negotiations—never happened. But all along Kissinger had intended a tough escalatory step—the mining of Haiphong harbor, part of the JCS bombing alternative. Then came the Korean shoot-down crisis,[46] to which the president responded by bombing Cambodia. Not wanting to move in different directions at once, Nixon delayed direct action against the DRV, setting a deadline and then extending it. Late in May the CIA's Richard Helms warned that mining without bombing would not work. On the eve of Nixon's departure for Midway there was movement at Paris, where delegation chief Henry Cabot Lodge met privately with DRV Politburo member Le Duc Tho, whose remarks suggested a fresh atmosphere, if not substantive change, in Hanoi. On Kissinger's staff, analysts pointed to Tho's statements as indicating fear of a U.S. escalation.

The Midway summit had been designed to showcase Vietnamization. The U.S. withdrawals and the upgrade of the ARVN entailed by that program were the central focus both there and at Honolulu, site of the president's preliminary get-together with the U.S. military. Nixon's NSC briefing book contained nothing regarding the threat strategy. The record of General Abrams's final MACV staff conference prior to attending also had nothing about Madman. But at the leaders' one-on-one session at Midway, according to the record made by Thieu's aide Nguyen Phu Duc, Nixon went out of his way to inform the Saigon leader the United States would shortly make new secret bombing raids in Cambodia, the biggest yet, striking several base areas at once. Kissinger emphasized that Nixon had rejected the advice to de-escalate. Later the president "observed that the greatest mistake of President Johnson was the gradualistic approach in military actions against North Vietnam. Now, it would be different." The broad hint of escalation was palpable. Nixon told Thieu his strategy was intended to demonstrate to Moscow that the USSR's interest lay in helping to end the war, a "top secret piece of information" that "only he, Nixon, and Kissinger were [in] on."[47]

Both Nixon and Kissinger noted the political problems in the United States, and the president congratulated Thieu on actions in Saigon that would help contain them, with Vietnamization being a big step in that direction. Thieu agreed.

A major headache with the Madman strategy flowed directly from the policy-as-conspiracy nature of the process. As in other instances of Nixon-era two-track gambits, time and attention were devoted to the artful business on the surface and drawn away from the secret course simultaneously pursued. With Vietnam, the Midway conference christened Vietnamization and negotiations as Nixon policy, and these aspects consumed an increasing proportion of the attention the White House lavished on Southeast Asia. The summer brought an extensive effort (covered in the next chapter) to refine the details of troop withdrawals. Kissinger and Nixon had to concern themselves with that to keep control of it. Escalation issues were muted.

Thus July brought a flurry of action, with NSSMs on troop withdrawal, Vietnamese politics, and internal security, plus fresh deliberations on the Paris talks following the NLF's creation of a new entity, the Provisional Revolutionary Government of South Vietnam, a gambit to claim national identity in the negotiations. The climactic encounter came aboard the presidential yacht *Sequoia* on July 7, when Nixon took his top brass for an evening cruise on the Potomac. The CIA estimate prepared for this occasion speculated on Hanoi's newly reduced military profile. The NSC briefing memo confined itself to Vietnamization. Before the *Sequoia* cruise Haldeman noted Kissinger as "discouraged" because Laird and Rogers were pushing for maximum withdrawals, while the security adviser's "plans for ending [the] war aren't working fast enough." Haldeman knew that Kissinger "wants to push for some escalation, enough to get us a reasonable bargain for a settlement within six months."[48] By Kissinger's account the *Sequoia* evening turned out as he had feared: "no one asked . . . whether the lull might not reflect the fact that our strategy was succeeding . . . It was decided to make a basic change in the battlefield orders for General Abrams."[49] The next morning Kissinger spilled the beans on Madman to Laird, telling him, "for his *own* use, the President has not excluded the possibility that he could take an option to the right in order to end the war quickly."[50]

Mr. Nixon himself dates his decision on the Madman strategy to July. He specifically recorded his fear of "a massive new antiwar tide" that could sweep the country when Congress and the colleges returned from summer vacation. "Unless I could build some momentum behind our peace efforts over the next several weeks, they might be doomed to failure by the calendar," Nixon wrote. "I decided to 'go for broke' in the sense that I would attempt to end the war one way or the other—either by negotiated agreement or by an increased use of force."[51] Morton Halperin and Winston Lord on the NSC staff collaborated on a succession of papers blandly titled "Vietnam Alternatives" that resurrected the proposal to "quarantine" North Vietnam by mining Haiphong harbor, this time coupled with a resumption of bombing. Another signal went to Hanoi, carried by Frenchman Jean Sainteny, now employed as an emissary.

While America and the world thrilled to the achievement of the *Apollo XI* astronauts who first landed on the moon, the president implemented his strategy. He began an around-the-world trip with a leg to the South Pacific to meet the returning astronauts, then went on to Bangkok and Saigon, seeing Nguyen Van Thieu at the presidential palace. The alternatives were plain enough. Thieu raised them, remarking that he saw two alternatives: "either for the U.S. to speed up the war or to help [South Vietnam] take over more of the war burden."[52] Nguyen Phu Duc also attended this private session. According to Duc's version, Thieu said, "We ha[ve] either to seek a military solution of the war, or prepare ourselves for a long war." The leaders discussed various aspects of U.S. support. "Should we make it clear to the other side we are not going to quit?" Nixon asked. The Saigon leader said yes. Nixon groused that negotiating had been expensive and had given the enemy time. According to Duc, "Nixon indicated that he was looking for another approach. He appeared to want a quick solution of the war."[53] The Saigon aide did not know the president had also used his Madman strategy as a tool to influence Moscow. On a further leg of this trip, Mr. Nixon signaled the Russians again, telling Romanian officials he would take new action if the Paris talks did not progress soon. "I never make idle threats," the president had said.[54] The channel to Hanoi through Sainteny was also used to transmit a letter from Nixon to Ho Chi Minh.

The administration posed its threat directly when Henry Kissinger held his first secret session with North Vietnamese diplomat Xuan Thuy. Arranged by Henry Cabot Lodge and Le Duc Tho as an alternative to the stalled public negotiations, the secret sessions were to become the main avenue for diplomatic exchange. At that first one, in Paris on August 4, Kissinger made a great deal of the upcoming one-year anniversary of negotiations in November. "He had been asked to tell them in all solemnity," the security adviser adverted, that "if by November 1, no major progress had been made toward a solution, we will be compelled—with great reluctance—to take measures of the greatest consequence." Kissinger did not specify what the United States might do, but Hanoi had erred gravely in trying to portray Vietnam as "Mr. Nixon's War," he said, because if it were, Richard Nixon would feel obliged to win it. "No one knows what the final result would be of such a series of events. We believe that such a tragic conflict to test each other can be avoided."[55]

In diplomatic usage this kind of representation is an ultimatum. Hanoi rejected it, using Ho Chi Minh's reply to Nixon's letter for that purpose. Washington learned of this on August 25 though U.S. officials in Paris and apparently received the text only five days later. Dr. Kissinger analyzed it for the president as "very tough, almost insolent."[56]

"After receiving this unpromising reply," Nixon recalled, "I knew that I had to prepare myself for the tremendous criticism and pressure that would come with stepping up the war."[57] The White House did not bother to await the hard copy. Kissinger had already begun agitating, telling Haldeman and Ehrlichman on August 18 that the option selected had to end the war in six to nine months. The security adviser had a plan, he told the others, but Nixon needed "to make [a] total mental commitment and really be prepared to take the heat."[58] On August 28 the advisers reviewed Henry's plan. One requirement, Kissinger noted, would be preparations to counter domestic upheaval. In early September the Pacific Command forwarded an Air Force scheme for aerial bombing of North Vietnam.

The fat now blazed in the fire. The world learned of the death of Ho Chi Minh on September 3, and NSC staffers predicted this might lead to moderation in Hanoi, but it made no difference. The president called a big strategy meeting for September 12. Dr. Kissinger had his people prepare a lengthy analysis of four possible courses of action. For the current strategy, as well as those of accelerating negotiations or Vietnamization, the paper advanced detailed criticisms; for escalation, there were none. Kissinger merely noted, "there are many problems associated with this policy but I will not concern you with them in this paper because they are being fully staffed elsewhere."[59] Officials met in the Cabinet Room at the White House for the entire morning. Ambassador Bunker, General Abrams, and Admiral John McCain, the Pacific commander in chief, all came home for these deliberations. They lunched with the president and then held additional discussions that afternoon in Nixon's hideaway in the Old Executive Office Building.

Despite the buildup, none of the talk actually dealt with the options, and Nixon made no decision. What was said that afternoon is not known. But three days earlier Kissinger told General Wheeler to ensure that all escalation planning be strictly confined within *military* channels—that is, kept from Mel Laird. A couple of days after the NSC discussion the Joint Chiefs sent a special group to Vietnam to create an operational concept. Headed by Admiral Frederic S. Bardshar, chief of the Joint Staff, the group conferred with CINCPAC planners at Honolulu, then went on to MACV. Shortly after they left CINCPAC, Admiral McCain cabled Washington to follow up on conversations he had had during his visit. The Kissinger staff adopted the code name "Duck Hook" to refer to the escalation plan. They envisioned a series of bold, imaginative actions against North Vietnam, each one distinct and conducted so as to achieve maximum political, military, and psychological shock at an increasing level of intensity, starting with mining Haiphong and the resumption of bombing. Staffer Anthony Lake and others pored over the list, noting that each escalation would be politically more difficult to justify in the United States, especially bombing the system of dikes along North Vietnamese rivers. They asked what would happen if the options had no effect.[60]

The military knew this as Operation "Pruning Knife." Admiral Bardshar, no fool, had flown carrier planes against the Japanese in World War II, commanded the aircraft carrier *Ticonderoga* during the Tonkin Gulf incident, and led U.S. naval air forces on Yankee Station during the final months of Rolling Thunder. But neither Bardshar nor the dozen or so officers with him could dream up anything new—the war had gone on so long that every option had been proposed at least once. General Abrams, when Bardshar checked with him, spoke enthusiastically about a "new ball game," but the concepts were not so fresh.[61] In addition, the air campaign plans bumped up against physical factors—Nixon's deadline coincided with the onset of the northeast monsoon, which would drastically reduce good flying weather over the North. Pruning Knife covered mining Haiphong, an aerial onslaught against the DRV, closing the Cambodian port Sihanoukville by blockade or mines, and ground forays into Cambodia, Laos, and the Demilitarized Zone.

The Pruning Knife planners' visit to Saigon coincided with a flurry of activity at the White House. Nixon wanted to cover his political flank by announcing a second troop withdrawal and, a few days later, draft call reductions of 50,000 over the next few months. Kissinger's staff discussed Duck Hook on September 20 and 24. The president had the Joint Chiefs to breakfast on the twenty-fourth, the first time during his presidency they had come to 1600 Pennsylvania Avenue as a group. On September 25 Bardshar delivered his Pruning Knife outline plan. Nixon went to Camp David on the twenty-seventh, bragging to aides that Hanoi had underestimated "the man"—he would not be the first president to lose a war—and "the time"— he still had more than three years left in his first term.[62] Aide Patrick J. Buchanan recorded Mr. Nixon as saying, "If for one month . . . everybody would 'shut up' about the war, we would be a long way toward getting it over." In fact, it would be over before the 1970 congressional elections, Nixon insisted. "We are going to be able by then to 'see the light at the end of the tunnel,'" he crooned.[63]

Nixon knew, though others did not, that a speech existed, already in its second draft, in which he would reveal Duck Hook to the nation as he hurled bombs at Hanoi. The text spoke of his "major decision" and "sober and considered judgment" that genuine talks had not occurred, a "tragic miscalculation of our will and purpose." Nixon would declare, "I was not elected to preside over the senseless attrition of American lives by a deluded foe." Saying nothing of the Madman Theory, he would insist this escalation was "limited" and sought no wider war.[64]

Kissinger saw Ambassador Dobrynin again that day, and in a bit of stage-managing, the president contrived to phone during their séance. Nixon called from Camp David, where he had just told nine Republican senators that he was thinking of blockading Haiphong and invading the DRV—scaring Congress and scaring the Russians, all at the same time. Dr. Kissinger's message to Moscow would be that Vietnam was *the* critical issue, that the United States "took seriously Hanoi's attempt to undermine the President's domestic position," and that "the train had left the station and was headed down the track."[65] Dobrynin's warnings of limited Soviet influence in Hanoi were ignored.

Immediately afterward Kissinger called Nixon back to report his impressions, and a key exchange occurred. Both men knew that a recently formed antiwar front, the New Mobilization to End the War in Vietnam, had called for a national moratorium with actions every month, starting with a mass march on Washington on October 15. The president clearly anticipated that his escalation would trigger a massive response. As they spoke in euphemisms for Duck Hook, Nixon referred to the demonstration. Kissinger, still pushing, opined that events of the past several weeks excluded a long-haul strategy: "The doves and the public are making it impossible." Nixon took the point. He asked Kissinger if they could pick up the pace and "make the tough move before the 15th of October . . . he doesn't want to appear to be making the tough move after the 15th just because of the rioting at home." Nixon was aware that the nation "is going to take a dimmer view after the move than before" and felt it better "to nip it before the first demonstration, because there will be another one on November 15." Henry warned only that this timing risked the deadline the United States had already given Hanoi, so "it will look as if we tricked them." The president was not dissuaded.[66]

Dr. Kissinger assembled his key aides on September 29 to hand out work assignments. This "September Group" included Soviet affairs expert Helmut Sonnenfeldt, who wrote the paper on probable Soviet reaction, and NSC China aide John Holdridge, author of the one on the Chinese. Authorship of the paper on Hanoi itself is not clear. Tony Lake, Roger Morris, and Peter Rodman collaborated on the draft presidential speech. No one was satisfied with the speech, and there were continuing doubts about the Duck Hook options themselves. That day Lake and Morris wrote a joint memo to the NSC military aide, Navy captain Rembrandt Robinson, arguing the basic paper needed extensive reworking to include more analysis, alternative military programs, and treatment of U.S. diplomatic objectives. The study, finished or not, went to the president on October 2. This was the paper that contained the "full coverage" of escalation absent from Kissinger's earlier analysis of Vietnam alternatives. The package contained a fresh draft of the speech and a list of questions to be answered before Duck Hook went forward. But the dozens of pages of projections and estimates ignored the political impact, except to say it was a question beyond the competence of NSC staff.

The next day the president pondered the plans during a visit to his Key Biscayne home. Away from Washington, closeted with his personal entourage (Kissinger, Haldeman, and Ehrlichman) instead of the usual administration officials, the chief executive sat in swim trunks and a sport shirt. Haldeman immediately picked up on the lack of any provision for domestic impact. Kissinger said the big question would be whether the president could hold the country together. Ehrlichman felt strongly that they ought to start getting ready, that "we can and should pre-program several routes on a [public relations] basis."[67] Nixon suddenly expressed fear that the escalation might not work, and he would be lost.

Over the next couple of weeks the entire Madman strategy would be abandoned. The questions are why and when. Some scholars date this to October 6, when the president ordered Laird to arrange for a major Strategic Air Command (SAC) nuclear war exercise that would surely be detected by the Russians.[68] It seems equally likely the SAC maneuver was first laid on as an element of Duck Hook, not a replacement for it. Both the NSC staff and the Pentagon continued to work on the escalation, including several more drafts for the speech, the earliest of which still contained Duck Hook. The final version of the bombing plan, "Pruning Knife Alpha," came as late as November 13 in a JCS paper to Laird. On October 9 the presidential speech was put on the official schedule—for November 3. According to Haldeman, Kissinger feared the president had decided against his plan, but Haldeman's own guess was that Nixon would enunciate U.S. attempts to mollify Hanoi, then wait for a reaction; if Hanoi escalated, "we move *fast* to heavy retaliation, mining etc., with this bad faith as basis."[69]

Several things had changed already. The president had abandoned the notion of carrying out Duck Hook before the October 15 moratorium. This kept his diplomatic deadline but further complicated the political problem. That equation also changed. The White House tried to project "cool contempt" toward the antiwar movement,[70] but Haldeman's diary vividly demonstrated Nixon's mushrooming anxiety. October 8: "Kept the doves at bay this long, now have to take them on." The president prevailed upon his vice president, Spiro Agnew, to give a series of speeches lambasting student protesters, which Nixon himself planned to follow up. October 9: "[The president] fears [he] can't hold the country that long at that level." October 10: "concern about schedule for next week after October 15, not strong enough." Nixon put speechwriter Price to work on something he could say about the protests. October 13: "Lot of concern about plans for Moratorium Day as it nears and heat builds." Nixon sent a letter to a student at Georgetown thundering that the democratic process would be destroyed if government accepted policies advocated by street demonstrations.[71] The day before the moratorium Agnew denounced a letter sent by Hanoi leader Pham Van Dong in support of the demonstrations and demanded that antiwar leaders repudiate it.

On October 11 Haldeman saw the president as nearing the final stages of his decision. Indeed, that day Laird and the full JCS spent three hours with Mr. Nixon. That Nixon still held book for Duck Hook is indicated by his telling them that contacts with legislators showed they could "'catch hell' from the Hawks as well as the Doves if we followed the long road." Yet casualty rates seemed to be falling, suggesting that a long-term approach like Vietnamization could be viable. Laird warned that Duck Hook itself should not be viewed as an immediate payoff strategy: "anything done in North Vietnam will take at least a year." Then Wheeler briefed Pruning Knife, declaring at the outset that he did *not* consider the plan militarily sound. At the end of his presentation the JCS chairman stated that the Chiefs as a whole thought Duck Hook flawed because it envisioned too short a period of attack. In between, Wheeler ranged over various problems from the impending monsoon to insufficient aerial refueling capability to the need to move additional aircraft carriers from Korean waters to Vietnamese. Admiral Thomas Moorer, the chief of naval operations, added that the target list and sortie allocations were merely illustrative, and much remained to be done. "The President then asked, 'What can we do in two weeks?'" Of course, the answer was the SAC aerial alert exercise. Mr. Nixon ordered that the Pruning Knife plans be refined and reformatted for week-long and fortnight-long aerial assaults.[72]

Clearly, no immediate "go" order was possible. Melvin Laird's role in this charade is notable but obscure. The Chiefs presented the plan to him several times. "I never understood why the Joint Chiefs of Staff were so enthusiastic about Pruning Knife," Laird recalled in an interview. But General Wheeler's White House briefing on October 11 indicated the polar opposite. Laird seems to have leaned on the Chiefs to get them to downplay the possibilities. So the SAC alert went ahead instead. There are suppositions but no clear evidence that the Soviets observed the SAC alert or drew any conclusions from it. However, Dobrynin returned to the White House on October 20 to deliver a note that plainly said the use of additional force in Vietnam was both misguided and extremely dangerous. Nixon's account here exults in the denunciation he dished up in return, but the fact remained that Moscow had put Washington on notice that it might well respond to an act of force. Kissinger ignored Nixon's demand he tell Dobrynin afterward that the president was out of control on Vietnam. This was one of those presidential orders his subordinates quietly torpedoed.

Publicly the protests held center stage. An ominous prelude took place in Chicago starting on October 8. This was the "Days of Rage" in which the most extreme faction of the SDS, which had all but broken up at its convention that summer, took to the streets to exact revenge for the 1968 police riot. Only a few hundred SDSers showed up, making impossible any real effort to support the Chicago Eight, then on trial, and the gathering degenerated into an aimless street fight. The rump SDS faction went underground and became known as the Weathermen. They would work assiduously to break down the middle-class values of upbringing that held members back from adopting violent tactics.

The big show on October 15 roiled across the nation. There were over *2 million* protesters—at least 50,000 in Washington, that many in New York, 100,000 in Boston—demonstrations in dozens of cities across the nation. At the White House the president ceremoniously held an early-morning NSC session. In the Old Executive Office Building suite of the NSC staff, William Watts labored on the latest draft of the speech. That night Nixon put a nail in Duck Hook's coffin, reflecting on the irony of this peace protest: "It had, I believed, destroyed whatever small possibility may have existed of ending the war in 1969."[73] The next day he convinced his chief congressional leaders, Gerald R. Ford in the House and Hugh Scott in the Senate, to call for a moratorium of their own—a moratorium on protest. Kissinger relates that on October 17 he advised the president—no doubt reluctantly—to put off a decision on Duck Hook. Two days later Agnew gave the first of his incendiary speeches attacking the Movement: student protesters were "an effete corps of impudent snobs," leaders were "hard core dissidents and professional anarchists." The Movement comprised trash with whom society could dispense.

From that point, Richard Nixon's unbending efforts were devoted to the speech he would give on November 3. Years later, retired and in disgrace, the former president gave three reasons why he had decided against escalation. First, Nixon doubted whether he could have "held the country together for the period of time needed to win in view of the numbers of casualties we would be sustaining." Second, he says, he had determined not to let Vietnam paralyze American foreign policy. Lastly, Nixon writes, "I knew a military victory alone would not solve our problem."[74]

The Duck Hook text morphed into something different, an effort to create a base of political support for the long haul. Price remained the lead speechwriter, but the Kissinger staff worked up a pair of drafts, and Nixon himself labored assiduously. A stack of all his scrawled, handwritten notes for the November 3 speech would be several inches high. There were at least a dozen drafts, with the precise number difficult to discern because of so many cut-

and-paste partial redrafts. Before a nationwide television audience that night the president conjured a "great silent majority" of Americans, claiming these people supported his Vietnam policy and rejected the position of the "vocal minority." Nixon repeated his earlier line that to withdraw from Vietnam because protesters urged it could destroy America as a free society. Mr. Nixon did not explain how extending the U.S. sojourn in the Vietnam quagmire, simply to defy protesters who expressed the national will embodied in the 1968 election, would perfect that free society.

Henry Kissinger characterizes response to the speech as "electric." He notes that from the moment it ended, "the White House switchboard was clogged with congratulatory phone calls," and there were 50,000 supportive telegrams and 30,000 letters. But the president took no chances. Even Kissinger conceded that "no doubt some of the enthusiasm was stimulated by Haldeman's indefatigable operatives who had called political supporters all over the country to send in telegrams."[75] In actuality, in testimony at a 1999 trial held to consider the fair market value of the original of this speech and its drafts, presidential aide Alexander M. Butterfield revealed that he had spent weeks prompting the response, arranging with labor unions, military retirees, the Veterans of Foreign Wars, the American Legion, millionaire entrepreneur H. Ross Perot, and others to generate it. "Everybody was spring-loaded to respond," Butterfield testified. "It truly was manufactured."[76] Nixon made a point of calling reporters into the Oval Office to photograph some of the telegrams and letters. Vietnam would be Richard Nixon's war after all.

It was a late summer day that I returned to New York, one of those bell-clear, glorious days that make you glad to be alive. The cab dropped me and my two suitcases on Amsterdam Avenue and 114th Street, right next to my dormitory, but actually at the worst possible place, since you could not enter the building there. John Jay Hall's entrance was inside, tucked away in a corner of the inner campus. Naturally I did everything wrong, lugging the suitcases two blocks up to College Walk, back around the main academic building, and into the dormitory quad. There had been a gate just up the street on 114th, as I learned soon enough. I was sweating profusely when I got to the dorm. Not an auspicious beginning, but I did not mind. New York was under my feet again. The dorm room turned out to be a nine- by twelve-foot cubicle facing up 114th toward the Hudson River. Until the 1968 student strikes, it had been occupied by two people. One reason for the strike that year became instantly apparent.

Vietnam had been the big issue at Columbia in 1968. It remained a live one when I arrived in 1969. Columbia strongly denied complicity, which was accurate, in that the university took no public stance supporting the war, and there was no on-campus ROTC program for aspiring officers. But the university was a major recipient of federal research money, many of those funds dedicated to military technology or scientific development. Columbia also stood among the founders of a university consortium working with the Institute for Defense Analyses. College Walk, the campus crosswalk that corresponded to 116th Street, witnessed many protests against the university's complicity and the war itself. These were a weekly, at times daily, occurrence. They were impossible to avoid.

I did not come to Columbia to participate in the antiwar movement. I had my doubts about the war, but also about political organizations. The events of 1968 had stunned me, from Tet right through the election; I had experienced a bombardment of successive challenges to my conventional thinking. But I rejected recruitment by Columbia's rump SDS chapter and other activists. Shortly after reaching New York I was scandalized by the sheer stupidity of the Days of Rage. But I also saw the press revelations of the U.S. bombing of neutral Cambodia. There seemed to be little wisdom on either side of this war.

The main lounge in my dorm had a TV set, the only one in the building at the time. We saw constant reports on the trial of the Chicago Eight, and the judge seemed as hell-bent on persecuting the protesters as the Chicago police had been on beating them up. Their offense had been to oppose a war I knew had never been declared, a war spiked by the Tonkin Gulf incident, which already seemed contrived. Defendant Bobby Seale, whose proceeding had been severed from that of the others, was shackled, restrained, and prohibited from speaking, without precedent in American justice. Rulings from the bench were arbitrary and quixotic, often betraying malice aforethought. The trial became an education in the arrogance of power. It contributed to the general ferment, not least at Columbia. Many upperclassmen, prompted by the Chicago trial, commented on the similar violence perpetrated by the New York Police Department at Columbia. The Nixon administration had declared its Vietnamization policy and announced the withdrawal of some American forces, but that little slice of 25,000 seemed merely cosmetic to me. I knew a lot about the U.S. military, and I knew that in a force the size of what we had in Vietnam you could pull that many out without much affecting anything. That turned out to be true. A new withdrawal shortly after I entered Columbia, another 35,000 troops, went further, but not much. Mr. Nixon seemed to be extending the war, not ending it.

In the fall of 1969 the New York Mets were in the World Series. The lounge in my dorm, and no doubt those in other Columbia residence halls too, was filled with students watching the games. The joy was great in Mudville when the Mets won the World Series. One could not avoid the news interspersed with the sports. Early in September, Army lieutenant William Calley was charged with premeditated murder for his unit's massacre of more than a hundred (later shown to be closer to 500) Vietnamese civilians at the hamlet of My Lai. Then, late that month, the Army dropped charges against eight Green Berets who had murdered one of their Vietnamese operatives. I had yet to learn the details, but both incidents showed that U.S. tactics were as misguided as the strategy, and immoral to boot. Reality obliged me to confront my reluctance to become engaged.

Presently, the death of Ho Chi Minh was followed by the president of the United States telling us that he refused to be influenced by protesters. I could read the newspapers as well as anyone, and I knew the dissenters were only voicing what the opinion polls showed to be the majority view. I looked favorably on those who participated in the October 15 moratorium, only to be told a few days later by the vice president that people like me were "effete impudent snobs." Agnew's rhetoric escalated from there. And in his November 3 speech, Nixon announced, contrary to everything I could see around me, that the real majority, the "great silent majority," favored the war. The extravagance of those claims struck me. I decided to listen to what the antiwar people had to say. Another moratorium march was coming up, in Washington on November 15. I went. That was my first antiwar demonstration.[77]

But my hopes the war might end were frustrated, along with those of all Americans who thought our country ought to be extracting itself from this tragic conflict. How bad it was would be revealed only gradually, painfully, starting the next year.

9   Dim and Flaring Lamps (1969–1971)

As Richard Nixon struggled to bring his strategy of threat to a head, the war went on in the paddies, jungles, and savannahs of South Vietnam. The administration needed an approach to that war, too, one inevitably defined by its perspectives, its diplomacy, and the shape of politics. Secretary Melvin Laird dubbed this strategy Vietnamization, but that served as shorthand for a broader, more complex evolution that encompassed many elements. As in every other aspect, individuals played key roles in creating the conditions under which the war progressed. Among the most important would be cigar-chomping, wisecracking General Creighton W. Abrams, America's field commander.

Little in the general's background suggested Abrams as a paragon of counterinsurgency warfare. Rather, his renown had been as an expert on armored and mechanized troops. The aggressive leader whose tank battalion first broke the German siege ring at Bastogne, in World War II's Battle of the Bulge, Abrams had led the way through the Siegfried Line. Like George Patton, under whom he served, Abrams loved his cigars—Ellsworth Bunker thought "Abe" had the best collection he had ever seen—but he was never a man of the boardroom. Abe was more suited to the plains of Germany, where the United States expected a Soviet invasion of Western Europe. He had, in fact, commanded V Corps of the U.S. Seventh Army in West Germany in the early 1960s, and an armored division before that. Nor did the general seem to be the brainy type, having graduated West Point in the bottom third of his class, with no academic training other than the higher service schools. Abrams had never been to the National War College, though he had passed through the Army's slightly less prestigious version.

Where he lacked academic chops, Creighton Abrams had something else—a feel for problem solving unfettered by conventional wisdom. Supple and flexible of thought, Abrams had employed radical means to keep his tanks running in World War II and radical tactics to fight the Germans. His quality had been recognized early—Patton was one admirer—and he soon appeared on the Army General Staff, including in its strategic nerve center, the War Plans Division. Abrams spent the entire Korean war as chief of staff for one Army corps after another. He had also been at the Pentagon in

charge of Army Reserve affairs; as director of civil affairs, then force development, later operations deputy for the General Staff.

No stranger to political problems, as a major general Abrams had been
chief of staff for the troops sent to the University of Mississippi in 1962
when African American James H. Meredith matriculated there—an important passage in the civil rights struggle. Abrams actually commanded the
federal troops alerted for possible intervention during civil rights protests at
Birmingham a year later. He became vice chief of staff of the Army upon returning from West Germany in August 1964. General Abrams had been on
the short list to lead MACV at that time, but Lyndon Johnson chose William
Westmoreland instead.[1]

By 1967 Abrams's number had come up again. President Johnson selected
him as Westmoreland's deputy commander. Saigon was about as foreign as it
could get for a man born and bred in western Massachusetts, but the work of
the Army staff already involved Vietnam to a considerable degree. Abe had
been there twice on inspections, receiving this appointment after a third.
The fifty-two-year-old Abrams did not miss a step in taking up the reins
when he arrived at Saigon on May 4, 1967. One measure of his performance
would be that many remember Abrams as MACV deputy commander,
whereas virtually no one recalls his predecessor, Lieutenant General John A.
Heintges.

Westmoreland gave Abrams responsibility for building up the South Vietnamese army, and he labored long and hard on ARVN equipment, performance, and U.S. advisory issues. Willing to listen to colleagues, whether
American or South Vietnamese, gracious in handling awkward situations, always coming across as friend and comrade, Abrams made great strides. The
list of unmet South Vietnamese equipment needs that JCS chairman
Wheeler assembled after Tet showed that much remained to be done, but in
less than a year General Abrams had filled many deficits and, equally important, changed MACV attitudes toward the South Vietnamese buildup, making this a major priority rather than just another program. In one
respect—provision of the lightweight M-16 assault rifle to the ARVN—even
Abrams's pleas had gone unanswered. But Tet changed that.

Another measure of Westmoreland's esteem came during Tet, when he
sent Abrams to Phu Bai to set up a forward headquarters for MACV and directly supervise the battles at Hue and along the Demilitarized Zone, as well
as the relief of Khe Sanh. The last, Operation Pegasus, was at its height when
LBJ took the final step, bringing Westy home and putting Abrams in his
stead. The official change of command took place on June 10, 1968, but
Abrams had already been de facto leader for several weeks. Among his first
acts was to order the evacuation of Khe Sanh.

If not already aware of political pitfalls, Creighton Abrams received an education during LBJ's last months, when he was drawn into Washington's in-fighting over the bombing halt. Johnson circulated Abe's private comments on a bombing halt as a press release at the height of the platform fight at the Democratic convention. That August, and again a month later, the MACV commander's assessment favored those opposed to a halt. But LBJ's changed direction became evident soon enough, and in October, Abrams reversed course, not only agreeing that bombing could end without disaster but also arguing that the aircraft thus freed could be used to better advantage over the Ho Chi Minh Trail. Abrams even came home to lend his weight to the president's efforts to open negotiations by ending the bombing.

Lyndon Johnson was fond of aphorisms, and one of his favorites concerned the camel: if you let him stick his nose into your tent, he would soon be entirely inside. Staff collected a list of some of Abe's sayings, and one of them was, "As to the camel in the tent—We patted him on the nose and said, 'Nice Camel.'"[2] The new MACV commander was a realist.

General Abrams would be universally acclaimed as a breath of fresh air after Westmoreland. Almost everyone agreed that Abe's flexibility; his readiness to work at convincing subordinates of the necessity of a thing, not merely to order it; plus his attentiveness to the intelligence flowing into MACV made the war effort far more effective from the first day he took command. General Andrew Goodpaster came to Saigon, after a brief stint on the U.S. negotiating team in Paris, to take up Abrams's old post as MACV deputy. Within weeks Goodpaster was on the phone to Walt Rostow—another of those back-channel communications Rostow swore he never engaged in—to tell him that Abrams's performance was "simply superb" and recommending he be awarded the Distinguished Service Medal.[3] Rostow reported the conversation to LBJ on October 8, 1968, just before the president began the frantic maneuvers that led to the October Surprise and the bombing halt. When the general appeared in connection with LBJ's final deliberations, President Johnson pinned the medal on his chest.

What Goodpaster reported to Washington flowed from events on the ground. After the collapse of the second wave of the Tet offensive and its third-wave strikes making barely a ripple, Hanoi changed strategy. The big units pulled back into their base areas. There were other redeployments too, with strength taken out of the Central Highlands and concentrated in the I Corps region or opposite Saigon. Abrams shifted his tactics as well, stopping the huge search-and-destroy operations, insisting that commanders focus on small-scale forays and patrol operations. The ARVN would take up the slack on big ops. Perceptive South Vietnamese complained about Vietnamization—they had been fighting this war long before the Americans came along—and for Saigon (as for Hanoi), this was a total war, not a limited one. What was there to Vietnamize? But the ARVN had been noticeably ineffective on pacification, which Abrams saw as creating the security to advance the village war. This became the hallmark of U.S. effort on his watch. Some might argue that the refocus was inevitable due to the need to restore pacification in the wake of Tet, and also because Hanoi's pullback perforce made the villages the big ballgame. This does not diminish Abrams's achievement in turning the U.S. military machine, organized and trained for the big operations, toward the kind of local action that had gotten only lip service during Westy's time. From here on out, the Americans would concentrate on local efforts.

New Strategy

Creighton Abrams succeeded in part because he had the resources for a broad security effort—not just U.S. and South Vietnamese troops, though there were plenty of those, but also practical, functional assistance of the type that freed soldiers for their new tasks without increasing the danger of fresh offensives by Hanoi. In a way, the operations conducted during this phase had not been possible earlier because the framework in which they proceeded did not yet exist.

First were the sinews of war, supplies for MACV and the ARVN. The U.S. deployments in 1965 had begun a race between troop arrivals and the port capacity to land them, plus storage and transport systems for the supplies.[4] Judgments on Westmoreland as field commander may vary, but one thing to which Westy paid great heed and at which he finally succeeded was to create the logistics capacity for the forces. Until the time of Tet, requirements had constantly run ahead of the ability to land, haul, and stock the supplies, and every South Vietnamese port had seen bunches of merchant vessels at anchor, waiting to unload their precious cargoes. The queues at Saigon and Cam Ranh sometimes numbered hundreds of ships. Abrams had no such problem. He could focus on operations, not logistics nightmares.

A second enabling factor stemmed from efforts by former secretary of defense McNamara and his widely reviled systems analysts to add a fourth company to each rifle battalion in MACV—a program Westmoreland had gladly accepted. This force augmentation had been accomplished by late 1967. By increasing rifle strength on the ground, the ability to inflict casualties would be improved and U.S. combat power increased, without the deployment of additional formations. In a security regime that emphasized pacification support, company-size clear-and-hold missions and patrol operations were the heart of the enterprise, and those fourth companies became a vital addition, permitting both a higher operational tempo and schedules that reduced pressure on the men. In August 1968 there were roughly 111 maneuver battalions with MACV. The fourth-company add-ons represented the equivalent of *25 extra rifle battalions* with U.S. forces.[5]

A third key development would be improvements in U.S. and Vietnamese intelligence. As chief of MACV intelligence in 1966–1967, Major General

Joseph McChristian had set up a Combined Intelligence Center Vietnam (CICV), with new estimating units and others to handle data from aerial photography and interrogations, along with a Combined Documents Exploitation Center (CDEC) whose special purpose was to translate enemy documents captured in combat or elsewhere. The CDEC had already provided useful information by the time of Tet, but the battles of 1968 brought a flood of National Liberation Front and North Vietnamese papers that furnished a new basis for understanding the adversary.

Meanwhile, in November 1967 U.S. signals intelligence had achieved a breakthrough on its intercepts of traffic in the "Vinh Window"—NSA slang for what it learned from recording unenciphered radio conversations between People's Army way stations on the Ho Chi Minh Trail and the base areas. First in the Ashau valley, then around Vinh, and then more widely along The Trail, the radio spooks were able to establish VPA routines and even crack the system Hanoi used to specify destinations for its infiltration groups. When the adversary introduced ciphers, the American cryptographers were able to solve them. Round-the-clock shuttles of electronic intelligence aircraft over both Laos and the Tonkin Gulf made the frontline intercepts; ground stations processed the traffic, and CINCPAC created a staff unit wholly dedicated to analyzing it, which also furnished raw meat for MACV J-2, its joint intelligence staff.[6]

By 1969 some 4,700 Americans were working on intelligence alone. Their sources provided a plethora of inside data on movements down The Trail, Hanoi's tactical techniques, its organizational structures, and its armament. Starting in 1968 CICV's special studies exhibited increasingly detailed knowledge and unprecedented sophistication. General Abrams benefited from these studies. At command conferences (begun during Westy's tenure) called Weekly Intelligence Estimate Updates (WIEUs) the new level of information resulted in an actual strategy, one to affect the adversary's logistics and therefore its offensive capability. The Nixon administration believed its data on Hanoi's infiltration down The Trail accurate to within 25 percent of the true figures. Even if the penetrations into North Vietnamese communications were lost, MACV would still be within 50 percent of reality. The data also enabled intelligence to warn General Abrams when he needed to reassemble units to fend off People's Army attacks.[7]

Another help to Abrams would be the existence of a U.S. command to manage pacification. President Johnson, who constantly harped on the "other war" in Vietnam, had sent his NSC sparkplug for these matters, Robert W. Komer, to mold the pacification command, which had been set up in 1967 and reached its stride after Tet. The CIA had previously taken the lead here, but it handed over its role to the new authority, including lending LBJ its Far East Division chief, William E. Colby, to be deputy director. The unit was known as CORDS, which originally stood for Civil Operations and

Revolutionary Development Support (following CIA nomenclature for "Revolutionary Development," one of its key programs); in deference to Vietnamese sensibilities, the unit was renamed Civil Operations and Rural Development Support.[8] CORDS handled the U.S. side of everything from village and district advisers to land reform, economic development, and attacks against what the allies called the "Viet Cong Infrastructure." Although the abrasive Komer made no friends with his bullish drive to activate CORDS—there would be jokes at Abe's command conferences about assassinating Komer should he ever show his face in Saigon again[9]—the heavy lifting had been done before Abrams took over. Colby succeeded Komer and worked closely with Abrams over the next three years.[10]

But no doubt the most important factor in Abe's success would be his own proclivities. Despite his background and MACV responsibilities during some of the most intense battles of the war, Abrams was attuned to the countryside and ready to make pacification his rallying cry. Perhaps this came from his background; he had grown up in Springfield, when it was still a small city surrounded by farms, with nearby Pioneer Valley and Amherst, the locale of the Massachusetts Agricultural College (today the University of Massachusetts). Or maybe Abrams the problem solver simply recognized pacification as the central strategic problem of the moment. MACV staff who thought in terms of massive sweeps watched in amazement as their boss became an evangelist for pacification and transformed U.S. tactics. He cut back the use of artillery and firepower in populated areas. Battalion-size operations, averaging about 120 during Westmoreland's last four months, dropped to 83 or fewer under Abrams, compensated by a huge growth in small-unit activity plus—dear to his heart—massive swelling of the ARVN effort (its large operations increased 75 percent over the same period and sustained an even higher pace for the rest of the war).

The evangelism was immediately evident in Abrams's reporting to Washington. When MACV tabulated enemy activity for the three weeks following LBJ's bombing halt, Abrams reported that 46 percent of targets attacked had tried to counter expanded allied population control, while another 29 percent had opposed clear-and-hold operations. He concluded that the enemy was now targeting pacification. Abrams stood ready to fight along those lines for longer than a summer.

■ ■ ■ The course of America's new strategy was set at Saigon on September 20, 1968. General Abrams customarily talked strategy at the WIEU meetings, and once a month he had senior leaders at the sessions, after which he held command conferences. On September 20 CORDS was set to brief at the WIEU, and Komer had Colby present their grand concept. Beginning with an overview of how Hanoi controlled its war and the National

Liberation Front controlled many villages in the South, the CORDS deputy used pacification data to show that enemy base areas corresponded to clusters of villages and districts where the cadres, not the Saigon government, reigned. Colby spoke of a "People's War" waged by Saigon this time, not the NLF, using self-defense, self-help, and self-government to give Vietnamese villagers a stake. The centerpiece would be a buildup of Regional Forces and Popular Forces—Saigon's local troop units—plus the creation of a new People's Self-Defense Force (PSDF), essentially a village militia. These forces would preempt Liberation Front efforts, making up one of four campaign concepts that Colby wanted to implement simultaneously. U.S. and Saigon forces would saturate problem sectors. The other elements were measures to strengthen Saigon's legitimacy—involving the U.S. embassy—and two more MACV initiatives: spoiling attacks on the clusters of enemy control, and interposing a security screen that would "harden" the villages against NLF inroads. The Colby plan included what CORDS termed an "Accelerated Pacification Campaign" to regain a thousand villages before the 1969 Tet new year.

Some experts, notably John Paul Vann, were suspicious of the timetable, fearing that a push for quick results would preclude doing the job right. However, MACV senior officers, including corps commanders General Robert Cushman and General Ray Peers, favored the scheme. Abrams tapped his cigar—Colby recorded that he did so "thoughtfully"[11]—then gave full approval. After a few weeks of detailed planning at CORDS the concept was presented to South Vietnamese president Nguyen Van Thieu, who also accepted it.

Before going further, a few words about *pacification* are appropriate. That word had come to encompass the array of things done with Vietnamese villagers as their object. Because the insurgency had been built on popular support, the contest for the "hearts and minds" of the Vietnamese became central to counterinsurgency. The available techniques consisted of population control, in which villagers were resettled and their identities and movements monitored as closely as possible; self-defense, including the creation of militias to involve villagers in their own security; civic action, in which security forces built community facilities, provided medical assistance, and liaised with hamlet authorities in an attempt to convince villagers the Saigon government cared about their concerns; economic aid; agricultural assistance; help with education; and direct efforts to root out NLF cadres among the people. In various combinations, all these methods had been tried over the years since Ngo Dinh Diem's time.

Americans and South Vietnamese had come up with some winning combinations, but the story of pacification in Vietnam is a record of successful local formulas that failed when replicated throughout the forty-four provinces. What made CORDS different was the creation of an entity designed to bring together all the threads, its chain of command integrated with the U.S. military and South Vietnamese at the regional level and with Saigon military and civil authorities at the province, district, and village levels. There had been embassy central managers before, but none with across-the-board authority. In addition, the CORDS organization tapped the U.S. military, with its enormous resources, for the pacification mission. With this new integration, regional and subordinate managers could funnel resources into needy areas, of which there were plenty. Even before Tet, the United States had assembled a list of eighteen provinces in South Vietnam for priority treatment, and now, of course, there were also the villages designated for the Accelerated Pacification Campaign.

Thus, by the end of the Johnson administration, the United States had rededicated itself to the pacification role, the military and civilian leadership were on board, and unprecedented resources had become available. Meanwhile, the adversary had suffered grievous losses.

One key difficulty continued to be measuring relative control of the villages by insurgents and government forces. In the early years, this measure had simply been based on estimates by Saigon's district and provincial officials, reviewed by American advisers. Such data were acknowledged to be soft, frustrating McNamara, who wanted something more objective. On one of his visits McNamara demanded action. Overnight, Agency for International Development official (and former CIA officer) Rufus Phillips came up with a scheme, refined by the CIA's George Carver plus other military and diplomatic officials, that became known as the Hamlet Evaluation Survey (HES). It required district advisers to complete monthly report cards, grading their areas on a number of socioeconomic, political, and security standards, each of them embodying even more minute criteria—ninety-seven in all. American advisers and Saigon officials signed off on the HES reports, but as a corrective, the U.S. advisers privately filed their own versions of the report card. There were six possible rankings: "A" villages were those under Saigon's secure control, with "B" ones slightly less well controlled. "C" villages were considered relatively stable, control was contested in the "D" and "E" categories, and a final group identified villages solidly controlled by the Liberation Front. The HES data were aggregated to create a South Vietnam–wide profile and became the official measure.

With the Abrams-Colby initiative, as had happened so often in the past, outcomes were limited by the available tools. The Accelerated Pacification Campaign is a good example. Much has been made of this, and indeed, great results were claimed for it. The campaign grew out of Operation Recovery, a frantic attempt to regain what had been lost at Tet. Before Tet, HES data had showed 67.2 percent of the villages as relatively secure (in the "A" to "C" categories). The offensive brought a steep drop. By June 1968 Recovery had restored the level to 63.3 percent. Recovery plus the Accelerated Pacification

Campaign would do even more: when Richard Nixon entered the White House, the HES "relatively secure" level stood at more than 75 percent.

But here the Vietnam data problem reared its ugly head. It turns out that after Tet, the HES criteria were changed in a way that skewed them toward military security. Six of the eleven major categories for grading were deleted: land reform, development of agriculture, eradication of disease, eradication of illiteracy, improvement of transportation lines, and good treatment of soldiers. Among the categories that remained, thirty-three of fifty-three pacification tasks were also dropped from the questionnaires. These included listing officials accused of corruption, organizing monthly rallies, creating village organizations, reconciling local differences, discouraging migration to cities, helping families return to the villages, mapping hamlets, and even listing residents known to be with the NLF. The deletions were justified at the time by the post-Tet emergency, but only a few of the criteria were ever restored. In short, HES failed to gather the data most relevant to where Saigon really stood in the struggle for hearts and minds.

There was also the question of subjectivity. At different times, HES data were compiled by U.S. advisers alone, Americans and South Vietnamese in unison, or both sides separately. In every case they represented advisers' personal opinions. At a White House meeting in the summer of 1969, Dr. Kissinger complained that when he asked advisers their criteria for judgment, "their answers ranged from the highly sophisticated to the appallingly crude."[12] And towering above everything were the differing commitments on the part of Washington and Saigon. The considered opinion of the CIA's official history of pacification is that U.S. officials *always* put more emphasis on incentives than did their Saigon counterparts. If so, the elimination of sociopolitical criteria from HES proved doubly damaging. The CIA notes, "After Tet 1968, as U.S. officials joined their [South Vietnamese] counterparts in relying on the reduction of the [NLF infrastructure] to pacify the countryside, the distinction between the two basic strategies, so important to pacification managers, began to evaporate."[13]

Small wonder that Bill Colby often said that he saw HES as an index of the direction of movement rather than a measure of control. John Paul Vann agreed, and he said so to the Senate Foreign Relations Committee in February 1970.[14] Nixon's NSC staff even drafted a directive (never issued) that would have ended the compilation of overall HES ratings from the individual indicators. Instead, the United States conducted an extensive review of HES discrepancies in late 1969, adding new questions and running both rating systems against each other for a few months. The result was a decision to regrade the figures at about five percentage points below then-current HES levels. Another review in 1971 dropped a couple more points of "progress."

But a worse shortcoming lay in the fact that the HES data were falsified. Throughout 1967–1968, about 20 percent of villages had never been evaluated, yet they were included in the "relatively secure" column when officials made their claims. Thus the 67.2 percent control HES showed in January 1968 was actually closer to 49 percent, as revealed when the United States released a new version of these data in 1972.[15] The proportion of villages not evaluated stood at 19 percent in January 1969 and remained high, 15 percent, in January 1970, when a HES review made a concerted effort to eliminate the unevaluated category (but failed to get it below 5 percent). Not until September 1970 did CORDS succeed in grading all of South Vietnam's villages. Naturally, questions regarding the reliability of the rankings persisted.

South Vietnamese officials, other than Thieu and some of his minions, were always more pessimistic than the Americans, and the Saigon side remained a key stumbling block. The Saigon government, slow to create a ministry for pacification in spite of "strategic hamlets" and all the rest, then repeatedly switched ministers and seemed to fire those the Americans considered most dynamic. When Komer and Colby took Accelerated Pacification to Thieu, they worried about the program's acceptability and whether it could be made to seem like a Saigon initiative. Thieu approved and appeared to be enthusiastic, making interior minister Tran Thien Khiem his point man. But commitment remained elusive. Saigon's rhetoric could be flowery, its actions sometimes dramatic—Khiem staged showdowns with corps commanders and even led a parade through Saigon at one point—yet its investment consisted primarily of recycled U.S. dollars. With CORDS under pressure to show equal efforts from both sides, the figures given to Congress displayed Saigon's proportion of expenses at nearly half, declining slightly from 50 percent (of $582 million) in 1966 to 49 percent (of $1.5 billion) in 1970. But in fact, the Thieu government spent 64.5 percent of its entire 1969 budget on the Ministry of Defense; total expenditures for "defense related civil programs," including pacification, stood at $112 million, about a sixth of Saigon's supposed contribution. The missing dollars could only have come from U.S. funds.[16]

For all that, the HES numbers did move. Here, Colby inserted a cautionary note. After accompanying President Thieu on a trip that reviewed pacification in each of Saigon's military regions, Colby told Abrams, "There is a little problem on the statistics thing here, because the president has stated that the [Saigon government] will not be in a position of admitting that the [NLF] control any part of the country, and therefore *he* has divided the total category of the country into two general classes: one, the areas in which the government has control; and the second, areas in which the government doesn't quite yet have *complete* control."[17] By early 1970 HES figures had more than 90 percent relatively secure (including the unevaluated villages). Thieu adopted goals such as moving villages to the secure "A" category. By 1971 HES showed no villages at all loyal to the Liberation Front, and only 5 percent contested. The records of the WIEUs are replete with expressions of satisfaction and cracks that the hapless NLF, condemned to pursuing villagers by tossing grenades at buses of schoolchildren or assassinating officials, could never succeed.

Terrorist incidents did increase steadily, more than doubling between 1968 and 1971, yet the number of those murdered or abducted each year held relatively steady. In 1971, the peak year for such incidents, the number of individuals affected dropped over 30 percent.[18] One can read this as growing NLF ineffectiveness, but also as the completion of Hanoi's strategic transition. Terrorism was a tactic to ensure that the villages did not shift their allegiance and to keep up the morale of the Front's cadres. Saigon and U.S. analysts favored claims of ineffectiveness. But according to the records of the U.S. senior adviser for Thua Thien province, which included Hue, the numbers of terrorist incidents and NLF armed attacks on the eve of the Easter offensive in 1972 were virtually identical to those in the month before Tet.

Economic assistance had always been important to pacification. Probably the most critical aspect lay in land redistribution, which in practical terms had largely been a preserve of the National Liberation Front and contributed to its political appeal. But despite Thieu's rhetoric and promises (in a February 1969 speech he declared a goal of distributing 625,000 acres that year), the Saigon leader did nothing until the Nixon administration gave money. The "Land to the Tiller" law Thieu signed in March 1970—after thirteen years of war—became the first true land reform by the Saigon government. By 1972, 400,000 peasants were given plots of land. Combined with U.S. agricultural assistance, including the introduction of so-called miracle rice (the IR-5 and IR-8 hybrid strains), this resulted in a real improvement in rural life. But the compensation payments to absentee landlords—who, due to the war, had long been unable to enforce their rents—may have been more important to Thieu. The payments served to ensure the loyalty of South Vietnamese elites.

Meanwhile, Bill Colby made strenuous efforts to show progress and achieve it, emphasizing the growing number of miles of secure roads and usable bridges, occasionally staging road trips at night or in notoriously "bad" areas to dramatize his point. One of Colby's major gambits was to enlist the peasantry by replacing appointed village leaders with elected officials. By 1970 this had largely been done, with local elections in more than 90 percent of hamlets and villages. Yet real authority lay at district and province levels, and those answered to Saigon. Thieu appointed the leaders or delegated that authority to regional commanders. Continually frustrated at the seemingly low effectiveness of Saigon's rural apparatus, Americans furiously compiled lists of ineffective or corrupt officials and asked that they be replaced. Thieu acted only sporadically, usually when Bunker or Abrams appealed to him personally. Corruption dominated all levels of the administration.

Another gambit was the attempt to neutralize the NLF's parallel hierarchy, with its own hamlet, village, and district committees and popular organizations. This began more or less spontaneously within the CIA, whose officers formed teams to fight the enemy apparatus, and then in Saigon, where agency officers conceived an Intelligence Coordination and Exploitation project to identify the Front's apparatus, enabling the CIA to target key cadres. CORDS transformed this into the "Phoenix" program (known as "Phung Hoang" to the South Vietnamese). Approved by President Thieu in 1968, Phoenix became a touchstone. Its Achilles' heels would be intelligence—and corruption. Intelligence remained a problem because, except in a few instances—based on imaginative local solutions that were not replicated—the data were confusing, repetitive, subject to manipulation, and rarely good enough to identify the really important NLF operatives. Corruption remained a problem because accusations fed the data pool, and Vietnamese officials of local Phoenix committees could exploit both these and the operational approval processes to demand bribes.[19]

So-called Provincial Reconnaissance Units (PRUs) were a main tool of Phoenix. Here a great deal depended on the South Vietnamese. In provinces where chiefs and district leaders were active and involved, the PRUs were effective; in others, they were not. Colby made at least one attempt to get rid of the units altogether, handing them over to Saigon's National Police, but the CIA trumped him. Yet the CIA station's own support for the PRUs was opposed by the covert operations high command in Washington and would be maintained for just one additional year past the originally planned mid-1970 termination.[20]

The PRUs acquired sinister reputations for high-handedness, and Phoenix would be tarred as an assassination program, generating controversies that dogged Colby for the rest of his life. He never stopped insisting that the facts were otherwise—that most neutralized members of the NLF had been arrested and that those who were killed had succumbed in the course of standard military operations. The CIA's official history concedes that many participants began to regard Phoenix as more trouble than it was worth after the 1970 hearings that first challenged Colby, and matters only got worse when more inquiries followed. When MACV pulled its military people out of Phoenix, CIA assistance evaporated as well. Saigon's proclivities as to methods and procedures remained.

But most of the real targets escaped; by CORDS's own figures, Phoenix neutralized only a handful of senior cadres in 1968. The next year, of the 19,534 enemy neutralizations claimed, just 150 were senior people (and only 81 were priority targets). The CIA's reporting indicated that PRU neutralization rates tumbled by 50 percent in the second half of the year, and the number of intelligence reports based on PRU-generated information declined similarly. Of the 22,341 neutralizations in 1970, there were fewer priority cadres than the year before (and among them, just 17 from COSVN and 357 from regional or subregional levels). The periodic target objectives fueled a cycle of arbitrary detention and corruption, and legality continually bumped into goals. Although captured documents and prisoner interrogations show the NLF and Hanoi feared Phoenix, there is no evidence it ever depopulated the NLF hierarchy. Lost cadres were replaced. The final story remains that the total of neutralizations claimed for the entire program, including its post-U.S. phase, does not add up to the estimate—70,000—that U.S. intelligence had used for the infrastructure during the order of battle dispute of 1967–1968.[21]

Claims by apologists that Phoenix did not operate on the basis of target goals are disingenuous. There is massive evidence on Phoenix goals, documentary as well as contemporaneous discourse and anecdotal recollections. President Thieu discussed goals with CORDS officials; MACV staff conferences were briefed on them—not once but *every* time pacification chiefs updated progress reports. Colby repeatedly told MACV that Phoenix had not attained desired goals—on October 4, 1969, for example, he termed it "kind of a wormy program."[22] General Abrams concurred, making similar remarks to staff at least twice by January 1970. Both saw Phoenix as important because it disrupted the NLF system—true enough, but a tactical result. Meanwhile, accusations of arbitrary detention and assassination were so controversial in the United States that Phoenix stimulated the antiwar movement, damaging public support for the war to an incalculable degree—perhaps even exceeding its impact on the Liberation Front.

After the war, all this led to a "lost victory" interpretation of Vietnam, in which former participants or observers claim the conflict had been won but the victory thrown away—with various culprits blamed. Henry Kissinger and Alexander Haig were among those holding this view. William Colby entered the debate with his book *Lost Victory*. Former Army officer and CIA analyst Lewis Sorley contributed this bon mot: "There came a time when the war was won."[23] The most recent commentators of this school call themselves "revisionists," arguing that Americans are wrong to believe they lost the Vietnam war. This is not revisionism, it is neo-orthodoxy.

Something happened in the countryside, but it was not Saigon's victory. Late-war village studies by anthropologists and social scientists, postwar recollections of Vietnamese, and scholarly studies confirm that the Liberation Front's hold weakened. Such accounts exist for Thua Thien province and for several in the Mekong delta.[24] But the record does not show happy peasants rallying to Saigon's flag. Rather, it indicates villagers hunkered down, oppressed equally by the NLF's terrorism and Saigon's security forces, with the PSDF, in effect, enrolling everyone who might have joined the NLF, affording Saigon one more means of keeping track of them. An early 1970 poll taken in Long An, one of the delta provinces, showed that 35 percent of the villagers would vote for Nguyen Van Thieu as president, 20 percent for the Liberation Front, if they could have, but fully 45 percent for someone opposed to both the United States and the Front.[25] At the same time, people left in droves for the cities, especially Saigon. The capital, with 400,000 residents in 1945, had nearly 3 million by the early 1970s. An awful lot of villagers were no longer on the land.

Official HES statistics may have projected zero villages loyal to the Liberation Front, but the Combined Intelligence Center Vietnam's studies of NLF and VPA base areas throughout this period show that not a single one, inside or outside South Vietnam, ever disappeared. At a minimum, one must question claims for pacification there. "We're supposed to be HESing them right out of business," a perplexed General Abrams told his staff in 1970, wondering how it could be he had reports that Front local committees had the time and security to set up medical stations in a district of Thua Thien, one of the "secure" provinces.[26]

■ ■ ■ The enemy's crisis came in 1969, not later. The Liberation Front insurgents, along with Hanoi's regulars, suffered heavy losses, efforts at a repeat Tet offensive collapsed, and cholera outbreaks were reported along the Ho Chi Minh Trail. Troop strength (by U.S. estimates) declined from about 260,000 to 226,000. Indications the enemy was deactivating regular units to reassign men to guerrilla formations fascinated U.S. commanders, who saw in them confirmation of defeat. Yet NLF armed attacks in 1969 totaled barely a hundred less than in the year of Tet. More than 47,000 cadres were recorded as defecting in 1969, but only 368 were army deserters. In Long An province, a key locale for the war against the infrastructure, almost 2,500 hoi chanh (defectors) were tabulated during 1969, but there were fewer than 1,000 in 1970. Optimists took the most favorable view: Long An defections were down because the NLF had been smashed; People's Army troops joined insurgents because there were no more recruits.

But defections dropped after 1969, and by 1971 there were fewer than in the year of Tet. In 1970 Hanoi still managed to send 103,000 fresh troops down The Trail. From then on, estimates of troop strength leveled off, staying about the same regardless of reduced infiltration, claimed casualties, defections, bombing of The Trail, and allied invasions of neighboring countries. The estimated proportion of VPA soldiers in NLF units also became essentially static (data are available through mid-1971), indicating that the Liberation Front *did* gather enough recruits to replace its losses. American and ARVN analysts overinterpreted the intelligence.

Again, the Vietnam data problem intrudes. In September 1969, reciting a long list of false U.S. appreciations—starting with pacification (now claimed as a huge success by the neo-orthodox)—security adviser Kissinger demanded the creation of a Vietnam Special Studies Group to tease out accurate information. The president approved. A few months later Kissinger would ask a senior pacification official whether the HES data were not slanted toward military indicators. He at least felt the need for a reality check. As Kissinger staffer Roger Morris said of the bad data and phony numbers: "It was just one great sort of crap game of fraud that was being perpetrated . . . *Everyone* was compromised . . . We had been lying to ourselves and others for so long about that problem that you just couldn't get decent, open analysis."[27]

Pacification did make gains under General Abrams and Ambassador Colby, but that success took place as the war itself changed. What had been central was becoming peripheral. By 1969 it was apparent in Hanoi that U.S. forces in the South were a diminishing quantity. North Vietnamese strategy reflected this. General Le Trong Tan returned to Hanoi for consultations that spring and assumed a field command in May. Tan's notebook was among the more interesting documents captured in 1969, taken from a bodyguard by soldiers of the ARVN 1st Division. Translated at the Combined Documents Exploitation Center, the notebook revealed Hanoi's orders for the Route 9 Front: Tan was to assert control over the mountain and rural areas of his command, rebuild his forces to a pre-Tet strength, and plant agents among the Saigon army and in the cities. He was to bend all efforts to help compel the United States to withdraw.[28] The village war did not figure in his instructions.

Not so for the Americans—or Saigon. Buddhists made up the peasantry, and in this sense, pacification figured in Saigon politics. An index of Saigon's methods can be taken from its treatment of Buddhists—still a problem in South Vietnam. The CIA station had made special efforts beginning in 1966 to keep its "Revolutionary Development" team members from joining the Buddhist "Struggle Movement," which intensified popular distaste for this CIA program. At one point armed Buddhists stormed the Thua Thien headquarters of the operation. The old Struggle Movement was gone now, splintered into factions that took several courses. One pursued electoral politics; another withdrew into religion; a third sought to play a humanitarian role, interposing itself between the government and the Liberation Front, uniting students and the religious to succor villages devastated by war. Saigon leaders did what they could to obstruct the Buddhist political enterprise; they pocketed gains represented by the bonzes who fell back on their meditations and sent the National Police after the humanitarians. Thich Tri Quang still led the remnants of the An Quang pagoda bonzes. Less anti-American than before, he gingerly put out feelers on forming a peace party but presently had to take asylum with the Americans. In late 1968, just prior to the Accelerated Pacification Campaign, National Police director Colonel Tran Van Hai had assessed the Buddhist issue as one of five major weaknesses (another was pacification itself) that, if not corrected, would give Hanoi victory.

President Thieu made no move to rectify any of these problems. Buddhist candidates won the most votes in both the Vietnamese Senate elections in August 1970 and those for the National Assembly a year later. Thieu's response was to try to emasculate the legislature.

The neo-orthodox commentators of the "lost victory" school make their claims as if the only important elements were pacification and Vietnamization, as if politics did not matter. Not only is this strange, given the kind of conflict—where supposedly everyone now understood the political to be paramount—but those same analysts take no account of Saigon politics. And South Vietnamese politics moved in a direction that portended extension of the war *because* there was no victory. In many ways this evolution, featuring Nguyen Van Thieu's consolidation of power, would be the most important development of all.

"This System Is Actually More the Control Mechanism"

The third major weakness identified by Tran Van Hai's analysis was corruption. The fourth was a constitutional system in shambles, which he attributed to "general Vietnamese indifference to the responsibilities of citizenship." The last was the government's failure to gain the allegiance of students—in effect, losing one of the greatest sources of energy and creativity in the society. President Thieu refused to solve the corruption and constitutional problems for a good reason: he depended on them to cement his control. As for the students, Thieu believed they were in league with the communists and considered it his duty to combat them. Thieu's actions and the lack thereof—nothing else—sealed the fate of South Vietnam.

By paying minimal attention to South Vietnamese politics, by presenting the Vietnam conflict as a two-sided struggle between Washington and Hanoi, former American participants as well as the neo-orthodox miss a crucial part of the equation and come to a distorted understanding of the war. This was not hidden but obvious, and it is perplexing why and how this can have occurred. The frequent refrain of American officials that they lacked "leverage" could mean only one thing—that Saigon stood at center stage, not in the wings, and its interests and actions were critical to the outcome. It could hardly be otherwise. Washington's war was for the future of South Vietnam, pacification about South Vietnamese villages, and the hearts and minds the counterinsurgents hoped to win were Vietnamese. The people looked to Saigon (or the NLF), not to Washington. To ignore the internal factors and present pacification as merely a matter of HES numbers and NLF neutralizations fails to capture the true processes at work here.

Much as Diem had set South Vietnam's trajectory during its first decade, Nguyen Van Thieu would dominate its last. Thieu had survived for a long time by appearing to be less than he was, and he talked a good game. From 1968 onward, "South Vietnamese" interests and calculations increasingly meant those of President Thieu. When he met Laird for the first time in March 1969, the Saigon leader mouthed all the appropriate phrases about the need for his government to have "a strong and broad political base." Complaining that South Vietnam had "more politicians than business-men"—surely an exaggeration in this land of the black market and system-atized corruption—Thieu said the problem lay in the inability of the politicos to come together.[29] Another time he told Richard Nixon that the politicians were sitting on the fence, waiting to see how the war and the ne-gotiations went. Creating the unity, mobilizing the politicians, was Thieu's challenge and his job, not merely the latest version of the old saw of "broad-ening the base" of Saigon's government, which Thieu never did.

At the time of *Tet Mau Than,* General Thieu, though president of South Vietnam, had no lock on power. Key officials were allies of Vice President Nguyen Cao Ky, who had people strategically placed throughout the appara-tus. In fact, Tet might have cost Thieu ground, as Ed Lansdale reported to Ambassador Bunker on June 7, 1968, at the height of the second wave of fighting. As head of the embassy's Special Liaison Office, Lansdale func-tioned as a kind of listening post, maintaining open channels to all manner of South Vietnamese and recording their opinions. Much could be said about Thieu, but Lansdale saw the possibilities clearly enough: "There ap-pear to be only two courses of action sufficient to solve present problems. One is for Thieu to take the lead in creating real teamwork among himself, Ky, Vien, Khang, and Loan; the other is for Thieu to consolidate full power himself."[30]

In a sensitive supplement to a study on Saigon nationalists, Lansdale opined that the four most powerful leaders after President Thieu were those just mentioned: Ky, police chief Loan, and generals Le Nguyen Khang and Cao Van Vien. None of them supported Thieu, Lansdale reported, and to some extent, each actively opposed him. Lansdale saw all four as angry that Thieu had stood back and let them bear the brunt of Tet but now took the credit—similar to the 1966 Buddhist crisis, when Thieu had also done noth-ing. Mistrust could be added to caution. General Vien headed the armed forces' Joint General Staff and, not especially political, might have been ig-nored save for suspicions that Thieu had helped spread malicious rumors of corruption on the part of Mrs. Vien. Proud and sensitive, Vien might not stand for that. But suddenly rumors began to circulate that Vien was about to be fired in favor of Do Cao Tri or, worse, Hoang Xuan Lam. For almost a year Vien was subjected to this innuendo. He subsided.

As for the others, the second battle of Saigon and the unfortunate friendly-fire incident on June 2 show their real import here. As noted earlier, Air Marshal Ky would have been present but for a dream, and the rocket strike directly neutralized General Loan, badly wounding him. The officers killed were allied with Ky, Loan, or Khang. The perfunctory South Vietnamese–U.S. incident investigation yielded the highly suspect conclusion that the strike had been an accident: the gunship helicopter supposedly suffered a short circuit in its fire control system, which launched the rocket. If true, this would have been an unusual malfunction and a spectacularly improbable unaimed shot. In addition, Ky's suspicion that Thieu loyalist Tran Van Hai had been aboard the chopper has been noted. In late July the widows of the victims accused Thieu of engineering the deaths. A CIA field report captured the dynamics well: "Thieu, aware of his weak position, refrained from challenging Ky until the post-Tet period . . . During the interim . . . Thieu planned the details of his new administration, made a start in removing a few Ky supporters in the middle echelons of government and refrained from compromising his constitutional position by working out a deal with Ky. . . . He became more sure of himself when several Ky stalwarts . . . were put out of action during the offensive."[31]

General Le Nguyen Khang led the Vietnamese Marines, as well as the Saigon Military District and III Corps since 1966. Khang resigned over the rocket incident—he even boycotted the change of command that installed General Do Cao Tri in his stead. Tri, though not known primarily as a political general, was very close to President Thieu and saw him two or three times a week (as often as did Ellsworth Bunker). The demise of Loan enabled Thieu to appoint Colonel Hai to the crucial police command. Thus, the fighting permitted Thieu to replace an entire echelon of opponents. Thieu also dismissed Ky's prime minister, Nguyen Van Loc, his failure certified by Tet. Tran Van Huong, who had once opposed Thieu, now offered to step up if given a free hand to eliminate corruption. Huong got the job. Among the cabinet Thieu installed General Khiem as interior minister. When U.S. agencies assessed the war in NSSM-1 they differed widely but, according to the NSC summary, agreed on one thing: "Some steps are being taken to strengthen the [Saigon government] politically but these are inadequate."[32]

Assassination as political tactic had been introduced onto the Saigon scene with the Diem coup. There is no direct evidence that Nguyen Van Thieu conspired at this incident, only suggestions raised by what happened. But on the other side of the coin, Thieu feared for his own life—at the hands of the CIA. In exile in London in 1976, the former potentate expressed that fear to aide Nguyen Tien Hung. The Nixon administration *was* tempted in that direction. Hung and American coauthor Jerrold L. Schecter subsequently published a book in which they cited evidence that Nixon and Kissinger had actually been presented with options for the "forcible removal" of Thieu by NSC staffers Roger Morris and Tony Lake in late 1969, and they quoted a Morris interview with Kissinger biographer Seymour Hersh in which he affirmed the reference had been to assassination. Although this is rather vague, on February 13, 1969, Kissinger had ordered the preparation of a plan for U.S. actions to be carried out "in the event of the assassination of the President of South Vietnam" in NSSM-22. Completely out of register with Washington's declaratory policy, this planning exercise has to raise questions. Defense Secretary Melvin Laird claims credit for quashing this initiative.[33]

Were anything to happen to Thieu, the key figures would be the commanders of South Vietnam's four corps areas, restyled as military regions in the summer of 1968. Ngo Dinh Diem had changed Saigon's military command forever by making the corps commanders directly responsible to the head of state. Thieu's underground bunker at Independence Palace would be crammed with radio equipment—more in fact than in Winston Churchill's World War II underground command center—precisely to enable him to reach beyond military communications channels. In Nguyen Khanh's time the corps commander had been given the predominant voice in selecting leaders in their areas, not just division officers but also province and district chiefs and even civilian officials. Edward Lansdale's description of this arrangement—not innuendo or press speculation, but official reporting in a secret document—needs to be quoted at length:

> The system developed of corps commanders selling these positions, the arrangements always being made through intermediaries (wives, aides, key staff assistants, etc.). The officer being appointed (for example, a province chief), in order to obtain the job and the personal profit which goes with it, agrees to make regular payoffs to his superiors, the division and corps commanders, and sometimes also pays a lump sum to the corps commander. The key money-collecting official in the system is the province chief, who makes regular payoffs to the division and corps commanders and often to regimental and battalion commanders associated with his province. The province chief's principal sources of money are juggling of official funds and payoffs from businessmen, medium and large, for protection or favors. No businessman can operate without at least the acquiescence of the government, and government favors can help business considerably. Thus virtually all substantial businessmen operating in a provincial capital pay a regular sum under the table through intermediaries to stay in business, and some pay more to obtain special privileges. The same system (i.e., payoffs by businessmen to government officials) is in effect at the district level in most districts and at the village level in many villages. Village chiefs pay part of the money collected to district chiefs, as do the latter to province chiefs.
>
> . . . This system is actually more the control mechanism for most of the [Vietnamese armed forces] and for most province and district chiefs, than the institutional channels of authority which appear on . . . organizational charts. Its damaging effects in terms of weakening discipline, esprit, and the overall effectiveness of the [government and armed forces] are obvious. It has become during the last three years a system with its *own momentum,* entrapping most senior officers and most middle-level managers.[34]

Thus the military region commanders held powerful and lucrative posts. For them the choice lay between acquiescing in Thieu's leadership and maintaining their advantages or supplanting the president to obtain even greater privileges. Since Thieu guarded himself carefully, the choice became an easy one.

Corruption helped Thieu consolidate his power. The case of Prime Minister Tran Van Huong provides a fine illustration. A Diem opponent, prime minister under Khanh, and one of the failed candidates in the presidential election Thieu and Ky had won, Huong was serious about ending corruption and tried to infuse new energy into the official inspectorate supposed to investigate it. Thieu interposed various obstacles, often through his operative General Khiem. In 1968, 25 province and 170 district chiefs were replaced. The United States had recommended firing 22 of the province chiefs and 91 of the district chiefs for either corruption or incompetence. By 1969 most were working again. That January education minister Le Minh Tri, an anti-corruption warrior, had been murdered. Equally serious, Huong himself narrowly escaped assassination in March. That July, a test case appeared when the inspectorate filed corruption charges against an ARVN division commander. With the bill of particulars about to appear, a majority of the lower house of the National Assembly, which Thieu controlled, suddenly produced a letter demanding that Huong be fired. Thieu asked the inspectorate to reconsider the charges against the general, but it confirmed them, though reducing the recommended penalty. Thieu did nothing about the charges and even promoted the general in question. Huong resigned. At that point Thieu appointed a new cabinet under General Khiem, who continued as interior minister. The Khiem government had strong military representation and a number of technocrats, but few political figures.

True, economic problems had sharpened Huong's difficulties. But those led in the same direction. The infusion of American cash based on few exports and little domestic production generated inflationary pressures in Saigon. Prices had risen steadily since 1965, but during Huong's year in office, inflation increased by a third or more. Much of that occurred in just three months. By 1970 the South Vietnamese piaster would have only a quarter of its 1964 value based on the official rate of exchange (at the black-market rate, it was worth much less). This corresponded to a year in which currency manipulation and diversion of merchandise from the U.S. post exchange (PX) system rose to monumental proportions. In only one month of 1969, some 600,000 gallons of gasoline were pilfered from just one of the U.S. pipelines feeding South Vietnam. For Thieu, the manipulations and diversions served as a safety valve for what could have led to rising discontent. U.S. authorities made strenuous efforts to bring PX corruption and currency manipulation under control but also stopped tracking Saigon retail prices among the statistics gathered in the standard database. It is no wonder that information problems persisted.

Three sectors that might have contributed to a change were the Buddhists, labor, and the students. Indeed, MACV staff were briefed at one point that enemy propaganda aimed at a Buddhist-labor alliance for peace. But Thieu checkmated the Buddhists, consistently using his security police against the activists' large demonstrations, including the self-immolation of monks. Thieu appeased conservative Buddhists with favors. He maneuvered against labor as well. A general strike of tens of thousands of workers in early 1970, when abolition of the government transport company laid off bus drivers, almost paralyzed Saigon. Thieu cracked down under antistrike laws he had promulgated, then co-opted the largest union, bringing it into his political front, dividing workers. The students were watched so closely—even more so than their American cousins—that political activism took place at great personal cost.

President Thieu coupled strong repression with monetary profligacy. The black market reduced political pressures, if only because the time needed to play in it took away from that available for politics. With ARVN soldiers on a fixed income—and forced to pay some of it for their own rations—participation in corruption seemed almost mandatory. The black economy also functioned like a magnet in the villages, irresistibly drawing peasants to the cities. "Miracle" rice may have doubled crop yields, but many Vietnamese considered it inferior. Although production increases enabled South Vietnam to export a few thousand tons of rice for a couple of years, before long, much of the land, redistributed or otherwise, lay fallow. The former villagers rode motorbikes in Saigon and traded in cigarettes or liquor. By 1974 South Vietnam was importing no less than 200,000 tons of rice. By then the piaster had fallen to about 20 percent of its 1970 value.

A manifestation of the stick behind the carrot came in the summer of 1968, when Truong Dinh Dzu, Thieu's opponent in the 1967 elections, was condemned to five years' hard labor for advocating a coalition government. The Interior Ministry threatened punitive action against anyone—individual, party, or religious group—who came out in favor of talks with the NLF. That fall, in the context of the October Surprise, newspapers that reported American complaints about Thieu, in particular those made by Secretary Clifford, were suppressed. The South Vietnamese press faced more frequent intervention. Papers were closed, or issues were seized. In February 1969 Buddhist Thich Thien Minh, alleged to be harboring draft dodgers and NLF agents, was sent to prison for ten years. A month later Thieu expelled more of Nguyen Cao Ky's allies from the government. Press restrictions tightened further, with newspapers ordered to provide copies of each issue to the Information Ministry at least three hours ahead of release, permitting the suppression of those the regime did not want Vietnamese to see. In April the manager of the *Saigon Daily News* was arrested for "activities beneficial to the communists," and in May three more newspapers were shut down by the security services.

Much of what the Vietnamese saw of their government, other than soldiers flitting about town, consisted of the maneuvers of the National Police, who the Americans often called "White Mice" for the color of their helmets. Thieu never relaxed his grip on the White Mice, after 1968, among the fastest-growing elements of South Vietnamese forces. Every successor to Ky's man in the front office would be a Thieu loyalist. Colonel Tran Van Hai was a solid supporter. In 1970 General Tran Thanh Phong took up the directorship. Phong was tied to Tran Thien Khiem by the marriage of one of his children to a relative of Khiem's wife. In September 1971 Colonel Nguyen Khac Bien became the last police director. Later promoted to general, Bien functioned simultaneously as chief of the Central Intelligence Organization, Saigon's version of the CIA, and enjoyed the strong backing of the Americans. He was Mrs. Thieu's nephew. By 1970 expansion of the White Mice, particularly its Phoenix-related Police Field Force, impinged on conscription for the ARVN. The generals were never able to rectify this because the police were especially important to Thieu.

Occasional gestures leavened the diet of restriction. In late 1968 Thieu invited Duong Van Minh ("Big" Minh, he of the Diem coup) to return from exile as a presidential adviser. Minh was never actually asked for any advice, but the act suggested liberalization. To celebrate South Vietnam's National Day (November 1, the day of Diem's overthrow), Thieu released several hundred political prisoners, among them Buddhist bonze Thien Minh (no relation to "Big" Minh). Within the tightly circumscribed spectrum Thieu permitted, parties or blocs were allowed to organize, and several emerged, some under longtime nationalists, and one under former general, now senator, Tran Van Don. Thieu later told Americans that Don and the Buddhists were behind his troubles with veterans and students. A dozen opposition leaders came together at the end of 1969 to charge that Thieu had created a military dictatorship, demanding he be tried for high treason. A few months later Prime Minister Khiem told Saigon's Senate that the government wanted a law enabling Thieu to rule by decree in case of economic or military crisis. Without much more emergency than business as usual, by 1971, President Thieu had begun using those powers.

Khiem's demand for emergency powers formed part of a yearlong back-alley struggle between Thieu and the legislature. In important ways the battle was framed by Thieu's assault on delegate Tran Ngoc Chau. A former ARVN officer, star of early 1960s pacification efforts, and sometime CIA asset, Chau had sought to reconcile South Vietnam's warring parties by meeting with his brother, an NLF official. Chau kept the U.S. embassy informed, and the Saigon government also knew of his contacts. Nothing came of them, but there were also no Thieu government objections. Then, barely a week after the legislators charged Thieu with treason, President Thieu accused Chau of being an NLF agent. The move was especially disturbing because Chau and Thieu had been comrades in the Vietminh after the August Revolution. Before moving into opposition, Chau had supported Thieu in the assembly. Now his parliamentary immunity was revoked, and White Mice arrested Chau in the assembly's sacrosanct halls. A military court sentenced him to twenty years. South Vietnam's high court threw out the verdict in May 1970 on the grounds that Chau's trial had been unconstitutional. Thieu demanded a new one. Chau received ten years at hard labor. While this controversy boiled, a "demonstration" took place at the National Assembly in which "protesters" invaded the hall and beat up lawmakers. Some accused Thieu of orchestrating this event. "Orchestration" befit the locale, for the assembly building was Saigon's converted opera house. Chau's intellectual successor in a way was Ngo Cong Duc, publisher of the Catholic opposition newspaper *Tin Sang,* Saigon's most frequently banned periodical.

Senate elections were held in the summer of 1970, with a fair number of opposition candidates and coalition blocs emerging, but the subterranean standoff persisted and Thieu retained control. Tran Ngoc Chau went to prison after all. His tragedy continued. The Americans spurned Chau when the time came to evacuate Saigon, and he traded his Saigon jail for a communist prison. Meanwhile, in 1971 Duc lost his assembly seat too and was arrested shortly thereafter. Another assembly figure, Phan Chi Thinh, would be stopped at Tan Son Nhut airport and found carrying pure heroin from Laos. Entrapment was suspected. Saigon officials portrayed the event as cracking down on drug trafficking and corruption.

What Nguyen Van Thieu lost in all this was the chance to build popular support. At first Thieu had no political party or mass movement. Efforts were made to correct that. On July 4, 1968 (an interesting choice of date), Thieu held a rally to inaugurate the National Alliance for Social Revolution (the "Lien Minh" Front), an entity intended to grow grass roots, with the elimination of corruption among its explicit core goals. The Americans helped—the Lien Minh Front became a CIA covert action project. It was approved by the 303 Committee, the U.S. government's central body for controlling secret operations, and CIA subsidies began in August 1968. Periodic shipments of cash were given directly to Thieu. The money became part of Thieu's "secret funds" in exactly the same way Ed Lansdale had handed cash to Ngo Dinh Diem during the sect crisis. The Lien Minh project was repeatedly reauthorized by the 303 Committee after the Nixon administration took office. It went nowhere. Update reports to the committee mentioned local initiatives in Saigon districts and efforts to organize committees in the provinces, but internal cleavages beset the Lien Minh, with labor unions constantly threatening to withdraw and its chief a virtually unknown figure.

Meanwhile, Thieu's promised backing failed to materialize. The CIA secret funds continued throughout 1969. More than $3 million poured into this political action, but hopes of recruiting 50,000 activists proved barren. Thieu aide and cousin Hoang Duc Nha later told CIA analyst Frank Snepp that he had been in charge of the money and that only a small portion had been used for the intended purposes.[35]

With fanfare, Thieu went to a higher level in May 1969, folding the Lien Minh into a new National Social Democratic Front that embodied five other small political parties or factions. The CIA project expanded to include this as well. But when Thieu appointed the Khiem cabinet in August, there were no Front ministers. The 40 Committee (the successor to 303) was updated on the project in February 1970, but there was little progress to cite. American officials were not enthusiastic. Ambassador Bunker nevertheless told Kissinger that CIA funding should go on—the Front played a "catalytic role" and should be treated like a "delicate plant which needs tender care."[36] The 40 Committee okayed more CIA funds on February 25, contingent on Bunker's approval and his pressing Thieu to desist from persecuting Tran Ngoc Chau, a public relations disaster in Washington if not Saigon. The money happened; the desisting did not.

Washington collaborated in Thieu's ascendancy in at least two more ways. One concerned the Saigon press. In classic political action style, the CIA subsidized one publication and paid for pro-government articles and editorials in others. Moreover, the agency worked to improve the distribution of publications considered favorable to the government (while doing nothing for others). An avowed intent to improve South Vietnamese journalistic standards cloaked this boosterism. This low-cost CIA project had substantial propaganda impact.

But the most important U.S. contribution to Thieu's consolidation of power was its general failure to pursue the very issues Washington knew to be central to Thieu's ability to win real support. For example, at the highest level, Bunker saw Thieu once or twice a week on average and had free run of the palace. A survey of declassified records—as yet only a small slice of what will eventually become available—shows easily a couple of dozen Bunker-Thieu conversations about various cases of corruption or their aspects. Among them are many initial conversations but few follow-ups, those primarily on currency manipulation and the PX scandal. Both of these were contentious in the U.S. Congress and therefore unavoidable for the embassy. Neither case was resolved, at least not as a result of Bunker's urgings of Thieu. Old diplomatic hands would say Bunker had "clientitis." As for Thieu, Bui Diem, a close observer, notes his standard procedure: "Thieu never refused anything. His usual way was to agree, to acquiesce and make promises, then to wait to see what would happen."[37]

On January 30, 1970, for example, Bunker told Thieu that corruption had become Saigon's number one problem, citing the PX scandal and merchandise diversions. Traffic in cigarettes alone, Bunker said, cost the Vietnamese 2.5 billion piasters a year, or more than $2 million at official exchange rates. Thieu replied that he knew about organized smuggling rings at Saigon's port and Tan Son Nhut airport, and Bunker observed that these rings were obviously being protected by top government officials. Thieu wanted to put together some ideas and talk again. Bunker reported that as progress.[38] The smuggling went on. It later emerged that an artillery battalion of the ARVN 18th Division was renting space in its depots for materials stolen from Saigon docks.

Personnel of Air Vietnam were caught smuggling currency. A stewardess was apprehended on the street carrying an airline bag full of heroin. The company's deputy director, targeted by corruption inspectors, got only a slap on the wrist. But the scandal became so pernicious the entire top management were put on leave. There followed an airline workers' strike at Tan Son Nhut. That, plus a strike by Saigon port stevedores, warned Thieu away from any major moves. Corruption was the price of doing business. Thieu depended on it. In 1973 he watched approvingly as his daughter married the chairman of the board of Air Vietnam.

Many cases were raised, then dropped. An exception was corrupt province chiefs, lists of whom the Americans provided regularly. From time to time Thieu relieved a few of the more egregious offenders, but the ARVN system being what it was, they were often recycled to other provinces or as unit commanders, where their corrupt activities continued. Drug smuggling proved especially poisonous since an acknowledged drug problem affected U.S. troops in Vietnam. Several senior Saigon officers were implicated at various times, including Air Marshal Ky and some corps commanders. There too, solutions were elusive. Thieu relieved one accused corps commander in 1972, but because he fought badly, not for corruption. Thieu later employed the same officer to head his delegation at four-power military talks. The Americans failed to set benchmarks or sustain what pressure they did exert.

Corruption not only weakened South Vietnamese society; it directly affected Saigon's military, to the extent of driving ARVN veterans into the streets. Disabled veterans in Saigon protested in March 1969 to dramatize the government's failure to help. White Mice busted up one march near the Veterans Ministry. Suddenly squatters' shacks appeared, built by disabled former soldiers. Soon there were veterans' settlements near the Pacification Ministry, at the French military cemetery, and in front of the residences of U.S. diplomats. By late March the situation had become so serious the government created a task force led by General Pham Van Dong, the minister for veterans affairs. But the task force never met with any protesters until after a demonstration in front of Doc Lap Palace. Police clashed with ARVN vets at this rally, which was followed by sit-ins at both the National Assembly and again at the palace. The disabled vets formed their own Veterans Struggle Committee and asked to see Thieu; they met with General Dong instead. Students went on strike to support the vets. Officials alleged that the veterans were controlled by the Buddhists (naturally), Nguyen Cao Ky (who did have a connection with one of the veterans' groups), and Tran Van Don. Thieu eventually proposed a Veterans Code, voted by the legislature, but politicians objected there was no money to pay for its generous provisions.

The Dong task force approved allotments of land to the vets and materials for them to construct real houses, and it promised government-built housing for disabled veterans who registered with the ministry. By August 1969 more than 4,000 vets registered, but none had been resettled. About 500 housing units were built in Saigon, but it is not clear when or if they were ever occupied. Veterans' protests spread outside the capital and turned against the Catholic Church when a priest in one village called on local People's Self-Defense Force militia to suppress a demonstration at his church. The winds of protest even reached Laos, where Laotian vets marched over the same issues. During August violence erupted at Nha Trang in Khanh Hoa province. In October a veterans' leader was assassinated, allegedly by a pro-government veterans' group. The Khanh Hoa protests were alleviated only by strenuous promises to furnish construction materials. The next summer the Khanh Hoa province chief was fired after investigation showed that 55 percent of the cement consigned to him at cost had been pilfered.

When Nixon's deputy national security adviser, Alexander Haig, visited Saigon in early 1970, Thieu resorted to his standard tactics. At their meeting, Thieu told Haig he worried about the plight of ARVN soldiers and offered that as the reason for the army's high desertion rate. Thieu said he wanted to provide amenities—such as education for dependents or increased food and housing allowances—rather than raise the soldiers' pay. Veterans' benefits were not mentioned. And Thieu never acted on the ideas he had broached.

Meanwhile, in late 1971 a soldier's weekly food allowance sufficed to buy a single bowl of soup at a roadside stand. Economic pressures blew inflation to new heights in mid-November, so much so that the period acquired the nickname "Autumn Revolution." Some food prices more than doubled. Rice cost nine times what it had in 1964. A dozen native oranges went for 4,000 piasters. An army private's basic pay (in 1972) totaled 13,750 piasters a month. A completely disabled ARVN veteran could expect an *annual* government payment of 10,420 piasters, plus a smaller amount for those with amputations of various body parts. Saigon's National Rehabilitation Center still had only 200 beds for disabled vets, with another 80 at the Vietnamese Red Cross. There were four convalescent centers, one for each corps, none of which ever had more than 200 beds. In 1971 all were required to open their doors to wounded from the military hospitals. Efforts by the U.S. Navy had recently made 230 more beds available, but this was merely a drop in the bucket. By then, somewhere between 200,000 and 250,000 disabled ARVN soldiers had been discharged. Saigon's idea of helping veterans secure employment was to encourage ministries and businesses to hire them as security guards—and then to draft those whose places they took. Walking the streets of the city much later, only months before the final collapse, NBC News reporter David Butler found disabled veterans begging on every street corner.

The dilemma of the disabled veterans would be eclipsed by the scandal over the Soldiers' Savings Fund. South Vietnamese soldiers were required to deposit 100 piasters a month in this fund, supposed to earn interest, although critics noted that commercial banks paid more. Then it became apparent that money had been skimmed from the fund and invested in businesses controlled by top officers. The scandal broadened. At this point, General Nguyen Van Hieu served as a special assistant to the vice president to fight corruption. Within four months, by June 1972, Hieu had traced the embezzlement to Tran Thien Khiem and General Dang Van Quang, Thieu's assistant for national security. Thieu eventually responded by firing a lesser figure, defense minister General Nguyen Van Vy, along with seven others. Vy's replacement would be Khiem, who was now defense minister, prime minister, interior minister, *and* pacification chief. When General Hieu continued to build corruption cases against Khiem and Quang, as well as against Cao Van Vien and, it is said, Thieu himself, he was suddenly transferred to the operations staff of III Corps.

Saigon politics was not conducive to the creation of a base of support that might have made pacification success meaningful. Buying officials and maintaining a permissive climate for corruption gained the loyalty of only a narrow, privileged segment of the people. Rather than viewing South Vietnam as "pacified" and loyal to Saigon, it would be more accurate to describe the society as metastable, similar to Romania in 1989, just before the upheaval that brought down the Ceausescu regime. Nguyen Van Thieu might have changed this with a forthright political program. It all came down to Thieu.

■ ■ ■ For all the comment and reporting and the constant American contact, Nguyen Van Thieu remained a cipher. His declarations were opaque, his speeches tepid. Here was a man who had convinced both Ngo Dinh Diem and the anti-Diem plotters that he was on their side, calculating but cautious. When a delegation of senior ARVN officers had visited the United States in the late 1950s, Thieu, relegated to handling the luggage, did so without a murmur. An American intelligence officer who met him at the time decided that Thieu was the ultimate survivor. Advisers who worked with Thieu from the early 1960s gave him high marks for competence but could not discern his attitude toward the regime. As for his view of the Americans themselves, Thieu was outwardly friendly, but a 1965 CIA profile noted, "His attitude toward the United States is difficult to determine."[39] Another report observed that, as a minister in Nguyen Khanh's government, "Thieu's specific position is somewhat ambivalent."[40]

Thieu was a product of central Vietnam, born in a village near Phan Rang in November 1924. The family followed Vietnamese custom in consulting the stars to select an auspicious birth date, and Thieu's would be reported as April 5, 1923. His father, a sometime fisherman and seaman, was a landowner—not rich but comfortable, able to send his oldest son to France for legal training and Thieu himself to a Catholic school at Hue. As a village official, Thieu's father at one point knew the young Ngo Dinh Diem. Thieu was the youngest of five children, three of them boys. He dreamed of the sea but farmed his father's land. After the August Revolution, Thieu joined the Vietminh and rose to become a district leader. He broke with them in 1946, disillusioned with Vietminh land reform and terrorist methods and bitterly opposed to communism. His dream of joining the merchant marine was shattered when Thieu discovered that the shipping company paid a Vietnamese less than his French colleagues. Thieu transferred to the Vietnamese Military Academy, recently established at Dalat. He was commissioned in 1949 and received advanced training at the French infantry school. Two years later he married a Catholic girl from My Tho, the daughter of a prosperous herbalist healer.

Nguyen Van Thieu made his early career in the French-sponsored Vietnam National Army (VNA) and benefited from its drive to showcase Vietnamese officers. After leading an infantry platoon and company—acquiring a reputation for caution—Thieu was selected for the first class of the new VNA General Staff course at Hanoi. After that he became operations staff officer for the key Hung Yen sector in the Tonkin delta. Promoted major, Thieu took command of a VNA battalion in central Vietnam, where he had the singular experience of leading an attack to dislodge guerrillas from his native village. Lore has it that Major Thieu used mortar and artillery fire to drive the enemy from his family's home. With the wholesale expansion of the VNA during the months before Dien Bien Phu, Thieu briefly led the 1st Infantry Division while functioning as deputy to the leader of I Corps. Later he acted as chief of staff of the army's Field Command and took staff training in the United States at Fort Leavenworth. Lieutenant Colonel Thieu would be commandant of the Dalat Military Academy for the first four years of the existence of the Army of the Republic of Vietnam. Cultivating a tobacco pipe, Thieu cut a suitably scholarly figure. During that time an entire generation of ARVN officers passed through Dalat, furnishing Thieu with many connections he drew on as general and president.

None of this suggested the Machiavellian image Nguyen Van Thieu acquired. Perhaps the succession of coups during the first half of the 1960s induced him to begin thinking in these terms. It is a measure of the political obsession that engulfed the ARVN that Thieu, who seemed an unlikely candidate, emerged as Saigon's leader. He favored hunting and fishing among a cadre of generals whose idea of relaxation was tennis at the Cercle Sportif. Thieu accepted a position as secretary of the generals' committee in its various guises, and he labored quietly in roles that indebted others to him. He relied on his dark-horse status. When the military had to present candidates for the 1967 presidential election, Thieu called in his chits. Nguyen Cao Ky, amazed at Thieu's sudden strength, was dissuaded from running independently by U.S. appeals plus arguments from the generals. Ky attempted to hem Thieu in with a secret compact, but once the time came to invoke it, Thieu's power became manifest and Ky was marginalized.

President Thieu functioned as both political leader and South Vietnam's supreme commander—in fact, he displayed a desktop plaque with two stars denoting his military rank. The politics, the diplomacy, economic management, and military command all fell to him. He relied on such advisers as cousin Hoang Duc Nha, foreign affairs adviser Nguyen Phu Duc, and General Dang Van Quang, a key operative among the military. Thieu combined caution and dexterity with intense suspicion—thus his hostility toward the Buddhists, which closed an avenue that might have led to real political gains, and his persecution of Truong Dinh Dzu and Tran Ngoc Chau. His infighting with Ky reached monumental proportions. General Lam Quang Thi, a successor as commandant at Dalat, sometimes attended official functions where Ky gave speeches or was merely present. Thi soon heard sinister rumors alleging he had been having secret meetings with Ky. Eventually a friend told Thi that an emissary had hinted it would be better for him if he stopped seeing Ky. The intermediary was Thieu intimate General Do Cao Tri.

Nguyen Van Thieu wore his various hats in succession or combination as he liked. Thus it was Thieu, not the prime minister of the day, who approved the Accelerated Pacification Campaign; it was Thieu, not Saigon's National Security Council, that delayed South Vietnam's response at the time of the October Surprise. Had Thieu truly committed himself to talks, objections elsewhere would have melted.

President's Thieu's attitude toward negotiations, unlike so many of his policies, remained crystal clear: the only acceptable settlement was one that removed the threat of Hanoi and the National Liberation Front. Thieu demonstrated his basic disposition as early as April 4, 1968—the day Lyndon Johnson revealed that talks would be held—when Thieu approved increases in the strength of the armed forces for 1969. Thieu feared a coalition government would end his dominance, and he feared a simple (in-place) cease-fire because it would leave Hanoi's troops in South Vietnam. Thieu wanted the negotiations to force an outcome that neither he nor Washington had been able to achieve by force of arms. Knowing the DRV would never accept such a settlement, he had to believe in military victory. That makes contradictory his steady refusal to do the things necessary to erect the base of support that was a prerequisite to a war effort that could match Hanoi's.

Nguyen Van Thieu tabled two specific peace programs in speeches delivered respectively on March 25 and July 11, 1969. Both amounted to demands for surrender. The Liberation Front could participate in elections if it disarmed and swore to abide by the law. Since "the law" featured Article 4 of Saigon's constitution, which made communism illegal, the NLF would also have to abandon its ideology. Reviewing Thieu's speech, William C. Sullivan, a key figure in U.S. Southeast Asia policy, remarked, "Thieu knew that the other side would not buy a winner-take-all proposition like national elections under the present constitution."[41] In 1970 he rejected proposals to revoke that article of the constitution. "Withdrawal" meant removing DRV troops not only from South Vietnam but from Cambodia and Laos too. Typically, in January 1971 Thieu told Melvin Laird he would present new proposals, then several months later informed Ellsworth Bunker he could make no fresh initiatives.

The CIA had early insight into this attitude, reporting just a day after talks were first announced that Thieu "is relying too much on things that might not happen."[42] That never changed. Years later, in his tearful final speech before fleeing Saigon, Thieu would say that his horoscope had forecast that all his days in power would be bad, and affirm that they had been.[43] But Thieu never made the choices that might have preserved South Vietnam.

To rewind to the outset of the talks, it needs to be said that the Americans were aware of this situation. Two months into his administration, Richard Nixon, visiting Paris, had diplomat Philip Habib update him on the talks. Among other things, Habib noted that all the members of Saigon's delegation, with the exception of Vice President Ky (whom Thieu had sent to Paris to get him out of the way), were under Thieu's thumb. Nixon took notes. At this point he wrote, "Some heavy going ahead."[44]

In one respect Thieu held a more realistic position. He feared abandonment by Washington, as well as the impact the Americans' departure would have on the South Vietnamese polity. But after 1968 the alternatives were exhausted. Thieu bent his efforts to preparing for that inevitable departure—portraying it in a positive light as the "replacement" of Americans by Vietnamese—and to extracting as much as he could in terms of compensation. Weapons and forces for the ARVN and aid for Saigon were his price for U.S. withdrawal. But President Thieu and his advisers recognized the U.S. troops were leaving. With qualms and varying fears, they watched that process begin.

Salted Peanuts

Among those who guided the powers during these fateful days, there was one who wanted to avoid the inevitable. For months Henry A. Kissinger fought a rearguard battle against a pullout. This began with the disappearance of unilateral withdrawal from the Nixon administration's policy review, but it did not end there. Kissinger muddied the meaning of terms, mixing one-sided with mutual withdrawal concepts, and argued against "de-escalation"—a code word for withdrawal—in a long series of memoranda. The position complemented Kissinger's search for ways to carry out the Madman strategy.

On March 8, 1969, with Defense Secretary Melvin Laird in Saigon actually assembling a framework plan for U.S. withdrawal, Kissinger sent Nixon a memorandum purporting to consider de-escalation in the light of overall U.S. strategy. "If we now de-escalate," the national security adviser wrote, "Hanoi will get for nothing what it has had to pay heavy, perhaps excessive casualties to obtain." Dr. Kissinger warned that officials would tell Nixon the United States could always resume military operations, but "every difficulty we have had in deciding whether the bombing halt 'understanding' had been violated will be compounded in the case of de-escalation." Kissinger concluded, "we should not agree to de-escalate now—all the more so if you plan to withdraw some forces in a few months."[45]

Kissinger's argument might be considered a short-term objection, particularly given its reference to an intention to actually begin withdrawals, except that virtually every time the issue arose, no matter the context, he offered similar counsel. When setting the U.S. negotiating position for the Paris talks, Kissinger wanted to make a U.S. withdrawal conditional on a North Vietnamese one. He noted, "It is hard to visualize concrete deescalatory proposals that would be truly reciprocal. Most suggestions would seem to favor the enemy militarily." Kissinger wanted detailed studies of unilateral possibilities, "in part to make clear the great difficulty of developing any concrete proposals."[46] At the March 28 NSC meeting that considered a negotiating strategy, Nixon called on his security adviser to cover de-escalation. There were two problems, Henry said: the game plan and mutual withdrawal. Kissinger noted a major disagreement over whether to de-escalate, and a contingent one whether negotiations should include withdrawal. Nixon clarified: de-escalation did not mean unilateral U.S. withdrawal. He simultaneously ruled out any reduction in the means of warfare such as Arc Light strikes.[47] If unilateral measures were ruled out, along with both forces and capabilities, there could be no de-escalation *except* through a peace agreement.

This same muddle applied to mutual withdrawal. Washington knew that Thieu, to the extent he was willing to countenance U.S. withdrawal at all, wanted a large residual force left in South Vietnam. But all the schemes that would be offered were predicated on a complete DRV withdrawal. Thus Nixon bucked for trading a partial U.S. withdrawal for the adversary's total one. Hanoi was not going to accept that, as was recognized at the time. Dr. Kissinger made this explicit. At the NSC meeting he said, "The alternatives are, should we negotiate a requirement for residual forces or should we opt to the listing of a series of conditions which we know won't be met, while speaking as though all forces will be withdrawn." It would be Richard Nixon who ended this discussion. "In my view," the president declared, "we should agree to total withdrawal of U.S. forces but include very strong conditions which we know may not be met."[48]

Quite consciously, President Nixon intended to seek a sham peace.

The final choice, embodied in National Security Decision Memorandum (NSDM) 9 on April 1, was that "there will be no de-escalation except as an outgrowth of mutual troop withdrawal."[49]

Americans could view Nixon's decision as pious or nefarious, depending on whether they considered the 1968 election a referendum on leaving Vietnam or even a choice between two candidates who both said they would end the war. But a refusal to de-escalate immediately clashed with political, economic, and military reality. The way to counteract adverse opinion trends was to give the impression of making progress, which meant either moving ahead in negotiations—impossible, given the choice just made—or reducing the burden of the fighting. Since capabilities were off the table, that left only force reductions. Withdrawal could also simplify Nixon's political problems by lowering draft calls. In addition, the Vietnam war had exacerbated U.S. economic woes. Budget deficits and a weakening dollar created an inflationary spiral that had to be met by cuts, which Nixon had promised in his election campaign. With the war among the biggest federal programs, costs *had* to be reduced. That dictated a need for force reductions. This calculation could come out only one way.

Pursuing Nixon's Madman Theory to the Duck Hook scheme, Henry Kissinger continued to take the other road. Kissinger wrote of the necessity for a "credible threat of serious consequences if no settlement is reached"[50]—which presupposed existing force levels. The president realized this could not be sustained. On April 10, only a week later, he ordered Laird to prepare a specific timetable for Vietnamization, acknowledging U.S. withdrawals by accepting the defense secretary's concept of a "termination day" ("T-Day") when there would be no American troops left in Vietnam. The assumptions Kissinger built into this study, NSSM-36, went the other way. It provided for "no deescalation in allied military efforts, except that resulting from phased withdrawals of US and other [allies'] forces."[51] Nixon wavered. On May 14 he gave a televised speech that rejected unilateral withdrawal, extolling a negotiated mutual one. Less than a month later at Midway, Nixon announced the first tranche of the unilateral American pullout.

When Secretary Laird produced his timetable to meet NSSM-36 in June, Dr. Kissinger hastened to point out—attributing the objection to Laird—that longer-range programs beyond the numbers announced at Midway would probably slow pacification, and shorter schedules (i.e., larger numbers at each stage) would balloon that problem.[52] This became Kissinger's mantra. At each stage he would recommend the minimum, or that a decision be postponed, based on whatever the situation might be at the moment. In July, at the *Sequoia* meeting that had so much to do with Duck Hook, the next increment of U.S. withdrawals was also discussed. Kissinger argued, "A too-rapid withdrawal might seriously shake the Thieu government . . . It might also create excessive optimism in the United States and make the withdrawal irreversible." Kissinger advised Nixon to postpone the decision.[53] Laird went back to the drawing board and produced a new set of timetables. These Kissinger opposed on several grounds—Hanoi would be encouraged, maintaining MACV morale would be harder, progress in the war would be progressively more difficult, the ARVN would not hold up, and, finally, one of Kissinger's more flagrant assertions: "Withdrawal of U.S. troops will become like salted peanuts to the American public: The more U.S. troops come home, the more will be demanded."[54]

Henry's objections served to promote his alternative, Duck Hook, the fight over which culminated at this time. He became notorious for his instrumental use of issues, to a degree that some colleagues refused to accept *any* Kissinger statement as reflecting a true core belief. Certainly the good doctor tacked to the wind of his president, and once Nixon had decided against Duck Hook, Henry's rhetoric became less strident. The Kissinger staff bid low on each stage of the U.S. withdrawal, but the security adviser gave up opposing the program outright.

Melvin Laird became Kissinger's foil in all this, and a worthy adversary. Schooled in alley-cat fights in the House of Representatives, Laird's escape routes remained a mystery to Kissinger, who decided it was foolish to start a scrap without closing them. Giving Laird orders was suicidal, Kissinger later wrote.[55] Laird had stalled on Duck Hook as much as he could, giving the Joint Chiefs enough on cross-border operations and "protective reaction" air strikes that, at the key moment, they spoke against the plan. On withdrawals, Laird educated Nixon to the political benefits, undercut Kissinger's objections, then started a competition with Nixon for the credit, which pulled the president into demanding drawdowns himself. Mr. Nixon liked salted peanuts too.

Creighton Abrams was the man on the spot, for MACV had to plan the details and manage withdrawal. A few days before Nixon's inauguration, Abrams and Bunker had seen President Thieu to discuss possible MACV reductions. Abrams was confident, telling staff the ARVN was doing very well, the American boys fighting for MACV magnificent, the air boys doing wonders over The Trail, and the intelligence better than ever. Success at breaking up Hanoi's 1969 Tet attacks confirmed his view. Soon Abrams would be helped more by Nixon's secret bombing of Cambodia. Abe showed a healthy skepticism on the data problem, telling associates they needed the statistics—"it's the way you get pointed, and the way you commit assets"—but warning, "we've got to fight *all the time* to look *past* those, and bear in mind what the *real* purpose is."[56] The records of MACV staff conferences at this time indicate an interest in going outside South Vietnam to engage the enemy. Abrams remembered Westmoreland's attempts to get the same approvals, which had always fallen afoul of the secretary of defense and then sunk without a trace at the White House. Generals Goodpaster and Davidson endeavored to convince him to try anyway. Davidson correctly appreciated that Nixon itched for action, though he seemed to think Kissinger did not. But withdrawal was already in the wind and Mel Laird about to arrive in Saigon.

"My guess," Phil Davidson told General Abrams on March 5, "is that the hidden theme this time, and there's no word of it on the agenda, is, 'When can you start withdrawing troops?'"[57]

Davidson proved exactly right. Laird did not simply visit; he blew into town like a whirlwind. Acting more like a Liberation Front proselytizer than a Washington official on a fact-finding mission, Secretary Laird did a lot of talking. He emphasized the need for a policy the administration could sell to Americans and spoke of the outcry at home, making the point that what was needed was to show commitment and progress plus "a program to reduce the United States contribution, not only in the form of men, but in casualties and materiel and in dollars." The notion of a U.S. residual force was explicitly discussed. Laird foresaw the program—and the schedule for withdrawals—being fleshed out over the next three or four months.[58]

General Abrams did not immediately fall into line. He objected that the instructions assumed nonexistent South Vietnamese capabilities. Then came the battle of Hamburger Hill (Ap Bia), which seemed to illustrate Abe's point (contemporaneous U.S. records show American troops took over a thousand casualties while ARVN losses amounted to three killed and four wounded, though the most recent accounts indicate the ARVN had a much greater role in the fighting). But Hamburger Hill touched off such a controversy in the United States that the Nixon administration recoiled. Bus Wheeler's back-channel cables to Abrams alarmed the MACV commander, who had an uncanny ability to read between the lines of the dispatches and got the meaning here. By May Abrams would tell the deputy chief of the U.S. delegation to the Paris talks that computerized T-Day planning was so solid the staff could display it in any format.

On July 26 senior MACV operations planner Colonel Donn A. Starry presented a detailed analysis of the initial U.S. withdrawals. Starry had known

Abrams for two decades, since commanding a company in his tank battalion. Abe trusted him implicitly. He had Starry assemble a tiny group—three majors—for the top-secret planning. Until the briefing, only Abrams's chief of staff knew. A month earlier, Starry recalled, Abrams had realized that the withdrawals would not stop at 200,000—the number they had been using for planning purposes. America was getting out. For Abrams, the key became accomplishing the mission in an orderly fashion that did not let the South Vietnamese down or collapse the entire system.[59]

The first phase sent home a Marine regiment deployed near the DMZ and a couple of Army brigades from the Mekong. Those were easy calls, since the ARVN's best troops manned the DMZ, and the enemy was weakest in the delta. In Washington new withdrawals were announced on September 16, when Nixon recalled 35,000 more troops. Selected this time were the rest of the 3rd Marine Division and the brigade of the 82nd Airborne Division that had gone to Vietnam as emergency reinforcements after Tet. Colonel Starry presented his view of conditions that would obtain following a third phase of withdrawals: at that stage, MACV would have "reached the point that we no longer have parity with the enemy as far as total maneuver battalions are concerned. After that the situation deteriorates."[60]

In addition to the force reductions themselves, over the last quarter of 1969, Washington shorted General Abrams by 7,000 individual replacements. Coming on top of the redeployment of 60,000 soldiers, this enabled the president to cancel all draft calls for November and December, a clear bid to lower the political heat. By now Laird had begun moving rapidly to eliminate the draft altogether and institute an all-volunteer military. He convened an expert panel to show that the force could be introduced effectively and economically, and by offering competitive pay, the military could attract sufficient enlistees away from the private sector. Laird induced Army chief of staff William Westmoreland to give a pair of speeches peddling the concept to key audiences such as the Reserve Officers Association. The Army conducted an experiment at Fort Ord, Washington, where it transitioned several infantry brigades from mixed personnel to a completely volunteer force. Laird simultaneously prepared a complete revamp of the Selective Service, basing the draft on a lottery and eliminating the deferment system. Dead set against the revision, General Hershey opposed it. Long past federal retirement age, Hershey was obliged to leave when those mandatory rules were suddenly invoked. Draft changes were announced in December, and a two-year extension of draft authority requested a month later. The all-volunteer military scheme would be ready to unveil in the spring.

General Abrams, who would be an enthusiast for the all-volunteer military during his subsequent tour as Army chief of staff, benefited immediately only from the changes in the draft. They could not come soon enough. The magnificent soldiers Abrams had admired showed signs of wavering.

Racial tensions, drug use, and the disciplinary problems that underlay frag-ging all indicated their brittleness. There was other evidence, too. For in-stance, in early 1969 soldiers of a Special Forces intelligence unit, in some murky collusion with the CIA, had murdered one of their Vietnamese agents who was suspected of spying for the enemy. Abrams pressed an investigation of this so-called Green Beret affair, but it evaporated once the CIA refused to testify at courts-martial. Simultaneously, more sinister charges were perco-lating up the chain of command that U.S. troops had massacred Vietnamese villagers at My Lai in March 1968. Higher-ups had covered up the atrocity, which emerged when helicopter pilots who had tried to save the villagers and enlisted men who had learned of the incident took their knowledge to Congress. Laird's office was aware of the incident by April, and Nixon knew by September. On September 5 Lieutenant William Calley, who had led the infantry platoon that entered My Lai, was formally charged with murder. His company commander and a few other officers were indicted for either the atrocity or the cover-up, though no one further up the line. These incidents could have only corrosive effects on morale in Vietnam. As far as Abrams was concerned, anything that could be done to ensure that soldiers who ar-rived in-country were more willing to serve was a plus for MACV.

December 1969 brought Nixon's announcement of a third drawdown of forces in Vietnam—this time a 50,000-soldier redeployment to be completed by mid-April 1970. Unknown to anyone at MACV, the White House had been playing with two options, one of them a mid-December announce-ment recalling 90,000 troops, which the president had been leaning toward. The other included the 50,000-man redeployment and also looked ahead to the recall of 85,000 troops in March 1970 and another 100,000 or more that August. Kissinger opposed the big numbers.

General Abrams had been working the possibilities for several months and had informed JCS chairman Wheeler in October that a 50,000-man reduc-tion would oblige him to give up a division base plus two combat brigades. Worried about a new enemy "high point" of activity, perhaps another Tet of-fensive, Abrams wanted to put off additional troop cuts as long as possible, at least until after Tet. He had MACV staff consider a huge reduction such as 100,000 or 150,000 in exchange for the freedom to time it, which he would use to delay any cuts at all for half a year or so. Abrams also had his planners prepare detailed justifications for every element of the MACV force struc-ture, hoping to convince Washington it was all needed. In November he told the White House, through Wheeler, that a withdrawal at this time would not be militarily sound. Nixon finally opted for the 50,000 immediate recall rather than the larger drawdown.

The actual pullout proved even more corrosive of U.S. capabilities than anticipated. The full 1st Infantry Division and more Marines left. By April 1970 MACV would be down to 434,000 troops. But MACV knew nothing of the White House plan for the president to make an announcement in April, followed by another later in the spring. When Laird returned to Vietnam in February 1970, Abrams hit him with the argument his planners had made: U.S. forces would no longer have parity with the enemy. It would be a "crunch" phase for Vietnamization. Laird professed not to understand. Haig, commenting on Laird's trip report, excoriated the secretary for a whitewash. But Nixon was not to be diverted.

During early deliberations on de-escalation, Richard Nixon had announced that capabilities other than troops were not on the table. More broken promises. Before his first year in office was half gone, Nixon had ordered B-52 sorties reduced from 1,800 a month to 1,600, and in 1970 they would be cut to 1,400. A pledge that tactical aircraft would be unaffected as the big bombers stood down evaporated with orders for a 20 percent reduction. Even naval gunfire support would be cut, by 22 percent. General Abrams absorbed the first round of cuts, avoiding adverse impact through technological and intelligence improvements that permitted better employment of existing capabilities. The sensor systems placed along the Ho Chi Minh Trail, their utility first demonstrated at the battle of Khe Sanh, were soon matched by similar ones around many installations in South Vietnam. Efficient target acquisition meant more damaging air strikes and artillery fire. Combined with the code breakers' detailed reporting on the destinations of Hanoi's reinforcements, MACV concentrated on the most serious threats.

But the degree to which lost capability could be offset was limited. And there were factors at work that made further reductions inevitable. General Wheeler explained the underlying situation to Abrams in October 1969. The JCS chairman noted that upon taking office, Nixon and Laird had almost immediately shaved $1 billion from the Pentagon budget. The budget proposed in January 1970 would contain a $1.2 billion increase, but due to inflation, previously committed spending, and the pay increases for the transition to an all-volunteer force, the new program actually meant even deeper cuts. In fact, those cuts entailed much greater reductions because of the way the Pentagon budgeted, with "obligational authority" requests to Congress for given programs, followed by actual appropriations of dollars in specific fiscal years. Meeting the required cuts in cash outlays necessitated canceling the equivalent of $14.5 billion in obligational authority. Yet there were big-ticket items in the defense budget that were absolutely necessary if the United States wanted to avoid yielding strategic superiority to the Soviet Union. These included land- and submarine-based multiple warhead missile systems, an expensive new class of nuclear attack submarines, and so on. The need for cuts was so great that the Army actually demobilized the first units to return from Vietnam and was seriously considering disbanding other major formations, including armored divisions slated to reinforce Germany in the event of war in Europe.[61]

In the context of the times, the pace of leaving Vietnam would be determined not just by the war's unpopularity and seeming stalemate but also by other exigencies of U.S. national security. Every American division redeployed put dollars back in the budget for other needs. Air sortie cuts were more questionable—field commanders and staff rightly pointed out that the "cost" of aircraft operations was a very fuzzy thing, depending more on the mission, distance and flight time, and ordnance than on sheer number of flights. Nevertheless, reduced sortie rates would have a budgetary impact at some level. At one point General Abrams toyed with recommending cuts worth a certain amount, say $100 million, in order to preserve capabilities of equal value, but he finally decided that if different packages were put on the table—suggesting they were negotiable—MACV would likely lose all those capabilities. His staff would stand on their justifications.

Creighton Abrams became the general who juggled the morass of war strategy, assistance to Saigon, realignment for pacification, measures to keep troops supple and responsive, and the withdrawal from the war. His was a huge job, and Abrams displayed superb leadership skill. Melvin Laird thought and still believes that Creighton Abrams did the impossible during these years. Abe kept his shoulder to the grindstone by focusing on the task in front of him at each moment. But with all the problems on his plate, it would hardly be surprising if something slipped past. What happened was huge. It began in the spring of 1970, an amalgam of more orders from on high coupled with unforeseen developments in Southeast Asia.

10   Die to Make Men Free (1970)

Not long after the events recounted here, the Nixon administration startled the world with its decision to abandon the Gold Standard, another measure this president adopted to cope with America's economic woes. The term *Nixon Shock* came to denote the huge impact of the action. The phrase applies equally to Vietnam. Duck Hook—had the president carried it out—would have been a Nixon Shock. As it happened, 1970 had come before the first of the Nixon Shocks in Vietnam. Creighton Abrams, great commander that he was, could not have avoided it. Richard Nixon would be the key mover, and his gambits played out from Laos to Washington, D.C. The events that were unleashed pulled in Abrams, led to the biggest American military venture of the Vietnam war, and ended by dashing the dreams that many in the military had long nurtured. This Nixon Shock brought near warfare to U.S. politics.

In truth, Abrams had no desire to avoid what his president would ordain. A centerpiece of MACV strategy since he took command had been what Abe called his "logistics offensive." This sought to constrain Hanoi by finding and destroying its supply stocks in South Vietnam while minimizing new materiel reaching the field through Laos or Cambodia. In addition, Abrams tried to reduce the number of troops that reinforced Hanoi's legions or replaced their losses. He relied on his improved intelligence to identify the flows and on his forces to attack them wherever and however he could. Nixon's orders built on that strategy. They began, finally, the chain of events that led the American government to fight its own veterans over a war that the president wanted and the country did not. This tragedy began to unfold before the New Year—the American one, not Tet.

■ ■ ■ For years the conflict in Laos had ground on, following its own pattern. Events there set the stage for the Nixon Shock, though they were not actually part of it. There were two wars, really. The one in the south, the so-called Laotian panhandle, centered on blocking the Ho Chi Minh Trail. It relied on bombing, armed reconnaissance by aircraft, high-tech sensor systems, forays by commandos of the MACV Studies and Observation Group (SOG), some CIA-recruited tribal units, and whatever Royal Laotian

Government (RLG) forces could be mobilized. The panhandle war waxed and waned daily, based on the vagaries of intelligence, enemy movements, and availability of assets. The conflict in the north was about the continued existence of Laos, or at least of the Lao government in its current form, and to a large degree it would be fought to enable the panhandle campaign to proceed. Despite its status as a neutral country, as internationally recognized by the Geneva agreements of 1962, Laos had been manipulated by every side in the Vietnam war. Its government was led by Prince Souvanna Phouma, who, though a neutralist by persuasion, could look the other way as the Americans fought in the panhandle because Hanoi had violated Laotian borders as much as the Americans or South Vietnamese had. Souvanna accepted American aid, plus technical and military assistance. Laos essentially functioned as a U.S. client state.

Hanoi had its own clients—the communist Neo Lao Hak Xat, or Pathet Lao, which had once been part of the neutralist government but were driven from it. The Pathet Lao had its own armed forces and political authorities, similar to the National Front for the Liberation of South Vietnam. They were stiffened by Vietnam People's Army troops. The North Vietnamese and the Pathet Lao were powerful enough to overthrow the royal government at almost any time—for years, U.S. intelligence estimates had reflected this projection. Not wanting to be in open breach of the 1962 Geneva accords, Hanoi tolerated the continued existence of the nominally neutralist RLG. In effect, the sides tacitly pretended Laos remained neutral while pursuing a bitter war there, one that waxed and waxed with the seasons

The Laotian army had numbers but poor morale and little fighting quality. Its soldiers were as likely to run from a battle as to fight it. Souvanna compensated by collaborating with the Americans, whose CIA ran a "secret army" of Hmong tribesmen—the best fighters in the country. The U.S. Air Force overmatched the enemy's firepower. During the rainy season, when Hanoi's heavy equipment bogged down, government forces would attack, spearheaded by the Hmong secret army and supported by airpower. The objectives were always designed to push the enemy as far away from the Mekong valley and the Lao lowlands as possible, where the country's population and commercial centers were located. In the dry season the People's Army and Pathet Lao counterattacked and regained whatever they could. This pattern replicated itself year after year, except that Hanoi gradually introduced more and heavier weapons, and the RLG forces added men, formed larger tactical units, and relied even more on American warplanes.

In early 1969 Hanoi's forces unleashed their usual offensive. They overran no fewer than thirty-four "Lima Sites," airstrips that were Hmong or RLG posts. Then they attacked Na Khang, near the Pathet Lao center in Sam Neua province. Laotian CIA station officers were divided, some warning that the enemy had become too strong. But Hmong commander Vang Pao determined to defend Na Khang, which had withstood big attacks twice in previous years. This time it fell. The Air Force carried out Operation "Rain Dance," a program of strikes designed to retard the North Vietnamese until the rainy season. Vang Pao attacked on the ground, gaining so much from the air strikes that his troops advanced virtually without fighting. One town they captured had not seen government troops since 1962. But they could not hold the positions, and the Hmong troops withdrew into their heartland.

Suddenly the Pathet Lao broke the pattern, attacking again in June, their first dry-season offensive of the war, striking directly at the RLG stronghold of Muong Soui. The Pathet Lao also used tanks—another first. A Laotian neutralist force (a third faction), but one aligned with the RLG, had a garrison of 4,000 men, stiffened by 100 Hmong and an artillery unit of Thai "volunteers"—introduced by the CIA. It failed to hold. In fact, more than 80 percent of the government troops deserted. The last Thais and Hmong had to be evacuated in a desperate airlift mounted by the CIA's Air America and all the Air Force helicopters that could be scraped together.

To put the enemy "off balance," Vang Pao executed an offensive with that code name. This operation, undertaken with mixed Hmong, neutralist, and RLG troops, became the first time the Lao government permitted its units to fight under Hmong control. The plan miscarried when neutralists again deserted. North Vietnamese reinforcements put the VPA in a position to strike the secret army's main base, the vaunted CIA city of Long Tieng, in the mountains behind a feature known as Skyline Ridge. To forestall this offensive the Americans planned a saturation air campaign modeled on the one carried out that spring and code-named "About Face." Vang Pao supported it with a three-pronged operation on the ground. About Face succeeded brilliantly, recapturing the Plain of Jars and Muong Soui. More enemy weapons and equipment were captured—including thirteen tanks—than ever before in Laos. But Vang Pao had reached his limits, and the North Vietnamese harried his outposts. The CIA secret army had been fine mounting quick strikes but was neither equipped for a static defense nor available in sufficient numbers. Vang Pao halted his advance but let pass the opportunity to withdraw in good order.

Meanwhile, in the Laotian panhandle, other CIA troops had had some success in different operations. One hit the "Sihanouk Trail," the extension of Hanoi's supply network that reached into Cambodia. Another regained some villages close to the Ho Chi Minh Trail stronghold Tchepone. Several Special Guerrilla Units (SGUs), as the agency dubbed its secret army semi-regulars, were involved. The Americans saw this as a complement to "Commando Hunt," the high-tech interdiction campaign against The Trail. Soon two remaining SGUs, as well as an RLG battalion, were pulled into the action. By late October they had reached the end of their resources, and most of one SGU deserted. More important, the Hmong and panhandle campaigns infuriated the North Vietnamese, who struck back with a ferocity unprecedented in this quiet war.

In Washington, beginning with Na Khang, individuals at the highest levels of the U.S. government spent a lot of time pondering Laos. The records of Kissinger's crisis unit, the Washington Special Actions Group (WSAG), burgeon with talk of the options. Optimism prevailed in the early months when the Hmong and other SGUs were on the attack. But the situation shifted. Washington discussions acquired a darker subtext. Hanoi, it is now known, ordered a major effort it called "Campaign 139" on September 13, 1969. A full division of People's Army regulars, the 312th, reinforced Hanoi's 316th, which had previously supplied the hard punch for the Pathet Lao and had been mauled in that year's fighting. Trying to blunt the move, or at least prevent the logistics buildup necessary for an attack, the Air Force flung 5,006 fighter-bomber sorties at northern Laotian targets in October, the peak rate for the entire war. In addition to utilizing tanks, the VPA began to engage in sapper attacks and used new, longer-range artillery. Before the new year the VPA regained almost all the positions lost earlier. They cleared the Plain of Jars and attacked toward Vang Pao's base at Long Tieng. Needing reinforcements badly, Vang Pao managed to get a couple of SGUs from other Lao military regions and recruit a few new Hmong. But it was not enough, especially when some of his fresh troops fled as the People's Army closed in. The CIA had created the secret army in 1960. After a decade bearing the brunt of the Laotian war, the Hmong were nearly fought out. Boy soldiers showed up in the ranks. The air support that had been a force multiplier had become a crutch. Without it, the SGUs were less and less effective.

Washington considered using Arc Light strikes in northern Laos—this option first arose in relation to a onetime bombing of Hanoi's headquarters in the Plain of Jars. Kissinger convened his crisis group to discuss this on January 26, 1970. The Washington agencies split. The question had yet to be resolved when the People's Army moved on the Plain of Jars and Souvanna Phouma asked the United States for B-52s. It was no longer a matter of a strike on some command post. By mid-February Nixon and Kissinger were discussing a program, which Secretary of State William Rogers still opposed. Rogers's argument that Congress was now watching closely and looking for signs of activity made it into briefing memoranda to the president. Nixon approved anyway. The news leaked immediately, appearing in the *New York Times* on February 19. It led to charges that Washington was escalating the war in Laos. Soon after a photograph of the CIA base at Long Tieng also showed up in the press.

Henry Kissinger's recounting of this episode—not modified in his more recent recasting of history—is another model of his subtle obfuscation.[1] For the most part, the security adviser's treatment of the assorted meetings and memoranda is accurate but his outline of surrounding events disingenuous. First, Kissinger writes as if this were a silly tempest over a single Arc Light strike. The B-52 missions over northern Laos would last four months and involve more than 4,200 tons of bombs. Kissinger does not note the reasons for domestic outcry, simply linking them to a series of complaints by senators. But the *reason* the senators expressed concern was that the secret B-52 bombing of Cambodia had already been added to the Vietnam controversy. Kissinger argues that the Senate and the media engaged in a sham campaign to get at the "truth," when the facts were already "widely known," for the purpose of forcing official acknowledgment of operations in Laos. But the facts were *not* widely known, and the administration stoutly resisted admitting them. Among its moves was an attempt to suppress the text of a 1969 Senate Foreign Relations Committee hearing that presented the most extensive discussion of the Laotian secret war there had ever been. Kissinger feared such an admission would "wreck what was left of the 1962 Accords" and give Hanoi a pretext for its own escalation. But Kissinger well knew—and said so in a February 27, 1970, memo to Nixon—that Hanoi had no need to "step up its aggression" to conquer Laos; it could do that anytime.[2] And if the truth about Laos was well known, as Kissinger claims, he fails to explain how admitting it would wreck the Geneva accords. *And* if the breakdown of Geneva *was* to become manifest, the most likely result would have been demands for an international conference on Indochina, providing a fresh venue to negotiate an end to the war—which negotiation was the administration's declared policy. Kissinger wanted secrecy on Laos to preserve freedom of action in Vietnam.

But by February 1970 that position had become untenable. Senator Stuart Symington, the Missouri Democrat who chaired the Laos hearings, had already threatened to release the transcripts by congressional action. When the NSC met to consider a public posture, Nixon, Laird, and Rogers all agreed something had to be said. The only issues were form and content. Kissinger, who had volunteered to discuss the pros and cons of revelation, remained mostly silent at the February 27 meeting. Nixon settled on a daytime television appearance—to keep the audience to 10 million instead of 70 million—and a short White House statement. In addition, a heavily expurgated version of the Symington hearings would be released.

Kissinger is directly misleading where he writes, "it is impossible to determine at this late date" why he agreed to draft the statement that would put Nixon and himself "in the direct line of fire on every factual dispute."[3] Rather, in his memorandum to the president, extensive portions of which are reprinted in his memoir (putting beyond doubt his use of the document), Henry argued that this "would allow us to control what is said, and how, without releasing sensitive information." He also noted the negative possibility that such an approach "would bring the White House directly into the controversy."[4] The dangers were squarely posed. Nixon rejected the caution and opted to control the document. The die had been cast.

What followed was a White House disaster. Kissinger assigned his newest aide to write the statement. Winston Lord collected what data he could. The national security adviser was in and out of the president's office on this— enough so that Bob Haldeman noticed—and he telephoned Nixon too. The two congratulated each other on taking the lead and not leaving the matter to the pansies at State. On March 6 Nixon appeared on television to say there were no U.S. combat troops in Laos. No Americans had been killed there. He made no mention of pilots or lost aircrews, the losses of numerous commando teams, or the five dead CIA men he had learned of at the NSC. Nixon gave a few details of the Americans involved in the secret war—leaving out those based in Thailand who commuted to their posts each day on Air America, and indeed, leaving out Air America itself. Nixon compared these small numbers to a huge figure for the North Vietnamese—terming the Pathet Lao insignificant—including not just Hanoi's troops in northern Laos but also everyone on the Ho Chi Minh Trail. Kissinger compounded the obtuse statement with a backgrounder, a press conference where he would be identified only as a "senior government official." In his memoirs Kissinger speaks of just *one* inaccuracy.

Within twenty-four hours the name of an Army officer killed in combat emerged; within days civilian casualties (CIA and Air America) were identified. Then the numbers involved in the Laos program were challenged, and it came out that Americans in Laos had been collecting combat pay since the beginning of 1966. It strained credulity to say there was no war in Laos—to the extent that the makers of the movie *Air America* could turn a clip of Nixon's TV appearance into a comedic scene in which the president speaks as explosions rip through the CIA's Long Tieng base as an aircraft breaks up overhead. Nixon suffered an eleven-point loss in the polls on his handling of the war. This wound was self-inflicted and entirely avoidable. On March 9 Kissinger admitted to Haldeman that he had *known* it was a mistake to claim no combat deaths.[5] Days later the White House chief of staff noted in his diary, "the credibility story is still riding."[6] Nixon's weakened position now put a premium on his actions on Indochina.

Battles in Laos continued but need not detain us. The North Vietnamese and Pathet Lao pressed their advantage and reached Skyline Ridge. Washington expanded the presence of Thai "volunteers" with the Hmong—first with an artillery unit, then infantry to compensate for the dwindling tribesmen— and threw tactical air strikes at the enemy. Long Tieng would be saved for that year. The WSAG still debated Laos at the very moment events in Cambodia brought the occasion for the first Nixon Shock.

The First Nixon Shock

The Laotian headache still afflicted Washington as a rush of events in Cambodia created a whole new situation. At the White House Nixon sought a way to escape the Laos fallout, and Cambodia quickly assumed the shape of an emergency in which he could stand tall, be seen in heroic terms, and take strong action. Richard Nixon's proclivities matched the desires of American field commanders: troop leaders itched to get at Hanoi's men in their sanctuaries across the border. In addition, they dearly wanted to do something about the supply flow to the adversary through the Cambodian port Sihanoukville. But the initiative came from the White House.

The U.S. military was highly exercised about Cambodia, or, more properly, Sihanoukville. Use of the port for Chinese arms shipments became the biggest intelligence dispute of the later stages of the war.[7] The Defense Intelligence Agency (DIA) and MACV intelligence types got into a regular donnybrook with CIA spooks over the issue. There were at least two interagency inquiries, one of which included an investigation on the ground, complete with queries to the Australians who represented U.S. interests in Phnom Penh and officials in Thailand and Laos. There was also a CIA econometric model of Sihanoukville port operations, and the agency sent its deputy director for intelligence to Saigon to nose out the question for himself. MACV set up a joint committee, known as "Vesuvius," just to monitor Cambodia intelligence, and its SOG made a special effort to collect data on supplies trucked out of the port. The Navy got into the act too, putting a submarine off Sihanoukville to watch ship traffic and setting up its "Sunshine Park" spy ring in an attempt to penetrate the Cambodian government and get to the bottom of the matter. The CIA had spy missions directed at Sihanoukville too, in both Indochina and Hong Kong. Military intelligence argued that virtually all the arms used by the enemy in the Saigon area and Mekong delta were coming from Chinese vessels that had docked there since 1966. The CIA considered the traffic much less important. This issue had been contentious in the NSSM-1 study too. Periodic MACV briefings on Hanoi's supply net constantly harped on Sihanoukville's role. But General Abrams believed the Operation Menu bombings and SOG's ground patrols were doing about as much as possible under the authority he possessed.

Kissinger's staff had not paid much attention to Cambodia once the bombing got under way, other than arranging for some Vesuvius maps and documents to be leaked to Prince Sihanouk to convince him of Hanoi's evil role, periodic reports to Nixon on Menu, and inclusion of the Sihanoukville dispute among Kissinger's bill of particulars condemning data on the war. There were some tentative thoughts about feelers to Phnom Penh—and one version of the Cambodia story features a secret mission there by Alexander Haig during his January 1970 Vietnam visit—but nothing of a concrete character materialized, at least at the Washington end.

The Nixon Shock began with a coup in Phnom Penh. The Byzantine quality of Cambodian politics fully rivaled that in Saigon. This text can barely touch on the rivalries reflected in the events of 1970. There are multiple versions of what transpired. In any case, Prince Sihanouk found himself under considerable pressure in the months before this crisis. Unable to solve the nation's economic problems, he made a deal with North Vietnam and China. Cambodia sold food and medical supplies to the DRV and NLF, and the communists could use the port. On June 11, 1969, Sihanouk had been among the first to recognize the NLF's Provisional Revolutionary Government, permitting it a full embassy in Phnom Penh.

Sihanouk, clever and politically astute, maneuvered between the sides. Faced with accusations of interfering in elections, Sihanouk stood by while the National Assembly came to be dominated by anticommunists. Moving to the right, in 1969 Sihanouk also acquiesced in Nixon's bombing and appointed a conservative government headed by General Lon Nol. The regrouping of North Vietnamese troops in Cambodian sanctuaries after Tet further complicated matters, making Hanoi's presence more difficult to disguise and aggravating Lon Nol's anticommunist proclivities. According to numerous U.S. intelligence reports, the general personally profited from the Sihanoukville traffic, and the most recent ones held that Sihanouk did too. Yet in the summer of 1969 the prime minister and the prince began to obstruct port traffic and eventually canceled the deal. Clashes between Cambodian and North Vietnamese troops dated from that time. The last Chinese ship bearing arms docked at Sihanoukville in August 1969 (one additional ship bearing foodstuffs arrived in the fall). Whether this represented an attempt to extract better terms from the communists, a Sihanouk political maneuver to cover his flank, a Lon Nol ploy to conceal his corruption, or the prince's resolve to move toward the United States is anyone's guess. Phnom Penh issued several releases documenting Hanoi's control of the border provinces and efforts of its diplomats to dictate to Cambodian officials. In Saigon, MACV briefers referred approvingly to the demarches and took credit for providing Phnom Penh with maps and other data.

Meanwhile, the deputy prime minister, Sisowath Sirik Matak, a cousin of Sihanouk's, actually bore some ill will toward the ruler, for his family had been frozen out when the prince became king during the French era. Prince Sihanouk customarily traveled to France in the early part of the year, and in 1970 he stayed longer, on the dubious excuse of dieting. General Lon Nol had also gone to France for medical treatment. With both top leaders away, Sirik Matak headed the government, and he used that opportunity to curb Sihanouk's income (closing the Phnom Penh casino). Shortly after Lon Nol's return, a monetary reform froze Hanoi's ability to spend its Cambodian currency and greatly exacerbated tensions with the North Vietnamese. On March 11, 1970, a swarm of protesters who could only have been assembled by the government ransacked Hanoi's and Beijing's embassies in Phnom Penh.

Sihanouk and Lon Nol were uneasy competitors, but in some versions of the Cambodian tale, the two conspired at a contrived coup that might enable Sihanouk to renew his power. The move, initiated by Cambodia's police director, the half-brother of Sihanouk's wife, first took the form of anti-Vietnamese riots, an excuse for police to take over key points in the capital. Lon Nol's motives were murky, but his power had grown. Stymied during the high years of neutrality, Lon Nol now had people throughout the government and army. During Sihanouk's heyday, that did not matter, but as the shadow of Hanoi and the NLF loomed, along with Chinese influence, Sihanouk had more need of military support. Both the officer corps and the urban elite chafed at Cambodia's delicate political and economic position, their dissatisfaction readily mobilized. As commander in chief, Lon Nol used troops to crush the police.

Had he been in Phnom Penh, Prince Sihanouk might yet have threaded his way through these shoals, but the prince delayed his return, tarrying in Moscow, and had yet to reach Beijing when the sword fell, spurred by the police chief's arrest. On March 18 the National Assembly voted to end the monarchy. Several battalions of troops and half a dozen Khmer army armored cars stood outside the parliament during the voting. No ally of the prince dared raise a hand.

The American role remains cloudy. Cautious to a fault, Lon Nol would have been loath to come out against Sihanouk without some assurances. And there is the curious role of the Cambodian nationalist troops, the Khmer Serei ("Free Khmer"), most of whom served the U.S.-led Civilian Irregular Defense Groups (CIDGs) in Vietnam, though some were in Thailand. They were widely believed to be CIA assets. Since the 1950s these Cambodians, under leader Son Ngoc Thanh, had battled for Khmer independence from France and alternately fought or supported Sihanouk, depending on his own political peregrinations. Lately the Khmer Serei had been in opposition. In 1969 a peculiar wave of Khmer Serei mass defections began in Vietnam, with hundreds at a time going home to join the Cambodian army or police. Three full battalions defected at the end of the year. A Special Forces sergeant along the Cambodian border trained a succession of these Khmer and understood their project to be aimed at Sihanouk. In February 1970 an American Special Forces officer in the Central Highlands got orders to send two companies of his CIDGs to Bu Prang camp to replace more Khmer Serei who had gone to Cambodia. The Khmer Serei would be the best troops in the Cambodian army. Son Ngoc Thanh met with Lon Nol about ten days before the coup. Thanh later recalled he had told a CIA officer about their conversation, and the agency man had said to go ahead. Only after Thanh's assurances did Lon Nol proceed. And in 1977 Kissinger confined his denial of U.S. participation to "the top levels."[8]

Sihanouk's rule quickly gave way to a Khmer Republic with Lon Nol at its head. The new ruler immediately ordered the Chinese, North Vietnamese, and Liberation Front (officially styled the Provisional Revolutionary Government of South Vietnam) embassies closed and soon demanded that all VPA and NLF troops leave Cambodia. His ultimatum gave them just seventy-two hours to get out, an impossibility that guaranteed war and raises the question of Lon Nol's understanding with the United States.

Memoirs and the declassified records available so far contain no evidence of collusion and indicate that Washington was surprised by the coup. Nixon instantly ordered military aid and, while awaiting those arrangements, instituted a CIA program to furnish off-the-shelf "man packs" of weapons, each sufficient to equip several battalions of troops. The ARVN first coordinated artillery fire with Khmer republican troops the day of the coup, and ARVN and Cambodian officers held meetings to plan cooperative measures the next day. The South Vietnamese began cross-border probes into Hanoi's base areas on March 20. Within a week U.S. helicopter gunships were supporting some of these ARVN incursions. The Pentagon ordered a stand-down and prohibited U.S. advisers from entering Cambodia with the ARVN units they normally accompanied. The White House concurred; Kissinger did not wish policy made by the local decisions of field commanders. But the respite would be strictly temporary.

According to Secretary of Defense Laird, the impetus for the Cambodian operation came from the White House. This tracks with the Abrams tapes, which contain no mention of Cambodia at the time of the coup or during the MACV briefings of March 21 and 28. Meanwhile, Haig met CIA director Helms to pass instructions on March 22. On the twenty-sixth JCS chairman Wheeler ordered Abrams to initiate planning that assumed the use of U.S. forces alongside the South Vietnamese and provided for offensives into several key base areas, including one thought to contain Hanoi's high command, COSVN. The Nixon Shock had begun to gather.

For nearly a month there were extended Washington maneuvers as President Nixon lined up subordinates for his preferred course. Nixon repeatedly complained about Helms and the CIA—their slowness in moving arms to Lon Nol's people, in setting up a station at Phnom Penh, and in preparing useful covert actions. He made similar complaints about the Pentagon, falling into his standard pattern of being more aggressive than the military. But the uniformed services were not Nixon's problem—Wheeler was happy to pass along Nixon's instructions and Abrams pleased to generate the operations plans. The president's real problem lay with top officials who, concerned about political and international conditions, warned Nixon against an invasion. The purpose of the lengthy NSC and WSAG meetings was for the White House to marshal Nixon's people and, equally important, induce them to get their hands wet with the Cambodia preparations, ensuring they could not disassociate themselves later. Both Rogers and Laird were key targets. On April 20, according to Haldeman, Nixon actually asked Kissinger if it would be possible to set up a back channel to give the military orders without going through Laird. But Rogers and Laird were hardly the only ones to worry. Nixon received warnings from White House aides John Ehrlichman and Charles Colson that a move into Cambodia would inflame the nation. Even Kissinger anticipated trouble with Congress.

Mel Laird and Bill Rogers continued to raise objections. In the middle of this debate came a sudden interruption—the *Apollo XIII* emergency, when a lunar mission came close to failure and U.S. astronauts almost died. The president flew to Hawaii to greet the brave astronauts, using the occasion to stage military briefings with Pacific commanders to answer the qualms of his subordinates. Nixon also covered his political flank with another 50,000-soldier withdrawal increment announced on April 15.[9] Rogers finally acquiesced. When Laird did not relent, he would be frozen out of the final decisions. Nixon was the president, after all. By late April Richard Nixon was ready to move, and Creighton Abrams had the troops in place.

A prime example of how Nixon's intricate maneuvers encouraged overzealousness was the series of decision memoranda (NSDMs) issued in the last days before the offensive. Believing he had surmounted the doubts of Rogers and Laird, Nixon immediately put out an order for the attack. Secretary Rogers was about to appear on Capitol Hill, and everyone knew he would be asked about Cambodia. Nixon had to delay implementation so Rogers could say truthfully that no decision had been made (just as the second Bush administration would repeatedly claim that no decisions had been made during its preparation for war with Iraq). The NSDM also prescribed decision-making channels different from those the president himself had already set. A new NSDM proved necessary.

With the president's speech in draft, the White House suddenly faced open revolt among NSC staffers, some of who fundamentally objected, wrote papers explaining their reasoning, and told Haig they would resign if the invasion went ahead. Here again, Nixon and Kissinger spurned warnings about the effect on antiwar sentiment. Finally Nixon stood ready with an April 30 speech that revealed his decision, even as American troops were crossing into Cambodia. The ARVN had started sooner, but its forays were cloaked by a news blackout. Nixon's concessions to his political liabilities were to limit the invasion in time (though he did not specify a duration in the speech) and scope (U.S. troops would not penetrate more than twenty miles into Cambodia) and to call the mission an "incursion" rather than what it was.

One of the primary goals was to get at COSVN, the enemy high command for the far south. Intelligence located COSVN in Base Area 353, ensconced in the border region known as the "Fishhook," target of the 1st Cavalry Division (Airmobile). It was not to be. Hanoi and Liberation Front leaders (the NLF and its provisional government kept their own headquarters close to COSVN) had already been put on notice by the Lon Nol coup, and there are indications the main camp had moved across the border, a short way into South Vietnam. On March 29 the NLF's camp, or at least one of its radio posts, was plastered by a B-52 strike.[10] COSVN immediately left its camps behind and began to trek deeper into Cambodia, with field commander General Hoang Van Thai deploying troops to create a corridor protecting the move. At one of the last big White House meetings on the invasion, Laird and Rogers argued that COSVN could not be caught, but Nixon fastened on this as one of his justifications for the operation. Senate committee staff who reached Saigon several days after the invasion began were told COSVN was the main objective of The Cav's part of the action. A week later the subject would not even be mentioned. The U.S.–South Vietnamese invasion had no real chance to catch COSVN, yet breathless pronouncements contributed to perceptions that the invasion, a breach of international law, had accomplished little.

The principal grounds for claiming success in Cambodia—that the invasion had helped the cause of Vietnamization—would be the tally of weapons and equipment seized in depots and caches in the base areas. The statistics became a chant, oft repeated then and later. There were plentiful numbers, including almost 23,000 individual weapons and 2,500 crew-served weapons captured. But there remains a question of why those weapons were there. If these were reserve stocks, the allies were affecting enemy strength. But if the weapons were merely surplus, their loss would have little impact. From 1966 through 1969 the Liberation Front and People's Army in the far south had acquired a new generation of firepower, rearming with modern AK-47 automatic rifles, heavier rocket launchers, guns, and a few tanks. The time frame coincides with that of the Sihanoukville arms shipments. There is no evidence that the weapons replaced had been taken out of Cambodia, either through Sihanoukville or up the Ho Chi Minh Trail. Why expend the energy? And the old weapons could still be given to the Khmer Rouge—Cambodian communists fighting Phnom Penh forces—or to fresh guerrilla troops. No doubt there were some modern weapons in the seized stocks, but the likelihood is that the bulk of what the United States and ARVN captured had been retired from service. The value of the weapons was a lot less than advertised. But the 8,200 tons of rice the enemy lost hurt a great deal.

Both Americans and South Vietnamese encountered some hard fighting during the invasion. At the base camp The Cav nicknamed "The City," and at the Cambodian towns of Krek, Mimot, and Snoul, there were pitched battles, the allies always victorious. The fighting was episodic but costly. Though

American forces were down—and losses fewer—total allied casualties from April to June still numbered 60 percent of the dead and 86 percent of the wounded of *Tet Mau Than*. Claimed enemy losses for the same months were less than half those at Tet. Except where necessary, it seems, the North Vietnamese avoided contact. When the ARVN began attacking into the Chup rubber plantation, III Corps commander General Do Cao Tri teased, "We'll be swimming in the plantation pool tomorrow." The next afternoon, to the embarrassment of French plantation managers, Tri did just that.[11]

Whatever the results, the political constraints compelled the United States to withdraw by the end of June. At that point the limited intervention left Washington with the need to support a new front in the war without the ability to rely on American troops. The ARVN did not have the same constraints, but it also lacked U.S. capabilities. When the Americans left, General Tri still had about a division's worth of soldiers in Cambodia, with eight helicopters to ferry them about. The Nixon administration tried to provision the new front with weapons shipments to Lon Nol, with organized military aid to Cambodia from Thailand and Indonesia, and by sending Khmer Serei to be incorporated into Lon Nol's army. A handful of U.S. advisers completed the package. If South Vietnam waged war on a shoestring, Cambodia's hung by a thread.

The White House's political problems were ultimately aggravated by the Khmer Serei, whose presence added to the impression that the United States had had something to do with Lon Nol's coup. Nixon handled the Khmer Serei's movement by top-secret, dead-of-night displacements into security-cordoned airfields—just like the CIA's weapons packs. Deployment of Son Ngoc Thanh's men became one of those few matters about which Abrams saved the dispatches in his papers, evidently as a sort of insurance policy. The State Department's cable traffic was classified "Top Secret/No Dis/Khmer," meaning the information was to be kept from Lon Nol. The Senate Foreign Relations Committee's investigators, on a fact-finding mission at the time, were given the runaround on both the weapons and the Khmer Serei. Their report is worth quoting:

> In the case of the Khmer CIDG soldiers, officials in Phnom Penh referred us to Saigon. There we requested a briefing from MACV or Special Forces on such details as how many Khmer had been sent to Cambodia, whether all had been serving with U.S. Special Forces, when the first had arrived, when the United States had stopped paying their salaries, and whether the United States had paid for their arms. Again, we were told that Special Forces in Saigon had "no authority" to brief us.
>
> We found in Phnom Penh that the arrival of the Khmer CIDG soldiers had first been discovered in the Cambodian capital by a correspondent who had spent years in Vietnam. He had noticed a Cambodian, who seemed to be

wearing an American uniform, walking in the center of town and had asked him, in English, whether he was from Vietnam. The Cambodian replied: "Say again, sir," and when queried further replied, "I am not authorized to speak to the press, sir." The correspondent had little difficulty in concluding from the language of these replies that the Cambodian soldier in question had worked closely with American forces. Another reporter told us that he had talked to one of the Khmer soldiers who had told him that he had been in Phnom Penh for 4 to 6 weeks which would mean that he had arrived there during the month of March.[12]

Nixon recalls his invasion decision in heroic terms, similar to those used in his memoirs to describe his November 3, 1969, speech. He awaited public reaction. Chief Justice of the Supreme Court Warren Burger came to him the night of the speech to say the invasion would surely be supported by Americans. Burger was wrong. The nation immediately erupted in a firestorm of protest. Congress broke with the president and passed legislation prohibiting the use of American troops in either Cambodia or Laos. Students took to the streets. Spiro Agnew called the protesters "psychotic and criminal elements" and "traitors and thieves and perverts." Richard Nixon called them "bums" who were "blowing up the campuses."[13] Nixon forged ahead, demanded action, insisted on maximum measures, and ignored the warnings of close advisers. He also broke federal regulations separating government from political action by making the State Department and the CIA pay the costs of responding to the political mail on Nixon's speech received at the White House.[14] The protesters had not created this situation. Cambodia became a Nixon Shock because he drove himself directly into the storm.

■ ■ ■ Tom Hayden and David Dellinger were in New Haven, Connecticut, the night the president went on TV to announce his invasion. Recently released on bail after their conviction in the Chicago Eight trial, the two activists were in a state of limbo, pending the day those convictions would be thrown out on appeal. New Haven was the scene of fresh controversy over the imminent trial of Black Panther leader Bobby Seale and eight others for murder and kidnapping, trumped-up charges like those already leveled at the Chicago defendants. A weekend of protests had been laid on, and the activists met Yale University officials that night. All agreed they preferred to avoid violence. Cambodia changed that. Speaking of the talks, which had included Yale president Kingman Brewster, Hayden recalled, "We sensed the beginning of one of the worst moments of recent history."[15]

New Haven stores were boarded up. The city appeared deserted, the atmosphere dark; 10,000 demonstrators were expected. Nixon officials had already huddled over whether to send troops. Attorney General Mitchell favored this but had been overruled. Now, with the Cambodia announcement, protests welled up in Philadelphia and New York, and more than 20,000 turned out for the Yale events, where Cambodia quickly overshadowed the original purpose. A bomb exploded on Yale's campus, fires were set, police clubbed protesters—a familiar story. Impelled by Cambodia, Yale student leaders called for a nationwide strike. Editors from student newspapers at ten colleges, including Yale and Columbia, met in New York to write a joint editorial widening the strike call, which they all published.

The dust had hardly settled from that weekend of agony in New Haven when the scene shifted to Kent State University in Ohio, where protests began the morning after Nixon's speech with a march of about 500 students. Concern about vandalism grew that night, and at another demonstration the next day, participants set fire to the Kent State ROTC building. Firemen retreated, deciding they needed police protection to fight the blaze. Ohio governor James A. Rhodes could have taken steps to calm the citizens of Kent but, engaged in a tough primary campaign against a candidate from an old-line Republican family (Robert Taft Jr.), chose to call out the National Guard instead. Police officials—ridiculously—talked of "sniping" as a protester tactic and threatened to shoot.[16] That night the Guard cleared the campus with tear gas and fixed bayonets. On Monday, May 4, Guardsmen used live ammunition to fire into a crowd of about a thousand protesters and bystanders. Four students were killed and nine wounded.[17] The nation gasped. A firestorm of protest ensued. Months later Mitchell proposed to convene a federal grand jury on Kent State, with the idea of proving that the students had incited the shooting. J. Edgar Hoover opposed him. Nixon rejected the scheme.

Those who would minimize the seriousness of these developments (and political developments they were) prefer to attribute what happened in the spring of 1970 to the excesses at Kent State, which they blame on a more or less innocent mistake. But Kent State served as catalyst, not cause. Police and security forces throughout the land were ranged against citizens. In fact, Guardsmen killed another student at Ohio State University, and state police killed two students (one a high schooler) and wounded a dozen more at Jackson State University in Mississippi. Either or both incidents would have had greater prominence but for Kent State. There were also major police actions against protests at the University of Oregon and dozens of other campuses. Any of them could have been Kent State. It was literally true that the government had gone to war against Americans to preserve its ability to make war in Southeast Asia. Absent National Guard depredations in Ohio, there would still have been a firestorm over Cambodia, and there is no telling if the tempest would have been any less fierce. Indeed, had Kent State *not* happened, something like it would have, somewhere, because the issue had been joined so fiercely. Government now stood just a step away from warring against its veterans.

Nor was Vietnam protest any more a matter of whether "mere" students liked strawberries. Opinion polls initially supported the invasion, but that effect wore off fast. Two days before Kent State, Bui Diem, still Saigon's ambassador to Washington, cabled President Thieu:

> Nixon's decision has provoked a very strong reaction here among liberal circles and it is still difficult to predict to what extent this new situation is going to tie the president's hands. . . . Observers here are of the opinion that it was a major political and military gamble. . . . On the internal political scene it is obvious that [Nixon] is running a lot of risk because the decision has not only provoked a split among the Republicans, it can also rekindle the blaring national debate.[18]

A few days later Diem reported the atmosphere as highly emotional, with Cambodia news dominating the media, protests everywhere, and vigorous debate in Congress.

A thousand lawyers, including judges and senior partners of Wall Street firms, converged on Capitol Hill to lobby their congressmen against the war. The Senate Foreign Relations Committee chose this moment to vote a repeal of the Gulf of Tonkin resolution. When repeal took effect, the U.S. government's sole remaining basis for waging war in Vietnam would be to recover American prisoners held by the enemy. Equally serious, the escapade impelled new resolutions limiting Nixon's freedom to act. The most important, sponsored by senators John Sherman Cooper and Frank Church, prohibited the use of American troops in Cambodia or Laos upon termination of the current operation. The Nixon White House lobbied strenuously, sending political maven Bryce Harlow into the breach to negotiate alternatives. FBI wiretaps yielded inside information on congressmen, but even that was not enough. The Cooper-Church amendment became a serious impediment to further Nixon ventures in Indochina.

State Department employees organized a petition campaign within the halls of the nation's own diplomatic service. Nixon ordered that everyone associated with it be fired—an impossibility under civil service regulations. Several hundred Asia scholars, led by Harvard great John King Fairbank, put out a hard-hitting analysis condemning the state of Vietnam scholarship in the United States. (The Nixon administration then put the Concerned Committee of Asian Scholars on the FBI's list of targeted "subversive" organizations.) Former Peace Corps volunteers invaded the agency's Washington headquarters, declared it a "liberated zone," and unfurled a National Liberation Front flag. Predictably, a call went out for a march on Washington on May 9.

Of special significance, American labor unions, most of which had long supported the war despite varying degrees of discomfort, now jumped off the bandwagon one by one. Until 1969 dissent among labor had been largely confined to individuals and union locals, such as Local 1199 of the Drug and Hospital Workers Union and District 65 of the Retail, Wholesale, and Department Store Workers Union, both AFL-CIO affiliates. They had opposed the war quite early, but big labor held the line, particularly AFL-CIO leadership and its president, George Meany, whom Nixon carefully cultivated. Some AFL-CIO senior people dissented, but Meany had prevented defections.[19]

With Nixon in office the Teamsters and United Auto Workers broke ranks to denounce the war, forming an Alliance for Labor Action in 1969. Cambodia accelerated the shift. The American Federation of State, City, and Municipal Employees (AFSCME) adopted a position against the war on May 7, 1970. United Auto Workers president Walter Reuther sent the White House a telegram to condemn the Cambodian invasion the same day, although organizational action would be delayed by Reuther's death in a plane crash. The Amalgamated Clothing Workers joined the exodus a few weeks later. As a major AFL-CIO affiliate, the clothing workers' action signaled that the Nixon administration was living on borrowed time. On May 18 the *San Francisco Chronicle* published a full-page ad signed by 450 union officials, executive board members, and shop stewards. The headline: "WE'VE HAD IT!"[20]

Richard Nixon went to the mat in response. His outburst about student "bums" had taken place the morning after his invasion speech, when the president had attended a Pentagon briefing and exhorted the brass to pull out all the stops. Nixon seemed positively manic, actually alarming some who witnessed this episode. Bob Haldeman saw Nixon himself as pleased. Kissinger feared that Nixon might waver even before he learned of Kent State, and he criticized Haldeman for informing the president of events on the campuses. After hearing of Kent State, the chief executive phoned Kissinger and told him the administration needed to get its people to speak out. The long-dormant American Friends of Vietnam suddenly publicized an eve-of-invasion report on a fact-finding tour by the equally moribund Citizens Committee for Peace with Freedom in Vietnam (that old Johnson-sponsored entity), which concluded by advising Nixon to "take firm immediate steps" to protect troops "seriously imperiled by current developments in Cambodia."[21]

George Meany publicly backed the invasion. Nixon visited AFL-CIO headquarters to express his appreciation. Not coincidentally, around this time Nixon had an hour-long telephone conversation with a friendly Labor organizer, Peter J. Brennan, head of the 200,000-member Building and Construction Trades Council of Greater New York. On May 8 several hundred

"Hard Hat" construction workers in the Wall Street area went on a rampage against antiwar protesters. More than seventy persons were injured. Witnesses observed individuals with walkie-talkies directing the Hard Hats. Television cameras recorded them wielding lead pipes and crowbars. The film appeared on the evening news the night before the big Washington march. The Hard Hats plus dockworkers formed the backbone of a 100,000-strong pro-war march that took place in New York on May 20. Brooklyn Republican activist William Sampol claimed credit for organizing both events. At the White House, Chuck Colson was point man for dealing with the construction workers. Nixon wanted Hard Hats and longshoremen at the White House to thank them. Colson begged the president not to but lost the argument. The resulting photo ops did the president harm.

The White House attempted to calm dissenters by listening to them. The president received a delegation of students from Kent State and another of university presidents. The university group included Nathan Pusey of Harvard and Charles J. Hitch of the University of California–Berkeley, who long ago had been one of Robert McNamara's "whiz kids." But Nixon did not so much listen as probe. Conceding "there is probably no question that the Cambodian action sparked a considerable amount of the current turmoil," the president asked what ought to be the "Federal role," referring to National Guard troops. None of the university officials took up that thread. One countered that "any repressive moves would be bad." Another objected that Nixon's questions about a long-term federal role were surprising, "analogous to discussing future insurance policies while your building was abalze [sic]." A third mused that the president's visit to the Pentagon after his invasion speech had been "unfortunate." Yet another likened Spiro Agnew to Joseph McCarthy—censuring without getting his facts straight. Several expressed fear the universities could not get through the week without more being killed. Pusey of Harvard warned, "no longer are we dealing with a small group of radicals, but rather a broad base of students and faculty who are upset. Even the conservatives are filled with anxiety." All this was ominous. "The situation on campus this week," Pusey declared, "seems new, different, and terribly serious." Henry Kissinger, who sat in, assured the group that they were listening to the students "and certainly have compassion with their anguish."[22] He did not repeat what he had told Nixon a few days earlier on the phone—that "the university presidents are a disgrace."[23]

Dr. Kissinger could hardly be said to be listening. He had not listened to his own NSC staff. One, Lawrence Lynn, left specifically because he considered the White House response to Kent State "hideous."[24] Lynn was appalled; his wife more so. In fact, it was on the day of Kent State that the White House ordered the FBI to wiretap Laird aide General Robert Pursley and senior State Department officials William Sullivan and Marshall Green. No doubt Nixon wanted to know whether and how Laird and Rogers were going to distance themselves from the Cambodia decision. A week later departed NSC staffers Tony Lake and Roger Morris were added to the wiretap list.

On May 6 Kissinger received students and faculty from Stanford and, after hearing them recite part of a resolution from its university senate, replied, "No one has a monopoly on righteousness." He assured the students that the president agreed with them: the war needed to end as soon as possible. They merely differed over the length of that interval, Kissinger felt, a matter that did not warrant "tearing up the country." Henry insisted the invasion had not expanded the war. "Too many professors," Kissinger said, "were more interested in being popular than in being right." As for the administration itself, "one does not always have the time or room to make the decision that is in the long-term best interests of world peace." One of the Stanford professors summarized campus concerns quite accurately: U.S. credibility would fall to zero unless the nation stopped the war, while academics feared too close an association with U.S. defense research, and the students more and more found Vietnam a racist war and an improper enterprise.[25]

Next Kissinger faced a delegation of his Harvard faculty colleagues. This group had lunched periodically with him and appreciated their access. They had supported Nixon on his "silent majority" speech and given Kissinger advice on issues ranging from arms control to Japan and European policy. The group included Francis Bator, a former deputy national security adviser to LBJ; Thomas Schelling, the sounding board for the Madman option during the presidential transition; and Adam Yarmolinsky, a senior official at McNamara's Pentagon. Bator, in particular, had advised talking to Hanoi through a secret emissary, which Nixon had already begun doing, with Kissinger as his envoy. Thirteen associates attended this confab, and their message was unrelenting. Henry was given to understand that his future at Harvard was threatened. That disturbed him profoundly, but he got over it. He never returned to Harvard.

Arguments about Kissinger's future employment aside, there is no doubt the Nixon Shock led to upheaval on America's campuses. The strike call was instantly heeded, and a national coordination center set up by students at Brandeis. Within forty-eight hours more than a hundred colleges had gone on strike. Before it was over, 1,350 colleges and universities would be affected; 536 shut down, and 51 never reopened that school year. Clashes between demonstrators and security forces occurred at more than two dozen campuses, and the National Guard would occupy 21 colleges. Almost 2 million students were affected. Nathan Pusey had been right—at Harvard the Center for International Affairs (now the Kennedy School) was trashed. Fires or bombs damaged ROTC facilities at 30 schools. Polls showed that protests or more serious actions took place at 80 percent of America's institutions of higher education.

Americans carried their message of dissent directly to Mr. Nixon on the weekend of May 9. Four million people protested nationwide, and 130,000 of them marched on Washington. Nixon tried to head off the worst by giving a televised press conference the evening before, spending the entire day at Camp David preparing a conciliatory message. On the spur of the moment he declared that all U.S. troops would be out of Cambodia by June 30. This uncounseled move, made for purely political reasons, imposed an operational constraint on General Abrams's troops. Stoically, Nixon claimed he had not been surprised at the vehemence of reaction to the invasion but insisted his decision had been made for the very reasons Americans protested—to reduce U.S. involvement and shorten the war. Nixon sympathized with the protesters, he said, but "I know that what I have done will accomplish the goals that they want."[26]

Spouting off to aides, Nixon told speechwriter William Safire, "If the crazies try anything, we'll clobber them." Safire remembered this as "the strangest, most impulsive and perhaps most revealing night of Nixon's Presidency."[27]

Trying to leave the White House after the president's performance, Bob Haldeman was hemmed in by troop trucks unloading a battalion of 82nd Airborne Division paratroopers, who waited in the basement of the Old Executive Office Building to back up the Secret Service and Washington police. Sixty buses were positioned bumper to bumper in a double ring to block access to the White House. Dr. Kissinger, whose apartment was picketed by protesters, slept in his West Wing office. Haldeman bedded down in the White House bomb shelter. To get to work, Colson had to be met outside the security cordon and guided into the complex. Young NSC staffer John Lehman had to crawl under the buses. As Kissinger put it, "Washington took on the character of a besieged city."[28]

The president got only a couple hours sleep. Valet Manolo Sanchez heard music from his room at 4:20 AM. Nixon told Sanchez to order up a limousine. Spirited out of the fortress, Nixon had himself driven to the Lincoln Memorial. There he struck up a conversation with students from Syracuse University. The three Secret Service agents who accompanied him were petrified.

The phone awoke Haldeman at about five o'clock. The president was at the Lincoln Memorial, John Ehrlichman gasped. They sent Egil "Bud" Krogh, Ehrlichman's assistant, chasing after him. Krogh found an eerie scene, with Nixon in campaign mode, as if he could wade into this crowd and shake hands. He talked of India, surfing, and football. This went on about an hour. "Unfortunately," Krogh observed, "the students were geared only for the kind of dialogue or rapping which hardly any of us are capable of doing."[29] Syracuse was on strike, its students typical of those protesting in Washington. Searching for common ground, Nixon discussed its football prospects. "I hope it was because he was tired," observed sophomore John Pelletier, "but most of what he was saying was absurd."[30]

Historian Melvin Small thinks this an unfair portrait of the president, and it may be. But it is drawn directly from the accounts of participants on the scene, including a student and a White House official. There has been no editorializing. Dr. Kissinger's own comment on Mr. Nixon at this time is worth citing here: "The President's statements, oscillating between the maudlin and the strident, did not help a volatile situation where everything was capable of misinterpretation."[31]

May 9 dawned bright and sunny, a beautiful spring day. The usual mix of top activists had been in on the planning—Fred Halsted recalled that few of them got much sleep—but the details hardly matter. Dave Dellinger wanted to stage civil disobedience, but the crowd never got the chance. There was no big confrontation, only a steady stream of determined marchers massing on the Ellipse behind the White House. Many were attending their first demonstration, and the number gathered in just a week's time was extraordinary. Both the White House and the South Vietnamese embassy sent out scouts, young people who could blend in with the crowd. The Vietnamese told Ambassador Diem the marchers were determined. He could also hear protesters outside his window. Late in the afternoon police used tear gas when some neared the White House, and Colson remembered hearing the GIs in the basement readying their gear. Late that night a disheveled Nixon walked into Haig's basement office. "We've had a tough day, Al," he intoned. "Things are bad out there. But we've got to stick to our guns."[32] Haig decided Nixon was trying to reassure him. "It seemed to me," Bui Diem wrote later, "that all Nixon's efforts to calm American opinion—withdrawals, Vietnamization, the masterly 'silent majority' speech—had become irrelevant. He had cast aside all his carefully arranged tactics of buying time."[33]

About the time Richard Nixon ordered up a limousine for his late-night journey, I was in New York boarding a bus. I do not know how many buses Columbia sent to the Cambodia march, but there were a lot. I might not have gone on this march but for the president's gibe that American youth were "bums," which offended me and everyone around me. It was he, not we, who had hurled armies across an international border and now epithets at those who opposed him. The Hard Hats' rampage had been on the evening news as we made final preparations.

In Washington the day was warm. I saw marchers who abandoned the rally for the waters of the Reflecting Pool, including some who stripped to the buff to wade in. There were little parties of protesters circulating throughout the downtown. At one point I was up in the Dupont Circle area—near the South Vietnamese embassy, though I did not know it then—and some protesters held placards with Vietnamese domestic themes. I saw no vandalism. What I did see—or, more accurately, feel—was steely determination among the antiwar crowd. But we did nothing in any way comparable to the Hard Hats in Lower Manhattan.

Cambodia was another turning point for average Americans, including me. For months I had wrestled with the question of what, as a responsible citizen, I should be doing about the Vietnam war. Cambodia made it apparent that more than protest had become necessary. The era of teach-ins had passed, at least at Columbia, where most had attained a fair degree of awareness. Instead we had films, readings, individual presentations by experts who spoke at lunchtime or in the evening. The SDS was gone too. Various antiwar groups formed and re-formed, and there were Columbia chapters of larger national organizations, a kaleidoscope of shifting and growing sentiment. I encountered assorted groups and learned the art of "rapping" that Bud Krogh so marveled at. Participatory democracy's main idea seemed to be for everyone to give a more or less lengthy statement that put the issue at hand in the context of their own lives. I understood this was necessary but chafed at endless meetings that produced little.

The opposite course—action without thought—was equally distasteful. I abhorred the Weathermen's "Days of Rage" in Chicago, thinking violence pointless. It reflected frustration, not constructive action, and played into the hands of those who wanted to paint the Movement as out of control. The Weathermen's violence may have exerted greater influence than their 150-odd number would otherwise afford, but their methods were not going to either end the Vietnam war or revolutionize society. On March 6, 1970, just a few weeks before the Cambodia crisis, a town house on West 11th Street in Greenwich Village blew up. It turned out bomb maker Ted Gold, formerly of the Columbia SDS, had made a fatal mistake in assembling some explosive device. The devastated home belonged to the father and stepmother of Weatherwoman Cathy Wilkerson, who survived and disappeared along with Katharine Boudin, but two others died in the blast, including Gold. Wilkerson, who notes that the radical group's leadership "seemed committed to the necessity of creating a new front on home soil," has confirmed that the bombs were intended to hit the officers' club at Fort Dix. Though it struck Wilkerson as "unbelievable," she realized "we were taking the first preparatory steps to going to war with the United States." With the town house explosion the bombing never took place.[34] But the strategy of these radicals shows how tightly woven had become the cycle of protest and repression in America. The incident gave the FBI and the police reason to go after anyone they could characterize as a dissenter. (Long after, a few days after 9/11, I was in a Greenwich Village bodega in search of sugar for my coffee, squatting down low to retrieve it from the shelf. I heard a voice and looked up to see a police officer towering over me. We had a pleasant conversation. Suddenly we were on the same side. I spent a good portion of that day reflecting on the divisions of Vietnam.)

The SDS had splintered. Its socialist progeny, known as the Progressive Labor Party, was active in the Columbia community through something called the

Worker-Student Alliance. Its operation was not overtly violent, making it more palatable than the Weathermen, but this did not stop the FBI from wiretapping the group. Progressive Labor activists were distrusted not only because they were suspected of using the war to recruit for another political agenda but also because they were "outside agitators," the very people authorities liked to blame for all protest. The Movement at Columbia was distinctively a community enterprise.

Others formed something called the December 4 Movement (D4M), named for the day African American activist Fred Hampton had been shot. A leader of the Black Panthers, Hampton had been asleep in his bed when deputies working for the Cook County (Chicago) district attorney raided his home, killing him. In the spring of 1970 a number of Panthers in New York went on trial. A Columbia trustee served on the grand jury that indicted them. The D4M first organized around getting the university to provide bail money for these people. Demonstrations took place on the Panther issue, but Vietnam predominated.

The Columbia atmosphere was not improved when, in late March, the Civilian Review Board announced its findings on New York Police Department (NYPD) conduct during the 1968 strike. The board concluded that senior officials had failed to control the police effectively, that the NYPD had used excessive force, and that police had both failed to warn bystanders and set up medical facilities for the injured. There were almost 200 complaints against the NYPD still pending.

The newspapers spoke of constant combat in South Vietnam. On the day the new president of Columbia, Dr. Andrew W. Cordier, was introduced to the world (and heckled by protesters), the papers reported U.S. battle deaths higher than at any time since the mini-Tet offensive of 1969. Ominously, they also recorded that American officers were in Cambodia, ostensibly for "protocol" purposes. Protests increasingly focused on Indochina. On April 15, 1970, a demonstration called by D4M to support the Panthers led to a nighttime rally. University president Cordier called on New York City police to clear the campus. The NYPD's large, specially trained Tactical Patrol Force (TPF), with a sinister reputation since 1968, came back to Columbia that night, resulting in a police action countered by stone throwing that left broken windows and doors at Butler Library and several other buildings. Students were chased through the campus, and many sought refuge in the student union or the adjoining dorm, Carman Hall.

University officials denounced outside agitators, but D4M was a Columbia group. The following day protesters tried unsuccessfully to shut down Columbia College's Hamilton Hall. These developments were debated fiercely. On my floor of John Jay Hall, students were divided. I tried to focus on my studies and work-study job at the Business School Library. There, the excitement centered on the New York Knicks playing the Los Angeles Lakers for the basketball championship. That was when Cambodia happened.

Columbia erupted immediately. Our strike story is representative of events on many campuses that year. The lopsided vote for a strike left no doubt where the students of Columbia College, Barnard College, and the graduate schools stood on Southeast Asia. Only the Business School students opted out. But in the view of the larger university community, there could be no business as usual as the Nixon administration extended the war into a new country. The Columbia strike began before the Kent State and Jackson State killings and was in full swing by the time of those unfortunate events. Columbia became a strike coordination center for the national effort. The Columbia Daily Spectator *carried reports on both local and national protests.*

Unlike the 1968 strike, students made no effort to take over the administration building, Low Library. We physically picketed Hamilton Hall; Butler Library; the physics building, Pupin Hall; the engineering building, Seeley Mudd; and others. Dr. Cordier threatened, cajoled, and demanded that the buildings be opened. Students kept them shut. I stood on picket lines in front of Hamilton and Butler. There were daily rallies at the Sundial, on College Walk in front of Low, an area known as Low Memorial Plaza. Among the more noteworthy people to address the multitudes from the Sundial was Arthur M. Schlesinger Jr., whose theories on Vietnam as a quagmire sucking in the United States now led him to condemn the Cambodian invasion.

Because the Columbia campus was private property, the TPF could not enter without a warrant or the permission of Columbia authorities. For days there were platoons of TPF beside each entrance gate. They followed us closely and lined the streets when we sortied for marches through Morningside Heights. Our protests were peaceful, though the neighborhood marches involved occasional dustups. After that first episode the NYPD never had cause to enter the campus. Columbia stayed closed through the end of the school year. In many ways the period proved even more academically productive than usual, because the best professors conducted a kind of open university, convening classes for students—plus anyone else who wanted to listen—on the grass or under trees around campus. The university ultimately gave students the option of accepting "pass-fail" grades for the semester.

One night during the strike I was asleep in my room at John Jay when a loud boom broke the silence. Hundreds of students, many in pajamas, spilled out of their dorms to find out what had happened. It was a little after four in the morning of May 15. Someone had planted a bomb in the statue of Alma Mater that stands halfway down the steps from Low Library. Its rear was blown out by the bomb, leaving a foot-wide gash in Alma Mater's back and a wider hole in the seated figure, moving the entire statue off its base by almost half a foot. This was the most violent action of the Columbia strike. A former student happened to be crossing the plaza with his girlfriend as the bomb went off. Standing just a flight of stairs below the statue, the couple were saved because they were on the side away from the blast, which was channeled in the opposite direction by the

folds of Alma Mater's dress. All Jim Wisniewski could think of was a nuclear attack. Wisniewski also believed he and his friend were the only ones in street
clothes, but he was wrong there too. I had gotten dressed, and so had a number
of others.

Students debated this bombing. Campus opinion, which I shared, was that it
was outrageous. Nevertheless, the message to Cordier was quite clear. The question of who planted the Alma Mater bomb was never resolved, and no one was
arrested. I would have guessed the Weathermen. Later there was an intrusion
and, if I remember right, another bombing at the construction site for the building going up for the School of International Affairs.

Along College Walk there were recruiting tables supporting every conceivable
cause, not just D4M and the Progressive Labor Party but also civil rights, social
justice initiatives, a nascent environmentalist movement, groups forming
around university issues, and more. One day I encountered a table for the Columbia Draft Collective. This turned out to be the university's draft counseling
group, with offices in Dodge Hall, the music building. This was something concrete, not rapping and not throwing bombs, and aimed directly at the administration's war capacity. I could do that. Dissent had kept pressure on Mr. Nixon,
but that had not translated into stopping the war. Something more seemed necessary. I had already decided to volunteer in the congressional elections of 1970
in hopes of returning a Congress more strongly committed to ending the war,
but that would be a slow and difficult endeavor at best. The Columbia Draft
Collective offered a new avenue, affecting the sinews of war. If the military could
not fill its ranks, the war would have to stop. I decided to become a draft counselor.

Columbia's draft counseling organization predated these troubles. It did not
result from the 1968 strike either, although it originated about that time. The
counselors first worked out of Earl Hall, the university chaplains' building, but
later moved to Dodge, where the draft specialists were part of Columbia's Career
Placement Office. In the fall of 1968 a notice of the availability of this service
had first been distributed to incoming students during freshman orientation.
The lead counselors, Jeff Green and Jack Lawson, worked closely with the American Friends Service Committee (AFSC), a Quaker group, and with the War
Resisters' League. The Quakers produced manuals on draft regulations and conscientious objection that were indispensable to our work. In conjunction with
the War Resisters' League, the counselors ran a storefront office in Morningside
Heights to reach out to the community, but it was not successful. By the time I
arrived, the storefront was gone. One key service was an effort to train other
counselors through workshops. Hundreds underwent this familiarization
course; former instructors estimated the total at between 200 and 500 freshly
minted draft counselors, who then worked all up and down the East Coast.
Quite a few were women. This was a place where women, though not subject to

the draft themselves, could make a full contribution to opposing it. The counseling was strictly legitimate and could not have been otherwise, since this was a university activity. The office, and especially the storefront, was regularly visited by people who seemed out of character for counselees. We viewed them as undercover members of the NYPD Red Squad or military counterintelligence operatives.

Jeff Green set the tone. Son of a psychologist, Green approached counseling from an interpersonal perspective. Ninety percent of the job was to understand the person and his reasons, 5 percent to know yourself, the rest to know the regulations. I believed in that myself. My routine started by asking the counselee exactly what he feared, advising him that there were many military specialties that did not include combat, and discussing the risks of attempting to avoid the draft. It was important to know there were alternatives, even within the military. As an almost Army brat, I was attuned to that. When counselees were just out of high school or were not college students, it was vital they have a full understanding of the possibilities, so I usually spoke of the educational benefits available after completing military service. These were not so generous as the GI Bill after World War II, but they were significant. (Whereas the GI Bill had paid all expenses for a full college program, a Vietnam veteran's benefit amounted to a partial stipend for up to thirty-six months, depending on length of service— veterans with three years or longer were entitled to the full amount, those with less duty to one month's benefit for each one of service. For a typical Army veteran with six months' training and a yearlong tour in Vietnam, that amounted to eighteen months, or two academic years.) Risks also needed to be understood. Getting caught evading the draft meant potential prison time, and a felony conviction had implications for job seeking, apartment rental or home buying (banks often asked about criminal records in mortgage applications), voting, holding political office, and more.

People looking at conscientious objection had to be told not only that it was difficult to obtain that status but also that a conscientious objector was not escaping anything; rather, he would be enlisting for alternative service for an equal period: minimum-pay jobs, many of them demeaning, chosen for him by Selective Service through the local draft boards. Counselors did not officially advise people to avoid the draft by leaving for Canada, but there were varying views on that. A few gave private advice outside the office when they wanted to speak of it; others did not. I did not.

Despite outreach efforts, the clientele was overwhelmingly white and not from Columbia. We received many referrals or calls from people who had simply heard about us. On an average day we got eight or nine inquiries; a very good day was twelve to fifteen. In comparison, a typical Boston counseling office in 1966–1967 fielded half a dozen or more inquiries a day and was staffed primarily by students from Brandeis and Boston University plus community activists.

Many people simply wanted to know what their draft status meant. We tried to meet personally with anyone who mentioned he was thinking of applying for conscientious objector status.

Our most visible activity was staging a weekly vigil outside the Selective Service induction center on Whitehall Street in Lower Manhattan. These were not mass demonstrations but rather a handful of people facing police and authorities who took a rather dim view of our efforts. We handed out leaflets listing individuals' rights at induction tests and information about our counseling center. The vigils made it clear to prospective draftees that help was available if they wanted it. The Whitehall actions probably accounted for two or three inquiries each week.

Since all American males of a certain age were subject to the draft, most of those we talked to had thought about what they would do if called up. They might be ignorant of the consequences of faking poor health on the physical examination, failing to respond to a draft notice, or fleeing to Canada or elsewhere, but many had some idea in mind. We never sent people to shady doctors or set up any means of evasion. There was only one time during the war when something like that happened, and then it was an enterprise of the entire Columbia community. That was around 1972 when a South African deserter asked university chaplains for sanctuary; he was sheltered for a time at St. Paul's Chapel, and hundreds of students shielded him. The deserter later moved to the City College of New York but was eventually apprehended by police.

At a certain point, before the Cambodia firestorm, the counseling office became a "collective," which meant we no longer received official support other than telephone service. This status somewhat broadened our ability to advise. It was the style of that age. Nick Maravel was our coordinator and had been with the office when the change to a collective occurred. My mentor in the counseling shop (and frequent bridge partner) was a class of 1972 Columbia College student, Gene Nathanson. Both Maravel and Nathanson were dedicated counselors and taught me much. The Dodge Hall office, near the Musicology Department, was a congenial place in spite of our grim volunteer work.

The major change that affected draft counseling had already happened. That was the institution of the draft lottery, embodied in Public Law 91-124, which extended authority for the Selective Service System, and the executive order President Nixon issued simultaneously on November 26, 1969. The new arrangement did not change individuals' classifications, but it radically altered the way men were summoned. There was much confusion for older men with previous deferments. Selective Service now held a lottery in which dates were drawn, and men's birth dates determined the order in which they would be drafted. Each person would be subject to call-up for one year, either with all others of his date of birth or immediately, once his deferment expired. Many questions now hinged on calculating one's relative chances of being drafted if one gave up a deferment right away, versus waiting. Currently deferred men

were a priority category if eligible in a year other than that of their age group—
oldest first. However, U.S. forces in Vietnam were now dwindling at a fairly
steady rate, and combat operations were being curtailed, which translated into
progressively lower draft calls and fewer birth dates being summoned.

A vital aspect was helping people with appeals. For a variety of reasons—
ranging from the amount of paperwork necessary to substantiate a given status,
to the willingness of schools, employers, or other authorities to produce relevant
documents, to the performance of the post office—many had trouble demonstrating their status to local draft boards. The boards themselves were quite arbitrary, sometimes refusing outright to reconsider decisions made due to simple
administrative errors. Appeals to the state level were then necessary. Presidential appeals were also possible, but I do not recall Columbia counselors dealing
with any of these during my time. In any case, until appeals were resolved, the
individual could not be inducted. This at least gave people time to put their affairs in order.

The other service we rendered had to do with helping those who wished to file
for conscientious objector (CO) status. This entailed an elaborate process, not
unlike a college application, which included an essay explaining personal beliefs, plus references and other materials for local boards to consider. Local
boards were notoriously loath to grant this status. There was also the problem of
selective versus universal objection to war. One successful CO from the 1968 period recalled Columbia's insight in advising him to use his foreign domicile to go
through Draft Board No. 100 in Washington, which handled all expatriates and
seemed to have no quota for inductees. Nathanson's recollection is that we
helped a number of men refine their arguments on beliefs. The latitude for
claims also widened after June 1971, when the U.S. Supreme Court ruling in
Muhammad Ali's CO case strengthened legal notification strictures. But because counselees typically got our help and then dealt with the boards themselves, we often did not learn the outcomes. Across the country as a whole,
however, the Pentagon's attitude shifted markedly: it was difficult enough keeping an effective force in the field; the military did not want those already disaffected. Almost half of CO claims (61,000 of 125,000) filed in fiscal year 1971
were granted.

As the war extended into 1972, the U.S. troops in Vietnam were restricted to
base and reduced to a low number. That year, estimates were that 40,000 might
be called, most after June, and that the total would be less than half the 1971
figure. In fact, only men with birth date numbers up to the high fifties were
called. There were more CO claims in 1972 than there were men drafted. At our
Columbia office the intervals between visits or calls became longer and longer.
The office was consolidated with other Columbia placement services in a single
building on campus. Eventually the collective disbanded.

A claim sometimes made about Vietnam is that the draft lottery and the all-
volunteer force emasculated the antiwar movement. There was an aspect of

weakening in the Movement into 1972, but as will be seen later, sufficient en-
ergy remained to generate storms. That argument ignores the degree to which
antiwar energies became enmeshed in the presidential election of that year and
the extent to which the Movement's aims had been incorporated into the na-
tional will. In the meantime, young Americans were still drafted and continued
to go off to war. And the Nixon administration still pursued its vendetta against
the people.

"The Fourth Amendment Did Not Apply to the President"

That the NYPD Red Squad visited Columbia draft counselors was symptomatic of the Nixon administration's approach to the
Movement. The president had not talked idly when he spoke of "creaming"
dissenters. Haldeman noted his boss's towering frustration with the (allegedly) poor intelligence gathered about dissenters. On June 5 the chief of
staff recorded in his diary the "historic" séance where Nixon called his intelligence chiefs into the Oval Office and ordered them to pull together and get
the activists.[35] Hoover of the FBI, Helms of the CIA, General Joseph Carroll
of the DIA, and Admiral Noel Gayler of the NSA all attended. Nixon made it
crystal clear that U.S. security services had failed. They were to meet among
themselves and craft a plan for the president. Nixon's point of contact would
be Tom Huston, a young former naval intelligence officer on Haldeman's
staff. Huston's name would forever be associated with this spy scheme, although he collaborated closely with the FBI's William Sullivan in this attempt at broader government surveillance.

At a series of encounters through the next month, intelligence officials
hammered out a plan, stapled to a report on the state of efforts against dissent. Chaired by Hoover in name but in practice by Sullivan, the group
demonstrated the administration's paranoia, its tunnel vision, and its contempt for due process and constitutional rights.

In a series of stunning assertions, the spooks manifested the faulty appreciation Nixon had accused them of—not because they lacked data but because they lacked the ability to look through anything but a restrictive
anticommunist prism. The Movement's dedication to fashioning a new society, in this construction, became the New Left "pointedly" advertising an objective to "overthrow our system of government by force and violence." This
was going to be achieved, the security services asserted, by student groups
whose activities were "somewhat autonomous and disjointed," with a shifting cast of characters because "the student body itself changes yearly." How
changing leaders who pursued disjointed actions were supposed to overthrow the government was not stated. The SDS continued to be pictured as
the heart of the Movement, even though Sullivan's committee acknowledged
its split. The Weathermen's New York town house explosion naturally featured as a data element, and the extremist faction was credited with at least

1,000 members. Abbie Hoffman's Yippie anarchists were presented as Weathermen supporters, even though the Sullivan committee found they had "no clearly definable ideology."

Further, Americans who had visited Cuba "must be considered as potential recruits for Cuban intelligence activities." Although "there have been no substantial indications that the communist intelligence services have actively fomented domestic unrest," the New Left was held to be open to manipulation. The campuses were a staging area. The underground press here represented the result of the New Left's inability to seize control of the media. The disaffection of Nixon's own civil servants (such as the diplomats who had rallied against Cambodia), the labor unions, and the media was pictured as the "limited success" of "efforts of the New Left aimed at fomenting unrest and subversion." There was a lot more.

The plan aimed to counter this by more vigorous security action. The spooks would take off the gloves supposedly holding them back. Strictures against break-ins, warrantless wiretaps, infiltration and provocation, and mail opening should all be removed. Much of the text on the "operational restraints" remains censored, but in every case, important advantages to ending the legal and constitutional barriers that prevented these intrusive methods were cited.[36]

Under questioning, Huston would tell senators, "It was my opinion at the time that simply the Fourth Amendment did not apply to the president in the exercise of matters relating to the internal security or national security" (similar to the Bush administration's claims regarding its powers in the war on terror). Richard Nixon had a perfect right, in this White House staffer's view, to do whatever he wanted. Huston recounted the threat: "We were sitting in the White House getting reports day in and day out of what was happening in this country in terms of the violence, the numbers of bombings, the assassination attempts, the sniping incidents—40,000 bombings, for example" (in December 1975 the FBI director enumerated 300 arsons and 14 bombings during *all* the years of the New Left COINTELPRO).[37]

Huston's plan would be defeated, ironically, by the FBI itself. J. Edgar Hoover objected to most of the proposed measures because they either conflicted with existing FBI operations or violated jurisdictional agreements among the agencies. More precisely, he wanted no one stepping on the Bureau's turf. Suggestions for illegal measures also towered as obstacles. The president could not be seen to be authorizing such activities and so left the paper untouched, neither ticking off the approval lines nor issuing any written authorization. Haldeman informed Huston *orally* that Nixon had approved and they should proceed. But absent an explicit mandate, Nixon's point man had no writ over the FBI or anyone else. When Huston passed along the orders, Hoover demanded written instructions. In late July Nixon and Mitchell met to decide what to do, and Nixon revoked his approval. Although Mitchell believed in the president's all-encompassing power—his position acquired the lofty title of the "Mitchell Doctrine"—as a political matter, there was no avoiding Nixon's liability were he to sign off on the Huston plan.

Tom Huston would be left in the dust, the White House coordinator of an Interagency Intelligence Committee that pushed paper but had no real role. But scrapping this extralegal spy scheme did not mean these things did not happen; it simply meant that Hoover wanted—and kept—control. In fact, operations against the Movement became more vital than ever because the FBI needed to demonstrate effectiveness or risk having its mission given to others. Athan Theoharis, FBI scholar, also points to another reason for Hoover's opposition: he wanted no part of illegal activity that put the FBI out on a limb simply to benefit other intelligence agencies.[38] In any case, the Bureau kept up its massive effort. On August 28 the FBI created a new "Student Agitation" (STAG) program directly aimed at dissenters.

The FBI became a major source of names of Americans (almost 1,000) whose overseas telephone conversations would be monitored by the NSA under Operations "Shamrock" and "Minaret." Many of those came from the Bureau's own wiretaps. A 1970 tap of a "Left-oriented campus group" yielded over 600 names during its first months, and 1,408 after six months. The tap remained in place for nearly a year. The FBI tapped the Progressive Labor Party's Worker-Student Alliance, as well as student, veteran, and black power groups. In 1970 the FBI installed 102 new taps along with electronic bugs in nineteen homes or offices, down slightly from 1969, but still a considerable increase over the number of wiretaps in Lyndon Johnson's last year.

Naturally, files were opened on all these people. In late 1970 the FBI created files on 2,500 alleged members of the SDS, 4,000 on other New Left individuals, and an equal number on African Americans. According to one account, almost half were people not associated with *any* group. A post-Vietnam investigation by the General Accounting Office sampled 797 FBI files and discovered that just 24 contained information derogatory enough to be referred to prosecutors; a follow-up sample of several hundred more files showed the same pattern. According to FBI observer Frank Donner, "90 percent of the Vietnam/civil rights era caseload represented investigations of individuals based largely on the fiction invoked to justify investigations of Communist Party members: No one could join (whatever that meant) a New Left group without accepting the necessity and desirability of violence as a tactic."[39] Apparently, the FBI had never heard of Mahatma Gandhi or his principles of nonviolence, which were at the very heart of the Movement's tactics of civil disobedience.

Interference with Americans' lives went beyond recording their conversations. The Bureau deliberately contacted people's employers, casting a pall on their service, and counted its success in getting people fired as an achievement—in the name of "counterintelligence." There were eighty-four of these persecutions, 3 percent of the overall COINTELPRO effort. Simultaneous with the invasion of Cambodia, the Pittsburgh FBI field office tried to get an academic in that city "removed" from his post, informing his college that the man had given up his draft card and twice been arrested (but never convicted). After its initial failure, the Bureau used an intermediary to try to get a foundation that supported the college to make an issue of the professor's "qualifications." Once the man had been convicted (with a suspended sentence) in one of the 1970 demonstrations, the Bureau tried again a year later. Similarly, FBI headquarters ordered its Minneapolis field office to inform city and state authorities of the alleged criminal infractions of another target. In St. Louis the Bureau's field office took credit for breaking up the marriage of two black activists by concocting phony evidence of the husband's philandering. In Atlanta the FBI planned to smear a Socialist Workers' Party candidate in the 1970 elections by revealing that she lived out of wedlock with a companion. The conspiracy collapsed when the woman announced at a political rally that she did not oppose premarital sex. Another FBI ploy, designed to disrupt relations between the Weathermen and Black Panthers, was to make incendiary phone calls to members of each organization, pretending to be from the other. There are many similar examples. That October FBI headquarters ordered fourteen field offices to carry out simultaneous "interviews" of persons thought to be connected to the group Revolutionary Union in an effort to chill their dissident efforts.

Other FBI actions were disruptive at a higher level. The Bureau's New York office discovered that the Episcopal Church intended to donate money to the SNCC for its project to create a "liberation school" in the ghetto, where government funding for education was sparse and helped keep the poor poor. Between June and August 1970 the FBI fabricated a series of letters, "leaked" to the church, purporting to show that the SNCC embezzled cash by soliciting false invoices for school supplies. The New York field office claimed credit for canceling the church's donation. By September the Philadelphia field office had opened up files on student activities at twenty-two local campuses, including community colleges. That October the Detroit FBI unit schemed to cripple New Left and Black Panther publishers with glorified stink bombs, asking headquarters if the FBI lab could synthesize a quart of solution (to be spread by aerosol sprayer) to duplicate the most foul-smelling feces possible. Washington nixed the idea, but less than two years later the bathroom at the national office of Vietnam Veterans Against the War would be impregnated with an undetectable chemical that caused severe itching. In December 1970 the Mobile field office targeted two local professors solely because they were influential in the publication of a student newspaper considered unfriendly to the administration.[40]

Efforts to counter opposition were national and were not confined to student protesters per se. By no means were all the schemes dreamed up by the FBI, although the censorship of declassified records and the nature of what was typically recorded in memoranda make it impossible to trace authorship in most cases. On July 25 Nixon told Haldeman to make sure Republican candidates in the upcoming congressional elections tied their opponents to hippies and youth, not just the Democrats. The president also talked of the need to "destroy" NBC news anchor Chet Huntley because that would have an effect on all other commentators. Two days later Haldeman assistant Larry Higby asked the FBI for data on contacts between members of Congress, their staffs, and certain foreign officials. On July 29 the FBI sent the White House a paper listing such contacts since January 1967. The Bureau added digests of embassy wiretaps for good measure. Tom Huston also tried to get the IRS to harass opponents by means of tax audits. In fact, it was during this period that the IRS created its first and only "intelligence" unit. Richard Nixon's notorious "enemies list," like his so-called national security wiretaps, were about chilling the opposition and hardball politics.

Meanwhile, the old FBI "Rabble Rouser Index" would be abandoned in 1971, partly due to political sensitivity, but also because it had become redundant—the Bureau now had a Priority Apprehension Program. Perhaps the height of folly came when the Bureau's Domestic Intelligence Division hit the original environmentalist action, Earth Day, with mail openings and surveillance teams. Senator Gaylord Nelson introduced a bill creating Earth Day in 1970, and it was recognized by the United Nations the next year. There were myriad observances throughout the land, including Senator Edmund S. Muskie as keynote speaker at Harvard and Nelson at Berkeley. Earth Day 1971 became an FBI target. Furious senators released Bureau records when they realized what had happened. Robert Mardian of the Bureau's newly reorganized Internal Security Division offered the lame excuse that the surveillance had been laid on because of an (alleged) assassination plot against Senator Muskie.

The FBI created a special unit known as Squad 47 specifically for break-ins in New York, initially aimed at the Weathermen. Though the Bureau claimed it had terminated break-ins in 1966, except for some foreign embassies (and stuck to that story when investigated by the Church Committee in the mid-1970s), a grand jury in 1977 returned an indictment for mail opening and wiretaps against the former head of Squad 47, special agent John J. Kearney. In the course of legal actions in that case, FBI director Patrick Kelley was obliged to admit the break-ins had continued. He claimed he had been misled. That indictment was substituted by another one a year later that directly implicated former FBI director L. Patrick Gray, Hoover's deputy and successor; W. Mark Felt, an FBI assistant director better known as the secret Watergate source "Deep Throat"; and senior official Edward Miller. Felt and Miller admitted the break-ins in grand jury testimony. Felt testified these had been authorized by the Nixon administration. A subordinate, special agent M. Wesley Swearingen, told federal prosecutors he had personally participated in more break-ins in Chicago than the FBI had admitted to the Church Committee as its all-time total for the nation as a whole. Two dozen special agents worked full time on break-ins in that city. Other black-bag jobs took place in Washington, D.C.; Los Angeles; Portland, Oregon; Newark; and San Francisco.

The administration's repressive campaign began to unravel—but only to a degree—in 1971, when a series of events combined to poke holes in either its secrecy or its legal rationale. Hints of spying by the military erupted into Senate hearings after the appearance of an article by former military intelligence officer Christopher Pyle that January. In California a court case found the Mitchell Doctrine of expansive presidential power unconstitutional. And at Media, Pennsylvania, antiwar activists took a page from the FBI playbook and broke into a Bureau office, hauling off a thousand pages of documents. Terrified that COINTELPRO would be blown, the FBI ended the program, although it continued to surveil activists.

Meanwhile, another FBI target over the years had been the American Friends Service Committee. Like the AFSC itself, draft evaders were perennial targets not only for FBI surveillance but also for apprehension. And the CIA seems to have taken part through its Project Merrimac; certain break-ins at the offices of the United Servicemen's Fund have been attributed to the agency. GI resistance remained on the radar screen. The Nixon administration needed its military to fight the war, though, as withdrawals proceeded, more and more it needed the South Vietnamese.

A New ARVN?

Many, but not all, Americans drafted were headed to Vietnam, though the need for them diminished. U.S. troops were supposed to be withdrawing in tandem with improvements in the South Vietnamese armed forces. But this rationale progressively attenuated as the American expeditionary force shrank, while the ARVN stayed about the same. It has become an article of faith among the neo-orthodox that Vietnamization produced a supple, effective Republic of Vietnam Armed Forces (RVNAF). That notion is identical to the assertions that filled a mountain of press releases at the time, not to mention official testimony, progress reports, statements at press conferences, South Vietnamese publications, and a plethora of materials flowing from U.S. sources in Saigon. But like everything else about the Vietnam war, that claim requires examination.

Figures packed the official releases, and from a statistical standpoint, much progress could be reported. An example from early in this period was *The ARVN*, a 1969 special issue of the *Vietnam Bulletin*, the slick magazine published by the South Vietnamese embassy in Washington. Reporting on the events of 1968, the magazine noted that the ARVN had inflicted more casualties on the enemy at Tet than had the Americans. It followed up: "The ARVN went over to the offensive at mid-year and has not lost the initiative since."[41] This was certainly correct from the standpoint of battalion-size operations, as indicated by the Pentagon's own statistics: in May 1968 ARVN operations had increased by a third, to more than 600, and never fell below that level. Large-scale South Vietnamese ops in 1969 peaked at 1,070 in July and averaged 950 a month. But even so, the ARVN did not meet the embassy's claims: a daily level of 40 to 60 efforts would amount to 14,600 to 21,900 battalion-size operations a year. The ARVN actually conducted 11,400 such operations in 1969, its most active year. Subsequently, operations declined to about 9,000 and stayed there. However, numbers of large-scale operations did not determine which side held the strategic initiative. The adversary still chose when to engage and when to avoid contact, even during the massive invasion of Cambodia when, pointedly, the North Vietnamese struck back with attacks in the Central Highlands.

The ARVN operations coincided with a general mobilization ordered by President Nguyen Van Thieu. Eligibility for Saigon's draft was expanded to males aged eighteen to thirty-eight (in the United States, those aged nineteen to twenty-six were eligible); seventeen-year-old youths and men from thirty-nine to forty-three were called up for the militia. Under the law, all males between the ages of sixteen and fifty were subject to some kind of service. Saigon intended to increase the RVNAF by 268,000 men by the end of the year and in fact obtained 220,000 fresh recruits before the summer was out. Of those, 161,000 volunteered, either enthused by Tet or attracted by the ability to choose their branch of service. But some 139,670 South Vietnamese soldiers deserted during 1968, and ARVN casualties numbered 27,915 dead, 70,696 wounded, and 2,460 missing. That amounted to almost 241,000 men and virtually wiped out the force increase anticipated with general mobilization. In mid-1968 there were 358,000 regulars in ten ARVN infantry divisions, one airborne division, and one of Marines. By year's end, the number of inductees had risen to 370,000.

About 100,000 South Vietnamese men reached draft age each year. Avoiding conscription became endemic, creating a whole social stratum of "cowboys," youths who buzzed around the cities on their motorbikes, many subsisting off the black market. Population flight from the villages increased the problem. Volunteerism dissipated after 1968, and South Vietnamese men had to be virtually vacuumed up to fill the ranks. A U.S. State Department report in May 1971 admitted that more than half of males aged fifteen to forty-nine in Saigon-controlled territory were in uniform.[42] That proportion was higher than in the United States at the height of World War II. The South Vietnamese, like the Hmong in the CIA's secret army in Laos, were resorting to child soldiers. As early as 1969, MACV projected that Saigon would be hard-pressed to maintain its force level, and so it proved. In a post-war monograph General Cao Van Vien conceded that even with an extra million in population, Saigon would have had trouble keeping up its force levels.[43]

All this led to zealous guarding of the chicken coop. For example, in 1969 the army was ordered to hand over 23,000 men to the National Police. Only 1,000 were provided. Conflicting requirements sharpened as the RVNAF grew, the demands of various elements increasing while the pool of recruits stayed the same. The ARVN, the Regional Forces (RF), and the Popular Forces (PF) relied on the same recruits, and competition among them worsened. Americans evaluated the RF-PF as more effective than the ARVN, but the latter took precedence. Conditions also impacted critical specialized functions such as intelligence. Draft calls threatened to denude U.S. intelligence of all its South Vietnamese civilian translators, for example, forcing leaders into various subterfuges to preserve capabilities. Demands for bodies in combat units also pressured the RVNAF's own intelligence people.

Desertion continued to be a problem, though also a poorly understood phenomenon. Peak rates coincided with the seasons for planting and harvesting rice, indicating that soldiers were going home to help on the farm. The lowest desertion rates (other than those for the Vietnamese air force and navy) were consistently posted by the RF-PF, who lived at home. These facts suggest that a more liberal leave policy might have substantially lowered desertion. Instead, the Joint General Staff adopted an antidesertion program in 1969. Service was lost altogether when deserters were imprisoned. That year there were over 123,000 deserters.[44] Many soldiers deserted units located far from home and enlisted in ones nearer to their families. About 150,500 soldiers deserted in 1970, but almost 24,000 of them returned one way or another. The RVNAF actually experienced its lowest desertion rate in 1966. Desertion fluctuated during the years of Vietnamization but was always far higher, especially in 1971.

Various measures were adopted to train the recruits who did enter the RVNAF.[45] The army had relied on a single basic training camp at Quang Trung, northwest of Saigon. With general mobilization, camps were added for each corps area, plus similar ones for RF and PF. After basic came advanced training for the various combat arms or specialties. Ones that required use of American technical manuals or extensive interaction with the Americans necessitated language skills, so English language courses began in Saigon. The ARVN's combat branches, divisions, and corps had their own tactical training areas to put battalions and other units through periodic refresher courses. The best ARVN units, such as the 1st Division, constantly rotated their maneuver units through this training. During the Korean war the United States had utilized a buddy system to help train South Koreans, but nothing like that was attempted in Vietnam. The Americans did, however, team up units to share know-how. In the spring of 1969, for example, MACV sent its 199th Light Infantry Brigade into the area of operations of the ARVN 18th Infantry Division, led by Brigadier General Lam Quang Tho, younger brother of Lam Quang Thi. The 18th, long considered among the worst South Vietnamese units (at the Midway conference, Nixon made special examples of the 5th and 18th Divisions), would improve markedly.

The ARVN force structure in January 1969 was close to what existed three years later.[46] Not until 1971 did the South Vietnamese add a division-size unit, and this would be done by taking its nucleus from another ARVN formation. Indeed, the Americans, whose major task was to assist RVNAF expansion, and who constantly monitored progress, noted at a 1969 MACV staff conference that the ARVN had reached its unit formation goals except for a few engineer battalions. In 1968–1969 the regulars formed seven rifle battalions, enabling the ARVN to add two regiments to its best unit, the 1st Infantry Division. Vietnamization added units at the margin.

The Airborne and Marine units were elite in part because they could fight anywhere in South Vietnam. With the exception of some ARVN Ranger units, other forces were all territorial. Families lived with or close to the soldiers. The divisions could not move to where the enemy threatened unless it was within their own region. Saigon lacked freely deployable forces. In 1971, when President Thieu rejected pulling the ARVN's 2nd Infantry Division out of its sector to reinforce the Laotian invasion, he was recognizing this fact. The next year, during the Easter offensive, the ARVN managed to send the 21st Division from the Mekong delta to aid defenders in a different military region, and the difficulty of that maneuver confirmed the basic problem. After the war General Vien theorized that creating large-scale units (regiments) from the RF would have freed the ARVN's divisions from their territorial defense responsibilities. But they still would not have been truly mobile without resolving the social issues.

By far the biggest increase in ARVN infantry forces during the period of Vietnamization came when the number of Ranger battalions more than doubled, starting in 1970, to twenty-five units. But this was not really a South Vietnamese force increase. Rather, the RVNAF took over the CIDGs the Americans had created and transformed them into Rangers. These units were composed of montagnards, who had been treated shabbily by the Saigon government for decades. In fact, montagnard groups (such as FULRO) that were opposed to the South Vietnamese government fled to Cambodia and became guerrillas just as the ARVN started up these Ranger battalions. This shows Saigon's error in not resolving the montagnard political imbroglio much sooner. Instead, in late 1971, Saigon's II Corps commander began uprooting montagnards from their villages and resettling them in camps.

The largest growth in the ARVN came in the specialized branches. The years of Vietnamization witnessed the expansion of artillery and armored forces. Artillery improvements were the most extensive.[47] Except for the Airborne and Marines, the South Vietnamese standard had been two artillery battalions per division (the U.S. Army fielded closer to five). The elite divisions, because they tended to be dispersed in operating areas, had just one artillery battalion each. By mid-1969 both elite divisions had been brought to the two-battalion standard, while half the ARVN infantry divisions fielded three. By 1972 all infantry formations had three light plus a medium battalion, and the elite divisions met the three-battalion standard. At that point the South Vietnamese army had 1,202 cannon.

Independent artillery units used by the military regions and the high command and to support local forces in the districts would also be greatly increased—by 150 percent in 105mm battalions and 100 percent in 155mm battalions in mid-1969. That added up to a lot of new units: ten 105mm and six 155mm formations were added to the ARVN in just one year. That same year there were numerous revisions in the plans for RVNAF modernization. For artillery this amounted to adding another pair of 105mm battalions plus one equipped with 155mm howitzers. Two battalions of 175mm guns were approved but not actually formed until 1971. The heavy gun force would later be doubled. The United States delivered 790 new 105mm howitzers to South Vietnam during 1969, meeting the requirements of the revised plans, but it faltered badly on 155mm weapons, managing to supply just 294 of the 701 field pieces. But having a large number of guns did not equate to having an effective artillery force. At the time of the Cambodian invasion, for example, only half the battery positions of the ARVN's III Corps had been surveyed, and 12 percent of its guns had never been calibrated, both of which significantly reduced the accuracy of artillery fire.

The need to support pacification and the local forces drained capabilities. A dedicated effort in the Central Highlands in 1969 to train CIDG personnel to man gun sections at the border camps and coordinate with larger artillery units showed the way. Eventually, there came a decision to form 176 artillery platoons of two guns each to be deployed within South Vietnam's districts and dedicated to local defense. The first hundred were created during 1970, though only half had been emplaced by the end of that year.

Training ARVN artillerymen and servicing the guns led to huge headaches. Expansion spread the skilled technicians thin. The South Vietnamese artillery school at Duc My, not far from Nha Trang, had plans to train 1,715 new personnel in 1970 but would actually enroll 2,327. The press of service demands diluted the training. American instructional programs imported from Fort Sill were pared back to essential elements. Much technical education would have to be done by American mobile teams roaming the ARVN's bases and by temporarily assigning Vietnamese artillerymen to U.S. units to gain specialized knowledge.

The South Vietnamese Armor Command and school were located at Thu Duc, north of Saigon. The corps began with armored cavalry units formed in the 1950s, equipped with a mix of light tanks and armored personnel carriers.[48] A squadron was attached to each ARVN corps, and one kept in the Saigon region. In 1962 the ARVN added pure tank squadrons for the first time, and by 1966 it had six armored cavalry squadrons. Elements of these units were later incorporated into the ARVN's infantry divisions, and five additional squadrons were activated in 1968–1969. Vietnamization added another five squadrons. It was in 1969 that reorganization created two actual armored brigades, grouping tank squadrons with the armored cavalry. One was assigned to the critical I Corps area, the other to the Mekong delta.

The Vietnamese air force and navy were greatly strengthened. The air force transitioned to an almost all-jet-fighter-bomber force, with a considerably augmented complement of helicopters and gunships. The South Vietnamese reached a force of about 1.1 million in 1969 (claims that the RVNAF reached this number earlier are not accurate). All these troops required leaders, and problems there were intractable. In 1969 half of all ARVN battalions were commanded by men ranked up to two grades below the stipulated level. This was *after* a sustained effort to promote qualified personnel, under which 2,653 officers reached field grade in the ten months ending in October 1969. Saigon's administrative system, which used officers to control most provinces, villages, and districts, was a major culprit here. At this time almost 40 percent of RVNAF officers were not even assigned to the military. Losses in battle only compounded the problem, as did the relief of officers for corruption. And there was no pool of reserves. With general mobilization, slightly more than 1,000 officers were recalled to duty, and that exhausted the supply.

The military academy at Dalat had 280 spaces for its entering class in 1966. That simply would not do. A new military academy was built and introduced a four-year program virtually identical to West Point's, alongside a two-year course for college-educated South Vietnamese. The reserve school at Thu Duc also ran flat out, training more than 11,000 officers in both 1968 and 1969—more than 90 percent of the ARVN's total. Dalat in 1969 graduated fewer than a hundred young officers. Efforts to encourage battlefield promotions yielded slightly over a thousand new leaders. By dint of extraordinary measures, the RVNAF met its officer goals in 1971. Yet in May 1971 a third of ARVN battalions were still commanded by captains, and almost two-thirds of infantry unit commanders had led their battalions for less than a year. During 1972 the ARVN actually reduced its infantry by fifteen battalions to economize on officer cadres and regroup troops into stronger units.

Corruption affected the RVNAF at every level—from the "ghost soldiers" who existed only on ARVN unit rosters and drew pay that disappeared into someone's pocket, to the gasoline pilfered from pipelines, to the antics of provincial and district officials and their effects on pacification. Some men paid commanders part or all of their pay to be somewhere else, showing up only when an inspection was held. Contributing to such attitudes was the fact that soldiers could hardly get out of the army. Disabling wounds were the only way. An anonymous ARVN captain, talking to reporter Gloria Emerson in 1970, recounted how he had already been wounded three times but needed to lose an arm or a leg to leave the army. He actually *wanted* to lose a limb. The officer was a regular who had graduated from Dalat.[49] American observers in 1971 speculated on the possibility that President Thieu might introduce a service limit of eight or ten years. He did not.

The high command presented problems too. In July 1970 Thieu issued a decree reorganizing the Joint General Staff, but he preserved the cumbersome system under which the JGS functioned simultaneously as the ARVN's authority, except that the actual chain of command ran from president to corps commanders. General Cao Van Vien asked to resign and go back to the paratroops. Thieu, who had targeted Vien a year earlier with gossip that he was about to be fired, refused his resignation, likely because he considered Vien a bulwark against any coup attempt. But Thieu had plenty on his own plate, so the regional commanders were left to function under general directives.

The JGS chief of staff advised Thieu on strategy, planned operations, sent out intelligence warnings, managed the force expansion, and administered the ARVN, but he could not issue an order. This became especially pernicious during intense fighting such as the Cambodian and Laotian invasions or the Easter offensive. Indeed, in his treatise on South Vietnamese military leadership, Vien notes that in the latter crisis the commander of a key front (I Corps) neglected to inform Saigon of the orders he had given. Why should he, if JGS would only complain? And Thieu himself bypassed his corps commanders to instruct their subordinates. The very last review by the American defense attaché in Saigon, rendered for the period January–April 1975, reported that events "amplified the lack of control by the JGS. There was a complete lack of knowledge at the working staff level of the JGS as to what the situation was at any given time."[50] The high command problem was never resolved.

Just as there were officers who had never served outside the Joint General Staff, there were division commanders who had no advanced training. Many of a certain age had been trained at French or U.S. schools, but it was not until 1969 that the ARVN itself had a Command and Staff College or a Political Warfare School (both of which were established at Dalat) and a National Defense College in Saigon, the most advanced course of all. Five classes took the defense college's yearlong course between 1968 and 1973. Of these 111 colonels and generals, fewer than a dozen showed up in key ARVN commands—divisions, corps staffs, combat arms branches, and the like. The problem of officer utilization, like that of leadership, persisted.

For all the statistics, the proof of Vietnamization lay in the fighting. American advisers—indeed, General Abrams himself—always put the best face on this, but the truth is that South Vietnamese performance remained uneven throughout. Every year brought new evidence. Abrams told Mel Laird in early 1970 that the ARVN's big battles the previous year had been in the Central Highlands. He cited four, all fights for Special Forces camps: Ben Het, Dak To, Bu Prang, and Duc Lap. Joint Chiefs of Staff historians agree that Ben Het, not Hamburger Hill or any of the U.S. battles, was the key engagement of 1969. Ben Het withstood siege for weeks without the ARVN sector commander (at Dak To) breaking up the enemy—so long, in fact, that the People's Army reached past the post to strike at Dak To itself. Hanoi failed to capture either place, despite using tanks at Ben Het, but the defenders were CIDG strikers, Special Forces, Nungs, and Americans. It took the ARVN four months to disengage the camp. Secret U.S. performance reports show desertions for the main unit in this sector, the ARVN 42nd Infantry, running 20 percent higher than for the ARVN as a whole. This battle was won by airpower, not ground troops, with the Americans furnishing all the Arc Lights and nine-tenths of the tactical air support. Bu Prang came under siege during late 1969, and here too the battle spilled over, to Duc Lap. The campaign featured the loss of several nearby firebases, with MACV putting out that it had deliberately withheld help, other than airpower, to "test" Vietnamization. Air saved the day again. When rescuers of the 23rd ARVN Division finally reached Duc Lap, the relief force commander accused the leader of the defending regiment of cowardice and expelled him and his troops. The ARVN largely failed in the Highlands campaign.

The Cambodian invasion formed the crown jewel for 1970 and would be widely portrayed as proving Vietnamization had worked. Without question, the ARVN did well. The South Vietnamese captured many weapons, inflicted losses, and sustained them. But several points must be made. The ARVN benefited from unprecedented amounts of U.S. artillery and air support. As noted, its own artillery was hampered by technical shortcomings. Meanwhile, American forces took the lead in every major assault save that into the Parrott's Beak. In places where the two allies worked in tandem, notably the Fishhook, U.S. troops tabulated the bulk of results. Indeed, in the second-phase exploitation there, ARVN losses tallied less than one-eleventh of American, and weapons captured totaled one-tenth of U.S. figures. The best ARVN results came from IV Corps attacks, where (with the exception of a sector north of the Mekong) Hanoi and the Liberation Front had much less strength.

In addition, there were the forgotten battles of 1970, again in the Central Highlands, where the Special Forces camps of Dak Seang and Dak Pek were besieged or assaulted. In the first campaign the ARVN displayed exactly the same weaknesses in risk taking it had shown the previous year. At Dak Pek the enemy overran more than half the camp, and U.S.-led Mike Force troops restored the situation before any South Vietnamese showed up. These battles again manifested leadership weaknesses. The campaign that would put all these problems in stark relief was about to begin. This time the South Vietnamese would take the lead. They invaded Laos.

Lyndon Johnson bites the bullet. At the White House on March 27, 1968, President Johnson listens raptly as Joint Chiefs of Staff chairman Earle Wheeler makes a point. Next to Wheeler is General Creighton V. Abrams, deputy commander of MACV, who was shortly to succeed Westmoreland in the top position. LBJ wrestled with the perennial questions of what to do about Vietnam. Within days he ordered a partial bombing halt over North Vietnam, began fresh diplomatic initiatives, and renounced any intention to seek reelection in 1968 (Johnson Library).

Hamilton Hall at Columbia University. Student protests at Columbia in April 1968 led to a strike that closed the university for the remainder of the school year. Police tactics in breaking the demonstrations further radicalized youth and contributed to antiwar opposition throughout the country, as well as in France, Germany, and Great Britain. Countervailing government surveillance then sharpened a vicious cycle that added to protests (author's collection).

A second round of Tet fighting took place in May and June 1968; the Liberation Front and Hanoi suffered their most serious losses yet. The most serious threat to Saigon actually took place here. South Vietnamese troops and U.S. battalions fought house-to-house to eject the enemy, with many districts in Cholon heavily affected. Here a South Vietnamese soldier, described as a twelve-year-old boy "adopted" by the ARVN Airborne, stands among ruins near Tan Son Nhut. Struggling to fill its ranks, the army would enlist younger and younger South Vietnamese (U.S. Army).

The French National Cemetery near Tan Son Nhut (its radomes visible in the distance) became the scene of a day-long pitched battle in May 1968. In it the slum settlement in the foreground would largely be destroyed. In the aftermath, disabled ARVN veterans desperate for housing would move into this area and become squatters. The Saigon government's treatment of its veterans would become a political issue (U.S. Army).

Lyndon Johnson's real attitude toward the 1968 elections remains obscure to this day. He may have had a private plan to run after all or he may have secretly favored Richard Nixon over his own party's candidate, Hubert Humphrey; both possibilities are supported by scattered evidence. Particularly suggestive is Johnson's display of charm toward candidate Nixon during this August 10, 1968, visit to the LBJ Ranch. Nixon is clearly highly amused with Johnson's repartee. Along the far side of the table the CIA's Richard Helms sits between Spiro T. Agnew and Nixon campaign official Jeb Magruder. In the foreground (third and fourth from the left) are John Ehrlichman and H. R. Haldeman. President Johnson is at the right, Lady Bird Johnson at the far end of the table (Johnson Library).

President Richard Nixon's initial National Security Council meeting on January 21, 1969, rehearsed arguments often heard on his watch. Nixon told the group he did not want any "coercive action with respect to the South Vietnamese" and that "he would rather take the heat now" to achieve an outcome he considered acceptable. Henry Kissinger sits at the left, flanked by General Andrew Goodpaster, David Kennedy, and Spiro Agnew. Richard Helms is at the end of the Cabinet table; next to him is Elliott Richardson. The president is at center, right, between William P. Rogers and Melvin Laird. General Wheeler is at the far right (Nixon Library).

Tet, 1969, brought another North Vietnamese offensive "high point." Here, near Bien Hoa on February 26, troops of the ARVN 5th Cavalry Squadron move toward enemy positions as the "Freedom Bird," the airliner that daily took GIs home and brought fresh personnel to South Vietnam, lines up on its final approach (U.S. Army).

The Cambodia invasion and Kent State brought another massive March on Washington on May 9, 1970. Officials' crowd estimates of 75,000 to 100,000 seemed far smaller than what one could actually see on the ground (author's collection).

Cadets march to class at South Vietnam's military academy in Dalat in December 1971. The Army of the Republic of Vietnam remained chronically short of officers. Expansion of the corps of cadets at Dalat represented only a drop in the bucket (U.S. Army).

Grass-roots organizing, the nickel-and-dime work of a host of activists throughout the nation, fueled the antiwar opposition. Here, sometime in 1971, Vietnam Veterans Against the War members Joe Bangert (right) and Clarence Fitch (conversing with an older woman beyond the table) reach out to the public at New York's Rockefeller Center (Bernard Edelman).

The strongpoint line below the Demilitarized Zone became a key target of Hanoi's 1972 Easter Offensive. This strongpoint, known as C-2, had been strengthened by U.S. engineers the previous summer. The improved defenses did not succeed in preventing heavy damage from North Vietnamese artillery. South Vietnamese troops withdrew from C-2 on April 2, among other things abandoning a sensitive intelligence bunker that provided read-outs from electronic sensors emplaced throughout the sector (U.S. Army).

The idea that the antiwar movement consisted just of college students is a misconception. These pickets from the Women's International League for Peace and Freedom in Miami during the Republican political convention in 1972 include not a single young person (Bernard Edelman).

South Vietnamese M-48A3 tanks of the ARVN 1st Armored Brigade resting and resupplying near the Dong Ha bridge in mid-April 1972. The brigade would nearly be destroyed in the battle for Dong Ha (U.S. Army).

North Vietnamese tank no. 843, a T-54 type famous for being the tank that broke through the gate at the Presidential Palace in the final battle for Saigon, is preserved today at the People's Army Museum in Hanoi (author's collection).

Historians John Prados (right) and Timothy Naftali (left) with former secretary of defense Melvin R. Laird in December 2006 on the occasion of the recording of Laird's official video history for the Nixon Library (Frank Kavanaugh).

Historian John Prados with former defense minister General Vo Nguyen Giap in Hanoi in June 1997 on the occasion of the "Missed Opportunities" conference between delegations comprising former officials and historians of both the United States and Vietnam (Monica Church).

11   Sound Forth the Trumpet (1971)

It was against a backdrop of stalled peace talks that South Vietnamese troops tested their mettle against Hanoi's. By 1970 the channels for negotiation had multiplied, with Henry Kissinger conducting secret meetings behind the public talks. One of those sessions had preceded the Cambodian invasion by weeks. The United States had a negotiating position, one closely matching Saigon's demand for an enemy surrender. A measure of the Nixon Shock's marginal impact on the war came in the talks. Rather than becoming more malleable after the offensive, the North Vietnamese hardened their stand. Having previously expressed a willingness to consider prisoner exchanges independently of overall progress, Hanoi now tied the issue to a general settlement. In the fall of 1970 the Provisional Revolutionary Government, the stand-in for the NLF, further complicated the talks when chief delegate Madame Nguyen Thi Binh produced negotiating points that made even more stringent demands for a rapid U.S. withdrawal.

It was Nixon who blinked first. Failing to achieve progress after another round of the secret talks, the Americans introduced a fresh proposal. That fall Washington settled on an offer of a cease-fire in place plus a defined timetable for withdrawal. Both were anathema to Nguyen Van Thieu. A withdrawal schedule might result in *all* American forces leaving South Vietnam, precluding the residual force Thieu hoped for. At least Hanoi would expect that. A cease-fire in place could mean abandoning Saigon's flat demand that Hanoi's troops abandon the South, Cambodia, and Laos. Thieu certainly interpreted it that way, and only American fast talk induced him to acquiesce, convincing him that the United States could fudge on residual forces and would continue to press for mutual withdrawal. Thieu succeeded in getting Nixon to delay a few weeks, but Kissinger tabled the proposal, initially framed as part of a mutual withdrawal. Nixon put the cease-fire formula in an October 1970 speech, offering to solve the political equation by holding elections in South Vietnam. Hanoi rejected the proposals. Mutual withdrawal was not acceptable to the North Vietnamese. But the standstill cease-fire stayed on the table.[1]

Anxious to encourage movement in the front channel at Paris, Washington induced Hanoi to agree to "private" discussions between U.S. delegation chief David Bruce and North Vietnamese representative Xuan Thuy. Wash-

ington also encouraged Saigon, which had offered almost no concrete proposals, to put forward the idea of a Vietnamese prisoner exchange. Since recovering American prisoners remained a key U.S. goal, this had the potential
to open the way toward a central objective. But Washington's interest lay
more in buying time than making progress. Once Thieu agreed in principle,
the South Vietnamese dragged their feet. Nixon officials let them do so.
Saigon's eventual proposal, delayed many months, would be cosmetic.

Hanoi also missed an opportunity in the negotiations, specifically with regard to prisoners. When the Nixon administration retreated to justifying the
war almost wholly on the basis of recovering American POWs, the DRV
could have called Washington's bluff simply by releasing them, all at once, no
conditions. That would have hopelessly bollixed up the American rationale
for war, leaving Nixon no practical reason to continue fighting. Doing so
would have led to immediate political upheaval in the United States. But,
cautious to a fault, Hanoi considered the POWs a kind of insurance instead,
an earnest of U.S. behavior in the negotiations. This is also a commentary on
the relative status of the DRV foreign ministry and its military: the latter
consistently held the upper hand in policy.

Military operations followed this diplomatic impasse. Nixon and
Kissinger could have put their weight behind an abiding effort to move the
diplomatic track off ground zero. Instead, they gambled that an offensive
would generate advantages and force Hanoi into concessions. Choices were
made here. The result became another Nixon Shock, hardly what had been
expected by either the president or his national security adviser. In fact,
Kissinger titled the relevant chapter of his memoir "Vietnam 1970–1971:
Forcing Hanoi's Hand."[2]

"Decisive Results with Respect to the Entire Conflict"

As the American ground war moved toward its seventh
year, the U.S. command in Saigon took a relaxed view. Both General
Creighton Abrams and pacification chief William Colby were pleased with
the apparent success of efforts to win the hearts and minds of the Vietnamese. On the military side, U.S. code breakers monitored a slower pace of
infiltration, estimating Hanoi's replacements as falling short of its 1970
losses. Airpower worked hard against the Ho Chi Minh Trail, and its pinball
wizards had fully deployed their electronic battlefield. The flow of enemy
weapons to Sihanoukville had been shut down. The ARVN had more men,
more weapons, U.S. support. It was not difficult to picture it as progressing,
Vietnamization as succeeding. Only the most acute observers noticed the
failures in the Central Highlands and questioned the ARVN's improvement.

American withdrawals continued. At the end of 1970 U.S. forces stood at
334,600, of which 274,000 were Army or Marine ground troops. A fresh increment of repatriations, to be completed by spring, would send home an-

other 60,000 servicemen and -women. General Abrams's troops were a steadily diminishing quantity. Presently they would be incapable of major offensive operations. At Pentagon East there was a definite sense of sand slipping through the hourglass. Abrams sought to maintain an orderly process—not too many withdrawals or too quickly—and to preserve the fighting ability of the troops he had. He was not particularly enamored of a scheme for an offensive.

It was in this climate that the invasion of Laos was born. Henry Kissinger obscures the chronology and structures his account to suggest that the idea for a Laotian offensive came from Abrams, Thieu, and Ambassador Ellsworth Bunker in Saigon. The reality is nearer to the pattern of Cambodia, where the White House maneuvered to have Saigon take responsibility for what it wanted, both to stymie opponents and to avoid blame if things went wrong. In the summer of 1970—on August 17, in fact—Kissinger had ordered up a Southeast Asia policy review. The specific context was to identify moves to follow the recently completed U.S. pullback from Cambodia. The review generated several options to support Lon Nol forces and continued ARVN operations in Cambodia, but also a "Strategy 4," which involved inserting troops into lower Laos to block the Ho Chi Minh Trail. Variants included commando forces working from South Vietnam, Thailand, and Cambodia or operations by the ARVN, crossing the Lao border in force. In Washington this review put a Laotian offensive on the table for the president.

As the Nixon administration debated options, the invasion idea grew from a raid to a full-blooded offensive. Pacific theater commander Admiral John McCain had a hand here.[3] McCain had played an exhortatory role in the Cambodia decision, and he had proposed missions into Laos as early as 1969, when the military was wrestling over Pruning Knife. In mid-October 1970 McCain asked Abrams to consider a major Laos operation. A month later he raised the possibility directly with Washington. On November 10 CINCPAC even gave Abrams a general concept for the offensive. Some U.S. planners preferred the old standby of invading North Vietnam around Vinh—which continued to have the same old drawbacks. Kissinger favored a renewed large-scale ARVN excursion into Cambodia.

At an NSC meeting on November 4, Nixon ordered the bureaucracy to redo its sums and produce fresh alternatives. It is worth noting that these instructions were issued four days after President Thieu, addressing the South Vietnamese National Assembly, reiterated his intransigence on negotiations. Thieu claimed that *he* could see the light at the end of the tunnel, even if others could not. With victory not so far away, Thieu would never accept a coalition government. Hanoi used talks to prolong the war. "Peace in victory," Thieu declared, would never come from the negotiations.[4]

On November 20 U.S. Special Operations forces struck at Son Tay, near Hanoi, in a major effort to liberate American prisoners. However, the prisoners had been moved elsewhere after Tonkin delta flooding. The raid failed. In the wee hours of that night, Nixon summoned Kissinger and declared he had settled on a new plan: "put real heat on North Vietnam."[5] The president spoke of taking the offensive, but specifically he mentioned only mining or blockading Haiphong. But blockade was not among the options being considered, and for a time, nothing more was said about it. Instead, Mr. Nixon shored up his public image with a White House dinner for the Son Tay raiders. On November 28 Nixon demanded the results of his strategy review.

By now Laos had a place on the front burner. Nixon sent Kissinger's deputy, recently promoted Brigadier General Alexander M. Haig, to shake up MACV's planners. On December 6, before Haig left, Admiral McCain sent General Abrams orders from the JCS to approach General Cao Van Vien and coordinate plans for a Laos operation. Two days later—still before Haig's departure—instructions went out for an invasion of the shape the offensive would finally take, along with an independent, smaller ARVN thrust into Cambodia. On December 10 JCS chairman Admiral Thomas Moorer cabled Abrams, ordering all preparations necessary to "carry the battle to the enemy to the greatest extent possible."[6] Haig departed Washington the next day. His memoir, at least, accurately ascribed authorship: "prodded remorselessly by Nixon and Kissinger, the Pentagon finally devised a plan."[7] Melvin Laird also confirms that the impetus for the Laotian operation came from the White House, not elsewhere.[8] Admiral McCain's cable forwarding the concept plan for Laos to the Joint Chiefs on December 15 plainly stated, "At my request General Abrams has developed a concept plan . . . for major ARVN ground operations into Laos panhandle."[9]

Abrams, who in late November had joked about higher-ups being steamed over MACV's handling of Laos, knew this was beyond wisecracks. On December 8 he summoned his intelligence people and senior commanders and asked each of them to plan a major operation in their area. In fact, only the plan of XXIV Corps—the U.S. formation now corresponding to Saigon's I Corps—was at issue. No doubt Abrams ordered up the others to preserve secrecy and ensure that no opportunities were missed in the drive for a Laos offensive. By December 12, the day after Haig arrived, the concept plan was essentially finished: U.S. forces would clear the way to the border, and South Vietnamese troops would make the attack, with American air, artillery, and logistics support. It envisioned a multidivision task force. On December 16 Kissinger gave Haig's preliminary comments to the president. "Operations now planned for the dry season," Kissinger reported, "will guarantee [the impossibility of Hanoi's reestablishing its sanctuaries] for at least another six months and have potential for achieving decisive results with respect to the entire conflict for Southeast Asia."[10] Beyond the anticipated military benefits, Nixon made his decision hoping to force Hanoi into concessions at the negotiations.

Nixon and Kissinger maneuvered just as they had before Cambodia. The memorandum recording Haig's meeting with Thieu on December 17 shows the emissary's care. Haig noted he had learned from Abrams that Thieu, the JGS, and MACV had a better idea than the Cambodian excursion concept he had brought from the White House. But the chief of the psychological warfare department of JGS told colleagues that "the Americans" had simply handed General Vien the plan to sign.[11] Once Haig returned to Washington, Nixon immediately invited him and Kissinger in to "chat" about "our operating plan in Laos," where "they're going to move the South Vietnamese in for a major attack."[12] A few days later Kissinger wanted Admiral Moorer to see Nixon because "he has to use [him] to force Laird and the military to go ahead with the . . . plans, which they won't carry out without direct orders."[13]

Secretary Laird and Admiral Moorer visited Saigon in early January. When Laird conferred with Thieu, the Saigon leader expressed reservations about the public explanation for the invasion—he suggested justifying it as "hot pursuit" of the enemy. U.S. troop levels also concerned Thieu; he wanted Nixon to preserve a MACV force of at least 165,000 through mid-1972, while Americans talked of being out of the war by then. Thieu emphasized that he did "not want a repeat of 1968 where U.S. domestic political considerations influenced decisions on troop levels which proved most damaging to the conduct of the war."[14] The troop objection dovetailed with Dr. Kissinger's predilections. He too argued for curtailed withdrawals in the U.S. election year. And an assumption in Abrams's Laos plan was that withdrawals would be halted while the offensive was under way. Parallel operations in Cambodia were another issue.

When Laird discussed his trip with the NSC on January 18, he noted that Thieu, like Nixon, had no confidence in the Paris talks but believed they must continue "as a means of posturing both the South Vietnamese and the U.S. Governments for the upcoming elections to be held in both countries." Presenting a proposal, as a means to claim progress, was exactly why Thieu was willing to go ahead and exchange wounded prisoners. Meanwhile, U.S. thinking on withdrawals looked toward a level of 100,000 to 120,000 for mid-1972. President Nixon wanted "the issue to remain somewhat obscure in terms of numbers." He intended "to end the United States combat role as soon as South Vietnam was ready." Vietnamization "was on schedule and it was as simple as that."[15]

Secretary Laird presented the dry-season offensive ideas, including a strike into Cambodia code-named "Toan Thang I-71," plus the Laotian offensive, "Lam Son 719." He seemed convinced the plan would work, but Laird warned that planners should assume Hanoi knew about the offensive. Moorer presented the military details. Haig's record of the meeting noted, "Dr Kissinger stated that if the enemy stood and fought, it would be to our advantage, adding that the enemy might be set back in its timetable by as much as a year." Nixon said the operations made sense but would pose domestic problems because of the charge that the United States had expanded the war into Laos. "There is no question but that we would get some real heat," he added.[16]

There were repeated replowings of this ground during the final days. Nixon became infuriated when Secretary of State William Rogers raised questions. Rogers, good lawyer that he was, couched his objections as innocent questions about definitions of things like "interdiction" versus "air support"—important in Cambodia, where there were legal limits on U.S. aerial activity—or discrepancies between what the administration had already said versus what it was about to do. He and Laird were to testify on Capitol Hill. Rogers and Nixon agreed the invasion would trigger a final break with Senator Mike Mansfield, whose support over the years had been invaluable to several presidents and who, on successively narrower grounds, had resisted going into opposition. Nixon could accept that. South Vietnamese attacks in Cambodia (Kissinger actually *was* getting his preferred option, in addition to the Laotian offensive) posed a special problem because massive air assaults there required U.S. helicopters and would breach understandings with Congress. The president and his advisers spent hours on that, with the Joint Chiefs repeatedly going over their calculations, only to concede there was no alternative. Washington expected the ARVN incursion to open with 7,000 troops, building to 20,000, and lasting three months. Nixon insisted on it. He repeatedly spoke of victory in the Cambodia attack and expected that victory to carry Nguyen Van Thieu to reelection in late 1971.

Laotian prime minister Souvanna Phouma might have saved Nixon from this venture. Early on, Souvanna looked favorably on the offensive, but the Lao neutralist got cold feet when he learned just how big the attack would be. The State Department raised objections based on these Laotian concerns. Nixon held more meetings. On January 26 and 27 he privately had Admiral Moorer to the White House to stage a dress rehearsal, then held an NSC meeting where Moorer presented his briefing. There was talk of limiting the operation to its initial phase, code-named "Dewey Canyon II," which U.S. troops would carry out, clearing the way to the Laotian border and reoccupying Khe Sanh. The president approved execution of the first phase only, but apparently as a device to get the operation in gear. Then General Abrams recommended cancellation after completing Dewey Canyon. Now President Thieu stepped in, postponing Lam Son on the grounds that his astrologer found the timing inauspicious. Saigon CIA chief Theodore Shackley bribed the astrologer to reverse himself. In Washington Nixon ordered full implementation.

Several things were apparent at the outset. There would be no surprises on either side. Senior American officials had discounted that more than six weeks earlier. The Vietnam People's Army had substantial strength in the objective area—both Washington briefings and military plans enumerated expected enemy forces in detail—and the People's Army had a substantial capacity to reinforce its initial disposition. Moreover, they had armor, heavy artillery, and both medium and heavy antiaircraft defenses that would impede U.S. air activity and, in a pinch, add to VPA artillery capability. Even the supply troops at the Ho Chi Minh Trail way stations were armed, which had not been the case earlier in the war. Meanwhile, ARVN forces were going to be affected by the absence of their American advisers, now prohibited by law from entering Laos. Finally, the crossing of the border would inflame American politics, a point Nixon himself made at least three times during the deliberations preceding the invasion.

In short, administration officials had no illusions about the probable consequences. As it had in Cambodia, the White House marched into Laos with open eyes. The key miscalculations were Nixon's and Kissinger's: that the adversary's concentrated combat power did not matter; that the South Vietnamese, given U.S. support, could not be defeated; and that military victory would trump the political consequences. Like Cambodia again, there were warnings beforehand. The CIA's Richard Helms raised questions. His agency provided an analysis on January 21 that predicted the scale and intensity of Hanoi's response remarkably accurately. Kissinger held the paper close; hardly anyone saw it. Undersecretary of State U. Alexis Johnson argued at WSAG against the attack, observing afterward, "The action was ill-conceived from the start. It required an unproven group of soldiers to strike at an objective that the enemy would defend stoutly in a region where it had superior logistics."[17] The president's miscalculations, reinforced by Kissinger's preferences, made Laos a Nixon Shock.

■ ■ ■ Gary Rafferty knew nothing of such matters of state. A young artilleryman with the 2nd Battalion, 94th Artillery (the 2/94), Rafferty was just a GI, one of those who would carry out the plans so blithely tossed around Washington. Already a 'Nam veteran, though not yet a "short timer," Rafferty had gone through the Army's transit center at Oakland, California, on the day of Kent State, thinking America on the verge of a civil war and himself on the wrong side of it. Arriving in Vietnam, he had been flown to join his unit at Dong Ha in Quang Tri province, just below the DMZ. The C-130 sustained a lucky hit from an enemy gunner who put a heavy machine gun round through its fuselage, instantly killing the GI sitting across from Rafferty, flooding the plane with the cold air from outside, and forcing the pilot into a steep dive to recover the aircraft and keep his passengers from freezing. It was Rafferty's third day in-country—an awful introduction to Vietnam.

Neither a rabble-rouser nor a racist, Rafferty was typical of MACV's troops at this point in the war. He described Vietnam as "a grinding down, a slow yet inexorable process wherein the very essence of who I was became mutated."[18] The frantic fear, the heat of battle, the craziness of Army regs, the exotic land, and the in-bred isolation of the Americans—all this shaped the soldiers General Abrams sent into Dewey Canyon II and used to shore up the ARVN for Lam Son 719.

The 2/94 had long played a role in the DMZ war. It had come to Vietnam in 1966 equipped with the Army's biggest weapons, 175mm guns. From Cam Lo and Camp Carroll, and with detachments sent to the outpost called the "Rockpile," the huge 175s had blown away targets all around the DMZ, helped defend the Marines at Con Thien, supported attacks around the Cua Viet River, and harassed the NLF wherever it could reach them. Batteries had fired in support of the Marines far to the west at Khe Sanh during the great siege of 1968. This battalion alone had shot more than 400,000 shells in anger in Vietnam.

Under Vietnamization, the unit ran fire control for much of the U.S. artillery in Quang Tri, ran the artillery battery school for XXIV Corps' 108th Artillery Command, and deployed its batteries to firebases and towns as required. Most of the firing batteries spent the fall of 1970 defending the approaches to Da Nang and Hue, particularly the Hai Van Pass, supporting the Americal and 1st Marine Divisions. Rafferty first worked at the fire control center but then joined A Battery. In early January XXIV Corps began positioning its units for Dewey Canyon and Lam Son. Sister unit C Battery moved to Dong Ha on January 17, and B Battery on the twenty-second. A week later, as five U.S. battalions with the 1st Brigade, 5th Infantry Division (Mechanized) began attacking toward Khe Sanh, A Battery went too, through Dong Ha, joining a large concentration of U.S. guns at Firebase Vandegrift. When A Battery arrived, the entire 2/94 was concentrated for the first time during Rafferty's tour with the unit.

This was a heavy artillery battalion with a mixture of 8-inch howitzers and 175mm guns. But it was just one of many. The South Vietnamese had their guns too. Lieutenant General James Sutherland, XXIV Corps commander, had been mulling over the possibilities with ARVN corps commander Hoang Xuan Lam since the end of December, and on January 21, a week after receiving MACV's concept, Sutherland unveiled his tactical plans. The troops, including Rafferty's battalion, were already assuming their positions. After that, things proceeded inexorably. On the appointed day the Americans moved out for Dewey Canyon led by Brigadier General John G. Hill of the U.S. Mechanized Brigade. The 7th Engineer Battalion began rebuilding the bridges and culverts on Route 9, the road on which everyone would depend. The 1st Battalion, 11th Infantry air-assaulted into Khe Sanh, while the 1st Squadron, 1st Cavalry scouted up the road, passing Khe Sanh and finally reaching the border at Lao Bao, recapturing the old Lang Vei Special Forces camp along the way.

Soon the Lao border became a concentration area. Specialist Rafferty got there on February 7. Three omens spooked him. A Battery's best powder man, a soldier who carried explosive propellant charges to the gun, impervious to the potentially lethal consequences of smoking cigarettes at the same time, fell off the back of their truck while trying to take a photo of his buddies. Then, as their convoy passed Quang Tri, a Vietnamese prostitute recognized them, calling them by unit number even though the GIs had removed their shoulder patches and vehicle identification. "You go Laos now! ARVN been gone four days!" The woman not only knew their identity; she knew their destination and South Vietnamese troop movements too! The third omen came courtesy of Armed Forces Radio. A Battery, briefly stopped at the unit's old base near Dong Ha, had found a ghost town, completely pilfered and stripped. The captain chose then to warn the men they were indeed headed for Laos, where the North Vietnamese had had twenty years to get ready. He expected hard fighting and heavy casualties. When they mounted their armored personnel carrier and turned on the radio, it spewed out the Credence Clearwater Revival hit "Bad Moon Rising."[19]

South Vietnamese Rangers, lifted by U.S. choppers, set up several firebases along the Lao border west and north of Khe Sanh to shield it, the key air link for Lam Son. Meanwhile, ARVN troops gathered for their invasion. Nixon gave his final approval for the Lam Son phase on February 2. The Vietnamese troops swept into Laos on the eighth. On the eve of the invasion a convoy of tanker trucks carrying gasoline to Khe Sanh was ambushed on Route 9, losing six of the big tractor-trailers, the shortage of which General Sutherland already considered his biggest logistical shortcoming. The ambush underlined the vulnerability of the supply line. It could be considered another omen.

Saigon's spearhead would be a task force built around the ARVN's 1st Armored Brigade, with a pair of cavalry battalions plus two of paratroopers. These were supposed to capture the intermediate objective of Ban Dong, a People's Army way station for The Trail, and then thrust ahead to Tchepone, Hanoi's key base. At Lao Bao, Rafferty watched trucks full of South Vietnamese soldiers drive past their gun positions for three straight days. But the ARVN tank commander, slow to reach Ban Dong, just sat there. Officials had been told that Tchepone would be taken on the fourth or fifth day of the offensive. It did not happen. Meanwhile, South Vietnamese Rangers and paratroops choppered into positions north of Route 9 to protect the flanks of the armored column, and airborne troops and Marines did the same to the south. Secure flanks did not encourage the armor. Various excuses were proffered: rain, unexpectedly heavy, began on the second day; the condition of Route 9 was terrible; the captured enemy supply caches required inventorying; and so on. Ban Dong became just another static firebase. The VPA assembled and began attacking the covering positions on both sides of Route 9. Tanks appeared in its assaults. Heavy artillery pounded ARVN and U.S. positions, while sapper attacks hit rear bases inside South Vietnam. More ambushes threatened allied supply lines. Lam Son went from the centerpiece of a brilliant offensive to a gathering disaster.

None of this played very well at home. The Nixon administration complicated its public relations problem with a scheme whereby journalists were told of the attack early and then prohibited from reporting it. The idea had been to prevent speculation while guarding security. When European and other media speculated anyway and their articles were recycled in the United States, Washington spokesmen began responding, opening a gulf between public relations at MACV and at home. The transition to Lam Son worsened the relationship with the media because the idea had been to give the lead to Saigon authorities, who were slow to provide any information and then purveyed highly skewed announcements. Early claims of the capture of Tchepone, reported by the incautious, proved to be inaccurate, souring the channel. Arrangements to limit coverage by permitting only press pools accompanied by escort officers increased reporters' suspicions. One of the first pools into Laos followed General Lam on a visit he made to forward bases. The reporters' chopper, carrying four experienced journalists plus an ARVN photographer, crashed, killing everyone. Only a few more groups of journalists were permitted into the area, satisfying no one. As Lam Son bogged down, there were efforts to claim that its objective had been merely to disrupt, not destroy, Hanoi's supply lines, further eroding credibility. The result was an increasingly skeptical press. Far from gaining a bonus from the invasion, Nixon saw his poll numbers fall by fourteen points during its first month. Another poll in the spring showed that 60 percent of respondents wanted all Americans out of Vietnam, even if it meant the fall of Saigon.

Nixon miscalculated who called the shots—one more episode in the American delusion that it had "leverage" in Saigon. On February 12 Thieu instructed General Lam to halt the offensive if he reached a level of 3,000 casualties. This gave Lam official sanction to halt the ARVN's armor at Ban Dong, and in fact, he stopped immediately. Suspicious, General Abrams intervened with Thieu and got empty assurances. A few days later Abrams conferred with Generals Lam and Sutherland at Dong Ha, where they cobbled together a plan to leapfrog the stalled tank column with helicopter assaults using the crack 1st Division, placing firebases near Tchepone that would then permit a ground thrust into that place. Nothing happened. In fact, Thieu ordered the troops to attack in an entirely different direction, toward the south. Regrouping them for the Tchepone mission took even more time.

Even Thieu became disgusted at General Lam's ineffectiveness. He recalled his stalwart, Do Cao Tri, from III Corps, where Tri had been leading the linked ARVN offensive in Cambodia, and ordered him to take over. But General Tri perished in a helicopter crash. After that, Thieu left Lam alone. Abrams, frantic to get the Vietnamese moving, tried to convince the Saigon leader to uproot the ARVN 2nd Division and send it into Laos. Thieu refused. Given the territorial basis of South Vietnamese army organization, Thieu was actually right—the 2nd probably would not have fought well in Laos. But the point is that Thieu made the decision and overrode the Americans. After meeting with General Lam on March 9, Thieu agreed to a complete withdrawal from Laos. On the eighteenth Thieu informed Lam that he was ordering the ARVN Airborne Division back to Saigon as soon as it could be gotten out of the combat zone.

If Creighton Abrams was frantic, the mood at the Nixon White House was first one of overconfidence, then of growing anxiety. In the Oval Office on February 18 Kissinger and Nixon were jocular, Henry almost congratulatory. "We expected Laos to be tougher," Kissinger said, and recommended a negotiating stance under which they would offer Hanoi a take-it-or-leave-it deal—U.S. withdrawal over one year, and DRV acceptance of a cease-fire and the handover of all its prisoners. Thieu would be told he had a year to get ready for the aftermath.[20] But the ARVN never budged from the initial positions it had gained. Like COSVN in Cambodia, Tchepone in Laos was an objective, then a receding goal, and finally an illusion. Richard Nixon had made a command decision, under no pressure from anyone, choosing to evade legal barriers erected precisely to avoid this sort of adventure and mindful of the probable political consequences. Now Saigon, to Nixon's mind, was making the desired outcome impossible.

Nixon's mounting anger is evident in Kissinger's cables, increasingly on the back channel and to Bunker in Saigon, demanding action from the Vietnamese and eventually condemning Abrams. On February 24 Kissinger told Nixon the military was infatuated with its plans. The next morning the president had Admiral Moorer in for another private chat, based on the new idea of throwing in the ARVN's 1st Division. That unit was led by Major General Pham Van Phu, a Vietnamese officer who had actually commanded a paratroop company at Dien Bien Phu, back in Nixon's Eisenhower-era salad days. Phu was considered a fighter, his background a plus. The real stake, Nixon told Moorer, was ARVN success—he could not countenance a sharp setback for Saigon. Nixon, too, had words about General Lam. He, Kissinger, and Moorer discussed the potential of air strikes on North Vietnam. The next day came a full NSC meeting. "If the South Vietnamese could just win one cheap one," the president groused, "take a stinking hill. . . . Bring back a prisoner or two."[21]

Only a couple of hours later the president learned that antiwar activists had called for mass civil disobedience on May 1, May Day, a protest they hoped might actually shut down the government. Nixon immediately began preparing a response. By March 1 Nixon and Haldeman were in recurrent conversations about May Day. Late that night a bomb placed by the Weathermen went off in a bathroom of the U.S. Capitol. Political troubles were accentuated by other developments, including congressional hearings into corruption within the military's PX system in Vietnam, a Senate inquiry into military spying in America, and the last stages of the court-martial of Lieutenant William Calley of My Lai infamy.

Unlike Nixon's objectives, Hanoi's armies were not illusory. The People's Army had created a field command, the 70B Front under General Le Trong Tan, specifically to fight in Laos, and Tan had plenty of troops. In a succession of attacks through the end of February, the VPA crumpled the line of firebases the Rangers and paratroops held above Ban Dong. Several ARVN battalions were obliterated. Southern soldiers fled the battlefield, some clinging to the landing skids of helicopters. Indeed, the enduring image of the invasion would be photographs of these men. An ARVN airborne brigade commander and his staff were overrun and captured on one post; a battalion commander fled with those who routed. North Vietnamese tanks were destroyed by Saigon's or by U.S. airpower, and People's Army regiments suffered big losses, but Tan's units maintained their integrity, while the South Vietnamese did not. Under the circumstances, the new attack by the ARVN 1st Division became a stunt. The ARVN briefly captured Tchepone on March 7, held it for a few days, then attempted an orderly withdrawal. By a South Vietnamese account, Thieu feared a repeat of Dien Bien Phu and told Lam, "You go in there just long enough to take a piss and then leave quickly."[22] Under the pressure of 70B Front attacks, the ARVN withdrawal barely avoided disintegration, and it would have collapsed except for U.S. airpower. On March 11, speaking to Kissinger, Nixon said this about the South Vietnamese: "We know what these people can or can't do. It's going to be close. They're going to take some racks. We've got to get the hell out of there."[23]

Meanwhile, the other prong of the dry-season offensive also ran into a meat grinder. A big ARVN task force entered Cambodia all right, led by helicopter assaults with South Vietnamese Rangers. Major fighting developed around the Chup plantation and then Snoul. By late February the ARVN there had grown larger than in Laos, but it fared no better. The North Vietnamese fought with two divisions. The death of General Tri eroded the ARVN's morale. A major attack on the ARVN supply line isolated its troops, who were obliged to await the rainy season for a breakout attempt. According to Hanoi's official history, only poor coordination due to the lack of a VPA higher headquarters saved the ARVN force. The North Vietnamese subsequently created a corps command called Group 301. By March 8 American sources in Saigon were telling journalists that the Cambodia offensive had foundered.

The president tapped Haig for an emergency mission. By Haig's account, Nixon ordered him to fly to Saigon and replace Abrams, who would be fired. That appeared ludicrous on its face—there were more than 200 generals senior to Haig who could aspire to that command—and Haig himself dissuaded Nixon. Although his instructions were to get Lam Son on the move again, once Haig reached Saigon, he realized the ARVN troops were actually on the verge of collapse. The key problem was to extract them from Laos in good order. Almost the only one to espouse a different view, Ambassador Bunker, argued that "success" had increased the ARVN's confidence. Meanwhile, General Lam's division commanders squabbled amongst themselves over who would get priority in the withdrawal, which had begun everywhere by March 19. Five days later the entire force would be out of Laos.

The air strikes Nixon had considered against North Vietnam were flown on March 20–21, 455 sorties against DRV air defenses covering the battle area and hitting road convoys. In the Lam Son sector itself there were more than 8,500 tactical air sorties (98 percent U.S.), 1,358 by B-52 bombers, and more than 20,000 helicopter gunship "sorties." Four times that many chopper "sorties" had made air assaults, carried troops or supplies, or picked up wounded.[24]

Supporting the South Vietnamese, the Americans of Dewey Canyon came under steady pressure. Many American convoys on Route 9 were ambushed, and shelling or mortaring of bases became a daily phenomenon. There were two battalions of U.S. guns at Lao Bao. The experience of A Battery was typical. Ground fog each morning provided a few hours respite when the men could nap, prepare equipment, or eat breakfast. Cooks supplied a steady diet of pancakes without butter, syrup, or trimmings, so unrelenting the artillerymen almost rebelled. It got worse when a mess truck was destroyed by North Vietnamese shells. After that, meals consisted of combat rations three times a day. Once the fog cleared the shooting began. GIs lived in constant fear, unable to build bunkers deep or strong enough to protect against the enemy's big guns. According to records, VPA artillery fire died down during the days of intense fighting along the Lam Son invasion front, but the enemy gunners resumed with alacrity after the first week of March. In an incident that spooked gunner Rafferty, four GIs at the end of their tours seemed to be bathed in an eerie white light as they climbed on a truck to begin their journey home to "The World." As soon as the vehicle got on the road, it was blown to pieces.

Sometimes a few shells harassed the Americans; other times came real bombardments, 100 to 200 rounds a day. The 2/94 battalion commander, reluctant to believe the enemy used 152mm guns, found shell fragments and made crater measurements that were undeniable. As at the siege of Khe Sanh, the North Vietnamese emplaced their guns carefully and used superior range to batter the U.S. positions. They had already sighted in the likely gun stands at Lao Bao and were bracketing them when 2/94 first arrived. Those U.S. guns that could reach the Vietnamese were not accurate enough to hit them, and the more precise weapons lacked the range. People's Army tanks hovered in closer. There were occasional ground attacks. The automatic weapons at the U.S. firebases—truck-mounted quad-.50-caliber machine guns and track-mounted 40mm automatic cannon—either were ineffective against tanks or could not see them in the jungle. For Gary Rafferty time itself dissolved under the shower of "incoming"—enemy shells.

The Americans tried every kind of device. Few worked. Artillery radar tracked the shells, but not quickly enough for the Americans to engage the VPA guns. A searchlight battery was deployed, but it merely attracted fire. It had to be taken out. Microphones to triangulate the enemy emplacements were disrupted often, damaged, then the tracking center destroyed. That battery, too, was withdrawn. Almost invariably, when the Americans began an artillery shoot, North Vietnamese shells began to fall before the GIs could loose more than a few salvos.

For five days beginning on March 18, Route 9 from Lao Bao to Khe Sanh became so saturated with ambushes it was impassable except to tanks. Engineers maintaining the roadbed could not work. On March 20 the Americans on road watch there—Lieutenant Colonel Gene L. Breeding's 1st Squadron, 1st Cavalry, equipped with thin-skinned armored personnel carriers (APCs)—got orders to relieve a scout patrol and recover their downed chopper. Moving forward, the patrol Breeding sent took casualties, and one of their "tracks," as the APCs were called, was damaged. Told to recover the APC too, the men refused—a mutiny among MACV soldiers. The episode was widely reported. General John Hill brought in the 1/77 Armor to guard Route 9.

That storied mutiny is known. Unknown were the daily insanities afflicting the U.S. troops. These led to a virtual mutiny by Gary Rafferty's artillery battery. The battalion commander played favorites, so B Battery would be the first to get orders to withdraw from Lao Bao at midafternoon on March 18. (B Battery was regarded as the 2/94's spit-and-polish Regular Army guys, whereas A Battery were the misfits.) For weeks, anything moving in daylight had been under observed artillery fire. Yet the GIs were ordered to form up a road convoy in plain sight. The VPA wasted no time, quickly hitting the first truck of the formation, then the last, then shooting the rest at leisure. Nine assorted vehicles plus an artillery prime mover, an engineer vehicle, the battery's fire control track, its mess equipment, a 175mm gun, and three trucks were blown up. Most of the 2/94's casualties for the entire campaign happened right there. Then the battalion commander ordered A Battery to form up too. Gunner Rafferty's comrades would have none of it. They ignored the orders to line up in a convoy, drove onto the road by ones and twos, took evasive measures, and escaped beyond the clear terrain before forming a column to speed through Ambush Alley en masse. The misfits lost just two trucks. The battalion's third element, C Battery, was recalled after this carnage. The batteries that had preceded it to Lang Vei set up their remaining guns and blasted back the tree lines on both sides of the road. The North Vietnamese countered with rocket-propelled grenade teams. When C Battery made its move, every one of its guns either broke down or was shot up in Ambush Alley. The battalion lost two-thirds of its guns in all, and although they were recovered later, only three could be repaired. Rafferty survived the maelstrom. His tour ended on April 9, and he headed for "The World" himself. The 2/94 Artillery learned of the end of Lam Son the next day—yet Saigon had officially terminated the operation on April 6 and had effectively ended it as of March 24.

Other American units faced comparable challenges, but none matched the sheer desperation and terror of the South Vietnamese in danger of being trapped in Laos. Washington and Saigon put their best faces on the disaster, claiming huge enemy casualties and supplies destroyed, yet the results were distinctly underwhelming, far less than in Cambodia in 1970. And these claims were not based on counted and inventoried munitions; the vast majority of the claim for enemy ammunition destroyed had been generated by a formula attributing tons of destruction to every observed secondary explosion. No doubt some of this was real, but it was impossible to know for sure. Saigon also inflated its lists by claiming such things as a handful of water pumps and electric generators. To make a different comparison, allied forces in South Vietnam in 1969, without this kind of major offensive, captured about twice as many weapons as were taken in Laos in 1971 (12,524 versus claims ranging from 4,877 to 7,133). And admitted U.S. battle deaths at the siege of Khe Sanh in 1968 are comparable to those for Laos, even though American troops had not actually fought in-country. Helicopter losses were enormous.[25]

Publicly, Nixon and Kissinger claimed victory—and proof of Vietnamization's success. Privately, Kissinger told a White House meeting that *Abrams* had oversold the offensive and the ARVN should have avoided Tchepone, "which was a visible objective but turned out to be basically a disaster." The president railed at Haldeman that Abrams ought to be fired, but U.S. withdrawals meant it no longer mattered who commanded MACV.[26] Perhaps the best index of the reality of Lam Son 719 is what happened at Khe Sanh. At the White House on March 26, as ARVN stragglers staggered across the border, Admiral Moorer told the president that the United States would probably hold Khe Sanh through May. In actuality, MACV pulled out of Khe Sanh on April 6. Nixon blamed the press for one-sided reporting. But he ordered more salted peanuts—a fresh withdrawal of 100,000 troops over the year to begin on May 1. These increments reflected Nixon's vulnerability. Significantly, Dr. Kissinger asked the Pentagon to evaluate whether the U.S. force remaining in Vietnam could be maintained solely on the basis of volunteers.

At Paris, the anticipated South Vietnamese offer to exchange long-held or wounded prisoners evaporated. Saigon now claimed it had no prisoners willing to be repatriated. President Nixon oscillated between acceptance of the political obstacles that forced him to continue U.S. withdrawals, with a contingent hope that this could be done within the framework of a negotiated agreement, and his desire to slam Hanoi. Kissinger stood with him. In the Oval Office on April 27, both agreed that airpower was the way—in fact, Mr. Nixon's chosen instrument.[27] The president would come to adopt what amounted to the Dien Bien Phu formula—that naval and air forces afforded unparalleled striking power unassailable by the enemy. For Nixon, the formula conveyed the possibility that U.S. withdrawals would reduce the war as an issue, which might enable him to exercise that power in an unfettered manner.

On May 25 the president again claimed success in Laos, alluding to a wider strategy. "This administration's policy is succeeding and bringing the war to an end," Nixon declared, "and bringing it to an end in a way which I believe will contribute to our goal of discouraging that kind of war, that kind of aggression."[28] This was not about negotiation. General Abrams, for one, knew that. A month earlier, speaking to the visiting secretary of the Army at MACV headquarters, Abrams had commented, "I think the president's made it fairly clear that *he's* got a plan to go all the way." With a sharp sense of the political constraints, now delimited by using the recovery of American prisoners to justify the war, Secretary Stanley Resor replied, "That's a little bit subject to the prisoners."[29] In early June, again with Kissinger, the president exclaimed, "We're gonna take out the [Red River delta] dikes, we're gonna take out Haiphong, we're gonna level that goddamn country!"[30] A month later, discussing a peace proposal from the NLF's Provisional Revolutionary Government that mentioned the American prisoners, Nixon objected when Kissinger observed that, with time, they might outnegotiate the other side. "We don't have it," Nixon said, referring to the necessary time and the impatience of the POW families. "You understand, I have problems with American public opinion."[31] Barely an hour later the president told Kissinger the North Vietnamese should settle because he, the man who had ordered Cambodia and Laos, might just escalate. Nixon's oscillations were a constant.

As for Hanoi, the "defeated" enemy went on the offensive in I Corps and the Central Highlands. An American firebase called "Mary Ann" was gutted by a sapper attack, and Da Nang hit hard with rockets. In the highlands near Dak To, an ARVN base on a hill (made infamous by a U.S. battle in the spring of 1967) almost fell, saved only by the intervention of a reconstituted ARVN airborne brigade. Abrams subsequently termed that battle a "fiasco." In both Laos and South Vietnam, captured documents contained exhortations to exploit the victory in Laos. Truck sightings averaged 2,500 a month, levels previously seen only at peak periods. Within days of the end of Lam

Son there was evidence that the People's Army was moving radars and SAM missiles right into Ban Dong. Seventh Air Force commander General Lucius D. Clay Jr. told Abrams, "They're right back in there, balls out."[32]

High Tide in Spring

The Laotian invasion and the travails of the GIs there energized the former servicemen of the Vietnam Veterans Against the War (VVAW). A large group of vets had been gathered in Detroit as Lam Son 719 got under way, holding a public event to bear witness to the realities they had seen on the ground in Vietnam. Five participants, coincidentally, were Marines who had been in the 1969 Dewey Canyon foray into Laos, unknown to Americans until the vets revealed it now, just as the new Dewey Canyon got under way. The Detroit event, known as the "Winter Soldier Investigation," marked a significant waypoint in the sudden rise of VVAW.

Veterans' emergence in the Movement had been slow. Every individual had his or her own tipping point. For a few, that had been the Democratic National Convention in Chicago, where they had gone in the guise of Vets for McCarthy. Assorted Veterans for Peace demonstrations had brought out others, as had draft resistance and the GI coffeehouses. Revelations of My Lai energized others. Cambodia became the catalyst. Until then, VVAW existed primarily as a mailing list of activist veterans plus some chapters on college campuses. Protest organizers typically phoned the group to try to get some vets to turn out for events. But Cambodia changed that. In Syracuse on May 20, Veterans for Peace and VVAW came together for a march through the city. When the Hard Hats busted heads in New York, Brooklyn vet Danny Friedman got knocked down, called a hippie, and assaulted by police. As happened time and again throughout the era, nothing radicalized like repression. Friedman became a stalwart of VVAW's New York chapter. The organizer of a VVAW chapter at Kent State, Tim Butz, had been standing on the other side of the building when the National Guard shot the students there. One of the victims was his roommate's girlfriend. Butz and Ohio Stater William Crandell, a tag team of energizers, fanned out to campuses throughout the area, creating new chapters. Organizing ramped up at universities in Texas, Arizona, Oregon, Florida, Alabama, and the Northeast.[33]

Actress Jane Fonda helped raise money for VVAW, generating both cash and publicity. Fonda's role deserves mention because of the controversy she generated, especially a year later. Along with so many others, Fonda had been stunned by Tet. Until 1968 Fonda had not been political. Suddenly she became an activist for American Indians; came out in support of Angela Davis, a University of California professor hounded for her political stance; then helped raise funds for the Black Panthers' inner-city children's breakfast program. The CIA opened a file on Fonda when its (illegal) mail-opening project discovered letters from her addressed to the North Vietnamese delegation at Paris. The FBI followed suit at the time of Cambodia, when Fonda first appeared on the platform at a peace demonstration. She became a victim of Bureau COINTELPRO when an FBI agent attempted to plant false allegations in the Hollywood press, exaggerating Fonda's role with the Black Panthers. Clumsy surveillance and harrowing events in Vietnam shaped Fonda's radicalism. In *Ramparts* magazine she read commentaries by former Green Beret—now VVAW member—Donald Duncan. Fonda met GI resistance organizer Fred Gardner at a Hollywood party and subsequently involved herself with the GI coffeehouses. Fonda and fellow actor Donald Sutherland created a road show variously called "Free the Army" or "Fuck the Army," which made the circuit of the coffeehouses in the style of a USO tour. Gardner's introduction, plus brushes with the law, put her in contact with lawyer (and JFK assassination author) Mark Lane and brought her together with VVAW, which Lane had encountered while gathering GI recollections for a book on the war.[34]

Meanwhile, protests by disabled GIs at Veterans Administration (VA) hospitals and VA efforts to squelch them drew in VVAW as a veterans' advocacy group. It is striking that these developments in the United States coincided with the similar efforts of disabled ARVN veterans. Cambodia brought new blood to the VVAW's national office, particularly Al Hubbard and Mike McCusker, who sparkplugged an intensification of outreach, and Scott Moore and Joe Urgo, who learned public relations on the job. Urgo busied himself creating a wall map with pins to signify new VVAW chapters. The map soon showed chapters nationwide.

Along the way, veteran "rap groups" began in about December 1970. There, GIs fought their post-traumatic stress disorder by telling comrades of their war experiences and getting their reassurance. Psychiatrist Robert Jay Lifton became a key figure, along with veteran Arthur Egendorf. Meanwhile, the dispatch of delegations to meet with other peace groups assumed new importance. As an African American, Al Hubbard could open channels to such groups as the Black Panthers, although meetings with the Panthers were mostly in the nature of consciousness-raising. African Americans and Latinos were underrepresented among the membership, but VVAW developed a style of relating to other organizations that served it well.

With growing membership came an interest in national actions. Bill Crandell got the idea of staging a mock "search-and-destroy" mission, a road march during which vets would mimic the kinds of things they had done in Vietnam. As the idea fleshed out it acquired the name Operation RAW, for "Rapid American Withdrawal," a three-day hike beginning at Morristown, New Jersey. Evoking the American Revolution—the vets rapidly became masters at using imagery—the march started at one of the encampments of the Continental Army and ended at George Washington's most famous campsite, Valley Forge, where Revolutionary War "winter soldiers" had survived the bitter cold of 1777. Despite problems securing parade and rally permits (which became commonplace) and a few altercations with pro-war locals, participants bonded in a way that made VVAW a surpassingly strong organization.

Performing guerrilla theater—mock "attacks" on towns along the line of march—more than 200 vets carried toy assault rifles and pretended to "arrest" or "interrogate" actors of the Philadelphia Guerrilla Theater (along for that purpose) or, in some cases, local citizens. Others distributed a leaflet that described their activities in the starkest terms:

A

U.S. INFANTRY

COMPANY JUST

CAME THROUGH HERE!

If you had been Vietnamese—

We might have burned your house

We might have shot your dog

We might have shot you . . .

We might have raped your wife and daughter

We might have turned you over to your government for torture

We might have taken souvenirs from your property

We might have shot things up a bit . . .

We might have done ALL these things to you

And your whole TOWN!

If it doesn't bother you that American soldiers do these things every day to the Vietnamese simply because they are "Gooks," *then* picture YOURSELF as one of the silent VICTIMS.

HELP US TO END THE WAR BEFORE THEY TURN *YOUR* SON INTO A BUTCHER

or a corpse.[35]

The vets saw the essence of their action in the march itself. To the media and the public (whose glimpse of Operation RAW was through the media), the Valley Forge rally was the central element. The rally certainly had star power, with Jane Fonda and Donald Sutherland in attendance. But also at the rally was veteran and former naval officer John Kerry. Enraged by Cambodia, Kerry, already an aspiring politician, had withdrawn from the race for a Massachusetts congressional seat won by cleric Robert Drinan. Kerry had served on a destroyer and as a Navy Swift boat skipper in the Mekong, and he had joined VVAW that spring. Hubbard recruited Kerry to speak at Valley Forge, and that speech, stark and powerful, impressed many. Fonda, for one, told an associate about Kerry and redoubled her efforts in behalf of VVAW.

Meanwhile, a whole other skein of antiwar action had developed: truth-telling by those who knew. There had been a certain amount of bearing witness earlier—notably, at an international war crimes tribunal presided over by Bertrand Russell in Stockholm in 1967, or by individuals speaking at demonstrations. Donald Duncan did this often. But after My Lai this kind of personal recounting took a standard form. In 1970 a Citizens Commission of Inquiry (CCI) made truth-telling a centerpiece of "hearings" in cities and towns across the nation, nine in all. Mark Lane was associated with the CCI movement and built bridges between the CCI and VVAW. The concept of testimony was familiar to vets, who did much the same thing privately in their rap groups. Public testimony would be just one step further.

The idea of a national hearing gathered steam through the latter part of 1970, although VVAW and CCI parted ways. Those in the CCI had developed an animosity toward Lane, both for his personal style and for the exaggerations in his Vietnam book. The Commission of Inquiry wanted the show to be in Washington, for political impact, whereas VVAW, interested in forging ties with the working class, favored a site somewhere in the Midwest, eventually deciding on Detroit. Beginning in the fall, a core of half a dozen vets worked full time preparing the event from a house VVAW rented in Detroit. The collective included Al Hubbard, Mike Oliver, Scott Moore, Tim Butz, Bill Crandell, and Arthur Flesch. Jane Fonda lent a hand, fund-raising specifically for this event. Playing on the Operation RAW imagery, the vets called this truth-telling the "Winter Soldier Investigation."

Beyond the split with the CCI, there were other obstacles. Anxious their testimony be absolutely authentic, organizers solicited abstracts of proposed remarks from VVAW members, then required participants to show their Department of Defense discharge papers. Vets had to overcome fear of speaking in public and qualms about disclosing military information. Organizers selected a representative cross section of the proffered accounts to show the commonality of experience among units from all over South Vietnam. As hard as this was—and the paper generated by the canvass filled several cartons—it proved the easy part. There were myriad logistical details, from arranging phone service to informing the press to finding the money and the venue. If the Nixon administration had had its way, the Winter Soldier Investigation would never have happened. The vets were bounced from their planned site at the last minute, prevented from securing a second one, and ended up at a Detroit Howard Johnson hotel. FBI intervention was instrumental in those headaches. Plans for testimony from Americans and Vietnamese in Canada were scotched when the Immigration Service cracked down on border crossings from Windsor, Canada, and the phone company refused its services.

Despite all obstacles, the Winter Soldier Investigation took place as scheduled. Panels of vets testified to hair-raising episodes of raw violence; standard procedures that lost, not won, "hearts and minds"; and casual arrogance for

Vietnamese, called "slopes" or "gooks."[36] The tone was set by Bill Crandell, who had been a lieutenant with the Americal Division:

> We went to preserve the peace and our testimony will show that we have set all of Indochina aflame. We went to defend the Vietnamese people and our testimony will show that we are committing genocide against them. We went to fight for freedom and our testimony will show that we have turned Vietnam into a series of concentration camps.
>
> We went to guarantee the right of self-determination to the people of South Vietnam and our testimony will show that we are forcing a corrupt and dictatorial government upon them. We went to work toward the brotherhood of man and our testimony will show that our strategy and tactics are permeated with racism. We went to protect America and our testimony will show why our country is being torn apart by what we are doing in Vietnam.[37]

The vets' accounts spanned years and regions, but it demonstrated all these things. Like it or not, antiwar vets or not, those days in Detroit distilled the common experience of the war.[38]

From VVAW's point of view, the worst aspect of Winter Soldier was that it failed to achieve the impact the vets sought. The testimony got limited coverage on television news and in national papers, though it did much better in local outlets such as the *Detroit Free Press*. Some of the best coverage, needless to say, was the FBI's, whose sources reported the testimony in detail each day. The vets would have done better had they followed the CCI notion of holding the event in Washington. Meanwhile, news of the Laotian invasion broke a few days later. The veterans began planning another action, one in Washington, the one that became Dewey Canyon III. John Kerry became a prime mover in Dewey Canyon III. He showed up at a planning meeting with a full proposal, complete with a briefing and easel charts. It looked good. Kerry soon joined the VVAW national leadership.

■ ■ ■ The nation may have been slow to notice the Winter Soldier Investigation, but the Nixon White House was not. When VVAW announced Dewey Canyon on March 16, Nixon's first Oval Office conversation about VVAW had already taken place. By then, the president's support was fraying at the margins—Haldeman noted the TV news had featured Hard Hats and Catholics protesting together when Nixon attended an Officer Candidate School graduation at Newport.

Lieutenant William Calley's court-martial verdict came through on March 29. Nixon's spokesman announced the president's intervention to ensure that Calley remained free (while the case was appealed) and his promise to review the final sentence. Frantically completing their preparations to march on Washington, VVAW actually took a mild stance on Calley, arguing that he had been singled out for egregious actions in Vietnam similar to those they had testified to at the Winter Soldier Investigation. Founder Jan Barry wrote of Calley in the *New York Times,* "to kill on military orders and be a criminal, or to refuse to kill and be a criminal is the moral agony of America's Vietnam war generation."[39]

The Laos offensive was collapsing. Nixon already knew of the upcoming May Day protests. He avoided the press and hid at San Clemente, much as Johnson had done at the LBJ Ranch. He spent days preparing a new speech justifying action in Vietnam, which he gave on April 7; it was amplified to a panel of the American Society of Newspaper Editors on the sixteenth. Seventeen years earlier, to the day, before the same group, then–Vice President Nixon had launched his trial balloon on U.S. intervention at Dien Bien Phu. This appearance would be controversial too, but in a different way. President Nixon declared that the United States would keep a residual force in Vietnam until Saigon could stand on its own. That sounded pretty open-ended.

Outside the New York hotel where Nixon spoke, demonstrators protested his appearance, shouting slogans and carrying signs. They simply walked behind police barricades, much like unionists picketing a building. At a certain point the police lifted the barricades, and the TPF and mounted police went after the protesters, who had done nothing more violent than hand out leaflets. A horseman pressed two up against the wall, and they barely escaped being crushed. The gratuitous police violence was symptomatic of America's increasingly bitter confrontation.

Nixon's men made careful preparations for the veterans' march and the mass protest to follow on April 24. Again, major units of troops deployed to Washington, and an alert force was stashed away at the Treasury Department to intervene, if needed, at the White House next door. Despite the extensive Senate investigations carried out just months earlier, military intelligence mobilized to watch the vets and minimize GI cooperation with VVAW. The Air Force would take overhead photographs of the marchers. The CIA lent its communications van and specialists to coordinate surveillance.

The VVAW action set the stage for the massive demonstrations that followed immediately afterward. The April 24 demonstration was organized by the National Peace Action Coalition (NPAC). As a result of strategy discussions almost a year earlier, this march had been separated from the May Day civil disobedience protest, which was sponsored by a different group, the People's Coalition for Peace and Justice, spearheaded by Dave Dellinger and Rennie Davis, among others. Even the peaceful event got official attention. FBI offices in San Antonio, New York, and Washington tried to obstruct some of the final planning conferences, without much effect. Nixon met with more delegations of students. "We have to sit here and talk to these little jackasses," he told Haldeman after one such session on March 25. He wanted to "scratch all this crap . . . all these meetings, this therapy meeting with the little assholes."[40] All his advisers urged Nixon to persevere. This president rejected public opinion. He preferred to control it.

For march organizers, the jealousies and cross-cutting purposes of the NPAC and May Day events were a headache. But preparations moved ahead. The mass march was truly that—Fred Halsted expected up to a million Americans, and later estimates put the figure at 650,000, the largest march in Washington so far. Some insist the million figure *was* attained. Another 300,000 or more turned out for a parallel demonstration in San Francisco. Alongside the usual suspects there were African Americans, Native Americans, welfare rights activists, Zionists and Palestinians, gay liberation and feminist groups, and many more.

I was there with the Columbia contingent. Laos had been over the top for me. Despite the political unacceptability of widening the Vietnam war at the time of Cambodia, the U.S. government had done it again. This was also the time and place where I became aware of VVAW vets, and their actions in the days before our arrival impressed me. If anything, the feeling of determination among protesters was stronger than at the May 1970 protest. Vehicles all headed to the same destination dominated traffic on Interstate 95 south to Washington. The Jersey Turnpike was bumper to bumper. Cars and buses full of people. I had never seen so many buses, even at the 1969 and 1970 marches, when, believe me, there had been plenty. Washington itself seemed like a parking lot for buses.

The throngs flowed like rivers to The Mall. Images of both protest and exuberance fill my memories of that day. Slogans shouted by so many voices they surely must have been heard in Baltimore. Protesters climbed statues and raised flags, some with the peace symbol, some American flags and some Vietcong, some American flags flown upside down. The huge mass called for an end to the war on the Ellipse, on the plain of The Mall beneath Capitol Hill, surrounding the Washington Monument. But the protest also proved amorphous; with so many groups and so many agendas, it lost some essential purpose. VVAW had been constant and consistent. May Day, in which I did not participate, would attempt to be so. Many who joined in the protests of those years lament that the Movement ultimately could not accomplish a social transformation. The reason was visible in microcosm that day, April 24, 1971: building a united front around one or a few issues simply became impossible in a universe of such diverse groups.

Nevertheless, the April 24 march carried its message on the war. Even an offensive with minimal U.S. involvement had become controversial, and Americans were willing to turn out in unprecedented numbers. The polls gave the president no comfort. Freedom of action for the White House had nearly disappeared.

Richard Nixon made himself scarce at Camp David, despite the fact that his retreat was in the throes of a huge renovation. He phoned the White

House periodically for updates from Haldeman, whose relief at the peaceful nature of the protest is evident in his diary. The president, Haldeman recorded, was "of course" mainly interested in making sure the protest "was downplayed as much as possible."[41] But others did not miss the implications. Saigon foreign minister Tran Van Lam happened to be visiting Washington, along with Vietnamese Senate president Nguyen Van Huyen. Ambassador Bui Diem drove them around in his nondescript beige sedan, "allowing them to see for themselves the flood of hatred and rage that had regularly washed the capital over the past several years." Skirting the main crowds, Diem still managed to give the dignitaries "close-up views of the ragged clothes and bitter faces of demonstrators and the stolid rows of police and national guardsmen." The foreign minister and the Saigon politician were "profoundly shocked."[42]

The message was driven home at May Day. When Nixon returned from Camp David, both the morning staff meeting and Haldeman's private conversation with the president were dominated by preparations to counter the May Day Tribe, as protesters styled themselves. Talking with Kissinger, Nixon worried about the impact the protests might have on Hanoi. On April 30 Nixon ordered the Pentagon to use federal troops against the demonstrators. At the event three days later, protesters shouted, "Stop the War or We'll Stop the Government!" The White House was ringed with buses again, and this time there were machine-gun nests on the president's lawn. Troops and police were on such a hair trigger that demonstrators were apprehended on sight. Some civil disobedience took place at government buildings, but in other cases protesters were busted virtually on arrival. Authorities arrested more than 8,000 people on May 3 alone, by White House count—up to 13,000, according to other estimates—cramming them into mass lockups at Robert F. Kennedy Stadium and the D.C. Armory with no legal proceedings whatever. At least 2,000 more were arrested outside the Department of Justice the next day. Efforts to deliver a "People's Peace Treaty" to Congress on May 5 led to another 1,100 arrests. The generally accepted figure for May Day participants is 50,000. On May 6 the South Vietnamese embassy would be surrounded by troops and police when protesters attempted to demonstrate there. Washington's mayor and police chief plus the military commanders responsible for these actions stepped into the Oval Office on May 8 to receive the president's thanks. But when the police actions came before the courts, the U.S. government was found to have violated the civil and constitutional rights of thousands and would be forced to pay huge amounts in damages.

One particular feature of May Day deserves mention. Those who planned civil disobedience joined "affinity groups," so that when taken into custody they would at least be with people they knew. One of these squads, intending to block streets, consisted primarily of members of the Concerned Committee of Asian Scholars, including Noam Chomsky, Fred Branfman, Marilyn Young, and Howard Zinn, plus associate Daniel Ellsberg. Ellsberg had been moving steadily into opposition, copying the text and documents of the Pentagon Papers study housed at the Rand Corporation. He had been a mover in creating a letter opposing the war that five Rand analysts published in 1969, and after Cambodia, Ellsberg had gone public at teach-ins. Hoping to trigger an intensive investigation of the conduct of the war, Ellsberg began giving material to Senator William Fulbright. Then Dr. Kissinger had had a talk with Ellsberg on the eve of Lam Son, assuring him the war was ending. Ellsberg woke up to news of invasion. Laos became the touchstone for Ellsberg. May Day marked his progression to civil disobedience. Ellsberg's affinity group was gassed. In fact, a policeman ran up out of nowhere and sprayed mace directly into his face, then Zinn's. At the time, they were simply standing on a corner, talking to a passerby.[43] Already aware the FBI was on his trail for the secret documents, he now saw Congress unwilling to move forward. Over the following weeks Ellsberg first approached the media, giving the Pentagon Papers to key newspapers.

Canny observers recognized that Nixon had gone to war at home. One Washingtonian went out to walk his dog only to find federal troops camped in the parkland that lay beyond Georgetown. That was no surprise; he had seen that before. Perhaps the troops deployed to face VVAW and May Day could be viewed as a reasonable precaution. What amazed him was to see troops camped out week after week. Reflecting on this period much later, an Army general remarked that the military had fielded the equivalent of a combat division to Washington several times, another to Chicago, two to Detroit, and a division to Miami later on. And those were merely the major deployments; not included were the endless summonses to the National Guard for actions from Kent State to New Haven. Every one of those confrontations pitted one American against another. There was no way this could continue.[44]

Dewey Canyon III, May Day, and the leak of the Pentagon Papers have special importance, not only as events but also because their combination set Richard Nixon on a course that both tied his hands on the war and led to a constitutional crisis. The Pentagon Papers were one key, exposing the conduct of the war up until Tet, but Nixon's efforts to suppress them, abetted by Kissinger and Haig, broke new ground in transgressions of the law by presidential fiat. May Day showed that the Movement would not be put off, that the president's measures so far had failed to defuse dissent or, worse, had been negated by his own Nixon Shocks. Dewey Canyon III represented the manifestation of a new wing of opposition, one uniquely qualified to hold the U.S. government to account. Nixon's efforts would rebound in an explosive fashion.

Richard Nixon was proactive, to adopt a later phrase. He had ordered the

State Department purged at the time of Cambodia and demanded a similar purge of White House staff at the height of the Laos disaster. In March, with Congress up in arms, Nixon dreamed up the idea of creating an organization of pro-war Capitol Hill secretaries and administrative aides. He had aimed broadly at Americans with his Huston plan. He had contrived an "enemies list." He had also been the architect of an alliance with the Hard Hats, and it was precisely now that the president brought union boss Peter Brennan to the Oval Office to thank him and reminisce "about the 'hard hat' parade last year."[45] Haldeman, Kissinger, all Nixon's top aides, had learned to hold off carrying out the president's more extreme orders. But sometimes they contributed to the excesses. It remains unclear whether Nixon, Kissinger, or some combination of them and staffers initiated all the warrantless "national security" wiretaps, but these too had targeted Americans. After the VVAW action in Washington, Nixon political aide Murray Chotiner suggested approaching John Kerry to turn him to the Republican side. Nixon dismissed that out of hand. A former CIA officer who now worked at the White House felt he was entering a building under siege, "an Alamo fighting not only the surrounding army but an internal uprising as well." These "halls were so deep in paranoiac sludge that we had to wade through it with boots."[46] The spring of 1971 threw up two new figures for Richard Nixon to smite: Daniel Ellsberg and John Kerry. Nixon went after them both.

■ ■ ■ The first installment of the Pentagon Papers appeared in the *New York Times* on June 13, 1971. Within hours Al Haig began pushing the president to suppress the revelations, and after a brief period of nonchalance, Henry Kissinger added his weight to the pile-on. Mr. Nixon hardly needed convincing. By the second day John Mitchell had given Ellsberg's name to the president, courtesy of the FBI. By the third the Justice Department was warning and then suing the *Times*, followed by the *Washington Post* and other papers that ran the material. The effort to suppress publication failed at the Supreme Court by a decisive six-to-three margin. The next day, on the phone to J. Edgar Hoover, Nixon denounced the "stinking," unbelievable Court decision and vowed to change the Court, mouthing epithets regarding several of the justices who had been in the majority.[47] That never happened, but the effort to attack and destroy Ellsberg continued—starting with a federal grand jury and eventually widening to investigate much more.[48]

On the evening of June 15, during one of his phone conversations on how to deal with the Pentagon Papers, Nixon told Chuck Colson to conjure up support from the administration's "constituent groups," including labor but also "veterans."[49] The timing is significant, since the next day the president met with John O'Neill, a representative of the Vietnam Veterans for a Just

Peace, one of Colson's special projects created specifically to counter VVAW. At their June 16 Oval Office meeting it was Nixon, not O'Neill, who brought up the Pentagon Papers, trying to elicit agreement that the leak had been treasonous. Having broached the subject of treason, Nixon seasoned the blend, adding Alger Hiss, whose persecution Nixon had ridden to prominence. The president had complained to Kissinger that VVAW spokesman John Kerry had been extremely effective. Now he exhorted O'Neill to go after Kerry, complimenting the visitor's pleasant manner, telling O'Neill he was perfect for the role, accusing the protesters of just running America down. The president said that O'Neill should just "give it to" Kerry. In a revealing slip of the tongue, Nixon told O'Neill that he was on the "winning side," but he instantly corrected himself and said the "right side."[50]

Colson described O'Neill to Bob Haldeman as an "emerging new hero" and dubbed him with the alias "Jack Armstrong," a reference to a 1947 Hollywood movie in which an All-American saves earth from an evil scientist's death ray. Indeed, O'Neill required no prodding to go after Kerry. Both had served in the same Navy riverine division on the Mekong, and O'Neill seethed at charges that his unit, or any U.S. forces in Vietnam, had engaged in war crimes, either routinely or otherwise. An Annapolis graduate with eighteen months in Vietnam, O'Neill left the service at the beginning of June 1971 and instantly began attacking Kerry and VVAW, first in announcing the creation of his own group, then in a series of television appearances, including on such programs as *60 Minutes, Face the Nation,* and *The Dick Cavett Show.* White House staff were ecstatic, thinking O'Neill even more articulate than the VVAW spokesman.

In 2004, when Kerry, then a U.S. senator, ran for president as the Democratic Party's candidate, O'Neill emerged from the shadows to attack Kerry again using a newly created vehicle called the Swift Boat Veterans for Truth. At that point the media focused light on the origins of O'Neill's first group, the Vietnam Veterans for a Just Peace, which O'Neill insisted had never been a creature of the Nixon White House, having started "a little bit before Colson knew who we were."[51] Asked about this, Chuck Colson confirmed that the White House had "formed" the group specifically as "a counterfoil" to VVAW. It is known that Colson had been assigned to rally veteran support for the president, and for months he circulated delegations from the American Veterans Association and the Veterans of Foreign Wars through the White House. Shortly after VVAW's Washington march, Colson took the lead—and Nixon followed—in denouncing Kerry as a "phony," and Colson had solicited denunciations of Dewey Canyon III from the VFW. The need for a counterfoil was evident. Bruce N. Kesler actually takes credit for forming the Vietnam Veterans for a Just Peace. Kesler, a former Marine corporal, had published a letter in *Time* magazine supporting Nixon's invasion of Cambodia, making him readily identifiable at the White House. Helping him was a Romanian émigré, Daniel E. Teodoru, also a Vietnam veteran and an outspoken character whose participation in this gambit is quite believable.

John O'Neill first appeared with the group when organizers announced its creation at a news conference on June 1, the day of his separation from the Navy, which certainly fuels speculation he had been handpicked for the role. The very next day at the White House, Haldeman told the president, "we've" got a veterans' group forming. Nixon thought they might be out in the hallway waiting to meet him, but Haldeman told his boss, "No, we don't want them to be able to see you yet."[52] By June 16 O'Neill had some TV appearances under his belt, and White House documents show its staff helped schedule more.

By far the most significant TV appearance took place on June 30, when O'Neill and Kerry actually duked it out on *The Dick Cavett Show*. O'Neill was in attack mode. It is clear from the transcript that he fastened on "war crimes" as specific acts by particular individuals, castigating Kerry for fabrications regarding their own Navy unit but also VVAW for its refusal to swear "depositions" at its Winter Soldier Investigation or afterward. Another sore point was Kerry's assertion in testimony on Capitol Hill that he spoke for a mass of Vietnam vets. As a debate, Kerry won the encounter. O'Neill could not demonstrate awareness of the Geneva Conventions Kerry relied on when he spoke of war crimes. O'Neill also resorted to the Nixon "silent majority" gambit, claiming the vast majority of soldiers in or back from Vietnam agreed with him. That fell flat. VVAW had had about a thousand vets in Washington at any given moment, perhaps 2,000 in all, but in the weeks since the Winter Soldier Investigation, its membership had ballooned to 20,000. What we know about Pentagon and MACV misgivings regarding the battle-worthiness of U.S. troops supports Kerry's claim that he spoke for more than himself and a few surly grunts. Despite the assertion that he represented a majority of veterans, O'Neill's organization had no mass membership; in fact, there was no evidence that Vietnam Veterans for a Just Peace consisted of more than a handful of persons, primarily O'Neill himself, Kesler, and Teodoru. (The largest known convocation of Vietnam Veterans for a Just Peace occurred at the 1972 Republican National Convention, when a dozen vets—not all of whom were members of O'Neill's group—were honored by Nixon's party.) Meanwhile, John O'Neill had told Richard Nixon at their meeting that he knew nothing about the Pentagon Papers, but on *The Dick Cavett Show* he invoked them twice—to blame the Vietnam war on Democrats.[53]

The best evidence that Vietnam Veterans for a Just Peace was a White House creature resides in its lack of a record. It did not even interest the White House. Except for "day after" ruminations on O'Neill's *Dick Cavett* performance, one mention a few weeks later, and one more late in 1972, when it was a question of drumming up vets' support for the administration's negotiations with Hanoi, O'Neill disappears from presidential discourse. Colson kept up contact, soliciting O'Neill when it seemed useful. O'Neill's cameo appearance at the 1972 convention helped nominate Nixon for reelection. But his group has no story, no string of accomplishments, whether it be marches, newspapers, conventions, or mass organizing.

There is one exception. On *The Dick Cavett Show* John O'Neill had charged that if Hanoi won in Vietnam there would be a bloodbath in the South, and untold numbers of Vietnamese would be executed. A year later Teodoru wrote a paper, "The Bloodbath Hypothesis: The Maoist Pattern in North Vietnam's Radical Land Reform," casting back to the period after the French war to substantiate the charge. Teodoru's paper exaggerated by a huge factor the number of deaths in North Vietnam during the 1950s land reform. In an indication of how tightly wound the whole pro-war apparatus had become, the Teodoru paper would be published by the American Friends of Vietnam in its newsletter *Southeast Asian Perspectives*.[54]

In contrast, VVAW remained in the forefront, anything but invisible. At the height of May Day, Mike Oliver, now Oregon regional coordinator, and other vets were arrested for dumping a hundred pounds of chicken excrement, which they had obtained from a Maryland farmer, on the Pentagon steps. The men styled themselves the "Chickenshit 20." Al Hubbard led them across the railroad bridge near the Pentagon, even counting cadence, while May Day marchers distracted the police with their mass parade across Memorial Bridge. In the middle of this action, the group discovered that Oliver had failed to check the train schedules, which could have been life threatening if a train had happened along.

John Kerry, always a moderate, deplored May Day's intention of actually shutting down the U.S. government, but he crisscrossed the country speaking on college campuses and at local protests, his themes being end the war and bring the boys home. Later that May the Boston chapter of VVAW held a protest on Lexington Common that was busted by police in the largest mass arrest in Massachusetts history. Of course, Lexington was the very place where American freedom began. VVAW was very good at imagery. Among those arrested was Gary Rafferty, who had joined immediately upon returning from Vietnam.

Founder Jan Barry began compiling material for the first of a series of Vietnam poetry collections that would feature VVAW contributors. When publishers showed no interest in the book, *Winning Hearts and Minds*, VVAW published it themselves.[55] The poetry attracted a great deal of attention, probably because no one had supposed grunts could write poetry. Vets attended a new international war crimes tribunal, and national coordinator Hubbard went to Paris to address an international antiwar conference. Joe Urgo traveled to Hanoi, the first GI to visit there during the war. Hopes the DRV might release some prisoners to his delegation were dashed. Another

VVAW activity centered around a Virginia farm, run as a de facto rehabilitation center for vets trying to cope with their trauma, a communal immersion for those who wanted to go beyond the rap groups. And local chapters struggled with VA hospitals, trying to obtain better medical care for the wounds of war.

■ ■ ■ The Movement's virtual spring offensive, most particularly VVAW's actions, led the Nixon administration not only to political manipulation but also to escalation on the surveillance front. Military contingency plans under "Garden Plot" and "Lantern Spike" were updated. Planning envisioned using forces of up to seven brigades of Army and National Guard troops—a contingent equivalent to more than two divisions, or, put differently, 20 percent of the peak U.S. force in Vietnam. The Army started a training course for officers, intelligence specialists, local police, and first responders. Between September 1971 and May 1975, at one training center alone, more than 4,000 persons attended the course. There were several such centers. Computerized files were compiled on 18,000 Americans, including members of Congress.

The Secret Service saw threats to Nixon behind every door. Rufus Youngblood, the stalwart who had defended LBJ, had been kicked upstairs to deputy director. He traveled with Mr. Nixon a few times, most notably on the trip to see Nguyen Van Thieu at Midway Island, but Youngblood would be largely isolated. The Secret Service's uniformed guards at the White House became something of a joke when Nixon tried to outfit them in ersatz European imperial uniforms, but they expanded greatly and became the Executive Protection Service. The Secret Service's list of those who had supposedly threatened the president's life had mushroomed to 50,000 names in 1969—a sevenfold increase over the Johnson years—and it doubled again by 1971. On a 1970 trip to California, President Nixon, code-named SEARCHLIGHT, faced such a tough crowd that his limousine ended up with ten dents from rocks thrown by protesters. Secret Service agent Marty Venker recalled, "Our Intelligence Division was getting word that the college whiz kids were wiring smarter bombs. Who knew what to expect? America was beginning to look like a tropical nation of juntas and coups where the victorious candidate was the one who survived until voting day." He began looking at crowds like herds of excitable animals ready to stampede.[56] The bombing reference no doubt referred to the Weathermen.

Youngblood reminisced, "the fact that you are a nonpolitical professional does not guarantee you immunity to the political intrigue that is constantly going on."[57] Venker confirmed that the vendetta against Youngblood bore Haldeman's fingerprints. Bob Taylor took over the White House detail. SEARCHLIGHT made many demands. Among them was Secret Service protection for national security adviser Henry Kissinger, code name WOODCUTTER. The Secret Service's view became jaundiced, its activity acquiring a political character. Typically, Joe Petro, a freshly minted agent ordered to stand post during a Nixon visit to Akron, Ohio, got orders from the agent in charge to seize a North Vietnamese flag from protesters outside the Holiday Inn where SEARCHLIGHT was staying. A Vietnam veteran, Petro refused the order, pointing out that such action went beyond personal protection and crossed constitutional boundaries. The superior turned to Petro's colleague, another vet, who rejected the demand too. In the end, the agent in charge could not get anyone to carry out his order. Petro thought the men on the White House detail were arrogant, reflecting the personality of their president. There were plenty of occasions when objections like these were overridden.

Attorney General John Mitchell instructed his Internal Security Division, led by Robert C. Mardian, to start an offensive of its own, driving the FBI to greater efforts. Mardian in turn had his litigations chief, Guy L. Goodwin, undertake a specific investigation of VVAW. At the time, Goodwin happened to be supervising FBI agents who used a provocateur to encourage resisters to plunder the Camden, New Jersey, draft board, with the Bureau furnishing gas, trucks, tools, and other equipment, and the FBI's informant training the resisters how to break into the draft board office.[58] Goodwin's tactics against VVAW would be similar. Several vets recount the same story—connected to both the national office and the New York chapter of VVAW—reporting they knew VVAW's phones were tapped when they tried to pay the bill and the utility company said it had already been taken care of, the "by whom" revealed with winks and nods. With typical aplomb, the vets promptly gave out their telephone credit card number to Movement groups all over, confident the FBI would pick up the tab.

Goodwin's orders went to the FBI's Domestic Intelligence Division, long led by William C. Sullivan, who now stood at Hoover's side as assistant to the director. The new division chief, Charles D. Brennan, had been Sullivan's top lieutenant. William R. Brannigan, then Robert L. Shackelford, headed the section responsible for "subversive" investigations. They became the field commanders of the Nixon administration's offensive against VVAW.

The foot soldiers were the FBI's special agents and their paid informants. Most of the latter were people who reported what the vets said at public functions, but some were actual members of the organization. Declassified FBI field reports displayed at VVAW's twenty-fifth anniversary reunion in 1992 provided virtual minutes of meetings of the New York chapter, clearly showing a Bureau presence on the inside.[59] The Secret Service got in on the act too. Three Secret Service agents—Joe Petro, Rick Zaino, and Holly Huffschmidt—were detailed to infiltrate VVAW at Dewey Canyon III, which led to the incongruity of Secret Service personnel handing out VVAW leaflets outside the White House, while the Executive Protection Service and White House detail shielded the president from them.

Surrounding the veterans with a web of agents and wiretaps furnished a wealth of information, but the surveillance hardly seems necessary. The truth is that VVAW conducted its affairs in the open, with the results of local, regional, and national meetings freely discussed and disseminated in mimeographed newsletters and sometimes in the group's paper, *First Casualty*. The most contentious debates of 1971 were certainly no secret because the former GIs bubbled with talk, attempting to recruit comrades to their factions. Leadership of the organization was exercised by the national staff in cooperation with a set of regional coordinators, all of whom met periodically as a steering committee. The most significant dispute pitted regional leaders against national ones over grassroots issues. Coordinators wanted local actions such as demonstrations at military posts, support for the GI coffeehouses, and speakers at rallies or teach-ins. The national office scrambled so hard to keep up with the flood of new members and chapters it simply lost touch. Staffer Scott Moore drove around the country that summer checking in on the regions and chapters and brought back a tale of discontent.

Some see this debate as a struggle between southern and northern wings of VVAW; others see it as pitting former sergeants (the regional coordinators) against officers (the national office). Neither is true. Certainly VVAW expanded rapidly in the South—particularly in Texas, Florida, and the Southwest—but there was no particular regional flavor to its cleavages. Similarly, it was not true that the national staff consisted of officers ranged against former NCOs. At the time, there were but a handful of former officer members anywhere. Hearing this charge, one VVAWer guffawed and replied there had been exactly *three* officers at Dewey Canyon. Important people at the national level—Hubbard being the obvious example—had been enlisted men. What was real was the feeling that the national office was disconnected. Its entire staff would turn over during 1971. The internal cleavages within VVAW—in common with other Movement organizations—sapped energy, reduced effectiveness, distracted activists from their real purpose, and add up to another reason why the strong organizations of the 1960s ultimately had a limited impact on America. But it is a distinction of VVAW that it rose above differences to get on with its work.

The personal differences between top-level officers Hubbard and Kerry were emblematic of the distractions. John Kerry's notoriety after Dewey Canyon III and his success at fund-raising, plus Al Hubbard's serious error in misrepresenting his past, gave Kerry a leg up. Kerry's proclivity for moderate tactics bumped up against Hubbard's more militant stance at the steering committee meetings held in June at St. Louis and that fall at Kansas City. The two hurled charges at each other. Kerry remained a spokesman without any leadership post. He failed to defeat Hubbard, and by late 1971 had increasingly come under siege. In addition, one of Hubbard's favored projects, the "Lifeline to Cairo"—a series of "convoys" taking supplies to besieged African American and civil rights activists in Cairo, Illinois—stayed on the books, even though Kerry opposed it and Scott Moore found it ineffective.

The leadership conference at Kansas City in November brought the crunch. As it had at St. Louis, the FBI monitored the Kansas City meeting. It had spies there, most notably Bill Lemmer, a former Green Beret from North Carolina recruited after a drug bust while joyriding with buddies in Leavenworth County, Kansas, a couple of months earlier.[60] (A pitch following arrest on other charges was a favorite FBI recruiting ploy.) Lemmer became a paid source. Courtesy of the FBI, Lemmer relocated to Arkansas for VVAW and had ample resources to travel, often showing up where Kerry spoke. He was at Kansas City when VVAW regional coordinators had it out at the steering committee, which met from November 12 to 14. So was another FBI source, Karl Becker. The FBI's extensive reports on the Kansas City meeting exhibit clear evidence of being compiled from information supplied by eyewitnesses—and they bear the weaknesses of that as well.

The most important result of the Kansas City meeting would be to shift power to VVAW's regional coordinators by adopting a measure requiring that a 60 percent majority approve of national actions. A motion to force the resignation of the entire roster of national executives failed by two votes, but several staff resigned anyway, including Kerry, who had his eye on a seat in Congress. Kerry promised to continue speaking for VVAW and made appearances in its behalf. Founder Jan Barry also left the leadership at this time. Joe Urgo was elevated to the national executive, along with Barry Romo and Del Rosario. Hubbard was not present and was not forced out, but he did resign later. The steering committee discussed actions to be taken at the end of the year, plus the Cairo convoy operation, and it began thinking about protests for the 1972 political conventions.[61]

When Kerry became a presidential candidate in 2004, critics made much of the Kansas City meeting, charging VVAW had adopted a plan to assassinate U.S. senators and John Kerry had participated. The FBI's own records do not support that charge. Rather, the FBI field report claims that the Southeast regional coordinator, Florida's Scott Camil, a former Marine sergeant, had a conversation at a party where he bragged about having a "training range" and allegedly advocated the formation of "Phoenix-type" squads that might eliminate the "governmental chain of command." Interviews with VVAW members indicate that this talk occurred among a small group sitting under a tree outside the house where the party took place. Kerry was not there, and there was no talk of specific plots. One FBI telegram records that Kerry arrived the next day.[62] As for the substance of the allegations, even the original FBI report notes that the steering committee refused to hear Camil's proposal. Camil apparently told writer Gerald Nicosia later that he began talking about "readiness groups" to counter what he felt were milquetoast and silly actions, and he eventually began to take it more seriously. He added that Bob Lemmer and Karl Becker encouraged him. But the Phoenix-like concept was deferred to a later conference, where it was roundly rejected— according to a national executive member, Camil himself voted against it. Although Camil was among the more militant members and liked guns, the evidence for these allegations is that of the FBI sources. And Lemmer would be the provocateur the FBI used to allege a violent VVAW plot less than a year later, which led to a trial in Gainesville, Florida. Becker also figured in that provocation. Bill Crandell, one of the regional coordinators, recalled that there were always people on "power trips," people "coming up to me and saying, 'I can get you guns,' or 'I can get you explosives.' But that wasn't where we were at. When they came to me I always sent them away. Scott Camil may have done that . . . but if so, why didn't it come out at Gainesville?"[63] That is a fair question, given that the Nixon people were hell-bent on nailing VVAW any way they could.

Real or not, the alleged comments at Kansas City enabled the FBI to escalate. The Bureau's Subversive Section chief, Robert Shackelford, advised Guy Goodwin and the White House of the ramped-up surveillance. Another bit of braggadocio at VVAW's Kansas City meeting had been that the convoys to Cairo carried more than food and clothing. So when VVAW sent another convoy of seven vehicles to Cairo in February 1972, the FBI pulled out all the stops to disrupt it, on the premise that the vets were running guns to civil rights activists. But the veterans engaged in no violence and no protests. By contrast, between 1969 and 1971 white supremacist snipers fired an estimated 174 times at activists or African Americans in Cairo. Four persons died for nothing more than a boycott of white-owned businesses, designed to dramatize the awful conditions in the ghetto and to protest repression. Hubbard considered the Cairo convoys one of the "crowning moments" among VVAW actions.[64]

While the FBI was all over the Cairo convoys, it completely ignored its own advance information on "Operation Peace on Earth," a set of actions mulled over in Kansas City and carried out after Christmas. Within the space of a few days, the vets staged another Valley Forge march, a protest at the Lincoln Memorial, a takeover of the South Vietnamese consulate in San Francisco, and occupations of the Betsy Ross House in Philadelphia and the Statue of Liberty in New York (some of these actions took place simultaneously). The newspapers printed photos of Lady Liberty with the flag flying upside down from her torch, generating powerful imagery for Barry's poetry collection. The vets succeeded in carrying out coordinated protests separated by thousands of miles. Their determination was enormous. Many admired them, though others denounced them. But their courage could not be disputed. *That* is what made them such a threat to Richard Nixon.

■ ■ ■ The Nixon White House would be content to let the FBI take the lead on VVAW, but it acted directly against Daniel Ellsberg. On July 1, 1971, the day after the Supreme Court overruled Nixon's attempt to quash publication of the Pentagon Papers, Chuck Colson recruited former CIA officer E. Howard Hunt, whom he knew as a fellow functionary of the capital's Brown University alumni chapter. By Hunt's account, the project began as a propaganda scheme to discredit the Kennedys with leaks of carefully doctored information about the Bay of Pigs and the Diem assassination. But the CIA refused to declassify the materials the White House wanted, in spite of repeated efforts by John Ehrlichman and measures taken by the president to strengthen the provisions of the Freedom of Information Act. (It is an irony of history that the first tough executive order restricting government secrecy would be a product of Richard Nixon's attempts to manipulate American politics.)

The main result of this effort would be a forgery, a State Department "cable" that Hunt created and Colson shopped to *Life* magazine. Hunt showed it to former CIA operative Lucien Conein in an effort to influence his commentary in a TV documentary. But as a result of the secrecy jam, Hunt's propaganda quickly took a backseat to work on a special investigations unit called the "Plumbers," who were ostensibly supposed to plug leaks but were actually out to destroy Ellsberg. In late July the White House intervened with the CIA to obtain false identity cards and disguise materials for Hunt to use. The agency also produced a psychological profile of Ellsberg for the White House. A few weeks later, disappointed that the CIA profile contained nothing that could be used to discredit Ellsberg, the Plumbers proposed to Ehrlichman that the offices of Ellsberg's psychiatrist be burglarized to obtain his case file. Egil B. Krogh, the chief Plumber, noted that when officials met to plan this act, no one even bothered to ask whether it might be illegal. The entire discussion dealt with the instrumental issues of how and when. The burglary took place in September 1971. It marked the beginning of another Nixon Shock, but one that long remained hidden, the one that would be known as Watergate.

"All This Could Have Been Avoided"
Richard Nixon's actions reflected his primordial concern with being reelected. The Plumbers, the vendetta against Ellsberg, and the drive to mobilize the FBI and CIA against the antiwar movement and VVAW, those things were all dressed up in the language of national security but were

really about dominating the American political scene going into the 1972 election season. Vietnam strategy had the same aim. A lost war, a stalled peace negotiation, or an eruption in Saigon politics could each threaten Nixon's prospects. The last of these matters stayed on the front burner through most of 1971, for Nguyen Van Thieu faced reelection before Mr. Nixon, and the October 1971 election in South Vietnam represented Washington's next challenge. Already, even during the planning of the ARVN offensives, Nixon justified some measures as a contribution to Thieu's reelection. As spring turned to summer, the South Vietnamese election became one of the two key Vietnam issues for the Nixon White House.

South Vietnamese law provided that no one could begin active campaigning until a month before the election, that is, in September. But Thieu effectively began his run with the victory parade held for Lam Son 719. That happened at Hue on April 17. General Abrams attended and thought it a splendid occasion. American adviser Don Walker, who witnessed President's Thieu's swing through Hue, felt otherwise. The Saigon leader avoided entering the city, flying his entourage directly into the Citadel by chopper. Thieu then staged a sort of parade, driving in highly decorated jeeps to the province chief's compound. Walker noticed that Thieu's bodyguards, hanging on the sides of the jeeps, were too tall to be Vietnamese. He decided they must be CIA Nungs or Koreans. After a couple of hours in conference, Thieu emerged for the celebration. Troops passed in review, wearing fresh, new uniforms. The parade's main feature would be the flyover of a large formation of helicopters right up the Pearl River. Walker overheard the spectators chattering away—what was missing, they gossiped, was a bunch of ARVN soldiers hanging from the choppers' landing skids. Thieu's campaign had an atmosphere of unreality.

Months before the election, key figures were jockeying for position. Vice President Nguyen Cao Ky was not invited to the Lam Son parade. Ky had offered to run again with Thieu, but Thieu's reply had been to make a public announcement of the ticket—himself plus Tran Van Huong. Huong's motives were complex, for Thieu had drummed him out of the government for his efforts to combat corruption. Enough of a realist to see that Thieu held the true power, Huong was also enough of a loyalist to play with Thieu again. Huong probably also believed that the election would free him to pursue his own agenda without fear.

Duong Van Minh represented a wild card. Thieu had permitted "Big" Minh to return from exile precisely because he had a political following that Thieu wanted to harness. Thieu subsequently ignored General Minh, who then lent himself to various third-force peace initiatives. When *Newsweek* polled South Vietnamese villagers in Long An province and found a plurality ready to follow a peace candidate, Minh was the obvious choice. Much of Big Minh's support remained shrouded, for no one wanted to take an open

stand and risk jail or worse. Typically, the chauffeur conducting a pack of reporters around Phuoc Long province that June spoke in a whisper when he
told an American journalist that 80 percent of the men in his militia unit
were ready to vote for Minh. As a Buddhist, the former general would have
had a natural base in Hue and Da Nang, which had voted against Thieu in
the previous election.

The skeleton in Minh's closet was, of course, the Diem coup, which General Minh had led. Diem's murder troubled many Vietnamese, especially the
politically dominant Roman Catholics. Predictably, Saigon swirled with
charges of Minh's complicity. The general defended himself, countering that
he had agreed to give Diem and his brother Nhu safe conduct into exile—a
plan that would have worked if the troops surrounding the presidential
palace had not permitted them to flee. Nguyen Van Thieu had been in charge
of those troops. President Thieu promptly called a news conference at the officers' club of the Joint General Staff to denounce Minh, accusing him of
slander. Thieu was flushed, his voice shrill.

Many believed that Thieu manipulated the electoral process. At the height
of the Minh fracas, Thieu rejected that charge, too, responding, "It is not
easy to rig the elections."[65] But the Saigon leader did exactly that, ramming a
revised election law through the legislature that required a presidential candidate to secure signatures from 40 National Assembly members or 100
provincial or municipal councilmen. This law aimed primarily at Nguyen
Cao Ky. With the concentration of former ARVN officers and third-force
politicians in the National Assembly, Minh had no difficulty passing the test.
But Ky had no equivalent power base, and the provincial officials, of course,
were Thieu appointees. Thieu's secret polls reportedly showed that 60 percent of the military backed Ky, but just 25 percent the Saigon leader himself.[66] Angling to reverse these attitudes, Thieu chose this moment to hand
out dozens of promotions. Thirty-nine-year-old Lam Quang Thi, for example, whose career had been stymied by the palace perception that he opposed
Thieu, suddenly received a promotion to lieutenant general. His brother was
promoted to major general in this shower of awards. Thi noted, "It was unheard of that a young officer without political affiliations, without a mentor
in the Army or the government, could rise to the second highest rank in the
Army."[67]

Vice President Ky failed to gain the required signatures to become a candidate. He condemned the new law in an open letter to President Thieu and
went to court to get it annulled. But the supreme court, going no further
than the text of the bill, ruled against Ky. Even American diplomats were
aghast at the prospect of Thieu in a one-man election. Ambassador Bunker
put tremendous pressure on Thieu to open up the process, and the Saigon
leader nudged the court to reconsider, just as he had forced corruption investigators to revisit their findings. The court reversed itself and declared Ky

a candidate. According to Ky himself, Ambassador Bunker approached him directly and offered him $2 million if he would stand for election. But Ky resented the idea and decided against running at all.[68] Journalist Stanley Karnow writes that the Americans "reportedly" offered money to Minh as well and actually did finance Thieu's political operation. Big Minh, who declared that the minimum requirements for a fair election were a halt to the seizure and suppression of South Vietnamese newspapers, a prohibition of the arrest of opposition campaign workers, and no switching of ballot boxes, was not satisfied. He too withdrew. The U.S. embassy got exactly what it most dreaded—a one-man presidential "election" in South Vietnam. "The unfortunate thing," Bunker told Abrams at a September 4 MACV staff conference, "is that all this could have been avoided."[69]

In Washington, the State Department had plumped for strict neutrality in the South Vietnamese election. But the White House held fast to supporting Thieu. Kissinger's memoir mocks the diplomats' desire for neutrality and pictures Thieu as a man of principle, deeply religious, patriotic, and strongly anticommunist. "Neither Nixon nor I," he wrote, "was prepared to toss Thieu to the wolves."[70] This says something about Nixon's strategy. An end to Thieu's leadership by means of electoral defeat would have added hugely to the administration's contention that South Vietnam was a democracy, and it would have removed an obstacle to peace negotiations with Hanoi. To pass up that advantage meant Nixon and Kissinger were prepared to tough it out, adding to the argument that they intended to end the Vietnam war by winning it. Ambassador Bui Diem supplies another valuable analysis here. "I thought Kissinger's position was unwise then, and I continue to think so," Diem wrote in 1987. "He wanted nothing so much as quiet from the unruly South Vietnamese. From his standpoint the elections were, in essence, an unfortunate disruption . . . But in opting to permit Thieu his methods, rather than unambiguously facing him with American requirements for reform and straightforward procedures, Kissinger invited the blossoming of one-man rule."[71]

President Thieu declared the election a referendum on his leadership and promised to resign if he received less than half the ballots. But Thieu had no doubt about the outcome. The day before the election, rather than wasting time campaigning, the Saigon leader hosted a lunch for visiting governor Ronald Reagan, joking about politics and Reagan's movies. The California governor was the serious one, asking how the war would end. Thieu replied expansively—Hanoi could either negotiate a peace deal, which it would not do, because it could not explain to its people a settlement on Saigon's terms, or the North Vietnamese would simply go away. Creighton Abrams sat through this conversation. He remarked later, "Thieu is either a greater actor than the Barrymores or he's a supremely confident man."[72]

Saigon authorities announced that all citizens had to vote in order to have their ration cards stamped for refugee assistance. In the election Thieu did worst in Buddhist Hue, where 63,000 voters delivered only 27,000 votes for him, and Da Nang (90,000 votes from 160,000 voters). Saigon's electorate of 675,000 gave Mr. Thieu 432,000 votes. But reports of ballot box tampering in the October 3 election were numerous. Officially, 87 percent of South Vietnamese participated, and Nguyen Van Thieu got 94 percent of the vote. The outcome proved identical to the "elections" in communist countries that the United States so often ridiculed. "In South Vietnam's brief history," Bui Diem observed, "the election was a point of no return, at which the search for a vivifying national purpose was finally discarded in favor of the chimerical strength of an autocrat."[73] Writing of Thieu's maneuvers, Ky expressed much the same sentiment: "His election sealed South Vietnam's fate."[74]

Washington noticed—or did not—at its peril. And indeed, Saigon's leadership remained an issue in another forum—the negotiations to end the war. There too the actions of the American president and his national security adviser bore directly on their strategic intent.

■ ■ ■ Three times during the war, members of VVAW visited the Democratic Republic of Vietnam. The first was Joe Urgo in August 1971. He traveled first to Japan, where two American delegations were melded into one for the Hanoi visit. They asked to meet with American prisoners held in the DRV but were never given access. Prisoners became a focus not only of peace negotiations but also of politics. Much has been made of an approach to the North Vietnamese by Senator George McGovern during this period.[75] Peace activists, politicians, and foreign intermediaries all became involved in the issue of prisoners precisely because negotiations seemed deadlocked, swamped in a marsh of sterile rhetoric, endlessly repeated. But unknown to the intermediaries or the public, for more than a year there had been ongoing secret negotiations, conducted by Henry Kissinger on behalf of the United States, with Hanoi representative Xuan Thuy and DRV Politburo member Le Duc Tho.

Since 1969, periodic secret meetings had been more substantive than the open talks in Paris but had made little progress. Only Washington and Hanoi participated, although the United States occasionally updated Thieu.[76] Nixon and Kissinger's conduct of the secret negotiations exhibits the same qualities of duplicity, striving for advantage, and self-deception as their management of the war. The standard diplomatic negotiation proceeds from common goals—in this case, ending the war in Southeast Asia—based on which the parties identify what they can agree on, devise formulas for issues on which they are willing to compromise, and agree to set aside matters that remain intractable. If the latter are serious enough, a solution is impossible.

The problem with the Vietnam negotiation, from the beginning, was that Hanoi and Saigon each had bottom lines unacceptable to the other. Washington, if sincere, *had* to settle because military victory had proved elusive and Americans had rejected the war. President Thieu wanted what he accused Hanoi of seeking—victory through negotiations. The NLF should disarm and Hanoi withdraw, and *after that* the southern resistance could participate in Saigon politics, with an American residual force in place to guarantee military superiority. Hanoi wanted a coalition government—driving Thieu from power—political norms to enable the Liberation Front to dominate, and a simple cease-fire that would permit a military solution if coalition failed. Hanoi also insisted on a "comprehensive" agreement including both political and military elements, since the lesson it drew from the 1954 Geneva negotiation had been that separating these had led to the failure to attain its goal of unifying Vietnam under DRV leadership.

The positions could not be reconciled. From the American standpoint, a settlement meant giving up on Saigon's demands, convincing Hanoi to give up its own, or fooling both. It is apparent from the development of the Nixon-Kissinger negotiating position in 1969 that Washington began by siding with Saigon. Thus, from the start, attaining such an agreement required military victory, since these goals meant that Hanoi must give up its own program.

There is an odd quality to the mountains of paper that document the secret Kissinger talks and the exchanges between the national security adviser and his president. In their comments about what was said at the talks or what new wrinkle Kissinger would offer, they repeatedly come back to the assertion that this or that element made an excellent "record," as if the purpose were to demonstrate appeal rather than reach a settlement. Such considerations permeate Kissinger's advisory memoranda and analyses of Hanoi or NLF positions, Nixon's and Kissinger's telephone calls, and the documents and tapes of their meetings on Vietnam diplomacy. There can be no doubt that the drive to build a "record" was significant and purposeful. Why create such a record? The reasonable inference is that Mr. Nixon foresaw a need at some point to use the fact of negotiations the same way he employed the echeloned U.S. troop withdrawals—as a mechanism to quiet dissent and buy time.

One other feature of the Nixon-Kissinger policy warrants mention: the endeavor to decouple Hanoi from its Soviet and Chinese allies. The notion of relying on Moscow to communicate with Hanoi dated to Lyndon Johnson's presidency, but Richard Nixon took it to new heights, expecting the Soviets to "deliver" Hanoi—that is, induce the DRV to agree with U.S. proposals. Dr. Kissinger called that "linkage," and he told the Russians that U.S.-Soviet bilateral relations depended on progress in Southeast Asia. Washington engaged Moscow in negotiations on trade and nuclear arms control that gave the Soviets some incentive to move away from North Vietnam. Nixon and Kissinger then made an effort to extend this tactic to the People's Republic of China (PRC) when, in 1971, the Americans moved to reopen relations with the Chinese. But Hanoi resisted pressure from the other two sides of the communist triangle, Washington overestimated the communist powers' influence in the DRV, and Nixon's own desire for foreign policy achievements with the USSR and China ultimately trumped his interest in using them to manipulate Hanoi.[77]

The president's envelope steadily narrowed. An increasingly frustrated and assertive Congress investigated more aspects of U.S. involvement, repealed the supposed justification of the Gulf of Tonkin resolution, and passed bills restricting military options in various ways. In mid-1971 a bill proposed by Senator Mike Mansfield that would have set a date for U.S. withdrawal, regardless of military factors or the progress of negotiations, narrowly failed to pass. It was only a matter of time until some similar device succeeded. Meanwhile, Nixon's troop withdrawals lost value as a political tool once MACV forces declined to a low level.

It is not coincidental that about the time the Gulf of Tonkin authorization met its demise, Nixon shifted his justification for continued hostilities to the recovery of American prisoners held by the enemy. The justification is notable for its circular logic, but the president proceeded anyway, and the records demonstrating White House reliance on the prisoner issue are enlightening. Administration relations with the families of POWs and those who were missing in action (MIA) became another of Charles Colson's peculiar portfolios. He played a significant role in creating the first groups of POW families and in scheduling White House events according them recognition. The White House then argued that the concerns of POW families had to be taken into account.[78]

As Mr. Nixon's options narrowed, the Kissinger secret talks accelerated.

The story of the negotiations is a tale of Washington's progressive peeling away of the layers of its—and Saigon's—original purposes, because military success remained elusive and Hanoi rejected compromise. Extending the talks—to provide more time for military measures to take effect—required new offers, and having something to offer meant stepping off elements of the initial bargaining position. As they moved deeper into this heart of darkness, Nixon and Kissinger were increasingly obliged to mislead South Vietnam. Saigon officials' accounts of this process share the common theme of American—that is, Nixon-Kissinger—betrayal. Senior diplomat Nguyen Xuan Phong, for example, recalled, "Our big negotiation was with the Americans, not the DRV."[79] National security adviser Nguyen Phu Duc, Kissinger's opposite number, wrote a book-length account demonstrating that in Vietnam, for the first time, "an ally of the United States was abandoned in the midst of a common struggle."[80] Thieu adviser Nguyen Tien Hung shows how, at successive stages of this process, Nixon sent the Saigon leader letters containing promises not capable of fulfillment.[81]

The attenuation of Washington's initial position began in September 1970, when Kissinger presented a proposal through the secret channel that included a standstill cease-fire in which all forces would remain in place (sometimes termed a "leopard-spot" cease-fire), implicitly conceding that North Vietnamese troops would not have to leave the south. The offer was revealed in Nixon's televised speech on October 7. The divergence with Saigon became apparent immediately, because Thieu gave his own speech connecting a cease-fire to the withdrawal of *all* foreign troops. Hanoi, of course, insisted it had no troops in the South, and even if it did, such troops would not be *foreign* but Vietnamese. The need to find a way through that thorny patch was obviated by the DRV's swift rejection of the peace plan.

The pace of change accelerated in 1971. Kissinger had another secret meeting with DRV representatives on May 31 where he offered a specific deadline for the withdrawal of U.S. forces, tied not to Hanoi's actions but to the release of American prisoners, with a cease-fire that would be separate from an overall political settlement. Hanoi rejected that out of hand because it was not "comprehensive." What is really interesting, however, is how Ambassador Bunker described the offer to President Thieu on June 3. According to the reporting cable, Thieu was informed only "in general terms" along the lines of the October formula, but including the "eventual withdrawal of all foreign troops from Indo-China."[82] No such element actually existed in the proposal Kissinger presented to Hanoi. The White House's real notion of how to achieve a de facto DRV withdrawal, referred to by Kissinger in press background briefings at the time of the October plan, was to strictly enforce provisions of the 1954 Geneva agreements that prohibited the crossing of borders or the Demilitarized Zone for military purposes, which presumably would lead to gradual attrition and final elimination of the DRV forces. Saigon officials thought Hanoi would not permit its expeditionary army to wither away, and in any case, violations would be very difficult to prove.

Pressing their demand for a coalition government, DRV negotiators told Kissinger for the first time on June 26 that they were prepared to release U.S. prisoners but wanted an even more rapid American withdrawal. Kissinger rejected the demand that Washington collaborate in the overthrow of Thieu but moved toward a "comprehensive" deal by agreeing to consider both military and political aspects. Some confusion was caused by the fact that both Hanoi and the Provisional Revolutionary Government suddenly issued formulas for agreement, but Kissinger noted that "in the fairy-tale atmosphere of Vietnam negotiations," the administration was thrilled that Hanoi had made a specific reply to an American proposal.[83]

Almost immediately after this exchange, Dr. Kissinger made the first of two secret visits to Beijing in preparation for Nixon's February 1972 visit to

China. PRC foreign minister Zhou Enlai asked quite pointed questions about the U.S.–North Vietnamese secret talks. Some of Zhou's questions indicated that Hanoi had not kept China up to date, and in his answers, Kissinger imparted information to the Chinese he had never given to Saigon. The mere fact of Americans meeting with the Chinese was certain to raise eyebrows in Hanoi, whose relations with the PRC had been worsening, to the extent that China had pulled its last troops out of North Vietnam in 1969. Beijing's reactions to the invasions of Cambodia and Laos had been notably tepid. On his way back from China, Kissinger stopped in Paris for another session with the DRV, without mentioning China. The North Vietnamese learned of that development a few days later when Nixon announced to the world that he was beginning a rapprochement with Mao Zedong's China and would soon visit there. Accounts of this period hardly notice the concatenation of these events or their role in Hanoi's thinking about what to do in South Vietnam.

A month later Kissinger had another secret meeting in Paris, with more talk of a withdrawal schedule and an overall settlement. In his report of the conversation Kissinger noted, "We are improving our already good negotiating record."[84] The results were otherwise minimal but at least kept the door open for another session in mid-September. In Kissinger's analysis, sent to the president on September 18, he judged the possibility of trading fixed withdrawals for American prisoners as "decisively unattractive." That had been the heart of administration offers since May 1971. He preferred to play out Vietnamization, which challenged the domestic front—a fatal flaw. The national security adviser concluded that one more push on major negotiations might end the war or brighten the prospects for an endgame based on Vietnamization.

At the September meeting Hanoi diplomat Xuan Thuy rejected the U.S. plan, arguing that the United States needed to do more than promise neutrality in a South Vietnamese political competition, and that American statements regarding a "total" withdrawal remained ambiguous. In fact, Xuan Thuy asked specifically about Washington's intentions regarding residual forces.

Hanoi's concerns were well placed. At the time, Kissinger's staff was working on a new formula, something to be framed as a comprehensive proposal and issued jointly with Saigon. This was, in fact, the big push he advocated. The draft of this "statement of principles" included a U.S. residual force, providing that on the "terminal date" of withdrawal there would be "a small number of technical advisers and logistic personnel who will have no combat or combat advisory role." This wording represented "language we would like" but entered an area "where disagreements remain" with Hanoi. Meanwhile, MACV's estimates of the U.S. force required following Vietnamization ranged up to 40,000, with 20,000 an often-cited number.

The agreed-on principles included a general cease-fire (note the step back from a standstill cease-fire—undoubtedly for Saigon's consumption), and the final version of this document had a promise that the South Vietnamese leader would step down a month ahead of an internationally supervised election in which a future government would be selected.[85] Thieu was asked to approve the document and told it was safe to do so because Hanoi would certainly reject it. Americans assured him that no use would be made of the paper other than to give it to DRV negotiators at a secret meeting. Thieu agreed. Without Saigon's knowledge, Dr. Kissinger promptly sent a note to Hanoi containing the substance of the proposal on October 11. Shortly before Hanoi accepted the idea of another secret meeting, Kissinger made a second visit to Beijing. The North Vietnamese called off the Paris meeting, claiming their chief negotiator had become ill.

Late in January 1972 Nixon gave another televised speech in which he revealed the secret negotiations. Washington and Saigon simultaneously issued their joint statement of principles. The whole exercise—exactly as Kissinger had argued in September—took advantage of the negotiating "record" the White House had carefully built. Typically, Thieu learned only now that a text of elements for a comprehensive agreement had been sent to Hanoi months earlier. But in Hanoi, the calculations were very different.

The Tides That Swirled

When Joe Urgo reached Hanoi in August 1971 he had no idea of the tides that swirled in the capital of the Democratic Republic of Vietnam. The VVAW activist and his companions attended a plethora of cultural events and met with officials who expressed appreciation for anti-imperialist efforts across the globe. The delegation was not permitted to see American prisoners. Despite later hints dropped by DRV diplomats in Paris to George McGovern, no prisoners were released to subsequent visitors either.[86] Hanoi's retreat on prisoners and its cancellation of scheduled talks with Kissinger were matters of high policy. The Democratic Republic of Vietnam had reached the last stage of preparing to cast the dice in a new attempt at a military solution, the "Nguyen Hue" offensive.

First, a few words about Hanoi and the American antiwar movement. Charges have been made over the years that North Vietnam controlled the Movement, used the protesters, subverted them, or duped them. Sometimes these charges are featured in analyses of how the United States lost the war. It is true that there had been a procession of delegations—Tom Hayden and Staughton Lynd, Women Strike for Peace, Rennie Davis and Tom Hayden (again), Dave Dellinger, now VVAW's Joe Urgo. There had been other delegations too. It is true that these or other groups met with Vietnamese counterparts in Czechoslovakia, Moscow, Paris, and elsewhere. But the best efforts of the CIA, the FBI, and military intelligence over years of working the subject never demonstrated a command link to Hanoi or any other communist capital.

The evidence adduced to support theories of this kind resided in Hanoi's statements, letters sent to organizations, articles in the Vietnamese press, and occasional speeches by senior officials. This material amounted to declarations of solidarity or exhortations to act in a common anti-imperialist enterprise, not command directives. It is significant that the Vietnamese publications directed at the outside world—the journal *Vietnam Studies* and the newspapers *Vietnam Courier* and *South Vietnam in Struggle* (the NLF organ)—were replete with communist views on the progress of the war or negotiations but light on commentaries about the Movement. Hanoi's radio and press contained much more about the war opposition than did the organs aimed abroad. Charges of Movement collusion with the DRV ignored the political importance of the antiwar movement in Vietnam—surely the aspect most important to Hanoi. In North Vietnam the appearance of Movement delegations and news of opposition to the conflict served to convey hope, showing Vietnamese that America was not unified on the war. Such news could also be used in South Vietnam to undercut claims of unwavering U.S. determination. These features ensured that war resistance in the United States would have been covered by the Vietnamese media regardless of whether Movement groups reached out to Hanoi. Meanwhile, the Movement's need and desire for the kind of firsthand information available only from direct contact virtually ensured that approaches would be made. That the Movement was enthralled with the heroism of people in a small country standing up to U.S. military might only made such contacts more likely.

What is missing is evidence of Hanoi Politburo decisions to *use* antiwar groups in military or political actions rather than for propaganda. Instead, the available Vietnamese documents, such as party resolutions and conference proceedings before Tet or the Nguyen Hue offensive, indicate a desire to *influence* war opponents among other factors driving decisions. In other words, the Movement was an audience Hanoi played to, not an element in its order of battle.

One place the North Vietnamese used allusions to the antiwar movement—tremendously frustrating to Kissinger—was in the secret negotiations. As already mentioned, when these talks resumed in May 1971, the United States presented a withdrawal plan that the DRV rejected, and some of its statements there referred to war opponents. Both the DRV and the NLF's Provisional Revolutionary Government answered with their own formulas. Hanoi cited opposition to the war to indicate American debility, countering U.S. officials who liked to think the DRV acted from weakness. The DRV aimed to make progress in the talks but had a military option if they failed. The negotiations stalled over the issue of a coalition government plus DRV suspicions that the United States sought to retain residual forces in the South. That put a military venture on Hanoi's table. As Le Duan put it in a letter to COSVN's Pham Hung in June, "To make the U.S. de-escalate further . . . , we should use political and diplomatic means in combination with military means." Le Duan specifically cited the Laotian invasion, not the antiwar movement, as opening up this possibility.[87]

North Vietnam's determination to seek a military solution grew with the revelation of Nixon's overture to China. The Politburo, already uncomfortable with its Chinese ally, saw a danger that the United States could neutralize their link. On one level, Beijing ought to have been reassured—the Chinese had criticized Hanoi in 1968 for agreeing to peace talks in the first place. In response, the PRC had ended its military participation in the DRV's air defense and transportation systems. But between Tet and the year of Laos, Beijing had turned inward, consumed by its Cultural Revolution. The Sino-Soviet split had nearly come to war, and private exchanges with the United States in Warsaw had indicated a softening in Washington's old China policy. Both Nixon and Mao took advantage. Henry Kissinger's two visits to Beijing were followed by one from Alexander Haig, who went to arrange the details of the Nixon-Mao summit. It was after the second Kissinger trip that the DRV canceled the Paris negotiating session scheduled for November 20. That same day North Vietnamese prime minister Pham Van Dong traveled to Beijing and asked the Chinese to give up the Nixon summit. Not a chance.[88]

Ironically, Nixon's Chinese gambit had the effect of facilitating Hanoi's military solution. Mao, eager to minimize the negative fallout of his rapprochement with the United States, made a fresh agreement on military aid to Hanoi just prior to Kissinger's July visit. In addition, as Le Duc Tho told French Communist Party officials a year later, China retained enough of its old proclivities to back a major offensive with enthusiasm. And knowledge of Nixon's new China gambit put Hanoi on notice that time was running out on its alliances, a fear already exacerbated when Moscow and Washington announced a 1972 summit conference of their own. Hanoi could well be decoupled from its erstwhile allies.

Under the Chinese arrangement, Beijing gave the DRV tanks for the first time and greatly increased deliveries of trucks—which the Americans were destroying in quantity along the Ho Chi Minh Trail. Military aid swelled to levels last seen in the year of Tet. Assistance in 1972, when Nixon actually visited China, continued at that high rate, with Beijing further increasing its provision of armor—220 tanks versus the 80 sent during 1971. Meanwhile, the North Vietnamese turned to the Soviet Union, disclosed their plans, and prevailed on the Soviets to sign accords increasing their aid as well. The Russians furnished large numbers of SAM missiles, aircraft, more armor, and petroleum products.

The Vietnam People's Army in the Nguyen Hue offensive would be transformed—far different from the army of Tet. The offensive marked the People's Army's attainment of a new level of sophistication and skill, hardly what the Americans anticipated. Indeed, MACV had seized on various reports—from Czech, Polish, and Soviet sources, plus the French military attaché in Hanoi—that North Vietnam had been badly damaged by the Laotian campaign. The CIA produced other reports out of Paris, said to originate from Hanoi officials, including a former private secretary to Le Duc Tho, that spoke of diminished morale and disillusioned youth. The reports may have been spurious, part of a deliberate deception, or accurate. We lack the sources to discern the truth in this matter. But no deterioration is evident from Hanoi's decisions. Instead, the Politburo gathered to assess policy on May 14, 1971, and determined to assume a strategic offensive posture and seek decisive victory the following year. By the time the Central Military-Party Committee met a month later to review Lam Son 719, Washington and Moscow had issued their joint declaration of intent to hold a summit conference, further cementing Hanoi's decision. Le Duan supervised efforts to upgrade command coordination and ordered improvements in combined arms cooperation. The committee adopted a preliminary plan for the Nguyen Hue offensive. In October General Van Tien Dung visited frontline zones in the DRV panhandle and Laos to check on local conditions and impart the latest Hanoi thinking. General Dung would exercise close control over VPA operations along the DMZ. At Group 559 headquarters Dung coordinated with General Dong Sy Nguyen on logistics for the offensive and informed the command that Hanoi had decided to strengthen its antiaircraft capabilities.

The North Vietnamese pursued their preparations with care, beginning with a seminar for midlevel and senior officers and some party officials that focused on Lam Son's lessons on large-unit operations, mobile warfare, and attacking fortified positions. Late in the year the army opened an exercise area near Haiphong that included a complete mock-up of a regiment-size base camp as used by U.S. forces and the ARVN. The VPA 308th Division conducted a four-day maneuver to practice capturing such a position. The General Staff combined Lam Son experience and the maneuver results to issue a revised field manual for attacks on fortified positions.

This attention to detail would be replicated across the board. Soviet aid included several new weapons, among them shoulder-fired SA-7 "Strella" antiaircraft missiles, AT-3 "Sagger" antitank missiles, and more of the long-range 130mm guns. The VPA conducted live-fire training with the weapons, along with tests; when the tests showed a need to adapt technology to local conditions, they put their scientists to work. Rockets were modified to extend their range, captured U.S. antitank weapons were modified to serve as air defense rockets, T-54 medium tanks were taken out of storage and their steering systems reconfigured.

Field preparations were extensive. Further development of the Ho Chi Minh Trail became necessary. Fresh transportation groups were created under Group 559, the command responsible for The Trail, which became a strategic coordination center. A pipeline that pumped oil to the South was extended from the border into Laos, saving the equivalent of many truckloads per day. Some 10,000 tons of gas and oil were shipped during the 1971 dry season. New roads were built, and existing ones given phony installations to deceive planes. Dong Sy Nguyen's trailblazers even contrived an answer to the U.S. gunships. A major thoroughfare, many miles long, was prepared entirely under a jungle canopy, invisible from the air. With four construction groups working from different points along the intended route, the building could be completed in record time. The covered way, almost 500 miles long, connected the Tchepone area with the Cambodian border. Group 559 sent its first convoy down the route on February 10, 1972, an infantry regiment destined for Nambo. Some 2,000 trucks—almost as many as the Chinese delivered—expanded the Trail's capacity by a third. Tactical commands added roads within their own areas to move troops onto anticipated battlefields. The Americans had become accustomed to witnessing North Vietnamese "logistics offensives" each fall. The one for 1971 occurred later than usual but was much more extensive.

The U.S. air forces remained the primary threat. Hanoi extended its air defense umbrella to the area of the DMZ and lower Laos. The Soviets furnished equipment for ten new SAM battalions. Beginning about November, the VPA deployed all of them to the combat theater, along with many antiaircraft units, radar for the large-caliber flak guns, and more 100mm, 57mm, and 37mm weapons. Eight antiaircraft regiments took the field. The concentration of antiaircraft forces in Laos more than doubled, to fifty-two battalions. North Vietnam established new commands—the 377th Antiaircraft Division for Laos and the 367th Division in the North Vietnamese panhandle. To counter Arc Light strikes, Hanoi's air force shifted MIG-21 interceptors to bases above the DMZ, extending its radar net to support them. MACV tallied almost eighty interception attempts against B-52s over the last months of 1971.

Preparing the troops was a key issue involving reorganization, new equipment, and training. In the COSVN area the People's Army trained specialized units. The 9th Division had the main attack mission and practiced fighting in cities and towns. Earmarked for siege warfare, assault, and mobile operations would be the 5th Division. The 7th Division prepared for mobile warfare too, along with ambushing relief columns. In central Vietnam's Military Region 5, the VPA 3rd Division retrained to conduct coordinated large-unit operations. In the Central Highlands' B-3 Front area, VPA units practiced for infantry-tank tactics, assault and envelopment techniques, and continuous intense fighting. The sector along the DMZ, where the Route 9

Front held sway, was a bit of an exception. Emplacements for heavy artillery and camps for big units were built but not occupied. Hanoi delayed moving up reserves until the last minute.

Many preparations involved units that were deployed at the front, sometimes even in combat. The People's Army worked training sessions into troops' daily routines. Units in South Vietnam rotated through base areas to get training. Political officers labored to ready the soldiers for the great sacrifices of the campaign. An example would be the 489th Sapper Company of Military Region 5. The unit withdrew from contact to train in the Quang Da Special Zone, where fresh men from the North increased it to a battalion, according to captured documents. The training took several months, lasting until the end of January 1972. Significantly, the entire process took place at a base *inside* South Vietnam. Allied pacification evidently did not prevent these VPA troops from conducting their complete training cycle in-country.

Reinforcing the combat fronts was another consideration. The B-3 Front received a full infantry division, the VPA 320th, and a battalion armed with "Sagger" antitank missiles. Military Region 5 formed a new division, the 711th, from two existing regiments. Replacements brought its 3rd Division up to strength. COSVN created an artillery division, the first in the People's Army. Four independent regiments shifted southward, including the 271st, taken from coast defense duty in North Vietnam and sent to Cambodia. Armor units in Laos abandoned their old light tanks, and the crews went North to bring new T-54 tanks to the front. Assorted battalions of armor, mechanized, transport, and artillery troops, twenty in all, also made the trek. To build NLF guerrilla formations, nine battalions and forty-four independent companies went South as well.

Coordinating the movement of reinforcements with the need for training became a particular headache. Requirements for men conflicted with the necessity for specialized training. Hanoi made a command decision to accept risks in current operations in order to prepare for Nguyen Hue. The result is evident in MACV's infiltration estimates, based on VPA communications intercepts and very accurate. During all of 1971 North Vietnam sent 67,400 soldiers down the Ho Chi Minh Trail, almost half during the first four months of the year (with 80 percent of those destined for the COSVN area; for the entire year, slightly more than 50 percent of infiltrators went to this "Far South" sector). After May the MACV estimates become quite revealing. Newly detected infiltrations averaged 3,000 men per week from January to May, but only 1,200 in June and July and 800 in August. American intelligence discovered *no* fresh infiltration at all through most of September, and the weekly average from October through mid-December fell to 640. Then, in one week, MACV found 20,700 fresh *bo dois* (as the Vietnamese call their soldiers) heading South. Over the next four months 63,000 more troops joined the flood, a number comparable to the *entire* infiltration estimate for

1971 and closely matching the rate just prior to the Tet offensive. These data show that Hanoi curtailed its replacement efforts beginning about the time it decided to launch the Nguyen Hue offensive. It made no particular effort to replace losses in the Lam Son 719 sector (based on MACV estimates, the total of replacement troops funneled into both the DMZ and Tri-Thien-Hue areas for the entire year amounted to only about 7,000 men)—another comment on claims of a Saigon "victory" there. Hanoi conducted minimal activity through the second half of the year, husbanding strength for the attack. The best interpretation is that People's Army soldiers were held back for training while the Ho Chi Minh Trail moved up supplies for Nguyen Hue.[89]

Four years after Saigon had done so, Hanoi now called for full mobilization. Protocols lowered the draft age by a year, to sixteen, and raised the end of eligibility by five years, to thirty-five. According to MACV intelligence, the DRV inducted 150,000 North Vietnamese into the People's Army. To cycle all these soldiers through its system, the army reduced the period of basic training from six months to five. Although this might indicate a decision to accept a lower level of training in order to put more troops in the field, U.S. intelligence surveys of prisoners captured during 1972 indicate that those who had passed through boot camp the previous year averaged six months of training, while 1972 inductees actually had slightly more (6.1).[90]

General Staff chief General Van Tien Dung exercised overall control under General Giap. He also supervised Major General Le Trong Tan, his own deputy and the victor of Lam Son 719, who commanded the VPA troops fighting in the northern provinces of South Vietnam. Party secretary on the special campaign committee for this front would be Major General Le Quang Dao, deputy chief of the VPA's General Political Department. With so many preparations and huge forces on the move, VPA commanders seem to have conceded the impossibility of attaining strategic surprise and made no effort at deception, unlike their actions before Tet. They focused on misleading Saigon and the United States as to the timing and scale of the operation.

Exactly as he had done before Tet, General Giap put out a series of articles and made at least one important speech. Under the slogan "Determined to Fight, Determined to Win," Giap analyzed circumstances, alluded to large-unit operations, called for sacrifice, and promised victory. Predicated on the idea that important changes had transformed the battlefield, his articles observed that armed struggle now held precedence over political *dau tranh* (proselytization efforts) and that main-force attacks were key, since only these could "conduct major enemy-annihilating campaigns, launch big attacks, strike directly at the enemy's strongest forces, and thereby, definitely weaken him." The articles carried the byline *Chien Thang*, translated as "the Victor," and declared, "The struggle requires that we make tremendous efforts toward new victories." U.S. intelligence interpreted the articles as implying that this would be a "final" effort. In a speech published in *Nhan Dan* on December 19, Giap called for increases in the armed forces, declaring, "All youth, regardless of past deferments, must serve." His climax? "We must fight with determination in order to ensure victory, which is near."[91]

Meanwhile, in mid-December COSVN issued a basic directive on operations that called not merely for actions to counter pacification programs but also for "strong, determined attacks" on South Vietnamese armed forces, referring to a "possible return to main force warfare." A few days later Hanoi and the Pathet Lao began an offensive in northern Laos, soon threatening the CIA base at Long Tieng. In a radio speech at Christmas, Prime Minister Pham Van Dong declared that "a total Communist victory is possible," stating it was now "possible to inflict a total defeat on the U.S. and to liberate the entire territory of the Indochinese peninsula."[92]

By January 1972 the pieces were in place and the preparations largely complete. The People's Army began the move that would inevitably telegraph its intentions—the deployment of almost all its divisions within the DRV down to Le Trong Tan's front at the Demilitarized Zone. Hanoi was all in, the cards had been drawn, and the curtain rose on the Democratic Republic of Vietnam's ambitious venture. There could be no doubt this operation would be decisive. The fates of both Hanoi and Saigon, and the outcome of Nixon's Vietnam war, hung in the balance.

12   Evening Dews and Damps (1971–1972)

At the Defense Intelligence Agency (DIA), the chief of current intelligence for Southeast Asia was a Marine officer, Peter Armstrong. He saw his role as projecting activities for the next six months, and the onset of the monsoon in September 1971 made prediction urgent, for with its end, the drying land would become suitable for operations. Armstrong had worked on Vietnam intelligence, gradually moving from the fringes toward the center, almost since the beginning of the American ground war, including at MACV and CINCPAC. Now he was responsible for the Pentagon's official prediction. Having arrived at the DIA after the Cambodian invasion, Armstrong would be having only his second go-round at reading the big picture in the tea leaves, but he was confident in his feel for the subject as well as his sources, except that Washington lacked anyone with direct knowledge of Hanoi's thinking. But the "observables" of troop movements, logistics, infiltration, and the like ought to suffice. The analysts went to work.

Hanoi's careful orchestration turned out to have an impact on the American and South Vietnamese spooks. When Armstrong's logistics specialists looked at supply movements, they found nothing ominous. His manpower analysts examined the infiltration indicators and saw nothing unusual there either. In September they identified no major units among the infiltrators and viewed the flow as keeping pace with U.S. estimates of VPA losses. Hanoi's public pronouncements added little. In early December the analysts expected business as usual. Armstrong looked forward to a quiet Christmas with family. Then his expert on the National Liberation Front butted in. The man was a mess—always late, recently divorced, overweight—but he had always provided excellent insights, and this time was no exception. He had noticed a strangely exuberant tone in NLF documents captured in the III Corps zone.

Colonel Armstrong ordered the analyst to redo his sums, this time with the help of other specialists. Within days other buttons were popping off the shirt too. The DIA's expert on order of battle discovered a dramatic increase in People's Army troops headed South. Shortly thereafter came evidence of units on the march. Then aerial reconnaissance returned pictures of a plain above the Demilitarized Zone parked solid with tanks. There had never been such an armor concentration. Armstrong's current intelligence people were soon in the office of DIA estimates chief Major General Richard R. Stewart, who heard them out, then ordered a fresh evaluation of Hanoi's intentions. It would be briefed to the Joint Chiefs and Secretary Laird the first week in January. Armstrong enjoyed the fact that his shop "was first on the street with the new estimate," because until then, there had been a close consensus among MACV, the CIA, the State Department, and the NSA—just about everyone.[1] Some might object, but the bottom line is that understanding Hanoi's intentions for 1972 came late and slowly.

One reason is that Washington and Saigon indulged themselves, believing their own victory rhetoric. The treatment of CIA analyses illustrates the problem. As ARVN troops straggled back from Laos, a paper sent to director Helms foresaw the high-point attacks Hanoi would in fact make, but it judged their purpose to be to demonstrate that the Laotian campaign had not damaged its capabilities. A month later a National Intelligence Estimate (NIE) offered a sober picture of a South Vietnam whose endurance was uncertain and that would require massive U.S. support for many years. The NIE predicted new Hanoi actions for 1972, but nothing like Tet. The agency's pessimism attracted no interest. Through the rest of the year no one asked Langley to follow up, and the CIA's field reporting fell in line with the rat pack.

At MACV, assumptions of success led officials to interpret each new piece of evidence as a further indication of the enemy's distress. A month after Lam Son 719, desertions (*chieu hoi*) tumbled by more than 60 percent (and would never recover). Staff took that to indicate that fewer enemy troops were left who could defect. General Abrams's experts observed that such reductions usually preceded offensives, but not only did they not perceive the VPA actions then under way as a riposte to the ARVN's failure in Laos, they told visiting officials to expect no major operations by Hanoi through mid-1972, although after that the picture seemed less clear. In August the intelligence staff noted that Hanoi's losses—including from Lam Son 719—were less than half those of 1968 or 1969, but then went on to argue that the adversary did not have the staying power to maintain an offensive posture over an extended period. Whenever the VPA or NLF pulled units back for training or other preparations for the offensive, U.S. intelligence saw more evidence of Hanoi's weakness. For example, in early September intelligence intercepted enemy orders for the front to become self-sufficient in food. Hanoi intended to focus its transport capability on the sinews of war. The spooks instead saw the Ho Chi Minh Trail way stations as starving, and Hanoi as having lost so many trucks it could no longer transport foodstuffs.

When Hanoi moved jet aircraft into the DRV's southern panhandle, reinforcing its air defenses, U.S. intelligence connected this to a simple desire to challenge B-52 raids. There were repeated briefings that larger amounts of supplies were moving down The Trail but smaller and smaller portions going into South Vietnam. The staffs saw this as a measure of the success of the air campaign, not as stockpiling for an offensive. The first break in this optimism came on November 13, when intelligence reported indications that "the enemy plans to initiate his dry season offensive earlier than he has in previous years, commencing in January or February."[2] Judging from the MACV briefings, that observation came virtually out of the blue.

Top leaders were less sanguine, and their views betrayed a significant shift in what the communists liked to call the "correlation of forces." That is, Hanoi suddenly held the initiative; its forces, not Saigon's, would make the next move. That too is evidence of the real result of Lam Son 719. On May 29, 1971, General Abrams told associates he felt that Saigon could "play out" the rest of the year, "but '72, I think, is different—'72 has some other *potential* in it for the enemy."[3] A month later MACV's intelligence chief, Brigadier General William Potts, was agreeing with Abrams that Hanoi had many more forces in southern Laos than previously. By July journalists were recording Saigon officials' belief that "1972 would be the year of decision."[4] Elsewhere President Thieu baldly told people there *would* be a 1972 offensive and it would be Hanoi's. When Henry Kissinger passed through Saigon on his way to secret talks in China, Thieu warned the envoy of an offensive, twice, and remarked that it would probably come along the DMZ because Hanoi "had more capability and opportunity there." Thieu asserted that although the Laotian operation had avoided "difficulty" for 1972, Hanoi's forces in Laos and above the DMZ necessitated the retention of South Koreans in Vietnam, and he could not agree to let them leave.[5] Early in December Thieu told Abrams he expected an offensive in the Central Highlands around Tet and along the DMZ in early April.[6]

The geographic focus of Hanoi's offensive is a key intelligence question. The sequencing of People's Army infiltrations pointed to operations in the Central Highlands, Hanoi's B-3 Front, and there is where the allies focused. When General Potts brought Abrams the first news of troop movements in late November, the MACV commander wondered, "That thing about the B-3 Front bothers me." On November 20 Abrams told top commanders, "We need to think about this quite a bit." Earlier, he had thought Hanoi's activity in the highlands aimed at forcing Saigon to commit its general reserves so it could move elsewhere, "but this portends something more than that." Intelligence chief Potts observed that the B-3 Front would be stronger than it had ever been. On December 3 Abrams remarked to staff, "I don't believe I quite understand the import of all this infiltration that presumably is going to the B-3 Front." A week later, having just read Lyndon Johnson's memoir account of Tet, Abe ruminated some more: "It won't be like Tet '68. It'll be limited to the B-3 Front. Now how far they'll want to *go* in Kontum and Pleiku, I just don't know." Vietnamese chief of staff Cao Van Vien agreed, expecting a big action in the highlands. Speaking to senior commanders on December 19, Abrams speculated that Hanoi's timing in the B-3 Front zone might have slipped. A serious threat to the DMZ suddenly reared its head. "And when it starts," Abe said of the anticipated offensive, "it won't look like anything that's ever started before." By the end of the year the MACV and ARVN staffs were huddling on measures to counter Hanoi's actions. General Abrams was headed to a party to mark the fifth anniversary of the "light at the end of the tunnel." He told associates, "What we're trying to paint here today is you can't see the end of the tunnel." It no longer seemed like such a victorious picture.[7]

When American and South Vietnamese officers met, the prospect of action at the DMZ began to get equal time with the threat to the Central Highlands. Saigon believed the newly created ARVN 3rd Infantry Division, now deployed along the Zone, would certainly be tested. Way down the chain of command, the American 101st Airborne Division had already taken precautions at its bases at Camps Eagle and Evans, even though most of its units were scheduled for repatriation soon. Specialist Donald M. Whaley, a lowly enlisted man but in charge of the Quang Tri desk on the division intelligence staff because of his expertise, assembled a special study compiling evidence from captured documents and agent reports. It was clear something was up. Whaley heard the report went to the White House.

Other appeals reached the White House from the CIA. Analyst Frank Snepp, then at Langley as the principal analyst on Hanoi leadership at the Office of Current Intelligence, recounted that he and several colleagues had detected ominous indications of an impending offensive, but CIA managers were not willing to commit to a judgment without checking with the White House.

The Kissinger staff saw some portents. On December 20 NSC Southeast Asia expert John H. Holdridge penned a summary for the security adviser. He cited "a quantum increase in enemy troops" in the highlands and "signs of a troop buildup in Quang Tri province," plus a supply buildup, as evidence "the Communists are apparently preparing for significantly increased military activity in early 1972." But the NSC was still infected with victory disease. In the face of all the evidence, Holdridge resisted concluding that Hanoi intended a strategic offensive. He saw more limited intentions: defense against a new Lam Son 719–type effort along the DMZ; in the highlands, defense of base areas, an attempt to overrun exposed ARVN camps for psychological effect, or the creation of "revolutionary bases" as part of a campaign to counter pacification.[8]

The intelligence picture in Washington began coming into focus the first week of January. That was when Armstrong entered the "Tank," the JCS conference room, to brief the Chiefs and Laird. By then MACV was solidly on board and the South Vietnamese agreed, although Washington still hewed to a different interpretation. The DIA argued the enemy would attack in the highlands and the Mekong delta but *not* along the DMZ. Laird was especially reluctant to accept these findings. He had been to South Vietnam recently and had come back mouthing the platitudes of the Lam Son 719 conventional wisdom. "I was a bit surprised," Armstrong recalled, "when Secretary Laird cast a baleful eye on me and seemed annoyed by what I was reporting. He interrupted repeatedly and questioned how conclusions had been reached."[9] But the DIA analysts had every answer, and within days came news of 11,000 more North Vietnamese troops trekking south.

On January 7 the State Department's Bureau of Intelligence and Research weighed in with its own analysis, predicting an offensive "somewhat larger in scale than in recent years" to begin around mid-February (Tet), center in the highlands and DMZ areas, and involve artillery attacks on ARVN installations, major ground attacks on highland firebases, and nuisance shellings of urban areas, but primarily targeting rural administrative centers and Saigon's territorial forces involved in pacification. State's analysts expected possible "multi-regimental attacks," but their picture, too, was cloudy: the paper predicted things the adversary had done in the past, not the coordinated operations by full divisions Hanoi was about to launch.[10]

Langley entered the lists on January 24 with an assessment by the CIA station in Saigon, its message a dark one: "The stage is thus set for the beginning of what seems likely to be the most ambitious enemy political/military campaign since the winter of 1968."[11] Headquarters followed with a paper of its own in early February. By then Hanoi's reserve divisions were on the move. In fact, the North Vietnamese press actually publicized news of troops heading South, complete with photographs—also unprecedented. The Office of Current Intelligence had no difficulty sizing this up as the antecedent to a major campaign that would begin soon. The CIA paper also pointed to Hanoi's using greater forces than expected in the Central Highlands. The agency anticipated the attack would begin either at Tet or during Nixon's late-February visit to China.

Meanwhile, there were problems in Saigon. On January 9 a MACV cable summarized the force balances in each of South Vietnam's four military regions. The only one sufficiently threatened to need reinforcement if the North Vietnamese attacked, MACV thought, would be the Central Highlands. Abrams's people were at least seeing the guerrillas in the trees. The same day briefers informed his deputy that the enemy was ready to go—now. "No one knows when or where they'll be committed," General Abrams told visiting Army secretary Robert F. Froehlke on January 10. "But the thing that *is* very clear is that he has made the decision."[12] The U.S. command had already begun bombing in an effort to blunt Hanoi's preparations. And in mid-January MACV finalized requests for a menu of new air options and changes in rules of engagement designed to help cope with the impending offensive.

The MACV commander's real frustration was with the Saigon leadership.

"Where we haven't gotten anywhere is with President Thieu," Abrams told the officers rehearsing a briefing for the Vietnamese leader. "Somehow, out of [all this], in my opinion, he's got to feel some sense of urgency."[13] The South Vietnamese seemed more concerned with demands the United States support formation of two more ARVN divisions for 1973. In December the Joint General Staff, displaying little urgency, did warn corps commands to expect something. General Vien issued a directive in early January for certain preliminaries, envisioning an attack around Tet, but did not follow up or monitor responses. General Hoang Xuan Lam, the I Corps commander who had been so ineffective in Lam Son 719, merely forwarded the JGS warning without comment. Creighton Abrams, at least, had no doubts. "The show is on!" Abrams announced to his staff. "The curtain's been drawn and we're in it."[14] The MACV commander could only agree with his deputy, General Fred Weyand, who had already remarked, "It's going to be a hell of a year, I think, because the enemy is going to have the initiative."[15]

Scorpions in a Bottle

Like scorpions in a bottle, the adversaries circled each other in a delicate dance of death that went on for weeks. Hanoi's proximity became palpable—a CIA field assessment late in January contained the first signs of movement by the DRV's general reserves. Three divisions started down the panhandle, with 34,000 fresh *bo dois* detected in infiltration estimates. Liberation Front instructions to cadres suddenly shifted from appeals to counter pacification to orders for determined attacks inflicting heavy casualties on the ARVN. Captives spoke of their expectation of a general offensive. The indicators were ominous at best.

The American command did not use its readouts on the Ho Chi Minh Trail merely for intelligence, nor did MACV quaver at the approaching enemy masses. Instead, it crafted a fresh aerial effort, "Island Tree," aimed directly at personnel infiltration. The pinball wizards of Task Force Alpha at Nakhon Phanom, who targeted strikes using their strings of electronic sensors along The Trail like players at an arcade game, had little enthusiasm for Island Tree but were knocked into line by CINCPAC. This program targeted B-52s at the enemy's way stations, called *binh trams*, on the basis of intercepts showing expected locations of People's Army infiltration groups. The Seventh Air Force put audio sensors near targets to learn what happened when the bombs fell. When staffers played the first tape recording of an attack in progress at MACV headquarters, orders shouted by VPA cadres and screams as the attack proceeded furnished graphic evidence of the power of this weapon. Island Tree, tested in November 1971, then applied in earnest, began with a pair of Arc Light strikes on December 6 against *binh trams* in the B-3 Front zone. Two more attacks struck at the VPA 320th Division a week later, then again on December 23. Tactical air came into action on

Christmas Eve. By New Year's four additional strikes had multiplied the destruction. General Abrams tried to keep Island Tree secret, according it priority above everything except missions in Laos. The embassy in Vientiane demanded those to save the CIA's secret army, threatened by Hanoi's attacks there. No doubt the strikes inflicted many losses, but results could not be verified by aerial photography or by communications intercepts, unless the People's Army did the United States the favor of reporting casualties, very rare. Admiral McCain, according to the Air Force's official history, "acknowledged that the actual impact on troop movements would almost certainly remain a matter of conjecture."[16]

The aerial onslaught against The Trail, the main business of the pinball wizards, continued simultaneously under Operation "Commando Hunt VII." Although the electronic battlefield had now become a well-integrated mechanism, and the AC-130 gunship offered great precision and firepower, redeployments had reduced the available aircraft, and Washington's budget crunch cut sortie numbers. Gunship strength had increased—to 18 AC-130s—but the 54 B-52s and 226 fighter-bombers amounted to one-half and one-third their strength, respectively, when Commando Hunt had begun back in 1968. People's Army air defenses were double what they had been—1,500 guns—and now SAMs strengthened the enemy. Bad weather also helped Hanoi, at least through December, and The Trail masters confounded the Americans by moving their trucks at dawn or in late afternoon rather than at night, when the AC-130s roamed. At those times flak gunners had better shots at the aircraft. Two of the scarce gunships were lost in early 1972.

None of this is meant to imply that the Americans did not throw tremendous weight into Commando Hunt VII. Southern Laos absorbed the bulk of the U.S. air effort in all of Southeast Asia. Between November and March 28,500 attack sorties were flown against The Trail. That meant 67,800 tons of bombs, not including the B-52s, which dropped another 58,500 tons, in all the equivalent of ten Hiroshima atomic bombs (at 12.5 kilotons) over a five-month period. Some 28 aircraft were lost to small-arms fire, flak, or SAMs; several were lost operationally; and 50 planes were damaged. Pilots were credited with 10,689 trucks damaged or destroyed, 7,335 of them by the gunships. This represents another manifestation of the Vietnam data problem, since the claims for destroyed vehicles exceed the total number of trucks working the Ho Chi Minh Trail. The data problem runs deeper: studies of VPA supply inputs versus consumption, plus U.S. destruction on The Trail, put Hanoi in negative numbers. There was less than nothing left—by *thousands of tons.* By that measure, there could be no offensive. The statistics were wrong.[17]

Meanwhile, General John D. "Jack" Lavelle, Seventh Air Force commander, mounted a parallel operation to wear down Hanoi's strengthened air defenses in the DRV panhandle, while incidentally blowing up tank and artillery concentrations above the Demilitarized Zone. Richard Nixon claimed he had ordered the strikes to respond to a rocket attack on Saigon, but that merely served as pretext.[18] This five-day air campaign began the day after Christmas. Some believe the timing aimed to minimize protests, since many college students would be home for the holidays, but the president noted that "domestic outcry was immediate and intense."[19] Over a thousand attack sorties made up the operation, code-named "Proud Deep Alpha," in which five aircraft and seven crewmen were lost. The most significant damage would be to fuel storage tanks, although MACV and CINCPAC disputed how much. One North Vietnamese airfield runway was cratered. Later intelligence suggested that Hanoi worried the United States intended to attack Haiphong. Another wave of these attacks took place on February 16–17, just after Tet, aimed directly at 130mm gun positions in the DMZ. These strikes ended the moment the president left for his state visit to the People's Republic of China. Both sets of strikes were clearly designed to disrupt Hanoi's concentration for the offensive.

A third initiative was Lavelle's so-called protective reaction strikes, more than two dozen in all, between November 1971 and March 9, 1972. Under the existing rules of engagement, these were supposed to counter attacks on U.S. aircraft and target only the particular enemy weapons involved. But numerous U.S. officials—including General Abrams, Admiral McCain, Admiral Moorer, and Secretary Laird—saw protective reaction as a device to reduce the enemy and encouraged Lavelle to stretch the rules. Recent releases of Nixon White House tapes indicate that on February 2 the president directly ordered Lavelle to conduct an attack program using protective reaction. Suppression of air defenses occurred when strikes hit enemy radars that had simply been switched on, and ground installations consisting of VPA artillery emplacements turned up among the targeted sites. A young airman of the 432nd Tactical Reconnaissance Wing, debriefing pilots after a mission, discovered violations of the standing rules and sent a letter to his congressman. On March 23 General Lavelle was recalled. None of those who had encouraged Lavelle or demanded that he act came to his defense. Mr. Nixon complained privately about the cashiering of Lavelle at a White House meeting on June 26 but told a news conference the general's actions had not been authorized. Lavelle was demoted and sent into retirement.[20] Aside from the political controversy, protective reaction never had the weight or duration required to affect Hanoi's offensive.

All this tried to preempt an attack whose timing allied intelligence never quite pinned down. Mid-January had been the early projection, but that came and went. Washington, Saigon, Ambassador Bunker, the generals, and the spooks next agreed that Hanoi would jump off at Tet. General Abrams ruminated about a March or April offensive at one point but gave his intelligence people their head, and they stuck with Tet. Despite captured documents from the delta province of Ben Tre that mentioned a general uprising, in early February MACV intelligence still held that COSVN had no offensive capability. When Tet came and nothing happened, the spooks pointed to agent reports and a February 17 intercept to predict the offensive for the twentieth. At a staff conference on the nineteenth, Potts exclaimed to Abrams, "Everyone agrees that tomorrow's the day!"[21] Potts explained that the delays in January were attributable to Hanoi's fear that Saigon was about to launch another Lam Son–style operation, and later to incomplete arrangements. By March 11, however, MACV believed the adversary ready to attack anywhere in South Vietnam. By that time infiltration was up to 76,500—already more than the previous year. The 525th Military Intelligence Group, MACV's main intelligence unit, released a captured document suggesting the NLF's general offensive plan had gone into effect the previous day.

The Nguyen Hue offensive was not going to be contested by American GIs. Withdrawals had reached the point that MACV no longer had significant ground capability. Of the 156,000 American troops in South Vietnam on December 31, 1971, three-quarters were Army, but the number included only a handful of combat brigades. By spring these would be reduced to just two. Nixon ordered another 70,000-person reduction on January 13, which, with the withdrawals already in progress, would bring MACV down to 69,000 by May and 47,000 in July. Washington's answer to Hanoi's attacks would come from the air.

American commanders consciously prepared for that eventuality. General Abrams requested new rules of engagement in January. Recommendations to reinforce air assets quickly followed. On February 2 the NSC considered this. Two days later the president ordered an aircraft carrier to join the Seventh Fleet, more fighters to Thailand, and enough B-52 bombers to Guam to permit 1,500 sorties per month, a level of capability absent since 1968. The carrier arrived in the South China Sea on March 4, bringing the number of these vessels on Yankee Station to four. Beginning on March 8 Abrams, the JCS, and then Secretary Laird asked to further widen the list of approved countermeasures. Laird, however, opposed JCS chairman Moorer's bid to resume bombing the panhandle of North Vietnam. Laird instead offered a series of short, sharp strikes along the lines of Proud Deep Alpha. On March 18, in a memorandum to the president, Kissinger sided with Laird, though he added a proposal that the DMZ be seeded with mines and cluster bombs. President Nixon approved the cluster bombs but none of the rest.

Meanwhile, Saigon's preparations had included the most important accretion of regular forces in the ARVN since the beginning of Vietnamization. This was the addition of the 3rd Infantry Division, announced in August 1971 and built around a regiment taken from the celebrated 1st Division, some rifle battalions from elsewhere, and some new formations. The division took over the old "McNamara Line" strongpoints below the DMZ. Although this has sometimes been pictured as an unalloyed force increase, in fact, the Third's formation indicated that the South Vietnamese were operating close to their limit. Many units were merely Regional Forces regraded as regulars. Also at this time, the Joint General Staff deactivated one battalion headquarters in *every regiment in the ARVN*. Some of the staffs went to 3rd Division units, while other officers were transferred to units that were short on commissioned strength because Saigon simply lacked enough officers. To a degree, South Vietnam merely rearranged its deck chairs.

When Henry Kissinger saw President Thieu in Saigon in July 1971, hopes for the 3rd Division were high, and much of their conversation regarding Vietnamization centered on improving the South Vietnamese air force and the ARVN's artillery arm. The next White House emissary to Thieu would be Al Haig in September, and by then the 3rd Division had become a source of complaint. The Saigon leader objected that U.S. deliveries of major equipment for the unit were behind schedule and the Third was being short-changed. By October the division had just begun to coalesce, and the Third lacked any logistics force at all. Much remained to be done.

Nixon administration spin doctors represented activation of the ARVN division as a tremendous success. Army public affairs chief General Winant Sidle—who had held the same job at MACV at the time of the Tet offensive—issued a press release to that effect. At that very moment, American reporters visiting the unit found ARVN officers mystified by their new U.S. equipment, the division's supply system faulty, and some of its soldiers unpaid for months. Artillery guns were scarce, radios too. Opinions on the 3rd's quality differed. General Ngo Quang Truong, who had had one of its regiments in his ARVN 1st Division, recorded that morale was high and the 3rd's leaders inspiring. Truong noted that many of its men came from the region—some had even served in the strongpoints they were about to occupy—and training seemed effective. The 3rd had not reached a point where it could confront a major conventional threat, but Truong thought no other ARVN unit better suited for the task. But Truong's old regiment was among those that had suffered the worst in Lam Son 719. The U.S. Marine colonel who advised the Vietnamese Marines, in line next to the 3rd, stated that the ARVN regiments along the DMZ—the very ones Truong referred to—were units "whose level of training and readiness was not the highest," or again, "marginally trained and unfamiliar with the terrain." American advisers no longer accompanied the ARVN battalions. The advisory presence extended no lower than the regimental level. There were none at all with the 2nd Regiment, as had been the case during Lam Son, when their absence had been a key weakness. The frontline units took position only a couple of weeks before the offensive.[22]

For many months both the South Vietnamese and U.S. commands had assumed that an offensive at the DMZ, if it occurred, could be met by troops from the general reserve and the Saigon or Mekong areas. At MACV General Abrams had spent hours in conversations that ranged back and forth over this prospect. But whether the troops would be available remained an open question. Parts of both the Marines and the Airborne were already committed elsewhere. Both Saigon's III and IV Corps had major forces in Cambodia, especially around the town of Krek, effectively absorbing any excess capacity they might have. Abrams tried to convince Thieu to recall the troops, restoring balance to ARVN dispositions. Thieu eventually agreed.

The degree of Hanoi's watchfulness is indicated by Le Duc Tho's order, as early as January 12, asking field commanders to assess the Krek pullback and advise how to counter it. North Vietnamese leaders also expected commando raids on the DRV panhandle—interestingly, the Pentagon prepared a menu of such raids in early 1972—as well as Nixon's effort to detach North Vietnam from its communist allies. The Central Military-Party Committee issued final instructions for the offensive in early March. In an accompanying letter Le Duan anticipated "a period of extremely ferocious and extremely complex struggles," resulting in heavy losses for the ARVN followed by a political crisis for the Thieu regime. The Politburo member hoped favorable results would drive the South Vietnamese peace faction to confront Thieu or to join Hanoi and the NLF "to some limited extent." (Prisoner interrogations in South Vietnam, agent reports, and captured documents confirm the authenticity of Le Duan's statements, providing half a dozen examples of orders to provincial committees or local units to prepare for urban uprisings.) Reprising instructions Hanoi had first issued in June 1971,[23] Le Duan declared the goal to be one of creating a situation in which there were two parallel governments in South Vietnam, "coexisting side by side."[24]

On March 25 the Party Secretariat issued orders alerting DRV air defenses, exhorting them to prepare for fresh U.S. attacks by strengthened forces. Another 11,000 *bo dois* were on the way South. The Politburo met on March 28, subsequently warning commanders that the United States and Saigon were aware of the impending offensive and had deployed reserves. The allies also knew that Hanoi's resources limited the duration of active operations. Behind the hard, fortified crust of Saigon's forces, Hanoi leaders believed in a weak rear area. Yet, they warned, "If the enemy is allowed to conduct a large-scale pullback and regrouping of his forces, the situation could easily develop into a hard, protracted, back-and-forth struggle." The Politburo thought in terms of destroying numbers of ARVN divisions. Hanoi expected a renewed U.S. air campaign against the North, either in waves or continuously.[25]

Le Duc Tho cabled his own thoughts to key commanders in the South on March 27. Tho noted that campaign-level logistics remained a problem in several areas but insisted supplies were adequate to sustain most planned operations. Hanoi's man also frankly admitted that the two weaknesses of the VPA and NLF lay in their limited ability to attack fortified positions and their inadequacies in fighting coordinated battles employing many units. The cable noted that the Liberation Front remained most feeble in South Vietnam's cities but expressed hope for the countryside and expressed confidence that mounting attacks over all battlefields for a sustained period would lead to opportunities to destroy pacification and expand political resistance in the South. Le Duc Tho referred to intractable problems with the U.S. economy and burgeoning opposition to the war as factors driving Nixon to leave Vietnam. "Clearly we are in the driver's seat," Tho declared. "We are in a posture of victory, we have the initiative, and we are on the rise."[26]

"I Intend to Stop at Nothing"

Along the Demilitarized Zone, the last days before the storm passed quietly. It was not peaceful, but there was no sign of what impended. Aerial photography disclosed fresh road construction and spotted new gun positions plus some tanks north of the DMZ. On March 26 the 525th Military Intelligence Group's daily summary pictured Hanoi's activity as slightly increased but still at a low level, well below capability. Shelling of South Vietnamese positions seemed to be the worst threat—in the five days ending on the twenty-seventh, the North Vietnamese had conducted fourteen bombardments, most of low intensity. On March 29 the 525th Group accented supply movements. The situation seemed tranquil enough for MACV's new senior adviser to the South Vietnamese Marines to fly to Quang Tri and make the rounds of two Marine brigades he was responsible for. They were stationed in the foothills, guarding the flank of the ARVN's 3rd Division. One Marine battalion had detected suspicious movements to the west, and some artillery and a B-52 strike had been aimed out there, but advisers could not convince the ARVN to take any ground action. That night it rained.

Brigadier General Vu Van Giai, the Third's commander, considered it sufficiently quiet for a troop rotation along the line. The next day the veteran 2nd Regiment would move up from the big base at Camp Carroll to replace the 56th at the front. General Giai, stretched to his limit, controlled the units of his own division plus the Marine brigades to the west. He had no time to spare. About noon on March 30, the critical phase of the troop rotation began. Both regiments shifted their command posts, turning off the radios. Suddenly all hell broke loose. Artillery rumbled in the distance. In the time it took Marine senior adviser Colonel Gerald Turley to run from the mess hall at 3rd Division headquarters to its tactical operations center, reports of heavy shelling had started to come in from all along the DMZ. The Nguyen Hue offensive had begun.

General Abrams thought this attack would be different. It was. The rockets and shells pitching into ARVN fortifications were the first of 13,500—a hurricane of fire beyond anything at Lam Son, Khe Sanh, or Con Thien. More than 5,000 rounds fell during the first day alone. South Vietnamese gun crews took cover, never to regain their poise. A battalion of the 56th Regiment, caught in the open during transfer, disintegrated. Another suffered badly. By nightfall the DMZ strongpoints were under pressure, even before northern assault troops had engaged. General Giai ordered one of his Marine brigades back to Dong Ha. At that point the North Vietnamese struck down Route 9.

The ARVN had built its defenses on the assumption that the People's Army would come from the hills, down Route 9 from Khe Sanh. But more than half the assault force thrust directly across the DMZ, backed by a regiment of sappers (the VPA had never before used a full regiment of these in a homogeneous assault) and another of tanks. The armor shocked as much as the artillery. Below the DMZ another northern division reached into the lowlands with a flanking maneuver. On the second day VPA troops closed in and a first firebase fell, quickly followed by another. The third day, April Fool's Day, the dam burst.

That day Saigon admitted to thirty-one ARVN soldiers killed. Anyone who believed that *was* a fool. Confusion prevailed, with refugees beginning to stream south from Quang Tri city and the surrounding villages. In the first major assault a Vietnamese Marine battalion lost Firebase Sarge in the Annamite foothills, while below the DMZ troops at the storied strongpoint Con Thien (now called A-4) evacuated at midmorning. By nightfall conditions had deteriorated so badly that General Giai ordered his entire force to pull back behind the Cua Viet and Cam Lo rivers. All the posts of the McNamara Line were abandoned. Giai moved his headquarters out of Ai Tu combat base (once Camp Eagle of the U.S. 101st Airborne) to Quang Tri city, leaving all his radios behind. Only Vietnamese Marines and arriving elements of the 1st Armored Brigade manned the forward defenses.

Hanoi's troops continued to advance on April 2. That afternoon the bulk of the 56th Regiment, holding strongly fortified Camp Carroll, long the anchor of the DMZ position, simply surrendered. About 1,500 ARVN soldiers marched into captivity, the biggest single loss to that point in South Vietnamese military history. With the base went the ARVN's heavy artillery and many other support weapons, and this immediately unhinged General Giai's new line. His 57th Regiment disintegrated while withdrawing. One bright spot would be that the Marines and U.S. advisers managed to destroy the bridge at Dong Ha before a VPA tank column could breach the river line. By April 2 even Ambassador Bunker had become concerned. He warned Washington that the ARVN was on the verge of collapse in Military Region 1.

The next day Radio Hanoi broadcast a surrender appeal from the captured leader of the ARVN units at Camp Carroll, Colonel Pham Van Dinh, something of a military hero for his role at Hue during the Tet offensive. South Vietnamese troops ignored the appeal but stopped the enemy. They set up a hasty defense along the river behind Dong Ha. Destruction of the bridge there—opposed by Giai as well as the ARVN tank commander—critically retarded the VPA advance. People's Army tanks were stuck, and their artillery had to move forward to be effective again. A successful Marine defense of Firebase Pedro also blunted General Le Trong Tan's infantry assaults. Quang Tri's defenses held, barely.

Many of General Giai's units were sent to reorganize while several Ranger groups plus the last of the Vietnamese Marines reinforced them. With the entire Marine Corps now in I Corps, Marine division headquarters moved north too. But corps commander Hoang Xuan Lam, still smarting over differences with Marine General Le Nguyen Khang during the Laotian invasion, refused to recognize the division leader. He left the defense in the hands of General Giai, who, with inadequate communications, was soon attempting to control far more than his original troops. The momentary reprieve due to Hanoi's repositioning masked this weakness. But Saigon chief of staff Cao Van Vien later concluded that Lam's decision to oblige Giai to overextend himself had been the key reason for Quang Tri's loss.

In the meantime, as at Khe Sanh during Tet, the much-anticipated attack on the Central Highlands did not come. There were probes and shelling, but mostly the People's Army remained hidden in the hills. Instead, on April 2 attacks began northwest of Tay Ninh city, near Saigon itself. This, too, proved a diversion when the main COSVN offensive opened against Loc Ninh and then An Loc. By then Saigon's Joint General Staff had sent ARVN's Ranger groups from here to reinforce the Quang Tri area, so III Corps had little to spare when COSVN struck with three full divisions reinforced by armor and artillery. On April 4 ARVN scouts encountered the enemy west of Loc Ninh and were almost wiped out. The scale of attack built rapidly, with tremendous assaults throughout the sector of the South Vietnamese 5th Division. An ARVN armored cavalry squadron surrendered, followed by the regiment commander and his bodyguard at Loc Ninh. These were disturbing losses, though not on the scale of what happened below the DMZ. Loc Ninh fell on April 7. Five U.S. advisers and a thousand ARVN soldiers were captured; two Americans went missing, never to be seen again.

In Saigon on April 7, President Thieu convened his military region commanders and senior advisers to consider the emergency. General Nguyen Van Minh, leader of III Corps and Military Region 3, argued that Hanoi's thrusts along the DMZ were a diversion and the real threat was to Saigon from the enemy flooding past Loc Ninh. Thieu rejected that reasoning but released ARVN's First Airborne Brigade from the general reserve to sustain III Corps, and he ordered Mekong delta commander General Ngo Quang Truong to prepare to send the 21st Division to Minh. Meanwhile, North Vietnamese leader Pham Hung's troops were closing in on An Loc, a key town on the road to Saigon. Troops from ARVN units ejected from Loc Ninh and elsewhere had drifted into An Loc, reinforced by Rangers and units from the ARVN's 5th and 7th Divisions. North Vietnamese artillery began bombarding An Loc and made initial probes on April 9. Beginning on the thirteenth, the People's Army launched full-scale assaults. From Hanoi, Le Duc Tho on April 15 ordered Hung to capture An Loc, no matter the cost. The town managed to hold out, and An Loc became South Vietnam's Stalingrad, the object of a siege that endured for weeks.[27]

Action in the center began on the coastal plain, not the Central Highlands, and again the sequence aimed at pulling ARVN forces out of position. In Binh Dinh province Military Region 5 threw a full division plus sapper units into attacks on key ARVN landing zones and firebases. These started at about the time Pham Hung activated his COSVN plans. The NLF enjoyed considerable success. Binh Dinh would soon be no-man's-land for the South Vietnamese. But the ARVN was not fooled, nor was American senior adviser John Paul Vann. Commanders kept their eyes on the main threat: the enemy B-3 Front with all its new forces. Vann convinced Thieu to post the bulk of his Airborne reserve to the Central Highlands; thus bolstered, ARVN II Corps assembled most of a division north of Kontum around Tan Canh and Dak To, the route People's Army tanks would have to take to enter South Vietnam.

In Hanoi the Politburo met on April 8 (one day after Thieu) to review initial results. Both along the DMZ and near Saigon attacks had progressed more quickly than expected. Hanoi also recognized the success in Binh Dinh and took note of the defections of ARVN units. The Politburo—and Le Duan in a dispatch the next day—thought there might be an opportunity for revolution in South Vietnam's cities. But, apparently referring to the halt in Quang Tri, Hanoi noted that supply factors were already impeding operations, and some units had incurred unnecessary losses due to overestimating the damage done to the ARVN. Politburo guidance was to press forward in a resolute and daring fashion. Shortly afterward the Central Military-Political Committee issued orders to attack the Central Highlands.

Existing accounts of the Easter offensive mostly overplay the simultaneity between what happened in the Central Highlands and on the other battlefields. This is because they lump together counterpacification attacks in Binh Dinh with B-3 Front operations, and because a probe at Firebase Delta on April 3 is deemed the start of the attacks. The Delta battle was a high point for U.S. adviser Vann, who intervened to help ARVN airborne troops hold on, but it was again only diversionary in nature.

In fact, General Hoang Minh Thao of the B-3 Front had yet to commit his main forces. He finally did so on April 13, when he flung his divisions against the Dak To–Tan Canh complex. Once that assault began, the ARVN's situation went critical almost immediately. Rocket Ridge, which loomed above Dak To and had become notorious as "Hill 1338," the focus of major battles in 1967, had a string of firebases oriented northwest to southeast and ending in Firebase Delta, an outlying position. Together they protected Highway 14 between Kontum and Dak To–Tan Canh, the center of a mass of roughly 10,000 ARVN troops. When the VPA attacked it wasted no time going for the jugular, ignoring Delta in favor of Rocket Ridge, where ARVN paratroops were driven from a firebase the second day. General Thao followed up his success by nibbling at the rest of the ridge. Once the ARVN focused there, he assaulted Firebase Delta, which the VPA captured on April 21. Two days later he sent a full division reinforced with tanks and "Sagger" antitank missiles barreling straight down the road to Tan Canh. By then the South Vietnamese were at a huge disadvantage. With new challenges in the north, Saigon had to pull both Airborne brigades from the highlands and send them to I Corps, along with Airborne Division headquarters. The only thing to replace them was a Ranger group already bloodied by fighting below the DMZ. Both the highlands corps commander and the ARVN 22nd Division leader were passive. Tan Canh and Dak To fell on April 24. Not even American AC-130 gunships could save them.

Back in Quang Tri, the North Vietnamese had resupplied and repositioned their troops by late April. That delay permitted the ARVN to re-form its defenses and saved Hue. Had the People's Army captured the Imperial City during the first few weeks, it would have shaken South Vietnam to its core. General Giai had time to try a counterattack, but this only exhausted his own men. Le Trong Tan at least extended his air defense umbrella and resumed attacking with three VPA divisions sweeping in from the flank. The South Vietnamese line held on the first day, April 18, but Giai had no reserves, limited artillery ammunition, and no coordinated battle plan. As the offensive progressed his ARVN troops were chewed up. The best I Corps could do was to exchange a Marine brigade reconstituted after the early fighting for one on the front. Saigon sent the Airborne Division, but it arrived too late to make a difference, being sucked into the direct defense of Hue. By April 28 the ARVN had lost Dong Ha and the entire river line but still held a narrow corridor along Highway 1 plus a bridgehead at Quang Tri. The Ai Tu combat base was forfeited on April 30. Next day the VPA surrounded Quang Tri. It fell on May 2.

These developments occurred despite enormous American airpower flung at Hanoi's forces. U.S. fighter-bomber sorties against targets in South Vietnam jumped from 400 in March 1972 to 10,526 in April. The Nixon administration had begun augmenting its air forces before the offensive began and immediately surged both tactical strikes and B-52 Arc Light operations. Though hampered by weather, especially in I Corps; by the vagaries of the buildup; and, briefly (until the arrival of additional aircraft), by resumption of the bombing of North Vietnam, airpower proved key in stopping Hanoi. Without it, Saigon's losses would have been much greater. At An Loc air support and resupply saved the position. In the highlands airpower slowed the North Vietnamese enough to permit the defense of Kontum city. In I Corps air held off Hanoi long enough for the supply factors to take effect again, and it would then spearhead Saigon's counteroffensive. Most important, the application of airpower would lead to a new Nixon Shock. As Quang Tri fell, that act of shock and awe already loomed.

■ ■ ■ The president sat in the Oval Office with Henry Kissinger and Bob Haldeman when an aide entered bearing a note for Dr. Kissinger. It was Thursday, March 30, and the note, from Haig, told of Hanoi's long-awaited offensive, now arrived. Nixon instantly went into crisis mode. Gone were the bureaucratic debates over permissible authorities for bombing. Kissinger complains it was difficult to get accurate information out of the Pentagon, but the truth is that for the first few days, MACV would be as confused as Washington. Nevertheless, on Good Friday Secretary Laird confirmed that Hanoi's operation was a major one. Nixon ordered strikes against North Vietnam—initially the air defenses protecting the invaders—right away. A few U.S. planes, including one of the AC-130 gunships, were lost early over the DMZ, and more during rescue missions sent to recover the crews. Focus on the battle area meant the northern bombing began as a tactical maneuver—but not for long. By April 3 the president ordered JCS chairman Moorer to concentrate air forces and wallop the North Vietnamese.

Nixon's stance reflected his strategic interests. Hanoi's offensive dashed the president's hope to head it off by his diplomacy with the communist world. He was scheduled to visit the Soviet Union for a summit conference a few weeks hence and blamed the Russians, along with the Chinese, for failing to dissuade the DRV. Had Nixon understood Vietnam better, he might have realized that the communist nations' leverage in Hanoi was no better than his own in Saigon. There was never any chance to avoid the offensive. Conversely, Nixon now worried that showing weakness might frustrate his designs on the bigger communist powers. And there was the upcoming U.S. presidential election in November, which Nixon intended to win at all costs. He could not afford to have Saigon go down the drain. "We're playing a Russian game, a Chinese game, and an election game," the president told Kissinger, to which his national security adviser replied, "That's why we've got to blast the living bejeezus out of North Vietnam."[28]

The plans for that already existed. They lay in files marked "Pruning Knife Alpha" and "Duck Hook," in vaults at both the Pentagon and the White House. Kissinger immediately called his Washington Special Actions Group into session. At the Pentagon the JCS worked late nights. On April 5 Admiral Moorer told the Chiefs the old rules no longer applied; the president wanted creative new options. The next day he proposed two plans. One, "Fremont Gambler," embodied a maximum-effort air strike against targets in the Haiphong area, along the lines of the summer of 1967. The other, "Pocket Money," would mine Haiphong harbor. Mel Laird forwarded both, observing that neither offered the desired military impact, but their political effect might be what was wanted. By then Mr. Nixon was already considering the full spectrum of Duck Hook actions, including both the mining and a sustained aerial bombardment. In fact, on April 6 the president met General John Vogt, the Joint Staff operations chief, to denounce the allegedly flaccid MACV response to the offensive. Vogt volunteered to fix the problem, which resulted in his being sent to Vietnam as commander of the Seventh Air Force.

America's armada of warplanes in Southeast Asia grew quickly. In March 1972 there had been roughly 600 aircraft in the theater, with more arriving. By April 13 there were over 900. Two additional aircraft carriers joined Task Force 77 on Yankee Station. The buildup would continue until almost 1,400 aircraft were in place by the end of July. In the midst of this, Nixon ordered a U.S. walkout from the Paris talks. When Hanoi, in turn, canceled a session of the secret talks, the president directed execution of the Haiphong strike plan. That sent fighter-bombers to both Hanoi and Haiphong, where four Soviet cargo ships were hit by U.S. bombs. Beyond the White House, Americans worried that the war might escalate beyond Southeast Asia.

The aerial reinforcements did not go unnoticed in the United States. In fact, antiwar veterans, who had good contacts with active-duty servicemen plus access through GI coffeehouses, were at the forefront, putting out information the media reported. A vet collective in Cambridge, Massachusetts, the Ad Hoc Military Buildup Committee, wrote a stream of reports and sent them to the Vietnam Veterans Against the War, which circulated them further. Their data went down to the micro level, noting departures of individual cells of planes from air bases in the United States and overseas. There were protests at many air bases, including Westover, Mountain Home, McGuire, Kirtland, and Offut, headquarters of the Strategic Air Command responsible for the Arc Light B-52 strikes. Aboard the aircraft carrier *Midway*, sixteen sailors signed an antiwar letter to President Nixon just before the vessel left for Yankee Station. Sailors and civilians protested the departures of the carriers *America* and *Oriskany*, and two dozen sailors refused to deploy with their ship when it steamed out of Alameda, California. That summer deployment of the *Forrestal* would be delayed more than two months by a massive fire set in the admiral's quarters, and the *Ranger*'s propulsion system was sabotaged. Later there would be a virtual mutiny aboard the carrier *Constellation*. Restiveness among the military had long since spread beyond the Army. The administration's surgical instrument for bombing the bejeezus out of North Vietnam was losing its edge by the day, even as the president unleashed the forces.

As had become his norm, Richard Nixon ignored all protest, forging ahead with ever more ambitious plans. Laird had objected that mining Haiphong would have little impact unless accompanied by a countrywide bombing campaign. The president promptly ordered plans for such attacks, which became Operation "Linebacker." Preparations for the Pocket Money mining were also in high gear by April 20. Senior admirals, including Moorer (chairman of the JCS), Elmo R. Zumwalt (chief of naval operations), McCain (CINCPAC), and Bernard A. "Chick" Clarey (commanding the Pacific Fleet), were in constant communication. Leader of the Seventh Fleet Admiral William Mack would go to his grave insisting his own staff had planned the mining, but their version differed from Pruning Knife—and earlier Haiphong mining schemes—only in fine details.

Tactical plans for the mining were updated from Duck Hook and complete by April 23, when Admiral McCain asked Washington to approve Pocket Money. Simple in concept and execution, Pocket Money was complex in its international fallout. Only one shipping channel led into Haiphong. Just a few strings of mines could close it (a mere thirty-six were used) because the DRV had no way to deal with sophisticated magnetic mines already aboard the U.S. aircraft carriers. Even diplomatic niceties could be accommodated, such as a warning to clear Vietnamese waters, because the "Destructor" mines had fusing mechanisms permitting activation (and, for that matter, deactivation) after a given interval. Some hundreds of mines would suffice to cover all the reseeding necessary for an extended campaign.

At this point Dr. Kissinger left for Moscow to make the final preparations for the planned summit. For weeks Nixon and Kissinger had mulled over the danger that actions in Vietnam might force its cancellation (and end any possibility of signing a nuclear arms control agreement), and the president had ordered Kissinger to threaten precisely that in his conversations with Soviet ambassador Dobrynin. Nixon's instructions to Kissinger for his Moscow trip have been declassified. They reveal that, despite certain outstanding issues on the nuclear arms agreement, Kissinger's primary task was to get the Soviets to do something about Hanoi's offensive. Trying to put the nuclear genie back in the bottle could take a backseat.

The mining of Haiphong became Nixon's hole card. Back during Duck Hook days, in September 1969, NSC staffer (and now official Nixon "enemy") Morton Halperin had predicted that the president would not go into the 1972 election without having mined Haiphong. That proved true. But there were significant political and diplomatic complications. Mining is an act of war under a series of international conventions with strictly defined rules of belligerency and notification. Since the United States had never declared war—and by 1972 its other legal claims were paper thin—in terms of international law, DRV allies would be perfectly justified in coming to Hanoi's aid. Mining would openly challenge the tacit limits under which the Vietnam war had been waged. More than the Moscow summit was at stake. The White House also understood that Americans would see these implications. Al Haig sent a memo to the president in which the deputy national security adviser pointed out, as Mr. Nixon recounts, "even more important than how Vietnam comes out is for us to handle these matters in a way that I can survive in office."[29]

At a barbecue held at the Texas ranch of Treasury Secretary John Connolly, a Nixon Democrat, conversations and questions from the audience spurred the president. From Floresville, Texas, he wrote Kissinger—before the fall of Quang Tri—demanding an even stronger air plan than the contemplated Linebacker. Nixon wanted a minimum three-day series of strikes on Hanoi by a fleet of at least a hundred B-52s. "We must *punish* the enemy . . . I intend to stop at nothing to bring the enemy to his knees." In Nixon's instructions to Kissinger for talks with Le Duc Tho, he told his emissary to offer only "settle or else" and used up much space demanding the application of more force. "Now is the best time to hit them," he insisted. "Forget the domestic reaction." Even Nixon recognized—explicitly, in this April 30 memorandum—that he was crossing a Rubicon.[30]

The NSC staff dealt with the assorted issues of foreign response and international law in a series of papers churned out in early May. Supervised by Haig, and by Kissinger once he returned from his futile encounter with Le Duc Tho, the analyses predictably concluded that the president faced risks but could make a case for his actions. To avoid any coalescence of opposition, Kissinger solicited comments from other officials individually. There was no mass circulation of the papers. He and the president then staged an NSC meeting where Laird and Rogers had their say, plus the usual audiences with congressional leaders and the Soviet ambassador, a Kissinger press conference, and a Nixon televised speech. Equally intricate staging required U.S. diplomats to advise close allies; notify dozens of seafaring nations, especially those trading with North Vietnam (including China, the USSR, Great Britain, and Japan); prepare a letter for the UN Security Council; and more. There was also a proclamation to satisfy international law insofar as possible.

Far down the food chain, the task of actually preparing the mines fell to Mineman Second Class Robert D. Gill Jr., sent to the carrier *Coral Sea* from his station at Charleston, South Carolina. Colleagues Roland Puscher and Tim Mercier rounded out the detail, supervised by the *Coral Sea*'s mine warfare officer, Lieutenant Commander Harvey Ickle. The job so easy the specialists could be flown in for the work, they arrived on Yankee Station on May 5 and the mines would be ready to go on May 8 (Washington date). Lieutenant Colonel Charles Carr of Marine Attack Squadron VMA-224 led a flight of nine aircraft to emplace the mines at 9:00 AM on May 9 (Vietnam time), coinciding exactly with the president's 9:00 PM (Washington time) televised speech to Americans.

With standard Nixonian aplomb, the White House announced afterward that telegrams ran 5–1 or 6–1 in favor of the mining. Reporting on Watergate for the *Washington Post* the following year, Bob Woodward and Carl Bernstein discovered that the Committee to Re-elect the President (CREEP), Mr. Nixon's campaign organization, had spent $4,400 to place a deceptive full-page ad in the *New York Times* suggesting wide public support. In addition, CREEP had used at least $8,400, mostly in hundred-dollar bills, to pay for the telegrams. Although the cash came from illegal campaign contributions, at least it was not U.S. government money—unlike in 1970, when the White House had strong-armed the CIA and the State Department. The journalists quoted a former Nixon campaign official: "We never do anything honestly. Imagine, the President sending himself telegrams, patting himself on the back."[31]

A Fabric of Deepening War

When the Easter offensive began, the antiwar scene in the United States was mostly quiet. Harrisburg, Pennsylvania, where seven were on trial for an alleged conspiracy to kidnap Henry Kissinger and attack draft boards, was the locale for the most serious organizing. The Harrisburg trial could have been a repeat of the Chicago Eight affair, this time targeting the Berrigan brothers—Philip, who was already in jail for a raid on a draft board in Catonsville, Maryland, and his brother Daniel, an unindicted coconspirator. In Harrisburg, however, the government's weak case foundered on the testimony of the FBI informant who became the star witness for the defense. In the first week of April the jury deadlocked, and the judge declared a mistrial. This episode illustrated a key flaw in the Nixon administration's efforts to suppress opposition by means of FBI infiltration: again and again the paid informants turned out to be the prime movers in the conspiracies the government alleged and prosecuted. The Harrisburg Seven were never retried. The incident marked a sorry end to the career of FBI czar J. Edgar Hoover, who had less than a month to live.

The day a mistrial was declared at Harrisburg, the United States resumed bombing North Vietnam. Suddenly there was an impetus for major protests. But the Movement did not respond as before. There were demonstrations, but protesters numbered in the hundreds or low thousands, nothing like the mass mobilizations for Cambodia or Laos. Even on April 15 and after, when the United States mounted heavy bombing raids in the Hanoi-Haiphong area, using B-52s there for the first time, the opposition called for campus strikes rather than marches on Washington. There were three main reasons. First, the American polity had turned decisively against the war, with Congress following suit, so there seemed to be less reason to take to the streets.

Second, Nixon's political strategy—moving to an all-volunteer military, cutting back in Vietnam, and thus radically lowering draft calls—had reduced the concerns of many American youths. Finally, 1972 was a presidential election year, leading to the hope that political differences could be settled at the ballot box. The net effect limited protests. These factors were quite evident at Columbia University.

As fighting intensified in Vietnam, earnest soul-searching consumed Columbia's Morningside Heights campus. Nixon's response to the Easter offensive made it more crucial than ever to do something, and all the participatory democracy and internecine quarrels did not prevent Columbia protests. On the night of April 17 there was a rally at the Sundial on College Walk, followed by a march to university president William McGill's residence at 116th Street and Morningside Drive. Protesters called on McGill to suspend business as usual. He expressed sympathy but insisted the university would stay open. Marchers crossed the campus to Broadway and went down it, only to be turned back by police at the little triangle where West End Avenue comes off Broadway at 107th Street. This became the first of a series of demonstrations or rallies held almost daily for weeks. Perhaps the longest would be a march to a Veterans Administration office at 24th Street, almost five miles.

On Tuesday the eighteenth there was a mass meeting at McIntosh Center, the Barnard College student union, across Broadway. This followed another neighborhood march. More than 2,000 students showed up for the meeting, where there was much talk of a strike. McGill addressed the crowd, retreating from his previous position, agreeing students could boycott classes on moratorium day, but still rejecting official closure. Columbia students' demands included the halt of work on Pentagon contracts (four or five faculty members participated in the JASON Group of consultants, which did a great deal of work specifically on Vietnam, including on bombing techniques, interdiction in Laos, and more); that professors at the School of International Affairs stop consulting for government agencies; and the divestiture of stock in companies linked to the war. Marchers focused on the physics building, Pupin Hall, and the newly opened International Affairs building.

Columbia was by no means the only school to respond this way. The National Student Association—ironically, financed for years by the CIA—called for a nationwide moratorium on classes for Friday, April 21. At Cornell, the university senate approved a moratorium and a call for a halt to military action. At Princeton, students voted to boycott classes, and the next day a large group took over the office of the dean of admissions; another occupied the Woodrow Wilson School. At Cambridge, Harvard students ransacked the Center for International Affairs (today the John F. Kennedy School). Police surrounded Harvard Square. The most incendiary action (literally) took place at the University of Maryland's main campus, where demonstrators burned four police cars; the governor called out the National

Guard and sent units to College Park. Demonstrations at the University of Texas–Austin were broken up by tear gas and riot batons. A VVAW chapter sparkplugged by veteran John Kniffen was in the forefront. There were also demonstrations at Boston University, the University of Michigan, the University of Wisconsin, Stanford, Syracuse, and Boise State. In addition to those already mentioned, there were strikes at Berkeley, Yale, Fordham, New York University, Tufts, Wisconsin, and other campuses. A couple of days before the mining of Haiphong, the presidents of sixty universities signed a letter to President Nixon deploring the U.S. surge in Vietnam. The presidents of the Ivies plus MIT issued their own statement. On May 17 the Ivy League university presidents met with Kissinger in the Roosevelt Room at the White House. One warned that they would be unable to run their institutions if the war continued, and all feared the upcoming fall semester.

Meanwhile, Thursday, April 20, brought new turmoil at Columbia. The university sought to head off a strike by obtaining a court order prohibiting the blockade of buildings. Protesters nevertheless gathered in the rain to picket the main entrance of the School of International Affairs on 118th Street, just off Amsterdam Avenue. Dr. McGill asked the New York Police Department to clear the area, which brought the TPF back to Columbia. Police took action despite the fact that, when read the court order, protesters agreed to open their picket line. That triggered a response McGill had not expected. The university senate was in session at the Business School, Uris Hall, even as police maneuvered just a couple of blocks away. Outraged students in magnified numbers marched on Uris. A few dozen pickets became a mass of 500. About a third entered Uris. Student senators convinced protesters not to invade the session, which had been declared closed, but notes were passed under the door. McGill, who presided over the senate, threw up his hands and declared the session adjourned. A shouting match ensued in which it became clear that a number of faculty and administration representatives, not to mention student senators, agreed with the protesters. McGill later declared that Columbia would be closed on moratorium day, but he refused to call it a moratorium, terming that word ambiguous. The act impugned his own credibility as well as the utility of the university senate, created as one of the reforms after 1968.

On moratorium day and through the weekend, Columbia simmered. The dorms, South Field, and College Walk saw vociferous debates on the war, on whether the moratorium should be extended into a strike, and on the sincerity of William J. McGill. There were rallies and marches. By Sunday a consensus emerged for another mass meeting, again at Barnard's McIntosh. After long hours of speechifying came a vote. More than a thousand students, a plurality, wanted to strike. But substantial numbers voted against that, unlike 1970, when feeling had been nearly unanimous. Disaffected antistrike students formed what they called the Majority Coalition. It held a few rallies, but its most important act was a legal one, threatening to sue Columbia if it failed to suppress the strike. In 1968 students opposed to the action had actively contested the strikers with blockades and fisticuffs; this time that did not happen.

A word on Pupin Hall is in order. Purists liked to call this building Pupin Laboratory, but most of Columbia knew Pupin as just another hall. It did, however, house a laboratory, and it was the bastion of the physicists who consulted for the Pentagon through the JASON Group. Strikers occupied the building and found papers that examined the efficiency of U.S. aerial bombing and interdiction. With fantasies of a Columbia version of the Pentagon Papers, historian Ronald Radosh looked at the materials and charged that the university was complicit in the war.[32] The Pupin occupation progressed to a blockade, and many people were shut inside, including physics students who had nothing to do with the strike. Food had to be smuggled in. Scientists later condemned the occupiers as nonphysicists, as if no member of the Columbia community other than a physicist had any right to be concerned about this work.

On April 24 picket lines closed the classroom building Hamilton Hall amid more demonstrations. Four more buildings were occupied. The daytime protests were desultory, but that night a very disturbing episode occurred. Students held a rally at the Sundial. Hundreds, perhaps more, were clustered on College Walk and South Field. At a certain point a mass of officers dressed in the uniforms of Columbia security guards emerged from Low Library. They lined up across the top of the steps behind the Alma Mater statue. Suddenly it became apparent the officers were accompanied by dogs. At a signal, the security forces began to descend. They swept the Walk and South Field with the dogs. Those not holding leashes held batons. Pandemonium ensued. Ralph J. Begleiter, later prominent as a broadcast journalist, was then a Brown University student moonlighting as a reporter for a Providence, Rhode Island, radio station. Begleiter also witnessed the chaos on College Walk that night. I have been unable to establish how many were injured. No one was arrested because, of course, Columbia security guards had no such power. The action was a pure show of force.

Except for the dogs, this maneuver replicated the methods of the TPF. Columbia security guards were not riot police and had no special training other than what they might have been given secretly just prior to this incident. Needless to say, Columbia University security had no attack dog unit.

The next day there was no further effort to disguise the police. It would later be reported that both New York mayor John V. Lindsay and acting police commissioner William H. T. Smith advised McGill against bringing police onto the campus. Lindsay argued that the police presence would have a polarizing effect. It did. President McGill, not dissuaded, met Smith that morning and summoned the police, already massed at 120th Street between Amsterdam and Claremont avenues. Accounts of these events put the numbers at about 150 uniformed officers plus 30 plainclothesmen drawn from ten different New York precincts. There were also 17 deputy sheriffs. Shortly after lunch a unit of Columbia security guards pushed their way through the pickets at Hamilton Hall *and used cutters to snip the chain shutting the doors. With New York's acting sheriff, Joseph P. Brennan, plus a posse of Columbia guards, McGill put in an appearance before the picketers at the School of International Affairs, demanding that they leave. Protesters marched away singing "Solidarity Forever." Later McGill's party entered Hamilton through a tunnel entrance.*

It was about 3:30 PM when McGill and his group appeared from inside Hamilton Hall. University guards pushed open the doors and shoved protesters aside to make space. I was standing among the crowd watching this, though not among the picketers. The guards were none too gentle. McGill himself later admitted that the first injury, to a woman student, occurred at this time. Sheriff Brennan read the university's court order and demanded that the picketers disperse. They did in fact move away, but the crowd began to surge, and McGill turned to Brennan. Apparently, this was the signal for the TPF, which appeared instantly. There was a tense standoff for ten or twenty minutes, with chants and slogans shouted at McGill. A few rocks and eggs pelted the helmeted police. Then someone threw a bottle. The police broke ranks and charged. Rock throwing began in earnest. Sheriff Brennan was hit on the head. The students were swept onto South Field. Protesters were beaten—five students and a faculty member were hurt seriously enough to require hospital treatment—and seven were arrested. Brennan and seven policemen also required treatment. McGill professed himself sickened and ordered the police off the campus.

Mayor Lindsay was exactly right. Following the Hamilton Hall fracas, enraged protesters broke windows and glass doors at the International Affairs building. Although the pickets had been cleared there and at Hamilton, before the night was over, protesters had reoccupied Hamilton and barricaded themselves inside. Others seized Kent Hall, the center for East Asian studies, and offices of the university registrar and bursar. On April 28 Columbia used a forklift plus security guards to overcome the barricaded doors at Kent. Dr. McGill met with university trustees and decided to ride out the storm. Columbia stayed closed for more than a week. Classes were held on the grass in South Field, in professors' apartments, at the nearby West End Bar, any suitable locale.

My problem with all this was that the student strikes absorbed attention and efforts that should have focused on Vietnam. Of course, antiwar protest remained a theme in every daily march, and Columbia students made some notable efforts to reach out to local labor unions as well as to students in high schools (my one experience as a true "outside agitator" consisted of doing a sort of teach-in and consciousness-raising session at a Nassau County high school). But the complaint that the University was not the War still resounded. I heard that in my dorm, on College Walk, and in the sixth-floor student lounge of the School of International Affairs building, where I had courses on Soviet foreign policy and on military technology. I had some sympathy for the argument, as well as misgivings about the events at Columbia, where controversy left the community divided and the strike much worse organized and focused than at the time of Cambodia. Strike sentiment weakened and petered out by early May. Students gave up the buildings one by one, the final holdouts being a group of African Americans in the office of the urban planning department—a different kind of protest aimed directly at the university, not the war. As a result, when Nixon made his major escalation on May 8, mining Haiphong harbor and risking confrontation with both China and the USSR, there was no energy for action at Columbia.

At the School of International Affairs I could see that the students, most of whom had their eyes on government jobs, were avoiding the issues. I resolved to confront them with information in a series of nonpolemical issue papers that simply laid out facts about the U.S. escalation. That became my private project for the rest of the semester. It consumed both money and many hours in the middle of the rush to complete term papers (in one of which I used the work of Gerald Hickey, John Donoghue, Harvey Meyerson, Robert Sansom, William R. Corson, and Don Luce for a study of pacification in the South Vietnamese countryside) and prepare for exams. It was my search for up-to-date data for these information papers that brought me into direct contact with the Vietnam Veterans Against the War. I had known who they were since Dewey Canyon III. The VVAW action at New Year's, taking place simultaneously in three cities, including at the Statue of Liberty in New York, had especially impressed me. I learned that the group's national office, then in New York City, had relevant material. I visited VVAW offices at 25 West 26th Street. There I discovered the reports of the Ad Hoc Military Buildup Committee.

The Ad Hoc Committee, formed on April 8, was typical of the myriad groups spawned by the Movement: it could only have existed in this environment. Frank Neisser, one of the founders, had been giving legal advice to people on active duty, somewhat akin to draft counseling. Ed Murray, another founder, was a VVAW member. Indeed, the Ad Hoc Committee and VVAW worked out of adjoining offices in Cambridge, an example of the way spontaneous outpourings could morph with surprising impact. When I encountered their product it was already being widely cited by journalists writing about Vietnam. An important milestone in gaining credibility came with the Nixon administration's mid-April bombings of Hanoi and Haiphong. Journalists who examined the committee's reports discovered that its analyses had included indications pointing to this attack two days before it took place. The committee petered out later that summer, as Washington completed its deployment of forces, but for some weeks the Ad Hoc Committee remained a key source. During those weeks the Nixon Shock of the mining became part of the fabric of a deepening war.

■ ■ ■ How Hanoi's allies would respond to the Haiphong mining had been a key consideration for the Nixon administration from the outset. Most obviously, the Nixon Shock called into question the summit between President Nixon and Soviet leader Leonid Brezhnev. Many thought it would be endangered. (Within Columbia's Political Science Department, a professor with the Institute of War and Peace Studies collected bets on the outcome from colleagues and students as a way to assess the reaction. The betting was overwhelming that the summit would be destroyed.) White House records declassified decades later show that Richard Nixon held the same view. In fact, the president wanted to discount a Soviet move by canceling the summit himself. Kissinger and Haig implored the president to let Brezhnev take the onus of cancellation.

Moscow had already protested the damage done to its ships during the mid-April U.S. bombing at Haiphong, in which five Russian seamen died. Now the Americans had upped the ante. Brezhnev was shocked, but according to Russian historian Ilya Gaiduk, his concern was the summit, not the DRV. Ambassador Anatoly Dobrynin confirms that Brezhnev hesitated. "The summit literally hung in the balance," Dobrynin recounted. Brezhnev's reply to the letter in which Nixon informed him of the mining denounced the U.S. move and said nothing about the summit. Dobrynin pointedly refused reassurances to Kissinger, despite the Nixon accolyte's strenuous efforts to get them. The Soviets' official statement condemned the mining as "inadmissible" and threatened to "draw the appropriate conclusions." A press statement from the official Tass news agency on May 11 called the Nixon Shock "fraught with serious consequences" and a single-handed attempt to impose U.S. rules on international navigation, a "gross violation" of freedom of the seas.[33]

The Soviet leaders did not all see Haiphong with the same eye. Politburo member Pyotr Shelest, president Nikolai Podgorny, and Central Committee secretary Dmitry Polyanski (who had helped engineer the overthrow of Khrushchev for alleged timidity in the Cuban missile crisis) favored responding. Army chief Marshal Andrei Grechko wanted to jettison the summit. Some reportedly favored sending a convoy to Haiphong. Party propaganda chief Mikhail Suslov hung in the middle. Others were uncertain too. Brezhnev overrode opponents, backed by premier Aleksei Kosygin, foreign minister Andrei Gromyko, and spy chief Yuri Andropov. According to Dobrynin, the deciding argument took Hanoi to task: since the DRV had been so circumspect in its relations with the USSR and had not taken Soviet interests into account in its decision for the offensive, Moscow was free to follow its own line.

The next morning Brezhnev plus a troika of his Politburo allies conferred with technical experts. The consultation would have taken place ahead of the Politburo meeting except that many Russians that day had been consumed with celebrations of the Soviet victory in World War II. One of them, Georgi Arbatov, an expert on the United States, recalled the debate as very serious and the decision difficult, but Brezhnev did not change his mind.[34] A Central

Committee Plenum meeting confirmed the decision. Washington's first hint of a break came when the Soviet minister for merchant marine made a U.S. visit as scheduled, and another Brezhnev-Nixon letter took a milder tone. Shelest's star began to fade at that time, as the Ukrainian party boss and former KGB chief became increasingly isolated in the Soviet leadership.

But the Soviets could not avoid *some* action. Navy commander Admiral Sergei Gorshkov recommended sending minesweepers to North Vietnam. There were seventeen Russian vessels in Haiphong at the time, with eight Soviet merchantmen en route, one already in the South China Sea, but most still in the Indian Ocean or exiting the Bosporus. From Vladivostok, headquarters of the Soviet Pacific fleet and several thousand miles from Haiphong, a cruiser and destroyer steamed out of port, headed toward the battle area. But, most ominously, the Soviets also sortied an Echo-II class cruise missile submarine, a warship with the ability to engage U.S. aircraft carriers. In a top-secret and highly dangerous cat-and-mouse game reminiscent of the movie *Hunt for Red October,* the American nuclear attack sub *Guardfish* detected the Soviet vessel passing through the Tsushima Strait and trailed it for a month, all the way to the South China Sea. Kissinger and Nixon were informed. The *Guardfish* later received a unit citation. But by June the Soviets had added two more Echo-II boats and an Echo-I class submarine to its squadron near Yankee Station. Brezhnev may have taken a soft line on the mining, but the Soviets had given themselves a capability for instant intervention. This had never been a factor in the past, and it was one that Kissinger's NSC staff papers had failed to predict; it signaled a potential escalation of the Vietnam war that U.S. policy had long sought to avoid.

The People's Republic of China reacted with strong rhetoric but no overt military moves. Radio Beijing broadcast a Chinese government statement on May 11 that declared, "This act of war escalation by U.S. imperialism seriously encroaches upon the territory and sovereignty of the Democratic Republic of Vietnam, grossly violates the freedom of international navigation and trade and wantonly tramples upon the Charter of the United Nations." Denouncing the "provocation," the Chinese reaffirmed their backing for the Vietnamese people and their determination to act as a "reliable rear area" for North Vietnam. A similar denunciation appeared from the PRC's representative at the United Nations, Huang Hua, who objected to circulating the U.S. message to the United Nations as a Security Council document.[35] Privately, at ongoing ambassadorial talks in Warsaw, a Chinese envoy conveyed a milder message, which Washington took to mean the Chinese would stand aside.

Amid the diplomacy, the horrors of war continued unabated. Richard Nixon remained the prodder in chief, goading subordinates on to greater efforts. On the telephone with Mel Laird on May 8 he demanded that oil be added to Linebacker targets to ensure the North Vietnamese "can't run those damn trucks." The secretary of defense assured him this was being done. Nixon repeated the exhortation to Admiral Moorer the next day on the phone and to Kissinger in a memo. In that paper Nixon returned to his idea of mass B-52 strikes on North Vietnam, complaining that the military was allocating too few sorties, evoking alleged "deary 'milk runs' which characterized the Johnson Administration's bombing." He added, "I cannot emphasize too strongly that I have determined we should go for broke." Nixon talked of a 500-plane raid. He needled Kissinger and Haig about ordering a mass tank attack. He wanted CIA "black" propaganda in North Vietnam—a subject he raised repeatedly in the days after Haiphong. On May 19 Nixon expressed disgust at the brass, contending they had repeatedly failed to carry out his orders over the years, and instructed Kissinger to convey to both the Joint Chiefs and the Air Force staff that "it is time for these people either to shape up or get out." The next day he told Haig he wanted at least 200 sorties a day aimed at the Hanoi-Haiphong area.[36]

The military did its best to comply. Attack sorties against the DRV tripled from April to May. The 1,895 fighter-bomber sorties (and 1,590 B-52 flights) in April—almost all near the DMZ—swelled to more than 6,000 fighter-bomber and 2,000 B-52 sorties every month through September. Linebacker peaked in August with 7,037 fighter-bomber and 2,307 B-52 attack missions, many aimed at Hanoi or Haiphong. After that the rate of effort dropped steadily due to U.S. budget problems and the sheer difficulty of maintaining the operational readiness required for these high sortie rates, even with the large number of American warplanes in the theater. With a unit of four aircraft carriers constantly on Yankee Station, the Navy flew roughly twice as many sorties as the Air Force. Through the end of the year there were a total of 44,494 fighter-bomber and 16,413 B-52 sorties flown, and they dropped somewhere around 240,000 tons of munitions. The B-52s alone deposited a greater weight of bombs on North Vietnam in Linebacker than all U.S. aircraft everywhere in Southeast Asia during 1966.[37]

New weapons also increased effectiveness, particularly the laser-guided bomb, first employed in warfare over Vietnam in 1972. At the time, the Seventh Air Force had only half a dozen of the sophisticated electronic pods needed to guide the bombs, and it employed mass escort tactics to protect the planes carrying them. Just two were lost during Linebacker. Officers bragged about the impact. For example, the multispan bridge over the Song Ma at Thanh Hoa, North Vietnam, had resisted efforts to destroy it throughout Rolling Thunder. No more than a span or two had ever been put out of action, and dozens of planes had been lost attacking it. Smart bombs destroyed most of this bridge at no cost. A wing of F-111 aircraft also deployed for Linebacker. These planes were supposed to fly so fast and at such low altitude as to be impervious. They depended on terrain-contour radar but could not discriminate the tall jungle vegetation of the triple canopies that soared above the hills. The mess-hall joke was that Vietnamese flak was 5 percent effective, but trees were 100 percent. Four planes crashed before crews acquired the knack for flying over the DRV. But the longer-range F-111s enabled the Air Force to withdraw many tanker aircraft previously needed for aerial refueling. New electronic jamming devices were also used to help U.S. aircraft evade SAMs, and communications intercepts warned strike commanders when the North Vietnamese detected their approach.

Nuclear weapons were considered but rejected. Nixon mentioned the possibility to Dr. Kissinger on April 25, possibly to startle him. By May 4 the president recognized that even using "the total power of this office," he could not resort to nuclear weapons "unless it's necessary." Such an action would have confronted the Soviets and the Chinese with the very dilemma to which they had refused to respond when the Americans mined Haiphong.[38]

Among the most controversial possible tactics was to attack the system of dikes in the Red River delta that provided irrigation to one of the DRV's main agricultural areas. Rupturing the dikes, Washington estimated, might drown more than 200,000 peasants. U.S. sources deny ever attacking the dikes. Hanoi insists that Washington did so and published elaborate maps and diagrams showing where dikes were hit and how this affected irrigation. Foreign diplomats, including the Swedish ambassador, reported personally witnessing dike bombings. Nixon's White House tapes contain a conversation—on April 25—in which the president himself said, "I still think we ought to take out the dikes now," suggesting, at a minimum, that such attacks were a recurrent subject at the highest level of government.[39] At the secret negotiations between Le Duc Tho and Kissinger on August 1, the DRV explicitly protested "the bombing against the dikes and heavily populated areas" as an escalation in violence. Presumably, Hanoi would not have done so unless it had a basis in fact.[40] Yet no record has emerged of damage assessment on dikes or of the kinds of orders or administrative messages one would expect if the dikes had been specifically targeted. The jury remains out, but the preponderance of evidence is that the United States did attack them.

For all the violence—and the exhortations of an embittered White House incumbent—Linebacker had its limitations. Some claim that the 1972 bombing was decisive in a way that Rolling Thunder had not been. The jury is still out on that too. One of the most popular charges against LBJ has been that he permitted exclusion zones around Hanoi and Haiphong and along the Chinese border. Nixon kept them for Linebacker. Like Johnson, Nixon reduced or restored the exclusion zones at whim, and strikes at targets within them required specific permission. Secretary Laird preapproved a hundred targets within the zones but afterward was parsimonious in adding new ones. Some of the same targets, such as the Hanoi thermal power plant and the Paul Doumer bridge, remained on the prohibited list. North Vietnamese documents admitted that the scale of bombing far surpassed LBJ's Rolling Thunder, but the day came when Mr. Nixon railed at the inefficacy of Linebacker just as he had condemned Johnson's bombing. An examination of official sortie records reveals that for the months of Linebacker the American air armada averaged a rate of 225 per day. Back in 1969 Pruning Knife Alpha had provided for 250 a day. Rolling Thunder's 1967 rate—for a full 365 days—had been 293 sorties a day. The main difference was the B-52 flights in the figures, but with a few exceptions, those were restricted to the panhandle throughout the campaign. Decisive or not, the Nixon war managers at full stride could not match the scale that had once been feasible.

A secret report to the Politburo during late May showed that the bombing plus mining had cut Haiphong's unloading capacity by two-thirds, from 6,500 tons per day to 1,000 or 2,000, and that a backlog of 60,000 tons of materiel had accumulated, of which the North Vietnamese were clearing about 2,600 tons daily. Underestimating the violence of the U.S. aerial response, the DRV had also prepared too few repair and backup capabilities, particularly in the panhandle, and supplies in some areas were critical. Food and petroleum were sufficient for five months, but gasoline stocks down to a month and a half. China immediately donated an extra 10,000 tons of gasoline, not including what it furnished directly to the People's Army. Industrial production declined.[41] But the available documents suggest that the impact was short term. After June the subject of supply difficulties disappears from the DRV documents. A message from the Lao Dong Party Secretariat to General Pham Hung reported some success clearing the mines, promising more determined supply efforts, though it conceded diminished industrial production.

For all the bombing, Hanoi did not flag. Under the heaviest of the interdiction, the VPA moved its last reserve division through the panhandle into South Vietnam and kept up the flow of supplies to the front. It also met its goal of raising 90,000 fresh troops for the People's Army, as well as improving transport repairs. Journalist Joseph Kraft wrote in the *New Yorker* in August that seafood remained in plentiful supply in Hanoi restaurants.[42] On August 11 the CIA supplied an analysis concluding that Linebacker would affect DRV industry but not its war capacity. A frustrated Henry Kissinger complained that he could not understand how a fourth-rate nation did not have a breaking point.

Hanoi sought propaganda value from visits by American delegations. Ramsey Clark, LBJ's former attorney general, led one delegation. He was appropriately horrified. But the most controversial visit was by a group that included actress Jane Fonda. On her July trip, Fonda brought mail for American prisoners and met with seven of them. She also recorded messages broadcast over Radio Hanoi and—most infamously—allowed her picture to be taken seated in the gunner's position of a North Vietnamese antiaircraft gun. It is a measure of the ferocity of the political debate over Vietnam that war supporters accused Fonda of treason.

Meanwhile, fighting continued in the South. Thieu declared martial law in June. He reformed the high command, finally firing General Hoang Xuan Lam at I Corps and also relieving his leader in the Central Highlands. But even now, Thieu did not actually rid himself of Lam, who became assistant to the prime minister for counternarcotics. Division commander Giai was dismissed and hauled in front of a board of inquiry. He went to jail. The leader of the forces at Dak To was also relieved and replaced by a more dynamic officer. Near Saigon the siege of An Loc was broken. In the highlands, Kontum would be saved by a combination of fresh ARVN leaders; the fighting qualities of montagnard troops, who bore the brunt of the Kontum city battle; and U.S. airpower. American adviser John Paul Vann fell in the fighting when his helicopter crashed. North Vietnamese documents of the period repeatedly voiced the hope of igniting the countryside to overcome Saigon's pacification gains, and COSVN received orders to send regular troops into the Mekong delta to augment local guerrillas. There was much fighting but no significant inroads.

An incident that occurred a week before Vann's death graphically illustrates how vulnerable Thieu felt. Ambassador Bunker had been urging him to get out of the presidential palace and be seen in public, especially in the highlands, where an appearance could bolster morale. But there was no airfield long enough for Thieu's personal aircraft, a C-118. One night at Tan Son Nhut, Sergeant Bob Laymon, crew chief of a C-47 in a U.S. squadron that shuttled VIPs, got the alert for a mission. Only after beginning to ready the plane did he learn the flight involved Thieu. ARVN officers said Thieu would not board an aircraft on the U.S. side of the field, so the pilot taxied the C-47 up to the civilian terminal. Snipers abruptly appeared on the roof. As Thieu's arrival neared, guards, watchers, and functionaries surrounded the plane. The Americans were scared. They had been told to expect Thieu to drive up, but instead the Vietnamese alighted from a helicopter that suddenly landed next to the C-47. Thieu boarded with a party of half a dozen. After accommodating the passengers, Laymon announced they would have to hand over any weapons—only the U.S. pilot and crew chief could be armed aboard an American aircraft. Laymon turned to Thieu and asked him directly, "So, are you carrying a weapon?" Thieu's eyes widened, then he shrugged, reached into a pocket, and pulled out a small pistol. A moment later he leaned over and took another gun out of his boot. His companions followed suit. Laymon found himself holding a dozen weapons. The C-47 took off and made a preliminary stop at Phu Cat, where Laymon asked Thieu where he wanted to go. Left would be the highlands, right to Qui Nhon. Thieu chose Qui Nhon. There they picked up John Vann. Thieu and Vann whispered in the back of the plane, chattering like teenagers. Then choppers appeared, and both Thieu and Vann departed, flying on to Kontum, leaving the C-47 behind. There, Thieu fired corps commander Ngo Dzu. When the copters returned to Qui Nhon, Thieu's C-118 unexpectedly materialized to take him back to Saigon.[43] Nguyen Van Thieu kept his security really tight.

The new commander in I Corps was General Ngo Quang Truong. He infused the northern front with confidence. In mid-May the ARVN began a counteroffensive toward Quang Tri. General Truong used new tactics, launching a series of small amphibious landings to hook around the VPA. More troops pushed up Highway 1. The decimated First Armored Brigade was rebuilt and stiffened the attack. Marines, Airborne, and Rangers made up the bulk of the assault force. Despite considerable artillery support and American air strikes, plus the ARVN's best forces, the advance had all the dynamism of World War I. It required almost two months for the South Vietnamese to push about ten miles to the outskirts of Quang Tri city, then two more for the fight there. Hanoi's Stalingrad? It is significant that in the course of the Easter offensive battles took place (An Loc, now Quang Tri) that so plainly revealed the boundaries of capability on both sides. The South Vietnamese flag rose over the ruins of the Citadel in Quang Tri on September 15. There was no question of recapturing the rest of the province or restoring the DMZ line. The ARVN had expended its offensive capacity. Without that ground strength, American airpower could not win the war—a point that goes all the way back to Eisenhower's 1954 scheme to win the French war while avoiding any commitment of troops. The outcome also shows the limits of Vietnamization. Nixon and Thieu had built a million-man South Vietnamese military machine that could not win the war. Fighting continued in a desultory fashion, merely lengthening the casualty lists. And the bombs fell, harder than ever.

13   Sifting Out the Hearts of Men (1972)

As the Easter offensive began, Hanoi's final directives envisioned reaching a decision on the battlefield, then making progress in negotiations—some in the summer, but more before the U.S. elections. Le Duc Tho followed that scheme in meeting Kissinger in Paris on May 2, a session the latter found especially frustrating. Hanoi's envoys rejected halting the offensive, and the United States held fast to its refusal to unseat Thieu. After this deadlock, Nixon ordered the diplomats to break off the official talks too, and Hanoi countered, canceling the next scheduled Kissinger-Tho conversation. Despite Linebacker and the Haiphong mining, it was Washington that blinked.[1] The Nixon-Brezhnev summit included an exchange on Vietnam, where Kissinger offered an important concession: the commission created to supervise South Vietnam's election of a new president could serve as an interim coalition government. The Soviets passed this on to Hanoi during a mid-June visit by Soviet president Nikolay Podgorny. As LBJ had done during other diplomatic initiatives—to much criticism—Nixon expanded the Linebacker exclusion zones around Hanoi and Haiphong. The Chinese took a hand as well, encouraging Hanoi to consider an arrangement that did not require Thieu's immediate ouster.[2]

It was also the United States, not the DRV, that issued the invitation to new talks. This led to a pair of meetings on July 19 and August 1 at which the long impasse began to break. Kissinger insists that Hanoi's military weakness forced it to deal and that he offered no concessions. By his own account, the U.S. presentation on August 1 "consisted mainly of cosmetic modifications."[3] Historian Jeffrey Kimball analyzes the evidence in some detail and argues otherwise.[4] Declassified transcripts of both sessions are now available and show the United States here agreed to include both political and military elements in an agreement—something Washington had resisted strenuously up to this point. The United States hoped to minimize this concession by reserving most political questions for a second stage of talks between the Vietnamese parties (in a commission created by the agreement). Kissinger also dangled the possibility of a bombing halt to advance the negotiation. He specifically said, "We believe that we have made a significant proposal." Nixon had already conceded a cease-fire in place, shortened—and here further reduced—the schedule for the U.S. troop withdrawal, and offered repa-rations. On August 1 Hanoi relented on its demand that Thieu be forced out (with the understanding he would resign before elections) and presented an outline framework of an agreement.[5]

After this, diplomacy began to move quickly. By August 10 the NSC staff had a draft Vietnam cease-fire agreement on paper, and further conversa-tions took place on August 14, where there were workmanlike efforts to hammer out acceptable language. Ten days later Dr. Kissinger visited Saigon to confer on the arrangements with President Thieu. Suddenly the sides were moving toward accommodation.

Why this agreement? Why now? Who was compromising with whom? The argument that Hanoi dealt from weakness founders on the military realities. Even though its bid for decisive victory had failed, Hanoi now held a strong position in the South, sustained in the face of U.S. mining and bombing as well as Saigon's counterattacks. It would be the American president who ran out of options. Mr. Nixon had no sharp tools left. Bombing was what it was. Without it, the battle lines would have been even worse. Withdrawal had run its course: Nixon had cleared the way for the mining with another increment in April, and two more afterward to still the disquiet. When they were com-plete, the U.S. force level would be 12,000. That card had played out. The public opinion spike Nixon gained from Haiphong itself was soft and evapo-rated when mining and bombing failed to produce visible results. Humani-tarian concern over attacking North Vietnam's dikes influenced the falling poll numbers. The ARVN bogged down in Quang Tri. Nixon had played out his string in Congress too. In late July a bill that would have strengthened his hand by locking the United States into the war, making exit contingent on an internationally supervised agreement, failed in the Senate. Another resolu-tion, one that *ordered* withdrawal if Hanoi simply returned U.S. prisoners, passed. The folly of justifying the war merely on the basis of the American prisoners stood revealed. Progress in the negotiations themselves became Nixon's only remaining card.

The key differences on the American side were between President Nixon and Dr. Kissinger. The national security adviser wanted to use the U.S. elec-tion as a cudgel to extract from Hanoi the best terms for a settlement. Kissinger actually told Le Duc Tho on August 1 that Nixon would be stronger after the election, implying a need to settle beforehand. Mr. Nixon also counted on being stronger after the election, so he preferred to string out the negotiations past then. For him, the election meant drawing a new hand he could play to his advantage. If agreement were achieved before the election, the president could use that to sway voters, but that was not his pre-ferred outcome. Suddenly American politics took center stage.

Marchers and Voters

By the summer of 1972 the presidential election had become a source of immense confidence at the White House and the object of intense hope, perhaps wishful thinking, among many others. Richard Nixon had done everything that was legal—and a lot that was not—to ensure his reelection. From his first day in the Oval Office, a great deal of posturing, staff work, public gestures, private maneuvering, assorted chicanery, and ultimately covert operations had been aimed at this very goal. President Nixon remains the only American chief executive ever forced to resign precisely because of the methods he used to seek office. With George W. Bush, Americans today have a new example of excessive zeal in a president, though it remains to be established whether irregularities in the 2000 and 2004 elections were parts of an orchestrated campaign. In 1968 observers spoke of advertising, public relations, and the selling of the presidency. And there was the matter of the October Surprise. But this time around Nixon spared no effort to choreograph the entire election. The campaign unfolded with a scripted quality. Richard Nixon wanted not only the greatest landslide in American history; he wished to have a procession to his reinauguration. This is not the place for a lengthy accounting, but a few points are in order to set the context for the disruption of his careful script by the Vietnam Veterans Against the War.

First, Nixon enjoyed unprecedented success in determining his opponent, and he eventually faced the weakest available Democratic candidate. This goes beyond the actions of acolytes of the Committee to Re-elect the President (CREEP) and the political "dirty tricks" of his campaign staff. The notorious "Canuck letter" was a dirty trick that led to the self-destruction of Nixon's most viable opponent, Senator Edmund Muskie of Maine. That was a CREEP activity, and one of its operatives was Muskie's driver. Much of the rest the president did himself. White House political records tell the story. The president had sharp analysts such as Patrick Buchanan compile in-depth summaries of the strengths and vulnerabilities of his opponents; then he acted to compromise those persons. For example, analysts pictured Hubert Humphrey, Nixon's 1968 adversary, as vulnerable on Vietnam. When Humphrey loyally made a statement backing U.S. action, Nixon telephoned to thank him and to encourage more of the same—then he had political operatives target Humphrey on those statements. Edward Kennedy might have been a strong opponent, but Kennedy was vulnerable due to his behavior in the Chappaquiddick incident, an accident resulting in the death of Kennedy's friend Mary Jo Kopechne. Nixon had Chuck Colson investigate Kennedy, and one of Howard Hunt's first White House assignments was to dig for dirt on Kopechne's death.[6]

Alabama governor George Wallace, a conservative, could have drawn off southerners and the blue-collar voters Nixon counted on. That is what he had done as a third-party candidate in 1968. John Mitchell's Justice Department developed a bribery case against Wallace's brother, after which a Nixon operative leaked the news to columnist Jack Anderson. The president had also had campaign contributions made to Wallace's gubernatorial opponent in the primary in 1970. When that failed to stop Wallace, Nixon tried to ensure that he stayed within the Democratic Party. In early 1972 the Justice Department dropped its investigation against his brother, and the next day Wallace entered the presidential lists as a Democrat. On May 15 Wallace suffered critical gunshot wounds from a would-be assassin. He would be paralyzed from the waist down and withdrew from the race. That left South Dakota's George McGovern, a liberal, as the leading Democratic contender, which was fine with the president.

Nixon's Watergate excesses stunned Americans later, but the important points here are their roots in Vietnam—the Plumbers formed to take out Daniel Ellsberg—and their commonality with other measures. The warrantless wiretaps ordered by the Nixon White House and the NSC against a variety of administration "enemies," plus some of its own officials, were not much different from the CREEP taps put on the Democratic National Committee at the Watergate building. Their discovery began the affair and gave it its name. The illegal cash collected for a slush fund, in excess of $2 million, was a massive extension of the tactic used against Wallace. Some of that money paid for the Haiphong mining telegrams. More of it went to finance the Plumbers.

The Republican nominating convention represented the start of Nixon's procession toward the inaugural, and he wanted it to be just right. The first fly in that ointment came when plans to hold it in San Diego collapsed. Miami became the new locale.

Nixon was highly concerned with image. His campaign events and rallies were a constant source of friction between White House and CREEP staff and the Secret Service. The Secret Service spent almost $6.4 million on security during the 1972 campaign, most of it for the president. At one point Bob Haldeman kicked up a ruckus with White House detail chief Bob Taylor over restraining ropes, which Haldeman wanted to drop so a crowd could surge forward in a "spontaneous" show of delight with the candidate. Taylor threatened to arrest the president's chief of staff, and he won that round. At the next rally, in Greensboro, North Carolina, CREEP advance people dropped the ropes themselves. Agents literally had to manhandle SEARCH-LIGHT onto Air Force One. In Cleveland, Haldeman wanted Nixon's motorcade to pass only cheering crowds, bypassing protesters, so enthusiasm would be the only emotion the TV cameras could record. Haldeman asked for a Secret Service radio in his limousine so he could monitor the post reports and direct the motorcade away from demonstrators. Logistics chief Dennis McCarthy refused. When the motorcade began, the White House detail discovered that a Haldeman aide with a walkie-talkie had been assigned to ride in their lead sedan. The Secret Service countered by having its agents use earphones, turning off the radio speakers. Taylor, jaundiced by Haldeman's animosity, eventually left the Secret Service.

The Secret Service also crossed swords with White House staff when Nixon's advance team wanted a checkpoint to keep protesters out of a Nixon rally. The Secret Service agreed to check for weapons but not to turn people away based on appearance. The campaign set up its own checkpoint beyond the real one and funneled protesters into a parking lot. Some of those denied entry sued the Secret Service, but legal proceedings established that White House staff had been the culprits. The Nixon campaign played it both ways. For a September rally at the Statue of Liberty, a package of fifty tickets appeared anonymously at VVAW offices. When a couple of dozen veterans attended, they were howled down by hundreds of Nixon partisans, and six were escorted away. That would be the televised image.

Various antiwar groups, including VVAW, announced their intentions to protest at the political conventions, particularly the Republicans'. Both the FBI and the CIA began frenzied efforts to divine Movement plans. James McCord of the White House Plumbers told Watergate investigators he had received almost daily reports. CIA records show that Project CHAOS began issuing evaluations as early as March 6. Given its charter, the CIA's reports purported to discuss "foreign support" for activities to disrupt or harass the conventions, but day after day they found "no direct indications" or that "indications remain limited." Instead, CHAOS analysts discussed *American* groups' activities. On March 21, when the Republican convention was still slated for San Diego, the focus was on "Expose 72," a multifaceted exhibit the San Diego Convention Coalition had planned at demonstrators' campsites. On April 24 CHAOS reported the protesters had received a letter of solidarity from North Vietnam but, more concretely, that the coalition had made an alliance with Mexican migrant workers and that the SDS had decided to participate. The next day the CHAOS situation report's lead read, "The spring fires of protest have been ignited on college campuses across the nation triggered in large part by the resumption of American bombing in North Vietnam." The analysts included a lengthy calendar of antiwar activities scheduled in various parts of the country through late May and observed: "American revolutionaries it seems will not pass up an opportunity to use the collective college protests as an additional lever to redress their grievances."[7]

The reporting ranged across the board. In May the CIA covered a visit to China by members of the Concerned Committee of Asian Scholars. In June the CIA noted that a Hanoi delegate to the Paris talks had expressed interest in learning about conditions in the United States from a traveler. In July there were reports on the New York–based People's Coalition for Peace and

Justice's plans for the Republican convention, now moved to Miami. In general, the CIA's reporting represented a hodgepodge of items, some relevant, many not.

Conspicuous for its absence was VVAW. Yet in his Watergate testimony, McCord singled it out as the "violent" organization of most concern as the convention neared. Hunt, who had taken his action team of Miami Cubans to check out McGovern campaign headquarters before doing the Watergate, undoubtedly would have been let loose on VVAW, except that the fumbled Watergate break-in of June 17 led to the Plumbers' arrest and the unraveling of the CREEP intelligence operation, eventually linked to the White House. Two Miami individuals, one in a sworn statement, later acknowledged being approached by the Plumbers' Barnard Barker in April and asked to sign on for an attempt to discredit VVAW. There is also evidence that, a month later, John Dean attempted to recruit a Department of the Interior official for undercover work on the Miami convention.

Veterans were honored guests at the Democratic convention that nominated George McGovern in July. Although the Nixon White House could not take the spotlight away from the Democrats, they did mount diversions. This would be the moment that Justice Department official Guy Goodwin chose to indict eight members of Vietnam Veterans Against the War for allegedly conspiring to attack attendees at the upcoming Republican convention. Southeast regional coordinator Scott Camil, already the subject of bogus drug and kidnapping charges, would be the lead defendant. At best, the indictment might preclude VVAW action in Miami. In any case, it would be an impediment and promised to bankrupt the organization by forcing it to spend money on legal fees.

The vets had long intended to put their weight into the balance. There had been many ideas about what to do. Some fantasized about a grand demonstration—a "triphibious" one—in which a few vets would parachute onto Miami Beach while others landed from the sea and a contingent marched onto the beach from the landward side. No one talked about attacking people. What they came up with was the "Last Patrol," the brainchild of Chicago members Bart Savage and Greg Petzel, in which road convoys of vets would converge on Miami from throughout the United States. Others would get there however they could, and the whole group would camp together and hold marches. The Midwest convoy departed Milwaukee led by John Lindquist, who had served with the Marines in the DMZ and had driven in road convoys to Khe Sanh. He left with fifteen vehicles, picked up more from Kansas City, St. Louis, and Chicago, and soon had forty. The East Coast convoy had thirty cars before it reached Maryland. The West Coast convoy was slowed by police, who stopped it in Arizona and Texas. The Secret Service, FBI, and local police shadowed them every step of the way. Lindquist continued to lead the main group, which grew to be a mile long. Some police harassment in Florida did not impede them. At Fort Pierce a party of vets dismounted for a "March Against Death" into the city.

Arrangements in Miami were made by Barry Romo, who secured a campsite at Flamingo Park, where other protesters also encamped. The place proved so chaotic that the vets closed their camp to the others and kept to themselves. The worst feature of the counterculture grab bag at the park was the presence of several dozen members of the American Nazi Party. The Nazis had swaggered around Miami Beach and now took over the stage, refusing to permit anyone else on the podium. Camp organizers begged VVAW to help. About forty vets responded and surrounded the stage, and Del Rosario of the national office asked the Nazis to leave. One of them hit Rosario from behind with a chair. Rosario struck back. The veterans overpowered the Nazis and passed them along a human chain to the edge of the park, where vet Fred Rosenthal, a really huge fellow, threw them out by the scruff of the neck. VVAW became the darling of Miami's Jewish community, many of them Holocaust survivors. Suddenly it was fine for the vets to move to a different part of the park to escape the chaos. Baskets of food, beer, and wine materialized as if by magic. When the Nazis tried to return later, the Jews themselves barred their way—little old ladies with garden hoses and men with shovels.

On the next day, August 21, VVAW marched to Miami Beach High School, being used to bivouac some specialists from the 82nd Airborne Division and 750 troops of a Florida National Guard battalion. Once again, the Nixon administration was treating the event as a threat to the nation. Almost 6,000 troops were deployed to Miami, including 500 Marines and 2,000 men of the 82nd Airborne. More than 1,000 state troopers had also been mobilized.

There was a definite potential for conflagration at the high school demonstration. California veteran Ron Kovic, a wheelchair-bound former Marine paralyzed in the war, made an impassioned speech, his message that in Vietnam the vets had discovered that America was on the wrong side of the war, and if it happened again, they would side with the people. The Guardsmen appeared to waver. Officers herded them back inside the school and shut the blinds so no one could see the street theater VVAW then staged. But the police log shows two servicemen appeared on the roof and flew the American flag upside down, a recognized distress signal. The Florida Guard's after-action report commented favorably on VVAW's conduct and discipline.

Discipline would be manifest the next day, too, when the vets mounted a "Silent March" up Collins Avenue to the Fontainebleau Hotel, where the president and many top Republicans were quartered. There were no shouts, no slogans, just vets arrayed in serried ranks, platoons arranged by state and guided by hand signals from disabled VVAWers who had been designated the leaders. Three vets in wheelchairs led the march—Kovic, Bobby Muller, and Bill Wyman. It was a haunting passage. Asked why there were no slogans, one vet replied, "There's nothing left to say."[8] In front of the hotel came another face-off, this time with Florida state troopers. The vets wanted to enter. Serving as march leader, Barry Romo ordered the group, consisting of 1,200 to 1,500 veterans, to sit down and block Miami's main street. They did. Mayhem was averted when California congressman Pete McCloskey arrived and invited the wheelchair-bound vets to come inside and await the president's arrival. Romo led the rest of the marchers through their planned speeches and a return to the campsite. Mr. Nixon actually arrived by helicopter, avoiding the vets altogether.

The Secret Service had rushed agents through training to have more of them in the field at the convention. It also went to the CIA to obtain the use of a Miami safe house for its operations, along with television recording equipment, special cameras, and half a dozen sets of false ID for undercover agents to use. A year later, Justice Department sources would leak that L. Patrick Gray, Hoover's successor at the FBI, had also yielded to demands for Bureau infiltrators among the protesters. By this time, Robert Mardian had left Justice's Internal Security Division and had joined CREEP. As a campaign official, he had no business in security planning for Miami, but it was Mardian who made the demand. According to the leak, infiltrators helped plan and foment the demonstrations put down by security forces. Miami assistant police chief Larry Cotzin, who actually controlled overall security at the convention, confirmed the infiltrations but denied knowing of provocateurs.[9]

Miami police responded to a variety of other incidents involving everyone from the SDS to Cubans to "Zippies" to the Nazis, who had moved their show to Key Biscayne. Larger groups numbered probably a thousand each, and there were a variety of smaller ones, somewhere between 5,000 and 10,000 activists. One night demonstrators attempted to harass delegates, and VVAW actually protected them, as well as a bus that seemed about to be set afire.

The Miami action climaxed on the night of August 23, when Richard Nixon accepted the nomination. Courtesy of Congressman McCloskey, there were four vets in the audience—Kovic, Muller, and Wyman, plus Mark Clevinger—assisted by some of McCloskey's staff. They were thrown out by security guards when they tried to shout out their opposition as Nixon began his speech. That was bad enough, but outside was pandemonium. VVAW tried to hold a march and a rally, but other demonstrators removed barricades, slashed tires, turned over a Volkswagen, blocked a street with sandbags, staged another sit-down on Collins Avenue, and threw rocks. Delegates on their buses going into the convention center rolled down their windows and shouted at state troopers to "get" the protesters and "Gas 'Em!" By 5:00 PM police were asking for reinforcements, by 7:30 they had begun using tear gas, and by 9:00 they were barricading Flamingo Park, surrounding it with a barrier of tear gas. The Dade County jail estimated 680 arrests; others put the number at 1,000. In the midst of the clubbing and gassing, members of the Miami Beach Jewish community threw their doors and hotel lobbies open to shelter the vets from the mayhem. Vet Danny Friedman recalled, "Some people think the only war we had to fight was over there—actually the one here was tougher."[10]

VVAW's strongest action involved nothing more than wire cutters and motor oil, a brainstorm of the California contingent. They chopped through a chain-link fence surrounding the convention center, then spread oil on the ramp going into it. The next bus promptly stalled. The ones following it crowded in, and the convention's entire entry system collapsed. The hall's garage door had been opened in expectation of the buses, then ground-level doors to admit delegates whose buses could not make it up the ramp. A remarkable thing happened: the wind changed direction, blowing tear gas right into the convention hall. VVAW had gotten inside after all. Spiro Agnew stopped halfway through his introduction speech, tears in his eyes. Richard Nixon later wrote, "My eyes burned from the lingering sting of tear gas as I entered the hall."[11] No doubt the president was furious.

By the summer of 1972, Nixon had arranged his White House processional to his satisfaction, and the opposition had been quieted by the demise of the draft and the seeming progress of the peace talks. At that point, the president still thought he could have his way. Refusing to view his tools of force as blunted, Nixon counted on a succession of triumphal images to give him the election, and he thought success at the polls would give him a free hand in Vietnam. A small band of veterans stood up to say it was not so, and they did that against the heaviest blows Nixon justice could throw at them. It would be an exaggeration to say that only VVAW stood between Richard Nixon and his Vietnam war, but it would not be far from the truth.

To me, the most important political task facing the country remained stopping the Vietnam war. That meant defeating Richard Nixon. The president negotiated with Hanoi but simultaneously hit North Vietnam hard, which looked like a policy of force majeure, not one of peace. Quite simply, George McGovern represented the best avenue to end the war. McGovern had captured the hopes of many of the nation's young people, including me. I became one of the multitude who made McGovern's campaign happen, at every level, everywhere. If ever there were a grassroots mobilization, this was it. Theodore White, who wrote a book on the 1972 elections, called us "McGovern's Army," a national mobilization of irregulars. "The army had an idea that could snare souls," White noted. "The idea was that politics could bring peace and justice, and the soldiers of the idea were pure."[12]

I would not go that far—I had no illusions that a McGovern win would solve all the nation's problems. But the war had to be stopped, and McGovern would do that. Vietnam was, however, just one among many issues, for the campaign became a joint enterprise of crusaders with a bewildering array of crusades, from working-class mobilization to Democratic Party reform to gender politics. In New York City there were feminists, a nascent gay political activism, major concerns among Jewish and African American groups ("black power" was more than a slogan in the City), and any number of other "isms." A succession of shifting coalitions, odd alliances, earnest debates, and minor headaches afflicted the campaign. For all the silliness, the level of honest motivation and adherence to political principles were among the highest I have ever seen. If all the wheels had been pulling in the same direction, and if we had had better traction, the result of the 1972 election might have been different. At least, that is the dream.

For New York State, the dream was probably just that. Embedded in the social topography of the place were factors that counted against McGovern. The same things that made him attractive in New York City were negatives in the conservative counties upstate. Even worse, Nassau and Suffolk counties on Long Island favored Nixon heavily and had many voters. Spillover of that population into the City's outer boroughs meant difficulty obtaining an overwhelming McGovern vote within the City itself. The liberal McGovern faced the absurd necessity of obtaining a plurality from upstate New York to balance the likely result on Long Island. The sole alternative was a huge McGovern win in New York City, which made the campaign there critical. The eventual result demonstrated the validity of that view.

Apart from this simple analysis, I cannot supply much of the big picture. I was just one of the unwashed masses of grassroots insurgents, a student from Columbia College who showed up one day at campaign headquarters. Like numberless others, I stuffed envelopes, reproduced leaflets, staffed telephone banks, and all the rest. I progressed to working with middle-level managers. Somehow it came out that I had experience with storefront political offices—in 1970 I had worked for candidate Joseph Duffy in Bridgeport, Connecticut. Such was the need in the McGovern campaign that my time at Bridgeport counted for something. At any rate, headquarters received numerous demands for help from all over the City. Sometime around mid-October I was sent to the Upper West Side of Manhattan to coordinate campaign efforts in a portion of the Sixty-ninth Assembly District, part of Representative Charles R. Rangel's congressional territory. My section amounted to a quarter of the whole. If memory serves (and since I have no records, it will have to), it ran from 65th Street to 79th and from Central Park West to the Hudson River. This was a solidly Democratic district, but McGovern needed maximum votes to offset losses elsewhere.

The nerve center for the effort would be the office of a reform Democratic club, the Park-Lincoln Democrats, a second-floor walkup on the south side of

72nd Street between Broadway and Amsterdam. What I remember most was the unusual picture window—an elongated oval shape that opened across half the width of the building and overlooked 72nd.

Almost immediately I discovered the truth about McGovern's Irregulars. There were cleavages everywhere. One, probably the most important, was between reform Democrats and more traditional members of the party machine. Party rules changes that had taken effect during the 1972 electoral season had helped McGovern win the nomination but angered many of the traditionalists. Some had no time for us now, and some of them held the keys to important levers of power in New York City or to data vital to our campaign. Some deliberately held back in ways that benefited the Nixon campaign. A few of the better folks put the past aside and worked hard; others, not willing to be seen helping, provided aid in quiet ways.

At the level of an assembly district, the absence (or lukewarm presence) of machine Democrats meant that we lacked a lot of know-how. The Park-Lincoln reformers were great on pressing for a modernist, honest party but weak on nuts and bolts. Efforts before I arrived had centered on voter registration and leafleting subway exits at rush hour. Eighteen-year-olds would be able to vote for the first time in 1972, and we presumed that much of the youth vote would go to McGovern. The machine people, who knew the political topography much better than we did, were an important missing link. Park-Lincoln volunteers could tell me how many hours we had people in the street and how many votes there had been in the last election but knew little about the relevant community groups, the buildings in the neighborhood, old versus young people, and so on.

It seemed clear that the McGovern campaign needed both better knowledge and a stronger presence in the streets. I lived on the Upper West Side myself, though not in that area, and I knew the physical layout as a result of driving a cab in the City. The obvious solution was a large-scale canvassing effort, going right into the apartment buildings and giving McGovern some visibility to voters other than those who commuted to work. I also asked volunteers to tell us about community groups they knew of or events they learned of. We tried hard to place people at those events to give McGovern visibility and learn the lay of the land. We did not rise to the level of Eugene McCarthy's 1968 "Get Clean for Gene" primary effort in New Hampshire, but we were aware that even on Manhattan's Upper West Side some of our more opinionated volunteers could potentially do more harm than good. I ended up developing different sets of volunteers for the canvassing, events, and leafleting and table activities.

I had experience canvassing in Bridgeport, but as a coordinator in the Sixtyninth District, there were problems I had never imagined. In Connecticut we had worked in a neighborhood of single-family homes; here, McGovern Irregulars needed to access large apartment buildings. In some places this was simply a matter of getting past locked doors, but other buildings were large enough or exclusive enough to feature closed-circuit monitors and doormen. Then, as now,

New Yorkers were very security conscious. The Irregulars resorted to a variety of subterfuges.

By far the best situation was where we had volunteers canvass their own buildings. Other tenants might know the person approaching them, or at least our Irregular could say, "I live here too!" Access became automatic. Once volunteers learned the technique in a familiar setting, they would have some idea what to do when working a different locale. The next best alternative was to have McGovern supporters who let Irregulars into their buildings. Beyond that, there were the excuses: that the volunteer was conducting an unspecified "survey" (only slightly disingenuous), making a delivery, doing a repair, providing consulting services, and so on. Several Irregulars who were students successfully combined the McGovern canvass with academic projects that involved sampling public opinion. Others proved successful with open declarations that they were working for George McGovern. Some Irregulars enlisted the aid of friends who lived in the buildings they were canvassing, which sometimes produced another Irregular for us. In addition, a number of folks simply showed up at the Park-Lincoln office and said they had decided to come in when canvassed by one of us.

Of course, there were times when nothing went right. One of our headaches was Lincoln Towers, a huge complex of a half dozen or so high-rise buildings west of Lincoln Center. These had television monitors and guards with a view of every floor. Our Irregulars were challenged repeatedly, often after working only a few floors, one floor, or just a few doors. But there were so many voters in the Towers the effort just had to be made. One of our people got in by telling guards she was selling magazine subscriptions to raise money for school. Another Irregular disarmed the guards by convincing them to accompany him, at least long enough to be reassured that the McGovern volunteer posed no threat. Still, coverage there remained the least satisfactory in our district.

I cannot say enough about the McGovern Irregulars. They were willing to move heaven and earth to turn the course of America. I got little sleep, and in the final week or so I virtually abandoned Columbia classes. I did not care a whit. Many student volunteers did the same. Two of our best Irregulars were "Gold Star Mothers." They had tremendous credibility and got past every challenge. Others brought their children to work with them. In fact, our best teams were parents accompanied by their children. High school students turned out in numbers. Not yet able to vote, these kids were nevertheless willing to leaflet or picket at any hour, in any weather. As election day neared our activists for particular "isms" even gave up their internal bickering and consciousness-raising to focus with one mind. The dedication of the Irregulars thrilled me. Their principle proved an inspiration.

Our major organizing tool would be a large wall map I made, with spaces for every building. While continuing to staff information tables and leaflet subway entrances, I set the goal of getting canvassing teams into every building in our portion of the district before election day. Ideally, we wanted to cover every building at least once a week during the final period. Neither goal was practical, but they gave us something to aim for.

Though we never quite achieved the coverage we wanted, the effort made a huge difference in every way. As we acquired data it became apparent there were buildings, even whole blocks, of especially strong support. New volunteers could be started in those places to break them in gently. There were also pockets where Nixon looked to be running well. I put my best people into those buildings and made sure leafleteers covered them, right outside the door. The results were inked on our wall map for all to see. More and more the Irregulars arriving at the office would cluster around the map, exchanging ideas about what to do and how to cover the ground. As the Irregulars saw concrete evidence of what they were accomplishing, morale rose perceptibly, despite McGovern's continuing weakness in national opinion polls. Some Irregulars approached me directly, asking to cover buildings to which they had access, even where this lay outside the scope of their usual campaign work. There were also very creative ideas about how to further the canvassing.

I posted the results in gross terms on the wall—so many apartments for McGovern, so many leaning, these buildings split, those for Nixon. The details—apartment numbers canvassed, voters' names and telephone numbers—went onto file cards. When we got another volunteer into a certain building, he or she was instructed to visit the apartments not yet canvassed or to return to those with leaning voters and provide particular information relevant to concerns those people had expressed earlier. It became possible to target our activities. For example, the intersection closest to one block with strong Nixon support became the object of a sustained information table and leafleting operation.

As far as City headquarters was concerned, as we derived data our reports sent downtown could add substance to the raw political polling results headquarters was getting for our district—data the City office had but we never saw. We also did a lot of work in response to New York headquarters. Many times we went out to encourage voters to turn out for rallies. The climax came a few days prior to the election, when George McGovern appeared at a rally in Manhattan's Garment District. There was also a big rally for vice presidential candidate Sargent Shriver. McGovern returned to New York the day before the election, but that time he appeared in other boroughs, Brooklyn and the Bronx.

As the campaign wound down to its final days, there came the incident of the abortive Vietnam cease-fire (discussed in the next section). In my district, people saw the exchange of charges between Hanoi and Kissinger on who was responsible for the breakdown primarily as a last-minute play for votes. It had echoes of the maneuvers just prior to the 1968 election, which I knew, but my Irregulars largely did not. When asked about it on the street, they discussed these events as a ploy. The Vietnam revelations did not have much of an impact in my district, but I suspect they helped Nixon in some of the other boroughs, especially conservative areas in Queens and Staten Island.

For the most part, the campaign in our area of the Sixty-ninth District pro-
ceeded straightforwardly. Given what was already known about Nixon cam-
paign "dirty tricks," not least the Watergate break-in, there was gossip about
what might happen at our level. As far as I recall, there were a couple of inci-
dents in which leaflets were grabbed or the Irregulars were shoved. There was
another episode in which one of our tables was overturned and the staff ha-
rassed. Those could have resulted from just random annoyances and alterca-
tions. There was also a problem with the rally for Shriver. We were supposed to
boost turnout for the event, but the buses hired to carry people downtown were
unaccountably canceled. Hundreds of potential attendees were without trans-
portation in our district, and older voters in particular, left to their own devices,
went home. City headquarters insisted it had laid on the buses and never
changed the order. I have no evidence this represented the other side in action,
but it could have been.

Nevertheless, enough happened around the country and the state to fuel spec-
ulation among my Irregulars. A storefront headquarters in Croton-on-Hudson
was vandalized no fewer than three times, another in New Rochelle hit twice. In
several parts of Westchester, people reported physical attacks, in particular, Mc-
Govern demonstrators holding placards who stood along the route of a Nixon
motorcade. Democratic Party officials and a town committeeman were beaten
by persons they believed to be taking orders from men wearing red lapel pins.
This kind of news sent shudders through our Manhattan volunteers. The jitters
climaxed a couple of days before the election when we learned that, as far away
as Kentucky, the state party headquarters had been broken into and its records
scattered.

Years later at a convocation marking McGovern's seventy-fifth birthday, at-
tended by many top officials from his national campaign, I asked whether they
had seen any pattern of Republican dirty tricks in the actual electoral operation.
None of the senior people recalled local harassment of McGovern organizations
as a serious problem. My Irregulars would have been grateful to know that for a
fact before election day.

That Tuesday, November 7, brought yet another manifestation of the McGov-
ern grassroots mobilization. In New York City the day dawned clear, crisp, and
cool. We had to keep up our street presence, get out the vote, mount a telephone
drive to contact voters identified in our canvass, provide poll watchers at an ar-
ray of individual precincts, and furnish transportation for those who needed as-
sistance getting to polling precincts. In Manhattan, where having a car is
actually a major hassle, the latter posed a real challenge. Given the hours the Ir-
regulars kept and the need to do all this until the polls closed at 8:00 PM, sched-
uling was a massive headache. But that proved the only headache. Getting the
necessary bodies, which I had expected to be our greatest difficulty, turned out to
be a breeze. The cars? No problem. McGovern's Irregular Army rose to the occa-
sion in splendid style. We had more than enough volunteers—enough, in fact, to

mount a last-minute leaflet blizzard into every one of the pro-Nixon pockets we had identified. We had so many vehicles that four times over the course of the day I was able to commandeer a car just to carry fresh supplies and leaflets to each of our polling places and check in with the Irregulars on the front line. There were no special problems at our precincts. Questioning of voters as they exited the polls indicated strong McGovern support. The Nixon campaign workers were very subdued, ours exuberant. Voters seemed to be turning out in good numbers.

My impressions of a perfect day would be shattered that night. That would also be the closest I ever came to the real powers in the New York City organization—I shared an elevator up to the McGovern reception with Robert F. Wagner Jr., whose father, the former mayor of New York, headed the City campaign. Of course, because of the poll work and scheduling it had been impossible to head downtown until fairly late, and the television networks had already projected Richard Nixon as the victor more than an hour before I arrived. The reception felt worse than a funeral wake, and I could not abide it. Very quickly I left.

I remain very proud of our work in the Sixty-ninth Assembly District and of the McGovern Irregulars who made it possible. George McGovern outpolled Richard Nixon in our district by a margin of more than 3–1, 37,388 votes to 11,099. Only three other Manhattan districts (one including Columbia, another Harlem), all with smaller voter lists, turned in better pluralities. For Manhattan as a whole, McGovern tallied 353,847 votes to 179,867 for Nixon. McGovern also carried the Bronx comfortably (245,757 to 197,941). But there it ended. The outer boroughs of New York City were too close to give McGovern the margin he needed. Brooklyn went for McGovern by just 10,000 votes, and he actually lost Queens and Staten Island. Overall, George McGovern won New York City by 1,341,164 votes to Nixon's 1,259,244. Still, the last New York Daily News opinion poll prior to election day had shown Nixon ahead in the City by 53 to 47 percent. I believe the McGovern Irregulars made the difference.

Nixon ran as strongly as predicted in Long Island and the suburbs, where he led by more than half a million votes. Upstate, McGovern fell short of hopes, if not expectations, and lost by more than 800,000. The Republican lead ultimately dwarfed whatever we had managed to accomplish in the City. In the end, Richard Nixon carried New York State by almost exactly the same number of votes he had gotten in the City itself.

None of these results should be held against the selfless and tireless efforts of McGovern's Irregular Army. The ingenuity, dedication, energy, and raw intelligence of the Irregulars were incredible. Coming out of nowhere they became a band of sisters and brothers who carried out a national campaign despite the absence, in places, of the traditional machine. I have wondered many times over the years what became of the Irregulars. But the day after Nixon's reelection, *more bombs fell on Vietnam. The war had not been solved. That struggle continued and still demanded our efforts.*

No Truce from Terror

Days before the election came a new kind of October Surprise—a peace that did not happen. This followed the breakthrough in the Kissinger-Tho private meetings that had begun in August. Who is to blame for the fiasco remains disputed, but what is certain is that somewhere in the middle of the president's triumphal procession to return to the White House, Richard Nixon and Henry Kissinger realized the game was up in Vietnam, for the climax took place within weeks of the vote. All this set the stage for yet another Nixon Shock.

This play centered around the prospect of a cease-fire, and it began with Kissinger, outline agreement in hand, visiting Saigon on August 17. Dr. Kissinger had no doubts about Nixon's strength in the presidential campaign. During their photo op, Kissinger mentioned that he had run into George McGovern. Beyond mere distress at the jet lag, Henry joked that McGovern had never recovered from his own Saigon visit in 1971. When they spoke privately, Kissinger told Thieu, "I have made a record that we are prepared to have a ceasefire. Now I will move off that . . . We believe it would be better for us not to have one." Nixon's emissary reviewed the talks, arguing that Hanoi had made a serious error by stalling in anticipation of the U.S. election while its military situation deteriorated. Now Washington would stall too. Kissinger presented a strategy to draw the talks out beyond the U.S. election and described how provisions in an agreement would benefit Thieu. After the vote, Kissinger said, "We will step up our air campaign and force a resolution." It was a point to which he would return. In describing the details of the proposal, the emissary said, "We will not have to go through another year of good will with our opponents." The situation would be totally new. "If we win the election," Kissinger declared, "we will settle the war one way or another." The next round of U.S. withdrawals got brief mention. There he affirmed that no naval forces would be sent home. "We want them for the campaign after November 7," Kissinger noted. "We don't want to bring them back."[13]

The next day, in a detailed response, Thieu exhibited his perennial concerns. He rejected any political commission, because that might evolve into some kind of coalition government. And Thieu, aware that "cease-fire" meant that troops would remain where they were—that is, Hanoi would not withdraw from the South—wanted one only "when the war is completely finished, everything is settled." In fact, Thieu specifically asked how the agreement would force Hanoi's withdrawal, and aide Nguyen Phu Duc recommended that the word "standstill" in the agreement be replaced. Kissinger preferred not to, though he let it seem that Duc had convinced him with some mumbo jumbo about Cambodia. Henry wished to leave ambiguous a phrase about "foreign" troops returning to their countries, which could then be claimed to include the North Vietnamese (but which the United States had separately agreed with Hanoi did *not* refer to its own forces, just as it had agreed that the political commission *could* serve as interim government). To reassure Saigon, Nixon's emissary then offered to continue the bombing through the U.S. election and asserted again, "Our strategy is that we are prepared to step up the military pressure on the DRV immediately, drastically and brutally one or two weeks after our election." Thieu was to be President Nixon's hole card. "We need your help to construct an ambiguous proposal," Kissinger told him. Dr. Kissinger also reassured Thieu that nothing here dismantled any part of the South Vietnamese government and that the other side could be stymied in the proposed committee on reconciliation. Kissinger encouraged Thieu to think about launching amphibious landings and commando raids into North Vietnam. The Saigonese could hardly believe their ears. "We saw it as a . . . lollipop treatment, you know," Thieu aide Hoang Duc Nha recalled for an associate. "It was a kind of joke to us."[14]

Kissinger also raised the possibility, twice, that Saigon could react to a U.S. proposal at the talks by declaring that Kissinger had gone beyond his authority. "I do not mind your attacking me," the national security adviser commented. "In this instance the choreography requires the impression of excessive reasonableness."[15]

Both Kissinger and Thieu expressed the belief that Saigon (and the United States) had nearly won the war. They agreed Hanoi would be even weaker in a year. The "brutal" escalation Kissinger spoke of would ensure that. Saigon accepted unquestioningly the complementary notion that the South Vietnamese army was capable of defeating Hanoi on its own. But the ARVN had not stopped the Easter offensive by itself, and even if it had, this was not the same as destroying Hanoi's military capability. Thieu and his national security advisers considered the U.S. proposals and delivered a response on August 28: they rejected U.S.-DRV talks as a valid forum to discuss political questions; no change in the Saigon government was acceptable, North Vietnamese withdrawal mandatory; and they were ambiguous on a Thieu resignation prior to a referendum on a new constitution. Such terms could be imposed only by force. Was this wishful thinking, belly talk? Perhaps.

Washington's calculations were complex. The new MACV commander, General Fred Weyand, had briefed Kissinger in Saigon that Hanoi's forces would have exhausted their capability in six months' time. But the CIA's appraisal continued to be that the DRV had absorbed the losses from the bombing and mining in its general economy; it would be able to fight on. The Joint Chiefs agreed, as Admiral Moorer confirmed to Congress in January 1973. About that time, a senior CIA official visited Saigon, convening a dozen or so of the agency officers who knew Vietnam best or had the closest contacts among the South Vietnamese. The group held nearly unanimously that without U.S. airpower, the ARVN was lost. In short, the Vietnam data problem persisted.

At the White House the president held to what had been his mantra since April—that Hanoi and Haiphong should be hit hard by B-52s. Kissinger can only have been reflecting Nixon during his talks in Saigon. But at this late date, the notion that one more round of bombing, however brutal, would break Hanoi's will can only be described as an opium dream—or the impression that Hanoi already hung on the ropes. Important people believed their own spin. Note also that choosing to bomb meant going outside the envelope of Nixon's diminished freedom to act. Thieu's adviser Nguyen Phu Duc, who constructs his retrospective of the entire negotiation around the assertions that Nixon and Kissinger engaged in duplicity and made preemptive concessions to Hanoi, fails to include the conversations described here, in which Kissinger and Thieu *agreed* on Hanoi's frailty and then Kissinger promised the bombing. Duc thus cannot explain why, if the Nixon White House was so hell-bent on a Vietnam agreement, Kissinger remained steadfast on a brutal bombing. The duplicity was real enough, but it seems more reasonable to conclude that Kissinger thought he could deliver Saigon because it had no alternative, while stalling Hanoi long enough to deliver a powerful blow that would leave Vietnam in some kind of shaky equilibrium as the United States exited the war.

The received history of these last months of negotiations is that Kissinger and Le Duc Tho held more talks and came to a draft accord, to which Saigon demanded a multiplicity of changes, ones that Hanoi rejected. Kissinger scrapped an itinerary in which he would have gone to Saigon to obtain Thieu's final clearance; to Hanoi, where he would initial the agreement; and then to Paris for a ceremonial signing. At that point Hanoi went public, releasing the text of the accord on October 26, and Kissinger answered with his own news conference. After a hiatus for the U.S. election, there were new exchanges in which Hanoi proved intransigent, and then the United States unleashed the destructive Christmas Bombing. Afterward North Vietnam meekly accepted changes to the agreement, which all parties signed in Paris on January 27, 1973.[16]

This version is a construct. Behind it lies a deeper story that involves Richard Nixon's longings plus inducements for South Vietnam. A fairly well-known part of this tale would be open shipments of military equipment to South Vietnam, which could be replaced on a one-for-one basis under the agreement. Operation "Enhance"—followed by "Enhance Plus"—aimed to put gear in South Vietnamese stockpiles—even if useless—on the principle that this would justify military aid *after* an agreement. For example, from Okinawa the United States shipped 63 working trucks to South Vietnam, but

1,350 that were broken. Similarly, none of the 175mm guns sent to Saigon were in working order. Aircraft additions included 80 jet fighter-bombers, 280 helicopters, 500 helicopter engines, 11 C-119 gunships, and 17 transport aircraft. There were supposed to be enough M-48 medium tanks and armored personnel carriers for a new ARVN armored brigade, plus guns, radios, mortars, quadruple .50-caliber machine guns, rifles, bombs, munitions, and more. All this was to be in place before anything was signed. The inducement was plain.

Less well known is Thieu's eleventh-hour attempt to head off the deal. When Al Haig visited at the end of September to check with Saigon on the latest evolution of the agreement, Thieu tried to break its momentum. He queried Haig on the U.S. response to his August note and the questions it had raised, pressed on why Washington had not kept South Vietnam better informed, and handed Haig a fresh memorandum with additional objections. Nixon's envoy could only bluster that the talks had gone beyond Saigon's concerns of August. Thieu tried to cobble together an alternative, using his proposition that a comprehensive agreement must encompass all the nations of Indochina as a basis to propose an international conference of Asian nations to negotiate the settlement, and incidentally demand withdrawal of foreign troops from those nations, neatly getting rid of the North Vietnamese in Laos with their Ho Chi Minh Trail, their troops in Cambodia, and potentially those in South Vietnam as well. Thieu's formula for a "Bandung-like" meeting would have stalled an agreement, by returning the dialogue to first principles, and it would have marginalized the United States. But Saigon could not interest anyone in the formula, even after Thieu publicized it in the *New York Times*. "We are not afraid of a cease-fire, nor do we evade it," he wrote.[17] But developments had isolated Saigon, whose only remaining bargaining chip was its signature on the settlement documents, with Kissinger on his way to Saigon even then, stopping in Paris for one last session with Hanoi diplomat Xuan Thuy.

One piece of the story has remained invisible and is reported here for the first time: the Christmas Bombing amounted to the same operation Kissinger had referred to in August and Nixon had demanded that spring. When Haig arrived in Saigon his briefcase contained a plan for bombing Hanoi from the Joint Chiefs of Staff. Worked out by Vice Admiral John P. Weinel of the Joint Staff, and so sensitive that Weinel hand-wrote it, this provided for "steady pressure air strikes concentrated on [northeast lines of communication] and [the] Hanoi-Haiphong complex," potentially lasting through May 1973.[18] An analysis for Haig by Jonathan Howe of the NSC staff noted that the plan "has the advantage of being [in] a period when the President will have a tremendous election victory and a Congress out of session."[19] Haig saw General John Vogt of the Seventh Air Force to discuss the plan privately. This all happened *before* any snags had developed in the peace talks.

A few weeks later Dr. Kissinger returned to Saigon himself, on the first leg of the trip that was supposed to take him to Hanoi to initial the agreement. In painful sessions with Thieu and his national security council, the South Vietnamese rebelled, refusing the cease-fire, demanding the same changes Thieu had insisted on previously. In a cable on October 20 Kissinger wrote of the South Vietnamese objections, "none of them [is] capricious," and "they are probably even right." A couple of days later he changed his mind and said of the demands, "almost all of them are nitpicks." At that point Kissinger was arguing that the entire top U.S. team—including Bunker and Abrams—considered the agreement the best that could be gotten. For days Kissinger maintained he should go on to Hanoi for the initialing, pressing the DRV for a few cosmetic concessions for which Saigon could then claim credit. On October 22 Kissinger referred directly to the Hanoi-Haiphong bombing plan: "While we have a moral case for bombing North Vietnam when it does not accept our proposals, it seems to be really stretching the point to bomb North Vietnam when it has accepted our proposals and when South Vietnam has not."[20]

Nixon had been pressing for this bombing for months. The military foreshadowed it with limited B-52 strikes in early and mid-November near the DMZ and in the North Vietnamese panhandle. The NSA's declassified history of the Vietnam war reveals that in Thailand, where Air Force radiomen had the task of following North Vietnamese air defense activity and warning the bombers, some airmen considered the strikes improper because the United States had announced a bombing halt. Their frustration would lead to difficulties not long afterward.[21]

Meanwhile, Nixon and Kissinger both knew that Saigon's basic objections were deal breakers. Moreover, Thieu was now furious. On October 17 he received a document the ARVN had captured in Quang Tin that contained Hanoi's instructions to its cadres for explaining the cease-fire agreement. Thieu saw that even low-level enemy cadres knew more about the accords than he did. He also discovered problems with the Vietnamese versus the English version of the text, with the Vietnamese one containing more sweeping provisions. Nixon had now thrown in his lot with Kissinger—or not. Nixon's letters to Thieu conflicted with his secret bombing preparations. But Kissinger, who admits to falling into the trap of advocating his own negotiation, hoped to initial the accord prior to the election. Afterward, at some point in November, it became clear to both men that an agreement *had* to be made. Why Nixon changed his mind remains shrouded in the welter of murky evidence. Publicly, his election was spun as a huge success owing to the 60.7 percent vote tally. But this landslide did not yield a Republican Congress. Nixon's party gained only a dozen seats in the House, leaving it under solid Democratic control, and actually lost two in the Senate. Within a week Nixon was demanding analyses of what he saw as a weak Republican campaign. And Watergate festered, a land mine that could explode at any moment. Kissinger calls this "the strangest period in Nixon's Presidency."[22] Far from Nixon being stronger after the election, his position remained tenuous. "The option of escalation—implied in going for broke after the election—was dramatic but not realistic," Kissinger wrote. "Shortly after our election Hanoi would rediscover not only our domestic fragility but also the budgetary pressures that would force us to reduce our forces unilaterally."[23]

By the hand of Al Haig, Nixon sent Thieu a letter commending the agreement. Haig's orders were to underline Congress's power to stop the war and argue that the time had come to settle. Nixon objected to Thieu's "continuing distortions of the agreement, and attacks upon it" as "unfair," and he warned, "We are in any event resolved to proceed on the basis of the draft agreement and the modifications which we are determined to obtain from the North Vietnamese."[24] He pictured Saigon starkly as playing into Hanoi's hands. Thieu rejected this advice, clear proof of the lack of U.S. leverage. The Pentagon Papers authors would have understood.

By Kissinger's analysis, the Saigon leader had either engaged in a game of chicken or set himself on a collision course. Replying on November 14, another Nixon letter argued the impossibility of obtaining Thieu's terms, specifically citing the withdrawal issue. Mr. Nixon also declared, "You have my absolute assurance that if Hanoi fails to abide by the terms of this agreement it is my intention to take swift and severe retaliatory action."[25]

This declaration, repeated orally and in several subsequent letters, underlies the claim that Richard Nixon secretly promised intervention during the talks. It is also the real reason that Hanoi would be bombed at Christmas, as a demonstration to Saigon of Nixon's sincerity. The president's long-standing demand for heavy B-52 bombing of the Hanoi-Haiphong complex also figured into the equation. The war would not end without Nixon exercising that option.

On November 18 Nixon told Bob Haldeman that he had instructed Kissinger to get the best deal possible "and then let Thieu paddle his own canoe."[26] On the twenty-third Nixon wanted to cable his emissary, now back in Paris, and reiterate the order to reach agreement no matter what. Haig's role is critical here, but obscure. After reconsidering, the president instead threatened new measures of force—alluding to the bombing plans—and recalled Kissinger. The envoy recited the darker portions of Nixon's cable to Le Duc Tho to induce Hanoi to cave. The DRV negotiator rejected the threat. The North Vietnamese were predictably outraged at the extent of the changes now being demanded. Although Hanoi itself reopened previously settled matters, the United States had opened the door by its actions on behalf of Saigon.

Henry Kissinger returned to the White House, where a series of meetings took place between November 29 and December 1 that defined the true diplomatic terrain of these events. Nguyen Phu Duc, whom Thieu had sent to oversee the Paris talks, came to Washington for these meetings. At the first of them, at midafternoon on the twenty-ninth, Nixon did most of the talking. He reiterated both the need to agree and, several times, his promise to retaliate.[27] President Nixon also laid out the bald fact that consultations with congressional leaders had convinced him that if agreement were not reached within ten days of the opening of the new Congress on January 3, 1973, America's lawmakers would defund the war. Republicans agreed with the Democrats. No alternative existed. Duc repeated Thieu's objections, also contained in a letter from the Saigon leader, and pleaded that an agreement would be politically acceptable in Saigon only if it were a victory. Kissinger pressed home the U.S. arguments in a discussion that continued into the evening.

This face-off resumed the next morning when the president again met with Duc. Prior to that Nixon had convened the Joint Chiefs plus Secretary Laird. With the Chiefs too, the president admitted the political realities. "The fact is," Nixon observed, "that the U.S. has stayed one step ahead of the sheriff, just missing fund cutoffs."[28] After January 3 that would no longer be possible. He ordered the Chiefs to prepare military options if the Paris talks broke off, plus retaliatory actions in case of violation. These became the specific instructions for the Christmas Bombing, issued (again) before any breakdown of talks with Hanoi. At his noontime meeting with Duc, the president reaffirmed his promise to use force and said he had just met the JCS on the subject. Mr. Duc argued repeatedly over these days that if the United States was so determined to leave the war it should simply make a deal with Hanoi for the POWs and get out. Collecting his thoughts on the plane back to Saigon, Nguyen Phu Duc says he was "not convinced by the presentation of the U.S. Government."[29]

■ ■ ■ Like adviser Duc, the American arguments moved neither Nguyen Van Thieu, his national security council, nor the key Saigon jurists and legislative leaders called on to consider the prospective accord. Space does not permit detailed recounting of the debate that raged in Saigon, the additional letters between presidents Thieu and Nixon, or the part played by supporting casts on both sides. Suffice it to say that Nixon became more strident on moving forward, and South Vietnamese objections changed not a whit. Saigon apparently never accepted the reality that if the Nixon administration halted aid, its refusal to accept would not matter. Available sources indicate that Saigon approached the issue as one of showing who bore responsibility for the demise of the regime. Thieu made some moves to lend weight to the Duc proposition that the United States should make its own deal, offering to release DRV prisoners in exchange for Americans, and calling for a lengthy Christmas stand-down. But then Thieu went before his National Assembly and put down a marker, publicly rejecting the Paris provisions he disliked.

Henry Kissinger had additional conversations with Le Duc Tho. The North Vietnamese yielded little and revisited more items that had seemed settled. Kissinger terminated the talks. On December 13 he recommended that Nixon approve massive bombing of the DRV. Haig concurred. Kissinger describes himself as melancholy, turning to military options reluctantly. Nixon never was. In his memoir Mr. Nixon retails the conventional wisdom: the bombing was Hanoi's fault, he had carried out a survey of lucrative targets and ended up with Hanoi and Haiphong, and says this was his most difficult decision of the war.[30] None of this is true. The president had plumped for B-52s on Hanoi-Haiphong since April, obtained a draft plan by September, mulled it over in November, and ordered the Chiefs to produce the final plan on December 1. The real audience sat in Saigon, not Hanoi. The president approved this Nixon Shock well aware of its cost in public opinion, a concern he had raised with Kissinger a month earlier.

The Christmas Bombing began on December 18 (east zone date) with 129 B-52 sorties supported by many fighter-bombers and missions by Navy A-6 aircraft. The lead bomber, piloted by Captain Hal Wilson, reported wall-to-wall SAMs ahead. His would be one of three lost that night, for Hanoi had made preparations of its own and fought the attackers. As early as 1968, during a visit to air defense headquarters, Ho Chi Minh had predicted the B-52s would come to Hanoi someday. The Central Military Party Committee concurred in the forecast and put specialists to work on finding ways to fight the big bombers. Concrete preparations, including a notice for troop training, began with the Easter offensive. Vo Nguyen Giap records they were largely complete by September 1972. General Van Tien Dung approved the final air defense plan for Hanoi on November 24 and ordered that everything be ready by December 3. On that day the mayor of Hanoi began to evacuate civilians from the city. The general staff daily briefing on December 18 noted an ominous stand-down in B-52 activities in the South, as well as interception of the report radioed by an American weather reconnaissance plane flying above Hanoi. Air defense forces went on high alert, and shortly after 7:00 PM General Giap learned that B-52s had taken off from both Guam and Thailand, the latter detected flying northward along the Mekong River. Slightly over an hour later Giap heard that a B-52 had been shot down by a unit of the 261st Missile Regiment. The battle was joined.

Day after day, with a brief thirty-six-hour pause on Christmas itself, massive B-52 formations and associated warplanes flew against Hanoi. The president recalled that he stunned Admiral Moorer when, on the second day, he phoned to say, "I don't want any more of this crap about the fact that we couldn't hit this target or that one. This is your chance to use military power effectively to win this war, and if you don't, I'll consider you responsible."[31] The North Vietnamese did everything they could to resist—mass SAM firings, missile launchings in unguided mode, fighter intercepts, even a fighter that deliberately collided with a B-52. Fifteen B-52s were lost and nine more damaged; most of these were the newer B-52G model, which, despite being designed to fly nuclear strikes against Soviet air defenses, had less effective electronic countermeasures than the older B-52D model. Seven tactical aircraft were also lost from 640 strike sorties. The losses added thirty-nine prisoners to Hanoi's cages, and thirty-five crewmen died or disappeared. In all there were 795 B-52 sorties that dropped more than 15,000 tons of ordnance, to which the smaller planes added their bombs.

Crews from the units most affected by the B-52 losses became restive at the pressures exerted by commanders. Some airmen reported that mutinies, or at least the refusal of orders, took place. The Air Force has repeatedly denied this contention. But an actual work stoppage did occur within air intelligence, as confirmed by the NSA's official history. Radiomen at two different bases, including both Air Force and Army operators, stopped processing the information that would warn the B-52s of North Vietnamese air defense activities. The incidents were hushed up.[32]

Among the factors adding to the political upheaval over the Christmas Bombing were charges that American planes were killing civilians and causing what officials euphemistically termed "collateral damage." Claims of damage to the Bach Mai hospital, on the outskirts of Hanoi, and to certain neighborhoods were rife. The Air Force piously insisted it was making precision strikes and even contrived accuracy estimates that it shared with Congress.

A few Americans could speak directly to that, including Barry Romo of Vietnam Veterans Against the War. Romo, along with singer Joan Baez and former Nuremberg prosecutor Telford Taylor, arrived in North Vietnam just as the bombing began. Driving south from Phuc Yen airfield, they stopped at the village of Duc Noi, where they were greeted by the inhabitants and entertained by local schoolchildren. The visitors wondered how the peasants could tell them from Russians. "Would Russians wear blue jeans and carry a guitar?" came the rejoinder. Beyond a stone wall that set off the village lay a rail yard, partly destroyed. "See? Precision bombing works," Taylor told Romo. The group continued into Hanoi, where their visit basically ended. They spent the next days in a bunker as the bombs fell, emerging in the daytime to view Bach Mai and a few other places that had been heavily damaged. Baez spent most of her time playing guitar. Taylor drank. Before the visit ended he was putting away nearly a bottle of bourbon every night. They left North Vietnam during the brief bombing pause, passing the same village on their way back to the airfield. Duc Noi had been completely obliterated, including the stone wall, nothing left except dead bodies and wreckage.

Romo said nothing, but he saw a single tear well up in Taylor's eye. For months after they returned to the United States, in every public talk he gave, Telford Taylor—already noted for his commentaries on the law of war, My Lai, and allegations of U.S. atrocities in South Vietnam—spoke incessantly of the brutality of indiscriminate bombing of North Vietnam.[33]

It has become almost an article of faith among war supporters that Linebacker II, as this aerial offensive was nicknamed, broke Hanoi. In particular, there have been claims that the DRV disarmed its own air defense forces, firing off all their SAMs, leaving only what could be brought in from the Soviet Union. Sir Robert Thompson has been quoted as saying that the United States won the war at that moment, even supplying a precise number of SAMs expended, 1,282 (most authorities cite figures between 800 and 1,000). Former pilot and Linebacker II veteran Marshall Michel has made the most careful study of this issue. He found North Vietnamese accounts that recorded firing only 239 SAMs and reports from U.S. support aircraft that generally support that number. He concluded that DRV forces had only about 420 missiles.[34] But, like stopping the Easter offensive, disarming Hanoi's air defenses, if it happened, did not equate to winning the war. Moreover, the true results were difficult to discern. Aerial photography posed a continuing problem throughout, making damage assessment difficult. In addition, the bombers focused on air defenses plus rail and industrial facilities, identical to the Rolling Thunder target lists, which had not defeated Hanoi in the 1960s any more than Linebacker II did now. The DRV's roads remained unaffected, as did its troops in the South. Linebacker II was intrinsically incapable of winning the war.

The other side of the equation is also frequently downplayed. The North Vietnamese believe they destroyed 31 B-52 bombers. They view Linebacker II as an "Air Dien Bien Phu." Their estimates for both aircraft shot down and the rate of loss are excessive, but the overall point is accurate: the United States could not afford strategic aircraft losses at a high rate over a long term. There were slightly more than 200 B-52s dedicated to the war in Southeast Asia, and the loss of 15 aircraft meant a rate of 7.3 percent. Many of the planes had been diverted from nuclear strike forces. General Giap records that in the weeks before Linebacker II Hanoi had sent hundreds of SAMs down to the North Vietnamese panhandle, missiles that could be recalled regardless of whether the Soviets delivered new ones. The Strategic Air Command could not tolerate either the diversion of B-52s or the losses for very long—even if the latter were at a much lower rate—before Vietnam affected its nuclear warfare capabilities.

At a 2006 conference at the Kennedy Library, Alexander Haig asserted that the Vietnam war could have been won, stating, "I saw it first-hand in the Christmas Bombing." Haig recounted that he had discussed this with Richard Nixon before his death, and the former president had replied that his greatest regret was not to have acted more forcefully. Another three or four months of B-52s (that is, the exact plan prepared by the JCS in September 1972), and Hanoi would have been ready to go back to the 1954 Geneva accords.[35]

Haig went on to say that Nixon had given up on the Christmas Bombing because his cabinet deserted him and there were threats of impeachment. But that was the point, of course. The bombing triggered a firestorm of dissent in the United States. Commentators charged the president had lost his mind. Protests surged. If Mr. Nixon thought Congress was about to defund the war—as he had told the South Vietnamese—what would it do in the face of an extended Linebacker II? The truth is that the Christmas Bombing was not politically sustainable. Beyond that lies the question of whether the B-52 raids were *militarily* sustainable. With aircrews and intelligence specialists restive in December 1972, who can say what their attitude would have been after months of going against Hanoi's air defenses?

Carrying out the bombing earlier in the war—the "perfect strategy" of some of the neo-orthodox—had not been diplomatically feasible because the United States had not detached Hanoi from its allies. The Joint Chiefs had proposed that "sharp blow" in the fall of 1965, and Lyndon Johnson had thrown them out of the Oval Office, specifically citing the danger of war with China. During the intervening time there had been no rationale for this go-for-broke measure because *American officials and generals thought they were winning.* Once more the Vietnam data problem intrudes.

The Christmas Bombing cost President Nixon at least as much in political support as he gained in military benefit. By early 1973 Gallup polls showed that more than two-thirds of Americans believed Nixon was not telling the truth about Vietnam, and 60 percent thought the war had been a mistake, with the majority favoring bombing by only a single percentage point (46–45), less than the poll's margin of error. The White House had no running room left.

Hanoi did return to the negotiating table. But the notion it agreed to whatever Kissinger proposed is a myth. A line-by-line comparison of the Paris agreement signed in January 1973 with the text Hanoi made public the previous October reveals minimal changes. The most significant was Hanoi's agreement that the new national council would not be an "administrative structure"—minimizing the possibility it could emerge as a coalition government—but Le Duc Tho had agreed to that on December 8, *before* the bombing. The other major change, language that assigned the Saigon-Hanoi committee responsibility for dealing with armed forces in South Vietnam, essentially punted the question of a DRV withdrawal to a committee that would predictably deadlock. Kissinger secured a change in format that would avoid Saigon's signing an agreement with the Provisional Revolutionary Government (thus not recognizing the NLF). Other changes were cosmetic. Insofar as Hanoi was concerned, the Christmas Bombing accomplished very little.

When the agreement was adopted, Nixon's standing in the Gallup poll instantly jumped fourteen points. After the Nixon Shock, President Thieu saw little alternative but to sign the accords. Entering the ground floor conference room at Independence Palace, where he customarily met with his national security council, Thieu complained to Nguyen Xuan Phong, the deputy chief of South Vietnam's Paris delegation. The Saigon leader told Phong of the agreement, "It is a sellout to the Soviets."[36] Richard Nixon coined his own slogan for the settlement. The White House called it "Peace with Honor."

There were a number of demonstrations against the war during the summer and fall of 1972. But having seen the dedication and discipline of VVAW, I was less and less happy with the amorphousness of the antiwar movement in general. At one protest in Union Square there were so many speakers on so many divergent issues that I wondered what the Movement had become. At one demonstration during the Christmas Bombing there was another confrontation with an NYPD horseman. Mostly, the protests accomplished an assertion of a presence, valuable, but frustrating to demonstrators who wanted results. By contrast, VVAW had mounted at least three coherent protests: at Dewey Canyon III, in the "Peace on Earth" series, and in Miami at the political convention. Early in 1973 VVAW created a nonveterans' section called the Winter Soldier Organization, and I joined. (Here, I continue to refer to this group simply as VVAW.)

Meanwhile, the VVAW's national office pulled up stakes and moved to Chicago. The New York chapter met at the former Washington Square Presbyterian Church at 137 West 4th Street in Greenwich Village, now converted into a condominium. There I encountered any number of unforgettable characters. There was Danny Friedman, hulking but jovial, a veteran of the armored cavalry who lived in Brooklyn. Mike Gold, another Brooklyn man, was quiet but efficient. Jim Duffy, a fiery redhead from the Bronx, had a virtual one-man campaign going against the VA hospital in his borough. Brian Matarese and Joe Hirsch had a strong veterans' effort under way at the SUNY campus at Old Westbury on Long Island. Joe Urgo, whom I already knew from the national office, stayed behind to continue his work in New York City.

The vets, along with many other groups, prepared for demonstrations to take place at Nixon's second inauguration on January 20, 1973. The plans were hurried, with just five days to concoct the final scenario before beginning practical preparations. Inauguration day proved cloudy and windy, though the thermometer reached forty-two degrees. The event turned into VVAW's largest ever, with about 5,000 rallying at Arlington Cemetery, where this time they gained access. Then they marched across Memorial Bridge to join a larger crowd massed on The Mall. The vets staged a symbolic signing of the Vietnam peace agreement, still to be finalized in Paris. As usual, the FBI furnished advance information, not difficult, since the vets in Washington to coordinate for the New York region were Brian Matarese from the City and John O'Neill from Buffalo, and both those chapters had been infiltrated. Some of the FBI's "Code Yellow" messages went right to the White House. Special agents in Cincinnati, Philadelphia, New York, and elsewhere were authorized to take direct action.

The vets tried to keep their march separate from other inaugural protests, but confusion abounded that day. There were separate demonstrations by the Yippies, the SDS, the National Peace Action Coalition (this NPAC demonstration was the largest, attracting upward of 45,000), and the Zippies. The Yippie-Zippie group brought a float, a huge papier-mâché rat they intended to burn in effigy. Around noontime police moved in and seized the rat, destroying it in front of the crowd. Police had also harassed a vigil meeting at the All Souls Unitarian Church the previous night. The vets expected trouble, and their arrangements for parade marshals went awry. At the end of the march a VVAW contingent mistakenly joined the NPAC crowd. Eventually the rest did too. No one ever knew whether they had been diverted by infiltrators. Some of the VVAWers wound up at 14th Street and Pennsylvania Avenue, where hundreds of protesters milled around. Police arrested a number in an attempt to deter them, but they were unable to clear the area. When the presidential motorcade passed, it would be pelted with eggs and rotten tomatoes. Mr. Nixon's limousine sustained several hits.

Within VVAW there were visible signs of the Nixon administration's continuing efforts to disrupt the Movement. There was the itching chemical incident at national headquarters, of which I myself had been a victim. I had to go home, shower, and change. I could never use those clothes again. Tapped telephones were routine. Years later an FOIA request to the FBI produced thousands of pages of surveillance reports on VVAW. Among them were accounts of the monthly meetings of the New York chapter. The FBI records were better than those of the VVAW chapter.

The other thing that happened was my entry into the publishing side of war gaming. That, too, was about Vietnam. There was a New York company called Simulations Publications Incorporated (SPI), which published board games plus a magazine, Strategy & Tactics, *each issue of which contained articles and a new game. One day at a Columbia dormitory I found a leaflet advertising this publication. Having long been a gamer, having designed my own, and having once contacted a publisher with some of my ideas, I thought it would be fascinating to see what a real game company looked like. So I decided to visit the SPI offices on 23rd Street. It so happened that a new multivolume edition of the* Pentagon Papers *(the Gravel edition) had just been published by Boston's Bea-*

con Press. The day I visited SPI, I brought one of the Gravel volumes to read on the subway. When I arrived, one of SPI's acolytes saw me with the Pentagon Papers under my arm. Instead of pushing me out the door, this fellow pulled me into a back room, where we had a long conversation about what was happening in Southeast Asia.

The editor of Strategy & Tactics had been trying to convince the publishers to do more on Vietnam, something completely unknown to me. At some point he entered our conversation and was impressed with my knowledge of the subject. It also emerged that I knew about board games, and the editor asked whether I had anything I could show him. The game I had designed on the French Indochina war was just the direction this editor was trying to pursue. The upshot would be that I demonstrated my French Indochina game and ended up with a contract for a game plus an article on the Easter offensive. The resulting material appeared in the November 1972 issue of Strategy & Tactics. It was my first published war game. I saw the project as part of my effort to bring information on Vietnam to Americans.

In keeping with everything about that war, my game proved one of the most controversial ever published by SPI, generating more editorial mail than anything before or after. I was pleased that virtually every letter from a Vietnam veteran or active-duty serviceman was very positive, but there was also a great deal of hate mail. The most odious piece, signed "Comrade Z," consisted of one line: "Madame Binh must be very proud of you." This had all the characteristics of the FBI's COINTELPRO red-baiting. Suddenly I was on someone's radar screen. That winter while I was in San Juan, the apartment I shared with four other Columbia students was burgled. The place contained a television, three stereos, typewriters, and several good cameras—great stuff to fence. But nothing was taken. Only my files were rifled. And my telephone began behaving weirdly too. Listening to someone on the line was like hearing them speak from the other end of a tunnel.

From my perspective, three other hopeful developments came out of the publication of my game. All emerged only later. The first was that elevator operators at the State Department played the game and had it set up where American diplomats could not fail to see it. Second, U.S. personnel with the military advisory group in Thailand played the game, substituting their classified knowledge for my open source information, but reaching the same conclusions. The third was that Canada, which sent personnel to Vietnam as part of the International Commission for Supervision and Control of the Indochina cease-fire that came out of the Paris accord, acquired copies of that issue of Strategy & Tactics for the briefing of its team.

In early March 1973, New York was the locale for a "Home with Honor" parade to mark the end of America's Vietnam war. High school bands, veterans' groups, police, and firefighters made up the parade. VVAW could not reasonably be denied a place in this procession, so it received a marching permit but was stuck at the tail end. The parade route started at Herald Square, passed through Times Square and the theater district, then went up through Columbus Circle and past a reviewing stand on Central Park West at about 60th Street. The unit of Army troops on the stand turned their backs on the vets, but the Color Guard of the Army Special Forces that had led the parade was also on the stand, and contingents of the procession passed it in review. A thrill went through our group when the Green Berets dipped their colors to VVAW marchers. On orders the Color Guard then turned their backs to the antiwar vets. But one of the Green Berets made the peace sign behind his back.

14   The Truth Comes Marching Home

The Paris peace agreement did not end the Vietnam war. Instead, it moved the conflict to a new phase, the so-called war of the flags, where the sides demonstrated their control over villages by flying the flags of Saigon or the NLF. Each accused the other of massive violations. Neither was innocent. Americans of the new Defense Attaché Office (DAO), which succeeded MACV, called the North Vietnamese and Liberation Front efforts Operation "Landgrab 73." General Lam Quang Thi, now commanding the elements of I Corps north of Hue, frankly recounts how, just days before the Paris agreement's signature, President Thieu ordered him to go on the offensive. Thi was supposed to seize the port of Cua Viet before the cease-fire went into effect. The South Vietnamese had already tried this and failed. This time the attack succeeded, but the ARVN managed to hold the town for barely a day before being driven back with heavy losses. There was another ARVN offensive in III Corps, up the road from Saigon toward An Loc. Hanoi and the Front tried their own grabs. The net effect seems about even, although General Giap concedes that Thieu's forces encroached on a number of liberated enclaves.

After that initial spurt, fighting continued at a reduced but significant rate. Liberation Front strategists warned that Saigon intended to flood the countryside with troops and espoused countervailing efforts. Hanoi initially sought to dampen their ardor. Its forces weakened by the 1972 campaign, with food shortages in some parts of the Mekong delta and the central coast plus wounds to lick in the North, Hanoi wished to establish a baseline of compliance with the Paris agreement. North Vietnamese planners envisioned an immediate political struggle, with military efforts more prominent later on. General Giap viewed the problem as one of disparities between local forces and regular troops and began an effort to rebuild the main forces. For the present Hanoi tried to implement a policy of the "Five Forbiddens"—it would be forbidden to attack the South Vietnamese, attempt to break up their land grabs, surround outposts, shell them, and build combat villages. The NLF saw a parallel with the abandonment of the resistance in the South after the 1954 Geneva agreements and wanted no part of that. Many of the early operations in the war of the flags were thus Liberation Front initiatives.

The four-power International Commission for Control and Supervision (ICCS) created by the Paris agreement could not regulate the fighting in any meaningful way. The ICCS, which supplanted the old International Control Commission and consisted of Canada, Indonesia, Poland, and Hungary, had teams stationed throughout South Vietnam to monitor the cease-fire and the one-for-one replacement of equipment permitted by the accords. It had no real enforcement power and could only issue reports. Even these required members' agreement, quite difficult to achieve. There were charges that the Hungarian mission collected intelligence on behalf of Hanoi, and ICCS teams were sometimes caught in firefights between the warring parties. After some of their people were nearly killed in the highlands, and angry at the Hungarians, Canada pulled out in the summer of 1973.

The accords also created two joint military commissions, one between Saigon and Hanoi, and the other consisting of those two plus the United States and the NLF. These commissions were supposed to act in concert with the ICCS and handle issues such as the exchange of Vietnamese prisoners, charges of cease-fire violations, and preparations for the creation of a National Committee on Reconciliation and Concord. The only practical effect of these provisions would be that Vietnamese communists were openly quartered near Saigon. Conversations among commissioners were completely sterile because the Vietnamese parties were each determined to win the war.

Although the Paris accords were sanctified by a general international conference some weeks later, including the participants of the 1954 Geneva conference, the war of the flags continued. The United States was no more forthcoming than Saigon. Washington assisted in clearing the mines from Haiphong and other harbors and got its prisoners back, but when Kissinger visited Hanoi for talks on healing the wounds of the war, which the DRV understood to mean reparations payments, the United States refused to make any commitments.

Going into the final phase of the negotiations President Thieu had asked to meet with President Nixon, undoubtedly to dissuade him from proceeding. Washington instead offered a Nixon-Thieu meeting after the agreement. This took place at Nixon's California residence at San Clemente in April 1973. The meeting satisfied no one save, perhaps, Mr. Nixon, who could be photographed shaking the hand of Saigon's leader, looking diplomatic, and claiming "Peace with Honor," while the Watergate scandal began to break all around him. At the beginning of April Nixon met with Thieu; by the end of that month he would be forced to accept the resignations of White House officials Bob Haldeman and John Ehrlichman, as well as Attorney General Richard Kleindienst.

For Nguyen Van Thieu, the San Clemente summit involved a series of calculated snubs—rejected dates, a meeting outside Washington, no state visit, an attempt (foiled) to avoid issuing a communiqué, food he did not care for, but most particularly, Nixon's refusal to convert his intervention pledge into a public commitment. The San Clemente meeting did not please the American public either, because it became the moment they learned of the secret pledge—in effect, a promise to resume the war. This leak, which the U.S. government refused to comment on and doubtless resulted from a South Vietnamese attempt to lock Nixon into his promise, became the only concrete result of the Thieu visit.

The agreement and its aftermath focused the Movement's efforts on ensuring that the Paris accords were carried out. The Indochina Peace Campaign, begun during the electoral season by activists that included Dave Dellinger, Dan Berrigan, Jane Fonda, Tom Hayden, and Cora Weiss, kept a spotlight on the conduct of the war, printing a digest of the Pentagon Papers and featuring talks by figures such as Daniel Ellsberg's wife Pat (Daniel stood trial for the leak), who now focused on the plight of political prisoners in South Vietnam. Prisoner bracelets, each bearing the name of someone held in Saigon's jails, mimicked the Nixon administration's own POW campaign, in which Americans had worn similar bracelets to support prisoners held by the NLF and North Vietnamese. The bracelets appeared all over during Thieu's visit. VVAW and others held demonstrations against continued bombing or any reintervention.

Broken-Backed War

Over these weeks the Nixon promises to Thieu came to a head. General Giap had visited the command centers in the DRV panhandle, Tri-Thien-Hue, and on the Ho Chi Minh Trail. He ordered improvement of The Trail for two-way all-weather motor traffic and began planning for a new route entirely *inside* South Vietnam. As an immediate stopgap measure, the People's Army sent 17,000 more troops down The Trail. Hanoi began one of those supply moves that General Abrams called "logistics offensives," replacing losses and reinforcing troops in the South. By some counts up to 223 tanks were on the move. Not long before Nixon appointed him White House chief of staff, Haig made a fresh foray to Southeast Asia to discuss retaliation. A round of bombing, including B-52 strikes, ensued. But on April 15 Air Force officers—a key indication of disaffection in the ranks of the military—along with New York lawyer Elizabeth Holtzman, filed suit in federal court to declare the bombing of Cambodia illegal, and on May 10 the Senate passed a measure terminating all funding for military intervention in or over Indochina. Nixon vetoed that legislation when a version of it reached his desk, but on the seventeenth the Senate began public hearings on the Watergate scandal, which hung a sword of Damocles over the president's head. Nixon's hands were now tied. Indeed, in August Congress voted to terminate the Cambodia bombing. A few months later, overturning Nixon's veto, it passed the War Powers Act.

Although beset by the Watergate scandal, the Nixon White House and the Justice Department attempted to pursue their vendetta against antiwar activists. The prosecution of Daniel Ellsberg for leaking the Pentagon Papers is an excellent example. In the months leading up his trial in San Diego, it emerged that Ellsberg's had been the second name on Nixon's enemies list and that the FBI had listened in to defense lawyers over its wiretaps. As a result of their guilty pleas in the Watergate break-in proper, White House officials were now suspected of somehow being connected to Ellsberg's persecution. On April 15 the government admitted that Gordon Liddy and Howard Hunt had been responsible for burglarizing Ellsberg's psychiatrist's office. News of that admission was delayed in reaching Judge Matthew Byrne, at the specific request of the president. Pressed by Byrne, the government admitted that Liddy and Hunt had been White House employees at the time, and Hunt told a grand jury that they drew on CIA support for the operation. White House counsel John Dean testified that he and Ehrlichman had ensnared the FBI director in a scheme to destroy Hunt's files on Ellsberg, which the Bureau had sequestered—an obstruction of justice. It then emerged that Ehrlichman had met with Judge Byrne and mentioned the possibility of his becoming director of the FBI, an obvious inducement, and that the Plumbers' goon squad had come to Washington, just before the Haiphong mining, to beat up Ellsberg during a rally outside Congress. Then, on May 10, prosecutors admitted that the FBI had listened in on Ellsberg himself as early as 1969. At that point Judge Byrne dismissed the charges against Ellsberg and codefendant Anthony Russo. Richard Nixon, frustrated but not deterred, made Ellsberg a target of his speech at the White House event he hosted for the returned POWs, excoriating those who stole secrets and published them in the newspapers. A few days after that, investigative reporters identified a connection between Haldeman and the Plumbers' actions against Ellsberg.

The same techniques employed against Ellsberg lay behind the Justice Department's persecution of Vietnam Veterans Against the War. In New Orleans, where for a time the chapter had but three members, all three had been FBI informants. In Jacksonville, Florida, which also had only three, two were infiltrators and stole materials from the third. In Miami, FBI and Dade County police broke into apartments, planted drugs, busted VVAW members, and then tried to recruit them. Guy Goodwin, the Washington director of this activity, shopped for the right jurisdiction and came up with a hanging judge in Gainesville, Florida, one Winston Arnow. Federal prosecutors stood before his bench and swore that a whole list of people slated to testify had no connection to the government. But the prosecution's leading witnesses—all of whom were on that list—turned out to be paid FBI informants. Others, the most militant VVAWers, were Miami police informers. One of the Plumber goons who had beaten Ellsberg, a Miami Cuban named Pablo Manuel Fernandez, similarly had been a police informer. Sent to elicit an overt act of conspiracy from veteran Scott Camil, Fernandez offered to get him military mortars. Camil's lawyer's office was also burglarized and his case file stolen. Goodwin, who attended the trial as a Washington overseer, was seen coaching a witness in the hallway, although he had no standing with the court. When John Mitchell appeared to deliver a bland denial that the government had done anything to set up the defendants, Judge Arnow eviscerated defense cross-examination, rejecting dozens of the questions posed. In the middle of the trial, courthouse employees caught two FBI agents servicing recording devices that had set been up to bug the defense conference room. Unlike the Ellsberg trial, that of the Gainesville Eight went to the jury, which found them innocent.

The vets worked hard to support their seven brothers (and one civilian) alleged to have participated in this conspiracy. Right after the Miami convention there had been a drive through the rain to Gainesville and a haunting march, the vets holding their hands on their heads in the manner of POWs, silent, then surrounding the courthouse and singing "When Johnny Comes Marching Home." In the summer of 1973 VVAW came back to support those on trial. A New York convoy filled a school bus and a number of cars. The bus, an ancient thing that had been found at a mission in Kansas, proved so decrepit it could barely make thirty miles an hour—downhill. Side missions took literature to a GI coffeehouse outside Fort Bragg. Some went just to escape the bus. In Gainesville there were local vets plus others from out of town, probably 200 in all. They marched every day, and protesters took turns attending the trial, providing a visible presence and observing Judge Arnow's conduct (he must have broken a box of pencils each day). Outside there were almost as many photographers as marchers, and only some of them were press. At night in camp, where military-style watches were mounted, noise and reflections from across the field made it clear there was close observation. But the war was supposed to be over. After the trial the VVAWers returned to their chapters, continuing the nickel-and-dime protests in many cities that pressured the Veterans Administration to deal with disabled 'Nam vets and the Nixon administration not to restart the war. Americans did not know the inside story of the differences between Nixon and Thieu at the time, and there was too much at stake in Southeast Asia to take much comfort from Watergate.

The Vietnamese settled into a strange sort of war after the initial burst of landgrabbing and a renewed truce agreed between Le Duc Tho and Kissinger in the summer. At the Han River, the front line in Quang Tri, there were South Vietnamese Marines and paratroopers on one bank and Hanoi's legions across the water. Each watched the other over the barrels of guns, but soldiers on both sides washed their laundry in the river, stood to stretch without fear of a bullet, and walked around. There was no point to a firefight between the armies in their heavily fortified positions. The Marine commander managed to accumulate a large reserve, rotating his units off the line and periodically sending them to home base for family visits. The ARVN paratroops, stretched thinner, had more trouble doing this. And the 1st Division, on its home ground, should have had no difficulty, yet both units were suffering morale problems before the end of 1973. Near Hue the North Vietnamese closed in on the lowlands. The ARVN could not drive them out of hills overlooking the air base at Phu Bai. Before the end of the year the Vietnamese Air Force had to stop flying combat missions out of Phu Bai, greatly complicating its air operations in the North.

In the Central Highlands, the Saigon region, and the Mekong, a rough jockeying for position continued. This was a war of posts and alarums. The VPA or COSVN would reach out a tentacle and capture or surround an old Special Forces camp or a minor base. The ARVN would eventually regroup and counterattack. In a number of cases, weeks or months passed before the South Vietnamese rallied to recapture the terrain. The highlands fighting related to Hanoi's decision to supplement the Ho Chi Minh Trail with a north–south route down the Vietnamese cordillera. The ARVN seemed unable to stop or significantly impede this construction. Cuba's Fidel Castro, who visited North Vietnam in 1973, bought specialized construction equipment in Hong Kong that he gave to Hanoi for the road project. Unprecedented resources were devoted to the project: more than 1,000 pieces of heavy equipment, including 200 bulldozers. Near Saigon the focus remained on Route 13 up to An Loc. In a few places the posts ended up as pockets of resistance, supplied by air for months until finally lost. An Loc, now held by ARVN Rangers, became one of these, though succored also by periodic road convoys. Another, Ton Le Chanh Ranger camp, would be besieged for a year until it fell in 1974. On the Mekong River the South Vietnamese protected boat convoys that fought their way to Phnom Penh to supply the Cambodians. The III Corps launched an offensive into Cambodia during the late spring. It would be the last major cross-border operation of the war. In the delta the ARVN enjoyed some success against COSVN's main forces, but the pacification situation that had been considered such a success in 1972 was now ignored, to the detriment of the South Vietnamese economy. Giap notes that NLF troops that had been hard pressed in 1971 now had no difficulty coping with an ARVN force twice the size.

Under these conditions Saigon had to endeavor to re-create itself. President Thieu at least knew he had to make an effort and put Nguyen Tien Hung in charge of economic reform. But the eradication of corruption remained perfunctory until 1974, when it was too late, and other necessary structural reforms failed or proved impossible to achieve. South Vietnam now lacked the money that had been pumped into its economy by all those American and Free World Forces troops, and the South Vietnamese who had worked directly for the United States (there had been 160,000 in 1969) were now largely unemployed. Only 20,000 Vietnamese remained on the American payroll in 1973. The rice harvest that year dropped by a quarter, while prices for cooking oil, laundry soap, brown sugar, gasoline, and kerosene all doubled. Military pay rates were unchanged. The National Bank of Viet Nam, it was rumored, traded half a million dollars a day in the black market to maximize its piaster holdings and sustain their value against inflation.

Oil—the getting of it, the having of it, and the use of it—became crucial to the entire exercise. Hanoi's real response to the mining of Haiphong had been to go after Saigon's fuel supplies; these had previously been left alone because illicit handovers in a sort of protection racket had helped fuel the Liberation Front and North Vietnamese. In late 1972 the United States intercepted communications indicating that a specially trained sapper unit was infiltrating specifically to attack the fuel supply, a large portion of which went up the Saigon River to Nha Be. In due course a tanker was attacked unsuccessfully with rocket-propelled grenades, then another sabotaged with limpet mines, also unsuccessfully. In 1973 the Nha Be facility itself was targeted by Naval Regiment 10 in a commando attack that almost completely destroyed it. Cong Ty Shell (the local subsidiary of Royal Dutch Shell), by dint of incredible improvisation, met its delivery contracts while rebuilding Nha Be. But this represented just one piece of the story.

Oil prices had been rising even before the October War in the Middle East brought an Arab oil embargo. The South Vietnamese had already imposed austerity measures—after 1972 their military consumption declined by about a third—with little slack left in the system. Independent of any government data, Shell's own delivery and price figures showed that by 1973 Saigon could hardly afford the costs of its own air operations. Shell discovered regular pilfering of whole barge-loads of oil and traced the action to Saigon's military. Similar thefts beset Caltex and Esso, the other oil companies active in South Vietnam. Even this merely put a dent in the shortfall.

With the Arab oil embargo the situation got worse, because one feature was a prohibition on oil exports for U.S. military activities. The Singapore refineries that supplied all of Saigon's oil imports interpreted this as applying to South Vietnam because the United States paid for the petroleum. A personal appeal from the head of Cong Ty Shell to the Saudi royal family restored the supply, but nothing shielded Saigon from higher prices.[1] Only 70 percent of its requests for oil money in fiscal year 1975, the last of the war, was budgeted in Washington. Less than the full Nixon administration aid request would actually be funded by Congress. Ironically, ARVN officers told soldiers that the oil crisis was good because South Vietnam's offshore deposits—hardly explored, much less opened for drilling—would make it like a rich Middle Eastern country. At a minimum, those conditions could not materialize for many years.

The South Vietnamese applied austerity measures everywhere they could, down to turning off lights in military bases after duty hours and packing up the lightbulbs and lamps in facilities turned over by the Americans. The top priority was ammunition consumption. For example, the ARVN cut its issues of 105mm and 155mm high-explosive artillery ammunition by 60 percent in 1973 and by half again the following year. Air force efforts were hobbled by not only fuel but also spare parts problems, and a significant number of planes were not flyable. The over-the-top Nixon deliveries of equipment in Operation Enhance and Enhance Plus compounded the problem, since the parts needed to rehabilitate broken gear ate up cash from the limited military aid funds. Half the ARVN's truck fleet had to be put up on blocks. There were some offsets, but off-budget ones. Saigon sold its captured Soviet and Chinese equipment for U.S. aid in kind, such as lumber and tin for military construction, no doubt paid for by the CIA and never included in aid budgets.

While Nixon was still at war, Saigon had pushed hard for the United States to underwrite the formation of two new ARVN divisions. General Abrams had opposed this idea as detrimental to pacification efforts, as well as contributing to the excessive mobilization of the South Vietnamese polity. Other U.S. officials had agreed with him. Their assessment of the basic limitations on Saigon had been accurate, as demonstrated when the ARVN created its 3rd Infantry Division. Without the Americans to object, Thieu went ahead with force increases in 1973, but he managed to add only a pair of fresh brigades, one each for the ARVN Airborne Division and the Vietnamese Marines, plus a couple of Ranger groups. A start was made toward reorganizing the Regional Forces to create some mobile groups. More deck chairs were moved to accomplish this with reduced spending: Thieu deactivated 100,000 Popular Forces troops.

Too much is made of the claim that U.S. aid to Saigon diminished while Soviet and Chinese aid to Hanoi increased. In the first place, the aid reductions were gradual, and during 1972–1973 Saigon remained ahead of the North: $2.3 billion versus $1 billion (by the highest estimate). With $1.2 billion more in fiscal year 1974, by any calculation, U.S. military aid to Saigon during the *calendar* year 1973 was greater than anything received by Hanoi. And it would be in 1973 that the key strategic development of the period occurred—Hanoi's completion of its new motor road and oil pipeline to the front lines. The ARVN's inability to prevent this changed the military balance. South Vietnam suffered key setbacks in 1973 not because Hanoi was better supplied, or because the ARVN did not fight hard, but because of the same rigidities that had long hampered it.

Equally important, communist aid to Hanoi has been overestimated. Both Chinese and Soviet assistance to North Vietnam declined after 1972. The amount of equipment supplied by the Chinese dropped by 25 to 33 percent in 1973 and perhaps another 20 percent in 1974, with the delivery of tanks down by 63.7 percent and aircraft almost disappearing from the supply flow. The total number of tanks China furnished to the DRV throughout 1973–1974 (200) was less than the number Hanoi was accused of sending South immediately after the Paris accords (223), a moment when it had as legitimate a claim to replace tanks used up in the Easter offensive as did the United States to substitute what it sent to Saigon under the Enhance programs. Overall aid to North Vietnam (both Chinese and Soviet) dropped even more than did U.S. assistance to Saigon. In a joint paper, the CIA and DIA estimated help to Hanoi at $1 billion in 1973 and $1.7 billion in 1974, but that was overwhelmingly economic aid. Of those totals, military aid amounted to $330 million in 1973—less than half the 1972 level of $750 million—and $400 million the next year. Equally telling, the dollar cost of ground-force equipment given to Hanoi dropped by almost two-thirds in 1973 and stayed at that level. Moreover, the Soviet side upped the *prices* of their equipment, meaning the dollars bought fewer weapons and less ammunition. For the last year of the war Hanoi received an estimated $170 million worth of ammunition, while the United States shipped Saigon $268 million in this category in fiscal year 1975. The total military aid to Hanoi for the entire period after the Paris agreement is comparable to the actual U.S. congressional appropriation for the last year alone ($700 million), which critics are so fond of lambasting as inadequate.[2]

Both sides continued their nibbling tactics through 1974. A key event occurred in the United States when Richard Nixon was obliged to resign the presidency to avoid impeachment over Watergate. One of the articles of impeachment would have indicted him for bombing Cambodia. Vice President Gerald R. Ford replaced him. Meanwhile, Thieu continued to insist his generals hold everywhere, at all costs. This was another root cause of defeat: the failure to realign Saigon's objectives. Thieu would finally do that, but he procrastinated for more than a year and then decided under pressure from a fresh North Vietnamese offensive. The ARVN high command also held a share of the responsibility. At Thieu's request, Nguyen Tien Hung attended national security meetings as rapporteur, where he observed Joint General Staff chief General Cao Van Vien in action. Hung found Vien passive, merely nodding his head in agreement with Thieu, who was typically careful to ask his views. Vien himself asserted that Thieu made all the significant decisions.[3] General Pham Van Dong, whom Thieu elevated to the top command in the Central Highlands in 1974, would grouse that in the October War the Nixon administration delivered more aid to Israel in three weeks ($2.2 billion) than it had given Saigon in all the months since the Paris accords. True enough, but Saigon resisted drawing the appropriate conclusions.

William Le Gro of the DAO, an acute observer of this period, later characterized much of the fighting in 1974 as "strategic raids." Two things were significant about the operations. First, most of them were North Vietnamese. Second, more often than not, the ARVN could not recapture lost ground. In Quang Nam and Quang Ngai provinces the enemy reached the edges of the coastal plain. The district seat of Thuong Duc fell, the first to do so since 1972. At Thuong Duc a VPA division defeated the ARVN's elite Airborne Division in the open field. Late that summer, district towns and important defense posts in the Central Highlands were lost as never before. Storied Special Forces camps such as Dak Pek, Tieu Atar, Plei Me, and Mang Buk disappeared into Hanoi's hands. The ARVN, able to move most of an infantry division into a threatened II Corps sector the previous year, was now limited to just a third of that force. In the Mekong delta a district capital fell for the first time, while the NLF made inroads in several provinces. Even U.S. ambassador Graham Martin, who had replaced Ellsworth Bunker and was Thieu's greatest American fan, began admitting setbacks in his dispatches to Washington.

That fall a group of Roman Catholic laymen and clergy issued a manifesto accusing Thieu of protecting, even benefiting from, corruption. If he lacked the support of the Catholics, so long the backbone of the regime, it was plain Thieu had lost the "mandate of heaven." Predictably, the government seized editions of three newspapers that printed the manifesto. Word spread anyway. And the Buddhists did not lag, forming what they termed a National Reconciliation Force. There were mass demonstrations. Thieu dismissed a corps commander, four cabinet ministers, and hundreds of army officers, but he cracked down on protesters. The White Mice even raided the Vietnam Press Club. And the military region commander he had relieved for corruption in the Central Highlands Thieu brought back as chief of III Corps, at the insistence of Ambassador Martin.

Hanoi noticed. And its forces in the South were stronger than ever. They had more tanks and more artillery, and their divisions were at virtually full strength. Hanoi regarded the ARVN's loss of Thuong Duc as a key indicator. Other operations also went better than hoped. The People's Army had formed its first mobile corps in October 1973. By the summer of 1974 it had three. The Central Military-Party Committee and Politburo concerted strategy together. What path to follow had been the subject of intense deliberations ever since the Paris agreement. Supervised by General Le Trong Tan, a group on the General Staff began elaborating plans. A concept for operations had been completed in June 1973. Since then it had gone through many iterations. By the spring of 1974 the planners were on their fifth draft. In July Le Duan felt comfortable enough to push for a decision. This led to a series of Politburo meetings that culminated on September 30 with the adoption of a strategic plan. Still suspicious of a U.S. reintervention, Hanoi decided on an intermediate approach—some major attacks in 1975 with the focus on the Central Highlands, but holding off a war-winning offensive until the following year. People's Army capabilities would be augmented by adding 150,000 recruits immediately, plus another 60,000 in 1975. The first attacks were set for Phuoc Long province, just below the highlands, partly in hopes of capturing stocks of artillery ammunition, which were in short supply in the VPA—a revealing commentary on the level of foreign support for North Vietnam. When these attacks succeeded beyond expectations, Hanoi modified its strategy and decided to go for broke. General Van Tien Dung went South to supervise as the North Vietnamese set all their forces in motion.

Phuoc Long province fell in early January 1975. This was a disaster for Saigon. Several thousand troops were lost, and for the first time an entire province had fallen to the adversary. At the critical moment Thieu froze, failing to make any decision at all on whether to reinforce or evacuate Phuoc Long. That may have been the decisive moment for Saigon morale. At this point the Joint General Staff finally proposed a strategic withdrawal under which the ARVN would abandon indefensible terrain. Thieu again resisted a decision. The JGS anticipated an offensive aimed at the cities, a sort of combination of 1968 and 1972, and it made ad hoc preparations for scratch combat units as extra reinforcements. But the moment passed, and the real enemy offensive looked nothing like what the JGS expected. Former ambassador Bui Diem, returned to private life as a newspaper publisher, believes Thieu still counted on U.S. intervention. Ford's NSC staff secretly surveyed the U.S. military potential to intervene, but the president was now bound by a War Powers Act and other statutes that prohibited the use of American forces in Southeast Asia. He faced an overwhelmingly Democratic "Watergate Congress" elected by a nation soured by Nixon's excesses. There was zero possibility of intervention, and not much better chances for a congressional vote on military aid. Ford had already asked for an extra $300 million for such assistance, but the request stalled in Congress.

Hanoi initiated its attack in Darlac province below the Central Highlands. The People's Army deployed a host of units to achieve an unprecedented 5–1 advantage. The March attack was a complete success. A second province fell. Only now did President Thieu, in concert with General Vien and his national security adviser, General Dang Van Quang, agree to strategic redeployment. Even so, he refused to designate specific positions to be held in I and II Corps, speaking vaguely of enclaves around key coastal cities. If they could not be held, the ARVN should retreat gradually to a bastion encompassing Saigon and the Mekong delta. Meeting his corps commanders on

March 14, Thieu ordered the withdrawal. The attempt to implement that plan led to the collapse of South Vietnam.

Except for the Saigon region itself, the North Vietnamese did not launch a strategic offensive so much as impede the ARVN's withdrawal, occupy the terrain it was abandoning, and pursue the routing troops. People's Army units quickly moved to block the passes out of the highlands the ARVN had to traverse, and the withdrawal was further hampered because, with air transport, those roads had not been used in years. The retreat from the Central Highlands turned into disintegration. In the middle of this, the communists overran Phnom Penh, ending the war in Cambodia. From Saigon, CIA station chief Tom Polgar sent Washington daily situation reports depicting the unfolding disaster. Polgar's lead analyst, Frank Snepp, who drafted these missives, worried that his reports were making Polgar's views seem even more pessimistic than they actually were. Polgar told Snepp not to worry, and he added language to each cable suggesting that more U.S. aid might save Saigon. One paragraph of Snepp's stark account is worth quoting at length:

> Whether he [Polgar] still believed this [that U.S. aid could save Saigon], I cannot say. In any case, I did not. But because of the incredible pressures of those days I did not attempt to debate him on the point. I merely amended the analyses as he wanted. In doing so, I helped him defeat one of our primary objectives. Instead of convincing colleagues in Washington of the gravity of the military situation, we succeeded in persuading them there was still an out. For the optimists back in the State Department and the CIA could always assure themselves after reading our analyses, "Well, yes, things are going badly out there, but Polgar and his boys say aid is still the answer." It was the beginning of a last fatal illusion.[4]

The Vietnam data problem endured until the very end, even as Hanoi's troops neared Saigon. The cable traffic for this period and Snepp's insider memoir of the tragedy contain literally dozens of examples of serious distortion in the information provided to Washington, as Ambassador Martin sought to avoid, then delay orders to begin an evacuation of Americans and Vietnamese nationals who were at risk if Saigon fell to the North Vietnamese.

General Frederick C. Weyand, now U.S. Army chief of staff, made a hasty visit and produced a report supporting the Ford administration's appeal for more money. Its assumptions were based on little more than whistling in the wind. On that basis Ford upped the ante and demanded $722 million to save Saigon. A new aid measure, if passed, could not have been applied in time. Vietnamese general Vien admitted that and wrote, "At that late hour, even if the . . . additional military aid had been approved, it would have been too late."[5] In fact, when Saigon fell, money already appropriated for military aid lay unspent in existing U.S. accounts. America's Vietnam intervention recycled in fast-forward, like some reflexive nerve signal, this time as farce. All the old arguments were deployed, and only the usual solutions were envisioned. Rallies and protests staged by VVAW and others put President Ford on notice that he had no free hand here, and groups such as the Indochina Resource Center—about which Martin complained in his cables—provided Congress and the public with information that went beyond government data.

Panic spread to I Corps when Ngo Quang Truong tried to fashion an enclave around Hue and Da Nang. The North Vietnamese thrust forward, breaking defense lines before they could be consolidated. Americans intervened all right—to evacuate Vietnamese (and their own) from Da Nang and other ports as the northerners approached, returning them to the Saigon area. Vietnamese Marines and Rangers, sent to guard Thieu's family grave outside Phan Rang, bulldozed it instead before fleeing on April 17. When President Thieu learned this, at the height of the crisis, he disappeared into an inner sanctum and was not seen for a day.

While engaged in pursuit in central Vietnam, the North Vietnamese and NLF launched an offensive against Saigon and the delta. The final hope lay in getting money for Thieu to defend this southern bastion. The concept was flawed from the beginning. North Vietnamese forces were concentrated, well supported by armor and artillery. Unlike 1972 they were well rehearsed in combined operations and had significant mobility plus great firepower. South Vietnamese defenses already in III and IV Corps were as rigid as ever, and the remnants from I Corps and the Central Highlands had barely begun reorganizing. They included almost all Thieu's elite general reserve forces. His heavy armor and artillery had been wiped out. Reconstituting them was not a short-term proposition. The South Vietnamese mounted an effective defense in one place, Xuan Loc, and delayed the enemy in a few sectors north and east of Saigon, but the defenses essentially collapsed. Saigon fell before Congress could complete its legislative action on the aid request, which was never formally rejected.

The last days of Saigon passed in a frantic effort to evacuate Vietnamese who had been American friends and allies. There were many acts of compassion, bravery, stupidity, and nobility—on both sides. At a key moment the North Vietnamese delayed their advance to give the Americans one more day to get aircraft out of Tan Son Nhut. Thanks to a combination of planes, convoys down the Mekong carrying refugees from the delta, and helicopter evacuations from Saigon—ending with choppers flying from the U.S. embassy and the roof of a CIA safe house—some 130,000 Vietnamese escaped the debacle. Nguyen Van Thieu resigned the South Vietnamese presidency on April 21 with a blast at the United States. He handed the reins over to

Tran Van Huong, who acceded to the presidency after all, seven years after running for that office. But Huong held the presidency only long enough to turn it over, in turn, to Duong Van Minh. That was ironic too. Senior ARVN commanders joined the flood of refugees, including General Vien. His replacement left as well. The de facto chief of the JGS on the last day of the war, according to Vietnamese sources, was actually a Liberation Front agent. North Vietnamese troops occupied Saigon. It was "Big" Minh who was left to surrender Doc Lap Palace on April 30, 1975. The American war in Vietnam ended that day.

Later Years

More Vietnamese came to America later—many as boat people, some by immigration—and their new lives would be very different. Vietnam remains a lost country to them. They miss it and idealize the South Vietnam they left. But North Vietnam won the war, and not by default. Saigon lost. Given its leadership, there is no combination of realistic measures that could have ensured the survival of that Vietnam. As for the United States, it did not betray South Vietnam so much as be ejected from a parallel war it could not win and could no longer fight. Other refugees included montagnards from the Central Highlands, Hmong from Laos, and Cambodians, all fleeing the horrors of the Southeast Asian war.

Those horrors were enormous. More than 58,000 American soldiers lost their lives, more than 303,000 were wounded, and somewhere between 1,400 and 1,900 are still missing and unaccounted for, despite strenuous efforts, especially since the mid-1990s. Civilian casualties, including those of the CIA, remain unknown. South Vietnamese battle deaths range somewhere between 220,000 and 244,000; North Vietnamese number about 800,000. As many as 300,000 northerners went missing in action, and Hanoi sustained about 600,000 wounded. Vietnamese government figures released in 1995 estimated approximately 2 million civilian deaths in each of the two regroupment zones of Vietnam. Some 700,000 Cambodians and 60,000 Laotians died as well, and Cambodians who perished at the hands of the Pol Pot regime may be as numerous as the South Vietnamese civilians lost. China admits to 1,446 combat deaths in North Vietnam and Russia to 16. The allies who fought alongside the United States suffered nearly 6,000 dead, more than 80 percent of them from South Korea and about 10 percent from Australia and New Zealand. In all, a huge butcher's bill.

President Gerald R. Ford passed away recently. He said little about Vietnam in his later years but looked on benignly as Henry A. Kissinger and Alexander M. Haig tried to make Congress the scapegoat for the loss of the war, an argument that Kissinger first made to Ford in office, penning a memorandum purporting to draw the "lessons" of Vietnam. Richard Nixon, driven from the White House, spent his last years trying to rehabilitate himself, reiterating the old arguments with enough success to impress the emerging neo-orthodox. He died in the spring of 1994. Lyndon Baines Johnson, bitter at his Vietnam experience, succumbed to his heart ailments on his way to San Antonio in January 1973. Despite his own opening of negotiations, LBJ had been furious when George McGovern ran on a platform of ending the Vietnam war. He survived Harry S. Truman by just one month. Truman left few reflections on what he had wrought in Indochina. Dwight D. Eisenhower, who gave us the Domino Theory, made critical commitments, and acted as Johnson's sounding board, never saw the end of the conflict, dying at Walter Reed Hospital in March 1969.

Nguyen Van Thieu went into exile in London and later moved to the United States, living in the Boston area. He died in 2001. Thieu nursed his bitterness at what he saw as betrayal, but except for interviews with close aides, never told his side of the story. His cousin Hoang Duc Nha and aides Nguyen Phu Duc and Nguyen Tien Hung remain active in the Vietnamese community in the United States. Nguyen Cao Ky and Nguyen Khanh both live in California. Ky has published at least two versions of a memoir, and Khanh, as of several years ago, was working on one of his own. Returning to visit Vietnam in 2004, Ky became the first of Saigon's former leaders to break the social barriers that have restricted contact between the overseas Vietnamese (*Viet kieu*) and their cousins in socialist Vietnam. Tran Van Huong spent two years in Saigon under house arrest by the new communist regime. He died in 1982. Duong Van Minh lived in Ho Chi Minh City, as Saigon has been renamed, and indulged his passion for raising orchids. He immigrated to France in 1982 and subsequently moved to California. He succumbed to complications from a fall in 2002.

Ambassador Bui Diem lives in retirement outside Washington, D.C. Thich Tri Quang was arrested by the communists after they took Saigon. Released later, Quang lived to see communist oppression of Buddhists in the new Vietnam. Nguyen Chanh Thi began his exile to the United States long before the war ended, spurned by Kissinger when the general sought to give advice. Thi worked as a custodian at a motel in Los Angeles and later managed a restaurant in Arkansas. He settled in New Jersey and died in June 2007. Ngo Quang Truong became an analyst for the American Railroad Association. He too passed away in 2007. Cao Van Vien, who got out of Saigon by helicopter on the last day of the evacuation, also came to the United States. Vien expired from cardiac arrest in January 2008. Both he and Truong contributed to the U.S. Army's Indochina Monographs series.

General Vo Nguyen Giap is the most prominent survivor of the Hanoi wartime leadership. His favorite story is still Dien Bien Phu. At the time of writing Giap was ninety-six years old. Madame Nguyen Thi Binh remains the most active. Since 1992 she has served as vice president of the Socialist Republic of Vietnam. Pham Van Dong died at age ninety-four in 2000. Le Duc

Tho preceded him, passing in 1990 after a severe illness. Le Duan retained his post as general secretary of the party, presiding over the 1976 reunification of South and North Vietnam and shepherding their joint path for a decade. He died in 1986. That would be a watershed year for the warlords. General Van Tien Dung's ascendancy did not survive Le Duan's death. Dung succeeded Giap as defense minister but was replaced as the head of the People's Army in the 1986 Politburo shakeup; he died in March 2002. Generals Tran Do, mastermind of Tet in Saigon, and Le Trong Tan, master of the DMZ who defeated Lam Son 719, took the zone once and for all in the Easter offensive and captured Da Nang in 1975; both died in 1986. Tan holds the distinction of having streets named for him in both Hanoi and Ho Chi Minh City. Tran Bach Dang was purged again, for the American contacts carried out at the behest of COSVN. As with Pham Xuan Anh, anyone who had had contact with the enemy was suspect. Anh submitted voluntarily to reeducation. Dang was eventually rehabilitated. Both lived quietly. When Dang passed he was at work on a grand history of the southern resistance. Anh died in Ho Chi Minh City in 2007. Most Vietnamese today were not yet born when Saigon fell.

Hubert H. Humphrey, the vice president so eclipsed by LBJ, and the senator manipulated by Richard Nixon, expired quietly in January 1978. Mike Mansfield, the U.S. Senate's Asia specialist, capped his career as ambassador to Tokyo from 1977 to 1988, an unprecedented run for any American diplomat. He died in October 2001. Senator J. William Fulbright, in decline in his later years, passed away in February 1995. The U.S. program under which American scholars visit abroad and foreign luminaries come to the United States is named in his honor. John F. Kerry, the Navy veteran and VVAW activist, entered politics and rose to the U.S. Senate. He was the Democratic Party's candidate for president of the United States in 2004. His nemesis John O'Neill emerged to denigrate Kerry's war record, coining the new verb "to swift boat." Kerry currently serves as junior senator from Massachusetts.

Only General Fred Weyand remains standing among the senior U.S. military commanders. He lives quietly in retirement in Hawaii and has long refused to talk about the war. Creighton Abrams had a tragically short tenure as Army chief of staff, dying in the saddle in September 1974. William Westmoreland went into retirement in 1972 and spent several decades trying to explain the light he saw at the end of the tunnel. Westmoreland walked at the head of the 1982 parade of Vietnam-era veterans who participated in the dedication of the Vietnam Veterans Memorial. Admiral U. S. Grant Sharp went to his death in December 2001 convinced that his bombers had never been given the green light to destroy North Vietnam. Admiral Thomas Moorer no doubt agreed, despite the Christmas Bombing; he passed away in 2004. General John Lavelle, who kept his counsel after being cashiered for doing too much for Nixon and Moorer, died in 1979.

Melvin Laird lives in retirement in Florida but remains active on health care issues in his home state of Wisconsin and still plays an elder's role in the U.S. House of Representatives. After long and honorable service, Clark Clifford became involved in a major bank scandal that tarnished his reputation. He passed away in 1998. Clifford's predecessor, the redoubtable Robert S. McNamara, disagrees with the air commanders. As one of the few top officials to have apologized for their roles in Vietnam—an apology not accepted by many Americans—McNamara at least sought answers, supplying a book with his interpretation of Vietnam as failure and participating in conferences with former enemies in Hanoi in an effort to discover what really happened. His polar opposite, Walt W. Rostow, apologized for nothing and spent the rest of his life justifying himself, responding to McNamara by arguing that the United States actually won, in a reverse Domino Theory, by buying time for other Asian nations to build strong economies. Rostow passed away in 2002. Dean Rusk would be more reflective. Though he never came to an apology, Rusk was clearly troubled by his role in the fiasco. He returned to his native Georgia and died of natural causes in December 1994. McGeorge Bundy also became reflective in retirement and clearly regarded Vietnam as a failure, perhaps even a mistake. Bundy was at work on a memoir when he died in 1996, and at least two efforts have been made to complete the work. Bundy later regretted his conspiracy with Rusk and McNamara to prevent LBJ from becoming infected with George Ball's criticisms of Vietnam policy. Ball firmly believed this past had another pattern and said so in the memoirs he published a dozen years before his 1994 death. Many in the antiwar movement admired Ball's forthrightness but deplored his refusal to resign in protest.

Among those who served in the White House, Anthony Lake followed his forthrightness in resigning over Cambodia with service as national security adviser to President Bill Clinton. He is currently a professor and farmer. Roger Morris, who resigned with Lake, became and remains an author. Chester L. Cooper, whose service spanned decades from the French return to Indochina to the LBJ peace feelers, died of natural causes late in 2005. Kennedy aide Michael V. Forrestal died of an aneurysm while chairing a meeting of the governing board of the Lincoln Center for the Performing Arts on January 11, 1989. General Maxwell D. Taylor had preceded Forrestal at Lincoln Center, of which he had been the first president. Taylor, who had served in the Kennedy White House, went on to chair the Joint Chiefs of Staff, and served as ambassador in Saigon before returning to the Johnson White House, died in April 1987.

Among the Vietnam characters from the CIA crowd, the foremost is probably William E. Colby. He perished on the Chesapeake Bay, probably of a stroke, while boating in 1996. George Carver died in 1994, victim of a heart attack while driving home from the airport. Sam Adams, the key figure in the notorious order of battle dispute, died at home of a heart attack in 1988.

Station chief Ted Shackley, who bribed Thieu's astrologer to get the Laos invasion going, passed away in late 2002. Roger Hilsman, once chief of State Department intelligence, lives at home in Connecticut but is in decline.

Opposition to the Vietnam war shaped many lives. The Berrigan brothers, Philip and Daniel, went on to struggle against nuclear weapons, as did Daniel Ellsberg. Philip died surrounded by family in December 2002. The others are still out there. Ellsberg has staunchly opposed the war in Iraq. Actress Jane Fonda married activist Tom Hayden, though they later divorced. Fonda avoided further political activism until she came out in opposition to the Iraq war in 2006. Hayden ran repeatedly for various California state and local offices and served eighteen years in the California assembly and senate. Dave Dellinger maintained his pacifist stance until his death in May 2004. The irrepressible Abbie Hoffman dipped into various issues. Incensed with U.S. intervention in Central America in the 1980s, Hoffman and presidential daughter Amy Carter were arrested in 1986 for obstructing CIA recruiting at the University of Massachusetts–Amherst. They were acquitted. Hoffman committed suicide in April 1989. Organizer Jerry Rubin did an about-face after his counterculture days and became a Wall Street investor. Rubin was hit by a car and killed while crossing the street in Los Angeles in November 1994.

The Vietnam Veterans Against the War continue their work. As a result of their efforts, post-traumatic stress disorder is now a recognized malady. VVAW organized several more marches on Washington on behalf of veterans and had a contingent at the Vietnam Veterans Memorial dedication in 1982. That was an amazing day for them, with a small group of VVAWers on a little hillock near The Wall, like Custer at his last stand, with some other vets hurling epithets. Yet at a local bar afterward, none of the VVAWers could buy a beer. The customers would not listen as they protested, "You don't understand, we were *against* the war!"

Today VVAW founder Jan Barry is a newspaperman in New Jersey. Danny Friedman is a veterans' affairs official in New York City. Al Hubbard is retired in the Southwest. Scott Camil still lives in Gainesville, Florida. David Connolly is a retired telephone lineman in South Boston. Gary Rafferty is a retired firefighter in New Hampshire. Both are poets, as is W. D. Ehrhart, who teaches at a Pennsylvania private school. Connolly also followed his musical passion by forming a band. David Cline, a key East Coast organizer, passed away in the summer of 2007. Barry Romo still leads the organization. They are as active as ever and have gained new energy from the war in Iraq. There were VVAW and Veterans for Peace contingents at every major march against the Iraq war and in many local protests throughout the nation.

The Justice Department officials who masterminded the Nixon administration's persecution of the vets are gone: Robert C. Mardian died of lung cancer in July 2006, and Guy W. Goodwin of a stroke in Washington on

December 20, 2007. The hanging judge of Gainesville, Winston E. Arnow, passed away in November 1994 after a long illness.

Vietnam Veterans Against the War celebrated its fortieth anniversary at a convocation in Chicago in August 2007.

The Reasons Why

American presidents involved the nation in the Vietnam conflict, primarily to wage the Cold War, and without understanding the Vietnamese revolution. Franklin D. Roosevelt, who died in office, can perhaps be excused. Harry Truman, with his deference to French explanations, and Dwight D. Eisenhower, because of his guilt over the siege of Dien Bien Phu, took the steps that set the commitment and cast in stone the limits on U.S. leverage. Eisenhower had fears of colluding with colonialism but let himself become ensnared by the arguments that had swayed Truman. John F. Kennedy, in his exuberance at the dynamism of his band of cold warriors and the efficacy of their solutions to Cold War problems, extended that commitment. Kennedy's acquiescence in the coup d'état against Ngo Dinh Diem transformed the relationship between Washington and Saigon. Lyndon Baines Johnson went the last mile, converting the links of military assistance into a wartime alliance. Until LBJ, there had been a succession of specific incidents or episodes that called the basic American enterprise in Vietnam into question, opportunities to raise the stark alternative of ending the commitment or, later, withdrawing from the war. Each president avoided that path. Presidents *chose* war.

Having unleashed the demons, presidents faced a succession of developments—influenced by their own political and strategic decisions—that progressively narrowed their freedom of action. Refusing to seek a declaration of war, financing the war off-budget through "supplementary" funding requests, manipulating American opinion instead of conducting a Great Debate on U.S. goals—all these acts had an impact. All would be replicated in Iraq. Vietnam became a war that lacked a solid legal basis, whose continuation sharpened existing problems in the American economy, the conduct of which created the perception of a credibility gap between government pronouncements and apparent reality. These features flowed from presidential and other official decisions. It was the lot of presidents from Eisenhower onward that they operated in an environment of increasing public awareness and activism, stimulated by the civil rights and antinuclear movements, and evolving into the social awareness of the 1960s. But presidents must lead in the milieu in which they live, and America was, and is, the product of a multiplicity of social, political, economic, and environmental dynamics that both transcend policy and set the stage on which decisions play out.

A key error by American leaders, in Vietnam as in Iraq, was their determination to avoid a general political debate. This had multifarious and pernicious effects. It restricted presidents to a narrow range of predigested advice. In Vietnam, that preempted any conclusion that the enterprise had failed. One more troop increment, one more dollop of treasure, one more massive bombing, and the war would be won. Lyndon Johnson abandoned the last opportunity to broaden the base of war support in 1964–1965 by failing to seek a congressional declaration, and in 1967 by eschewing any national mobilization. Determination to avoid debate also led to the information practices that undercut credibility and to the security policies that treated opponents as enemies of the state, creating conditions for a war in America over the war in Vietnam. To blame this on the press, the intellectuals, the "liberal establishment," or the antiwar movement is to put the egg before the chicken. Presidents buttered the bread they lay in.

Both government lying and security crackdowns contributed powerfully to the rise of the antiwar movement, *making* the war reach into the lives of individual Americans. In my own case, a typical American was converted from an unquestioning supporter of U.S. policy into an antiwar opponent purely by observing the discrepancies between what the government said and what I could see. That I, a worm in the Movement, a rank-and-file member at best, could be subjected to wiretapping, an intrusive black-bag job, and COINTELPRO-style red-baiting for my puny efforts shows how deeply the apparatus of government surveillance reached. Countless Americans experienced some part, all, or more of these intrusive measures. Government tactics created more opposition than they eliminated. Surely that is the root meaning of the rise of the GI resistance, VVAW, and the veterans' antiwar movement. Those tactics were another choice and did not evolve by random selection. LBJ might complain of being a prisoner in his big white jailhouse, but he built the prison himself. Richard Nixon complained incessantly, and when he tried to get even, he ending up destroying his own presidency.

As the war continued, the Movement grew, and America's internal problems mushroomed, presidents' range of choice narrowed further. The combination of their actions set a framework within which the war played out, effectively against a time clock. The military strategy failed to achieve outright victory. Eventually, Tet blew open the credibility gap and fused Americans' basic views. After that there remained only two essential possibilities: get out of Vietnam, or try to break out of the deadlock. Lyndon Johnson recognized this. Although he remained torn by the temptation to try to win the war, LBJ opened negotiations to end it and began the preparations to withdraw American troops.

By the fall of 1968 the political reality was such that no one who overtly expressed a maximalist view on winning the war could become president. At that point the clock had begun to run out. Richard Nixon spoke softly, and Americans thought his plan was to get out of the war, but his approach proved more insidious. As president, he adopted a declaratory policy of pursuing negotiation and devised instruments to reduce antiwar protest, to put more time on the clock. But his bargaining position that demanded Hanoi agree to its own defeat reveals different intentions. Trapped by the politics of the war, Nixon oscillated between a desire to end the mess with victory and the recognition that there was no alternative to abandoning the war.

Covering his flanks, the president tried to break out of the policy box with his Nixon Shocks. It is highly significant that in every one of them Mr. Nixon was aware beforehand that his preferred choice would outrage Americans. Duck Hook would have been the first Nixon Shock but proved abortive. That was significant too. The policy box could not, in fact, be breached, and the lesson was apparent less than a year after his inauguration. Duck Hook also gives the lie to the proposition that Nixon might have won by executing the Christmas Bombing earlier—there was no window of impunity. He moved to isolate Hanoi by building bridges to its communist allies. The subsequent Nixon Shocks—the invasions of Cambodia and Laos, the Haiphong mining, and the Christmas Bombing itself—cost the president any progress he had made in neutralizing opposition. The Shocks cut the time left on Nixon's clock. Meanwhile, the president's relationship with his legislature deteriorated, to the point that Congress essentially told Mr. Nixon the war was over. Once that happened, the Paris agreement followed swiftly.

After January 1973 the president's hands were tied. No doubt Nixon's promises of a brutal intervention against any Hanoi violation of the cease-fire were sincere, but his excesses in the war, not least the Christmas Bombing itself, would have made any such move a Nixon Shock. Despite his sincerity and the building of a record to justify future action, Nixon's promises were empty because his political position had eroded. And, in turn, Nixon's personal vulnerability arose from the very measures he had taken to destroy Ellsberg and the antiwar movement, while ensuring his reelection. The road to Watergate lay through Vietnam. Richard Nixon never escaped the box. His circle became a vicious one.

Gerald R. Ford inherited the shards of a Vietnam policy and a broken-backed war. A full analysis of Ford's war is not possible here. But attempts to blame the final failure on Congress were hollow arguments that only helped ensure the persistence of debate over Vietnam. The aid requests came from the White House, not Congress. They were based on assessments by the U.S. government. The aid reductions began with Nixon. Congress cut requests but also *increased* economic aid. Despite charges against Congress, there was unspent money in aid accounts when Saigon fell. And there was no prospect of victory. Those who make these charges are equating victory with the purchase of a little more time. That is disingenuous.

The truth is that as of the spring of 1975, Saigon had yet to put its own house in order. South Vietnamese forces retained the weaknesses that had always impeded their effectiveness. International economic trends, in particular the skyrocketing price of oil, affected ARVN operations at least as much as reductions in U.S. aid. Equally to the point, had Thieu taken the U.S. aid he *did* receive and used it to put Saigon's economy on a sounder basis, rather than persisting in the corruption that benefited him (this is not to say that Thieu was personally corrupt, but that the corrupt system cemented his power), Saigon would have had a better chance of survival. The purpose of American aid had always been to construct a self-sustaining entity in South Vietnam, but Saigon had not used it for that. Absent such a transformation, South Vietnam's defeat was never more than a matter of time. And that had run out.

■ ■ ■ That American officials failed to understand Vietnam or the Vietnamese is well appreciated, and nothing more needs to be said on that score. Plentiful evidence on the theme appears in this narrative. But that *South Vietnamese* failed to understand *Americans* requires comment. General Nguyen Khanh's constant coups and cabinet reshufflings were gambits he thought had no effect on his relations with Washington. Khanh believed his only problem was with Maxwell Taylor. Not so. Saigon leaders, including Khanh, Diem, and Thieu, all resorted to making promises they had no intention of fulfilling—broadening their governments is the most prominent example, but only one. Those promises had a cost. Each of the Saigon leaders chose not to try to explain Vietnam to Americans. The whys and wherefores of Saigon politics were obscure to most Americans, especially those who had the president's ear. To the extent that, at the time of the negotiations, Thieu reflected true societal concerns in rejecting moderation and in insisting that Saigon politics required any agreement to seal victory, he paid a very heavy price for not educating Washington. The Vietnam data problem began early and persisted through the war and beyond. If anything, the data problem for Saigon leaders was worse than for the Americans. In the South Vietnamese system, ARVN commanders considered it acceptable to tell Saigon nothing while their fronts collapsed. There were even fewer incentives for accurate reporting than on the U.S. side.

The Vietnamese told Americans what they thought Washington wanted to hear, but they were not the only ones. For the United States, the data problem was pernicious. Observers compiled statistics ad infinitum but could never be sure of their accuracy, except those of least import, such as air sorties flown or bomb tonnage expended. Numbers of troops under arms did not equate to military power; the enemy's order of battle did not reflect the true distribution of force; the number of enemies surrendered or neutralized, or the number of weapons captured, did not signify the collapse of Hanoi's military machine. The body counts were so nebulous as to be laughable. Collectors of data collaborated to craft even more subjective measurements, such as the Hamlet Evaluation Survey ratings. Measures of merit substituted for evidence because no one could agree on what constituted a valid indicator. Worse, the subjective data were then relied on as hard fact in making decisions of real importance in both Washington and Saigon.

Presidents from John Kennedy onward would have experienced fewer political problems had they been able to fight the war effectively. Here a different set of considerations applies. The data problem is a starting point, but there existed both intractable elements in the nature of the conflict and intrinsic difficulties in attaining a proper triangulation for a winning military-political strategy. Intractable elements included the physical geography and international status of the nations of Indochina after the 1954 Geneva agreements, which endowed South Vietnam with a porous border, beyond which the nations made neutral by Geneva formed natural approaches. In addition, a primitive South Vietnamese port and road system limited the rate at which the United States could move forces into the combat theater, a factor that was not immutable but took several years to solve. An intractable policy element was the lack of U.S. leverage, the continued inability of Washington to convince Saigon leaders to follow through on their promises. Another problem lay in Saigon's rigidity, which hampered its own war effort. Hanoi's determination was considerable, and its policies were certainly intractable, which imposed heavy burdens since the DRV proved capable of matching each American escalation. This was especially crucial because Hanoi and the NLF drove the pace of the fighting by committing to or refusing engagement. These elements reduced the impact of presidents' actions.

Intrinsic difficulties included the basic structure of the U.S. military, its doctrine, and its style of warfare, all of which were designed for major conventional or nuclear war and were obliged to undergo a ponderous transformation to cope with insurgency. Early U.S. commanders failed to change their way of thinking. President Kennedy's efforts to instill a more dynamic approach to counterinsurgency had only limited effect. General Westmoreland chose to rely on existing forces and doctrine, which led to conventional operations in the face of a guerrilla threat. Military organizations changed gradually, and General Abrams took advantage by dedicating forces quite explicitly to a pacification role, but by that time, Hanoi had shifted to focus on conventional operations. In addition, the deterioration in the quality of the U.S. forces, rent by racial and antiwar sentiments, created a fresh weakness that substituted for the earlier problem of conventional orientation. Thus the mismatch continued. At the same time, Saigon's lesser dedication to pacification retarded progress in that area, even as the clock ran down. Meanwhile, commanders were unable to devise a truly effective aerial campaign. Worse, the political necessity for the White House to extend the time on the clock forced the withdrawal of U.S. forces. The final formula of a reliance on naval and air power to back a South Vietnamese force suffered from the same inadequacies General Matthew Ridgway had criticized at Dien Bien Phu: remote intervention lacked traction without U.S. boots on the ground. And by 1972 the envelope for action had become so narrowly circumscribed by America's war over the war that troops were out of the question. There was no strategy capable of producing victory. The combination of intractable elements and intrinsic difficulties crippled military approaches to the war.

One point cannot be emphasized enough. All this discussion presumes that beyond the specifics that applied to Vietnam there existed, somewhere in theory, a strategy that would have worked. But all along, presidents made their decisions against larger historical tides. The whole world, not just Vietnam, underwent a metamorphosis after 1945, acknowledging nationalism, banishing empires, and recognizing sovereignties, communist or not. The Vietnamese revolution flowed with that tide. America's intervention struggled against it. The overlay of Cold War ideology among U.S. officials became an impediment to understanding those dynamics. A transformation within American society, one that enshrined individual activism in service of social goals, one that presidents turned against themselves, also hampered their efforts. These forces posed huge obstacles to U.S. victory. No mere military strategy could succeed without taking them into account, and no proposed strategy ever did.

Since the military, in particular the Joint Chiefs of Staff, has been accused of dereliction of duty, it must be recorded that the charge is misleading. This arose from Lyndon Johnson's 1964–1965 incremental decisions on bombing and troops, where the Chiefs stand accused of being tacticians rather than strategists. Surveying military advice over the broad span of the war reveals a different picture. The advice of the JCS, and that of specific Chiefs, varied. Truman's military advisers took an essentially neutral position, while Eisenhower's were divided. His JCS chairman, Arthur Radford, was definitely in step with his president, saved from disaster by a brave Army chief of staff who sacrificed his career to do it. Even with Radford, Eisenhower's Chiefs united to warn him that Indochina was devoid of any decisive strategic objectives worth fighting for. That was not tactical advice. It was also the opposite of dereliction.

In the Kennedy-Johnson period the Chiefs were less imaginative but, I think, not derelict. The argument that the Chiefs should have fallen on their swords for "decisive" intervention founders on the realities of logistics and geography. Given the existing South Vietnamese road and transport network, the U.S. troop deployment, incremental as it was, proved about as rapid as it could have been. That the Chiefs did not threaten resignation to force national mobilization is also understandable: their role was to furnish political-military advice, not military advice only, and by 1967 Johnson had amply shown where his political boundaries lay. Different arguments are possible: the Chiefs lacked imagination, evolving a litany of proposals they trotted out on each suitable occasion, or, alternatively, trying to stay close to their presidents, the Chiefs put White House goals ahead of military ones. If the Joint Chiefs were derelict, it was in not understanding Vietnam and not warning their presidents that pursuit of the war conflicted with global U.S. commitments, and that if the extra troops were not available, the time had come to phase out.

Early on, Army Chief Harold Johnson went some distance toward that position, telling LBJ that half a million men might be necessary, but he left the president to draw his own conclusions and did not fight the issue through the full JCS. Nevertheless, the Army chief's action flies in the face of the claim that the Joint Chiefs restricted themselves to "tactical" advice. So does the Chiefs' 1965 proposal for intensive bombing of Hanoi-Haiphong, which LBJ rejected. The Chiefs' failure was one shared by the whole U.S. bureaucracy, which never squarely confronted the president with the choice of going ahead versus getting out. As the neutralization of George Ball's objections and the handling of the Nixon transition policy review show, the bureaucracy actively worked to suppress the withdrawal option. The one time a president was given this alternative, when Bundy and McNamara alluded to it in their "fork in the road" memorandum, withdrawal was posed as a false choice and set up for rejection.

During Richard Nixon's presidency the Joint Chiefs of Staff could not be aggressive enough to satisfy the White House. Admiral Thomas Moorer and his predecessor General Earle Wheeler were clearly in tune with their presidents, and they suggested aggressive actions but displayed appropriate caution too, such as when the JCS argued against Duck Hook at the last minute. The Chiefs were telling the president what he did *not* want to hear. They were also making strategic arguments, not tactical ones. Was that derelict? Mr. Nixon constantly ran ahead of his military commanders in demanding action.

Dien Bien Phu merits special comment. That crisis is more than an analogy and of greater import—critical as that is—than simply the battle that ended the French colony of Indochina. Rather, this 1954 climax of the Franco-Vietnamese war had a fundamental importance, laying down a sort of genetic code. It influenced everything that followed. Dien Bien Phu not only shaped some of the intractable elements of the second war (through the Geneva agreements); it led Dwight D. Eisenhower to accept an obligation to a local ally certain to renew the war and, in the 1955 sect crisis, to the United States giving up its leverage over the situation. Dien Bien Phu conditioned the thinking of key players, including three American presidents, Thieu and his commanders, many of Hanoi's leaders, and even principals in the antiwar movement. The crisis led to creation of the SEATO alliance, which gave

American leaders a false sense that intervention would enjoy support at home and abroad. Dien Bien Phu also produced significant military results that generals on both sides would aspire to emulate. It furnished a model and strategy for a specific key battle of the American war—Khe Sanh—and appreciation of its import led Hanoi to frame the crucial deception for the most important campaign, Tet. Dien Bien Phu gave Richard Nixon the strategic concept he adopted as U.S. troops left the war—a return to air and naval power. And it would be invoked repeatedly on all sides of the conflict—by American generals advocating bombing strategy, others mesmerized by the potential for repetition as they tried to interpret the evidence for Tet, and North Vietnamese planners of the Easter offensive, not to mention Hanoi's air defense officers extolling their efforts to blunt the Christmas Bombing.

Other key passages of this history range from the well marked to the hardly noticed. The Diem coup, the failure to hold post-Geneva elections in 1956, and the Tet offensive are among the former. Less known, though attracting more attention recently, is Truman's inattention to Ho Chi Minh's nascent Vietnamese state in 1945–1946, when some judicious prodding of France might have prevented the Indochina wars in the first place. Virtually unknown is the decision made in 1945 to supply Allied shipping for the transport of a French Expeditionary Corps to the Far East. Technical military experts thought of soldiers only in terms of an invasion of Japan, but the potential for French forces to reimpose colonial control over Indochina should have been obvious in Allied political councils. Again, a simple measure would have completely avoided the Indochina war, though in this case the matter may have fallen through the cracks due to confusion in the interregnum between Roosevelt's presidency and that of his successor. Truman's decision to accord military aid to France in Indochina in 1950, based on Cold War considerations, represents acquiescence to French efforts to paint black hats on the Vietminh, framing the Vietnamese revolution as an anticommunist crusade. Washington never escaped from this characterization, and it limited subsequent opportunities to appreciate Vietnamese realities, contributing to the Vietnam data problem, among other things.

Vietnam histories, including those of the antiwar movement, have failed to appreciate the full import of the fall 1967 march on the Pentagon. That became the moment that Lyndon Johnson built the big white jailhouse that trapped him and his successors. Ordering a war against the American people was not a formula for success. With the inception of the FBI's "New Left" program, the CIA's Project CHAOS, the NSA's Operations Shamrock and Minaret, and the DIA's military intelligence infiltration of the Movement, *every* element of the U.S. intelligence apparatus, not to mention local police, operated against Americans. The Johnson administration burned the bridges that might have led to a national consensus even if a Great Debate had been conducted. Presidents themselves narrowed the envelope for their actions.

The range of what was acceptable is well illustrated by the question of a U.S. withdrawal from Vietnam. Dwight Eisenhower forfeited the option in the 1955 Saigon crisis and ended by eliminating U.S. leverage. John Kennedy tried but failed to use the threat of withdrawal to regain that leverage. His move toward early Vietnamization has caused deep confusion among JFK fans, who insist Kennedy was on the brink of pulling out, but the claim is not sustainable in the face of the president's simultaneous escalation in Laos. Lyndon Johnson toyed with withdrawal, but only rhetorically as a product of his frustrations with Saigon leaders. Richard Nixon actually implemented a withdrawal, but for the purpose of gaining a free hand for military measures and because he had no political alternative. With the possible exception of Kennedy, on whom further evidence may yet emerge, none of these men considered simply getting out of Vietnam because the game was no good. That reluctance, in itself, locked them into an increasingly ferocious, increasingly frustrating war.

Some developments that might have marked key passages were inconclusive. Pacification is one. Flooding South Vietnam with U.S. troops and bombing the North, along with early efforts at pacification, generated little momentum in the village war until the Vietnamese squandered their National Liberation Front at Tet. Thereafter a new dedication under a visionary commander achieved considerable progress. Had it happened in 1962 or 1964, a pacification breakthrough might have been an important milestone. But if, to take the hypothetical, General Abrams had been appointed to MACV in 1964, he would have been hampered by the conventional war orientation of U.S. forces, yet to learn that their tactics were inadequate, and distracted by managing the U.S. deployment. Despite his insight, Abrams might not have done any better than Westmoreland. The later success of pacification proved misleading because Tet changed the texture of the war itself, because the data problem conveyed a mistaken impression of actual conditions, and because South Vietnamese society also mutated.

At the conventional level, Washington invaded Cambodia in 1970 but could not sustain the operation due to the political upheaval it triggered. A year later a full-scale effort to isolate the battlefield by cutting the Ho Chi Minh Trail failed in Laos with the collapse of a South Vietnamese offensive. And in 1972 when the North Vietnamese captured territory in the South, Saigon could not eject them. The trend in those developments is plain. Expecting South Vietnam to turn the tide without the United States when it had not been able to do so with the Americans at its side was wishful thinking.

Artfully concealed was the impact of the 1971 invasion of Laos. That Nixon Shock impelled the antiwar movement to its own unprecedented spring offensive, one that brought to the forefront the new shock troops of

VVAW and signaled that the Washington clock had just about run out. In treating the Laotian failure primarily as a public relations problem, the Nixon administration was obliged to handle the South Vietnamese performance gaps the invasion revealed as simple technical matters—things to be resolved by equipment and money. In truth, this fiasco uncovered fundamental flaws in Vietnamization at a moment when Washington and Saigon still had a year or more to recast the ARVN as a truly supple and effective instrument. Continuing business as usual meant Saigon would confront Hanoi in the post-U.S. period with armed forces outmatched by the adversary. If, in fact, U.S. officials did not perceive the flaws of Vietnamization— ones openly discussed within the antiwar movement—that only compounds the error here.

The other Nixon Shocks scared the hell out of the American people but largely accelerated existing trends. Cambodia led to important restrictions on the subsequent employment of U.S. forces, but those limits were in the cards anyway as MACV strength fell and Nixon's desire to avoid American casualties continued. A possible exception might be the Haiphong mining, because it showed that China and the Soviet Union had become less enamored of Hanoi, but the revelation did not lead to freedom of action for Nixon because his operational envelope had virtually disappeared. Thus these Shocks do not rise to the level of turning points.

A word is necessary on Hanoi's alliances and their impact on U.S. strategy. Any escalation to a superpower conflict was an unacceptable consequence of action in Vietnam, as Eisenhower recognized as early as Dien Bien Phu.[6] No subsequent president deviated from that rule. The Soviets had troops in North Vietnam throughout the American war, until the Paris agreement. China had forces in the DRV from 1964 through 1969. The chances of Soviet or Chinese intervention, and later of counterescalation, were incalculable, but more important, they were *unknown*. In Washington, U.S. presidents had intelligence estimates of the probability of counterintervention, but that was all they had. National security advisers such as Walt Rostow or military figures like Admiral Moorer could argue that it was not likely but could never prove their case. In the face of this uncertainty, President Johnson was right to avoid actions that might trigger forceful involvement by the Soviets or Chinese. Nixon followed suit. The option of an invasion of North Vietnam—which the CIA evaluated as *likely* to bring counterescalation—was never really on the table. Both Johnson and Nixon flirted with the idea, most directly LBJ in 1967, but there was only one possible answer when a president asked what the communist response would be. The likelihood was simply unknown; therefore, all possibilities had to be taken into account. In the face of that uncertainty, and cued by press leaks that any invasion would shock Americans, Johnson dropped the idea. There is no gainsaying his decision. And for all the period until the Cambodian invasion, Hanoi managed to avoid any overt break with its allies and even, in the face of the Sino-Soviet split, succeeded in keeping them both pretty closely aligned with it. As late as 1972 the Soviet Union was willing to deploy a counter–aircraft carrier capability (in the form of cruise missile submarines) in the South China Sea on the occasion of the mining of Haiphong. The threat of intervention was submerged but very potent. Nixon, significantly, chose to elicit a measure of bilateral cooperation with both Moscow and Beijing *before* feeling secure enough to try the Christmas Bombing. Lyndon Johnson had rejected that same option in September 1965, and for the same reason—the small but incalculable danger of a wider war.

To this day, war defenders and neo-orthodox historians have been unable to propose a convincing argument for how the Vietnam war could have been won. "Decisive" intervention, pacification, and bombing were options that had to be carried out in the context of specific diplomatic, geographic, logistical, and doctrinal conditions; with a given force posture; and subject to the intractable elements and intrinsic difficulties that applied to Vietnam. The perfect strategies revolved around options that were always on the menu and were either tried and found wanting or never really practical. Divorcing the options from their political and military context to claim feasibility is not acceptable analysis. And in the moment, befuddled by the Vietnam data problem, faced with contradictory advice from aides whose understanding of the requirements of insurgency warfare was imperfect, while confronting a running clock, presidents could never achieve a proper strategy.

Failing to get past these conundrums, some of the defenders and the neo-orthodox have resorted to the proposition that the United States *did* win in Vietnam. Aside from the fact that Hanoi's troops ended the conflict by marching into Saigon, and not the other way around, this claim ignores a plethora of evidence. In explaining the actual outcome, proponents are forced into a stab-in-the-back argument: Congress lost the war, the Movement lost the war, the press, or whatever. These explanations trivialize historical forces: the social, political, and economic dynamics at work in Vietnam, the United States, and the world. They also distort the political and military events that defined its actual course. The atomization of the history of the war has, until now, made trivialization and distortion easier. Triumph was not forsaken in Vietnam, nor victory lost; there was no day that the war was won, except for Hanoi on April 29, 1975, when its troops marched into Saigon.

■ ■ ■ That debate is past and ultimately sterile. More useful is to ask why the North won. There are levels and layers of reasons, some of Vietnamese agency, some larger, and some the obverse of elements discussed earlier. One vital reason is that Hanoi had the power of an idea on its side, unmatched and unmatchable in the South: the goal of reunification of the nation. That idea had already powered the French war and captured the hopes and dreams of Vietnamese. From the day the Geneva agreements were abrogated by refusal to countenance the 1956 unification elections, those hopes and dreams stood ready to be harnessed in a renewed effort to attain the same goal. Considering the privations to which the North Vietnamese and Liberation Front fighters were subjected—at home under the bombing, infiltrating down The Trail, and in the field in the South—the tactical disadvantages they tolerated, the U.S. and South Vietnamese firepower they had to withstand, and the endless duration of service at the front, *only* a dream could have fueled their efforts. No system of oppression or inculcation of communist ideology would have sufficed to maintain morale in the face of those obstacles. Moreover, the Vietnamese goal—and here is the larger dynamic—flowed in tandem with the global tide of decolonization and the U.S. endeavor against it. This weakened the Americans in their war, making it more difficult to recruit loyal allies and easier for Hanoi to call on the peoples and governments of third countries both to oppose the Americans and to press for peace.

On a practical level, Hanoi achieved and preserved a closer integration of political and military elements throughout. These included the creation and work of parallel hierarchies of administrative structures that matched Saigon's government apparatus in the South, the popular associations that enrolled all manner of people in the struggle, the coordination of political and military activities, and the *dau tranh* proselytizing, which, for whatever insincerity, coercion, and hype it featured, at least represented constant attention to the people. South Vietnamese and U.S. counterefforts wavered and came late, hampered by their own insincerity, corruption, cultural inappropriateness, and, of course, the Vietnam data problem.

On the military side, the system of political indoctrination applied within the Vietnam People's Army and the People's Liberation Armed Forces, irrespective of communist ideology, created tightly knit units of combat forces with cohesion superior to those of Saigon and—beginning with the decline of the American forces in the late 1960s—the United States as well. The fact that the VPA and PLAF had to build their capability under the gun, as a result of U.S. efforts to interdict them, also meant that forces in the field already represented a hard kernel of effectiveness. The ARVN, operating openly, was softer. The insurgents, except for the local PLAF guerrillas, also did not have to worry about, or defend, their families, as did the ARVN. And over time the People's Army increased its capabilities until it could match the ARVN in conventional warfare.

At the strategic level, Hanoi exhibited a willingness to make and execute necessary decisions in a timely fashion, in contrast to Saigon, which resisted making key changes. The contrast is palpable between Hanoi's willingness to retrench in the post-Tet situation, after sustaining major losses, and Saigon's refusal to do this in 1973–1975 until the moment when withdrawal meant rout. As a result, the VPA and PLAF were able to ride out the crisis of confidence in 1968–1969, while in the later instance Saigon collapsed. Hanoi made seven major strategic decisions during the war: in 1959 to support the southern insurgents, in 1964 to commit regulars, in 1965 and afterward to match U.S. escalation, in 1967 to mount the Tet offensive, in 1968 to reorient itself toward conventional operations, in 1971 to undertake the Easter offensive, and in 1974 to begin the probes that became the rolling offensive that ended the war. In each case the decisions exhibited a deliberative process that weighed the potential benefits with some realism, a willingness to accept risk, and careful and precise implementation.

This is not to say that Hanoi did everything right. The Tet decision clearly overestimated political support in the South for the Liberation Front. The idea that a general uprising would occur was either wishful thinking or based on poor intelligence. While we are on the subject, the Tet aftermath also provides a clue to the true status of the war situation. Having lost so many fighters put Hanoi in its weakest position of the war, its morale as low as it would get. The Americans were still at peak strength, and into 1969, troop reductions had yet to bite much. The South Vietnamese had gained confidence from enduring Tet. The United States had its best field commander at the helm and had finally installed a comprehensive pacification organization. If ever there were a moment to win the war, that was it. Yet the VPA and NLF weathered the crisis, for three reasons in my view. First was Hanoi's timely decision to pull back into the base areas. Second came the equally well-managed shift to tactics of commando attack plus bombardments behind a screen of main-force units as the primary mode of offensive operations. Third—and back to the Vietnam data problem—Hanoi had been stronger going into Tet than Washington gave it credit for.

At the operational level, a significant mistake occurred in 1972, when People's Army forces along the Demilitarized Zone halted after their initial breakthrough instead of pressing on to Hue. This lull gave the ARVN precious time to recover its balance. Some of this hiatus was undoubtedly required to reposition troops and equipment, but the halt proved excessive. The reasons are open to debate but likely relate to the fact that although the VPA had made the transition, it remained as yet inexperienced at conventional war.

Hanoi's allies were not the source of its victory. The Soviet Union and China exercised an important influence in several ways, however. The DRV's alliances in themselves prevented the United States from attempting such options as invading North Vietnam, a big plus. Their military equipment armed the DRV's air defenses against U.S. bombing, which raised the cost of Washington's interdiction campaign and provided the means to motorize infiltration. They also played a key role in providing Hanoi with the types of equipment that facilitated the shift to conventional warfare after 1968. But at no time in the war—including after the Paris agreements—did communist aid to North Vietnam overmatch the amount of aid Saigon received from the United States. The DRV's alliances helped accelerate the war, but they did not change the distribution of forces.

The North Vietnamese suffered from their own version of the Vietnam data problem. Cadres under pressure to produce results consistently filed exaggerated reports on U.S. and South Vietnamese losses, population control, and the rest, which became a source of the Tet error. But on the whole, Hanoi was well informed. Despite its lack of good strategic intelligence on Washington decision making, the DRV had the Saigon government so thoroughly penetrated that no major South Vietnamese move could occur without it knowing. Exemplified by the activities of Pham Xuan Anh, the work of DRV and NLF spies made allied war strategy almost an open book for Hanoi and COSVN.

North Vietnamese diplomacy may have been the weakest link in Hanoi's apparat. Historian Robert K. Brigham has used the phrase "guerrilla diplomacy" to describe Liberation Front efforts in this area, but the concept can be applied more widely than that.[7] The key point is that Hanoi trained its diplomatic corps in the bush, during the French war. With little experience and no diplomatic tradition, the corps was drawn primarily from the ranks of the military. Colonel Ha Van Lau, a key negotiator at Geneva in 1954 and an ongoing participant in the diplomacy of the 1960s, furnishes a case in point. For Hanoi, diplomacy took a backseat to political-military strategy. The ideological strictures of communism did not help when it came to the finesse of statesmanship. But the rigidities of DRV negotiators also relate back to the dream of reunification, and as a result, only a narrow range of outcomes was ever acceptable to Hanoi. The most that could be accomplished—and was—would be a truce that postponed the day of reckoning. A true peace, a diplomatic settlement of the American war, lay beyond reach.

■ ■ ■ If that was Vietnam, what is Iraq? The analogy between the two is uncommonly apt, though not in the way President Bush would have liked. This narrative has encountered numerous instances in which processes for making decisions, laying down strategies, creating data problems, manipulating public opinion, and forfeiting leverage over the local ally in the current war mimic those of the past one. There are many more that have not been specifically underlined. This is disturbing not only because it happened at all but also because President Bush and his colleagues saw themselves as *avoiding* the mistakes of Vietnam and putting to rest the "Vietnam syndrome." The Bush administration was fortunate in that its adversaries lacked the coherence and organization of those in Vietnam. It is too soon to speak of outcomes in Iraq, but the outlook at this writing is for a continuing and grinding stalemate, with the Iraqi government using the cloak of U.S. power to prop it up as it settles accounts with hated religious and ethnic groups. Like Vietnam, where intervention was itself a distraction from America's Cold War conflict, the Iraq fixation kept Washington's focus away from the real central front of the terrorism war in Afghanistan. Iraq is already more expensive in treasure than Vietnam, and the jury remains out on how costly it will be in blood and sacrifice. Yet it seems clear this war will ultimately contribute as little to U.S. security as did the tragic Southeast Asian conflict. Indeed, the deteriorating American position in the parallel war in Afghanistan suggests that Iraq's contribution will be a negative one.

People, legislatures, and media in the United States and elsewhere, in both wars, were reactive, not in control. In Vietnam, at least, the awakening of individuals in many places—in the military command and the bureaucracies, among the public, in the ranks of the armed services—to the insanity of an effort to reverse the tide of history shortened a war that proceeded with unimaginable violence and no possibility of a different outcome. People are the unsung heroes of the Vietnam war. In Iraq the game is still afoot. Presidents and generals drove the diplomatic and military machinery through much of the American war in Vietnam and all of the Iraqi conflict so far. Theirs is the ultimate responsibility.

Notes

.

Abbreviations

The following abbreviations are used in the notes. Also see the list of acronyms for additional terms used in both the text and the notes.

CFVN	Country File: Vietnam
CO	country
DCI	director of central intelligence
DDEL	Dwight D. Eisenhower Library
EBB	Electronic Briefing Book (of the National Security Archive)
FOIA	Freedom of Information Act
FRUS	*Foreign Relations of the United States*
GRFL	Gerald R. Ford Library
GRFP	Gerald R. Ford Papers
HQ	headquarters
LBJL	Lyndon Baines Johnson Library
LBJP	Lyndon Baines Johnson Papers
MSS	Manuscript Series (at SHSW)
NARA	National Archives and Records Administration
ND	National Defense
NIACT	night action (cable priority)
NLP	Nixon Library Project (of NARA)
NSAF	National Security Adviser's Files
NSF	National Security File
PHF	President's Handwriting File
POF	President's Office File
PPF	President's Personal Files
SHSW	State Historical Society of Wisconsin
WHCF	White House Central Files
WHSF	White House Special Files
WSO	Winter Soldier Organization

In the following notes I attempted to make the materials as accessible as possible for scholars. Therefore I cited documents from the most widely available sources, such as the *Foreign Relations of the United States* series or other sets of collected documents, in preference to the archival locations of the materials, because the books are widely held in libraries and are even available in part on the Internet. Although the archival citations look good, and other scholars and I did much of the spadework in filing the declassification requests that led to the opening of many of these materials, this course is preferable to enable others to retrace the research. Beginning in 1977 I filed thousands of requests to release Vietnam material from the National Archives and every presidential library save Truman's (where I pursued different research interests) using procedures for Mandatory Declassification Review, from agencies using the FOIA, and directly or through colleagues at the National Security Archive using both mechanisms. I do cite some archival or FOIA materials below, primarily where they are not available from more accessible sources or where the original documents are more complete than their published versions.

April 1971: Veterans at War

1. H. R. Haldeman, *The Haldeman Diaries: Inside the Nixon White House* (New York: G. P. Putnam's Sons, 1994), 261.

2. The U.S. operation to clear the Vietnamese side of the border to support a South Vietnamese invasion had been called Dewey Canyon II. The original Dewey Canyon, carried out in early 1969, had been a foray into southern Laos by a U.S. Marine Corps battalion intent on blocking North Vietnamese troops moving on the Ho Chi Minh Trail.

3. VVAW national office, *Newsletter* 71, no. 1 (March 1971): 1, SHSW, Collection MSS-370/VVAW, box 13, folder "10: Programs: Dewey Canyon III, 1971 April, General Information."

4. The quote is from a speech Agnew gave on September 30, 1969. See Charles DeBenedetti with Charles Chatfield, *An American Ordeal: The Antiwar Movement of the Vietnam Era* (Syracuse, NY: Syracuse University Press, 1990), 258. Agnew continued to use highly inflammatory rhetoric, attacking youth and the antiwar movement on numerous occasions.

5. Quoted in Andrew E. Hunt, *The Turning: A History of Vietnam Veterans Against the War* (New York: New York University Press, 1999), 88.

6. FBI, Washington Field Office–Director, Telegram 100-47162, April 15, 1971, FBI files, HQ 100-448092 section 2 (declassified October 29, 1993).

7. Nixon Oval Office telephone conversation 42-54, April 16, 1971, 11:06 AM, NARA, NLP, Tape Subject Log.

8. White House memorandum, "Telephone Call Recommendation: Frank Sinatra," March 2, 1971, NARA, NLP, WHSF, PHF, box 6, folder "President's Handwriting, March 1–15, 1971."

9. Quoted in Tom Wells, *The War Within: America's Battle over Vietnam* (Berkeley: University of California Press, 1994), 447. Colson's bragging seems misplaced, since the students delivered an antiwar petition, not an expression of support. Nixon complained about them after they left. Elsewhere, the National Student Association had friendly relations with other Movement groups and shared office space with some.

10. White House memorandum, Charles W. Colson–Richard Nixon, April 7, 1971, NARA, NLP, WHSF, PHF, box 10, folder "President's Handwriting April 1–15, 1971."

11. UPI dispatch, UPI-75, April 16, 1971, from FBI files.

12. Quoted in John Kerry and Vietnam Veterans Against the War, *The New Soldier,* ed. David Thorne and George Butler (New York: Collier, 1971), 96.

13. Quoted in Hunt, *Turning,* 97.

14. This story was first related by columnist Mary McGrory a few days later and first appeared in a book by *New York Times* reporter Gloria Emerson, *Winners and Losers* (New York: Random House, 1976), 331. It has appeared in every subsequent account of Dewey Canyon III. McGrory commented that the vets were probably no more bedraggled than those of George Washington's Continental Army in the American Revolution, whom the DAR venerated. See Gerald Nicosia, *Home to War: A History of the Vietnam Veteran's Movement* (New York: Crown, 2001), 111.

15. Quoted in Glenn A. McCurdy, "The Last Patrol," *Washington Star Sunday Magazine,* June 6, 1971.

16. Ibid.

17. According to VVAW organizer Frank Toner, the vote was 494 to 464 to stay on the Mall (interview, June 4, 1994). Other sources record the vote, which was by a show of hands, at about 480 to 460. VVAW organizers met with police officials and agreed that if an arrest were attempted, they would leave peaceably. The District of Columbia Police Department, which itself included many Vietnam veterans, was not anxious to carry out such an order. McCurdy quotes one D.C. officer whose beat was the Mall: "These guys have paid their dues in full. If you think I'd shove some wounded guy out on the street or in a wagon, forget it!"

18. Joe Urgo interview, New York City, May 25, 2002.

19. *Washington Daily News,* April 22, 1971.

20. Haldeman, *Haldeman Diaries,* 278.

21. U.S. District Court for the District of Columbia, Civil Action 688-69, transcript of proceedings, April 22, 1971, pp. 8–9, SHSW, MSS-370, VVAW-WSO, box 13, folder "12: Programs: Dewey Canyon III, 1971 April: Transcript of Court Hearings."

22. Nixon Oval Office telephone conversation no. 42-63, April 21, 1971, 2:31 PM.

23. This is a reference to a 1970 speech by Agnew in which the vice president stated, "Some glamorize the criminal misfits of society while our best men die in Asian rice paddies to preserve the freedom which most of those misfits abuse."

24. John Kerry testimony before the Senate Foreign Relations Committee, *Congressional Record,* April 23, 1971, S5550–5551.

25. William Crandell, "They Moved the Town," in *Give Peace a Chance: Exploring the Vietnam Antiwar Movement,* ed. Melvin Small and William D. Hoover (Syracuse, NY: Syracuse University Press, 1992).

Chapter 1. A Splendid Little War

1. Treatments of these issues include Christopher Thorne, *Allies of a Kind: The United States, Britain, and the War against Japan, 1941–1945* (New York: Oxford University Press, 1978), and Edward R. Drachman, *United States Policy toward Vietnam, 1940–1945* (Rutherford, NJ: Fairleigh Dickinson University Press, 1970). These issues are also touched on by Richard D. Aldrich in his *Intelligence and the War against Japan: Britain, America and the Politics of Secret Service* (Cambridge: Cambridge University Press, 2000).

2. The best French accounts of the period are General Georges Catroux, *Deux Actes du Drame Indochinoise* (Paris: Plon, 1959); Admiral Jean Decoux, *A la barre de l'Indochine* (Paris: Plon, 1952); General Gabriel Sabattier, *Le Destin de l'Indochine: Souvenirs et documents, 1941–1951* (Paris: Plon, 1952); and Philippe Devillers, *Histoire de Vietnam de 1940 a 1952* (Paris: Editions de Seuil, 1952). In English see Joseph Buttinger, *Vietnam: A Dragon Embattled* (New York: Praeger, 1967), and David G. Marr's several works: *Vietnamese Anticolonialism, 1885–1925* (Berkeley: University of California Press, 1971); *Vietnamese Tradition on Trial, 1920–1945* (Berkeley: University of California Press, 1981); and *Vietnam 1945: The Quest for Power* (Berkeley: University of California Press, 1996). Marr is currently working on a project that will extend his account through the beginning of the French war and the formation of the Vietnam People's Army.

3. Documents and records of the OSS in Indochina have been declassified and are now available at the National Archives. A selection of these records has long been available in U.S. Congress, Senate Foreign Relations Committee, *Hearings: Causes, Origins and Lessons of the Vietnam War* (Washington, DC: Government Printing Office, 1973). For a memoir of this OSS experience, see Archimedes L. Patti, *Why Viet Nam? Prelude to America's Albatross* (Berkeley: University of California Press, 1980). A detailed history is Dixee R.

Bartholomew-Feis, *The OSS and Ho Chi Minh: Unexpected Allies in the War against Japan* (Lawrence: University Press of Kansas, 2006).

4. See Hoai Thanh et al., *Days with Ho Chi Minh* (Hanoi: Foreign Languages Publishing House, 1962); Vo Nguyen Giap, *Unforgettable Days* (Hanoi: Foreign Languages Publishing House, 1978); Truong Chinh, *Primer for Revolt: The Communist Takeover in Vietnam* (New York: Frederick A. Praeger, 1963); John T. McAlister Jr., *Viet Nam: The Origins of Revolution* (New York: Alfred A. Knopf, 1969); Stein Tonnesson, *The Vietnamese Revolution of 1945: Roosevelt, Ho Chi Minh, and de Gaulle in a World at War* (London: Sage, 1991); and Marr, *Vietnam 1945*.

5. A recent account that shows the difficult situations throughout the SEAC area as well as in China is Ronald Spector's *In the Ruins of Empire: The Japanese Surrender and the Battle for Postwar Asia* (New York: Random House, 2007).

6. The best account of these events is Peter M. Dunn, *The First Vietnam War* (New York: St. Martin's Press, 1985).

7. Contemporary OSS reports noted that the weapons had been given to the Vietminh by the Japanese, but historians David Marr and Stein Tonnesson both reject this suspicion. Marr notes that the Japanese furnished the Vietminh with a certain number of *French* weapons. Some Japanese soldiers also deserted to the Vietminh; estimates of the total range up to 4,500 (Patti, *Why Viet Nam,* 341, puts the number at 4,000), but a few hundred fighters seems to be the most reliable figure (Bartholomew-Feis, *OSS and Ho Chi Minh,* 274–277). The most extensive inquiry into this issue is Christopher Goscha's "Belated Asian Allies: The Technical and Military Contributions of Japanese Deserters (1945–1950)," in *A Companion to the Vietnam War,* ed. Marilyn B. Young and Robert Buzzanco (Malden, MA: Blackwell, 2002), 37–64. Also see John T. McAlister, *Vietnam: The Origins of Revolution* (Garden City, NY: Doubleday Anchor, 1971).

8. Quoted in Bartholomew-Feis, *OSS and Ho Chi Minh,* 290.

9. Department of State memorandum, James C. Dunn–Edward R. Stettinius, April 23, 1945, quoted in Lloyd C. Gardner, *Approaching Vietnam: From World War II through Dien Bien Phu* (New York: W. W. Norton, 1988), 58.

10. Quoted in *The Senator Gravel Edition: The Pentagon Papers: The Defense Department History of United States Decisionmaking on Vietnam* (Boston: Beacon Press, [1971]), 1: 16–17 (hereafter *Gravel Pentagon Papers*).

11. In fact, although France was an American ally, it consistently followed an independent course and actually proved much less pliant on the German occupation than Truman might have expected. For example, France held out for its own occupation zones, disputed where in Germany these should be, refused to join these zones into a common area, and opposed rearming Germany to meet the Soviet threat, all elements going back to France's historical conflicts with the Germans. How much Truman gained by favoring Paris is questionable.

12. Franco-Vietnamese agreement, March 6, 1946, in *Gravel Pentagon Papers,* 1: 18–19.

13. State Department cable, December 5, 1946, in *Gravel Pentagon Papers,* 1: 20–21.

14. Jean-Pierre Rioux, *The Fourth Republic, 1944–1958,* trans. Godfrey Rogers (Cambridge: Cambridge University Press, 1987), 94.

15. Quoted in Leclerc report, January 1947, in *Gravel Pentagon Papers,* 1: 24–25.

16. State Department cable, May 13, 1947, in *Gravel Pentagon Papers,* 1: 31–32.

17. State Department cable, July 1948, in *Gravel Pentagon Papers,* 1: 33–34.

18. During 2001–2002, I made an effort to address the Vietnamese revolution as an independent variable, presenting at least four talks to historians, including one to a mixed audience of secondary school teachers and university professors at a summer study workshop, one to a college history class, the others to professional groups. I argued that the Cold War context was not necessary to the evolution of events in Indochina. In every case this thesis proved highly controversial. Lacking empirical evidence, one might infer that the French

were amazingly successful in their campaign to cast Indochina as a Cold War battlefield or, more likely, that from the Americans' perspective, it is more comforting to view the Vietnam conflict as a battle lost amid a war that was won. See Arthur M. Schlesinger Jr., *The Bitter Heritage* (Greenwich, CT: Fawcett, 1967). An early discussion of underlying causes is in Noam Chomsky and Howard Zinn, eds., *The Pentagon Papers: The Senator Gravel Edition,* vol. 5, *Critical Essays* (Boston: Beacon Press, 1972). For a more recent exegesis, see Jeffrey Kimball, ed., *To Reason Why* (Philadelphia: Temple University Press, 1990).

March–July 1954: Dien Bien Phu, Geneva, and the Harnessing of American Power

1. John Prados, *Operation Vulture* (New York: iBooks, 2002), 105–107, 129–133, 160–166, 190–192, 200–203.

2. Chalmers M. Roberts, "The Day We Didn't Go to War," *Reporter,* September 14, 1954, 31–35.

3. For example, Melvin Gurtov, *The First Vietnam Crisis: Chinese Communist Strategy and United States Involvement, 1953–1954* (New York: Columbia University Press, 1967); Frank R. Brophy, "The Failure of US Policy toward Viet-Nam, 1953–1954" (master's thesis, Columbia University, 1962); Robert A. Devine, *Eisenhower and the Cold War* (New York: Oxford University Press, 1981); Richard Ned Lebow, *Between Peace and War: The Nature of International Crisis* (Baltimore: Johns Hopkins University Press, 1981). A more recent approach tends to take the conventional interpretation and build on it, as in John P. Burke and Fred I. Greenstein (with Larry Berman and Richard Immerman), *How Presidents Test Reality: Decisions on Vietnam, 1954 and 1965* (New York: Russell Sage Foundation, 1989), or in Yuen Foong Khong, *Analogies at War: Korea, Munich, Dien Bien Phu and the Vietnam Decisions of 1965* (Princeton, NJ: Princeton University Press, 1993). Historians Richard Immerman and Gary Hess represent transitional figures here, publishing papers on John Foster Dulles, Eisenhower's decision making, the "Bao Dai solution," and other Indochina issues that move closer to the view advanced here.

4. Dwight D. Eisenhower, *The White House Years,* vol. 1, *Mandate for Change, 1953–1956* (New York: New American Library, 1963), 420–421.

5. This point passed with little comment when I originally made it in 1983 in my book *The Sky Would Fall* (New York: William Morrow, 1983). I had worked from Eisenhower's papers and had observed his handwriting on drafts of the Dulles speech. Later, in his study of nuclear crises, McGeorge Bundy noticed the claim and checked with NSC and presidential secretaries, who confirmed that the handwriting was Eisenhower's. See McGeorge Bundy, *Danger and Survival* (New York: Random House, 1988), 264. The content of the changes Eisenhower made, such as converting conditional statements into positive assertions, is unmistakeable.

6. Quoted in Prados, *Operation Vulture,* 127.

7. Roberts, "The Day We Didn't Go to War," 105.

8. Quoted in Eisenhower, *Mandate for Change,* 419–420.

9. White House, *Public Papers of the Presidents: Dwight D. Eisenhower, 1954* (Washington, DC: Government Printing Office, 1955), 382.

10. Eisenhower's response also referred to Indochinese production of tin, tungsten, and rubber, affording some ammunition for proponents of an economic cause of the Vietnam war, but aside from this statement at a press conference, the administration's secret records contain no studies of Indochina's economic importance at this time, and documents bearing on security issues barely register economic interests. Bolivia was a much larger producer of tin than Indochina, and Malaya a more important producer of rubber; also, by this point in the 1950s, synthetic rubber was being widely produced, supplanting the natural product. Con-

versely, Eisenhower did not mention oil—which *was* a key product from Southeast Asia (Indonesia)—at all. In addition, the more important sources of these raw materials (Malaya, Indonesia) would be at risk only if other "dominos" actually fell. This suggests that Eisenhower's motives were other than economic.

11. Prados, *Operation Vulture*, 208–215, provides the most detailed discussion of this matter.

12. John Prados, "Ike, Ridgway, and Dien Bien Phu," *MHQ: The Quarterly Journal of Military History* 17, 4 (Summer 2005): 16–23.

13. Note that this interpretation follows my own work in *The Sky Would Fall* and *Operation Vulture*. The older, conventional view, first advanced by Chalmers Roberts and reiterated in 1988 by Melanie Billings-Yun in *Decision against War: Eisenhower and Dien Bien Phu, 1954* (New York: Columbia University Press, 1988), is that Eisenhower used his "hidden hand" tactics to configure obstacles to intervention to make this impossible. My view is that the evidence—in particular, the persistence of action schemes long after the fall of Dien Bien Phu and in spite of Washington's inability to recruit allies—presented here in some detail, renders that interpretation obsolete. It is worth noting that Roberts, who wrote a highly laudatory review of *The Sky Would Fall* in the *Washington Post,* telephoned me to express his admiration for that work and indicated that he himself no longer held the views expressed in his 1954 article and his 1973 book *First Rough Draft* (New York: Praeger, 1973). Roberts marveled that a "young" man could have captured so well the sense of the time and the inside story. He also said that his piece in the *Reporter* had been largely based on interviews with the legislators who attended the April 3, 1954, session with Dulles and Radford. He had no access to Eisenhower administration records, including its white paper on Indochina. Because Roberts's article had been so influential at the time, I think many later writers strove to reconcile the evolving evidence with that interpretation rather than letting the material speak for itself. The issue was further clouded because so much relevant material was declassified only between the mid-1980s and early 1990s, much of it the result of requests I filed during my own research.

14. The Cold War International History Project and Cornell University Cold War Project (with the Asia Program of the Wilson Center and the George Washington University Cold War Group), held a workshop titled "Reconsidering the 1954 Geneva Conference" in Washington, DC, on February 17–18, 2006, to assess these materials. Work is presently under way on both a collection of the Chinese documents and a set of papers that reflect the new evidence.

15. George C. Herring, *America's Longest War: The United States and Vietnam, 1950–1975* (New York: McGraw-Hill, 1996), 40.

16. The most recent statement of this version is advanced by Mark Moyar in *Triumph Forsaken: The Vietnam War, 1954–1965* (New York: Cambridge University Press, 2006). 28.

17. Philippe Devillers and Jean Lacouture, *End of a War: Indochina 1954* (New York: Praeger, 1969).

18. Prados, "Ike, Ridgway, and Dien Bien Phu."

19. Johnson's newsletters and constituent mail are in his prepresidential papers at the Johnson Library in Austin, Texas. The discussion here follows and quotes from Prados, *Operation Vulture*, 124–127.

20. A perceptive analysis of what Nixon carried away from Dien Bien Phu is provided by Jeffrey Kimball, *Nixon's Vietnam War* (Lawrence: University Press of Kansas, 1998), 23–24.

21. My view here is notably different from that of D. Gareth Porter, whose latest book, *The Perils of Dominance: Imbalance of Power and the Road to War in Vietnam* (Berkeley: University of California Press, 2005), argues that Eisenhower, Kennedy, and Johnson were *all* opposed to intervention in Vietnam both in 1954 and later and were trapped into it by their advisers. I believe that all these presidents harbored misgivings, but that is far from being ac-

tively opposed. I have presented *direct* evidence that this was not true for either Eisenhower or Johnson. In addition, in Eisenhower's case the notion that he was against intervention in Vietnam does not square with his treatment of either his adviser most opposed—General Ridgway—or the one most in favor—Admiral Radford. I believe that such a construction understates the identity of view between Eisenhower and Dulles and overstates the secretary of state's independence in the administration.

22. See Robert Buzzanco, *Masters of War: Military Dissent and Politics in the Vietnam Era* (Cambridge: Cambridge University Press, 1996). For Ridgway's own account, see Matthew B. Ridgway, *Soldier* (New York: Harper & Row, 1956).

23. "Agreement on the Cessation of Hostilities in Viet-Nam," July 20, 1954, and "Final Declaration of the Geneva Conference," July 21, 1954, in Allan W. Cameron, ed., *Viet-Nam Crisis: A Documentary History,* vol. 1, *1940–1956* (Ithaca, NY: Cornell University Press, 1971), 288–307.

24. Chester L. Cooper, *In the Shadows of History: 50 Years behind the Scenes of Cold War Diplomacy* (Amherst, NY: Prometheus, 2005), 113.

25. Geneva conference, verbatim record of the Eighth Plenary Session on Indochina, July 21, 1954, in Cameron, *Viet-Nam Crisis,* 314.

26. Ibid., 309–310.

27. One can debate whether a "solemn protest" as opposed to an outright rejection—which the Saigon government did not assert—carries any weight in international law as nullification of an agreement. The corollary question of whether a state that lacks de jure sovereignty has standing to reject an international agreement is also relevant here. But the framers of the Geneva agreements, by structuring them the way they did (as an international declaration not voted on or signed, along with a formal undertaking between the respective French and Vietminh high commands), made the question of rejection moot.

Chapter 2. Many Roads to Quagmire (1954–1960)

1. David L. Anderson, *Trapped by Success: The Eisenhower Administration and Vietnam, 1953–1961* (New York: Columbia University Press, 1991), 68–71.

2. *The Senator Gravel Edition: The Pentagon Papers: The Defense Department History of United States Decisionmaking on Vietnam* (Boston: Beacon Press, [1971]), 1: 215–217 (hereafter *Gravel Pentagon Papers*); Anderson, *Trapped by Success,* 71.

3. Quoted in John Prados, "The Numbers Game: How Many Vietnamese Fled South in 1954?" *VVA Veteran* 25, 1/2 (January–February 2005): 4 (http://www.vva.org/The Veteran/2005_01/feature_numbersGame.htm). Note that Eisenhower was already—deliberately—calling South Vietnam a "country."

4. Quoted in ibid., 8.

5. Letter, President Dwight D. Eisenhower–Prime Minister Ngo Dinh Diem, October 23, 1954, in Allan W. Cameron, ed., *Viet-Nam Crisis: A Documentary History,* vol. 1, *1940–1956* (Ithaca, NY: Cornell University Press, 1971), 349–350.

6. Quoted in John Prados, "Too Many Cards to Play: The First Diem Coup," *VVA Veteran* 20, 9/10 (October–November 2000): 10, from the declassified memorandum of the conversation.

7. A good account of this period is in Cecil B. Currey, *Edward Lansdale: The Unquiet American* (Boston: Houghton Mifflin, 1988), 145–147, 167–169.

8. General J. Lawton Collins's papers on this period are located at the Dwight D. Eisenhower Presidential Library of the National Archives and Records Administration in Abilene, Kansas. Declassified mostly in the last ten years, the Collins papers were not available to David Anderson, Cecil Currey, or most previous scholars of this period, but they are an eye-opening set of source materials. The best recent account of the events related here is in Seth

Jacobs, *America's Miracle Man in Vietnam: Ngo Dinh Diem, Religion, Race, and U.S. Intervention in Southeast Asia* (Durham, NC: Duke University Press, 2004), 172–216. Jacobs puts more emphasis on American officials (Collins) and Frenchmen acting in neocolonial fashion than I do, and he portrays John Foster Dulles as more uncertain than pictured here, but we are in close agreement on most points.

9. Untitled, undated memorandum ("*Problem:* To prepare plans for relieving the Binh Xuyen of control of the police and surete functions in the Saigon-Cholon area," [early 1955]), DDEL, J. Lawton Collins Papers, box 27, file "Binh Xuyen." Compare memorandum, Francis E. Meloy Jr.–J. Lawton Collins, "Alleged American Plan," February 14, 1955, ibid.

10. J. Lawton Collins memorandum, "Conversation with General Ely, March 29, 1955" (declassified July 25, 1987), Collins Papers, box 29, file "Memoranda for the Record."

11. CIA memorandum for the DCI, "The Crisis in Saigon," April 4, 1955, 5, in Office of the Director of National Intelligence, National Intelligence Council, *Estimative Products on Vietnam, 1948–1975,* NIC 2005-03, April 2005, document on attached CD-ROM.

12. Department of State cable, Washington–Saigon, 4330 (NIACT/EYES ONLY), April 4, 1955 (declassified April 7, 1987), Collins Papers, box 26, folder "Monthly Papers, April 1955 (3)."

13. John Foster Dulles notes, "Telephone Call to Mr. Allen Dulles," April 11, 1955, 11:15 AM, DDEL, John Foster Dulles Papers, Telephone Calls Series, box 3, folder "Conversations March 7–April 29, 1955 (2)."

14. State Department revised draft cable, Washington–Saigon, April 11, 1955, in Department of State, *FRUS, 1955–1957,* vol. 1, *Vietnam* (Washington, DC: Government Printing Office, 1985), 237–238.

15. Department of State cable, Saigon–Washington no. 4663, April 19, 1955, in U.S. Congress, House Armed Services Committee, *United States–Vietnam Relations 1945–1967* (Washington, DC: Government Printing Office, 1971), 10: 921 (hereafter *U.S.-GVN Relations*). The only experience from the time of the French war was the record of *French* intransigence in the face of U.S. advice. The powerless Bao Dai government had not been capable of compromise or indeed of taking any action at all.

16. Department of Defense, Record of Conversation, "Department of State Debriefing of General Collins," April 25, 1955, in *U.S.-GVN Relations,* 10: 937–940; quote from 937.

17. NSC, "Memorandum of Discussion at the 246th Meeting of the National Security Council, Washington, April 28, 1955, in *FRUS, 1955–1957,* 1: 307–312.

18. Central Intelligence Agency, "The Current Saigon Crisis," SNIE 63.1-2/1-55, May 2, 1955, in *U.S.-GVN Relations,* 10: 955–958; quote from 956.

19. William Doyle, *Inside the Oval Office: The White House Tapes from FDR to Clinton* (New York: Kodansha International, 1999), 86. Eisenhower presented himself as "one of the ones around here that was against the American air force going in."

20. *Gravel Pentagon Papers,* 2: 280. Actually, the Pentagon Papers analysts studied the sect crisis but, contrary to Gelb's assertion here, failed to consider its impact on "leverage" or to draw the relevant conclusion. The Pentagon Papers themselves thus become a further example of the phenomenon Gelb describes.

21. Eisenhower also had his records from the Dien Bien Phu period culled and the most sensitive material gathered in a "Project Clean Up" set for special handling. Of the many crises in the Eisenhower period, including nuclear brinkmanship between the United States and the Soviet Union over Berlin and Suez and between the United States and China over the Taiwan Strait, only records related to Dien Bien Phu were sequestered in this fashion.

22. "How Near We Came to War," *U.S. News and World Report,* August 6, 1954.

23. Chalmers M. Roberts, "The Day We Didn't Go to War," *Reporter,* September 14, 1954.

24. Quoted in Don Oberdorfer, *Senator Mansfield: The Extraordinary Life of a Great American Statesman and Diplomat* (Washington, DC: Smithsonian Books, 2003), 128.

25. Ibid., 136, 138.

26. Kathryn C. Statler, *Replacing France: The Origins of American Intervention in Vietnam* (Lexington: University Press of Kentucky, 2007), 143–144, 183–191. Also see Mark A. Lawrence, *Assuming the Burden: Europe and the American Commitment to War in Vietnam (From Indochina to Vietnam: Revolution and War in a Global Perspective)* (Berkeley: University of California Press, 2005).

27. Quoted in Statler, *Replacing France*, 139.

28. Joseph G. Morgan, *The Vietnam Lobby: The American Friends of Vietnam, 1955–1975* (Chapel Hill: University of North Carolina Press, 1997), 15–26. Also see Jacobs, *America's Miracle Man in Vietnam*, 229–240.

29. Quoted in Robert Mann, *A Grand Delusion: America's Descent into Vietnam* (New York: Basic, 2001), 172.

30. Ibid., 200.

31. Arthur Marwick, *The Sixties: The Cultural Revolution in Britain, France, Italy and the United States, c. 1958–c. 1974* (New York: Oxford University Press, 1998). Marwick finds a surprising degree of commonality among developments in the four countries, and his exposition is quite interesting, but the point here is that strands of social and political development that arose in the United States in the late 1950s grew and broadened right through the next decade and beyond.

32. It is impossible to recount here the story of the civil rights struggle in the detail it deserves. For an excellent account of the life and times of Martin Luther King Jr., see the three-volume biography by Taylor Branch: *Parting the Waters: America in the King Years, 1954–1963; Pillar of Fire: America in the King Years, 1963–1965;* and *At Canaan's Edge: America in the King Years, 1965–1968* (New York: Simon & Schuster, 1988, 1998, 2006). Stokely Carmichael's recollections are in his memoir, *Ready for Revolution: The Life and Struggles of Stokely Carmichael (Kwame Ture)* (New York: Scribner, 2003).

33. Lawrence Wittner, probably the foremost student of the antinuclear movement, observes that "pacifist organizations exhibited extreme caution when dealing with Communists, and consequently shunned all participation in Soviet-inspired 'peace initiatives.'" Lawrence S. Wittner, *Rebels against War: The American Peace Movement, 1933–1983* (Philadelphia: Temple University Press, 1984), 205.

34. In addition to Wittner's *Rebels against War,* see Lawrence Wittner, *The Struggle against the Bomb,* vol. 2, *Resisting the Bomb, A History of the World Nuclear Disarmament Movement, 1954–1970* (Stanford, CA: Stanford University Press, 1997).

35. For the Eisenhower administration's efforts with regard to the test ban, see Robert A. Divine, *Blowing on the Wind: The Nuclear Test Ban Debate, 1954–1960* (New York: Oxford University Press, 1978). I conducted extensive research in Eisenhower's nuclear records for my book *The Soviet Estimate: U.S. Intelligence and Soviet Strategic Forces* (Princeton, NJ: Princeton University Press, 1986).

36. See U.S. Congress, Senate Select Committee to Study Governmental Operations with Respect to Intelligence Activities [Church Committee], *Hearings* (Washington, DC: Government Printing Office, 1976), particularly bk. II of its report and bk. III of its detailed supplementary staff reports. On the Women's International League for Peace and Freedom specifically, see Susan Dion, "The FBI Surveillance of the Women's International League for Peace and Freedom, 1945–1963," *Journal for Peace and International Studies* 3, 1 (Winter 1991).

37. "Aid to South Vietnam," n.d., Lyndon Baines Johnson Library, LBJ Papers, Country File Vietnam, box 76, folder "2H(4): Strategic Reappraisal, 4/68–12/68." The distribution of

aid monies should be regarded with a certain amount of caution. The general impression among historians is that U.S. assistance during this period was more military than economic. For example, Anderson (*Trapped by Success*, 133, 154, 156) finds that 78 percent of U.S. aid from 1956 to 1960 went to Saigon's military, that the United States. financed about 85 percent of South Vietnam's military budget (and 66 percent of its overall budget, plus 75 to 85 percent of its imports), and that the commercial import program—a source for between $1 billion and $2 billion—was considered by many "as more a means of financing a large military force than of promoting economic development." It is possible that military pay and certain other security expenditures were carried in economic aid accounts in the U.S. budget, and it is probable that much of the military equipment recovered from the French and then turned over to Saigon was not included at all.

38. State Department cable, July 12, 1956, quoted in Philip E. Catton, *Diem's Final Failure: Prelude to America's War in Vietnam* (Lawrence: University Press of Kansas, 2002), 52.

39. Po Dharma (with Mak Phoeum), *Du FLM au FULRO: une lutte des minorities du sud indochinois, 1955–1975* (Paris: Les Indes Savants, 2006), 28.

40. Piero Gheddo, *The Cross and the Bo Tree: Catholics and Buddhists in Vietnam* (New York: Sheed & Ward, 1970), 71, 99. According to Gheddo, 619 priests and 5 bishops accompanied their flock, a rather small number to minister to the claimed 700,000 migrants.

41. John Prados, *The Hidden History of the Vietnam War* (Chicago: Ivan Dee, 1995), 60–70.

42. Lam Quang Thi, *The Twenty-five Year Century: A South Vietnamese General Remembers the Indochina War to the Fall of Saigon* (Denton: University of North Texas Press, 2001), 92.

Chapter 3. Loose the Fateful Lightning (1961–1964)

1. Theodore H. White, *The Making of the President, 1960* (New York: Atheneum, 1961).

2. Ibid., 377.

3. Lansdale Report, "Vietnam," January 17, 1961. The report, submitted to the secretary and deputy secretary of defense by Lansdale's Office of Special Operations, was passed along to Robert S. McNamara, Kennedy's incoming secretary of defense. U.S. Congress, House Armed Services Committee, *United States–Vietnam Relations 1945–1967* (Washington, DC: Government Printing Office, 1971), bk. 2, sec. IV.a.5, pp. 66–77; quotes from 66, 68, 76 (hereafter *U.S.-GVN Relations*)..

4. Quoted in Arthur H. Schlesinger Jr., *A Thousand Days: John F. Kennedy in the White House* (Greenwich, CT: Fawcett, 1967), 14.

5. See *US-GVN Relations*, bk. 2, sec. IV.a.4.

6. Brigadier General James Lawton Collins Jr., *Vietnam Studies: The Development and Training of the South Vietnamese Army, 1950–1972* (Washington, DC: Department of the Army, 1975), 9.

7. On the South Vietnamese military generally, see Robert K. Brigham, *ARVN: Life and Death in the South Vietnamese Army* (Lawrence: University Press of Kansas, 2006).

8. *US-GVN Relations*, bk. 2, sec. IV.a.4, p. 4.1.

9. An excellent treatment of the origins of the National Front for the Liberation of South Vietnam is Carlyle Thayer, *War by Other Means: National Liberation and Revolution in Vietnam, 1954–1960* (London: Routledge, 1990). For North Vietnam and the NLF together and apart, see most recently Cheng Guan Ang, *The Vietnam War from the Other Side* (London: Taylor & Francis, 2002). The works of Christopher Goscha are also of great importance, although so far, his book-length treatments have focused on Laos and the period up to 1954 (he is currently editing a multifaceted dissection of the Geneva conference of 1962). David Marr is working on the development of the Vietnam People's Army. For earlier treatments of these

subjects, see the works of King C. Chen, Robert Turner, Allen Goodman, and John T. McAlister. Dated but still useful are Douglas Pike, *Viet Cong: The Organization, Tactics, and Techniques of the National Liberation Front of South Vietnam* (Cambridge, MA: MIT Press, 1966), and, from the Hanoi perspective, William J. Duiker, *The Communist Road to Power in Vietnam* (Boulder, CO: Westview Press, 1981).

10. Quoted in John Prados, *The Blood Road: The Ho Chi Minh Trail and the Vietnam War* (New York: John Wiley's Sons, 1999), 30.

11. Schlesinger, *A Thousand Days,* 496–497.

12. Quoted in Roger Hilsman, *To Move a Nation: The Politics of Policymaking in the Administration of John F. Kennedy* (Garden City, NY: Doubleday, 1967), 420.

13. Quoted in Schlesinger, *A Thousand Days,* 501.

14. Ibid., 502.

15. In particular, see Philip E. Catton, *Diem's Final Failure: Prelude to America's War in Vietnam* (Lawrence: University Press of Kansas, 2002), and Edward G. Miller, *Grand Designs: Vision, Power and Nation Building in America's Alliance with Ngo Dinh Diem, 1954–1960* (Cambridge, MA: Harvard University, 2004, University Microfilms Inc. code 3149576), 216–226. Both these scholars used records of the former South Vietnamese government archived by the Socialist Republic of Vietnam in Ho Chi Minh City. However, the actual materials cited consist of speeches, articles, and other basic public records; these are not the kinds of declassified government analyses, position and option papers, or other records considered de rigueur for archival research. Consequently, arguments drawn from these sources command no greater standing than those based on the public record. Granted that Diem's thinking drew from Vietnamese traditions and cultural values distinct from those of the West, these explanations do not seem more persuasive than previous attempts to validate personalism. Also see Howard Jones, *Death of a Generation: How the Assassinations of Diem and JFK Prolonged the Vietnam War* (New York: Oxford University Press, 2003).

16. Some recent scholars analyzing personalism do indeed come out in favor of the older interpretation that Diem's philosophical basis was a patchwork of obscure tenets difficult to translate into policy. See Seth Jacobs, *Cold War Mandarin: Ngo Dinh Diem and the Origins of America's War in Vietnam, 1950–1963* (Lanham, MD: Rowman & Littlefield, 2006), 87–88.

17. Hilsman, who was later my professor at Columbia, and whom I have known for many years, spoke often and intimately of the Kennedys. There can be no doubt he had the access and clout to sell this program.

18. Hilsman, *To Move a Nation,* 427–444, quote from 432; Catton, *Diem's Final Failure,* 117–161.

19. Military History Institute of Vietnam, *Victory in Vietnam: The Official History of the People's Army of Vietnam, 1954–1975,* trans. Merle L. Pribbenow (Lawrence: University Press of Kansas, 2002), 107–114.

20. Ibid., 118.

21. *The Senator Gravel Edition: The Pentagon Papers: The Defense Department History of United States Decisionmaking on Vietnam* (Boston: Beacon Press, [1971]), 2: 154–157, tables.

22. Colby argues this in his book (with James McCargar) *Lost Victory: A Firsthand Account of America's Sixteen Year Involvement in Vietnam* (Chicago: Contemporary Books, 1989). He made the same claims at conferences at the Cantigny Museum and the Vietnam Center of Texas Tech University in 1996, just weeks before his death. Colby's most extreme formulation (in his speech at Texas Tech)—that there was a "turning point" for victory in almost every year of the war—begs the question that if there were so many opportunities for the United States to win the Vietnam war, how could it possibly have been lost? In a way, this proposition indicts Washington war managers even more strongly. Taking up the victory thesis

most recently is scholar Mark Moyar in *Triumph Forsaken: The Vietnam War, 1954–1965* (New York: Cambridge University Press, 2006). This book structures its argument that the war was won (but the victory thrown away) during this early period around the dubious statistics, North Vietnamese accounts, and the claim that Diem's pacification was successful. The North Vietnamese accounts are suggestive, but they acknowledge difficulties, which is different from conceding defeat. In public appearances associated with the release of his book, Moyar also significantly mischaracterized the intelligence disputes of 1963 that brought the Vietnam data problem to the fore, representing them as a quarrel between the military and CIA (which were allegedly correct—and allied) versus the (misguided) press and State Department. As the present narrative makes clear, the U.S. military disputed every other interpretation of the status of the war in Vietnam, and in 1963 it was never aligned with the CIA.

23. Taking the statistics for NLF deserters and prevailing estimates of PLAF strength, the monthly rate of guerrilla and regular desertions in January 1962 was about 1 in 250, whereas in April 1963 the much higher number of deserters equated to a monthly average of 1 in 270—not much different. The deserters, of course, included a proportion of intelligence agents being deliberately inserted into the South Vietnamese structure. Also, the number of infiltrators from the north coming down the Ho Chi Minh Trail more than made up for all the deserters. The actual raw numbers of defections recorded was 3,955 in 1962—less than in 1961—and another 2,592 from January to September 1963. Records show that ARVN desertions were greater than those of the PLAF: 11,203 in 1962 (plus 18,721 from militia forces), and 6,489 (plus 15,877 militia) for the stated period in 1963.

24. John M. Newman, *JFK and Vietnam: Deception, Intrigue, and the Struggle for Power* (New York: Warner, 1992).

25. Neil Sheehan, *A Bright Shining Lie: John Paul Vann and America in Vietnam* (New York: Random House, 1988).

26. David Halberstam, *The Making of a Quagmire* (New York: Random House, 1964); Malcolm Browne, *The New Face of War* (New York: Bobbs-Merrill, 1965). Also see William Prochnau, *Once upon a Distant War: Young War Correspondents in the Early Vietnam Battles* (New York: Random House, 1995).

27. Harold P. Ford, *CIA and the Vietnam Policymakers: Three Episodes, 1962–1968* (Washington, DC: CIA/Center for the Study of Intelligence, 1998), 9.

28. George W. Allen, *None so Blind: A Personal Account of the Intelligence Failure in Vietnam* (Chicago: Ivan Dee, 2001), 134–136.

29. Quoted in Willard C. Matthias, *America's Strategic Blunders: Intelligence Analysis and National Security Policy, 1936–1991* (University Park: University of Pennsylvania Press, 2001), 188.

30. Ibid.

31. John Prados, *Lost Crusader: The Secret Wars of CIA Director William Colby* (New York: Oxford University Press, 2003), 104–107; Ford, *CIA and the Vietnam Policymakers,* 11–20; Matthias, *America's Strategic Blunders,* 185–191.

32. Louis G. Sarris, "McNamara's War and Mine," *New York Times,* September 5, 1995, A17.

33. John Prados, "The Mouse That Roared: State Department Intelligence in the Vietnam War," National Security Archive website, Electronic Briefing Book no. 121.

34. The two tribal leaders were Y Bham Enuol and Paul Nur. They were released in January 1963 on the order of ARVN II Corps commander General Nguyen Khanh, with the encouragement of the CIA's Gilbert Layton.

35. Moyar, *Triumph Forsaken,* 186–205, barely concedes Ap Bac as an ARVN failure. He argues that it was exaggerated by American reporters abetted by John Paul Vann and contends it was not a real defeat because the strategic epicenter of the war lay in the Central Highlands. This misconstrues the significance of Ap Bac, which is that an NLF unit fought

(rather than melting into the countryside), held, and defeated a far superior South Vietnamese force. As for the primacy of the Central Highlands, this might carry some weight as a geostrategic proposition, but in January 1963 neither South Vietnamese nor American commanders regarded the mountains as anything more than one of many battlefronts. It is quite plausible to argue, in fact, that Ngo Dinh Nhu was willing to acquiesce in the CIA montagnard project precisely because he saw the highlands only as a secondary theater of conflict. The most exact study of this engagement, based on contemporaneous field reporting, is by professional Army officer David M. Toczek in *The Battle of Ap Bac, Vietnam* (Westport, CT: Greenwood Press, 2001). He concludes for a number of reasons that the action was a major setback for Saigon.

36. For an informed view of the ARVN at this point in time, see Trinh Minh Nguyen, "Army of the Republic of Vietnam: At War and in Politics, 1954–1963" (master's thesis, University of Calgary, 2005).

37. Quoted in Allen, *None so Blind,* 152.

38. Lam Quang Thi, *The Twenty-five Year Century: A South Vietnamese General Remembers the Indochina War to the Fall of Saigon* (Denton: University of North Texas Press, 2001), 92.

39. Nguyen Cao Ky with Marvin J. Wolf, *Buddha's Child: My Fight to Save Vietnam* (New York: St. Martin's Press, 2002), 77.

40. CIA cable TDCS DB-3/656,252, August 24, 1963, contains General Tran Van Don's account of these events given to the agency; see Department of State, *FRUS, 1961–1963,* vol. 3, *Vietnam, January–August 1963* (Washington, DC: Government Printing Office, 1991), 614–620. Don named the generals who met on August 18, outlined some of their discussion, and recounted how the crackdown proposal had reached Diem. Don stated his *personal* opinion that the Buddhist crisis could have been solved except for the fact that NLF agents had "penetrated" the Buddhist movement, and he said that the "generals" had told Diem the crisis was affecting ARVN morale. Moyar's account of this sequence (*Triumph Forsaken,* 231–232) is strained on several points, and because of the importance of the pagoda attacks in Diem's fall, it cannot pass without comment. Moyar relates that neither Diem nor Nhu attended the August 18 meeting, whereas Don, according to the CIA, "did not say who brought the generals together" and made no reference to whether Nhu attended. Another U.S. cable, which Moyar also cites and was therefore aware of, contains a confusion of dates, which suggests that Nhu may indeed have been present. The assertion that the generals believed the crisis had gone on too long is the *interpretation* of an American diplomat in a source document. A *different* cable reported General Tran Thien Khiem's statement that ARVN morale would suffer if the crisis went on much longer. General Don *alone* said this in meeting with Diem. No assertion that the Buddhist leaders would not relent until Diem had been swept from power appears in the documents. Nor is there reference to the 1955 sect crisis. In short, the Moyar account misrepresents the source material, attributes information to the documents that they do not contain, and weaves together statements from different sources that are not cited. This example is typical of his handling of source material throughout. In addition, the statement that the majority of the generals meeting on August 18 were Buddhist is not accurate: the breakdown is even for those on whom such information is available; the religious affiliations of two are not known. Tellingly, two of the ten "converted" to Catholicism under Diem. In particular, General Ton That Dinh was Catholic. Elsewhere, in discussing the original May incidents, Moyar makes the blanket statement that the majority of South Vietnamese citizens supported the crackdown, based on no evidence at all.

41. Galbraith's son James, also a noted economist, has argued in a variety of fora and in several papers that the evidence for the Kennedy withdrawal is conclusive. Jones's *Death of a Generation,* the most detailed recent study of this period, reaches a similar though less confident conclusion. D. Gareth Porter, *The Perils of Dominance: Imbalance of Power and the*

Road to War in Vietnam (Berkeley: University of California Press, 2005), 165–179, also argues the Kennedy withdrawal thesis. In general, these analysts treat McNamara as a surrogate or stand-in for Kennedy in the bureaucratic action over withdrawal. Porter does not even touch on the alternative view that withdrawal talk was itself a veiled threat to Diem to rid himself of the Nhus.

42. See David Kaiser, *American Tragedy: Kennedy, Johnson, and the Origins of the Vietnam War* (Cambridge, MA: Harvard University Press, 2000), 36–149.

43. "Memorandum from the Chairman of the Joint Chiefs of Staff (Taylor) and the Secretary of Defense (McNamara) to the President," October 2, 1963, in *FRUS, 1961–1963*, vol. 4, *Vietnam, August–December 1963,* 336–346, quote from 337. For the cited tape, see the recording of the NSC meeting of October 4, 1963, available from the John F. Kennedy Presidential Library or the Miller Center of the University of Virginia.

44. As late as January 27, 1964, Secretary McNamara testified to the House Armed Services Committee that the goal of the United States remained to withdraw "most" of its troops from South Vietnam by the end of 1965, saying that it was reasonable "to expect that after four years of . . . training, we should be able gradually to withdraw," but that some Americans must "stay until the counterinsurgency operation has been successfully completed." Quoted in Lester A. Sobel, ed., *South Vietnam: U.S.-Communist Confrontation in Southeast Asia, 1961–1965* (New York: Facts on File, 1966), 92. This statement testifies to McNamara's agency, not Kennedy's, and it clearly indicates that the design of this program was for a form of Vietnamization, not a total U.S. withdrawal.

45. U.S. Congress, Senate Foreign Relations Committee, *Background Information Relating to Southeast Asia and Vietnam,* 7th rev. ed. (Washington, DC: Government Printing Office, 1975), 250.

46. Quoted in Joseph G. Morgan, *The Vietnam Lobby: The American Friends of Vietnam, 1955–1975* (Chapel Hill: University of North Carolina Press, 1997), 100.

47. The audiotape (in CD format), introductory notes, and a full transcript of this key meeting are available in John Prados, ed., *The White House Tapes: Eavesdropping on the President* (New York: New Press, 2003), 92–150.

48. Ibid., 110–111. Robert Kennedy was probably thinking of the CIA operations in Iran in 1953 and Guatemala in 1954, although he did not express it quite that way.

49. Robert McNamara's analysis of the role of Kennedy's advisers in his Vietnam memoir is instructive. He faults General Maxwell Taylor for not pushing to resolve the problems with Vietnam data; Dean Rusk for not riding closer herd over the diplomats, particularly Ambassador Lodge; and himself for not forcing debate of such basic questions as whether the United States could win with Diem, whether there was a better replacement, whether neutralizing Vietnam (similar to Laos) was preferable, or whether "withdrawing on the grounds that South Vietnam's political disorder made it impossible for the United States to remain there." Robert S. McNamara with Brian VanDeMark, *In Retrospect: The Tragedy and Lessons of Vietnam* (New York: Times Books, 1995), 70. By asserting that this option had not been effectively debated, McNamara undercuts claims, some of them his own (see *In Retrosepct,* 96), that President Kennedy had decided to get out of Vietnam.

50. In Hue, Ngo Dinh Can evaded arrest and fled to the U.S. consulate but was later handed over to the South Vietnamese military junta. He was tried, sentenced to death, and executed on May 9, 1964. Brothers Ngo Dinh Luyen, serving as an ambassador, and Archbishop Ngo Dinh Thuc, as well as Madame Nhu, were abroad at the time and escaped death. Ironically, Tran Thi Xuan, who became Madame Nhu, had been a school classmate and rumored former lover of General Tran Van Don, one of the principal coup plotters.

51. Bill Moyers's recollections at the Musgrove conference on the Vietnam war, April 2005. I was present and discussed these recollections with Moyers. Jamie Galbraith attended this conference as well.

52. CIA memorandum, "South Vietnam—Where We Stand," December 6, 1963, in *FRUS, 1961–1963,* 4: 682.

53. John E. Mueller, *War, Presidents, and Public Opinion* (New York: John Wiley & Sons, 1973), 81. Most poll figures cited in this narrative up through 1971 are from Mueller's exhaustive study.

August 1964: The Last Mystery of the Tonkin Gulf

1. The most authoritative account of the Tonkin Gulf incident is Edwin E. Moise, *Tonkin Gulf and the Escalation of the Vietnam War* (Chapel Hill: University of North Carolina Press, 1996). The Navy's official version is Edward J. Marolda and Oscar P. Fitzgerald, *The United States Navy and the Vietnam Conflict*, vol. 2, *From Military Assistance to Combat, 1959–1965* (Washington, DC: Naval Historical Center, 1986). Important contemporary accounts include Eugene G. Windchy, *Tonkin Gulf* (Garden City, NY: Doubleday, 1971), and Anthony Austin, *The President's War: The Story of the Tonkin Gulf Resolution and How the Nation Was Trapped in Vietnam* (Philadelphia: J. B. Lippincott, 1971).

2. Captain Norman Klar, USN (ret.), "How to Help Start a War," *Naval History* 16, 4 (April 2002): 40–42. Klar was the officer in charge of the NSG unit on Taiwan and the person who assured the *Maddox*'s captain, Commander Herbert L. Ogier, that his ship would not be attacked. It was Klar's van aboard the destroyer and his unit, augmented by communications personnel from other detachments in the Far East, that staffed the mission.

3. The whale remark was first reported by Joseph C. Goulden, *Truth Is the First Casualty: The Gulf of Tonkin—Illusion and Reality* (Chicago: Rand McNally, 1969).

4. At the same conference a lower-level official, General Nguyen Dinh Uoc of the Vietnamese Institute of Military History, gave an identical affirmation that the August 2 naval sortie had been carried out at the initiative of the local naval district command. (See chapter 4, note 27, for details on this conference in Hanoi.)

5. See John Prados, *The Hidden History of the Vietnam War* (Chicago: Ivan B. Dee, 1995), 48–59. This discussion first appeared as an article in the *VVA Veteran* in August 1989.

6. NSA, *United States Cryptologic History,* series VI, *The NSA Period: 1952–Present,* vol. 7, *Spartans in Darkness: American SIGINT and the Indochina War, 1945–1975* (CCH-E05-02-03) (Fort Meade, MD: Center for Cryptologic History, 2002), 200–214.

7. Lyndon B. Johnson, *The Vantage Point: Perspectives on the Presidency, 1963–1969* (New York: Holt, Rinehart & Winston, 1971), 113. Actually, the missions were conducted by South Vietnamese Special Operations forces under U.S. control, not by the South Vietnamese navy. They were specifically programmed as U.S. "unilateral" operations under the directive NSAM-273, which President Johnson approved in November 1963. LBJ also approved the actual mission program in January 1964. In fairness to Johnson, he notes that the United States had a "supporting role" in 34-A, although this remark obscures the fact that the United States chose the targets, supplied and maintained the weapons and naval craft, funded the program, trained the Vietnamese commandos, and did everything except crew the raiding boats. There are, in fact, accounts from two former U.S. special warfare people who claim to have actually participated in the August 2 missions. Johnson also writes that "it was later alleged that our destroyers were supporting the South Vietnamese naval action," and he denies that. He is correct in that assertion, and if those are the grounds for LBJ's contention that the missions were not connected, in that narrow sense, the claim is accurate. However, the question of support really runs the other way: by striking the North Vietnamese coast, the 34-A raid supported the Desoto patrol by giving North Vietnamese commanders reason to activate their radar and radio networks, whose emissions the *Maddox* could then record.

8. George W. Ball telephone notes, TELCON, Bundy, Ball, 8/3/64, 10:40 AM, National Security Archive, Robert McNamara Donation, box 1, "Documents, Chapter 4—Tonkin

Gulf." These documents represent the source materials for McNamara's memoir *In Retrospect* and form part of the archive's collection on the 1997 Hanoi conference "Missed Opportunities."

9. Michael Beschloss, ed., *Taking Charge: The Johnson White House Tapes, 1963–1964* (New York: Simon & Schuster, 1997), 493.

10. John Prados, ed., *The White House Tapes: Eavesdropping on the President* (New York: New Press, 2003), 185; disk 5, track 1.

11. Ibid., 188.

12. A few minutes later came an intercept fixing the position of the U.S. Desoto patrol. These and other cables are located in the Lyndon Johnson Papers. See LBJL, LBJP, NSF, CFVN, box 77, folder "3A(3) Gulf of Tonkin, 8/64." Note that the Desoto patrol position referenced in the second intercept corresponds roughly to the position of the *Maddox* on August 2 not long before it was attacked. Other messages in this series indicate activities known to have happened in the earlier incident, which is no doubt why senior NSA officials believed that the communications concerned the earlier engagement. Why these cables reached Washington on August 4 remains unknown.

13. Telephone conversation, Johnson–McNamara, August 4, 1964, 9:43 AM, in Prados, *White House Tapes,* 193–194.

14. Telephone conversation, Johnson–McNamara, August 4, 1964, 10:53 AM, ibid., 196.

15. McGeorge Bundy notes, "4 August, Lunch," National Security Archive, Hanoi Conference Papers, Robert McNamara Donation, box 1, folder "Docs, Ch. 4, Tonkin Gulf."

16. Memorandum, McGeorge Bundy–George Reedy, August 7, 1964, LBJL, LBJP, NSF, NSC Histories, box 38, folder "Gulf of Tonkin, v. I (Tab 9) [2 of 2]."

17. Daniel Ellsberg, *Secrets: A Memoir of Vietnam and the Pentagon Papers* (New York: Viking Press, 2002), 10–12.

18. Quoted in Robert Dallek, *Flawed Giant: Lyndon Johnson and His Times, 1961–1973* (New York: Oxford University Press, 1998), 150.

19. William Y. Smith, Memorandum for the Record, White House Staff Meeting, August 5, 1964, 8 AM, in Department of State, *FRUS, 1964–1968,* vol. 1, *Vietnam* (Washington, DC: Government Printing Office, 1992), 631.

20. U.S. Senate, *Executive Sessions of the Senate Foreign Relations Committee, 1964* (Washington, DC: Goverment Printing Office, n.d.), 291–292. McNamara's artful statement attributed the 34-A operations to the South Vietnamese, as did LBJ in his memoir. This was true only in the sense that U.S. special warfare units, not the Navy per se, bore direct responsibility. The Navy, however, provided the attack boats and their maintenance, and the Desoto patrol was indeed kept informed of the raids on a current basis. This is totally beside the point, since the alleged North Vietnamese attack of August 4 never happened. The secretary of defense's statement amounted to a falsehood.

21. The NSA's Vietnam history, declassified in 2007, maintains that NSA officials compiling a Tonkin Gulf chronology at the time of the incident and another one some months later fudged the data from intercepts, did not follow standard procedures for compiling these reports, and referred to only a small portion of the traffic—in fact, only those messages supporting the two-incident version, including the mistranslated intercept from Phu Bai. The author, NSA historian Robert J. Hanyok, contends that the notion that NSA analysts were pressured to do this cannot be substantiated. The Johnson and, to a lesser extent, Nixon administrations then relied on the flawed chronologies in defending the original version of events. The intercepts used in the false arguments were not declassified until early in the twenty-first century, and the full traffic was declassified only in 2005. See NSA, *Spartans in Darkness,* 214–218, 222–223.

Chapter 4. Burnished Rows of Steel (1964–1965)

1. Quoted in Stanley Karnow, *Vietnam: A History* (New York: Viking, 1983), 357.

2. Nguyen Cao Ky with Marvin J. Wolf, *Buddha's Child: My Fight to Save Vietnam* (New York: St. Martin's, 2002), 112.

3. William C. Westmoreland, *A Soldier Reports* (New York: Dell, 1980), 90.

4. NSC Staff, "Memorandum of a Meeting, White House," September 9, 1964, 11:00 AM, in Department of State, *FRUS, 1964–1968,* vol. 1, *Vietnam 1964* (Washington, DC: Government Printing Office, 1992), 752.

5. Michael Beschloss, ed., *Reaching for Glory: Lyndon Johnson's Secret White House Tapes, 1964–1965* (New York: Simon & Schuster, 2001), 38–39.

6. It is worth mentioning that in both 1945, when Bull Halsey's Third Fleet operated against the Japanese in Indochina, and again in 1954, when a U.S. task force sailed the Gulf of Tonkin in anticipation of intervening at Dien Bien Phu, American aircraft and warships recorded spurious radar returns in these waters. U.S. aircraft carriers actually vectored planes to investigate the sightings and found nothing.

7. Quoted in H. R. McMaster, *Dereliction of Duty: Lyndon Johnson, Robert McNamara, the Joint Chiefs of Staff and the Lies that Led to Vietnam* (New York: HarperCollins, 1997), 148, 326.

8. John Prados, *The Blood Road: The Ho Chi Minh Trail and the Vietnam War* (New York: John Wiley's Sons, 1999), 61–68.

9. Quoted in Westmoreland, *A Soldier Reports,* 161.

10. John Prados, ed., *The White House Tapes: Eavesdropping on the President* (New York: New Press, 2003), 155.

11. Beschloss, *Reaching for Glory,* 137.

12. Lyndon B. Johnson, *The Vantage Point: Perspectives on the Presidency, 1963–1969* (New York: Holt, Rinehart & Winston, 1971), 119.

13. Leslie H. Gelb and Richard K. Betts, *The Irony of Vietnam: The System Worked* (Washington, DC: Brookings Institution, 1978).

14. David Halberstam, *The Best and the Brightest* (New York: Fawcett, 1972).

15. Leslie H. Gelb, *The Irony of Vietnam: The System Worked* (Washington, DC: Brookings Institution, 1979). Betts coauthored the paper that originally proposed this thesis.

16. D. Gareth Porter, *The Perils of Dominance: Imbalance of Power and the Road to War in Vietnam* (Berkeley: University of California Press, 2005), 287–288.

17. Daniel Ellsberg, *Papers on the War* (New York: Simon & Schuster, 1972). Ellsberg's model is stated in bare-bones form on pp. 132–135 but explicated in detail on pp. 47–131. He actually wrote in response to Arthur Schlesinger's historical interpretation that the United States slid down a muddy slope into the quagmire of Vietnam. See Arthur M. Schlesinger Jr., *The Bitter Heritage: Vietnam and American Democracy, 1941–1966* (New York: Fawcett, 1968).

18. OPLAN 34-B remains a tantalizing mystery of the Vietnam war. It is mentioned in documents from early 1964, and the context definitely suggests the cross-border operations that became known by the code name "Shining Brass." But to this day, no further information on 34-B has emerged.

19. The story of the demise of the chance for peace in what he terms "the long 1963" is admirably recounted in Fredrik Logevall's *Choosing War: The Lost Chance for Peace and the Escalation of the Vietnam War* (Berkeley: University of California Press, 1999).

20. Quoted in Richard Goodwin, *Remembering America: A Voice from the Sixties* (Boston: Little Brown, 1988), 231.

21. Michael Forrestal told me this story on March 11, 1988. I quote it here from my *Keep-*

ers of the Keys: A History of the National Security Council from Truman to Bush (New York: William Morrow, 1991), 215.

22. Johnson, *Vantage Point,* 121.

23. Memorandum, McGeorge Bundy–Lyndon Johnson, "Basic Policy in Vietnam," January 27, 1965, in Department of State, *FRUS, 1964–1968,* vol. 2, *Vietnam, January–June 1965* (Washington, DC: Government Printing Office, 1996), 95–97.

24. James C. Thomson Jr. Oral History, LBJL (AC 81-98), 1, 18.

25. Chester L. Cooper, *The Lost Crusade: America in Vietnam* (New York: Dodd, Mead, 1970), 257.

26. Westmoreland, *A Soldier Reports,* 146.

27. CIA Memorandum for the Record, John McCone, "Meeting of the National Security Council, ex President," February 8, 1965, in *FRUS, 1964–1968,* 2: 197.

28. The conference, "Missed Opportunities: Former U.S. and Vietnamese Leaders Re-examine the Vietnam War, 1961–1968," was jointly sponsored by the Thomas J. Watson Institute of Brown University and the Institute of International Relations of the Ministry of Foreign Affairs of Vietnam. Robert McNamara led the U.S. delegation. Unfortunately, no formal conference proceedings have ever been published. Bits and pieces, along with some materials from preparatory sessions and from the follow-up meeting at Bellagio, Italy (July 28–31, 1998), appear in Robert McNamara et al., *Argument without End: In Search of Answers to the Vietnam Tragedy* (New York: Public Affairs, 1999). The primary sources specifically recording the June 1997 meeting are John Prados, "Looking at the War from Both Sides Now," *VVA Veteran* 17, 7–8 (August–September 1997); John Prados, "Letter from Hanoi," *MHQ: The Quarterly Journal of Military History* 11, 1 (Autumn 1998); David K. Shipler, "Robert McNamara and the Ghosts of Vietnam," *New York Times Magazine,* August 10, 1997; and George C. Herring, "Missed Opportunity: A Participant's Reflection on the June 1997 Hanoi Conference on the Vietnamese-American War," *Kentucky Historical Register* 95 (Summer 1997). Chester Cooper was also present at the Hanoi conference, though not at the "military lunches." For his opinion, see *In the Shadows of History: 50 Years behind the Scenes of Cold War Diplomacy* (Amherst, NY: Prometheus, 2005), 221. As the historian on the American delegation most conversant with the military side, I helped initiate these military lunches and served as rapporteur. The Socialist Republic of Vietnam today celebrates February 7 as the day North Vietnamese forces came to the aid of their brothers in the South.

29. Quoted in Halberstam, *Best and Brightest,* 646.

30. The best treatment of this aspect of U.S. policy is in George McT. Kahin's *Intervention: How America Became Involved in Vietnam* (New York: Alfred Knopf, 1986).

31. These South Vietnamese decisions remind us that Saigon, not Washington, ultimately called the shots on pacification. Some analysts of the U.S. defeat in Vietnam argue that a 1963 "victory" was lost because the *United States* halted the strategic hamlet program.

32. See Thich Nhat Hanh, *Lotus in a Sea of Fire* (New York: Hill & Wang, 1967).

33. Lam Quang Thi, *The Twenty-five Year Century: A South Vietnamese General Remembers the Indochina War to the Fall of Saigon* (Denton: University of North Texas Press, 2001), 113.

34. Ky, *Buddha's Child,* 102, 106.

35. U. Alexis Johnson with Jef Olivarius Oliver, *The Right Hand of Power: The Memoirs of an American Diplomat* (Englewood Cliffs, NJ: Prentice-Hall, 1984), 414–415.

36. Quoted in Westmoreland, *A Soldier Reports,* 93.

37. Bui Diem interview, Lubbock, TX, October 20, 2006.

38. A fine account of the early antiwar movement is in Thomas Powers, *The War at Home: Vietnam and the American People, 1964–1968* (New York: Grossman, 1973).

39. *Boston Globe,* December 18, 1964.

40. Charles DeBenedetti and Charles Chatfield, *An American Ordeal: The Antiwar Movement of the Vietnam Era* (Syracuse, NY: Syracuse University Press, 1990), 101.

41. Robert R. Tomes, *Apocalypse Then: American Intellectuals and the Vietnam War, 1954–1975* (New York: New York University Press, 1998).

42. Department of State, *Aggression from the North: The Record of North Vietnam's Campaign to Conquer South Vietnam* (Department of State Publication 7839, February 1965).

43. Cooper, *Lost Crusade,* 265.

44. I. F. Stone, "A Reply to the White Paper," *I. F. Stone's Weekly,* March 8, 1965, 1–4.

45. Lyndon B. Johnson, "A Plan for Peace in Southeast Asia," *Department of State Bulletin,* April 26, 1965, 606–610.

46. Adam Garfinkle, *Telltale Hearts: The Origins and Impact of the Vietnam Antiwar Movement* (New York: St. Martin's, 1995), 1–2, 56–79.

47. Max Frankel, "Military Pledge to Saigon Is Denied by Eisenhower," *New York Times,* August 18, 1965, 1.

48. White House, "President Johnson's Notes on Conversation with President Eisenhower, August 18, 1965," LBJL, LBJP, Transcripts of Telephone Conversations, transcript no. 8555a.

49. David S. Broder, "Eisenhower Backs Stand on Vietnam," *New York Times,* August 20, 1965, 1.

50. Irwin Unger, *The Movement: A History of the American New Left, 1959–1972* (New York: Harper & Row, 1974), 51–81.

51. Staughton Lynd, "Coalition Politics," *Liberation,* June–July 1965, quoted in Nancy Zaroulis and Gerald Sullivan, *Who Spoke Up? American Protest against the War in Vietnam, 1963–1975* (New York: Holt, Rinehart & Winston, 1984), 42.

52. *The Senator Gravel Edition: The Pentagon Papers: The Defense Department History of United States Decisionmaking on Vietnam* (Boston: Beacon Press, [1971]), 3: 105.

53. Ibid., 430.

54. Westmoreland, *A Soldier Reports,* 158.

55. Robert S. McNamara with Brian VanDeMark, *In Retrospect: The Tragedy and Lessons of Vietnam* (New York: Times Books, 1995), 175.

56. MACV cable, MAC JOO 19118 Westmoreland–Sharp (CINCPAC), June 7, 1965, in *FRUS. 1964–1968,* 2: 733–736.

57. McNamara, *In Retrospect,* 188.

58. Among Vietnam records, these 1965 NSC meetings are some of the first to be handled in this fashion. The compilation of verbatim transcripts later became quite common. Johnson in 1968 and Nixon in 1971 added tape recordings of meetings to this mountain of records.

59. George W. Ball, *The Past Has Another Pattern* (New York: W. W. Norton, 1982), 389.

60. Ibid., 392.

61. Department of State, George W. Ball–Lyndon B. Johnson, "Keeping the Power of Decision in the South Viet-Nam Crisis," June 18, 1965, in *FRUS, 1964–1968,* 3: 16–21.

62. NSC, McGeorge Bundy–Lyndon B. Johnson, "France in 1954, and the U.S. in 1965 — A Useful Analogy?" June 30, 1965, ibid., 79–85; emphasis in original.

63. McNamara, *In Retrospect,* 191.

64. Henry F. Graff, *The Tuesday Cabinet: Deliberation and Decision on Peace and War under Lyndon B. Johnson* (Englewood Cliffs, NJ: Prentice-Hall, 1970). I studied with Graff at Columbia not long after he wrote that book, and considerably later he sat on my dissertation defense committee. The wealth of detail in his stories about LBJ confirms that Graff had sufficient contact with Johnson to appreciate the president's anguish.

65. Beschloss, *Reaching for Glory,* 381–384.

66. Logevall, *Choosing War.*

67. McNamara, *In Retrospect,* 115.

68. Joint Chiefs of Staff, Joint Staff, Report of the Ad Hoc Study Group, "Intensification of the Military Operations in Vietnam: Concept and Appraisal," July 14, 1965 (declassified December 10, 1985), LBJL, LBJP, NSF, CFVN, box 20, folder "Vietnam, v. 37, Memos (c)."

Chapter 5. A Hundred Circling Camps (1965–1967)

1. Nguyen Cao Ky with Marvin J. Wolf, *Buddha's Child: My Fight to Save Vietnam* (New York: St. Martin's Press, 2002), 144.

2. William C. Westmoreland, *A Soldier Reports* (New York: Dell, 1980), 179.

3. Military History Institute of Vietnam, *Victory in Vietnam: The Official History of the People's Army of Vietnam, 1954–1975,* trans. Merle L. Pribbenow (Lawrence: University Press of Kansas, 2002), 158.

4. Robert Mason, *Chickenhawk* (New York: Penguin, 1983), 226. The account of Ia Drang is based on a number of sources from all three sides. Mentioned in the text is Harold C. Moore and Joe Galloway, *We Were Soldiers Once . . . And Young* (New York: Random House, 1992). There are several good accounts of the 1st Cavalry Division's arrival and deployment, including J. D. Coleman, *Pleiku: The Dawn of Helicopter Warfare in Vietnam* (New York: St. Martin's, 1989), and Shelby Stanton, *Anatomy of a Division: The 1st Cav in Vietnam* (Novato, CA: Presidio, 1987). For the view of another battalion commander, see Kenneth D. Mertel, *Year of the Horse—Vietnam—1st Air Cavalry in the Highlands* (New York: Exposition Press, 1968). On the "Headhunters," see Matthew Brennan, ed., *Hunter-Killer Squadron* (New York: Pocket, 1992). For the role of Special Forces Detachment B-57 at Duc-Co and Plei Me, see Charles Beckwith and Donald Knox, *Delta Force* (New York: Harcourt Brace Jovanovich, 1983). Official sources include John M. Carland, *The United States Army in Vietnam: Combat Operations: Stemming the Tide, May 1965 to October 1966* (Washington, DC: U.S. Army Center for Military History, 2000), 95–150. Also see John J. Tolson, *Airmobility in Vietnam: Helicopter Warfare in Southeast Asia* (New York: Arno Press, 1981), first published as a volume of the Army series "Vietnam Studies." For the ARVN airborne attack into the Chu Pong, see H. Norman Schwarzkopf with Peter Petre, *It Doesn't Take a Hero* (New York: Bantam, 1993). Also see Vinh Loc, *Why Pleime?* (Pleiku: privately printed, 1966). Several relevant ARVN after-action reports appear in Tin Nguyen, *General Hieu, ARVN: A Hidden Military Gem* (New York: Writers Club Press, 2003). On the North Vietnamese side, see Military History Institute of Vietnam, *Victory in Vietnam,* and Nguyen Khac Vien, ed., *Face to Face with the Enemy,* Vietnamese Studies no. 54 (Hanoi: Foreign Languages Publishing House, 1978).

5. The CIA issued periodic reports, which became more regularized in 1967, that tracked merchant ships calling at North Vietnamese ports. These consistently showed Great Britain as the leading carrier other than the Soviet Union, China, and Poland.

6. Fredrik Logevall's *Choosing War: The Lost Chance for Peace and the Escalation of the Vietnam War* (Berkeley: University of California Press, 1999), is best on the French negotiating effort. Surveys of many nations' positions on the war can be found in Lloyd C. Gardner and Ted Gittinger, eds., *International Perspectives on Vietnam* (College Station: Texas A&M University Press, 1999), and Andreas Daum, Lloyd C. Gardner, and Wilfred Mausbach, eds., *America, the Vietnam War and the World: Comparative and International Perspectives* (London: Cambridge University Press, 2003).

7. On the Free World Forces in general, see Robert M. Blackburn, *Mercenaries and Lyndon Johnson's "More Flags": The Hiring of Korean, Filipino and Thai Soldiers in the Vietnam War* (Jefferson, NC: McFarland, 1994); Stanley R. Larsen and James Lawton Collins Jr., *Allied Participation in Vietnam* (Washington, DC: Department of the Army: Vietnam Stud-

ies, 1975). On Japan specifically, see Thomas R. H. Havens, *Fire Across the Sea: The Vietnam War and Japan, 1965–1975* (Princeton, NJ: Princeton University Press, 1987).

8. Peter Edwards, *The Official History of Australia's Involvement in Southeast Asian Conflicts, 1948–1975: A Nation at War: Australian Politics, Society and Diplomacy During the Vietnam War, 1965–1975* (Canberra: Australian War Memorial with Allen & Unwin, 1997), 20–51. On Ted Serong, see Anne Blair, *There to the Bitter End: Ted Serong in Vietnam* (Sydney: Allen & Unwin, 2001). For a popular military history, see Frank Frost, *Australia's War in Vietnam* (Sydney: Allen & Unwin, 1987).

9. President Lyndon B. Johnson's News Conference, July 26, 1965, White House, *Weekly Compilation of Presidential Documents,* August 2, 1965.

10. I met and discussed these issues with Blair Seaborn in Vancouver in September 2002. He confirmed that although his American interlocutors had not said so directly, they were well aware his mission was other than peaceful. He stated that the Canadian prime minister had also known this and had asked him to go outside his neutral International Control Commission role as a favor to President Johnson.

11. George C. Herring, ed., *The Secret Diplomacy of the Vietnam War: The Negotiating Volumes of the Pentagon Papers* (Austin: University of Texas Press, 1983), 5, 10, 44. The Herring edition was assembled from two separate, partial texts (one his own, one Morton H. Halperin's) and contains numerous redactions. As a result of my own declassification requests, the full text of the negotiating volumes was finally released in 2000. It now forms part of the National Security Archive's "Vietnam II" microfiche set and part of the Digital National Security Archive collection; the paper copy is also available for research at the archive. Because the Herring edition is published and more widely available, I cite that version.

12. David Kaiser, "Discussions, Not Negotiations," in *The Search for Peace in Vietnam, 1964–1968,* ed. Lloyd C. Gardner and Ted Gittinger (College Station: Texas A&M University Press, 2004), 50. U Thant is quoted from *UN Monthly Chronicle,* May 1965.

13. Herring, *Negotiating Volumes,* 79.

14. General Cooper witnessed this argument because he was in the room holding the map display the Chiefs used to present their plan. Christian Appy records his account in *Patriots: The Vietnam War Remembered from All Sides* (New York: Viking, 2003), 121–123, quote from 122. However, the timing of the tale is not entirely clear: Cooper recalls the meeting as being in the Oval Office at precisely 2:00 PM on an early November day. Lyndon Johnson's daily diary, a sort of logbook, records no meetings with the full JCS between September 14 and December 10. General Wheeler met with Johnson in the Oval Office on November 19 for a little over twenty minutes, but this was in the morning (11:25 AM), not the afternoon. No other JCS members are recorded as being present. The only time the Chiefs were with Johnson at 2:00 PM was on December 10—but that was at the LBJ Ranch. For September 14, however, there is a clear case: on the thirteenth McNamara informed President Johnson that the Chiefs were proposing these measures, on September 14 they met with LBJ, and on the fifteenth McNamara sent the JCS a memorandum rejecting their proposal, specifically citing the risk of a U.S.-Chinese confrontation. The bombing program involved, incidentally, was Rolling Thunder 32/33.

15. Department of State, press release, "U.S. Official Position on Vietnam," January 3 and 7, 1966; U.S. Congress, Senate Foreign Relations Committee, *Background Information Relating to Southeast Asia and Vietnam,* 7th rev. ed. (Washington, DC: Government Printing Office, 1974), 285–286.

16. Former NSC staffer and Harriman assistant Chester Cooper, for example, in his last volume of memoirs, recalls the moment at the 1997 conference in Hanoi when he raised the fourteen points and argued that all had been negotiable: "Three decades later, I quoted Rusk's proposal to the North Vietnamese participants . . . Although they had been personally in-

volved and seemed to be steeped in the history of this period, they were unaware of and taken aback by the concessions inherent in the secretary's proposal" (Chester L. Cooper, *In the Shadows of History: 50 Years behind the Scenes of Cold War Diplomacy* [Amherst, NY: Prometheus, 2005], 229). I well remember that moment in Hanoi. The Vietnamese group included their deputy foreign minister of the time as well as several of his senior negotiators. When Cooper came out with this sally, there was almost a collective sigh from the historians on the U.S. delegation. It was definitely *not* the consensus among American analysts that the fourteen points were what Cooper claimed. George Herring, for example, another historian on the delegation, writes in his classic Vietnam account, "in fact the administration's 'Fourteen Points' offered few concessions" (George Herring, *America's Longest War: The United States and Vietnam, 1950–1975,* 3rd ed. [New York: McGraw-Hill, 1996], 183). See footnote 28, chapter 4, for information on the Hanoi conference.

17. Chester L. Cooper, *The Lost Crusade: America in Vietnam* (New York: Dodd, Mead, 1970), 296.

18. Cooper, *In the Shadows of History,* 224.

19. Thomas Powers, *Vietnam: The War at Home* (Boston: G. K. Hall, 1984), 68. Bundy sought to trap Morgenthau by reference to the Geneva Protocol of 1962, and the analyst conceded error, but in truth, the Kennedy and Johnson administrations' private calculations were not much different. Moreover, Morgenthau proved to be correct after 1975, when the communist Pathet Lao in fact took over Laos.

20. For Rusk, see *Department of State Bulletin,* May 10, 1965, 697; August 2, 1965, 188; and Nancy Zaroulis and Gerard Sullivan, *Who Spoke Up? American Protest against the War in Vietnam, 1963–1975* (New York: Holt, Rinehart & Winston, 1984), 42. Rusk went so far as to claim on one of these occasions that "no one" seriously believed the National Liberation Front had any real strength in South Vietnam, while at the same time, the administration secretly debated sending hundreds of thousands of troops to Vietnam to combat the NLF. For McNamara, see Zaroulis and Sullivan, *Who Spoke Up?* 46, and Robert S. McNamara with Brian VanDeMark, *In Retrospect: The Tragedy and Lessons of Vietnam* (New York: Times Books, 1995), 322.

21. The meetings of August 3 and 4 are best covered in William Conrad Gibbons, *The U.S. Government and the Vietnam War: Executive and Legislative Roles and Relationships,* vol. 4, *July 1965–January 1968* (Washington, DC: Government Printing Office, 1994), 30–32. This study was republished more widely by Princeton University Press in 1995.

22. McNamara, *In Retrospect,* 216.

23. Westmoreland, *A Soldier Reports,* 199.

24. Ibid.

25. Paul Starr with James F. Henry and Raymond P. Bonner, *The Discarded Army: Veterans after Vietnam* (New York: Charterhouse, 1973), 10.

26. Lyndon B. Johnson, *The Vantage Point: Perspectives on the Presidency, 1963–1969* (New York: Holt, Rinehart & Winston, 1971), 237.

27. Cooper, *Lost Crusade,* 291–292, recounts events of December 27 that suggest ad hoc action. That is the same day McNamara went to Texas for an hours-long private meeting (McNamara, *In Retrospect,* 225–226). But official documents (Department of State, *FRUS, 1964–1968,* vol. 3, *June–December 1965* [Washington, DC: Government Printing Office, 1996], 576–721) make it clear that the long pause was always intended, extensively discussed, and fully staffed. The events of December 27 also relate to a last-minute attempt by Westmoreland to obtain a decision to renew the bombing.

28. Cooper, *In the Shadows of History,* 230.

29. Johnson, *Vantage Point,* 237.

30. Graham A. Cosmas, *The United States Army in Vietnam: MACV: The Joint Command*

in the Years of Escalation, 1962–1967 (Washington, DC: Center for Military History, 2006), 255.

31. Quoted in Ky, *Buddha's Child,* 187.

32. Embassy cables and MACV dispatches show that Ky discussed the troop move with Ambassador Henry Cabot Lodge and that the American diplomat acceded to the request (Department of State, *FRUS, 1964–1968,* vol. 4, *Vietnam 1966* [Washington, DC: Government Printing Office, 1998], 318–319). Ky relies on these for his own account (*Buddha's Child,* 205–207). The U.S. Marine Corps' official history for this period also confirms the use of U.S. aircraft (Jack Shulimson, *U.S. Marines in Vietnam: An Expanding War, 1966* [Washington, DC: Headquarters, U.S. Marine Corps, History and Museums Division, 1982], 82). General Westmoreland, however, insists that he denied the use of U.S. planes (*A Soldier Reports,* 222).

33. Henry F. Graff, *The Tuesday Cabinet: Deliberation and Decision on Peace and War under Lyndon B. Johnson* (Englewood Cliffs, NJ: Prentice-Hall, 1970), 68–108.

34. Johnson, *Vantage Point,* 247.

35. White House, Jack Valenti, "Notes of a Meeting, Washington, April 2, 1966, 1:30 PM," in *FRUS, 1964–1968,* 4: 317.

36. White House, Jack Valenti, "Notes of a Meeting, Washington, April 4, 1966, 7:10–8:35 PM," ibid., 323–325; quote from 324.

37. The best analysis of this period is in Robert J. Topmiller, *The Lotus Unleashed: The Buddhist Peace Movement in South Vietnam, 1964–1966* (Lexington: University Press of Kentucky, 2002), 93–142.

38. U. S. Grant Sharp, *Strategy for Defeat: Vietnam in Retrospect* (Novato, CA: Presidio Press, 1978), 108–111 and passim. On discussions of purpose, as well as aerial strategy, see James C. Thompson, *Rolling Thunder: Understanding Policy and Program Failure* (Chapel Hill: University of North Carolina Press, 1980), and Mark Clodfelter, *The Limits of Air Power: The American Bombing of North Vietnam* (New York: Free Press, 1989). For a discussion focused more on signaling and other aspects of the air campaign, see Wallace J. Thies, *When Governments Collide: Coercion and Diplomacy in the Vietnam Conflict, 1964–1968* (Berkeley: University of California Press, 1980).

39. A good account of the air campaign is in Wayne Thompson, *To Hanoi and Back: The U.S. Air Force and North Vietnam, 1966–1973* (Washington, DC: Smithsonian Institution Press, [2000]). This book apparently resulted from the private publication of a concluding volume of the Air Force official history that was not published by the U.S. government. The first volume of that history is Jacob Van Staaveren, *Gradual Failure: The Air War Over North Vietnam, 1965–1966* (Washington, DC: Air Force History and Museums Program, 2002). The Navy included its air campaign in an official history for the years 1965–1968 that has never been published. For a summary overview, see Ronald B. Frankum Jr., *Like Rolling Thunder: The Air War in Vietnam, 1964–1975* (Lanham, MD: Rowman & Littlefield, 2005).

40. On the munitions shortage, see Van Staaveren, *Gradual Failure,* 263–265, and John Prados, *The Blood Road: The Ho Chi Minh Trail and the Vietnam War* (New York: John Wiley's Sons, 1999), 158–160. It is worth reiterating the point I made there: had the air war in Southeast Asia been freed of all restrictions, it still could not have been waged effectively because the U.S. military did not have the munitions necessary to conduct it.

41. "Man of the Year: The Guardians at the Gate," *Time* (Latin American edition), January 7, 1966, 15.

42. Quoted in "The War: The Hawaii Conference," *Time* (Latin America edition), February 11, 1966, 5.

43. Quoted in "The War: Cards on the Table," *Time,* May 5, 1967, 11.

44. "What Dayan Says About Vietnam," *U.S. News and World Report,* June 26, 1967, 58.

45. "To Hanoi With Candor," *Time* (Latin America edition), May 26, 1967, 7.

46. "War at Crisis—Mobilization Ahead?" *U.S. News and World Report,* June 12, 1967, 29–30.

47. "McNamara's Mission," *Newsweek,* June 26, 1967, 50.

48. Clarence R. Wyatt, *Paper Soldiers: The American Press and the Vietnam War* (New York: W. W. Norton, 1993).

49. William Hammond, *The Army in Vietnam: Public Affairs: The Military and the Media, 1962–1968* (Washington, DC: Center for Military History, 1988).

50. Gibbons, *U.S. Government and the Vietnam War,* 4: 157.

51. Quoted in *The Vietnam Hearings* (New York: Vintage, 1966), 170. That volume reprints the most important parts of the Fulbright hearings. For General Gavin's Vietnam position, which draws explicitly on his Dien Bien Phu experience, see James M. Gavin, "A Communication on Vietnam," *Harper's,* February 1966.

52. Melvin Small, *Johnson, Nixon, and the Doves* (New Brunswick, NJ: Rutgers University Press), 80; Charles DeBenedetti with Charles Chatfield, *An American Ordeal: The Antiwar Movement of the Vietnam Era* (Syracuse, NY: Syracuse University Press, 1990), 143; Adam Garfinkle, *Telltale Hearts: The Origins and Impact of the Vietnam Antiwar Movement* (New York: St. Martin's, 1995), 89.

53. Quoted in J. Y. Smith, "Post Editor J. Russell Wiggins Dies at 96," *Washington Post,* November 20, 2000, B7.

54. The force balance and logistical aspects of moving troops to South Vietnam are discussed in detail in John Prados, *The Hidden History of the Vietnam War* (Chicago: Ivan Dee, 1995), 102–110.

55. CIA, "Intelligence Memorandum: Reactions Abroad to Vietnam Protest Demonstrations in the U.S.," October 26, 1965 (declassified June 15, 1993), Texas Tech University, Vietnam Center Archive, CIA Collection, item 04108114004.

56. Seth Rosenfeld, "The Campus Files: Reagan, Hoover and the UC Red Scare," *San Francisco Chronicle,* special ed., June 9, 2002, http://sfgate.com/cgi?f=/chronicle/archive/2002/06/09/MNCFLEADIN.DTL. See additional headings for subsidiary articles and FBI documents.

57. Daniel C. Tsang, "The Few, the Proud, the Spies," *OCWeekly,* July 8, 1999, http://www.ocweekly.com/columns/columns/the-few-the-proud-the-spies/18186/.

58. Historian James Hershberg is at work on what will undoubtedly be the definitive examination of all the events surrounding Marigold. For an interim report of his findings, see "Who Murdered Marigold?—New Evidence on the Mysterious Failure of Poland's Secret Initiative to Start U.S.–North Vietnamese Peace Talks, 1966" (written with the assistance of L. W. Gluchowski), Cold War International History Project, Working Paper no. 27, February 2000.

59. Joan Morrison and Robert K. Morrison, *From Camelot to Kent State: The Sixties Experience in the Words of Those Who Lived It* (New York: Times Books, 1987), 107–111, quote from 107.

60. Christian Appy, *Working Class War: American Combat Soldiers in Vietnam* (Chapel Hill: University of North Carolina Press, 1993).

61. Gibbons, *U.S. Government and the Vietnam War,* 604.

62. NSC note, Walt Rostow–Nicolas deB. Katzenbach, March 22, 1967, with attachment, letter and "Preliminary Thoughts" paper, Abbott Washburn–Walt Rostow, March 22, 1967, LBJL, LBJP, NSF, CFVN, box 42/1, folder "Vietnam: Memos, v. 68 (3/20–31/67) [2 of 2]." Also see Kenneth T. Downs–Walt Rostow, March 28, 1967, LBJL, LBJP, NSF, CFVN, box 42/1, folder "Vietnam: Cables, v. 68 (3/20–31/67)," which shows Washburn and Kermit "Kim" Roosevelt in active contact with Rostow and another version of the proposal.

63. NSC memorandum, Walt W. Rostow–President Lyndon Johnson, March 29, 1967,

11:00 AM, LBJL, William C. Gibbons Papers, box 25, folder "March 1967 [8 of 8]." Contrary to Gibbons's conclusion that the idea did not go forward (*U.S. Government and the Vietnam War*, 606), in fact it did. Many members of the group that *Time* identified in its coverage of the statement issued were the same individuals suggested in the original proposal memorandum. The group appears to have morphed into the American Security Council.

64. White House memorandum, Harry McPherson–President Lyndon Johnson, quoted in Gibbons, *U.S. Government and the Vietnam War*, 606; emphasis in original.

Chapter 6. Trampling Out the Vintage

1. Harrison E. Salisbury, *Behind the Lines—Hanoi, December 23, 1966–January 7, 1967* (New York: Harper & Row, 1967). Also see Salisbury's retrospective account in *A Time of Change: A Reporter's Tale of Our Time* (New York: Harper & Row, 1988).

2. Phil G. Goulding, *Confirm or Deny: Informing the People on National Security* (New York: Harper & Row, 1970), 54. Critics such as Guenther Lewy subsequently attacked Salisbury for using details drawn from Vietnamese pamphlets that obviously had a propaganda purpose; see Guenther Lewy, *America in Vietnam* (New York: Oxford University Press, 1978), 398–404. However, such data were the only figures available from DRV sources, and critics would have attacked any DRV "official" statistics with equal alacrity for the same reason: reports of civilian casualties created pressure for restrictions on bombing that threatened to reduce its effectiveness. Critics assume—and I lack the space to engage that argument here—that the bombing of North Vietnam actually could have been successful, which is pure speculation. It is worth noting that postwar histories, including U.S. official histories, have used Vietnamese sources and data of the same type.

3. Harry Ashmore and William C. Baggs, *Mission to Hanoi: A Chronicle of Double-Dealing in High Places* (New York: Bantam, 1968), 54.

4. Ibid., 7.

5. The best account of the Sunflower episode remains Chester L. Cooper, *The Lost Crusade: America in Vietnam* (New York: Dodd, Mead, 1970), 342–368. Johnson administration officials later sat for interviews for a semiofficial account by journalists David Kraslow and Stuart H. Loory, *The Secret Search for Peace in Vietnam* (New York: Random House, 1968), 186–198. Cooper's Johnson Library oral history is also eloquent on this experience. The Pentagon Papers account of Sunflower is in George H. Herring, ed., *The Secret Diplomacy of the Vietnam War: The Negotiating Volumes of the Pentagon Papers* (Austin: University of Texas Press, 1983), 371–516. Also see the official documents collection in Department of State, *FRUS, 1964–1968*, vol. 5, *1967* (Washington, DC: Government Printing Office, 2002), 75–181.

6. There remains some uncertainty regarding the nature of this DMZ buildup. CIA reports, including triangulations of VPA division headquarters by NSA code breakers, show the three divisions. In contrast, U.S. orders of battle for the adversary show this number of divisions in the area both before and after this date, and JCS official historians cite U.S. Marine intelligence reports that quote Hanoi's strength along the DMZ after the pause at 20,560, just 3,780 more than in June 1966. JCS Historical Division, *History of the Joint Chiefs of Staff: The Joint Chiefs of Staff and the War in Vietnam, 1960–1968, Pt. III* (Washington, DC: JCS Joint Secretariat, July 1, 1970), 42–39 (declassified May 25, 1994), copy in National Security Archive, Vietnam II Collection.

7. Department of State, Office of the Ambassador at Large (Chester Cooper), "Re 'A Package for Hanoi' (Rewrap No. 1)," December 4, 1966 (declassified January 24, 1987), Library of Congress, W. Averell Harriman Papers, Subject Series, box 520, folder "Vietnam, General, October–December 1966."

8. Chester L. Cooper, *In the Shadows of History: 50 Years behind the Scenes of Cold War Diplomacy* (Amherst, NY: Prometheus, 2005), 248.

9. Schlesinger's journal, December 7, 1967, quoted in Arthur M. Schlesinger Jr., *Robert Kennedy and His Times* (New York: Ballantine, 1979), 884.

10. Andrew F. Krepinievich Jr., *The Army and Vietnam* (Baltimore: Johns Hopkins University Press, 1986); James W. Gibson, *The Perfect War: The War We Couldn't Lose and How We Did* (New York: Random House, 1986); and Cincinnatus (Cecil B. Currey), *Self-Destruction: The Disintegration and Decay of the United States Army During the Vietnam Era* (New York: W. W. Norton, 1981) all give powerful testimony along these lines, although they focus on combat types and tactics rather than the officers' experiences.

11. Lyndon B. Johnson, *The Vantage Point: Perspectives on the Presidency, 1963–1969* (New York: Holt, Rinehart & Winston, 1971), 257.

12. LBJ cites the document in ibid., 258. The NLF figure corresponds rather closely with numbers in MACV's monthly "Population and Area Control Report," which estimated that between July 1965 and September 1966, Vietnamese under Saigon's control increased by 1,486,000. See *The Senator Gravel Edition: The Pentagon Papers: The Defense Department History of United States Decisionmaking on Vietnam* (Boston: Beacon Press, [1971]), 4: 375, table (hereafter *Gravel Pentagon Papers*).

13. *Gravel Pentagon Papers,* 4: 405.

14. Ibid., 387.

15. Ibid., 322–387. Cf. Graham A. Cosmas, *The United States Army in Vietnam: MACV: The Joint Command in the Years of Escalation, 1962–1967* (Washington, DC: Center of Military History, 2006), 411–416.

16. MACV cable MAC 09101, March 18, 1967, in *FRUS, 1964–1968,* 5: 253–255. Cf. *Gravel Pentagon Papers,* 4: 426–431 (*FRUS* does not print the parts of the cable detailing the "minimum essential force" or the sectors where it would be deployed). Troops would have totaled 678,248 if extra personnel spaces already requested to fill out the units in Program 4 were included.

17. *Gravel Pentagon Papers,* 4: 432.

18. Joint Chiefs of Staff, "Movement of a Corps-Size Force to South Vietnam," JCSM-148-67, March 17, 1967 (declassified May 17, 1996), National Security Archive, FOIA.

19. James Reston, "Tougher Johnson Stance," *New York Times,* March 16, 1967.

20. Marquis W. Childs, "Johnson's Image as War Leader," *St. Louis Post-Dispatch,* March 18, 1967.

21. Richard Dudman, "Mansfield Issues Warning against Invading North Vietnam," *St. Louis Post-Dispatch,* March 17, 1967.

22. Walter Lippmann, "Guam, Prelude to Escalation," *Washington Post,* March 21, 1967.

23. Milton Leitenberg, memo, "Record of Phone Conversations Concerning Purported Invasion of North Vietnam," n.d. (c. March 23, 1967), copy courtesy of Milton Leitenberg.

24. Taylor Branch, *At Canaan's Edge: America in the King Years, 1965–68* (New York: Simon & Schuster, 2006), 581–604.

25. There are several records of this crucial meeting. One is a set of notes attributed to press secretary George Christian (*FRUS, 1964–1968,* 5: 349–352). The typescript copy of these notes bears the handwritten notation "McNaughton," however ("Notes on Discussion with the President," April 27, 1967, LBJL, William C. Gibbons Papers, box 26, folder "April 1967 [4 of 5]"). These notes also exist in John McNaughton's office files. Another record is a set of handwritten notes attributed to Walt Rostow ("Meeting with President, Morning 10:30 AM—4/27/67," ibid.). There is also a record of the meeting in Westmoreland's diary ("General Westmoreland's History Notes, 10–30 April 1967," 14–17, LBJL, William C. Westmoreland Papers, box 11, folder "History File v. 15 (April 10–30, 1967)." Several participants also wrote about the meeting: Walt W. Rostow, *The Diffusion of Power* (New York: Macmillan,

1972), 512–513; William C. Westmoreland, *A Soldier Reports* (New York: Dell, 1980), 298–299; Robert S. McNamara and Brian VanDeMark, *In Retrospect: The Tragedy and Lessons of Vietnam* (New York: Times Books, 1995), 265.

26. This account draws on the sources cited in note 25; all quotes are from the Christian–McNaughton (?) notes.

27. NSC memorandum, Walt W. Rostow–Lyndon Johnson, April 27, 1967, 2:45 PM (declassified May 12, 1993), LBJL, LBJP, NSF, CFVN, box 43, folder "VN: Cables v. 70 (4/25–5/8/67)."

28. "Westmoreland's History Notes," April 27, 1967.

29. Rostow, *Diffusion of Power,* 513.

30. Department of State memorandum, William P. Bundy–Nicholas deB. Katzenbach, "Thoughts on Strategy in Vietnam," May 1, 1967 (declassified January 11, 1991), LBJL, Paul Warnke Papers (John McNaughton Files), box 2, folder "McNTN III — Drafts 1967 (2)." Bundy also believed that an invasion would "stabilize the internal Chinese situation at least temporarily, that is, halt Beijing's paralysis amid the Cultural Revolution." His assessment of the Laos option was that sending an ARVN division into Laos "would almost certainly be ineffective" and would lead to immediate demands for more troops while seriously compromising Laotian prime minister Souvanna Phouma's position. Bundy was responding to Katzenbach's request for a review of strategies in play as a result of Program 5 issued on April 24.

31. "Westmoreland History Notes," 16; Douglas Pike interview, Wheaton, IL, March 7, 1996.

32. Arthur M. Schlesinger Jr., *Journals: 1952–2000,* ed. Andrew Schlesinger and Stephen Schlesinger (New York: Penguin, 2007), 260.

33. Richard Dudman, "Invasion of North Vietnam Debated," *St. Louis Post-Dispatch,* May 7, 1967.

34. Department of Defense, Robert McNamara, "Future Actions in Vietnam," May 19, 1967 (declassified June 9, 1989), LBJL, LBJP, NSF, CFVN, box 81/82, folder "VN 3E(1)b Future Military Operations, 6/65–12/67."

35. NSC memorandum, Walt Rostow–Lyndon Johnson, May 20, 1967, 4:30 PM, National Security Archive, Robert S. McNamara Donation, box 2, folder "Vietnam Documents, Chapter 9."

36. Anatoly Dobrynin, *In Confidence: Moscow's Ambassador to America's Six Cold War Presidents* (New York: Times Books, 1995), 165.

37. Quoted in Ashmore and Baggs, *Mission to Hanoi,* 39.

38. Vo Nguyen Giap, *Big Victory, Great Task* (New York: Frederick A. Praeger, 1968), 101–102.

39. Quoted in William Broyles Jr., *Brothers in Arms: A Journey from War to Peace* (New York: Knopf, 1986), 97.

40. Merle L. Pribbenow, "General Vo Nguyen Giap and the Mysterious Evolution of the Plan for the 1968 Tet Offensive," *Journal of Vietnamese Studies* 3, 2 (Summer 2008): 1–33.

41. For an important discussion of the Anti-Party affair in relation to the Tet offensive, see Lien-Hang T. Nguyen, "The War Politburo: North Vietnam's Diplomatic and Political Road to the Tet Offensive," *Journal of Vietnamese Studies* 1, 1–2 (Spring 2006): 4–55.

42. Quoted in Odd Arne Westad et al., eds., *77 Conversations Between Chinese and Foreign Leaders on the Wars in Indochina, 1964–1977,* Cold War International History Project, Working Paper no. 22 (Washington, DC: Woodrow Wilson Center for International Scholars, May 1998), 103.

43. As a matter of fact, contemporaneous CIA memoranda accurately reported Thanh's cause of death as a heart attack. CIA, Directorate of Intelligence, Intelligence Memorandum, "Problems Posed for North Vietnam by Death of Politburo Member Nguyen Chi Thanh," no.

1365/67, July 11, 1967 (declassified February 13, 2001), LBJL, LBJP, NSF, CFVN, box 86, folder "VN3(L)1: North Vietnam Leadership Attitudes." This CIA memorandum is probably one source of the conventional wisdom that the locus of Hanoi's strategic debate lay in a dispute between Thanh and Giap.

44. For a more detailed discussion of these points, see John Prados and Ray W. Stubbe, *Valley of Decision: The Siege of Khe Sanh* (New York: Dell, 1993), 197–199. Cf. John Prados, *The Blood Road: The Ho Chi Minh Trail and the Vietnam War* (New York: John Wiley's Sons, 1999), 234–237.

45. Giap, *Big Victory, Great Task,* 58, 90, 94, 105, 198–199.

46. Ngo Vinh Long, "The Tet Offensive and Its Aftermath," in *The American War in Vietnam,* ed. Jayne Werner and David Hunt (Ithaca, NY: Cornell University Southeast Asia Program, 1993), 31–33.

47. Historian Jeffrey Kimball argues that although developments in the antiwar movement encouraged the North Vietnamese, Hanoi understood that the U.S. government was capable of continuing the war despite public doubts. See Jeffrey Kimball, *Nixon's Vietnam War* (Lawrence: University Press of Kansas, 1998), 46.

48. Westmoreland, *A Soldier Reports,* 296.

49. Charles DeBenedetti with Charles Chatfield, *An American Ordeal: The Antiwar Movement of the Vietnam Era* (Syracuse, NY: Syracuse University Press, 1990), 176–180, 191.

50. These and preceding details are taken from the Church Committee's 1976 report: U.S. Congress, Senate Select Committee to Study Governmental Operations with Respect to Intelligence [Church Committee], *Final Report: Book III: Supplementary Detailed Staff Reports on Intelligence Activities and the Rights of Americans* (Washington, DC: Government Printing Office, 1976).

51. Johnson, *Vantage Point,* 169–170.

52. Tom Hayden, *Reunion: A Memoir* (New York: Random House, 1988), 143.

53. *Report of the National Advisory Commission on Civil Disorders* [Kerner Commission] (New York: Bantam, 1968).

54. Department of the Army, Robert E. Jordan III, Secretary/Undersecretary of the Army, memorandum, "Review of Civil Disturbance Intelligence History," n.d.; U.S. Congress, Senate Government Operations Committee, *Hearings: Legislative Proposals to Strengthen Congressional Oversight of the Nation's Intelligence Agencies* (Washington, DC: Government Printing Office, 1974), 176.

55. Church Committee, *Final Report: Book II: Intelligence Activities and the Rights of Americans* (Washington, DC: Government Printing Office, 1976), 83, n. 363.

56. Fred Halsted, *Out Now! A Participant's Account of the American Movement against the Vietnam War* (New York: Monad Press, 1978), 293.

57. Kirkpatrick Sale, *SDS* (New York: Vintage, 1974), 321.

58. Jessica Mitford, *The Trial of Dr. Spock, the Reverend William Sloane Coffin, Jr., Michael Ferber, Mitchell Goodman, and Marcus Raskin* (New York: Vintage, 1970), 53–54.

59. According to Tom Hayden, Bratislava flowed from an invitation to himself and Dave Dellinger for a seminar-style meeting (*Reunion,* 206–210, 213–237), which he saw as "a confusing success" (208). Activist Todd Gitlin was another attendee at Bratislava. His account of the conference makes it clear that the activists were in no way under North Vietnamese control and were in fact meeting the Vietnamese for the first time. Some groaned when Dellinger observed that, like the Vietnamese, Americans loved their country. Gitlin records the excess of enthusiasm that led someone to proclaim that the Movement was like the NLF behind LBJ's front lines. See Todd Gitlin, *The Sixties: Years of Protest, Days of Rage* (New York: Bantam, 1987), 270–273. In later years Gitlin felt distaste for this episode: "Questions that might have emerged in calmer times about the political nature of 'the other side' felt like distractions and were swept into the shadows" (273). The post-Bratislava tour of the DRV by

these Americans led to the first North Vietnamese release of U.S. prisoners. The Bratislava meeting would be a subject of major interest in the CIA's November 15, 1967, report to the president. Deletions in the source document, which are virtually identical in versions declassified in 1979 and in 2001, suggest that although the agency had inside sources at the conference it uncovered "little information . . . beyond discussion of the planned demonstrations" ("International Connections of US Peace Groups," 25, LBJL, LBJP, NSF, Intelligence File, box 3, folder "US Peace Groups"). There is a sense that the CIA believed there had to be more, however, such as some communist control mechanism. Incidentally, the sole difference between the 1979 and 2001 redactions of this document is the statement that the only connection the CIA could find between the peace groups and the Communist Party of the United States—which was assumed in the document to be passing along substantial Soviet advice and applying influence—was that the party "possibly" gave activists some airline tickets (13). The agency's statement that "contact between Hanoi and the leaders of the US peace movement has developed to a point where it is now almost continuous" (2) was true only in the sense that a procession of activists went to Paris to meet Hanoi's representatives, and two delegations had by this time visited North Vietnam itself. The U.S. Secret Service, which opened an office in Paris to watch activists, and the CIA itself, which surveilled the North Vietnamese legation there, had more continuous "contact" than did the peace movement.

60. Quoted in Nancy Zaroulis and Gerald Sullivan, *Who Spoke Up? American Protest against the War in Vietnam, 1963–1975* (New York: Holt, Rinehart & Winston, 1984), 131–132.

61. Abbie Hoffman, *The Best of Abbie Hoffman* (New York: Four Walls, Eight Windows, 1989), 26. This material first appeared in Hoffman's 1968 book *Revolution for the Hell of It*.

62. Department of Defense memorandum, "The President's Meeting with: Secretary Mc-Namara, Attorney General Clark, Under Secretary Katzenbach, et. al," undated, attached to memorandum, Solis Horwitz-Warren Christopher, September 30, 1967 (declassified July 27, 1984), National Security Archive, Robert McNamara Donation, box 2, folder "Vietnam Documents, Ch. 8, March on Pentagon."

63. White House, Tom Johnson memorandum, "Notes of the President's Meeting with Educators from Cambridge, Massachusetts Colleges and Universities," September 26, 1967, LBJL, LBJP, Tom Johnson Meeting Notes series, box 2, folder "September 26, 1967."

64. National Security Agency, DIRNSA cable, October 21, 1967, reprinted in Church Committee, *Hearings,* vol. 5, *The National Security Agency and Fourth Amendment Rights* (Washington, DC: Government Printing Office, 1976), 147–148. Material from earlier in the paragraph is drawn from the Church Committee's detailed staff reports on the NSA. It is notable that the subject of NSA domestic surveillance has gone untouched in the Vietnam histories and monographs this agency has declassified.

65. Christopher H. Pyle, *Military Surveillance of Civilian Politics, 1967–1970* (New York: Garland, 1986), 52–69; Norman Mailer, *Armies of the Night* (New York: New American Library, 1968); Tom Wells, *The War Within: America's Battle Over Vietnam* (Berkeley: University of California Press, 1994), 184–191. Paul Nitze's comments are from an undated interview excerpt in the McNamara papers cited above. The data on the Army Security Service is from Church Committee, bk. III, 808–809.

66. Quoted in Paul Hendrickson, "McNamara: Specters of Vietnam," *Washington Post,* May 10, 1984, B1.

67. Hoffman, *Best of Abbie Hoffman,* p. 29.

68. Halsted, *Out Now!* 338.

69. Mailer, *Armies of the Night.*

70. Halsted, *Out Now!* 339.

71. White House memorandum, Jim Jones-Lyndon Johnson, "Luncheon Meeting with

Secretaries Rusk and McNamara, Walt Rostow, CIA Director Richard Helms, George Christian and Jim Jones," November 4, 1967, in *FRUS, 1964–1968,* 5: 989.

72. For example, Admiral Sharp told a Washington conference on November 9, 1995, held specifically to comment on McNamara's book, "We had the forces we needed to win . . . we weren't allowed to use them." General Westmoreland told the same audience, "In the final analysis we must have done something right." Former Vietnam pacification official and senior CIA official William E. Colby attributed defeat to McNamara's "faulty plans and policies" (Marc Leepson, "Perspectives: At a Conference on McNamara's Book *In Retrospect,* Military Heavyweights Lined up to 'Knife the Mac,'" *Vietnam,* December 1996, 62). Rostow went so far as to argue that the United States had, in fact, *won* the Vietnam war, save for the "wild card" of the antiwar movement ("The Case for the Vietnam War," *Parameters* [Winter 1996–1997]: 39–50). These unreconstructed war managers retailed the view that has become the rallying point for the so-called Vietnam revisionists whom I term neo-orthodox, but they were not the only ones denouncing McNamara's memoir. Former *Ramparts* editor Robert Scheer's perspective was titled "Sorry, Mac—You're Not Forgiven," *Los Angeles Times,* April 16, 1995. Wartime draft evaders in Canada complained of an apologia too little and too late (Charles Trueheart, "Deserters Bemused," *Washington Post,* April 22, 1995, A1, A21), and Americans on both sides of the politics of the war expressed anger (B. Drummond Ayres Jr., "Belated Regrets About Vietnam Create a Consensus of Antipathy," *New York Times,* April 15, 1995, 7). Conservative columnist Wesley Pruden railed, "Mr. McNamara insists that American arms could not win a victory, and yet complains that every time Hanoi seemed ready to talk peace the moment was ruined by the success of American arms" ("Trying to Clean up the Meat Grinder," *Washington Times,* April 11, 1995, A4). From the antiwar side, Rusk's son Richard contributed "Did He Help with the Healing?" *Washington Post,* April 26, 1995, A23. This sampling is only a fragment of the public mulling over of the McNamara memoir.

73. Stanley Karnow, "An Antiwar Protester Comes out of the Closet," *New York Times,* April 16, 1995, E3.

74. W. Averell Harriman, file memorandum, "Memorandum of Conversation with Secretary McNamara," October 10, 1966 (declassified January 30, 1986), Library of Congress, W. Averell Harriman Papers, Subject Series, box 520, folder "Vietnam, General, October–December 1966.

75. Author's notes, conversation with Robert McNamara.

76. Admiral U. S. Grant Sharp, CINCPAC cable, n.d., quoted in *Gravel Pentagon Papers,* 4: 193.

77. William W. Momyer, *Airpower in Three Wars* (Maxwell Air Force Base, AL: Air University Press, 2003), 29.

78. White House, Tom Johnson memorandum, "Notes of a Meeting," July 12, 1967, in *FRUS, 1964–1968,* 5: 609.

79. U.S. Congress, Armed Services Committee, Preparedness Investigating Subcommittee, *Hearings: Air War against North Vietnam, Part 2* (Washington, DC: Government Printing Office, 1967), 191. This hearing is printed in five parts plus a committee report.

80. Robert D. Joffe, letter to the editor, *New York Times,* April 13, 1995, A24.

81. McNamara, *In Retrospect,* 261.

82. Daniel Ellsberg, *Secrets: A Memoir of Vietnam and the Pentagon Papers* (New York: Viking, 2002), 141–142.

83. Tom Johnson, "Notes of a Meeting," July 12, 1967.

84. "The War: Taking Stock," *Time,* July 14, 1967, 18–19.

85. Quoted in Clark Clifford and Richard Holbrooke, *Counsel to the President, A Memoir* (New York: Random House, 1991), 447.

86. Armed Services Committee, *Hearings: Air War against North Vietnam, Part 4,* 280.

87. Department of State, Averell Harriman, "Memorandum of Conversation with Secretary McNamara," July 1, 1967 (declassified April 7, 1998), W. Averell Harriman Papers, Subject Series, box 520, folder "Vietnam, General, July–December 1967."

88. Department of State, W. Averell Harriman, "Personal and Top Secret: For Personal Files Only: Memorandum of Conversation with Secretary McNamara," August 22, 1967 (declassification date illegible), ibid.

89. Quoted in Larry Berman, *Lyndon Johnson's War: The Road to Stalemate in Vietnam* (New York: W. W. Norton, 1989), 89–90.

90. White House memorandum, Harry McPherson–Lyndon Johnson, October 27, 1967, 11:05 AM, LBJL, LBJP, NSF, CFVN, box 127, folder "Vietnam [March 19, 1970 Memo] (1)."

91. Quoted in Clifford and Holbrooke, *Counsel to the President,* 457.

92. Ibid.

93. All the commentaries, bearing various dates in November 1967, are contained in the same file of the Lyndon Johnson Papers as the McNamara memorandum itself. See note 90.

94. Department of State, Nicholas deB. Katzenbach, "Memorandum for the President, Subject: Vietnam," November 16, 1967 (declassified July 29, 1994), ibid. Larry Berman (*Lyndon Johnson's War,* 117–118) was the first to draw attention to this important Katzenbach analysis. Berman was working from an incomplete redaction. The 1994 release is more complete and even more impressive.

95. White House, Lyndon Johnson, "Memorandum of President for File," n.d. [December 18, 1967], ibid. See note 90.

96. McNamara, *In Retrospect,* 311.

97. NSC memorandum, Walt W. Rostow–Lyndon Johnson, March 17, 1967, LBJL, LBJP, NSF, Memos to the President series, box 14, folder "Rostow, v. 24 (March 16–31, 1967)."

98. White House, Jones–Johnson memorandum, November 4, 1967.

99. Melvin Small wrote about the VIG in 1988 in *Johnson, Nixon, and the Doves* (New Brunswick, NJ: Rutgers University Press, 1988), and I covered the unit in much greater detail in my NSC history *Keepers of the Keys* (New York: William Morrow, 1991). However, between 1971, when Don Oberdorfer included a garbled version of the unit in his work *Tet!* (Garden City, NY: Doubleday, 1971), and 1988 there was nothing. For example, in a very reputable study of 1967–1968, Larry Berman (*Lyndon Johnson's War*) includes a full chapter on "The Big Sell" (114–138) without once mentioning the VIG. Beginning with William Conrad Gibbons's exhaustive volumes on Washington (Congress and the presidents) at war, it has been common to mention the VIG in the context of the antecedents of Tet, but even today the VIG's continuing and wider impact is ignored, as is the fact that the VIG continued to operate during the Nixon and Ford administrations.

100. For books, see the account by the CIA officer at the center of the controversy, Sam A. Adams with Thomas Powers, *War of Numbers: An Intelligence Memoir* (South Royalton, VT: Steerforth, 1994); C. Michael Hiam, *Who the Hell Are We Fighting? The Story of Sam Adams and the Vietnam Intelligence Wars* (Hanover, NH: Steerforth, 2006); Philip B. Davidson, *Secrets of the Vietnam War* (Novato, CA: Presidio, 1990); and George W. Allen, *None So Blind: A Personal Account of the Intelligence Failure in Vietnam* (Chicago: Ivan Dee, 2001). Probably the best among many sources on the trial is Bob Brewin and Sydney Shaw, *Vietnam on Trial: Westmoreland vs. CBS* (New York: Atheneum, 1987). The television documentary that led General Westmoreland to file his lawsuit was *CBS Reports: The Uncounted Enemy* (1982). For the lawsuit, court records, and related materials, see *Westmoreland v. CBS Inc., et al.,* 752 F2d 16 (2nd Circuit, 1984). Sam Adams and General Daniel O. Graham, antagonists in the dispute, also testified during the Pike Committee investigations of U.S. intelligence in 1975. An official CIA account is in Harold P. Ford, *CIA and the Vietnam Policymakers: Three Episodes, 1962–1968* (Washington, DC: CIA/Center for the Study of Intelligence,

1998), 85–104. The narrative here follows primarily Ford's account and my own in John Prados, *The Hidden History of the Vietnam War* (Chicago: Ivan Dee, 1995), 121–128.

101. NSC memorandum Harold Kaplan–Walt Rostow, November 9, 1967 (declassified June 29, 1984), LBJL, LBJP, NSF, CFVN, box 99, folder "VN7E(2) Public Relations Activities, 11/67."

102. NSC memorandum, Walt W. Rostow–Lyndon B. Johnson, November 15, 1967, 12:15 PM, in *FRUS, 1964–1968,* 5: 1027–1028.

103. NSC, untitled attachment to memorandum, Robert N. Ginsburgh–Walt Rostow, September 26, 1967, LBJL, LBJP, NSF, CFVN, box 99, folder "VN7E(1)a: Public Relations Activities, 9/67–10/67."

104. Transcript, Ambassador Bunker on *Face the Nation, Department of State Bulletin* 57, 1484 (October 2, 1967): 416–421.

105. NSC memorandum, Art McCafferty–Marvin Watson, with attachment, December 5, 1967, LBJL, LBJP, WHCF, Confidential File: ND 19/CO 312, box 73, folder "Situation in Vietnam, October–December 1967."

106. NSC memorandum, Richard Moose–Bill Bundy et al., November 21, 1967, attachment 1, LBJL, LBJP, NSF, Komer-Leonhart Files, box 16, folder "Monday Group (2)."

107. For example, Berman, *Lyndon Johnson's War,* 114–125, 137–138.

108. Melvin Small is a welcome exception, having devoted significant attention to this effort. In addition to *Johnson, Nixon, and the Doves,* cited earlier, see his *Covering Dissent: The Media and the Anti-Vietnam War Movement* (New Brunswick, NJ: Rutgers University Press, 1994). Also see Chester Pach, "The War on Television: TV News, the Johnson Administration and Vietnam," in *A Companion to the Vietnam War,* ed. Marilyn B. Young and Robert Buzzanco (Malden, MA: Blackwell, 2002), 450–469.

109. Don Oberdorfer, "Statistics on War Fail to Show Real Progress," *Washington Post,* November 24, 1967, A1.

110. Don Oberdorfer, *Tet! The Turning Point in the Vietnam War,* 2nd ed. (Baltimore: Johns Hopkins University Press, 2001), 99–101.

111. Joint Chiefs of Staff, Wheeler–Westmoreland, Cable JCS 9566 Nov 67, 081512Z, LBJL, William Westmoreland Papers, Eyes Only Message File, box 37, folder "From 1/11/67–30/11/67."

112. Westmoreland, *A Soldier Reports,* 303.

113. William C. Westmoreland speech (prepared text), "Progress Report on the War in Vietnam," National Press Club, November 21, 1967, LBJL, Westmoreland Papers, box 14, folder "History File, v. 25."

114. MACV cable, Westmoreland–Abrams, HWA 3445, 252203Z Nov 67, ibid.

115. Westmoreland, *A Soldier Reports,* 306–307.

January–May 1968: *Tet Mau Than*

1. David Maraniss, *They Marched into Sunlight: War and Peace, Vietnam and America, October 1967* (New York: Simon & Schuster, 2003).

2. Quoted in "Death Among the Rubber Trees," *Time,* November 10, 1967, 23.

3. Military History Institute of Vietnam, *Victory in Vietnam: The Official History of the People's Army of Vietnam, 1954–1975,* trans. Merle L. Pribbenow (Lawrence: University Press of Kansas, 2002), 212.

4. Le Cao Dai, *The Central Highlands: A North Vietnamese Journal of Life on the Ho Chi Minh Trail, 1965–1973,* trans. Lady Borton (Hanoi: Gioi Publishers, 2004), 185.

5. William C. Westmoreland speech, "Progress Report on the War in Vietnam," National Press Club, November 21, 1967, LBJL, Westmoreland Papers, box 14, folder "History File, v. 25."

6. Admiral U. S. Grant Sharp and General William C. Westmoreland, *Report on the War in Vietnam (as of June 30, 1968)* (Washington, DC: Government Printing Office, [1968]), 156. Rosson's objections are noted in Edward F. Murphy, *Dak To: America's Sky Soldiers in South Vietnam's Central Highlands* (New York: Pocket, 1993), 329.

7. MACV cable, Westmoreland–Wheeler (MAC 11956), December 10, 1967 (declassified May 11, 1984), LBJL, Westmoreland Papers, box 15, folder "History File, v. 26."

8. Patrick J. McGarvey, *CIA: The Myth and the Madness* (New York: Saturday Review Press, 1972), 126.

9. NSA history by Robert J. Hanyok, *United States Cryptologic History,* ser. 6, *The NSA Period: 1952–Present,* vol. 7, *Spartans in Darkness: American SIGINT and the Indochina War, 1945–1975* (CCH-E05-02-02) (Fort Meade, MD: Center for Cryptologic History, 2002), 340–347 (declassified 2007).

10. For a more detailed discussion, see John Prados, "The Warning That Left Something to Chance: Intelligence at Tet," in *The Tet Offensive,* ed. Marc J. Gilbert and William Head (Westport, CT: Praeger, 1996). This originally appeared as a paper in the *Journal of American–East Asian Relations* in 1993. The overall issue is treated at length in Ronnie E. Ford, *Tet 1968: Understanding the Surprise* (London: Frank Cass, 1995), and James J. Wirtz, *The Tet Offensive: Intelligence Failure in War* (Ithaca, NY: Cornell University Press, 1991). The NSA attack warning was revealed in a declassified NSA postmortem of Tet released subsequent to all these studies. For the original document, see the Vietnam (I) collection at the National Security Archive, which I edited.

11. Pham Gia Duc, *Su Doan 325 (1954–1975), tap 2* [325th Division, 1954–1975, vol. 2], trans. Robert DeStatte (Hanoi: People's Army Publishing House, 1986), 56, in Ray W. Stubbe, ed., *B5-T8 in 48 QXD: The Secret Official History of the North Vietnamese Army of the Siege at Khe Sanh, Vietnam, Spring 1968* (Wauwatosa, WI: Khe Sanh Veterans, 2006); copy courtesy of Ray W. Stubbe.

12. Ha Dang, ed., *Van Kien Dang, Toan Tap 29, 1968* [Collected party documents, vol. 29, 1968], trans. Merle Pribbenow (Hanoi: National Political Publishing House, 2004), 1–68; copy courtesy of Merle Pribbenow. All quotes are from the Fourteenth Plenum Resolution, 41–68.

13. Lieutenant General John A. Chaisson, U.S. Marine Corps Oral History, 1975 (Marine Corps History and Museums Program, Washington, DC), 217.

14. MACV cable, Westmoreland–Wheeler (MAC 01333), January 31, 1968, LBJL, LBJP, NSF, NSC Histories, March 31st Speech subseries, box 47, folder "v.2: Tabs A-Z and AA-ZZ."

15. Author's notes of Ambassador Bui Diem's comments at the conference "Remembering Tet," Salisbury State University, Salisbury, Maryland, November 20, 1992.

16. Quoted in Nguyen Cao Ky with Marvin J. Wolf, *Buddha's Child: My Fight to Save Vietnam* (New York: St. Martin's Press, 2002), 260.

17. General Phillip B. Davidson, LBJL Oral History 85-66, p. 44.

18. Kim Willenson et al., eds., *The Bad War: An Oral History of the Vietnam War* (New York: New American Library, 1987), 95. Komer, however, subscribed to the "desperate gamble for Hanoi" school of thought on Tet, and what most surprised him about the offensive — aside from debunking his idea that pacification had made great progress by the end of 1967 — was that the DRV seemed to have abandoned gradualism in progressing from guerrilla to mobile warfare to the general uprising, per the classic Mao Zedong model.

19. Larry Berman, *The Perfect Spy: The Incredible Double Life of Pham Xuan An, Time Magazine Reporter and Vietnamese Communist Agent* (New York: Smithsonian Books/Collins, 2007), 153–180.

20. Quoted in Ky, *Buddha's Child,* 262.

21. Don Oberdorfer, *Tet!* (Garden City, NY: Doubleday, 1971), 34.

22. Interview, Lieutenant Barry Romo, Washington, DC, January 27, 2007.

23. Quoted in Oberdorfer, *Tet!* 251.

24. Peter Braestrup, *Big Story: How the American Press and Television Reported and Interpreted the Crisis of Tet 1968 in Vietnam and Washington* (New Haven, CT: Yale University Press, 1977). Braestrup's claims about the wearing impact of reusing particular images, such as the Loan photograph, pictures of the C-130 that crashed at Khe Sanh, and so forth, should not be taken seriously. The fact is that the press always uses repetitive and stock imagery; it did so in reporting every military action by the United States in the last half of the twentieth century. No one objected to stock images of the Gulf War or Panama, and those of the Iraq war have been repeated without qualms as well. In fact, the case of Iraq is instructive, because the images remained unobjectionable even as the public's view of the conflict reversed itself. This suggests that the interpretation of the images is what changes as political context varies, rather than the images themselves molding opinion in a given direction.

25. Clarence R. Wyatt, *Paper Soldiers: The American Press and the Vietnam War* (New York: W. W. Norton, 1993), 188.

26. Willenson, *Bad War,* 97.

27. Bui Diem's comments at "Remembering Tet," November 20, 1992.

28. Robert R. Tomes, *Apocalypse Then: American Intellectuals and the Vietnam War, 1954–1975* (New York: New York University Press, 1998), 167.

29. William M. Hammond, *Reporting Vietnam: Media and Military at War* (Lawrence: University Press of Kansas, 1998), 122.

30. William C. Westmoreland, *A Soldier Reports* (New York: Dell, 1980), 427.

31. Bui Diem's comments at "Remembering Tet," November 20, 1992.

32. Department of Defense, "Statistics on Southeast Asia (Unclassified), 1972," reprinted in Rafael Littauer and Norman Uphoff, eds., *The Air War in Indochina,* rev. ed. (Boston: Beacon Press/Cornell University Air Power Study Group, 1972), 269.

33. Quoted in Clark Clifford and Richard Holbrooke, *Counsel to the President, A Memoir* (New York: Random House, 1991), 475.

34. Shana Alexander, "What Is the Truth of the Picture?" *Life,* March 1, 1968, 18.

35. Willenson, *Bad War,* 95.

36. Vietnam Veterans Against the War, *Winter Soldier Investigation* (Boston: Beacon Press, 1971), 169.

37. Andrew E. Hunt, *The Turning: A History of Vietnam Veterans Against the War* (New York: New York University Press, 1999), 18.

38. Westmoreland would later be convinced that General Wheeler had mousetrapped him into an exaggerated request through his back-channel cables and their conversations. As Army chief of staff a few years later, Westmoreland assigned aides specifically to track down the paper trail here and assemble a report he could use to prove the manipulation. The MACV commander commented obliquely about this matter in his memoir (*A Soldier Reports,* 467–472), but he also leaked the data to a young Harvard student, James Henry, who penned two articles much more critical of Wheeler. Clark Clifford noted, "I do not believe the accusation" (Clifford and Holbrooke, *Counsel to the President,* 481). Contrary to Westmoreland's insistence that he requested only the creation of capabilities (except for an initial wave of reinforcements)—in effect, to put troops "on the shelf" (*A Soldier Reports,* 468)—Washington officials who met to consider the request on February 27 were told specifically that the general wanted 105,000 men by May 1 and another 100,000 in two tranches by September 1 and December 31. White House, Harry McPherson, "Notes of a Meeting," February 27, 1968, in Department of States, *FRUS, 1964–1968,* vol. 6, *Vietnam, January–August 1968* (Washington, DC: Government Printing Office, 2002), 260. The actual Wheeler post-Tet trip report, dated February 28, 1968, appears in the LBJL Tet NSC history files cited in note 14; a short summary memo is in *FRUS, 1964–1968,* 6: 263–266.

39. Clifford and Holbrooke, *Counsel to the President,* 473–474.

40. According to Don Oberdorfer, the *Times* discovered the number from a congressional staffer on Capitol Hill after one of its reporters learned of high-level dissent over the request while attending a party (*Tet,* 266–271). Colonel Herbert Y. Schandler, who authored this segment of the Pentagon Papers and later wrote a book on Tet and its sequel, believed that senators briefed by the president himself divulged the number, which they put at 206,000. See Herbert Y. Schandler, *The Unmaking of a President: Lyndon Johnson and Vietnam* (Princeton, NJ: Princeton University Press, 1977), 201. Rostow's view was that "the materials were mainly gathered from medium-level officials in both State and Defense who oppose the sending of more troops to Vietnam," and that this was "the product of dangerous insubordination" (NSC memorandum, Rostow–Lyndon Johnson, March 10, 1968, 11:20 AM [declassified February 25, 1998], LBJL, LBJP, NSF, CFVN, box 98, folder "VN 7D (2), News Media Coverage").

41. Daniel Ellsberg, *Secrets: A Memoir of Vietnam and the Pentagon Papers* (New York: Viking, 2002), 197–206.

42. Harry McPherson, *A Political Education: A Washington Memoir* (Austin: University of Texas Press, 1995); Clifford and Holbrooke, *Counsel to the President,* 506.

43. Clifford and Holbrooke, *Counsel to the President,* 512–519, quote from 513.

44. Lyndon B. Johnson, *The Vantage Point: Perspectives on the Presidency, 1963–1969* (New York: Holt, Rinehart & Winston, 1971), 416.

45. Quoted ibid., 435.

46. Anatoly Dobrynin, *In Confidence: Moscow's Ambassador to America's Six Cold War Presidents* (New York: Times Books, 1995), 170–174.

47. Todd Gitlin, *The Sixties: Years of Protest, Days of Rage* (New York: Bantam, 1987), 281. Gitlin is correct to note that the "Prague Spring"—the seeming loosening of Czechoslovakia's bonds to the Soviet Union—also contributed to this impression among Movement stalwarts.

48. Here the narrative follows the Cox Commission recitation of these events. Archibald Cox et al., *Report of the Fact-Finding Committee Appointed to Investigate the Disturbances at Columbia University in April and May 1968,* reprinted in Cox Commission Report, *Crisis at Columbia* (New York: Vintage, 1968). The best account is in Jerry L. Avorn et al., *Up against the Ivy Wall: A History of the Columbia Crisis* (New York: Atheneum, 1969).

49. Government professor Herbert Deane, who would be named university provost not long after the 1968 revolt, had said on the occasion of a 1967 referendum on the IDA, "Whether students vote 'yes' or 'no' on an issue is like telling me they like strawberries." James S. Kunen, *The Strawberry Statement: Notes of a College Revolutionary* (New York: Avon, 1968), 140.

50. Christopher H. Pyle, *Military Surveillance of Civilian Politics, 1967–1970* (New York: Garland, 1986), 218.

51. Zbigniew Brzezinski, *New Republic,* June 1, 1968, 23. Brzezinski enlarged on this theme in his book *Between Two Ages: America's Role in the Technetronic Era* (New York: Penguin, 1971).

52. Quoted in Randall B. Woods, *LBJ: Architect of American Ambition* (New York: Free Press, 2006), 844.

53. Quoted in Kirkpatrick Sale, *SDS* (New York: Vintage, 1974), 449–450.

54. Tom Hayden, *Reunion: A Memoir* (New York: Random House, 1988), 282.

55. Quoted in Nancy Zaroulis and Gerald Sullivan, *Who Spoke Up? American Protest against the War in Vietnam, 1963–1975* (New York: Holt, Rinehart & Winston, 1984), 165.

56. Dan Berger, *Outlaws of America: The Weather Underground and the Politics of Solidarity* (Oakland, CA: AK Press, 2006), 47–51.

57. Jeremy Varon, *Bringing the War Home: The Weather Underground, the Red Army*

Faction, and Revolutionary Violence in the Sixties and Seventies (Berkeley: University of California Press, 2004), 26.

58. Dobrynin, *In Confidence,* 173.

59. 1968 DRV documents (see note 12), 210.

60. Military History Institute of Vietnam, *Victory in Vietnam,* 224, 228, 231.

Chapter 7. Terrible Swift Sword (1968–1969)

1. Chicago Study Team of the National Commission on the Causes and Prevention of Violence [Walker inquiry], *Rights in Conflict: The Violent Confrontation of Demonstrators and Police in the Parks and Streets of Chicago During the Week of the Democratic National Convention of 1968* (New York: Bantam, New York Times ed., 1968), 10.

2. Todd Gitlin, *The Sixties: Years of Protest, Days of Rage* (New York: Bantam, 1987), 265.

3. Daniel Ellsberg, *Secrets: A Memoir of Vietnam and the Pentagon Papers* (New York: Viking, 2002), 220.

4. Kirkpatrick Sale, *SDS* (New York: Vintage, 1974), 450.

5. Lyndon B. Johnson, *The Vantage Point: Perspectives on the Presidency, 1963–1969* (New York: Holt, Rinehart & Winston, 1971), 543.

6. Carl Rogers comments at memorial to David Dellinger, VVAW Fortieth Anniversary Conference, Chicago, August 5, 2007.

7. Gitlin, *Sixties,* 319.

8. Norman Mailer, *Miami and the Siege of Chicago: An Informal History of the Republican and Democratic Conventions of 1968* (New York: New American Library, 1968), 131.

9. David Farber, *Chicago '68* (Chicago: University of Chicago Press, 1988), 157.

10. Quoted in Nancy Zaroulis and Gerald Sullivan, *Who Spoke Up? American Protest against the War in Vietnam, 1963–1975* (New York: Holt, Rinehart & Winston, 1984), 194.

11. Ibid., 199.

12. Clark Clifford and Richard Holbrooke, *Counsel to the President, A Memoir* (New York: Random House, 1991), 565.

13. George M. Elsey notes, August 30, 1968, LBJL, Papers of George M. Elsey, box 1.

14. Ibid.

15. Harry G. Summers Jr., "Duty, Duplicity, and Design: The Army's Reaction to Tet" (paper presented at Naval Historical Center, Eleventh Colloquium on Contemporary History, September 29, 1998). Also see Harry Summers, *On Strategy: A Critical Analysis of the Vietnam War* (New York: Dell, 1982). This book is a slightly altered version of the extended monograph Colonel Summers wrote for the Army War College.

16. Fred P. Graham, "Arrests for Threats to the President up Sharply Since the Assassination," *New York Times,* January 7, 1968, 59.

17. George Rush, *Confessions of an Ex–Secret Service Agent: The Marty Venker Story* (New York: Donald Fine, 1988), 65.

18. Richard H. Melanson with Peter F. Stevens, *The Secret Service: The Hidden History of an Enigmatic Agency* (New York: Caroll & Graf, 2002), 299.

19. White House, *Public Papers of the President: Lyndon B. Johnson, 1968–1969* (Washington, DC: Government Printing Office, 1970), 2: 1155.

20. George C. Christian, *The President Steps Down: A Personal Memoir of the Transfer of Power* (New York: Macmillan, 1970), 68.

21. *New York Times,* October 17, 1968, 4.

22. Johnson, *Vantage Point,* 516.

23. Department of State, Cable Saigon 29468, June 8, 1968, LBJL, LBJP, NSF, Memos to the President series, box 35, folder "Rostow, v. 81."

24. John Prados, "The Shape of the Table: Nguyen Van Thieu and Negotiations to End the Conflict," in *The Search for Peace in Vietnam, 1964–1968,* ed. Lloyd C. Gardner and Ted Gittinger (College Station: Texas A&M University Press, 2004), 355–370.

25. CIA intelligence report, "Discussion Between President Nguyen Van Thieu and Vice-President Nguyen Cao Ky to Discuss Coup Rumors and the General Vietnamese Situation," September 16, 1968, in Department of State, *FRUS, 1964–1968,* vol. 7, *Vietnam, September 1968–January 1969* (Washington, DC: Government Printing Office, 2003), 43–44.

26. John Prados, "October Surprise," *VVA Veteran* 18, 3/4 (August–September 1998).

27. Henry A. Kissinger, *Ending the Vietnam War: A History of America's Involvement in and Extraction from the Vietnam War* (New York: Simon & Schuster, 2003), 52.

28. White House, Tom Johnson's notes of meeting, August 10, 1968, in *FRUS, 1964–1968,* 6: 946–949.

29. Clifford and Holbrooke, *Counsel to the President,* 563.

30. Jeffrey Kimball, *Nixon's Vietnam War* (Lawrence: University Press of Kansas, 1998), 58.

31. Henry A. Kissinger, *White House Years* (Boston: Little, Brown, 1979), 10.

32. Anna Chennault, *The Education of Anna* (New York: Times Books, 1980), 185.

33. Richard Moser, *The New Winter Soldiers: GI and Veteran Dissent During the Vietnam Era* (New Brunswick, NJ: Rutgers University Press, 1996), 93.

34. This narrative relies on a range of sources, starting with Moser, *New Winter Soldiers.* Additional key sources on the rise of disaffection in the military are David Cortwright, *Soldiers in Revolt: The American Military Today* (Garden City, NY: Doubleday, 1975); Colonel Robert D. Heinl Jr., "The Collapse of the Armed Forces," *Armed Forces Journal,* June 1971; Colonel George Walton, *The Tarnished Shield: A Report on Today's Army* (New York: Dodd, Mead, 1973); Robert Sherrill, *Military Justice Is to Justice as Military Music Is to Music* (New York: Harper & Row, 1970); Cincinatus (Cecil B. Currey), *Self-Destruction: The Disintegration and Decay of the United States Army During the Vietnam Era* (New York: William Morrow, 1980); and Richard A. Gabriel and Paul L. Savage, *Crisis in Command: Mismanagement in the Army* (New York: Hill & Wang, 1978). Guenther Lewy presents a contrary view in *America in Vietnam* (New York: Oxford University Press, 1978), 153–161. On the draft, see Lawrence M. Baskir and William Strauss, *Chance and Circumstance: The Draft, the War, and the Vietnam Generation* (New York: Random House, 1978); and *Report of the President's Commission on an All-Volunteer Armed Force* [Gates Commission] (Washington, DC: Government Printing Office, February 1970). I also used memoranda to and from Secretary of Defense Melvin R. Laird but do not quote them. The discussion among former Army officers referenced here occurred at a plenary session toward the end of the 1996 triennial conference of the Vietnam Center at Texas Tech University.

35. White House memorandum, Frank Borman–Richard Nixon, "Report of Vietnamese Trip," December 26, 1969, NARA, NLP, WHCF, Subject File: Country Series, box 84, folder "CO 165 Vietnam 8/1/69–12/8/70 [2 of 2]."

36. Arnold Abrams, "South Vietnam: Everybody USA," *Far Eastern Economic Review,* February 12, 1970, reprinted in U.S. Congress, Senate Foreign Relations Committee, *Hearings: Vietnam: Policy and Prospects, 1970* (Washington, DC: Government Printing Office, 1970).

37. David Hackworth, "When No One Wanted to Fight," *Newsweek,* February 24, 1969, 24.

38. Guenther Lewy (*America in Vietnam,* 155) attempts to minimize this entire situation by citing only "several" cases of refusal to engage in combat. He does this by restricting himself to the 1971–1972 time frame. He also makes a distinction between ordinary refusals and "politically motivated" ones (156)—for which he finds no evidence. This distinction is fatuous, since combat refusal for any reason reduced the dependability of troop units and thus

MACV offensive capability. And Lewy draws the completely unsupported conclusion that "greater damage to morale than that caused by the antiwar movement probably resulted from the feeling among many servicemen that people back home did not appreciate their sacrifices" (159). Aside from the fact that it was the war and what they could see around them, not the antiwar movement, that caused disenchantment, servicemen would not encounter the phenomenon of Americans' support or the lack thereof until they returned home from the war. Soldiers' impressions at the time of their enlistment or drafting were surely secondary to what they encountered in the Vietnam combat theater and the treatment they experienced from the U.S. military itself.

Chapter 8. Crush the Serpent under Heel (1969)

1. Melvin R. Laird, Richard M. Nixon Presidential Library Video/Oral History Interview, December 19, 2006.

2. Daniel Ellsberg, *Papers on the War* (New York: Simon & Schuster, 1972), 23–24. See also Ellsberg's more expansive account in his memoir *Secrets: A Memoir of Vietnam and the Pentagon Papers* (New York: Viking, 2002). Cf. Jeffrey Kimball, *Nixon's Vietnam War* (Lawrence: University Press of Kansas, 1998), 91–94.

3. Rand Corporation, Daniel Ellsberg, "Alternative Vietnam Options," memo no. 8868, December 20, 1968 (copy courtesy of Daniel Ellsberg), compared to "Vietnam Options 1969," January 8, 1969, LBJL, Morton H. Halperin Papers, box 10, folder "Vietnam Options"; all quotes are from the latter.

4. NSC, "Minutes of National Security Council Meeting," January 25, 1969, in Department of States, *FRUS, 1969–1976,* vol. 6, *Vietnam: January 1969–July 1970* (Washington, DC: Government Printing Office, 2006), 23–41, quotes from 39, 38, 40.

5. Quoted in H. R. Haldeman with Joseph DiMona, *The Ends of Power* (New York: Dell, 1978), 121–122.

6. Jeffrey Kimball in *Nixon's Vietnam War* (63–86) provides a detailed exegesis on the background of the Madman Theory. Haldeman later denied Nixon had made the remark he himself quoted, and some scholars have disputed the whole concept. Kimball collected declassified documents, transcribed Nixon's pertinent telephone conversations, and revisited the issue in his book *The Vietnam War Files: Uncovering the Secret History of Nixon-Era Strategy* (Lawrence: University Press of Kansas, 2004), 53–61. I wrote about this myself in *The Blood Road: The Ho Chi Minh Trail and the Vietnam War* (New York: John Wiley's Sons, 1999), 287–289.

7. Henry A. Kissinger, *White House Years* (Boston: Little, Brown, 1979), 237–238.

8. National Security Study Memorandum 1, c. March 1969, reprinted in *Congressional Record,* May 10, 1972, E16749–16836, E4976–5005; May 11, 1972, E5009–5066; quote from E16752. The originals of the study can be found in Part II of the National Security Archive's collection *U.S. Policy in the Vietnam War* (2005). A condensed version of the summary memorandum appeared in the *New York Times,* April 26, 1972, 10.

9. Haldeman, *Ends of Power,* 139–140.

10. Kissinger, *White House Years,* 239–240.

11. NSC, memorandum of conversation, January 30, 1969, in *FRUS, 1969–1976,* 6: 44.

12. Kissinger, *White House Years,* 242.

13. NSC memorandum, Henry Kissinger–Richard Nixon, "Consideration of B-52 Options against COSVN Headquarters," February 19, 1969, in *FRUS 1969–1976,* 6: 68–74, quote from 73–74. There are dozens of similar examples of Kissinger's parsing of the official records in crafting his memoirs, as well as in his more recent version, *Ending the Vietnam War: A History of America's Involvement in and Extraction from the Vietnam War* (New York: Simon & Schuster, 2003). I note only the most important ones.

14. Telephone conversation, Kissinger–Nixon, March 8, 1969, 7:10 PM, in *FRUS 1969–1976*, 6: 96.

15. U.S. Congress, Senate Armed Services Committee, *Hearings: Bombing in Cambodia* (Washington, DC: Government Printing Office, 1973), 345.

16. Lewis B. Sorley, ed., *Vietnam Chronicles: The Abrams Tapes, 1968–1972* (Lubbock: Texas Tech University Press, 2004), 115–154, quote from 141.

17. Telephone conversation, Kissinger–Laird, March 16, 1969, 9:00 PM, in *FRUS 1969–1976*, 6: 125.

18. Kissinger, *White House Years*, 244.

19. Richard Nixon, *RN: The Memoirs of Richard Nixon* (New York: Warner, 1978), 1:471.

20. The sortie figure is from an Air Force official history: Bernard C. Nalty, *Air War Over South Vietnam, 1968–1975* (Washington, DC: Air Force History and Museums Program, 2000), 130. A postwar Pentagon study put the number of B-52 sorties against Cambodia during March 1969 at only forty-eight: Department of Defense, "Sensitive Operations in Southeast Asia, 1964–1973," n.d. (declassified December 5, 1990, FOIA). The bomb tonnage is from the second source.

21. Both Kissinger (*White House Years*, 316–321) and his military assistant Haig (Alexander M. Haig with Charles McCarry, *Inner Circles: How America Changed the World* [New York: Warner, 1992], 204–209) raged at Laird's action—or the lack of it. According to Laird, he was suspicious of initial reports and delayed responding; in fact, he established that the EC-121 aircraft involved in the incident actually had blundered into North Korean airspace (Laird, Nixon Library Videohistory Interview, December 19, 2006). Laird claims that statements in memoirs by Kissinger, Nixon, and Haig that the plane never left international airspace are not accurate.

22. William Beecher, "Raids in Cambodia by U.S. Unprotested," *New York Times*, May 9, 1969, 1.

23. It is curious that the Beecher story gained much of its notoriety only after the fact, when the illegal wiretaps became known. As evidence of U.S. military action against a neutral nation, the story ought to have raised eyebrows, especially in Congress. Yet there was little media follow-up and no congressional inquiry. A combination of Pentagon denials and deference to a new president seems to have warded off the attention the administration dreaded.

24. Kissinger, *White House Years*, 299.

25. Anthony Summers with Robbyn Swan, *The Arrogance of Power: The Secret World of Richard Nixon* (New York: Penguin, 2000), 24–26. Nixon's most recent biographer, Conrad Black, disputes this view. See Conrad Black, *The Invincible Quest: The Life of Richard Milhous Nixon* (Toronto: McClelland & Stewart, 2007).

26. Quoted in Summers, *Arrogance of Power*, 26.

27. Haig, *Inner Circles*, 194.

28. William Safire, *Before the Fall: An Inside View of the Pre-Watergate White House* (New York: Belmont Towers Books, 1975), 8.

29. Nixon, *RN*, 1:464.

30. Henry Kissinger, "The Vietnam Negotiations," *Foreign Affairs* 47, 1 (January 1969): 211–234. The fate of this Kissinger paper is revealing. Almost immediately after his accession to the White House staff, Kissinger gathered a selection of his papers, including this one, in *American Foreign Policy* (New York: W. W. Norton, 1969). The piece condemned Johnson's peace efforts for their "excessive reliance on tactical considerations," foresaw a need to get the Vietnamese parties talking directly to one another, and declared that U.S. foreign policy interests could be satisfied by a decent interval between American withdrawal and the end of the conflict, even if that entailed final success for Hanoi. The paper's strategic propositions amounted to Vietnamization. The idea of the Vietnamese talking to each other was

woven into the fabric of the moment, when in fact, the sides were arguing over the shape of the table. Meanwhile, preoccupation with tactical considerations would be the very essence of the Nixon-Kissinger Vietnam negotiations, and the "decent interval" became identified with the way the war ended. It was even used by CIA officer Frank Snepp for his highly critical memoir *Decent Interval* (New York: Random House, 1977). Kissinger dropped this paper from *American Foreign Policy* when it was republished in 1977 and kept it out of subsequent editions. He does not mention it in his memoirs and neglects it in works such as *Ending the Vietnam War* and *Diplomacy,* which also deal with this period.

31. Tom Wells, *The War Within: America's Battle Over Vietnam* (Berkeley: University of California Press, 1994), 309.

32. *Nixon: The First Year of His Presidency* (Washington, DC: Congressional Quarterly, 1970), 93-A.

33. Interview with John Ehrlichman, transcript, Cable News Network, *The Cold War,* episode 16, "Détente," broadcast February 7, 1999, http://www.gwu.edu/~nsarchiv/coldwar/interviews/episode-16/erlich.

34. Quoted in Wells, *War Within,* 307.

35. Ibid., 315.

36. Ibid., 323, from *Washington Post,* June 4, 1969.

37. Nixon, *RN,* 1:430.

38. NSC, Kissinger memorandum, "Actions Resulting from National Security Council Meeting of January 25, 1969," January 29, 1969, in *FRUS, 1969–1976,* 6: 43.

39. Department of Defense memorandum, Melvin Laird–Henry Kissinger, February 21, 1969, National Security Archive, EBB no. 81, item 2 (FOIA from National Archives, Nixon Presidential Materials Project, National Security Files, Alexander Haig Files, Vietnam series, box 1007).

40. Attachments to ibid.

41. NSC memorandum, Henry Kissinger–Melvin Laird, "Memorandum Enclosing Preliminary Draft of Potential Military Actions re Vietnam," March 3, 1969, ibid.

42. Anatoly Dobrynin, *In Confidence: Moscow's Ambassador to America's Six Cold War Presidents* (New York: Times Books, 1995), 200.

43. NSC, Henry Kissinger–Richard Nixon, "Memorandum of Conversation with Ambassador Dobrynin, April 3, 1969," April 3, 1969, in *FRUS 1969–1976,* 6: 185–186. Kissinger makes no mention of this exchange in his memoirs. The Soviet record of this conversation is available from the Cold War International History Project and is in the most recent *FRUS* volume, which collects both U.S. and Soviet records of the Kissinger-Dobrynin contacts throughout this period. Some of the documents cited here are also reprinted or excerpted in Kimball's *Vietnam War Files,* which has the additional virtue of his transcriptions of a number of the Nixon tapes, as well as entries from the full Haldeman diaries (which were condensed for publication).

44. NSC, Henry Kissinger–Richard Nixon, "Memorandum of Conversation with Dobrynin, April 14, 1969," April 15, 1969, in *FRUS, 1969–1976,* 6: 199–203.

45. Kissinger, *White House Years,* 268.

46. On April 15 an American electronic reconnaissance plane, an EC-121M from naval air squadron VQ-1, was shot down over the Sea of Japan by North Korean MIG interceptors. The president ordered a naval concentration off the Korean coast and made plans to retaliate against the Democratic People's Republic of Korea. This crisis has an involved story of its own that is not germane here, except that Nixon's motives for the initial bombing of Cambodia began to include an additional aspect—signaling to communist nations, including North Korea, that the United States was not to be trifled with.

47. Nguyen Phu Duc, *The Vietnam Peace Negotiations: Saigon's Side of the Story,* ed. Arthur J. Dommen (Christiansburg, WV: Dalley Book Service, 2005), 216. These comments

go beyond what is in the U.S. record of this meeting. See NSC "Memorandum of Conversation, Midway Island, June 8, 1969," June 13, 1969, in *FRUS, 1969–1976*, 6: 248–252.

48. H. R. Haldeman, *The Haldeman Diaries: Inside the Nixon White House* (New York: G. P. Putnam's Sons, 1994), 69–70.

49. Kissinger, *White House Years*, 276. The security adviser notes that this was "symptomatic of the intellectual confusion of the period." Kissinger himself was among those confused. His pre-meeting paper for Nixon had declared, "I believe that we need to change in some way the instructions to General Abrams" (July 7, 1969, memo, "*Sequoia* NSC Meeting on Vietnam," in *FRUS, 1969–1976*, 6: 283–288, quote from 285). Worse, copies of the draft and final memoranda in Morton Halperin's papers reveal that Kissinger *reversed* his advice, advocating in the draft version that Abrams's orders not be changed (LBJL, Morton H. Halperin Papers, box 3, folder "Halperin Chronological File, March–July 1969," items 61 and 63).

50. Telephone conversation, Kissinger–Laird, July 8, 1969, 10:40 AM, in *FRUS, 1969–1976*, 6: 283n2.

51. Nixon, *RN*, 1:486. Note the choice of language—"one way or the other"—identical to that used with the Soviet ambassador months earlier. Jeffrey Kimball (personal communication) objects, reasonably enough, that historians should not use the Nixon and Kissinger memoirs when there are so many actual records and tapes showing their attempts to spin the story. I agree that the memoirs are not reliable. I used Nixon's in this instance because the former president knew what would eventually emerge from the record and thus admitted to what he believed would correspond to those documents. Nixon's minimalist scriblings demonstrate that he was aware he could not get away with pretending Madman never happened, however euphemistically his presentation was structured. In general I use the Nixon and Kissinger accounts to show what they themselves admitted to and tried to elide or obfuscate, or for details of daily activities and general opinions.

52. NSC, "Memorandum of Conversation," Saigon, July 30, 1969, in *FRUS, 1969–1976*, 6: 321–326, quote from 322–323.

53. Quoted in Duc, *Vietnam Peace Negotiations*, 228–229.

54. NSC, Memorandum of Conversation, Richard Nixon–Nicolae Ceaucescu," August 3, 1969, excerpted in Kimball, *Vietnam War Files*, 96–97.

55. NSC, "Memorandum of Conversation, Paris, August 4, 1969," c. August 6, 1969, in *FRUS, 1969–1976*, 6: 331–343, quote from 333.

56. NSC memorandum, Henry Kissinger–Richard Nixon, "Response from Ho Chi Minh," August 31, 1969, ibid., 351.

57. Nixon, *RN*, 1:491.

58. *Haldeman Diaries*, August 18, 1969, 81.

59. NSC paper, "Vietnam Options," September 11, 1969, in *FRUS, 1969–1976*, 6: 376–390, quote from 390. Kissinger's treatment of this paper in his memoir was sparse, limited to his argument that a strategy based entirely on Vietnamization would not work (*White House Years*, 284); he reproduced just one paragraph of his exegesis (1482n12). This appeared in the original as part of Kissinger's discussion of domestic political factors, in which he argued that any options other than escalation "carry potential problems with our other audiences, the [South Vietnamese government] and the enemy" (*FRUS, 1969–1976*, 6: 381).

60. The NSC staff commentaries of September 16 and 17 are examples of key documents that were left out of the *FRUS* series. Kimball commendably includes them (*Vietnam War Files*, 102–104).

61. MACV cable, Bardshar–Wheeler, "Pruning Knife Status Report no. 2," 211335Z Sep 69, repeated to CINCPAC in MAC 12408 Intel, 230143Z Sep 69. U.S. Army Military History Institute, Creighton V. Abrams Papers, box "1969–1970." Also see Prados, *Blood Road*, 290–294.

62. *Haldeman Diaries,* September 27, 1969, 90.

63. White House, Patrick J. Buchanan, "Note for the President's File," September 27, 1969, in Department of State, *FRUS, 1969–1976,* vol. 1, *Foundations of Foreign Policy, 1969–1972* (Washington, DC: Government Printing Office, 2003), 109.

64. NSC, "Draft of a Presidential Speech, 2nd Draft," September 27, 1969, GRFL, GRFP, National Security Adviser's Files: West Wing Office Series, box 34, folder "Mr. 'S' File (5), 9/1/69–9/30/69."

65. NSC, Henry Kissinger, "Memorandum of Conversation," September 27, 1969, NARA, NLP, NSC Files, box 489, folder: "Dobrynin–Kissinger 1969 (2)."

66. Telephone conversation, Kissinger–Nixon, September 27, 1969, 4:40 PM, in *FRUS, 1969–1976,* 6: 312–413.

67. *Haldeman Diaries,* October 3, 1969, 95.

68. This is the thesis of William Burr and Jeffrey Kimball in several well-argued papers. See their "Nixon's Nuclear Ploy," *Bulletin of the Atomic Scientists,* January–February 2003, 28–37, 72–73; "Nixon's Secret Nuclear Alert: Vietnam War Diplomacy and the Joint Chiefs of Staff Readiness Test, October 1969," *Cold War History* 3, 2 (January 2003): 113–156; and "New Evidence on the Secret Nuclear Alert of October 1969: The Henry A. Kissinger Telcons," *Passport,* April 2005, 12–14. Burr and Kimball also collaborated on a pair of National Security Archive EBBs (81 and 195) that made available a selection of the documents relevant to this matter.

69. *Haldeman Diaries,* October 9, 1969, 97–98.

70. Safire, *Before the Fall,* 172.

71. *Haldeman Diaries,* 96–100.

72. Chief of Naval Operations, Admiral Thomas Moorer memorandum for the record, "JCS Meeting with the President, Saturday, 11 October 1969," October 11, 1969, in *FRUS, 1969–1976,* 6: 454–460, quotes from 456, 457.

73. Nixon, *RN,* 1:499.

74. Richard Nixon, *No More Vietnams* (New York: Arbor House, 1985), 102.

75. Kissinger, *White House Years,* 307.

76. Associated Press, "Nixon 'Manufactured' Response to Speech, Former Aide Says," *Boston Globe,* January 23, 1999, A7.

77. Meanwhile, work at Columbia and the New York Public Library affirmed my reasons for coming to New York. The sources on French Indochina were everything I could have wished for—I even discovered the biweekly news bulletins of the Colonial Ministry of France. Materials on current events were equally plentiful. Eventually, I declared a history major at Columbia College and pursued my interest in Southeast Asia, complete with an independent-study project at one point. I took a job in the library of Columbia's business school and later worked as a research assistant to professors who needed someone to track down elusive source materials, increasing my proficiency at what became my calling. Later I visited Cornell in Ithaca, New York, where I got a crack at the Southeast Asia holdings in Cornell's great Eccles Library, the best collection on the subject on the East Coast. It was there that I first met scholars George and Audrey Kahin and D. Gareth Porter.

Chapter 9. Dim and Flaring Lamps (1969–1971)

1. For a full biography of Abrams, see Lewis B. Sorley, *Thunderbolt: General Creighton Abrams and the Army of His Times* (Washington, DC: Potomac Books, 1998).

2. MACV Staff, "Quotations from General Creighton W. Abrams," n.d., University Press of America, Microfilm Collection, Records of the Military Assistance Command Vietnam, part 1, reel 1, frame 0452.

3. NSC memorandum, Walt W. Rostow–Lyndon B. Johnson, October 8, 1968, 12:05 PM (declassified February 1, 1993), LBJL, LBJP, NSF, Memos to the President series, box 40, folder "Rostow, v. 97 (October 1–4, 1968) 2 of 2."

4. John Prados, *The Hidden History of the Vietnam War* (Chicago: Ivan R. Dee, 1995), 102–110.

5. This was the figure by four-company organization. By three-company organization, the force would have been equivalent to thirty-seven rifle battalions. A full infantry division in the Vietnam war contained ten maneuver battalions (nine infantry and one armored). With appropriate support troops, this mere addition of rifle companies could have made up four additional infantry divisions.

6. NSA history by Robert J. Hanyok, *United States Cryptologic History,* ser. 6, *The NSA Period: 1952–Present,* vol. 7, *Spartans in Darkness: American SIGINT and the Indochina War, 1945–1975* (CCH-E05-02-02) (Fort Meade, MD: Center for Cryptologic History, 2002), 110–116, 381–382.

7. On the CICV and its subordinate centers, see Major General Joseph A. McChristian, *Vietnam Studies: The Role of Military Intelligence, 1965–1967* (Washington, DC: Department of the Army, 1974), 21–93. Specific developments on Abrams's watch are best covered by Lewis Sorley in *A Better War: The Unexamined Victories and Final Tragedy of America's Last Years in Vietnam* (New York: Harcourt Brace, 1999), 32–37, 45–58, 131–134, 310–311, 344–346. Numerous specific examples of intelligence briefings from these sources are contained in the transcribed proceedings of the WIEU conferences reprinted in Lewis Sorley, ed., *Vietnam Chronicles: The Abrams Tapes, 1968–1972* (Lubbock: Texas Tech University Press, 2004).

8. There has been confusion over the CORDS acronym because some observers are seemingly unaware that "Revolutionary Development" was ever part of its name. As late as the fall of 1968, the MACV publication *Troop Topics,* produced to explain the war and their role in it to soldiers arriving in South Vietnam, carried "Revolutionary Development" as a section heading.

9. At a MACV command conference in November 1970, after hearing a sarcastic reference to Komer, General Abrams remarked, "Actually my aide just took my pistol away. Otherwise — ." Later Abrams added, in reference to the possibility Komer might return to Vietnam, "I'd say it would be a very unhealthy thing for him to do" (Sorley, *Abrams Tapes,* 505).

10. On CORDS, see Robert W. Komer, *Bureaucracy at War: U.S. Performance in the Vietnam Conflict* (Boulder, CO: Westview Press, 1986), and Thomas W. Scoville, *Vietnam Studies: Reorganizing for Pacification Support* (Washington, DC: Center of Military History, 1982). The section of the Pentagon Papers on pacification is also an important source; it is more amply reproduced in the U.S. government edition of this document than in the Gravel edition. A useful general history is Richard A. Hunt, *Pacification: The American Struggle for Vietnam's Hearts and Minds* (Boulder, CO: Westview, 1985). Colby's own account is in William Colby and James McCargar, *Lost Victory: A First-Hand Account of America's Sixteen-Year Involvement in Vietnam* (Chicago: Contemporary Books, 1989). For a biography of Colby, including his role in pacification, see John Prados, *Lost Crusader: The Secret Wars of CIA Director William Colby* (New York: Oxford University Press, 2003).

11. Colby and McCargar, *Lost Victory,* 254.

12. White House, NSC, minutes of Vietnam Review Group meeting, July 10, 1969, in Department of States, *FRUS, 1969–1976,* vol. 6, *Vietnam: January 1969–July 1970* (Washington, DC: Government Printing Office, 2006), 300.

13. CIA historical study by Thomas L. Ahern Jr., *CIA and Rural Pacification in South Vietnam* (CIA, Center for the Study of Intelligence, August 2001), 404–405 (declassified, Historical Review Program, October 2006).

14. U.S. Congress, Senate Foreign Relations Committee, *Hearings: Vietnam: Policy and Prospects* (Washington, DC: Government Printing Office, 1970), 194–195.

15. Compare the chart "Population Status in South Vietnam" in the CINCPAC/MACV publication *Report on the War in Vietnam* (Washington, DC: Government Printing Office, 1968), 199, with the same chart reproduced in Walt W. Rostow's *Diffusion of Power* (New York: Macmillan, 1972), 442.

16. Senate Foreign Relations Committee, *Vietnam Policy and Prospects, 1970,* tables on 630, 708.

17. Colby at the WIEU conference, February 8, 1969, quoted in Sorley, *Abrams Tapes,* 123. Colby told the group that Thieu had essentially added up all the villages in the "A" to "E" categories regardless of their assessed pacification status.

18. Department of Defense, "Statistics on Southeast Asia (Unclassified), 1972," reprinted in Rafael Littauer and Norman Uphoff, eds., *The Air War in Indochina,* rev. ed. (Boston: Beacon Press/Cornell University Air Power Study Group, 1972).

19. This discussion draws on my own work in *Lost Crusader* (188, 194–197, 203, 207–232, 235–236). Other sources on the program include Dale Andrade, *Ashes to Ashes: The Phoenix Program and the Vietnam War* (Lexington, MA: D. C. Heath, 1990); Douglas Valentine, *The Phoenix Program* (New York: William Morrow, 1990); and Mark Moyar, *Phoenix and the Birds of Prey: The C.I.A.'s Secret Campaign to Destroy the Viet Cong* (Annapolis, MD: Naval Institute Press, 1997). Moyar is responsible for the assertion that there were no Phoenix neutralization goals, despite the mountain of evidence that exists about them. The CIA official history (Ahern, *CIA and Rural Pacification*) discusses those goals as well.

20. Ahern, *CIA and Rural Pacification,* 361–366.

21. Prados, *Lost Crusader,* 227–228.

22. Colby at an MACV briefing for General Wheeler, October 4, 1969, quoted in Sorley, *Abrams Tapes,* 273.

23. Sorley, *Better War,* 217.

24. These works include Le Ly Haislip with Jay Wurts, *When Heaven and Earth Changed Places* (New York: Penguin, 1993); Duong Van Mai Elliott, *The Sacred Willow: Four Generations in the Life of a Vietnamese Family* (New York: Oxford University Press, 1999); James Trullinger, *Village at War: An Account of Conflict in Vietnam* (Stanford, CA: Stanford University Press, 1994); Eric Bergerud, *Dynamics of Defeat: The Vietnam War in Hau Nghia Province* (Boulder, CO: Westview, 1991); William R. Andrews, *The Village War: Vietnamese Communist Revolutionary Activities in Dinh Tuong Province, 1960–1964* (Columbia: University of Missouri Press, 1973); Jeffrey Race, *The War Comes to Long An: Revolutionary Conflict in a Vietnamese Province* (Berkeley: University of California Press, 1972); Robert L. Sansom, *The Economics of Insurgency in the Mekong Delta* (Cambridge, MA: MIT Press, 1970); and David Elliott, *The Vietnamese War: Revolution and Social Change in the Mekong Delta, 1930–1975,* 2 vols. (Armonk, NY: M. E. Sharpe, 2003). Also see Don Luce and John Sommer, *Vietnam: The Unheard Voices* (Ithaca, NY: Cornell University Press, 1969). The wonderfully detailed volumes by David Elliott, a wartime Rand analyst engaged in these issues, are the current standard. Duong Van Mai Elliott is David's wife.

25. "Finally Their Own Way Out?" *Newsweek,* February 9, 1970, 38.

26. General Creighton Abrams at MACV briefing, January 12, 1970, quoted in Sorley, *Abrams Tapes,* 337.

27. Quoted in Tom Wells, *The War Within: America's Battle Over Vietnam* (Berkeley: University of California Press, 1994), 327.

28. John Prados, *The Blood Road: The Ho Chi Minh Trail and the Vietnam War* (New York: John Wiley's Sons, 1999), 324–325.

29. Department of Defense, memorandum of conversation, Melvin R. Laird–Nguyen Van

Thieu et al., March 8, 1969 (declassified March 15, 2001), LBJL, Morton H. Halperin Papers, box 10, folder "Vietnam."

30. Department of State memorandum, Edward Lansdale–Ellsworth Bunker, "Sensitive Supplement," June 7, 1968 (declassified September 22, 1994), National Security Archive, Edward Lansdale Papers, box 2, folder "1968."

31. CIA cable (IN 27249), June 9, 1968 (declassified May 2, 2001), LBJL, LBJP, NSF, CFVN, box 243, folder "VN: CIA Cables for June 1968 (1)."

32. NSC report, "Summary of Agency Responses to NSSM 1," March 22, 1969, in *FRUS, 1969–1976,* 6: 146.

33. Quoted in Nguyen Tien Hung and Jerrold L. Schecter, *The Palace File: The Remarkable Story of the Secret Letters from Nixon and Ford to the President of South Vietnam* (New York: Harper & Row, 1986), 81; cf. 27, 78–82. Their citation is to Seymour Hersh's *The Price of Power: Kissinger in the Nixon White House* (New York: Summit Books, 1983), 128. For NSSM-22, see White House, NSC memorandum, "Contingency Plans for Vietnam," NSSM-22, February 13, 1969 (declassified February 27, 1981), NARA, Records Group 273, Records of the National Security Council, folder "NSSMs." Laird claims to have terminated this planning in his video history for the Nixon Library, December 18, 2006.

34. Lansdale–Bunker memo, "Sensitive Supplement," emphasis in original. This document is also significant because it shows that U.S. officials were already aware of this problem in 1968. By 1971 individuals in the Nixon administration were testifying in Congress about the *average prices* South Vietnamese were paying for their appointments. Neither the succession of high-level visitors from Washington nor Bunker, Colby, and Abrams, apart or together, could make much of a dent in this corruption. The entire matter has been treated gingerly in postwar accounts. Former South Vietnamese military officers are among the more forthright, but within limits. For example, Lieutenant General Dong Van Khuyen, in his extensive 1980 monograph on the Republic of Vietnam Armed Forces (RVNAF), includes a full chapter on corruption but terms it "a media issue." He is silent on corruption cases among senior officers, barely mentions the disabled veterans' problems, and leaves untouched the Soldiers' Savings Fund scandal. See Dong Van Khuyen, *Indochina Monographs: The RVNAF* (Washington, DC: Center of Military History, 1980), 341–378, quote from 341. Although he fails to comment on many cases, Khuyen properly notes that a key step to counter corruption would have been "decentralization of the presidential power to make appointments and transfers by giving the Prime Minister and Minister of Interior authority over directors general and province chiefs, and the Minister of Defense or the JGS the same authority over general officers" (377). The question is whether Thieu, who relied on his power of appointment, would have permitted such a step. It is safe to say he would not.

35. Frank Snepp, *Decent Interval: An Insider's Account of Saigon's Indecent End Told by the CIA's Chief Strategy Analyst in Vietnam* (New York: Random House, 1977), 15n.

36. Department of State cable, Ellsworth Bunker–Henry Kissinger, Saigon 681 (backchannel), January 28, 1970, in *FRUS, 1969–1976,* 6: 569n. For progress reports and other documentation regarding this covert project, see ibid., 61, 161–163, 569–570.

37. Bui Diem with David Chanoff, *In the Jaws of History* (Boston: Houghton Mifflin, 1987), 276–277.

38. Department of State cable, Ellsworth Bunker–William Rogers, Saigon 1515, January 31, 1970, in *FRUS, 1969–1976,* 6: 552–555.

39. CIA, Office of Central Reference, Biographic Register, "Nguyen Van Thieu: Republic of Vietnam, Second Deputy Premier," n.d. (declassified June 9, 1976), LBJL, LBJP, NSF, International Meetings Series, box 29, folder "McGeorge Bundy Trip to Saigon, 2/4/65, v. IV (1 of 2)."

40. CIA report, "Brigadier General Nguyen Van Thieu," January 29, 1965 (declassified December 5, 1977), ibid.

41. NSC memorandum, "Minutes of Review Group Meeting: Vietnam Negotiations and Internal Security," July 10, 1969, 2:25–3:40 PM, in *FRUS, 1969–1976,* 6: 292–302, quote from 294.

42. CIA cable (IN 85773), April 5, 1968 (declassified February 5, 2001), LBJL, LBJP, NSF, CFVN, box 243, folder "VN: CIA Cables for April 1968."

43. Thieu Resignation Speech, April 21, 1975, in *Historic Documents of 1975* (Washington, DC: Congressional Quarterly, 1976), 295.

44. White House, "Notes by President Nixon of a Meeting," March 2, 1969, in *FRUS, 1969–1976,* 6: 81.

45. NSC memorandum, Henry Kissinger–Richard Nixon, "Reflections on De-escalation," March 8, 1969, ibid., 97–99.

46. NSC paper, "Vietnam Negotiations Issues for Decision," undated (March 1969), ibid., 158–161.

47. NSC, "Minutes of National Security Council Meeting," March 28, 1969, ibid., 164–176, especially 171–173.

48. Ibid., 173.

49. NSC memorandum, "Vietnam," NSDM-9, April 1, 1969, ibid., 179–180. In NSSM-37 the administration sought to define more clearly its goals and prospective timetables for a "mutual" withdrawal. The plans provided for a residual force with the equivalent of two divisions of combat troops (100,000 men) plus another 60,000 as a support and advisory group for the South Vietnamese (ibid., 280).

50. NSC memorandum, Henry Kissinger–Richard Nixon, "Vietnam Problems," April 3, 1969, ibid., 181–184, quote from 182.

51. NSC memorandum, "Vietnamizing the War," NSSM-36, April 10, 1969, ibid., 195–196.

52. NSC memorandum, Henry Kissinger–Richard Nixon, "Vietnamizing the War (NSSM 36)," June 23, 1969, ibid., 261–263.

53. NSC memorandum, Henry Kissinger–Richard Nixon, "*Sequoia* Meeting on Vietnam," July 7, 1969, ibid., 283–288, quote from 286. It is a testament to the realism, or lack thereof, in Kissinger's thinking that in July 1969 he still thought that American withdrawals from South Vietnam were "reversible."

54. NSC memorandum, Henry Kissinger–Richard Nixon, "Our Present Course on Vietnam," September 10, 1969, ibid., 370–374, quote from 372.

55. Henry A. Kissinger, *White House Years* (Boston: Little Brown, 1979), 32–33.

56. General Creighton Abrams at WIEU conference, February 15, 1969, in Sorley, *Abrams Tapes,* 127.

57. General Phillip Davidson at MACV briefing, March 5, 1969, ibid., 138–139.

58. Secretary of Defense MACV briefings, March 6–10, 1969, ibid., 140–154, quote from 141.

59. General Donn A. Starry Oral History (Abrams Oral History Project), December 14, 1976, 34–36, U.S. Army Military History Institute, Creighton Abrams Papers, box "B."

60. Colonel Donn A. Starry at MACV briefing for General Abrams, September 8, 1969, in Sorley, *Abrams Tapes,* 256.

61. General Earle Wheeler at MACV briefing for Wheeler, October 4, 1969, ibid., 269–272.

Chapter 10. Die to Make Men Free (1970)

1. Henry A. Kissinger, *White House Years* (Boston: Little Brown, 1979) , 451–457, quote from 453. See also Henry A. Kissinger, *Ending the Vietnam War: A History of America's In-*

volvement in and Extrication from the Vietnam War (New York: Simon & Schuster, 2003), 122–126.

2. NSC memorandum, Henry Kissinger–Richard Nixon, "National Security Council Meeting to Consider Public Posture on Laos," February 27, 1970, in Department of State, *FRUS, 1969–1976*, vol. 6, *Vietnam: January 1969–July 1970* (Washington, DC: Government Printing Office, 2006), 635.

3. Kissinger, *White House Years,* 455.

4. Kissinger–Nixon memo, February 27, 1970, in *FRUS, 1969–1976,* 6: 637. Notes on the NSC meeting itself appear at 638–646.

5. NSC, telephone conversation, Henry Kissinger–H. R. Haldeman, March 9, 1970, 8 PM, in *FRUS, 1969–1976,* 6: 650.

6. H. R. Haldeman, *The Haldeman Diaries: Inside the Nixon White House* (New York: G. P. Putnam's Sons, 1994), 136–137, quote from 137.

7. For greater detail see John Prados, "Port of Entry: Sihanoukville," *VVA Veteran* 25, 6 (November–December 2005).

8. Quoted in Wilfred P. Deac, *Road to the Killing Fields: The Cambodian War of 1970–1975* (College Station: Texas A&M University Press, 1997), 66–67. Also see John Prados, *Presidents' Secret Wars* (Chicago: Ivan R. Dee, 1995), 301–303. The Green Beret sergeant's comment is more recent and is recorded this way: "His team, he said, had trained a succession of groups of Khmer mercenaries who later supported Lon Nol's coup. He added that his team took for granted that this program was meant to overturn the Sihanouk government and that it had begun before his time in Vietnam" (William Pfaff, "The Ill Fate of US-Backed 'Uprisings,'" *Boston Globe,* June 26, 2000, A11). As the flow of Khmer Serei to Lon Nol's army continued during the Cambodian war, a top Khmer general recorded, "What we knew at the time was that these 'Special Forces' were under direct U.S. command in South Vietnam" (General Sak Sutsakhan, *The Khmer Republic at War and the Final Collapse* [Washington, DC: Center of Military History, 1980], 55). On charges of U.S. complicity in the coup—and much else besides—see Seymour Hersh, *The Price of Power: Kissinger in the Nixon White House* (New York: Summit, 1983).

9. Jeffrey Kimball, *Nixon's Vietnam War* (Lawrence: University Press of Kansas, 1998), 182–183, argues that Nixon and Kissinger sought to control the pace of withdrawal to avoid undermining their negotiating strategy with Hanoi, in effect, holding U.S. forces as a bargaining chip. Although I agree that this was a tactic in the original negotiating strategy, I believe tension existed from the beginning between bargaining for withdrawals and using them for political gain, and the latter concept won out rather quickly. Mr. Nixon did like his salted peanuts. The bargaining chip notion fell in the face of budget strains and the headaches of maintaining the draft. Further, using the force as a bargaining chip does not track with the notion, articulated by Nixon and Kissinger in March 1969, of imposing so many conditions on an agreed mutual withdrawal as to give the United States reason to abandon its side of the withdrawal.

10. Since a front command headquarters had been hit by B-52s near Khe Sanh in 1968, Hanoi had evolved new security measures, which now included locating actual headquarters away from communications posts, using dispatch riders to carry messages to groups of radio units that took turns being the communications link, and relocating the other radio facilities when they were not in action.

11. Quoted in Jerry Van Drew, "Close-up: LTG Do Cao Tri," *Hurricane,* September 1970, 46. The *Hurricane* was the slick magazine produced for GIs by the II Field Force in Vietnam. Van Drew was a staff sergeant and military journalist given access to Tri. A copy of this magazine is in the author's collection.

12. U.S. Congress, Senate Foreign Relations Committee, *Staff Report: Cambodia: May*

1970 (Washington, DC: Government Printing Office, 1970), 11–12. The congressional staffers were James G. Lowenstein and Richard M. Moose, widely attacked by Nixon administration supporters for reporting negative information. Reading their paper, one can appreciate their frustration. Despite possessing all the appropriate security clearances, they were turned away at many corners, not just on the matter of the Khmer Serei. Without bogging down on this issue, it needs to be said that declassified cable traffic demonstrates conclusively that Washington gave U.S. officials in Vietnam, Cambodia, and Laos explicit instructions what to tell the staffers and what to keep from them.

13. Agnew quoted in Tom Wells, *The War Within: America's Battle Over Vietnam* (Berkeley: University of California Press, 1994), 424–425; Nixon quoted in Melvin Small, *The Presidency of Richard Nixon* (Lawrence: University Press of Kansas, 1999), 79, citing *New York Times*, May 1, 1970. The president quickly explained that by "bums" he was referring to extreme radicals, such as those who may have been responsible for an April 24 fire at Stanford University's Center for Advanced Study in the Behavioral Sciences that destroyed research materials, including the work of almost a dozen scholars. Small happened to be in residence at the center at the time, but fortunately, his own work escaped destruction. See Melvin Small, *Johnson, Nixon, and the Doves* (New Brunswick, NJ: Rutgers University Press, 1988), 201, 283n19.

14. In 2007 the government declassified the long-suppressed CIA "Family Jewels" compendium, compiled in 1973, which contains documents that reveal an extended dialogue between the Nixon White House and the CIA over what the latter's share of these costs would be. The CIA reimbursed that amount to the White House even though it never had any role in actually answering the mail, choosing the contractor that did so, or monitoring the claimed expenses.

15. Tom Hayden, *Reunion: A Memoir* (New York: Random House, 1988), 416.

16. Until 1970 sniping had never been a protest tactic, and there had never been a sniper incident at an antiwar rally. Sniping had occurred in the urban riots of the 1960s, and black power advocates, who considered themselves at war with authorities, had adopted a certain gun culture and threatened a resort to violence. But construing the Kent State protesters as such a threat was gratuitous.

17. For detailed accounts of Kent State, see William A. Gordon, *Four Days in May: Killings and Coverups at Kent State* (Buffalo, NY: Prometheus, 1990); James A. Michener, *Kent State: What Happened and Why* (New York: Random House, 1971).

18. South Vietnamese embassy, Washington, cable, Bui Diem–Nguyen Van Thieu, May 2, 1970, quoted in Bui Diem with David Chanoff, *In the Jaws of History* (Boston: Houghton Mifflin, 1987), 274.

19. For a detailed analysis based on research in AFL-CIO records, see Edmund F. Wehrle, *Between a River and a Mountain: The AFL-CIO and the Vietnam War* (Ann Arbor: University of Michigan Press, 2005).

20. The ad is reproduced in Philip S. Foner, *American Labor and the Indochina War: The Growth of Union Opposition* (New York: International Publishers, 1971), 6.

21. American Friends of Vietnam, "Focus on Vietnam: Vietnam Revisited, April 1970," Reprint no. 10, May 1970, 4, Texas Tech University, Vietnam Archive, Douglas Pike Papers, "Assessment & Strategy" series, folder "4/70."

22. White House, Edward L. Morgan, memorandum for the President's File, "Mid-Day Meeting in the President's Office with Eight University Presidents," May 7, 1970, NARA, NLP, POF, WHSF, Memos to the President series, box 80, folder "Beginning May 3, 1970."

23. NSC, telephone conversation, Richard Nixon–Henry Kissinger, May 4, 1970, 4:45 PM, in *FRUS, 1969–1976*, 6: 929.

24. Wells, *War Within*, 432.

25. NSC, memorandum of conversation, "Mr. Kissinger's Meeting with Eleven Students

and Five Faculty Members of Stanford University," May 6, 1970, 3–4:15 PM, in Department of State, *FRUS, 1969–1976,* vol. 1, *Foundations of Foreign Policy, 1969–1972* (Washington, DC: Government Printing Office, 2003), 211–217.

26. Text, President Nixon's news conference, May 8, 1970, in U.S. Congress, Senate Foreign Relations Committee, *Background Information Relating to Southeast Asia and Vietnam,* 7th rev. ed. (Washington, DC: Government Printing Office, 1974), 417–422, quote from 417.

27. Quoted in William Safire, *Before the Fall: An Inside View of the Pre-Watergate White House* (New York: Belmont Towers Books, 1975), 203, 202.

28. Kissinger, *White House Years,* 511.

29. White House, Egil Krogh Jr., memorandum for the President's File, "President's Visit with Students," May 9, 1970, NARA, NLP, POF, WHSF, Memos to the President series, box 80, folder "Beginning May 3, 1970."

30. "Mr. Nixon's Home Front," *Newsweek,* May 18, 1970, 27.

31. Melvin Small comment on manuscript. Kissinger, *White House Years,* 511.

32. Quoted in Alexander M. Haig with Charles McCarry, *Inner Circles: How America Changed the World* (New York: Warner, 1992), 239.

33. Diem, *In the Jaws of History,* 275.

34. Cathy Wilkerson, *Flying Close to the Sun: My Life and Times as a Weatherman* (New York: Seven Stories, 2007), 340–341.

35. *Haldeman Diaries,* June 5, 1970, 172.

36. White House, "Special Report, Interagency Committee on Intelligence (Ad Hoc), Chairman J. Edgar Hoover," June 1970, reprinted in Church Committee, *Hearings,* vol. 2, *The Huston Plan,* 141–188, quotes from 146, 151, 150, 159, 147.

37. Huston testimony, ibid., 20, 32. Even statistics given out at the time fall short of Huston's claims. The Justice Department at one point announced there had been 862 bombings between January 1969 and April 1970, while the Bureau of Alcohol, Tobacco, and Firearms later estimated something over 5,000 bombings during the war (Kirkpatrick Sale, *SDS* [New York: Vintage, 1974], 632). Bombings (and firebombings) were of course highly controversial and reported in the news. Living through the period and attentive to the news, I personally do not remember bombings being reported at a rate that could account for these large numbers.

38. Athan Theoharis, *Spying on Americans: Political Surveillance from Hoover to the Huston Plan* (Philadelphia: Temple University Press, 1978), 29.

39. Frank Donner, *The Age of Surveillance: The Aims and Methods of America's Political Intelligence System* (New York: Random House, 1980), 152.

40. Most of this detail comes from the Church Committee's 1975 investigations. The best monograph treatments of the FBI operations are in James K. Davis, *Assault on the Left: The FBI and the Sixties Antiwar Movement* (Westport, CT: Praeger, 1997), and David Cunningham, *There's Something Happening Here: The New Left, the Klan, and FBI Counterintelligence* (Berkeley: University of California Press, 2004).

41. Embassy of South Vietnam in the United States, *The Vietnam Bulletin: The ARVN: The Armed Forces of the Republic of Vietnam,* Special Issue, December 1969, 7; copy in the author's files.

42. Department of State, Bureau of Public Affairs, "Progress of the Armed Forces of the Republic of South Vietnam Exceeds Expectations," P-412-570, May 1970, Texas Tech University, Vietnam Center Archives, Douglas Pike Papers, "War" series, folder "5/70."

43. Cao Van Vien, *Leadership* (Washington, DC: Center of Military History, 1981), 100.

44. There are many sets of desertion numbers and much confusion on the matter generally. Some figures reflect "net" desertions, or the number of deserters after subtracting soldiers who returned to their units; other figures simply reflect those who left. Many authors fail to specify which they are using. Figures here are from James Lawton Collins Jr., *Vietnam Stud-*

ies: The Development and Training of the South Vietnamese Army, 1950–1972 (Washington, DC: Department of the Army, 1975), 93. For a different set of figures, see Dong Van Khuyen, *Indochina Monographs: The RVNAF* (Washington, DC: Center of Military History, 1980), table, 140. The most recent treatment is Robert K. Brigham's *ARVN: Life and Death in the South Vietnamese Army* (Lawrence: University Press of Kansas, 2006). Brigham makes the connection between the rice planting and harvesting cycle and desertion. His interviews with ARVN veterans constistute the best source on recruitment and mobilization, life on base, relations to families, and other practical aspects of the South Vietnamese military experience, along with comparisons with NLF soldiers.

45. See, in general, Collins, *Development and Training*.

46. Nguyen Duy Hinh, *Indochina Monographs: Vietnamization and the Cease-Fire* (Washington, DC: Center of Military History, 1980).

47. David E. Ott, *Vietnam Studies: Field Artillery, 1954–1973* (Washington, DC: Department of the Army, 1975), 190–203.

48. Timothy J. Kutta, "Fighting Forces: The ARVN's Armored Corps Rose from Humble Beginnings in 1950 to Play a Major Role in the Final Battles of the War," *Vietnam* 11, 2 (August 2000): 12, 70–71.

49. Gloria Emerson, "A Saigon Captain Sees War Devouring His Life," *New York Times,* July 21, 1970, 7.

50. Defense Attaché Office Saigon, "RVNAF Final Assessment: Jan thru Apr FY 75," June 15, 1975 (declassified February 26, 1976), 13–1, Department of Defense FOIA Reading Room, document no. 64.pdf.

Chapter 11. Sound Forth the Trumpet (1971)

1. The work of Jeffrey Kimball is the essential source on Vietnam negotiations. For the exchanges leading up to the October 1970 formula, see Jeffrey Kimball, *Nixon's Vietnam War* (Lawrence: University Press of Kansas, 1998), 230–236. Kimball offers supplementary material and documents in *The Vietnam War Files: Uncovering the Secret History of Nixon-Era Strategy* (Lawrence: University Press of Kansas, 2004). For a differently nuanced view, see Larry Berman, *No Peace, No Honor: Nixon, Kissinger and Betrayal in Vietnam* (New York: Free Press, 2001), 76–80. Despite differences in interpretation, the key point remains that in October 1970 the United States retreated from the demand that Hanoi remove its troops from South Vietnam. For an earlier study of the negotiations that contains some interesting points, see Allen E. Goodman, *The Lost Peace: America's Search for a Negotiated Settlement of the Vietnam War* (Stanford, CA: Hoover Institution Press, 1978). On Hanoi's side the essential source is Luu Van Loi and Nguyen Anh Vu, *Le Duc Tho–Kissinger Negotiations in Paris* (Hanoi: Gio Publishers, 1996). Loi quotes from DRV records of conversations and often presents a very different view from that in U.S. sources. Loi was an assistant to North Vietnam's foreign minister and translated at some of the Kissinger meetings. He participated in the 1997 conference in Hanoi on the Vietnamese delegation.

2. Henry A. Kissinger, *White House Years* (Boston: Little, Brown, 1979), 968.

3. Admiral McCain was the father of Commander John McCain, then a prisoner in Hanoi, subsequently a U.S. senator and Republican candidate for president in 2008.

4. Quoted in U.S. Congress, Senate Foreign Relations Committee, *Background Information Relating to Southeast Asia and Vietnam,* 7th rev. ed. (Washington, DC: Government Printing Office, 1974), 130.

5. H. R. Haldeman, *The Haldeman Diaries: Inside the Nixon White House* (New York: G. P. Putnam's Sons, 1994), November 20, 1970, 212.

6. JCS dispatch, Admiral Thomas Moorer–General Creighton Abrams, December 10,

1970, quoted in James H. Willbanks, *Abandoning Vietnam: How America Left and South Vietnam Lost Its War* (Lawrence: University Press of Kansas, 2004), 97 (I do not identify the specific source document because it appears to have been inaccurately recorded in Willbanks's otherwise thorough work).

7. Alexander M. Haig and Charles McCarry, *Inner Circles: How America Changed the World* (New York: Warner, 1992), 273.

8. Melvin Laird, Nixon Library Video Oral History, December 19, 2006.

9. CINCPAC cable, Admiral John McCain–Admiral Thomas Moorer, 150236Z Dec 70, NARA, NLP, NSC Records, Al Haig Trip File, box 1012, folder "Haig TripVN-Phnom Penh, 11–18 Dec 1970."

10. NSC memorandum Henry Kissinger–Richard Nixon, "Situation in Southeast Asia," December 16, 1970 (declassified), NARA, NLP, Al Haig Trip File, box 1011, folder "Dec. 1970 Haig Trip [1 of 2]." Kissinger repeated this precise language in a different memo sent to the president two days later.

11. Nguyen Tien Hung and Jerrold Schecter, *The Palace File: The Remarkable Story of the Secret Letters from Nixon and Ford to the President of South Vietnam* (New York: Harper & Row, 1986), 43.

12. *Haldeman Diaries,* December 18, 1970, 222.

13. Ibid., December 22, 1970, 224.

14. NSC, Alexander M. Haig, memorandum for the President's File, January 18, 1971 (declassified), NARA, NLP, WHSF, POF, Memos to the President Series, box 83, folder "Beginning January 17, 1971."

15. Ibid.

16. Ibid.

17. U. Alexis Johnson with Jef Olivarius Oliver, *The Right Hand of Power: The Memoirs of an American Diplomat* (Englewood Cliffs, NJ: Prentice-Hall, 1984), 533.

18. Gary Rafferty recollections (ms., February 2000), used by permission.

19. Ibid.

20. Richard Nixon, White House tapes, conversation 451-23, February 18, 1971, 9:56–10:09 AM, excerpted in Kimball, *Vietnam War Files,* 144.

21. Richard Nixon, White House tapes, conversation 459-2, February 27, 1971, 9:35–11:57 AM, quoted in Robert A. Dallek, *Nixon and Kissinger: Partners in Power* (New York: HarperCollins, 2007), 260.

22. Quoted in Hung and Schecter, *Palace File,* 43.

23. Richard Nixon, White House tapes, conversation 466-12, March 11, 1971, after 4:00 PM, reprinted in Kimball, *Vietnam War Files,* 145.

24. Sorties are in quotation marks here because the conventional meaning of the word was strained in Laos by the tremendous pace of air activity. So urgent was the situation that crews simply flung themselves into the work. Because the Air Medal was awarded for the completion of a certain number of missions (sorties), keeping track of sorties became paperwork that got in the way of need. Many pilots simply dispensed with conventional procedures and recorded one "sortie" each time they had to return to base to refuel and rearm, no matter how many flights (sorties) they had made. I have heard this about Lam Son 719 from both Army and Marine helicopter pilots.

25. Official U.S. losses for the siege of Khe Sanh were 205 killed, 1,668 wounded, and 1 man missing in action. Posted losses for Lam Son 719 were 214 killed, 1,149 wounded, and 38 missing in action. As for helicopters, the United States admitted to 108 lost and 618 damaged. But helicopters were counted as merely damaged if recovery crews succeeded in salvaging only the aircraft number panel. An unknown but significant proportion of the damaged choppers never flew again.

26. *Haldeman Diaries,* March 23, 1971, 259.

27. White House, Oval Office conversation 488-15, Richard Nixon–Henry Kissinger, April 27, 1971, 10:19–11:43 AM, extracted in Kimball, *Vietnam War Files,* 158–160.

28. Quoted in Henry S. Bradsher, "Saigon Expecting New Offensive," *Washington Star,* June 10, 1971, A6.

29. MACV, briefing for the Secretary of the Army, April 26, 1971, in Lewis Sorley, ed., *Vietnam Chronicles: The Abrams Tapes, 1968–1972* (Lubbock: Texas Tech University Press, 2004), 605.

30. White House, Oval Office conversation 508-13, June 2, 1971, 9:45 AM–12:04 PM, extracted in Kimball, *Vietnam War Files,* 161–166, quote from 163. Kimball, who listened to the tape, describes Nixon as shouting and pounding his desk.

31. White House, Oval Office conversation 534-2, Nixon–Kissinger and Haig, July 1, 1971, 8:45–8:52 AM, in Kimball, *Vietnam War Files,* 175–182, quote from 176–177.

32. Abrams commented on the Central Highlands battle on December 28, 1971 (Sorley, *Abrams Tapes,* 728); General Clay spoke of the enemy resurgence on April 3 (ibid., 584).

33. The presence of veterans on college campuses and their active organizing there should not be attributed to the student movement. Rather, the vets were concentrated on the campuses due to the Vietnam-era GI Bill, so the colleges became natural venues for organizing.

34. A basic biography is Fred L. Guiles, *Jane Fonda: The Actress in Her Time* (New York: Pinnacle, 1982). For a pro-Fonda account, see Mary Hershberger, *Jane Fonda's War: A Political Biography of an Antiwar Icon* (New York: New Press, 2005). An anti-Fonda view is Henry M. Holzer and Erika Holzer, *"Aid and Comfort": Jane Fonda in North Vietnam* (Jefferson, NC: McFarland, 2002). For Fonda's own story, see *My Life So Far* (New York: Random House, 2005).

35. VVAW "Operation RAW" leaflet, copy in author's files.

36. Vietnam Veterans Against the War, *The Winter Soldier Investigation: An Inquiry into American War Crimes* (Boston: Beacon, 1972).

37. Ibid., 1.

38. Cf., for example, Eric Bergerud, *Red Thunder, Tropic Lightning: The World of a Combat Division in Vietnam* (Baltimore: Penguin, 1994). Bergerud's work is an oral history of the 25th Infantry Division compiled by an author who came on the scene long after Vietnam and had no stake in the politics of the war. In fact, he takes the position (in a different book) that pacification worked in Vietnam. Many of these veterans' recollections contain some of the same imagery and even phrases as those who testified at the Winter Soldier Investigation.

39. Quoted from an op-ed column in the *New York Times,* April 23, 1971, in Nancy Zaroulis and Gerald Sullivan, *Who Spoke Up? American Protest against the War in Vietnam, 1963–1975* (New York: Holt, Rinehart & Winston, 1984), 355. On the Calley trial in general, see Michal R. Belknap, *The Vietnam War on Trial: The My Lai Massacre and the Court-Martial of Lieutenant William Calley* (Lawrence: University Press of Kansas, 2003).

40. Quoted in Dallek, *Nixon and Kissinger,* 306, from a March 25, 1971, conversation.

41. *Haldeman Diaries,* April 24, 1971, 279.

42. Bui Diem with David Chanoff, *In the Jaws of History* (Boston: Houghton Mifflin, 1987), 286.

43. Howard Zinn's account of this episode is in his *You Can't Be Neutral on a Moving Train: A Personal History of Our Times* (Boston: Beacon Press, 1994), 141–148. Shortly afterward, near Washington's Dupont Circle, Zinn saw a group of youths ambling along, singing "America the Beautiful." They were set upon, spread-eagled against police cars, then arrested (147).

44. Lieutenant General John Cushman interview, Lubbock, TX, April 19, 1997.

45. White House, Charles W. Colson, memorandum, "Meeting with Peter Brennan on July 2, 1971," NARA, NLP, WHSF, POF, Memos to the President series, box 85, folder "Begin-

ning June 27, 1971." A note Colson prepared for the president in advance of this meeting judged that the "demonstration in May of last year . . . scared the hell out of the leftists" (ibid.).

46. Howard Hunt with Greg Aunapu, *American Spy: My Secret History in the CIA, Watergate & Beyond* (New York: John Wiley's Sons, 2007), 178.

47. Walter Pincus, "Nixon, Hoover Bashed Justices in '71 Phone Call," *Washington Post,* September 28, 2007, A7.

48. Legal maneuvers related to the Pentagon Papers, transcripts of Nixon's telephone conversations on the leak and on Ellsberg, an analysis of the truth of the claims of secrecy advanced about portions of the text of the papers, and much more can be found in John Prados and Margaret Pratt-Porter, eds., *Inside the Pentagon Papers* (Lawrence: University Press of Kansas, 2004).

49. White House, telephone transcript, Richard Nixon–Charles Colson, June 15, 1971, 6:21 PM, ibid., 108.

50. White House, Charles Colson, "Memorandum for the President's File: Meeting with John O'Neill, Spokesman for Vietnam Veterans for a Just Peace," June 16, 1971, NARA, NLP, WHSF, POF, Memos to the President series, box 85, file "Beginning June 13, 1971." For quotes from the conversation, see Nixon conversation 523-5 of June 16, 1971 (4:30 PM).

51. O'Neill quoted in Michael Dobbs, "After Decades, Renewed War on Old Conflict," *Washington Post,* August 28, 2004, A6.

52. White House, Nixon conversation 508-19, June 2, 1971, 2:25 PM.

53. Transcript, *The Dick Cavett Show,* June 30, 1971.

54. See Daniel E. Teodoru, "The Bloodbath Hypothesis: The Maoist Pattern in North Vietnam's Radical Land Reform," *Southeast Asian Perspectives* 9 (March 1973): 78–79, for the exaggeration of deaths in North Vietnam. The AFV, it will be recalled, supported the Cambodian invasion by publishing a favorable report from the pro-war "citizens" group the Johnson White House had created, another false "mass" organization.

55. Larry Rottman, Jan Barry, and Basil T. Pacquet, eds., *Winning Hearts and Minds: War Poems by Vietnam Veterans* (New York: First Casualty Press, 1971). Another anthology, edited by Barry with W. D. Ehrhart, followed later: *Demilitarized Zones: Veterans after Vietnam* (New York: East River Anthology, 1976).

56. George Rush, *Confessions of an Ex–Secret Service Agent: The Marty Venker Story,* (New York: Donald Fine, 1988), 42.

57. Rufus W. Youngblood, *20 Years in the Secret Service: My Life with Five Presidents* (New York: Simon & Schuster, 1973), 242.

58. Writers friendly to the FBI marveled that the arrests had been so well planned. The Bureau had been able to erect floodlights surrounding the entire area, which they flipped on as the bust began, as if this were coincidental and had nothing to do with foreknowledge. The Camden 28 went to trial in 1973. They were acquitted. The FBI provocation became an issue during the Church Committee investigations. See U.S. Congress, Senate Select Committee to Study Governmental Operations with Respect to Intelligence Activities [Church Committee], *Hearings: Federal Bureau of Investigation* (Washington, DC: Government Printing Office, 1976), vol. 6, 143–144. *Time* magazine carried Robert Hardy's story on April 17, 1972. Hardy, the FBI informant, procured the materials used for the break-in, gave the radicals whatever training they had, and encouraged the action. He had been assured by the FBI the radicals would be arrested when they rehearsed the break-in but afterward was told the orders to arrest the culprits in the act had been directly based on White House preferences. Hardy felt remorse when his daughter was shot and killed by police and FBI agents as they arrested the draft board raiders.

59. The documents included accounts of meetings that I attended and exchanges that I remembered. The spy's "take" was awfully sparse, however. There were no grand conspiracies,

only lengthy discussions of preparations for the next demonstration, accounts from those in touch with other peace groups, and endless headaches about dealings with the Veterans Administration. The Bronx VA hospital remained an especially hostile terrain for Vietnam veterans and framed the subject for many of these conversations. As for the documents themselves, I do not know the scholar who got them declassified and have been unsuccessful so far in tracing them.

60. Frank Donner, "The Confession of an FBI Informer," *Harper's,* December 1972, 54–66.

61. FBI report, "Vietnam Veterans Against the War (VVAW) Steering Committee Meeting, Kansas City, Missouri, November 12, 13, 14, 1971—Internal Security–New Left," November 18, 1971 (declassified December 19, 1995), FBI, FOIA Reading Room, file "HQ 100-448092, Section 11."

62. During the 2004 presidential campaign, John Kerry said he could not remember attending the Kansas City meeting, but he accepted the truth of the FBI reports that said he had. However, those reports also placed Al Hubbard at the meeting, and Hubbard says he did not attend (interview, August 5, 2007). VVAW national office representatives at Kansas City were Scott Moore, Joe Urgo, and Barry Romo. Romo does not recall Kerry or Hubbard being there either, although they attended a previous session in St. Louis (Barry Romo interview, March 24, 2004).

63. FBI report, "VVAW Steering Commmittee Meeting, Kansas City," 2, 3, 5; Gerald Nicosia, "Veteran in Conflict," *Los Angeles Times Magazine,* May 23, 2004; Bill Crandell interview, April 1, 2004; Barry Romo interview, March 24, 2004. Romo is 99 percent sure the vote went 100 percent against the proposal.

64. Andrew E. Hunt, *The Turning: A History of Vietnam Veterans Against the War* (New York: New York University Press, 1999), 125; Gerald Nicosia, *Home to War: A History of the Vietnam Veteran's Movement* (New York: Crown, 2001), 213. FBI reports on the Cairo surveillance can be found in file folders under HQ 100-448092, sections 2, 11, and 13.

65. Quoted in Alvin Shuster, "Thieu Terms Minh a Liar and Defends Role in Diem Coup," *New York Times,* July 20, 1971, 1.

66. "The Mudslingers," *Newsweek,* August 2, 1971, 38.

67. Lam Quang Thi, *The Twenty-five Year Century: A South Vietnamese General Remembers the Indochina War to the Fall of Saigon* (Denton: University of North Texas Press, 2001), 257.

68. Nguyen Cao Ky with Marvin J. Wolf, *Buddha's Child: My Fight to Save Vietnam* (New York: St. Martin's Press, 2002), 318.

69. Quoted in Sorley, *Abrams Tapes,* 687.

70. Kissinger, *White House Years,* 1035.

71. Diem, *In the Jaws of History,* 292.

72. Sorley, *Abrams Tapes,* 678–679.

73. Diem, *In the Jaws of History,* 293.

74. Ky, *Buddha's Child,* 319.

75. See Berman, *No Peace, No Honor,* 82–101.

76. Kimball, *Nixon's Vietnam War.* Kimball follows the secret negotiations in great detail, working primarily from cables and fragments of the discussions available at the time. Declassification of the actual transcripts largely took place after Kimball compiled his study, but they confirm his analysis. Dated but interesting accounts of the secret negotiations include D. Gareth Porter, *A Peace Denied: The United States, Vietnam and the Paris Peace Agreement* (Bloomington: Indiana University Press, 1976); and Tad Szulc, *The Illusion of Peace: Foreign Policy in the Nixon Years* (New York: Viking, 1978).

77. For the USSR, see Ilya V. Gaiduk, *The Soviet Union and the Vietnam War* (Chicago:

Ivan R. Dee, 1996). For China, see Qiang Zhai, *China and the Vietnam Wars, 1950–1975* (Chapel Hill: University of North Carolina Press, 2000).

78. The thorny question of whether American prisoners were left behind at the end of the Vietnam war, and whether and what proportion of those American servicemen listed as missing in action were also prisoners left behind, has been a source of controversy ever since. Many American veterans have taken up the cause originally championed by the POW families, and private efforts, Pentagon inquiries, and congressional hearings have never fully resolved the issue. If Americans *were* left behind, that was an action of the Nixon administration. For a recent recapitulation of the POW-MIA abandonment thesis, see the investigative report by journalist Sydney Schanberg, "McCain and the POW Cover-up," *The Nation Institute,* September 18, 2008, http://www.nationinstitute.org/p/schanberg09182008pt 1, and pt2 (accessed September 21, 2008).

79. Ambassador Nguyen Xuan Phong, presentation at the Fifth Triennial Symposium of the Vietnam Center, Texas Tech University, March 18, 2005.

80. Nguyen Phu Duc, *The Vietnam Peace Negotiations: Saigon's Side of the Story,* ed. Arthur J. Dommen (Christiansburg, WV: Dalley Book Service, 2005), xi. Duc's view of the Nixon-Kissinger negotiation is unrelentingly negative, more so than appears justified. For example, he charges that at his first private session with Xuan Thuy in August 1969, Kissinger abandoned the possibility of a U.S. residual force in South Vietnam by offering "complete" mutual withdrawals (286). The U.S. documentary record makes clear that the Kissinger offer deliberately obscured a U.S. intention to maintain residual forces, and Vietnamization planning also continued to be predicated upon the existence of such a force.

81. Hung and Schecter, *The Palace File*.

82. Department of State, Saigon Backchannel Cable 0144, Bunker–Kissinger, June 3, 1971 (declassified January 11, 1996), GRFL, GRFP, NSAF, NSC Convenience File, Embassy Saigon Series, box 1, folder "Saigon to Washington, 12/15/69–12/16/71."

83. Kissinger, *White House Years,* 1023. In the fairy-tale atmosphere of the Kissinger memoirs, the national security adviser completely omits his visit to Saigon and meeting with President Thieu on July 4, where, according to Nguyen Phu Duc, he characterized the Paris conversation with Hanoi's Le Duc Tho as "nothing new" and promised that the United States would not discuss South Vietnamese political issues in the talks. He also advised Thieu to look into Hanoi's latest formula, the "Nine Points" and not reject them out of hand (Duc, *Vietnam Peace Negotiations,* 266).

84. NSC memorandum, Henry Kissinger–Richard Nixon, "My Meeting with the North Vietnamese, August 16, 1971" (declassified December 16, 1992), NARA, NLP, NSC Files, Paris Talks series, box 189, folder "Paris Talks, August 1970–."

85. NSC, "Draft Agreed Statement of Principles for Negotiated Settlement for Indochina," August 10, 1971 (declassified April 24, 1996), GRFL, GRFP, NSAF, NSC Convenience File, Embassy Saigon Series, box 1, folder "Saigon to Washington, 12/15/69–12/16/71." Cf. "U.S.–South Vietnam Proposal for Settlement in Indochina," January 25, 1972, *Department of State Bulletin,* February 14, 1972, 185–186.

86. According to FBI surveillance reports on VVAW, Hubbard had similar conversations in Paris a few months later. Hubbard terms the claim an "FBI fantasy." The reports had the timing of his visit wrong and inaccurately had him speaking with Hanoi officials rather than the PRG delegate Madame Binh; Hubbard insists there was no conversation about prisoners. His reason for the trip was to address an international conference of war opponents meeting at Versailles. Hubbard spoke in King Louis XIV's famous Hall of Mirrors at the palace. His speech was based on notes by Fred Branfman, another American attendee who was not from VVAW (Hubbard interview, Chicago, August 5, 2007).

87. Letter, Le Duan-Pham Hung, June 29, 1971, excerpted in Kimball, *Vietnam War Files,* 175.

88. Qiang Zhai, *China and the Vietnam Wars*, 193–198.

89. Infiltration data were compiled by the author from MACV J-2 estimates presented periodically at command briefings and recorded in Sorley, *Abrams Tapes*.

90. Stephen P. Randolph makes the argument for the command decision in his fine history *Powerful and Brutal Weapons: Nixon, Kissinger, and the Easter Offensive* (Cambridge, MA: Harvard University Press, 2007), 38. The figures for actual training experience are taken from MACV, "The Nguyen Hue Offensive," J-2 study, undated (declassified January 7, 1977), E-1-1, University Press of America Microfilm Collection, Records of MACV, pt. 1, reel 19, frame 001 et seq.

91. General Abrams's reporting cable to Admiral Moorer, February 22, 1972, quoted in Dale Andrade, *America's Last Vietnam Battle: Halting Hanoi's 1972 Easter Offensive* (Lawrence: University Press of Kansas, 2001), 25. Also quoted in Sorley, *Abrams Tapes*, 786, 791, 757.

92. Quoted in Sorley, *Abrams Tapes*, 765, 743.

Chapter 12. Evening Dews and Damps (1971–1972)

1. Colonel Peter F. C. Armstrong, "Capabilities and Intentions," *Marine Corps Gazette* 70, 9 (September 1986): 45.

2. MACV, Weekly Intelligence Estimate Update conference, November 13, 1971, in Lewis Sorley, ed., *Vietnam Chronicles: The Abrams Tapes, 1968–1972* (Lubbock: Texas Tech University Press, 2004), 693.

3. MACV, Commanders' Weekly Intelligence Estimate Update conference, May 29, 1971, ibid., 633.

4. Orr Kelly, "U.S. Foresaw the Offensive by Hanoi, Review Shows, *Washington Star*, May 14, 1972, 20.

5. NSC, memorandum of conversation, Kissinger, Thieu, et al., Saigon, July 4, 1971, 2–3, 7–9, 14, NARA, NLP, NSC Records series, Al Haig Special File, box 1021, folder "Kissinger and Haig Memcons with Thieu [4 of 4]." Incidentally, in this same conversation Thieu confirmed that Lam Son 719 had not surprised Hanoi: "Returnees and prisoners said that the North Vietnamese had been prepared for a South Vietnamese offensive in Laos for eight months, since . . . Cambodia. They had been prepared psychologically, politically, and technically, for at least six months" (12). Thieu also said that the upcoming South Vietnamese presidential election would be better organized and fair and that the election law he had just promulgated was aimed at "fantasist" candidates, not at Nguyen Cao Ky (15). Thieu, like the Americans, could play games of deception. In fact, his presidential palace had one ornate room set aside for gambling.

6. MACV, B-3 Front Assessment Briefing, December 8, 1971, in Sorley, *Abrams Tapes*, 707.

7. MACV, Southeast Asia Assessment for COMUSMACV, November 18, 1971, ibid., 694; Commander's Weekly Intelligence Estimate Update conference, November 20, 1971, ibid., 696; Weekly Intelligence Estimate Update conference, December 4, 1971, ibid., 704; Special Assessment Briefing, December 10, 1971, ibid., 715; Commander's Weekly Intelligence Estimate conference, December 19, 1971, ibid., 724; COMUS and Commander's Update briefing, December 28, 1971, ibid., 733.

8. NSC memorandum, John Holdridge–Henry Kissinger, "Communist Dry Season Intentions in South Vietnam," December 20, 1971 (declassified February 2, 2000), GRFL, GRFP, NSAF, NSC Staff series, Vietnam Information Group subseries, box 9, folder "North Vietnam-Military 1967–1972 (6)."

9. Armstrong, "Capabilities and Intentions," 45.

10. Department of State, Bureau of Intelligence and Research paper, "South Vietnam:

Hanoi Plans a Winter/Spring Offensive," REAN-2, January 7, 1972 (declassified February 2, 2000), GRFL, GRFP, NSAF, NSC Staff series, Vietnam Information Group subseries, box 9, folder "North Vietnam-Military 1967–1972 (7)."

11. CIA, Saigon Station, "Situation Appraisal: VC/NVA Capabilities and Intentions During the Tet 1972 Season," January 24, 1972 (declassified June 1, 2001), ibid., box 6, folder "NLF/PRG (5)."

12. MACV, briefing for Secretary of the Army Robert F. Froehlke, January 10, 1972, in Sorley, *Abrams Tapes,* 746.

13. MACV, Southeast Asia assessment briefing, January 4, 1972, ibid., 741.

14. MACV, Weekly Intelligence Estimate Update conference, February 5, 1972, ibid., 775.

15. MACV, COMUS and Commander's Update briefing, December 28, 1971, ibid., 732.

16. Bernard C. Nalty, *The War against Trucks: Aerial Interdiction in Southern Laos, 1968–1972* (Washington, DC: Air Force History and Museums Program, 2005), 202.

17. The Seventh Air Force reviewed the statistics, attributing high confidence to its figures for tonnage entering The Trail and for what arrived in Cambodia and South Vietnam, and it concluded that the amount destroyed had been exaggerated by at least one-third (Nalty, *War against Trucks,* 219–221). As for truck numbers, North Vietnamese histories record 1,970 assigned to Group 559 at the beginning of the season, another 1,571 with transport units, and 4,775 arriving later. These sources record losing 4,228 trucks. Stephen P. Randolph, *Powerful and Brutal Weapons: Nixon, Kissinger, and the Easter Offensive* (Cambridge, MA: Harvard University Press, 2007), 55–56.

18. Richard Nixon, *RN: The Memoirs of Richard Nixon,* vol. 2 (New York: Warner, 1979), 57. Even Nixon noted the North Vietnamese buildup in the DMZ in the immediately preceding sentence.

19. Ibid.

20. See Aloysius Casey and Patrick Casey, "Lavelle, Nixon, and the White House Tapes," *Air Force* 90, 2 (February 2007). For congressional hearings into this affair, see U.S. Congress, Senate Armed Services Committee, *Hearings: Nomination of John D. Lavelle, General Creighton W. Abrams, and Admiral John S. McCain* (Washington, DC: Government Printing Office, 1972). The report was issued in December. Armed Services Investigating Committee, *Report: Unauthorized Bombing of Military Targets in North Vietnam* (Washington, DC: Government Printing Office, 1972). At the White House in June, Nixon railed at Laird for taking action against Lavelle instead of protecting him. Laird in fact accepts this responsibility. In his 2007 videotaped oral history for the Nixon Library, Laird admits he actually threatened JCS chairman Admiral Moorer, himself close to retirement, with court-martial unless he took care of the Lavelle mess.

21. MACV, Weekly Intelligence Estimate Update conference, February 19, 1972, in Sorley, *Abrams Tapes,* 788.

22. William M. Hammond, *Reporting Vietnam: Media and Military at War* (Lawrence: University Press of Kansas, 1998), 265–266; Ngo Quang Truong, *Indochina Monographs: The Easter Offensive of 1972* (Washington, DC: U.S. Army Center of Military History, 1980), 19–20; George H. Turley, *The Easter Offensive: Last American Advisors in Vietnam, 1972* (Novato, CA: Presidio Press, 1985), 20, 57.

23. The timing of the original instructions furnishes additional evidence of the outcome of the Lam Son 719 offensive, since absent a favorable military situation in the south, Hanoi would have no expectation of being able to hold ground within South Vietnam, which would have been required to install a provisional government.

24. DRV letter, Comrade Le Duan–COSVN and Regional Party Committees, March 10, 1972, in Nguyen Thi Nhan, *Van Kien Dang Toan, Tap 33, 1972* [Collected party documents, vol. 33, 1972], trans. Merle Pribbenow (Hanoi: Nha Xuat Ban Chinh Tri Quoc Gia, 2004),

187, 188, 189 (hereafter *Collected Party Documents, 1972*); copy courtesy of Merle Pribbenow.

25. DRV Politburo cable no. 182/B, March 29, 1972, ibid., 224–228, quote from 227.

26. DRV cable no. 119, Le Duc Tho–Key Commanders, March 27, 1972, ibid., 206–223, quote from 209.

27. For a fine account of the siege, see James H. Willbanks, *The Battle of An Loc* (Bloomington: Indiana University Press, 2005). Willbanks was an American adviser with the ARVN in this sector.

28. Quoted in Robert A. Dallek, *Nixon and Kissinger: Partners in Power* (New York: HarperCollins, 2007), 372. Kissinger had used the identical phrase in an Oval Office conversation on April 27, 1971, which Jeffrey Kimball transcribes in *The Vietnam War Files: Uncovering the Secret History of Nixon-Era Strategy* (Lawrence: University Press of Kansas, 2004), 158–160. On that occasion Mr. Nixon had exclaimed, "Don't worry, we're not going out whimpering; we're gonna blast the goddamn hell out of them!"

29. Quoted in Nixon, *RN*, 2: 77. The use of pronouns and verb tenses here appears to be in the moment, suggesting an entry from the Nixon diary, but the material is formatted as part of the text of Nixon's retrospective memoir.

30. The first quote is from John Prados, "America's Ultimate Plan to End the War," *VVA Veteran* 7, 7 (September 1987): 25. Nixon's comment on timing, domestic opposition, and crossing the Rubicon is from White House memorandum, Richard Nixon–Henry Kissinger, April 30, 1972 (declassified), NARA, NLP, POF, PPF, box 3, folder "Memos, April 1972."

31. Quoted in Bob Woodward and Carl Bernstein, "Nixon Fund Used to Laud War Tactics," *Washington Post,* April 25, 1973, A1. In a recently released telephone conversation from May 8, 1972, Colson told Haldeman that, on one front of this operation, "the guy" had called from Vermont to report "they can't get into [the] Western Union office." Looking ahead, Haldeman had responded, "We'll have to find a new method of communication" (American Radio Works, "The President Calling," transcripts).

32. Ronald Radosh, *Commies: A Journey through the Old Left, the New Left and the Leftover Left* (San Francisco: Encounter, 2001), 113–115.

33. Ilya V. Gaiduk, *The Soviet Union and the Vietnam War* (Chicago: Ivan R. Dee, 1996), 237–238; Anatoly Dobrynin, *In Confidence: Moscow's Ambassador to America's Six Cold War Presidents* (New York: Times Books, 1995), 247–248. See also, "Text of Soviet Statement on Vietnam," *New York Times,* May 12, 1972, 18.

34. Georgi K. Arbatov, *The System: An Insider's Life in Soviet Politics* (New York: Times Books, 1992), 182–183.

35. "Texts of Chinese Statement and Letter," *New York Times,* May 12, 1972, 18.

36. White House memoranda, Richard Nixon–various mentioned recipients, May 9, 10, 15, 18, 19, 20, 1972 (declassified), NARA, NLP, POF, PPF, box 4, folder "Memos, May 1972."

37. All these data are derived from Joint Chiefs of Staff, Historical Division, Joint Secretariat, "Sensitive Operations in Southeast Asia, 1964–1973," n.d. (declassified December 5, 1990, FOIA). Ronald B. Frankum Jr., in *Like Rolling Thunder: The Air War in Vietnam, 1964–1975* (Lanham, MD: Rowman & Littlefield, 2005), 162, presents different, lower numbers based on studies done by civilian consultants for the Air Force.

38. Jeffrey Kimball best summarizes this evidence and transcribes the relevant White House tapes in *Vietnam War Files,* 214–218, 220.

39. Conversation in the Old Executive Office Building, no. 332-35, April 25, 1972, 12:00–12:28 PM, quoted in Kimball, *Vietnam War Files,* 145.

40. NSC, memorandum of conversation, Henry Kissinger–Le Duc Tho et al., August 1, 1972 (declassified), 30, NARA, NLP, NSC series, Winston Lord subseries, box 864, folder "1." When Le Duc Tho raised the issue of the dikes a second time, Kissinger replied, "As for

the dikes, I have noted what you have said and we will pay special attention to the avoidance of floods" (52). Kissinger did not *deny* bombing the dikes, and he promised to manage the program more carefully, all of which suggests the dike attacks were real.

41. Lao Dong Party Secretariat, "Report on Recommendations to Shift the Direction of Activities and Urgent Operational Duties to Be Completed in Response to the Current New Situation," May 18, 1972, in *Collected Party Documents, 1972,* 272–305.

42. Joseph Kraft, "Letter from Hanoi," *New Yorker,* August 12, 1972, 58–72.

43. Robert Laymon interview, Lubbock, TX, October 18, 2006.

Chapter 13. Sifting Out the Hearts of Men (1972)

1. Jeffrey Kimball, *Nixon's Vietnam War* (Lawrence: University Press of Kansas, 1998), 318–320.

2. Kimball's *Nixon's Vietnam War* remains the most authoritative source, modified on only some points by subsequently declassified documents. For this period, see pp. 306–308, 318–329.

3. Henry A. Kissinger, *White House Years* (Boston: Little Brown, 1979), 1315.

4. Kimball, *Nixon's Vietnam War,* 320–323.

5. NSC, memorandum of conversation, Henry Kissinger–Le Duc Tho et al., August 1, 1972 (declassified). NARA, NLP, NSC series, Winston Lord subseries, box 864, folder "1"; Kissinger is quoted from p. 50.

6. A good summary of these maneuvers is in Melvin Small, *The Presidency of Richard Nixon* (Lawrence: University Press of Kansas, 1999), 241–267.

7. CIA, "Situation Information Report," April 25, 1972 (declassified April 1996), Texas Tech University, Vietnam Archive, CIA Collection, item 04112154006.

8. Quoted in John Prados, *The Hidden History of the Vietnam War* (Chicago: Ivan R. Dee, 1995), 287.

9. Donald M. Rothberg, "Say FBI Helped Plan Convention Protests," *New York Post,* May 10, 1973.

10. Danny Friedman telephone interview, June 4, 1994.

11. Richard Nixon, *RN: The Memoirs of Richard Nixon,* vol. 2 (New York: Warner, 1979), 174.

12. Theodore H. White, *The Making of the President, 1972* (New York: New American Library, 1973), 125.

13. White House, NSC, memorandum of conversation, Henry Kissinger–Nguyen Van Thieu et al., August 17, 1972, 4:35–6:40 PM (declassified), 4, 10, 18, 21, 30. NARA, NLP, NSC Records, Al Haig Special File, box 1021, folder "Kissinger and Haig Memcons with Thieu [4 of 4]."

14. Quoted in Nguyen Tien Hung and Jerrold L. Schecter, *The Palace File: The Remarkable Story of the Secret Letters from Nixon and Ford to the President of South Vietnam* (New York: Harper & Row, 1986), 67.

15. White House, NSC, memorandum of conversation, Henry Kissinger–Nguyen Van Thieu et al., August 18, 1972, 10:00 AM–1:30 PM (declassified), 6, 8, 25, 25. NARA, NLP, NSC Records, Al Haig Special File, box 1021, folder "Kissinger and Haig Memcons with Thieu [4 of 4]." The possibility of ARVN invasions of North Vietnam is discussed at pp. 14–15.

16. The most recent recitation of this story is in Pierre Asselin, *A Bitter Peace: Washington, Hanoi, and the Making of the Paris Agreement* (Chapel Hill: University of North Carolina Press, 2002). Asselin quotes some of the exchanges given here (63–64) but maintains the conventional interpretation. In an otherwise very good account, Asselin apparently lacked the crucial documents on U.S. secret plans for the bombing that are cited below. On the

bombing itself, see Marshall L. Michel III, *The 11 Days of Christmas: America's Last Vietnam Battle* (San Francisco: Encounter, 2002).

17. Nguyen Van Thieu, "Mr. Thieu Calls for a Bandung-like Conference of Asian Nations to Find Peace. He'd Include North Vietnam," *New York Times,* October 17, 1972. Even here Thieu outlined a hard-line position that North Vietnam would have to "withdraw all its tools of aggression to the North" and pay reparations to South Vietnam. He insisted these proposals were "open-minded, broadened, and sensible and reasonable" and that they were "maximum concessions."

18. JCS (Admiral John P. Weinel), untitled outline plan, n.d. (c. September 27, 1972), 3. NARA, NLP, NSC Records, Al Haig Trip File, box 1017, folder "Haig Vietnam Trip, September 29–October 4, 1972 [2 of 6]."

19. NSC memorandum, "Contingency Plan," Commander Jonathan Howe–General Alexander Haig, September 27, 1972, ibid.

20. See NSC, cable HAKTO 24, Henry Kissinger–Richard Nixon, 20115Z (October 20, 1972), for "they are probably right." The later quote is from HAKTO 43, 221600Z (October 22, 1972). NARA, NLP, NSC Records, Vietnam 10-72 HAKTO file, box 25, folder "TO-HAK-HAKTO: California Before Elections."

21. NSA history by Robert J. Hanyok, *United States Cryptologic History,* ser. 6, *The NSA Period: 1952–Present,* vol. 7, *Spartans in Darkness: American SIGINT and the Indochina War, 1945–1975* (CCH-E05-02-02) (Fort Meade, MD: Center for Cryptologic History, 2002), 418 (declassified 2007).

22. Kissinger, *White House Years,* 1406.

23. Ibid., 1348.

24. White House, letter, Richard M. Nixon–Nguyen Van Thieu, November 8, 1972, reprinted in Hung and Schecter, *Palace File,* 383–384.

25. White House, letter, Richard M. Nixon–Nguyen Van Thieu, November 14, 1972, ibid., 386.

26. H. R. Haldeman, *The Haldeman Diaries: Inside the Nixon White House* (New York: G. P. Putnam's Sons, 1994), November 18, 1972, 538.

27. Nguyen Phu Duc maintained that in this succession of meetings Nixon and Kissinger also offered the information that the United States had reached private understandings with the Soviet Union and the People's Republic of China on their aid to Hanoi. Nguyen Phu Duc, *The Vietnam Peace Negotiations: Saigon's Side of the Story,* ed. Arthur J. Dommen (Christiansburg, WV: Dalley Book Service, 2005), 353, 355, 358. As presently redacted, the available U.S. records, including transcripts and memoranda of conversation, do not support this claim.

28. White House, NSC, Alexander M. Haig Jr., "Memorandum for the President's Files: President's Meeting with the Joint Chiefs of Staff," November 30, 1972 (declassified January 7, 1998). NARA, NLP, WHSF, POF, Memos to the President Series, box 90, folder "Beginning Nov. 26 [1972]."

29. Duc, *Vietnam Peace Negotiations,* 360.

30. Nixon, *RN,* 2: 239–252.

31. Quoted ibid., 242.

32. Hanyok, *Spartans in Darkness,* 418. Some airmen maintain that secret courts-martial took place on Taiwan.

33. Barry Romo interview, Chicago, August 6, 2007.

34. Michel, *11 Days of Christmas,* 248–249. Sir Robert Thompson's claim appears in an official Air Force monograph: Brigadier General James R. McCarthy and Lieutenant Colonel George B. Allison, *Linebacker II: A View from the Rock* (Maxwell Air Force Base, AL: Air War College, 1979), 173.

35. Conference "Vietnam and the Presidency," John F. Kennedy Presidential Library, March 10–11, 2006. I attended the conference and witnessed Haig make these remarks.

36. Ambassador Nguyen Xuan Phong, Statement to the Fifth Triennial Vietnam Symposium of the Vietnam Center, Texas Tech University, March 18, 2005.

Chapter 14. The Truth Comes Marching Home

1. Louis Wesseling, *Fueling the War: Revealing an Oil Company's Role in Vietnam* (London: I. B. Tauris, 2000), 107–112, 165–168.

2. The Chinese figures are from Qiang Zhai, *China and the Vietnam Wars, 1950–1975* (Chapel Hill: University of North Carolina Press, 2000), table, 136. The overall numbers, which include Soviet aid, are from CIA/DIA, "Communist Military and Economic Aid to North Vietnam, 1970–1974" (unclassified). GRFL, GRFP, NSAF, East Asia and Pacific Staff series, CFVN, box 12, folder "March 1–7, 1975." The paper notes that information on imports to Hanoi was always incomplete and "substantially better" on civilian aid than military and that, within the military, ammunition figures were the least firm. However, the paper was extensively massaged within the NSC staff to provide the most alarming view possible, and it was produced at a time when the Ford administration had the greatest incentive to exaggerate the situation. The massaging of the paper included the figures quoted for aid to Saigon. Somewhat different numbers are supplied in postwar writings by ARVN generals. See, for example, Cao Van Vien, *Indochina Monographs: The Final Collapse* (Washington, DC: Center of Military History, 1983), 46–53, and Dong Van Khuyen, *Indochina Monographs: RVNAF Logistics* (Washington, DC: Center of Military History, 1980), table, 416. Both point out that expenses for the U.S. Defense Attaché Office had to be subtracted from the aid under U.S. budget rules and that Saigon's air force consumed a portion of the money, but even their figure for bottom-line support to the ARVN, $458 million, exceeds total communist military aid to Hanoi by a considerable margin.

3. Nguyen Tien Hung and Jerrold Schecter, *The Palace File: The Remarkable Story of the Secret Letters from Nixon and Ford to the President of South Vietnam* (New York: Harper & Row, 1986), 226–227.

4. Frank Snepp, *Decent Interval: An Insider's Account of Saigon's Indecent End Told by the CIA's Chief Strategy Analyst in Vietnam* (New York: Random House, 1977), 214–215.

5. Vien, *Final Collapse,* 129. It is important to note that the experts on the Weyand mission who recommended the $722 million arrived at that figure simply by calculating the cost of reequipping four ARVN divisions and supplying them for sixty days of combat (Snepp, *Decent Interval,* 307). That would merely have pushed the moment of Saigon's crisis forward to sometime in the summer of 1975; it would not have saved South Vietnam. Moreover, the ARVN's calculation of the time required to refurbish its broken units—which General Vien pegged at fifteen days for a regiment or a brigade (*Final Collapse,* 125)—would have ensured only that minimally reorganized South Vietnamese units, in imminent danger of running out of supplies, would face powerful VPA formations flush with triumph. The Weyand program should be seen as the desperate formula that it was. The probability of its success would have been greater than zero, but not much. And, even assuming *complete success,* what was being discussed was preserving a rump portion of South Vietnam for a short period, *not* victory in the Vietnam war.

6. Eisenhower's 1954 refusal to countenance general war because of what was happening in Indochina was implicitly a decision to divorce Vietnam from the Cold War, making it arguable that Eisenhower stepped back from the brink of bringing the Southeast Asian conflict into the Cold War. This alludes to the point raised early in this narrative regarding whether the Vietnamese revolution ought to be seen as part and parcel of the Cold War or as an inde-

pendent event on the periphery. Subsequent presidents utilized anticommunist rhetoric in common with their Cold War stances, but their repeated decisions not to court outside intervention by expanding the war strengthen this point. Nixon's mining of Haiphong, with its challenge to Moscow for a Cold War–type response, makes the point in reverse. It is instructive that in 1972 Soviet leaders declined to make that same kind of decision, preserving the limited character of the conflict.

7. Robert K. Brigham, *Guerrilla Diplomacy: The NLF's Foreign Relations and the Vietnam War* (Ithaca, NY: Cornell University Press, 1999).

Bibliographic Essay

Let me first describe in more detail my own work on Vietnam. I began studying the subject in the mid-1960s and have never stopped. At first focusing on the French colonial period and the Franco-Vietnamese war, I also gained knowledge on the American war, accumulating clipping files and whatever books were available. At Columbia University, where I attended both Columbia College and the Graduate School of Arts and Sciences and was physically present from 1969 to 1980, that research burgeoned using both the university's extensive libraries and the New York Public Library at 42nd Street. I also traveled to Cornell University and the University of California–Berkeley and used their Southeast Asia resources. My collection of Vietnamese biographies began in about 1970. I created a card index where I noted information on various figures whenever I encountered it. That collection was powerfully enhanced in about 1973 when Gareth Porter gave me copies of a similar card file that David Marr, a Marine intelligence officer in Vietnam, had compiled on South Vietnamese generals. Later I succeeded in getting declassified a series of Defense Intelligence Agency biographies of ARVN officers down to middle rank. I have added much to the card files since and have continued to mine all available source material on Southeast Asia.

As is apparent from various comments in the narrative, I was a historian member of the American delegation to the 1997 conference "Missed Opportunities in the Vietnam War," sponsored in Hanoi by the Watson Institute of Brown University and the Institute of Military History of Vietnam. I compiled the documentary briefing book for that conference and initiated and served as rapporteur at a series of "military lunches" between American officers and their Hanoi counterparts. Later I participated at several other Watson Institute "directed oral history" conferences.

My first writing on Vietnam appeared in 1972, in the conflict-simulation magazine *Strategy & Tactics* and the VVAW newspaper *First Casualty*. I used my biographical files to assemble a paper, published in 1973 by the Indochina Resource Center, profiling the social origins of South Vietnamese generals. Through the 1970s I contributed various articles on Vietnam, mostly related to the French war, as well as on Algeria, which appeared primarily in the conflict-simulation literature. My first book-length study was of U.S. diplomacy and the battle of Dien Bien Phu (*The Sky Would Fall: Operation Vulture: The U.S. Bombing Mission in Indochina, 1954* [New York: Dial Press, 1983]). A revised edition of that book with considerable additional material, especially on U.S. military activity based on my interviews with veterans, appeared in paperback in 2002 (*Operation Vulture* [New York: iBooks, 2002]). Presidential decision making and White House advice were major themes in my study of the National Security Council published in 1991 (*Keepers of the Keys: A History of the National Security Council from Truman to Bush* [New York: William Morrow, 1991]). Actual tape-recorded conversations of Presidents Kennedy, Johnson, and Nixon were featured in my book-CD collection *White House Tapes: Eavesdropping on the Presidents* (New York: New Press, 2003). Together with Margaret Pratt-Porter I wrote and edited a book including recollections, taped presidential conversation transcripts, and analyses of content and legal proceedings on the Pentagon Papers (*Inside the Pentagon Papers* [Lawrence: University Press of Kansas, 2004]). Various aspects of Vietnam intelligence were themes in my works on CIA covert operations (*Safe for Democracy: The Secret Wars of the CIA* [Chicago: Ivan R. Dee, 2006] and *Presidents' Secret Wars: CIA and Pentagon Covert Operations from World War II through Iranscam* [New York: William Morrow, 1988]) and my biography of William E. Colby (*Lost Crusader: The Secret Wars of CIA Director William Colby* [New York: Oxford University Press, 2003]). A multilevel analysis of decision making, international history, North and South Vietnamese accounts, and military operations was at the heart of my reframing of the story through the lens of the Ho Chi Minh Trail (*The Blood Road: The Ho Chi Minh Trail and the Vietnam War* [New York: John Wiley, 1999]). Vietnam battle actions were the primary focus in my books *The Hidden History of the Vietnam War* (Chicago: Ivan R. Dee, 1995) and, with coauthor Ray W. Stubbe, a Navy chaplain and veteran of this battle, *Valley of Decision: The Siege of Khe Sanh* (most recently available in a paperback edition from the U.S. Naval Institute in 2004).

At the National Security Archive, among other things I direct our Vietnam Documentation Project and am responsible for two microfiche document collections on Vietnam, as well as a number of Electronic Briefing Books, including ones on Kissinger and Nixon, the Gulf of Tonkin, the Diem assassination, the Pentagon Papers, and State Department intelligence during the war. Since 1987 I have contributed feature articles (forty, at last count) on the war to *VVA Veteran,* a publication of the Vietnam Veterans of America. Some are referenced in the notes. My Vietnam articles have also appeared in *MHQ: The Quarterly Journal of Military History, Diplomatic History, New Republic Online,* and *Against the Odds.* In addition, my academic papers or articles on the war appear in fourteen edited books, and I supplied entries on Vietnam in three reference works. I have also published three board games on Vietnam and designed several others.

What follows is my tabulation of good basic sources on aspects of the Vietnam war. A number of excellent works that belong in a general bibliography on the war are not included to avoid redundancy with the endnotes.

Pride of place as a general history, because it has figured so prominently, has to go to Stanley Karnow's *Vietnam: A History* (New York: Viking, 1983). Contemporary with that, and also based primarily on interviews, is Michael Maclear's *The Ten Thousand Day War* (New York: St. Martin's, 1981). A more recent account incorporating a good deal of presidential audiotape evidence is by the former *New York Times* bureau chief in Saigon, A. J. (Jack) Langguth, *Our Vietnam: The War 1954–1975* (New York: Simon & Schuster, 2000). A somewhat more rigorous historical treatment is Marilyn Young's *The Vietnam Wars, 1945–1990* (New York: HarperCollins, 1991). Another important survey history is Robert D. Schulzinger's *A Time for War: The United States and Vietnam, 1941–1975* (New York: Oxford University Press, 1996). A standard now in its third edition is George C. Herring's *America's Longest War: The United States and Vietnam, 1950–1975* (New York: McGraw-Hill, 1996). Whereas Herring's vision is more oriented toward Washington, one more oriented toward the South Vietnamese perspective is Anthony J. Joes's *The War for South Vietnam, 1954–1975* (Westport, CT: Praeger, 2001). A period account that was influential in its time and is still worth reading is George McT. Kahin and John Lewis, *The United States in Vietnam: An Analysis in Depth of the History of America's Involvement in Vietnam* (New York: Delta, 1967). A magnificent history, especially good on the French colonial period but truncated by its appearance at the same time as Kahin and Lewis's work, is Joseph Buttinger's two-volume *Vietnam: A Dragon Embattled* (New York: Praeger, 1967). Complementing Buttinger is a standard on the French colonialization of Vietnam, John Cady's *The Roots of French Imperialism in Indochina* (Ithaca, NY: Cornell University Press, 1954).

There is no good English-language history of the Franco-Vietnamese war. Strong on the British handover to the French in the south is Peter M. Dunn's *The First Vietnam War* (New

York: St. Martin's, 1985). Stein Tonnesson illuminates the opening moments of the war in *The Vietnamese Revolution of 1945: Roosevelt, Ho Chi Minh and DeGaulle in a World at War* (Newbury Park, CA: Sage, 1991). Most accounts either are episodic, skipping through events, or focus overwhelmingly on either the military or the political side. Examples of the former include Edgar O'Balance, *The Indochina War, 1945–1954: A Study in Guerrilla Warfare* (London: Faber & Faber, 1964), and Lucien Bodard, *The Quicksand War* (Boston: Houghton Mifflin, 1967). Bodard's book appears in three volumes in the French edition, which is much better than that in English. Bernard Fall's classic *Street Without Joy* (Harrisburg, PA: Stackpole, 1961) is also episodic; much of its material is drawn from the Expeditionary Corps' monthly magazine *Indochine Sudest Asiatique*. Ellen J. Hammer's book *The Struggle for Indochina, 1945–1955* (Stanford, CA: Stanford University Press, 1966), long regarded as the standard political and diplomatic account, neglects military aspects and could have done more on the political development of the South Vietnamese state. Two classics that do better are Denis J. Ducanson's *Government and Revolution in Vietnam* (New York: Oxford University Press, 1968) and Donald Lancaster's *The Emancipation of French Indochina* (New York: Oxford University Press, 1961). As might be expected, French-language sources are richer for this period. What may now be the French standard is General Yves Gras's *Histoire de la guerre d'Indochine* (Paris: Plon, 1979). The best work on the developing American interest in Indochina is Lloyd Gardner's *Approaching Vietnam: From World War II Through Dien Bien Phu, 1941–1954* (New York: W. W. Norton, 1988). The handful of earlier works that existed were surpassed by Gardner's opus.

Dien Bien Phu is a subject of special importance and has a literature all its own. Bernard Fall is an important contributor here too, and his book *Hell in a Very Small Place* (New York: J. B. Lippincott, 1966) remains an important account, along with Jules Roy's *The Battle of Dien Bien Phu* (New York: Harper & Row, 1965). Roy's work, though rendered very nicely into English by translator Robert Baldick, is significantly better in French; that edition also contains a documentary appendix that is entirely absent from the English version. An account from an American eyewitness is Howard R. Simpson's *Dien Bien Phu: The Epic Battle America Forgot* (Washington, DC: Brassey's, 1994). General Vo Nguyen Giap, who wrote a history of this battle in 1962, has far surpassed his earlier work with his rewritten (with Huu Mai) *Dien Bien Phu: Rendezvous with History: A Memoir* (Hanoi: Gioi Publishers, 2004). A new English-language account that will become a classic history is Martin Windrow's *The Last Valley: Dien Bien Phu and the French Defeat in Vietnam* (New York: Da Capo, 2004). Unfortunately, the most authoritative history has never appeared in English. That is Pierre Rocolle's *Pourquoi Dien Bien Phu?* (Paris: Flammarion, 1968). The Geneva negotiations are covered by Jean Lacouture and Philippe Devillers in *The End of a War, 1954* (New York: Praeger, 1969); again, the French edition is superior to the English. Lacouture also provides insights into this negotiation in his biographies of Pierre Mendes-France and Ho Chi Minh. A book that focuses on a textual analysis of the diplomatic documents is Robert Randle's *Geneva, 1954* (Princeton, NJ: Princeton University Press, 1969). Many of those documents are available in Allan W. Cameron, ed., *Viet-Nam Crisis: A Documentary History,* vol. 1, *1940–1956* (Ithaca, NY: Cornell University Press, 1971).

Knowledge of South Vietnam is presently evolving, impelled by a new generation of historians who are working with the Vietnamese sources that are starting to open up in Ho Chi Minh City. This skein of writing, so far devoted primarily to Ngo Dinh Diem, is discussed in the text and cited in the notes and is mentioned only briefly here. Older but still useful treatments of Diem include Denis Warner's *The Last Confucian* (New York: Macmillan, 1963) and Anthony T. Bouscaren's *The Last of the Mandarins: Diem of Vietnam* (Pittsburgh: University of Pittsburgh Press, 1965). The main English book-length treatments of Diem's consolidation of power are David Anderson, *Trapped by Success: The Eisenhower Administration and Vietnam, 1953–1961* (New York: Columbia University Press, 1981); Edward G. Lansdale, *In the Midst of Wars* (New York: Harper & Row, 1972); and Anthony Arnold, *The First Domino: Eisenhower, the Military, and America's Intervention in Vietnam* (New York: William Morrow, 1991). I expect that historian Kathryn Statler will presently overturn these older interpretations. Bernard Fall's articles written in the mid-1950s on the political-religious sects are seminal; they are reprinted in his book *Vietnam Witness, 1953–1966* (New York: Praeger, 1966). A nuanced view of the sects is in Hue-Tam Ho Tai's *Millenarianism and Peasant Politics in Vietnam* (Cambridge, MA: Harvard University Press, 1983). For the Michigan State University vision of Vietnam, see Richard W. Lindholm, *Vietnam: The First Five Years* (East Lansing: Michigan State University Press, 1959); Wesley R. Fishel, *Problems of Freedom: South Vietnam Since Independence* (East Lansing: Michigan State University Press, 1961); and Roy Jumper and Nguyen The Hue, *Notes on the Political and Administrative History of Vietnam, 1802–1962* (East Lansing: Michigan State University Group, 1962). Political development in general, plus a similar treatment of North Vietnam, is offered by Bernard Fall in *The Two Vietnams: A Political and Military Analysis* (New York: Praeger, 1967). This second edition, published the year he died, climaxed Fall's work. Another important treatment, from a conservative perspective, is Robert Scigliano's *South Vietnam: Nation under Stress* (Boston: Houghton Mifflin, 1964). Journalist Robert Shaplen was an acute observer of the Saigon scene. His articles from *New Yorker* magazine are collected in *The Lost Revolution* (New York: Harper & Row, 1966) and *The Road from War, Vietnam 1965–1970* (New York: Harper & Row, 1970). Another acute observer was Frankie FitzGerald, and her *Fire in the Lake: The Vietnamese and the Americans in Vietnam* (Boston: Little, Brown, 1972) was very influential. Key studies of Saigon electoral politics are Allen E. Goodman's *Politics in War: The Bases of Political Community in South Vietnam* (Cambridge, MA: Harvard University Press, 1973) and John C. Donnell and Charles Joiner's *Electoral Politics in South Vietnam* (New York: Lexington, 1974). Also interesting are Richard Critchfield's conspiracy theories in *The Long Charade: Political Subversion in the Vietnam War* (New York: Harcourt, Brace, 1968) and Zalin Grant's *Flight of the Phoenix: The CIA and the Political Defeat of the United States in Vietnam* (New York: W. W. Norton, 1991). Interesting observations about life in Saigon, related in the course of telling a spy story, are in Larry Berman's *Perfect Spy: The Incredible Double Life of Pham Xuan An,* Time *Magazine Reporter and Vietnamese Communist Agent* (New York: Smithsonian Books, 2007).

There are no English-language memoirs or biographies of Duong Van Minh, Nguyen Khanh, or Nguyen Van Thieu. Thieu's aides Nguyen Tien Hung and Nguyen Phu Duc wrote books (cited in the notes) on aspects of the peace negotiations or Thieu's relationship with Richard Nixon. The magazine *Vietnam Bulletin,* published by the South Vietnamese embassy in the United States during the Thieu period, is also a useful source. Nguyen Cao Ky produced two memoirs: *Twenty Years and Twenty Days* (New York: Stein & Day, 1977) and, with Marvin J. Wolf, *Buddha's Child: My Fight to Save Vietnam* (New York: St. Martin's, 2002). The second is more reflective, and I have cited it in the notes in preference to the first. Ambassador Bui Diem also produced an important reflection that I quote in this narrative. Significant as well is Tran Van Don's *Our Endless War: Inside Vietnam* (Novato, CA: Presidio Press, 1978).

On the military side, General Lam Quang Thi's memoir is cited in the notes. One of the few sources on Saigon's air force, from the perspective of a boy (who grew up to be an American fighter pilot) watching his father, is Quang X. Pham's *A Sense of Duty: My Father, My American Journey* (New York: Ballantine, 2005). There is a substantial Vietnamese-language literature, but not much in English. Exceptions range from wartime tomes such as General Vinh Loc's *Why Pleime?* (Pleiku, Vietnam: privately published, 1966) to Tin Nguyen's *General Hieu, ARVN: A Hidden Military Gem* (New York: Writer's Club Press, 2003). One historical publication was issued by the Joint General Staff during the war: Pham Van Son and Le Van Duong, eds., *The Viet Cong Tet Offensive* (Saigon: Republic of Vietnam

Armed Forces, 1969). A collection of comments by ARVN officers after the war is contained in Stephen T. Hosmer et al., *The Fall of South Vietnam: Statements by Vietnamese Military and Civilian Leaders* (New York: Crane Russak, 1980). General Cao Van Vien reflected on the war in *The Final Collapse* (Washington, DC: Government Printing Office, 1983). Vien and other ARVN generals contributed what is the most important compendium of material on the South Vietnamese army, given that its records were lost in the fall of Saigon. That led to the series of a dozen or so studies commissioned by the U.S. Army Center of Military History and called the *Indochina Monographs*. Several are cited in the notes. Another U.S. official publication of note is General James L. Collins Jr.'s *Vietnam Studies: The Development and Training of the South Vietnamese Army, 1950–1972* (Washington, DC: Department of the Army, 1975). An important recent account is Robert K. Brigham's *ARVN: Life and Death in the South Vietnamese Army* (Lawrence: University Press of Kansas, 2006).

The countryside was crucial in the war, but virtually the only direct Vietnamese accounts of life in the villages are Le Ly Haislip with Jay Wurts, *When Heaven and Earth Changed Places* (New York: Penguin, 1993), and Duong Van Mai Elliott, *The Sacred Willow: Four Generations in the Life of a Vietnamese Family* (New York: Oxford University Press, 1999). Also see Don Luce and John Sommer's *Vietnam: Unheard Voices* (Ithaca, NY: Cornell University Press, 1969). James Trullinger's *Village at War: An Account of Conflict in Vietnam* (Stanford, CA: Stanford University Press, 1994) is based on extensive interviews with villagers near Hue. For provinces in the Mekong delta, see Eric Bergerud, *Dynamics of Defeat: The Vietnam War in Hau Nghia Province* (Boulder, CO: Westview, 1991); William R. Andrews, *The Village War: Vietnamese Communist Revolutionary Activities in Dinh Tuong Province, 1960–1964* (Columbia: University of Missouri Press, 1973); Jeffrey Race, *The War Comes to Long An: Revolutionary Conflict in a Vietnamese Province* (Berkeley: University of California Press, 1972); Robert L. Sansom, *The Economics of Insurgency in the Mekong Delta* (Cambridge, MA: MIT Press, 1970); and David Elliott, *The Vietnamese War: Revolution and Social Change in the Mekong Delta, 1930–1975*, 2 vols. (Armonk, NY: M. E. Sharpe, 2003). Sansom is especially instructive on aspects of "rice warfare," a subject largely ignored in analyses of pacification, and the Race book has been highly influential. Elliott's work may become the new standard; he was a Rand analyst at the time and an admirer of Vietnamese culture. For the central part of South Vietnam, see any of the writings of anthropologist Gerald Hickey, in particular his *Village in Vietnam* (New Haven, CT: Yale University Press, 1964), and Michael E. Petersen, *The Combined Action Platoons: The U.S. Marines' Other War in Vietnam* (Westport, CT: Praeger, 1989). The long-recognized standard has been Alexander Woodside's *Community and Revolution in Modern Vietnam* (Boston: Houghton Mifflin, 1976). A typical wartime view is Samuel Popkin's *The Rational Peasant: The Political Economy of Rural Society in Vietnam* (Berkeley: University of California Press, 1979). For a history of pacification that ties much of this material together, see Richard A. Hunt's *Pacification: The American Struggle for Vietnam's Hearts and Minds* (Boulder, CO: Westview, 1995). For a related subject, see Douglas Valentine's *The Phoenix Program* (New York: William Morrow, 1990), Mark Moyar's *Phoenix and the Birds of Prey: The CIA's Secret Campaign to Destroy the Viet Cong* (Annapolis, MD: Naval Institute Press, 1997), and Dale Andrade's *Ashes to Ashes: The Phoenix Program and the Vietnam War* (Lexington, MA: D. C. Heath, 1990). Two of the *Indochina Monographs,* one on pacification and the other on territorial forces, as well as one of the U.S. Army's "Vietnam Studies" series, also bear on this issue. The CIA's official history on pacification, recently declassified, is referenced in the notes. Most readers know this subject courtesy of Neil Sheehan's *A Bright Shining Lie: John Paul Vann and America in Vietnam* (New York: Random House, 1988).

North Vietnamese documents and records are only gradually becoming available in published collections and official histories. There is still little available in archives. I am indebted to Merle Pribbenow for supplying translations of the North Vietnamese sources cited in the notes as well as others that informed the analysis but were not actually quoted. Pribbenow also translated the Vietnam Institute for Military History official history volume cited in the notes. During and after the war I made considerable use of the primary (but not "official") texts offered by the U.S. Foreign Broadcast Information Service (FBIS; subsequently the Joint Publications Research Service [JPRS]) and the BBC World Digest of Reporting. I also studied the North Vietnamese journals *Vietnam Studies* and *Hop Tac* (as translated by the FBIS), the periodicals *Nhan Dan* and *Quan Doi Nhan Dan* (again in FBIS translation), *Vietnam Courier, South Vietnam in Struggle,* the press releases of the Khmer Rouge "GRUNK" government, and others. Chronological but of general relevance is Cuoc Chien Chong, Chong My, and Cuu Nuoc, *The Anti-U.S. Resistance War for National Salvation, 1954–1975: Military Events* (JPRS translation 80968, June 3, 1982). Early decisions are officially revealed in published proceedings: *Third National Congress of the Vietnam Workers Party* (Hanoi: Foreign Languages Publishing House, 1961).

Writings from the DRV side include Vo Nguyen Giap's classic *People's War, People's Army* (New York: Praeger, 1967) and his *Big Victory, Great Task* (New York: Praeger, 1968). Truong Chinh's work was collected in the West in *Primer for Revolt* (New York: Praeger, 1963). A volume of his selected works appeared in Hanoi from the Foreign Languages Publishing House in 1977. The inside view of a communist who went over to Diem is Hoang Van Chi's *From Colonialism to Communism* (New York: Praeger, 1966). A defector to the Chinese, former senior diplomat and Politburo member Hoang Van Hoan, published *A Drop in the Ocean: Hoang Van Hoan's Revolutionary Reminiscences* (Beijing: Foreign Languages Publishing House, 1988). Ho Chi Minh's writings have been collected and issued in multiple volumes by Vietnam, but in the West at the time they were reflected in a book edited by Bernard Fall: *Ho Chi Minh on Revolution: Selected Writings, 1920–1966* (New York: Signet Books, 1967). Le Duan's collected works and his *Letters to the South* exist in various editions in Vietnamese and French. On the military side, General Hoang Van Thai wrote *The Decisive Years: The Memoirs of Senior General Hoang Van Thai* (JPRS translation 346718, June 23, 1987). Probably the best-known military memoir is that of General Tran Van Tra: *History of the Bulwark B2 Theater,* vol. 5, *Concluding the 30 Years War* (JPRS translation 82783, February 2, 1983). There is also a Vietnamese history of the Ho Chi Minh Trail, which I used in Spanish (but an English edition exists): General Dong Sy Nguyen with Duy Truong and Ky Van, *La ruta de Truong Son* (Hanoi: Gioi Publishers, 2007). Several other Vietnamese generals, including Nguyen Don, Cao Pha, and Nguyen Huu An, have memoirs as yet unavailable in English. For the interesting perspective of a figure who moved in and out of the military, edited the newspaper *Nhan Dan,* and finally became disillusioned with the entire Hanoi enterprise, see Bui Tinh's *Following Ho Chi Minh: Memoirs of a North Vietnamese Colonel* (Honolulu: University of Hawaii Press, 1995).

The fall of Saigon and end of the war are favorite subjects for the North Vietnamese participants. This is reflected in the Tra memoir cited above. Widely known in the West is Van Tien Dung's *Our Great Spring Victory* (New York: Monthly Review Press, 1977), collected from a series of articles that first appeared in *Vietnam Courier.* Giap published his own pamphlet on these events, *How We Won the War* (New York: Reconstruction Press, 1976), and more recently wrote an important work from a high-level perspective, *The General Headquarters in the Spring of Brilliant Victory* (Hanoi: Gioi Publishers, 2005). Hoang Van Thai also contributed his own account in *How South Vietnam Was Liberated* (reprint; Hanoi: Gioi Publishers, 2007). Other memoirs still available only in Vietnamese include those of generals Hoang Cam and Dang Vu Hiep. One secondary work worth including, because it is a virtual oral history from Hanoi's side, is Wilfred Burchett's *Grasshoppers to Elephants: The Viet Cong Account of the Last 55 Days of the War* (New York: Urizen, 1977). Burchett, an Australian journalist, enjoyed special access to Hanoi officials throughout the war and wrote a number of other books that are also worth a look.

General histories include Nguyen Khac Vien's *The Long Resistance, 1858–1975* (Hanoi: Foreign Languages Publishing House, 1975) and, of course, the official *Outline History of the Vietnam Workers Party, 1930–1975* (Hanoi: Foreign Languages Publishing House, 1975). Key sources on the development of the party include Huynh Kim Khanh, *Vietnamese Communism, 1925–1945* (Ithaca, NY: Cornell University Press, 1982); Robert F. Turner, *Vietnamese Communism: Its Origins and Development* (Stanford, CA: Hoover Institution Press, 1975); P. J. Honey, *Communism in North Vietnam* (Cambridge, MA: MIT Press, 1962); and William J. Duiker, *The Communist Road to Power in Vietnam* (Boulder, CO: Westview, 1981). Not to be missed is David G. Marr's definitive trilogy on the origins of the Vietnamese revolution: *Vietnamese Anticolonialism, 1895–1925; Vietnamese Tradition on Trial;* and *Vietnam 1945: The Quest for Power* (Berkeley: University of California Press, 1971, 1981, 1995). For a biography of Ho Chi Minh, I like William J. Duiker's *Ho Chi Minh: A Life* (New York: Hyperion, 2000), although it is notably short on the period after about 1960. Period biographies include Jean Lacouture, *Ho Chi Minh: A Political Biography* (New York: Vintage, 1968), and Nguyen Khac Huyen, *Ho Chi Minh: Vision Accomplished?* (New York: Collier, 1971). A private reflection by Jean Sainteny is in his *Ho Chi Minh and His Vietnam: A Personal Memoir* (Chicago: Cowles, 1972). Life in North Vietnam is exhaustively studied by Edwin Moise in *Land Reform in China and North Vietnam: Consolidating the Revolution at the Village Level* (Chapel Hill: University of North Carolina Press, 1983). Also see Gerard Chailland's *The Peasants of North Vietnam* (Baltimore: Penguin Books, 1969). For the role of women, there are two major sources: Sandra Taylor, *Vietnamese Woman at War: Fighting for Ho Chi Minh and the Revolution* (Lawrence: University Press of Kansas, 1999), and Karen G. Turner and Phan Thanh Hao, *Even the Women Must Fight: Memories of War from North Vietnam* (New York: John Wiley & Sons, 1998). On the Vietnamese military and the National Liberation Front, see Douglas Pike's books *PAVN: People's Army of Vietnam* (Novato, CA: Presidio, 1986) and *Viet Cong: The Organization and Techniques of the National Liberation Front of South Vietnam* (Cambridge, MA: MIT Press, 1966). On Hanoi's impressive foreign relations, see Donald Zagoria's *The Vietnam Triangle: Moscow/Peking/Hanoi* (New York: Pegasus Books, 1968). Hanoi's side in the negotiations is presented by Lu Van Loi and Nguyen Anh Vu in *Le Duc Tho–Kissinger Negotiations in Paris* (Hanoi: Gioi Publishers, 1996). Loi, who participated as a translator, makes use of Hanoi documents and records not available elsewhere.

The origins of the National Front for the Liberation of South Vietnam are elucidated by Carlyle A. Thayer in *War by Other Means: National Liberation and Revolution in Vietnam, 1954–1960* (Sydney: Allen & Unwin, 1989). The official version is Tran Van Giau and Le Van Chat's *The South Viet Nam Liberation National Front* (Hanoi: Foreign Languages Publishing House, 1962). At this writing we are near the publication of an official history from the Council for the History of the Southern Resistance. For a U.S. view, see Michael C. Conley, *The Communist Insurgent Infrastructure in South Vietnam: A Study of Organization and Strategy* (Washington, DC: Department of the Army Pamphlet 550–106, March 1967). Two important memoirs are Truong Nhu Tang with David Chanoff, *A Viet Cong Memoir: An Inside Account of the Vietnam War and Its Aftermath* (New York: Vintage, 1985), and Nguyen Thi Binh, *No Other Road to Take: Memoir of Mrs. Nguyen Thi Binh* (Ithaca, NY: Cornell University Southeast Asia Studies Program, 1976). On NLF foreign relations, the standard is Robert K. Brigham's *Guerrilla Diplomacy: The NLF's Foreign Relations and the Vietnam War* (Ithaca, NY: Cornell University Press, 1999).

On Hanoi's allies I must salute the Cold War International History Project of the Smithsonian Institution's Woodrow Wilson International Center for Scholars, which has spearheaded the effort to make documentary sources available for China, Russia, and the Eastern European nations. A key exemplar here is Working Paper no. 22, the most significant primary source on the subject: Odd Arne Westad et al., eds., *77 Conversations Between Chinese and*

Foreign Leaders on the Wars in Indochina, 1964–1977 (Cold War International History Project, May 1998). The key book is Qiang Zhai's *China and the Vietnam Wars, 1950–1975* (Chapel Hill: University of North Carolina Press, 2000). A broader Chinese policy study is Chen Jian's *Mao's China and the Cold War* (Chapel Hill: University of North Carolina Press, 2001). The most important account of Nixon's opening to China, containing a perspective on its importance for Vietnam, is Margaret Macmillan's *Nixon and Mao: The Week That Changed the World* (New York: Random House, 2007). On the Soviet side, see Ilya V. Gaiduk's *The Soviet Union and the Vietnam War* (Chicago: Ivan R. Dee, 1996). The only primary account is the memoir of Soviet ambassador Anatoly Dobrynin, *In Confidence: Moscow's Ambassador to America's Six Cold War Presidents* (New York: Times Books, 1995). The memoirs of Soviet foreign minister Andrei Gromyko are frustratingly thin on Vietnam. Material on both countries appears in journal articles and in the proceedings of a conference at the Lyndon Baines Johnson Library edited by Lloyd Gardner and Ted Gittinger, *International Perspectives on Vietnam* (College Station: Texas A&M University Press, 2000). This volume also contains material on Germany, South Korea, Japan, and India. There is a specific monograph on Japan and the war: Thomas R. H. Haven, *Fire Across the Sea: The Vietnam War and Japan, 1965–1975* (reprint; Princeton, NJ: Princeton University Press, 2007). The German Historical Institute (a German Marshal Fund entity in the United States) has made a special effort to advance European perspectives on Vietnam through its conferences and proceedings. One example is Andreas Daum, Lloyd Gardner, and Wilfrid Mausbach, eds., *America, the Vietnam War, and the World: A Comparative Perspective* (Cambridge: Cambridge University Press, 2003). On 1968 specifically, see Ronald Fraser, ed., *1968: A Student Generation in Revolt: An International Oral History* (New York, Pantheon, 1988). I also studied French and German sources on the events of 1968 in those countries. On the American allies in South Vietnam, see Robert M. Blackburn, *Mercenaries and Lyndon Johnson's "More Flags": The Hiring of Korean, Filipino and Thai Soldiers in the Vietnam War* (Jefferson, NC: McFarland, 1994). On Australia, see Jeff Doyle et al., eds., *Australia's Vietnam War* (College Station: Texas A&M University Press, 2002). I also used three of the seven volumes of the Australian history, *The Official History of Australia's Involvement in Southeast Asian Conflicts, 1948–1975*. The best source on the Australian antiwar movement is one of these works: Peter Edwards, *A Nation at War: Australian Politics, Society and Diplomacy During the Vietnam War, 1965–1975* (St. Leonards, Australia: Allen & Unwin with the Australian War Memorial, 1997). It is a commentary on their government and people that the Australians chose to devote an official history volume to a movement to stop a war, and that they produced one that treated the Movement evenhandedly.

In the course of my research I interviewed, talked to, conferenced with, or met White House and Pentagon officials; South and North Vietnamese negotiators; military people from generals to frontline soldiers of the U.S., South Vietnamese, North Vietnamese, and French armies; veterans, antiwar protesters, and politicians; analysts of the CIA, DIA, and South Vietnamese intelligence services; and other participants. I also utilized dozens of oral history interviews conducted by the presidential libraries, Stanley Karnow, Brian VanDeMark, Columbia University, the U.S. Naval Institute, the U.S. Army War College, and the State Department.

On the U.S. side, the importance of documentary sources cannot be overstated. Among the collections of papers I used were those of presidents Harry S. Truman, Dwight D. Eisenhower, John F. Kennedy, Richard M. Nixon, and Gerald R. Ford. These include the files of their subordinates such as Henry Kissinger, Alexander Haig, Walt Rostow, McGeorge Bundy, and others, including the NSC staff; secretaries of defense Thomas Gates, Robert S. McNamara, and Clark M. Clifford; officials Robert C. Cutler, Dillon Anderson, Gordon Gray, Robert F. Kennedy, John McCone, William E. Colby, Arthur M. Schlesinger Jr., Roger Hilsman, Donald Ropa, James C. Thomson, Robert Komer, William K. Leonhart, John T. Mc-

Naughton, Paul C. Warnke, George M. Elsey, Morton H. Halperin, Douglas Pike, and Maxwell Taylor; generals Creighton V. Abrams, Earle Wheeler, Edward G. Lansdale, J. Lawton Collins, and William C. Westmoreland; Admiral Arthur W. Radford; and individuals John Newman, William C. Gibbons, Daniel Ellsberg, Larry Berman, Douglas Valentine, and a number of GIs who served in Vietnam. Other collections I consulted were the papers held by the National Security Archive, including donations from Robert McNamara, Gareth Porter, Mark Perry, and others; papers of the U.S. Supreme Court; record groups at the National Archives pertaining to the Department of State, the Department of Defense, and the CIA; separate collections of CIA records held by the Vietnam Center of Texas Tech University; electronic reading rooms of the Department of Defense, FBI, and CIA; records of the Combined Documents Exploitation Center Vietnam held by the Joiner Center at the University of Massachusetts, Boston, and by Texas Tech; papers of the Vietnam Veterans Against the War held by the Wisconsin State Historical Society; papers of VVAW members held by the Wisconsin Veterans Museum; documents from Electronic Briefing Books prepared by the National Security Archive; and many documents directly obtained through the Freedom of Information Act and other official declassification mechanisms.

I have used audiotapes of presidents Kennedy, Johnson, and Nixon, which provide some of the most recent and interesting evidence. I gathered a few of these and showcased them in my collection *The White House Tapes,* but I consulted many more. And I benefited from the work of others, including Philip Zelikow, Ernest May, et al., *The Presidential Recordings: John F. Kennedy: The Great Crises,* 3 vols. (New York: W. W. Norton, 2001); Michael R. Beschloss, *Taking Charge: The Johnson White House Tapes, 1963–1964* (New York: Simon & Schuster, 1997), and *Reaching for Glory: Lyndon Johnson's Secret White House Tapes, 1964–1965* (New York: Simon & Schuster, 2001); Stanley I. Kutler, ed., *Abuse of Power: The New Nixon Tapes* (New York: Free Press, 1997); Robert Dallek, *Nixon and Kissinger: Partners in Power* (New York: HarperCollins, 2007); William Doyle, *Inside the Oval Office: The White House Tapes from FDR to Clinton* (New York: Kodansha International, 1999); and the Watergate Special Prosecution Force.

Important official collections (aside from the *Foreign Relations* series and the FBIS/JPRS materials) include the series *Vietnam Documents and Research Notes* issued by the U.S. embassy in Saigon, as well as State Department public information releases. U.S. military field manuals are a key source of doctrinal and other information. Among those I consulted were ones covering pacification and stabilization operations; maneuver; civil affairs operations; airmobile operations; air cavalry troop tactics; logistics; supply and service reference data; intelligence and interrogation; training lesson materials on the Geneva Convention; country manuals on South Vietnam, North Vietnam, and Laos; and ethnography manuals for minorities in the Republic of Vietnam and the Democratic Republic of Vietnam.

Three decades after the end of the Vietnam war, only the Marine Corps and Air Force have completed their official histories of the war. The Marine Corps history includes a volume on the early years, annual volumes for 1964 through 1968, one volume for 1969–1970, one for 1971–1973, and a bibliography volume. The Air Force history includes a thematic series and a topical one; the first covers types of aircraft (such as air engagements and aces, air transport, or gunships), and the second focuses on campaigns (one on Rolling Thunder, two on the air war in South Vietnam, two on interdiction in Laos, one on base defense and services). The Air Force also produced a separate set of monographs on specific topics, plus a book-length study on base defense; during the war, the so-called CHECO reports were an early cut at the same ground. The Navy history has a volume for 1945–1959 and one for 1960–1965. Its volume covering Rolling Thunder operations from Yankee Station has been written but not issued. The Navy also published two separate overview volumes—one general, and one with an important focus on riverine operations. No other Navy materials are available. The Army compiled an early set of "Vietnam Studies," individual monographs on subjects including everything from Free World Forces to systems analysis, communications, intelligence, engineering and combat support, combat arms (such as mounted operations, air mobility, artillery, riverine operations), and some studies on campaigns such as Cedar Falls–Junction City or the war in the northern provinces. There are roughly a dozen of these monographs. The Army's official history, like that of the Air Force, consists of both thematic and operational volumes. For the most part, the thematic ones were done first, with two volumes on advice and support to the ARVN, two on the military and the media, one on communications, one on combat photography, and so on. One volume on MACV has been released, and the second one is close. A volume on SOG has been written and is in process. So far, two volumes of combat history have taken the story only as far as October 1967. The volume for the year of Tet is being written. The Joint Chiefs of Staff history, in multiple volumes consisting of multiple parts, is complete. I have inserted a full set of the JCS histories in the National Security Archive's Vietnam microfiche collections. Official historians, however, are now rewriting the JCS histories to incorporate the plethora of other material that has become available since they were written, nearly contemporaneous with events in Vietnam. I used all this official history in this book.

The CIA histories remain classified except for the volume on pacification, which was released in October 2006. The agency has published a separate monograph on several Vietnam episodes, a collection of its Vietnam National Intelligence Estimates, and a number of articles from its journal *Studies in Intelligence* (including one, by Army general Bruce Palmer, that consumed an entire issue evaluating the agency's intelligence production), and it has declassified the notorious "Family Jewels" collection of documents on domestic activities. But there is no overall CIA Vietnam history currently available. I am informed that additional volumes of CIA history will be released about the time this book appears. Some CIA memoirs exist, and certain books on Laos deal with the agency in some detail. The National Security Agency has monographs on Southeast Asia that it prepared contemporaneously and in the years soon after the war. Some progress has been made under the Freedom of Information Act in getting these declassified, primarily by myself and cryptography scholar Matthew Aid. The NSA's release of Gulf of Tonkin materials constituted its first major opening of Vietnam records. In terms of publications, the NSA's official Vietnam history appeared in 2007 (it is cited in the notes). Another NSA account—quite good—is a study of North Vietnamese cryptography.

Analyses of this war have focused to a great degree on presidents and their decisions. I will not endeavor to list all this literature or all the sources I consulted. David Halberstam takes top billing with *The Best and the Brightest* (New York: Random House, 1972). For the Kennedy period, see John Newman, *JFK and Vietnam: Deception, Intrigue, and the Struggle for Power* (New York: Warner, 1992); William J. Rust et al., *Kennedy in Vietnam: American Vietnam Policy, 1960–1963* (New York: Charles Scribner's Sons, 1985); David Kaiser, *American Tragedy: Kennedy, Johnson, and the Origins of the Vietnam War* (Cambridge, MA: Belknap, 2000); Lawrence Freedman, *Kennedy's Wars: Berlin, Cuba, Laos and Vietnam* (New York: Oxford University Press, 2000); Roger Hilsman, *To Move a Nation: Politics and Policymaking in the Administration of John F. Kennedy* (Garden City, NY: Doubleday, 1967); and the Kennedy biographies by Arthur M. Schlesinger Jr. and Theodore Sorensen. A neglected but important work is Paul Kattenburg's *The Vietnam Trauma in American Foreign Policy, 1945–1975* (New Brunswick, NJ: Transaction, 1980); Kattenburg had a front-row seat on these events. Views from the Saigon embassy during this period include John Mecklin's *Mission in Torment* (Garden City, NY: Doubleday, 1965) and Frederick Nolting Jr.'s *From Trust to Tragedy* (Westport, CT: Greenwood, 1988). A commentary on an ambassador is Anne Blair's *Lodge in Vietnam* (New Haven, CT: Yale University Press, 1995). For the Diem assassination, see Howard Jones, *Death of a Generation: How the Assassinations of Diem and JFK Prolonged the Vietnam War* (New York: Oxford University Press, 2003);

Ellen J. Hammer, *A Death in November* (New York: Oxford University Press, 1987); and my own *Lost Crusader*. A transitional account that moves from the end of the Kennedy period through the failure of neutralization schemes is Fredrik Logevall's *Choosing War: The Lost Chance for Peace and the Escalation of the War in Vietnam* (Berkeley: University of California Press, 1999).

Many of the officials and military officers of this period have produced memoirs. They include Dwight Eisenhower, Lyndon Johnson, Richard Nixon, Gerald Ford, Robert McNamara, Clark Clifford, Melvin Laird, Dean Rusk, Henry Kissinger, George Ball, Victor Krulak, Maxwell Taylor, William Westmoreland, Bruce Palmer, U. S. Grant Sharp, Arthur Radford, Matthew Ridgway, Lewis Walt, Walt Rostow, William Bundy, John Kenneth Galbraith, U. Alexis Johnson, Paul Nitze, Chester Cooper, William Colby, Alexander Haig, Elmo Zumwalt, Jack Valenti, Joe Califano, Harry McPherson, Richard Goodwin, Horace Busby, George Christian, Phillip Goulding, H. R. Haldeman, John Ehrlichman, William Safire, Ray Price, Charles Colson, and more. McGeorge Bundy was at work on a reflection at the time of his death, and efforts are being made to complete it, most recently by Francis M. Bator. Some figures, such as Kissinger, Haldeman, Cooper, Valenti, and Colby, have produced multiple volumes of memoir materials. Biographies exist for many of these individuals and others as well. On Johnson I prefer Robert Dallek's *Flawed Giant: Lyndon Johnson and His Times, 1961–1973* (New York: Oxford University Press, 1998), and Randall Wood's more recent *LBJ: Architect of American Ambition* (New York: Free Press, 2006). Robert Caro's multivolume LBJ biography, at three volumes so far, has not even touched Vietnam. In fact, it is puzzling that such an in-depth study never engages Johnson's role at Dien Bien Phu.

For obvious reasons, Johnson's decision to commit U.S. ground troops to South Vietnam has attracted a very great deal of historical attention. General accounts of the process include Arthur M. Schlesinger Jr., *The Bitter Heritage: Vietnam and American Democracy, 1941–1966* (Greenwich, CT: Fawcett, 1967), and Leslie H. Gelb with Richard K. Betts, *The Irony of Vietnam: The System Worked* (Washington, DC: Brookings Institution, 1979). Among the more notable specific treatments of the troop decision are George McT. Kahin, *Intervention: How America Became Involved in Vietnam* (New York: Knopf, 1986); Ralph Stavins, Richard J. Barnett, and Marcus G. Raskin, *Washington Plans an Aggressive War* (New York: Vintage, 1971); Larry Berman, *Planning a Tragedy: The Americanization of the War in Vietnam* (New York: W. W. Norton, 1982); David Barrett, *Uncertain Warriors: Lyndon Johnson and His Vietnam Advisers* (Lawrence: University Press of Kansas, 1993); and Brian VanDeMark, *Into the Quagmire: Lyndon Johnson and the Escalation of the Vietnam War* (New York: Oxford University Press, 1991). A wider-ranging analysis of LBJ on Vietnam is Frank E. Vandiver's *Shadows of Vietnam: Lyndon Johnson's Wars* (College Station: Texas A&M University Press, 1997). It is interesting that this reflective study is the work of a scholar of the American Civil War. The H. R. McMasters study of the Joint Chiefs of Staff, discussed in the text and cited in the notes, also focuses on this period, beginning with the Tonkin Gulf incident.

On the Tonkin Gulf, the best source is Edwin Moise, *Tonkin Gulf and the Escalation of the Vietnam War* (Chapel Hill: University of North Carolina Press, 1996). Anthony Austin's *The President's War: The Story of the Tonkin Gulf Resolution and How the Nation Was Trapped in Vietnam* (Philadelphia: J. B. Lippincott, 1971) is of continuing importance. Both were published before certain NSA communications intercepts sent to the White House were declassified (at my request). I posted a National Security Archive Electronic Briefing Book on the fortieth anniversary of the Tonkin Gulf that presented the new evidence. During the following year the NSA declassified and released its entire set of Tonkin Gulf intercepts, along with official history monographs, interview records, chronologies, and certain documents bearing on the incident or its investigation. These added much to our knowledge. The Tonkin Gulf awaits an intrepid researcher's new comprehensive account.

That incident, along with the OPLAN 34-A operations, involved what was then called "coercive diplomacy." That concept was formalized by Alexander L. George, David Hall, and William E. Simons in *The Limits of Coercive Diplomacy: Laos, Cuba, Vietnam* (Boston: Little Brown, 1971). That concept also lay at the heart of U.S. bombing strategy. This is elucidated in some detail in Wallace J. Thies's *When Governments Collide: Coercion and Diplomacy in the Vietnam Conflict, 1964–1968* (Berkeley: University of California Press, 1980) and Robert L. Galucci's *Neither Peace nor Honor: The Politics of American Military Policy in Vietnam* (Baltimore: Johns Hopkins University Press, 1975). On bombing policy directly, see the work of Mark Clodfelter, *The Limits of Airpower: The American Bombing of North Vietnam* (New York: Free Press, 1989). Another interesting policy analysis is James C. Thompson's *Rolling Thunder: Understanding Policy and Program Failure* (Chapel Hill: University of North Carolina Press, 1980). A participant's view is Earl H. Tilford Jr.'s *Crosswinds: The Air Force Setup in Vietnam* (College Station: Texas A&M Press, 1993). Critics who believe airpower was never allowed to do its thing are best represented by operational commander Admiral U. S. Grant Sharp in his memoir. Critics on the other side are Raphael Littauer, Norman Uphoff, and the Air War Study Group of Cornell University in their *The Air War in Indochina*, rev. ed. (Boston: Beacon Press, 1972). A handy compendium of air war data is in Ronald B. Frankum's *Like Rolling Thunder: The Air War in Vietnam, 1964–1975* (Lanham, MD: Rowman & Littlefield, 2005). Sources on the Christmas Bombing are cited in that section of the narrative.

The Tet offensive is another special subject. The standard there remains Don Oberdorfer's *Tet!* (Baltimore: Johns Hopkins University Press, 2001). A recent addition of note is James H. Willbanks's *The Tet Offensive: A Concise History* (New York: Columbia University Press, 2007). A policy overview is Larry Berman's *Lyndon Johnson's War: The Road to Stalemate in Vietnam* (New York: W. W. Norton, 1989). A campaign history of the year 1968 can be found in Ronald Spector's *After Tet: The Bloodiest Year in Vietnam* (New York: Free Press, 1993). The dean of battle histories here is probably Keith W. Nolan, who has written on the fighting at Hue and in Saigon and the second-wave battle of Saigon. There are at least two other book-length accounts of the battle of Hue. The standard on Khe Sanh remains Stubbe's and my *Valley of Decision*. Through the Khe Sanh veterans' association, Stubbe has also produced a collection of Marine veterans' reminiscences and a compendium excerpting North Vietnamese official histories in translation. Earlier visions of Khe Sanh include Robert Pisor's *The End of the Line: The Siege of Khe Sanh* (New York: W. W. Norton, 1982) and Eric Hammel's *Khe Sanh: Siege Above the Clouds: An Oral History* (New York: Crown, 1989). Captain Moyers Shore also produced a monograph on Khe Sanh in the Marine Corps' official history program, and Air Force historian Barnard Nalty produced a similar one in the Air Force's program.

Negotiations have a literature of their own, richer for the Nixon period than for LBJ's. A key starting point is the (expurgated) Pentagon Papers negotiating volumes edited by George C. Herring: *The Secret Diplomacy of the Vietnam War: The Negotiating Volumes of the Pentagon Papers* (Austin: University of Texas Press, 1983). This text contains deletions and confusions resulting from the fact that it was melded from two different copies with different redactions. A full set of the negotiating volumes has been declassified to the National Security Archive and forms part of our Vietnam (II) microfiche set. Lloyd Gardner and Ted Gittinger's edited work *The Search for Peace in Vietnam, 1964–1968* (College Station: Texas A&M University Press, 2004), which resulted from a conference held at the Johnson Library, marked an important advance in our knowledge, especially of the third-country peace feelers. A book that Johnson administration officials privately cooperated on and then complained about is David Kraslow and Stuart H. Loory, *The Secret Search for Peace in Vietnam* (New York: Random House, 1968). Hungarian defector Janos Radvanyi provides insight into a few of the third-country peace feelers in his *Delusion and Reality: Gambits, Hoaxes and Diplo-*

matic One-upmanship in Vietnam (South Bend, IN: Gateway Editions, 1978). An important document collection on the Nixon era is Jeffrey Kimball's *The Vietnam War Files: Uncovering the Secret History of Nixon-Era Strategy* (Lawrence: University Press of Kansas, 2004). Kimball also provides a narrative account in his *Nixon's Vietnam War* (Lawrence: University Press of Kansas, 1998). Larry Berman has a different view in his *No Peace, No Honor: Nixon, Kissinger, and Betrayal in Vietnam* (New York: Free Press, 2001).

Mr. Nixon's war has barely begun to be documented, save for the preemptive bids to structure the history by the president himself, Kissinger, and Haig. In great part this reflects the late emergence of archival records, both paper and audiotape. A period piece with continuing utility is Tad Szulc's *The Illusion of Peace: Foreign Policy in the Nixon Years* (New York: Viking, 1976). Szulc is also the author of two important articles in *Foreign Policy* that were the first to delve into the Kissinger–Le Duc Tho secret negotiations. A second-generation account by a well-placed observer is William P. Bundy's *A Tangled Web: The Making of Foreign Policy in the Nixon Presidency* (New York: Hill & Wang, 1998). There are many works on Kissinger written during those years and several biographies of him, most notably by Marvin and Bernard Kalb and by Walter Isaacson. For a second-generation view, see Jussi Hanhimaaki's *The Flawed Architect: Henry Kissinger and American Foreign Policy* (New York: Oxford University Press, 2004). Kissinger's telephone transcripts have been declassified and are available at the National Security Archive. They have been featured in a few Electronic Briefing Books, and I believe William Burr intends to edit a collection of them, similar to his earlier work reproducing the transcripts of conversations from the Kissinger-Nixon visits to China. Kissinger aide Peter W. Rodman has a useful Vietnam chapter in his wider-ranging book *More Precious Than Peace: The Cold War and the Struggle for the Third World* (New York: Charles Scribners', 1994). Melvin Small's nicely done biography of Richard Nixon is *The Presidency of Richard Nixon* (Lawrence: University Press of Kansas, 1999). Anthony Summers presents a more colorful vision in *The Arrogance of Power: The Secret World of Richard Nixon* (New York: Viking Penguin, 2001).

Congress is critical to understanding the history of the war. The authority on this aspect is William Conrad Gibbons, whose five-volume *U.S. Government and the Vietnam War: Executive and Legislative Roles and Relationships* spans the period from the onset of the war to 1968. This work began as an internal history by the Congressional Research Service for the Senate Foreign Relations Committee but was republished by Princeton University Press from 1986 to 1995. Unfortunately, Gibbons was never able to extend his study through the Nixon administration. One who did is Robert Mann, *A Grand Delusion: America's Descent into Vietnam* (New York: Basic, 2001). There are several biographies of J. William Fulbright. The best is Randall Woods, *Fulbright: A Biography* (Cambridge: Cambridge University Press, 1995). Don Oberdorfer supplies an excellent biography of Mike Mansfield in *Senator Mansfield: The Extraordinary Life of a Great American Statesman and Diplomat* (Washington, DC: Smithsonian Books, 2003). For the legal and constitutional issues raised by the war, see John Hart Ely, *War and Responsibility: Constitutional Lessons of Vietnam and Its Aftermath* (Princeton, NJ: Princeton University Press, 1993). There have been many discussions of war powers during and since the passage of the War Powers Act. See the writings of legal scholar Richard Falk, an authority on both war powers issues and international law as it applied to the war in Vietnam; read John Norton Moore for the opposing viewpoint.

A key source on the war and the media disputing the Peter Braestrup thesis (cited later) is Clarence R. Wyatt's *Paper Soldiers: The American Press and the Vietnam War* (New York: W. W. Norton, 1993). More in the media's own style of presenting the facts is Daniel C. Hallin's *The "Uncensored War": The Media and Vietnam* (New York: Oxford University Press, 1986), which demonstrates censorship in operation. Also quite important is the condensation of the U.S. Army's two-volume official history of dealings with the media, William M. Hammond's *Reporting Vietnam: Media and Military at War* (Lawrence: University Press of Kansas, 1998). For a reporter's commentaries on the government's efforts against him, see Jack Anderson with Daryl Gibson, *Peace, War, and Politics: An Eyewitness Account* (New York: Tom Doherty Associates, 1999). Neil Sheehan's life of John Paul Vann, already cited, contains material on the government's war on reporters during the Kennedy years, and that is the subject of William Prochnau's *Once Upon a Distant War: Young War Correspondents and the Early Vietnam Battles* (New York: Random House, 1995). Profiles of women journalists are in Virginia Elwood-Akers, *Women War Correspondents in the Vietnam War, 1961–1975* (Metuchen, NJ: Scarecrow, 1988). Journalists' memoirs include ones by David Halberstam, Keyes Beech, Richard Tragaskis, Margueritte Higgins, Malcolm Browne (he has two), Morley Safer, Peter Arnett, Michael Herr, John Laurence, Richard Dudman, Gloria Emerson, Peter Boyle, and David Butler. Also worth attention is Donald Kirk's *Tell It to the Dead: Memories of a War* (Chicago: Nelson Hall, 1975).

Naturally, there is a huge array of sources on the battle history of the war. These range from accounts of campaigns and battles, such as the siege of Khe Sanh, Tet offensive, invasion of Laos, and Easter offensive, to individual fights. For a general one-volume history, I still prefer William S. Turley's *The Second Indochina War: A Short Political and Military History, 1954–1975* (Boulder, CO: Westview, 1986). Phillip Davidson's *Vietnam at War* (Novato, CA: Presidio, 1990) suffers from being a participant's defense of strategy; he manages to get through the entire account of the French war without identifying a unit. Robert Asprey devotes little space to Vietnam in his massive compendium on guerrilla warfare (*War in the Shadows*, 2 vols. [Garden City, NY: Doubleday, 1973]), but he does as well as or better than Davidson's lengthy history. A campaign history that focuses on the U.S. Marines is Edward F. Murphy's *Semper Fi: Vietnam: From Da Nang to the DMZ, Marine Corps Campaigns, 1965–1975* (Novato, CA: Presidio, 1997). He is also the author of a fine battle history of the 1967 actions around Dak To. An overview of the last phase of the war appears in Lewis B. Sorley's *A Better War: The Unexamined Victories and Final Tragedy of America's Last Years in Vietnam* (New York: Harcourt, Brace, 1999). Equally impressive is James H. Willbanks's *Abandoning Vietnam: How America Left and South Vietnam Lost Its War* (Lawrence: University Press of Kansas, 2004). A campaign history in statistics is Thomas C. Thayer's *War without Fronts: The American Experience in Vietnam* (Boulder, CO: Westview, 1985).

An early representative of the school I term the neo-orthodox was Peter Braestrup, whose book *Big Story: How the American Press and Television Reported and Interpreted the Crisis of Tet 1968 in Vietnam and Washington* (Boulder, CO: Westview, 1977) argued for a strategic victory thrown away. Following him came Guenther Lewy's *America in Vietnam* (New York: Oxford University Press, 1978), influential in its time. More recent works on this theme include C. Dale Walton, *The Myth of Inevitable U.S. Defeat in Vietnam* (London: Frank Cass, 2002), and Michael Lind, *Vietnam: The Necessary War: A Reinterpretation of America's Most Disastrous Military Conflict* (New York: Free Press, 1999). Other proponents of this school focus on the protest movement (Adam Garfinkle) and the media (Peter Rollins). A contrary view that centers on the military is James W. Gibson's *The Perfect War: The War We Couldn't Lose, and How We Did* (New York: Atlantic Monthly Press, 1986). A broader perspective is presented by Gabriel Kolko in his *Anatomy of a War: Vietnam, the United States and the Modern Historical Experience* (New York: Pantheon, 1985).

There are two biographies of William C. Westmoreland. The better one is Samuel Zaffiri, *Westmoreland* (New York: William Morrow, 1994). Zaffiri is also the author of the only history of the 1969 battle of Hamburger Hill. The only biography of Creighton V. Abrams is Lewis B. Sorley's *Thunderbolt: General Creighton Abrams and the Army of His Time* (New York: Simon & Schuster, 1992). Sorley is also author of the campaign history referenced earlier and the transcriber of the Abrams tapes, which appear in *Vietnam Chronicles: The Abrams Tapes, 1968–1972* (Lubbock: Texas Tech University Press, 2004). In addition, he wrote a biography of Army chief of staff Harold K. Johnson: *Honorable Warrior: General Harold K. Johnson and the Ethics of Command* (Lawrence: University Press of Kansas, 1992). Maxwell D. Taylor is profiled by his son in John Taylor's *General Maxwell D. Taylor: The Sword and the Pen* (New York: Doubleday, 1989). On the Joint Chiefs of Staff, read Mark Perry's *Four Stars* (Boston: Houghton Mifflin, 1989) and Robert Buzzanco's *Masters of War: Military Dissent and Politics in the Vietnam Era* (New York: Cambridge University Press, 1996).

Shelby Stanton deserves special mention for his work on Vietnam. Author of a standard reference work, *Vietnam Order of Battle* (Washington, DC: News Books, 1981), Stanton has also contributed *The Rise and Fall of an American Army: U.S. Ground Forces in Vietnam, 1965–1973* (New York: Ballantine, 2003); *Green Berets at War: US Army Special Forces in Southeast Asia, 1956–1975* (New York: Dell Books, 1991); and *Anatomy of a Division: The 1st Cav in Vietnam* (New York: Warner, 1989). The Cav has been a favorite subject, at least for publishers. There are a good half dozen accounts of its Ia Drang battles, including two by battalion commanders, as well as works by helicopter pilots, grunts, and recon men. See, for example, Robert Mason's *Chickenhawk* (New York: Viking, 1983). Probably the best known is General Harold G. Moore and Joseph L. Galloway, *We Were Soldiers Once . . . And Young* (New York: HarperCollins, 1993). On Cambodia, read J. D. Coleman's *Incursion* (New York: St. Martin's, 1991); Coleman also produced a fine book on Ia Drang. See also John M. Shaw's *The Cambodian Campaign: The 1970 Offensive and America's Vietnam War* (Lawrence: University Press of Kansas, 2005). For a grunt's view, there is Keith Nolan's *Into Cambodia: Spring Campaign, Summer Offensive, 1970* (Novato, CA: Presidio, 1990). A most influential book soon after the war was William Shawcross's *Sideshow: Nixon, Kissinger, and the Destruction of Cambodia* (New York: Simon & Schuster, 1979). For an important work produced in the heat of the moment, see Donald Kirk's *Wider War: The Struggle for Cambodia, Thailand, and Laos* (New York: Praeger, 1971). The only campaign history for Cambodia, aside from one of the Army's *Indochina Monographs*, is Wilfred P. Deac's *Road to the Killing Fields: The Cambodian War of 1970–1975* (College Station: Texas A&M University Press, 1997). Sources for the Easter offensive are cited in the chapters that deal with it.

There is a huge array of other Vietnam battle histories, accounts from the perspective of MACSOG, GI and airman memoirs, and CIA stories, plus a vast quantity of articles on the same themes. Some of these I consulted at various points, and all of them I read. I apologize to all those whose works have not been mentioned here.

The U.S. military conducting all these operations changed over the course of the war from a professional force to one consisting primarily of draftees. GI resistance rose in tandem with antiwar protest. On the forces themselves, see Christian G. Appy, *Working-Class War: American Combat Soldiers and Vietnam* (Chapel Hill: University of North Carolina Press, 1993). James E. Westheider covers blacks in *Fighting on Two Fronts: African Americans and the Vietnam War* (New York: NYU Press, 1997). Tom Holm discusses consequences for Indians in *Strong Hearts, Wounded Souls: Native American Veterans of the Vietnam War* (Austin: University of Texas Press, 1996). For Mexican Americans, see George Mariscal's *Aztlan and Vietnam: Chicano and Chicana Experiences of the War* (Berkeley: University of California Press, 1999).

GI resistance is represented mostly in data on military discipline. Decades later, few studies exist. Most recent is the fine book by Richard Moser, *The New Winter Soldiers: GI and Veteran Dissent During the Vietnam Era* (New Brunswick, NJ: Rutgers University Press, 1996). The origin of the species is David Cortright's *Soldiers in Revolt: The American Military Today* (Garden City, NY: Doubleday, 1975). Also see Robert S. Rivkin's *GI Rights and Army Justice: The Draftee's Guide to Military Life and Law* (New York: Grove Press, 1970), a GI guide similar to the Quakers' draft guides. For some relevant data, see William T. Allison's *Military Justice in Vietnam: The Rule of Law in an American War* (Lawrence: University Press of Kansas, 2007).

On the consequence of war experiences, see Murray Polner, *No Victory Parades: The Return of the Vietnam Veteran* (New York: Holt, Rinehart & Winston, 1971); Paul Starr et al., *The Discarded Army: Veterans After Vietnam* (New York: Charterhouse, 1973); John Helmer, *Bringing the War Home: The American Soldier in Vietnam and After* (New York: Free Press, 1974); Bob Greene, *Homecoming: When the Soldiers Returned from Vietnam* (New York: Ballantine, 1990); Jerry Lemcke, *The Spitting Image: Myth, Memory, and the Legacy of Vietnam* (New York: NYU Press, 1998); Ellen Frey-Wouters and Robert S. Laufer, *Legacy of a War: The American Soldier in Vietnam* (Armonk, NY: M. E. Sharpe, 1986); Jonathan Shay, *Achilles in Vietnam* (New York: Simon & Schuster, 1994); Joel O. Brende and Erwin R. Parson, *Vietnam Veterans: The Road to Recovery* (New York: New American Library, 1985); Robert Jay Lifton, *Home from the War: Vietnam Veterans: Neither Victims Nor Executioners* (New York: Simon & Schuster, 1973); and Arthur Egendorf, *Healing from the War: Trauma and Transformation After Vietnam* (Boston: Shambhala Publishers, 1985). The last two cover the efforts of Vietnam Veterans Against the War to establish techniques for treating post-traumatic stress disorder.

Best on the draft in general remains Lawrence M. Baskir and William A. Strauss's *Chance and Circumstance: The Draft, the War and the Vietnam Generation* (New York: Knopf, 1978). I used the specialist studies on reauthorizing the draft in 1967, the proceedings of the Benjamin Spock trial, the study on the all-volunteer Army in 1969, the Army monograph on its Fort Ord experiment, and my old draft counseling handbooks but do not cite them here. On draft policy in general, see George Q. Flynn's *Lewis B. Hershey, Mr. Selective Service* (Chapel Hill: University of North Carolina Press, 1985). There is no general history of draft resistance, but a start in that direction was made by Michael S. Foley in *Confronting the War Machine: Draft Resistance During the Vietnam War* (Chapel Hill: University of North Carolina Press, 2003). Resisters and conscientious objectors figure in many of the oral history collections from Vietnam, but they are center stage in two books: Sherry G. Gottlieb's *Hell No We Won't Go: Resisting the Draft During the Vietnam War* (New York: Viking, 1991) and James W. Tonelson's *The Strength Not to Fight: An Oral History of Conscientious Objectors of the Vietnam War* (Boston: Little Brown, 1993). There is, however, an excellent monograph on fleeing to Canada: David S. Surrey's *Choice of Conscience: Vietnam Era Military and Draft Resisters in Canada* (South Hadley, MA: J. F. Bergin/Praeger, 1982).

Primary sources on Vietnam Veterans Against the War are its newspaper *First Casualty* and its later newspaper *Winter Soldier.* The proceedings of its Detroit action were published as *The Winter Soldier Investigation: An Inquiry into American War Crimes* (Boston: Beacon, 1972), and its account of the Dewey Canyon III march on Washington is in John Kerry and the Vietnam Veterans Against the War, *The New Soldier,* ed. David Thorne and George Butler (New York: Collier Books, 1971). Some VVAW poetry collections are cited in the text and notes. There are several more. An excellent oral history is Richard Stacewicz's *Winter Soldiers: An Oral History of the Vietnam Veterans against the War* (New York: Twayne, 1997). Among nonfiction writing by VVAWers, Donald Duncan's *The New Legions* (New York: Random House, 1967) was influential in the formation of the antiwar movement. Postwar writing includes John Ketwig's *And a Hard Rain Fell* (New York: Macmillan, 1985), W. D. Ehrhart's *Marking Time* (New York: Avon Books, 1986) and his revised *Passing Time* (Jefferson, NC: McFarland, 1989), plus Robert McLane's *Stop War America* (n.p.: Corps Productions, 2005). Kenneth J. Campbell contrasts his Vietnam experience with Iraq in *A Tale of Two Quagmires: Iraq, Vietnam, and the Hard Lessons of War* (Boulder, CO: Paradigm Publishers, 2007). Scott Camil recounts his travails in "Undercover Agents' War on Vietnam Veterans," in *It Did Happen Here,* ed. Bud Schultz and Ruth Schultz (Berkeley: University of

California Press, 1989). Bill Crandell tells of Operation Rapid American Withdrawal and Dewey Canyon in "They Moved the Town," in *Give Peace a Chance: Exploring the Vietnam Antiwar Movement*, ed., Melvin Small and William D. Hoover (Syracuse, NY: Syracuse University Press, 1992). My favorite history is Andrew E. Hunt's *The Turning: A History of Vietnam Veterans Against the War* (New York: NYU Press, 1999). Also noteworthy is Gerald Nicosia's *Home to War: A History of the Vietnam Veterans Movement* (New York: Crown Publishers, 2001). Richard Moser's book on GI resistance also tries to cover VVAW. Biographies of John Kerry include Michael Kranish et al., *John F. Kerry: The Complete Biography by the* Boston Globe *Reporters Who Know Him Best* (New York: Public Affairs Press, 2004), and Douglas Brinkley, *Tour of Duty: John Kerry and the Vietnam War* (New York: William Morrow, 2004).

Most Americans lacked the veterans' experience of war. We had to learn secondhand and depended on witnesses who could describe events or analysts who could interpret them. There are a host of such sources. Representative of the anti-imperialist genre is Noam Chomsky's *At War with Asia* (New York: Pantheon Books, 1970). Approaches that center on human rights are typified by Telford Taylor's *Nuremberg and Vietnam: An American Tragedy* (New York: Quadrangle Books, 1970). The rise and impact of the Movement are chronicled in Nancy Zaroulis and Gerald Sullivan's *Who Spoke Up? The American Protest Against the War in Vietnam, 1963–1975* (New York: Holt, Rinehart & Winston, 1984), and Charles DeBenedetti and Charles Chatfield's *An American Ordeal* (Syracuse, NY: Syracuse University Press, 1990). The contrary view is espoused by Adam Garfinkle in *Telltale Hearts: The Origins and Impact of the Vietnam Antiwar Movement* (New York: St. Martin's Press, 1995) and by Kenneth J. Heineman's *Put Your Bodies Upon the Wheels: Student Revolt in the 1960s* (Chicago: Ivan R. Dee, 2001). Shifts in public opinion are ably explored—and compared to Korea and World War II—by John E. Mueller in *War, Presidents, and Public Opinion* (New York: John Wiley & Sons, 1973). An account that goes into the Johnson and Nixon administration responses as well is Tom Wells, *The War Within: America's Battle Over Vietnam* (Berkeley: University of California Press, 1994). An earlier effort to cover this same ground is Melvin Small's *Johnson, Nixon and the Doves* (New Brunswick, NJ: Rutgers University Press, 1988). Rhodri Jeffreys-Jones segments his account by interest groups, such as women, labor, and so on, in *Peace Now: American Society and the Ending of the Vietnam War* (New Haven, CT: Yale University Press, 1999). Broader treatments of the Movement as a whole include Terry H. Anderson's *The Movement and the Sixties: Protest in America from Greensboro to Wounded Knee* (New York: Oxford University Press, 1995) and Edward P. Morgan's *The 60s Experience: Hard Lessons About Modern America* (Philadelphia: Temple University Press, 1991). Many studies focus on the decade of trauma, such as Milton Viorst's *Fire in the Streets: America in the 1960's* (New York: Simon & Schuster, 1979) or Kim McQuaid's *The Anxious Years: America in the Vietnam-Watergate Era* (New York: Basic Books, 1989). Political reporter Jules Witcover takes on 1968 in *The Year the Dream Died: Revisiting 1968 in America* (New York: Warner Books, 1997). So does David Caute, whose *The Year of the Barricades: A Journey Through 1968* (New York: Harper & Row, 1988), covers Europe, Japan, and Mexico in addition to the United States. Also international in scope is Carole Fink, Philipp Gassert, and Detlev Junker, eds., *1968: The World Transformed* (Cambridge: Cambridge University Press, 1998). For a survey of culture and society in the 1960s, read Arthur Marwick's exhaustive *The Sixties: Cultural Revolution in Britain, France, Italy, and the United States, c. 1958–c. 1974* (New York: Oxford University Press, 1998).

Journals, pamphlets, leaflets, speeches, and books of all kinds fueled the Movement. In addition to the massive literature on aspects of the Movement and many oral history collections, there is a wide array of studies on everything from methods to specific groups. On drama, see Henry Lesnick, ed., *Guerrilla Street Theater* (New York: Avon Books, 1973). The origins of marches on Washington are the subject of Lucy G. Barber's *Marching on Washing-*

ton: The Forging of an American Political Tradition (Berkeley: University of California Press, 2002), which centers in part on VVAW and the 1971 peace offensive. Grassroots outreach is covered in Wini Breines's *Community Organization in the New Left, 1962–1968: The Great Refusal* (South Hadley, MA: J. F. Bergin/Praeger, 1982). For the mobilization of women, see Jo Freeman's *The Politics of Women's Liberation* (New York: Longman, 1975). On labor, Philip Foner's treatise is cited in the notes. For the role of intellectuals, see Robert F. Tomes's *Apocalypse Then: American Intellectuals and the Vietnam War, 1954–1975* (New York: NYU Press, 1998). On academics, see David L. Schalk's *War and the Ivory Tower: Algeria and Vietnam* (New York: Oxford University Press, 1991), which has the important virtue of directly comparing the cross-cultural responses of American and French society to specific cases of military involvement in operationally similar combat environments. On religious groups, DeBenedetti is very useful, but Stanley Rothman and S. Robert Lichter zero in on the subject in *Roots of Radicalism: Jews, Christians, and the New Left* (New York: Oxford University Press, 1982), based on extensive survey data. For the transition from civil rights and antinuclear efforts to the war, see Irwin Unger's *The Movement: A History of the American New Left, 1959–1972* (New York: Harper & Row, 1974), or Maurice Isserman's *If I Had a Hammer . . . The Death of the Old Left and the Birth of the New Left* (New York: Basic Books, 1987). There are important memoirs by, among others, David Dellinger, Fred Halsted, Stokely Carmichael, Eldridge Cleaver, Jerry Rubin, Abbie Hoffman, Jane Fonda, Angela Davis, David Harris, Daniel Ellsberg, James Carroll, and Howard Zinn. Arthur M. Schlesinger Jr.'s diary has just been published, posthumously. For the aftermath, read A. D. Horne, ed., *The Wounded Generation: America After Vietnam* (Englewood Cliffs, NJ: Prentice Hall, 1981).

The Students for a Democratic Society have a literature all their own. Their premier observer is Kirkpatrick Sale, author of *SDS* (New York: Random House, 1973); he must have done an even better job of collecting SDS leaflets than did the FBI. A key recollection—part theory, part memoir—is James Miller's *"Democracy Is in the Streets": From Port Huron to the Siege of Chicago* (New York: Simon & Schuster, 1987). Tom Hayden's memoir is cited in the notes. Hayden stopped short of joining the Weather Underground, capping his activism with the Indochina Peace Campaign. The official theoretical tract of the Weathermen is *Prairie Fire: The Politics of Revolutionary Anti-imperialism: Political Statement of the Weather Underground* (n.p.: Communications Company, 1974). Bernardine Dohrn, Bill Ayers, and Jeff Jones retrospectively compiled *Sing a Battle Song: Poetry, Statements, and Communiqués of the Weather Underground* (New York: Seven Stories Press, 2006). Bill Ayers published his recollections in *Fugitive Days: A Memoir* (Boston: Beacon Press, 2001). Cathy Wilkerson also has a memoir, *Flying Close to the Sun: My Life and Times as a Weatherman* (New York: Seven Stories Press, 2007). Mark Rudd has an autobiography forthcoming. The Weathermen are studied by Dan Berger in his *Outlaws of America: The Weather Underground and the Politics of Solidarity* (Oakland, CA: AK Press, 2006). They are compared with German radicals who emerged from 1968 in Jeremy Varon's *Bringing the War Home: The Weather Underground, the Red Army Faction, and Revolutionary Violence in the Sixties and Seventies* (Berkeley: University of California Press, 2004).

A huge surge in government surveillance activities preceded and accompanied the rise of the Movement. The Church Committee investigation, cited in the notes, inquired deeply into these efforts and became the bedrock source for a number of significant texts. In my view, the best are James K. Davis, *Assault on the Left: The FBI and the Sixties Antiwar Movement* (Westport, CT: Praeger, 1997); Athan Theoharis, *Spying on Americans: Political Surveillance from Hoover to the Huston Plan* (Philadelphia: Temple University Press, 1978); and Frank Donner, *The Age of Surveillance: The Aims and Methods of America's Political Intelligence System* (New York: Vintage Books, 1981). The most recent addition to this literature is David Cunningham's *There's Something Happening Here: The New Left, the Klan, and FBI*

Counterintelligence (Berkeley: University of California Press, 2004). Also significant are Alexander Charns, *Cloak and Gavel: FBI Wiretaps, Bugs, Informers, and the Supreme Court* (Urbana: University of Illinois Press, 1992), which has resonance with Bush administration surveillance efforts today, and Richard E. Morgan, *Domestic Intelligence: Monitoring Dissent in America* (Austin: University of Texas Press, 1980). The FBI's COINTELPRO efforts are the specific subject of Ward Churchill and Jim Vander Wall's *The COINTELPRO Papers: Documents from the FBI's Secret Wars Against Dissent in the United States* (Boston: South End Press, 2002). Collections that focus on COINTELPRO against the Socialist Workers' Party, civil rights groups, and Native Americans also exist. Some material on the FBI's programs against dissent appears in Mark Riebling's *Wedge: The Secret War Between the FBI and the CIA* (New York: Knopf, 1994). A recent reminiscence on the White House Plumbers is E. Howard Hunt with Greg Aunapu, *American Spy: My Secret History in the CIA, Watergate, and Beyond* (New York: John Wiley & Sons, 2007). For a broader perspective, read Michael Linfield's *Freedom Under Fire: U.S. Civil Liberties in Times of War* (Boston: South End Press, 1990).

A special category is Secret Service protection for U.S. presidents. Remarkably, there is no standard source on the subject. The information presented in this narrative was pieced together from the periodical literature and individual memoirs. Philip H. Melanson and Peter F. Stevens, in *The Secret Service: The Hidden History of an Enigmatic Agency* (New York: Carol & Graf, 2002), cover the Kennedy assassination and the attempted murders of Gerald Ford and Ronald Reagan, but they are very thin on Lyndon Johnson and Richard Nixon. For Secret Service memoirs, see V. E. Baughman and Leonard W. Robinson, *Secret Service Chief* (New York: Popular Library, 1962); Rufus W. Youngblood, *20 Years in the Secret Service: My Life with Five Presidents* (New York: Simon & Schuster, 1973); Denis V. N. McCarthy with Philip W. Smith, *Protecting the President: The Inside Story of a Secret Service Agent* (New York: Dell Books, 1985); Joseph Petro with Jeffrey Robinson, *Standing Next to History: An Agent's Life in the Secret Service* (New York: St. Martin's Press, 2005); and George Rush, *Confessions of an Ex–Secret Service Agent: The Marty Venker Story* (New York: Donald F. Fine, 1988).

Index